BOTTOM LINE YEAR BOOK 1994

BY THE EDITORS OF

Bottom Line
PERSONAL

Copyright © 1993 by Boardroom Reports, Inc.

10 9 8 7 6 5 4 3 2 1

Boardroom® Classics publishes the advice of expert
authorities in many fields. The use of a book is not
a substitute for legal, accounting, or other professional services. Consult a competent professional for
answers to your specific questions.

Library of Congress Cataloging in Publication Data
Main entry under title:

Bottom Line Yearbook 1994.

    1. Life skills—United States.   I. Bottom line
personal.
ISBN 0-88723-067-9

Boardroom ® Classics is a registered trademark of
Boardroom ® Reports, Inc.
330 W. 42nd Street, New York, NY 10036

Printed in the United States of America

Contents

3 • MONEY MANAGEMENT FOR TOUGH TIMES

4 • INSURANCE SAVVY

5 • TAX SAVVY

6 • SUCCESS IN THE OFFICE

7 • RETIREMENT PLANNING

8 • ESTATE PLANNING

9 • INVESTMENT SAVVY

10 • SUCCESSFUL LIVING

11 • YOUR FAMILY, YOUR HOME

12 • NUTRITION, FITNESS, AND EXERCISE

13 • YOUR CAR

19 • TECHNOLOGY 1994

20 • DID YOU KNOW THAT...

21 • THE NEW TAX LAW LOOPHOLES

1

Healthy Secrets

What's Coming In Health Science

Over the next year or two, we can expect further dramatic advances in cracking the genetic code. There are supercomputers working in several different parts of the world under the Human Genome project led by Dr. James Watson, the cofounder of modern molecular genetics.

The original projection was that they would crack the entire human genetic code by the year 2005. Now it's been pushed up to 2003 and there's a good chance it will happen before the end of this decade.

There are 24 chromosomes...that is, 22 plus X and Y—and we've already completely mapped chromosome No. 22, which is the smallest one next to the Y chromosome.

Every day there are announcements of the discovery of new genetic markers for disease and for various tendencies and traits.

The technology is moving at a terrific clip plus the marriage of genetic research with brain research and other kinds of pharmaceutical research, means that within two years we're going to see huge barriers come down in our ability to understand and intervene in conditions like Alzheimer's disease, heart disease, childhood diseases like muscular dystrophy and cerebral palsy, and some types with tendencies toward cancer. Even baldness...

This will have an enormous impact on the pharmaceutical and medical testing businesses. Every year, for example, new research is leading to a greater ability to test fetuses for possible genetic problems and, increasingly, to intervene prenatally or during the early stages of childhood to genetically alter or reverse those conditions.

These advances will also increase our ability to manage our own personal exposure to health problems so as not to trigger the risks we carry in our genes. We will be moving more toward prevention instead of treatment. If you knew, for example, that a tendency toward multiple sclerosis lurked in your genes, you might reduce your risk by altering your diet.

Another result of this combination of genetic research and brain research, together with the implications of hormone research, is that we are increasingly recognizing homosexuality as a biological phenomenon, not a life style choice, for the majority of homosexuals. First came brain research showing that the embryonic development of the brain when it's exposed to an abnormal quantity of a hormone in the womb, say testosterone, can give a female fetus a more male patterned brain. Now the genetic marker for homosexuality has also been found.

While there are still many ethical and moral questions surrounding the area of possible intervention with fetuses, there's no doubt that homosexuals will feel much better about themselves as a result of this knowledge. Moreover it will have an impact on how the rest of society views homosexuality. It will be harder to discriminate against people who represent a natural biological deviation from the norm—not just some offbeat life style that they have adopted.

Combined with a breakdown in government oversight over such things as water supplies, I would not be surprised to see more cholera, malaria and even typhoid in the US.

In pharmaceuticals, the next year or two will see better targeting of drugs, so that they zero in on the problem area of the body or do a certain task, without causing as many unwanted side effects. Also, we will increasingly be able to administer drugs ourselves.

We don't expect a cure for AIDs to be developed in the next two years, and I worry that we could see resurgences of infectious diseases in the industrial world that we thought we had conquered after the turn of the century.

Several forces are coming together to cause this problem: The enormous amount of illegal immigration…the breakdown of the health infrastructure in Africa, which people constantly travel to and from, and the importation of both people and goods from the tropics. People in Northern climates have limited natural immunity against tropical organisms.

Some diseases, like tuberculosis and syphilis, have also become increasingly resistant to antibiotics.

The pharmaceutical liability crisis has also stopped a lot of pharmaceutical companies from wanting to be in the vaccine business.

Finally, we have crowding and homelessness which is creating Third World conditions—including the spread of disease—in many of our large cities.

Source: Edith Weiner is president of Weiner, Edrich, Brown, Inc., futurists and strategic planning consultants, 200 E. 33 St., New York 10016.

About Your Immune System

The immune system can be compromised by many things—from an ordinary cold to deadly cancers. *That's the bad news.*

The good news is that your immune defenses regularly repair themselves, and there are simple measures you can take to assist them when they have been breached.

Basically, your immune system is a thriving swarm of billions of white blood cells, all with just two goals…
- Recognize germ invaders.
- Respond to the threat.

When bacteria enter your body—for instance, through that razor nick you got yesterday—specialized cells called neutrophils rush to the scene to virtually devour the marauders. Other cells soon come by to clean up any bacterial fragments.

Against viruses—which are more insidious than bacterial infections because they sneak into our cells and commandeer them for their own evil purposes—your immune system dispatches antibodies to tackle the attacking aliens.

More important, your immune system has memory cells that look at the viral perpetrators and remember those particular villains for the rest of your life. When antibodies recognize and defeat a virus, your system has established an immunity.

Vaccines and medications may be thought of, in a sense, as backups that assist a person when the immune system is overloaded.

There are a lot of microscopic threats out there. But, don't worry. We have plenty of memory cells—enough to recall every virus, bacteria, or toxin that is in existence.

Why it fails:

Without an immune system, even the mildest infection would be lethal. Under normal circumstances, our immune system serves us admirably. When it does malfunction, it is usually for one good reason or another...

•Stress. Chronic, unrelieved stress is probably the most severe threat to your immune system. Along with depression, grief, and anxiety, stress can trigger chemical changes, stimulating the release of neuropeptides, which adversely affect the operation of your immune system.

•Exertion extremes. Moderate exercise is necessary for basic health, of course, and that includes maintaining a healthy immune system. But, too much exertion—for instance, marathon running, mountain climbing in arctic conditions, or other such strenuous activities—has been shown to temporarily depress immune system functions.

•Malnutrition. The relationship between nutrition and the immune system is still a puzzle. We do know, though, that those with poor diets are more susceptible to illness and infections, increasing the burden on their immune systems.

•Rapid and excessive weight loss, through quirky diets or periods of starvation, also drastically reduces your immune system's effectiveness.

It is natural to want to keep your immune system operating at its peak efficiency. Remember, though, that it has gotten you this far without much attention. As with a smoothly running computer, tinkering with your immune system can do more harm than good.

Routine maintenance:

•Keep stress at a reasonable level. Stress reduction is critical for your immune system to function well. If you're not addressing this common problem, make it a health-care priority.

•Vaccinations. These are key to preventing "sneak attacks" on your immune system. Follow the vaccination schedule your child's pediatrician recommends. You may be due for a tetanus booster yourself. When traveling internationally, seek medical advice on specific vaccinations you may need.

•Follow a balanced diet. Sustaining a fit immune system is another good reason for healthy eating. But, avoid the temptation to "boost" immunity defenses through fad diets or the currently popular vitamin or mineral therapy. Such self-treatment can have serious consequences. Large doses of iron, for example, can cause dangerous digestive tract problems. And, while vitamin A is crucial to combat infections, massive supplemental doses can actually suppress vital immune functions.

•Follow your physician's advice exactly when you are ill. Take *all* medication prescribed, especially antibiotics, which we tend to discontinue using immediately after symptoms disappear.

Give your immune system time to fight your illness and recover afterward. Finally, realize that we often have unrealistic expectations for our health. A few colds a year is not a sign that something is wrong with your life style. Being sick occasionally is just a part of being alive. Thanks to your immune system, so is getting well.

•Stay happy. Just as depression and anxiety can adversely affect all aspects of your health, a happy and optimistic outlook will contribute to a healthier immune system. Recent studies show that this may not be entirely psychological, but may have a neurological basis as well.

Source: David S. McKinsey, MD, codirector of epidemiology and infectious diseases at the Research Medical Center, 2316 E. Meyer, Kansas City, Missouri 64132.

How to Protect Yourself Against Disease Mongering

When it comes to treating cancer, heart disease, severe trauma, and other life-threatening ailments, the American health-care system is second to none. Our doctors are highly trained, our drugs carefully screened, our hospitals chockablock with sophisticated medical equipment.

Still, it pays to remember that a desire to aid the afflicted isn't the only motive driving our health-care system. *Also at work:* A powerful and unrelenting urge to maximize profits.

In order to remain in business, doctors, hospitals, diagnostic facilities, drug and medical equipment makers, insurance companies, and other recipients of our health-care dollars all need one thing—patients with health insurance. The greater their number, the sicker they are, the more drugs they take, the more tests they undergo…the bigger the industry's profits.

Problem: To get more patients, the health-care industry often resorts to an insidious form of exploitation known as *disease-mongering.*

Disease-mongering takes many forms…

•It's the surgeon who insists upon treating a minor heart ailment with costly and often risky bypass surgery—just to earn more money.

•It's the drug maker that uses manipulative ads to portray the common cold as a debilitating ailment in need of drug therapy.

•It's the diagnostic clinic that sells mammograms even to women for whom there's no evidence that they work.

•It's also the medical journalist who earns his or her keep by hyping minor illnesses as plagues.

No matter what form disease-mongering takes, however, the result never varies—*healthy people are led to believe they're ill or at risk of becoming ill…and persons suffering from minor ailments are led to believe they're seriously ill.*

The health-care industry knows that once we're instilled with fear, we'll take action—scheduling costly medical checkups and diagnostic tests at the merest hint of trouble…using cold remedies, painkillers, and other drugs for conditions that clear up even without treatment…gobbling prescription drugs with nasty and potentially harmful side effects…and submitting to surgery that is risky and of questionable benefit.

Watch out for trouble:

•Manipulative ads. Television, newspapers and magazines are filled with ads for sinus remedies, arthritis pills, headache relievers—and, of course, even baldness cures.

The more often we encounter these ads, the more firmly we're convinced that we need the products they promote. *Reality:* Minor aches and pains, as well as occasional cold or flu symptoms, are a normal part of life. There's no good reason to visit the drugstore every time you sneeze.

To avoid being manipulated: Each time you choose to read a health ad, ask yourself who really stands to benefit from its message—you or the makers of the product. Are there alternatives? What would happen if you took no action? *Use only those products truly beneficial to you.*

•"Man-made" diseases. While there's no doubt that broken bones and heart attacks need prompt treatment, not all medical conditions require treatment.

Example: Mild hypertension. The cutoff between "normal" and "high" blood pressure has been set arbitrarily low in this country—as a result, inflating the ranks of the "ill" and maximizing the profit potential for doctors and companies selling antihypertensive drugs. In fact, a blood pressure reading treated in this country with an aggressive drug regimen might be considered normal in England.

Blood pressure isn't the only such "man-made" disease. Elevated cholesterol level is considered a heart disease risk factor—and rightly so. But often even mildly elevated cholesterol is treated as a disease in its own right. *Result:* People who feel perfectly fine are urged to take harsh and costly drugs, even though evidence of their value is controversial.

And in an effort to sell more estrogen, drug makers are now trying to turn menopause from a natural process into a deficiency disease that needs treatment. The list goes on and on.

To avoid trouble: If a doctor says you're at risk for or already have a particular disease and urges aggressive treatment, follow the advice only if there's solid evidence that the treatment will cut your risk. Get a second opinion, and do your own research.

•Needless diagnostic tests. Doctors order far too many diagnostic tests. Each time you have a mammogram, stress test, cholesterol test, AIDS test, etc., *you're taking a risk.* Not only that you'll hear bad news, but your test results could be wrong. The test might indicate you're okay when you're really sick, for instance, or that you're sick when you're healthy.

Danger: A "false positive" causes not only needless anxiety, but also labels you as "sick" and thereby jeopardizes your insurability. It can even lead you to seek risky treatments.

Example: There have been cases in which people died during heart surgery scheduled after stress tests mistakenly indicated that they had heart disease. Similarly, mammograms are often urged for women under 40—even though young breasts are usually too dense for accurate X ray readings.

To avoid trouble: For anyone already at reasonably high risk for a particular condition, the potential benefits of being tested generally outweigh the risk of inaccurate results. But if your risk for the ailment is very low, avoid being tested. Ask your doctor to explain your level of risk when making the decision.

Make sure the doctors with whom you discuss your case have no financial stake in performing the test.

Scandalous: Though the conflict of interest in such an arrangement is obvious, many doctors now own their own CAT scanners, MRI scanners, and other diagnostic equipment. The more tests they schedule, the more money they make.

•Free screening clinics. These days, free screening is being offered for everything from prostate cancer to high blood pressure. It sounds like a good idea. But in many cases these clinics are set up to bring in more patients...and are more beneficial to their sponsors than to the general public.

Problem: Unreliable readings. Some serious medical problems are missed entirely, while problems are diagnosed in persons who are actually perfectly healthy.

To avoid trouble: Be tested in a doctor's office or a diagnostic facility specializing in medical tests. Make sure the person who interprets the test results is highly experienced.

•Needless surgery. A surprisingly large percentage of operations in this country are performed needlessly—up to 25% by some respectful estimates. Certain procedures are especially likely to be performed inappropriately, including hysterectomy, back surgery, caesarean sections, and bypass surgery. *Result:* Needless expense, discomfort, and even the risk of fatal complications—all because a surgeon was eager to operate.

To avoid trouble: Always get a second opinion before agreeing to surgery. Many problems frequently treated with surgery can be resolved more cheaply and safely via exercise, changes in diet, physical therapy, and other nonsurgical methods.

•Overbearing doctors. Americans tend to be much more deferential toward doctors than toward lawyers, accountants, and other professionals we employ—and doctors rarely do anything to stop us.

Explanation: Most of us started seeing doctors when we were kids, and we still behave like kids in the presence of them.

Better way: Instead of blindly accepting your doctor's advice, make it a point to discuss all your available options.

Helpful: Calling your doctor by his/her first name—especially if the doctor calls you by yours. Doing so reminds you that you're on an equal footing with one another—that you're hiring the doctor, not the other way around.

•Overly aggressive treatment. Every good doctor knows that too much medical care is just as deleterious as too little. Unfortunately, patients often demand aggressive treatment.

Problem: While such treatment might be warranted for serious ailments, most conditions do just as well with minimal or no treatment. In fact, few medical conditions call for urgent intervention of any kind.

Certainly you should see a doctor right away for obvious injuries, severe pain or high fever. In many cases, however, it's not only safe to wait a few weeks before seeking medical care, *it's the smartest course of action.*

Reason: Many conditions improve or disappear without treatment, saving you money, aggravation and more.

Source: Lynn Payer, former editor of *The New York Times Good Health Magazine* and author of several books on medical topics, including *Disease-Mongers: How Doctors, Drug Companies, and Insurers Are Making You Feel Sick*, John Wiley & Sons, 605 Third Ave., New York 10158.

Hospital Bill Self-Defense

Over 90% of hospital bills contain errors—most of which are in the institution's favor, we hear from Charles Inlander. *Self-defense:* During your stay, keep a log of doctor visits and the medications, tests, and equipment you receive. When checking out, request a *detailed* bill listing these products and services. At home, compare the bill with your notes. Hospitals are usually quick to adjust or remove disputed charges.

Source: Charles Inlander is president of the People's Medical Society in Allentown, Pennsylvania, and author of *Take This Book to the Hospital With You*, Wings Books, 40 Engelhard Ave., Avenel, New Jersey 07001.

Coronary Disease Treatments

Quick fixes for coronary disease are not permanent. *Angioplasty* uses tiny balloons inserted in blocked arteries to remove plaque causing the blockage. *Bypass surgery* actually routes blood around blocked arteries. But the underlying problems that created these blockages are not cured by either procedure. *Better:* Aggressive lowering of blood-cholesterol levels…and modification of other risk factors, such as smoking and obesity, that can lead to coronary disease.

Source: K. Lance Gould, MD, professor of medicine, University of Texas Medical School at Houston, reported in *University of Texas Lifetime Health Letter*, 1100 Holcombe Blvd., Houston 77030.

Mouthwash Danger

High-alcohol mouthwashes may raise a person's risk of developing oral cancer by as much as 60%. *Danger threshold:* Mouthwashes with an alcohol content of 25% or higher (as indicated on their labels) have been implicated in mouth, tongue, and throat cancers. *Theory:* Alcohol acts as a solvent in the mouth, making tissues more vulnerable to carcinogens.

Source: Research by the National Cancer Institute, reported in *Working Mother*, 230 Park Ave., New York 10169.

Surprising Cause Of Gallstones

Very low-calorie, low-fat diets can cause gallstones. Half of those on weight-loss diets who ate less than 600 calories and 3g of fat a day (4.5% of calories from fat) developed gallstones. *Reason:* Low intake of calories and fat lead to cholesterol buildup in the gallbladder, a factor in gallstone formation. *Self-defense:* Eat at least 1,200 calories a day…and make sure one meal contains between 5g and 10g of fat.

Source: Steven Heymsfield, MD, deputy director of the Obesity Research Center at St. Luke's–Roosevelt Hospital in New York City.

Benefits of Soybeans

Japanese women have fewer hot flashes and other menopausal symptoms than American women. *Possible reason:* They eat about two ounces a day of foods made from soybeans, such as tofu (bean curd) and miso (soybean paste). Soybeans are rich in isoflavinoids, which are converted during digestion to estrogen-like substances that can help prevent hot flashes.

Source: Barry Goldin, PhD, and Sherwood Gorbach, MD, Tufts University School of Medicine and Herman Adlercreutz, MD, Helsinki University, Finland.

Very Wise New Way To Treat Arthritis

Of all chronic diseases, few are as common, as physically and emotionally debilitating or as financially destructive as serious arthritis. This family of diseases now afflicts more than 37 million Americans, resulting each year in 45 million lost work days and $35 billion in medical care and lost wages...*and untold suffering*.

If you experience one or more of the warning signs—joint pain, stiffness and swollen joints—for more than two weeks, *see a doctor immediately*.

Sad: The average arthritis patient waits four years before seeking medical attention, enduring needless pain and possibly permanent joint damage.

Knowledge is power:

Arthritis patients traditionally have controlled their symptoms using some combination of exercise, rest, surgery and—most important—drug therapy.

Many different medications are now available, from aspirin and other nonprescription painkillers to a variety of prescription anti-inflammatories. Recently, however, scientists have realized that one of the most effective weapons against arthritis is *knowledge*.

Patients who learn as much as possible about arthritis gain a sense of mastery over the illness. This mastery gives them an upbeat attitude about their illness. More important, it enables them to manage their symptoms rather than simply respond to them.

Bottom line: Knowledgeable patients seem to fare much better psychologically than those who remain largely ignorant of their illness.

Here at the University of Texas, we're exploring this finding with a special training program for arthritis patients. In this program, conducted in Dallas, patients receive a sophisticated education in joint anatomy, inflammatory processes and other topics they need to know in order to discuss their symptoms with their doctors. We also teach them how to conduct a joint exam. It is crucial for keeping track of their illness.

Result: Instead of simply complaining to their doctors that their knuckles are swollen, for example, participants can report that their *metacarpophalangeal joints have active synovitis*.

Surprisingly, this simple ability to discuss arthritis in scientific terms is an emotionally liberating experience for most patients—especially those who've been in the dark about their illness for years. Some participants actually break down and cry upon discovering that there are specific names for what's been going on inside their bodies.

Upon returning home, most participants in our program pass along their knowledge to other arthritis patients and even to medical students and practicing physicians. Helping others in this way isn't mere charity—doing so helps confer a sense of purpose upon arthritis patients whose symptoms may have put an end to their previous careers.

However, if you can't come to Dallas, much of the material that we cover is available from health publications* and medical textbooks.

One of the best sources of arthritis information is your local Arthritis Foundation chapter. It provides free literature and conducts arthritis support groups, exercise classes and a six-week self-help course. Participants learn how to control not only arthritis symptoms, but also the fatigue and depression that often accompany the illness. If there's no Arthritis Foundation chapter in your community, contact the foundation's Atlanta headquarters at 800-283-7800.

Beyond a thorough education of arthritis, several other tools are available to keep your symptoms in check. *Most important:*

Accurate diagnosis:

Osteoarthritis and rheumatoid arthritis are by far the most common forms of arthritis—16 million and two million sufferers respectively.

Scientists have now identified more than 120 different forms of the disease, including gout and spinal arthritis.

The methods of treating these diverse illnesses vary widely. Without a proper diagnosis, you're unlikely to get the form of treatment

*Recommended reading: *The Arthritis Helpbook* by Kate Lorig, RN, DrPH, and James F. Fries, MD, Addison-Wesley Publishing Co., Jacob Way, Reading, Massachusetts 01867.

best suited to your particular case. While a simple blood test is available to identify rheumatoid arthritis, most other forms of arthritis are identifiable only via X rays and a skilled examination of the affected joints.

Keeping a diary:

Arthritis symptoms typically wax and wane according to the time of day and your activity levels.

Problem: Patients whose symptoms repeatedly catch them by surprise often become frustrated, depressed, and reclusive.

Strategy: A diary will help you learn to "forecast" your arthritis symptoms. Use one to record how you feel at different times of the day, during and after different activities, etc. Review your comments periodically and try to detect a pattern connecting your activities and how you feel. Discuss your findings with your doctor. Changes in the pattern might suggest the need to switch to another medication or to change dosages of your current medication.

Assistive devices:

If your symptoms make everyday tasks difficult or impossible, find ways to simplify those tasks.

Example: If arthritic hands make it hard to open doors in your home, use a handle instead of a door knob—or use a loop of cloth… it is especially helpful for refrigerator doors.

For other helpful ideas, ask your doctor or physical or occupational therapist. Many mail-order catalogs* now sell assistive devices—clothing that fastens with Velcro rather than buttons, tools for grasping hard-to-reach objects, electric can and jar openers, etc.

Rest:

Besides being painful, arthritis is very tiring. Many arthritis patients think it lazy or self-indulgent to take an occasional time-out. In fact, it's remarkably prudent. Always pace yourself. If you start to tire, sit quietly for a few minutes or take a nap.

Use of heat and cold:

Try both to see which you find more soothing.

Exercise:

Jogging and other bone-jarring exercises aggravate arthritis symptoms. However, swimming, walking, low-impact aerobics and other

*The J.C. Penney Easy Living catalog is one.

gentle forms of exercise ease pain and increase joint mobility.

Especially effective: Warm-water exercise (aquatics) classes. These and other exercise programs are offered free of charge by many YMCA's and Arthritis Foundation chapters.

Weight control:

The more you weigh, the greater the stress on your joints. If you're overweight, shedding a few pounds will help alleviate your symptoms.

Source: Valerie Branch, director, patient educator program, division of rheumatic diseases, The University of Texas Southwestern Medical Center, 5323 Harry Hines Blvd., Dallas 75235-8884. An arthritis patient herself since 1982, Ms. Branch also serves on the board of directors of the North Texas chapter of the National Arthritis Foundation. For more information about the patient educator program, contact Ms. Branch at the address above.

Faster Healing

Heal faster—by increasing your intake of zinc. Cuts, scrapes, blisters, and minor burns heal about one-third faster in those who take a minimum of 15 mg. of zinc daily. Fast healing decreases the chances of infection, scarring and stiffness. *Best:* A multiple vitamin-mineral supplement containing zinc rather than plain zinc tablets, which sometimes cause heartburn or indigestion.

Source: *Prime Time: A Doctor's Guide to Staying Younger Longer* by John E. Eichenlaub, MD. Prentice-Hall, Route 9W, Sylvan Ave., Englewood Cliffs, New Jersey 07632.

Surgery Self-Defense

Checking out a surgeon before you go under the knife makes perfect sense, but obtaining accurate information can often prove to be exceedingly difficult. *Possible information sources:*

• The surgeon. Ask how many similar or identical procedures he/she has performed in the past. What sort of success rate has he had performing these procedures. All other things being equal, the greater the number of similar procedures the surgeon performs each year and the higher the success rate, the better the surgeon.

•Previous patients. Ask the surgeon for the names of patients on whom he performed the identical surgery and call them. *Ask:*

•Do you regard the surgeon as competent and professional?

•Were the results good?

•Were there any unusual problems or complications?

•The surgeon's colleagues. Although doctors are notorious for their reluctance to speak ill of other doctors, many will give you an accurate reading of a reputation.

•Does this surgeon do good work?

•Is he friendly and generally accessible to his patients?

•Does he have any problems that might interfere with good work?

•The state medical board. Boards vary widely in their responsiveness to inquiries, but it doesn't hurt to ask:

•Has the board ever taken disciplinary action against the surgeon?

•Is there any record of patient complaints? Malpractice lawsuits?

•Hospital administrators. As with state medical boards, hospital administrators vary in their willingness to discuss individual surgeons. But it is possible to find out if the surgeon has ever been reprimanded, had certain privileges revoked, etc.

Source: Ingrid VanTuinen, a former staff researcher with the Public Citizen Health Research Group, a Washington, DC–based consumer rights group founded by Ralph Nader, 2000 P St. NW, Washington, DC 20036.

The Truth About Health Scares

The leading environmental causes of premature death in the United States are now—and have long been—smoking…drinking…and consuming too much fat.

Tragically, many smart, health-conscious Americans are more concerned about pesticide residues in our food and water, toxic dump sites, invisible fields from power lines and other items on an ever-growing list of "modern scourges."

Reality: In virtually every case, the threats posed by these "scourges" are either almost nonexistent or are completely nonexistent.

•ALAR. This synthetic chemical, used to regulate the growth of apples, was used for years with no apparent ill effects. Then a study showed high rates of cancer among rodents fed ALAR, and the ensuing hysteria forced the compound from the market. In fact, the study was inconclusive. Only one type of rodent fed ALAR developed cancer at higher-than-normal rates. Others were unaffected by the compound. In addition, the rodents who developed cancer did so only after eating enormous quantities of ALAR—roughly 290,000 times higher than a human who regularly ate apples might be expected to ingest. At these levels, about half of *all* chemicals—both synthetic and natural—will cause tumors in laboratory animals. Because most food comprises a great number of chemicals, the ALAR standard would require banning virtually all nutrition.

•Power lines. Recent studies in the US and Sweden suggest that the electromagnetic fields (EMFs) given off by power lines may cause certain forms of cancer, especially childhood leukemia—a finding thoroughly reported in the popular media.

There are also several recent studies that have found no such cancer link, yet the media has almost completely ignored them. That the EMF-cancer studies have been conducted since 1979 and are still far from producing a conclusion indicates that if a connection is ultimately found, it will be a very slight one—a very tiny risk that is much smaller than many of the risks to children that parents routinely ignore, such as diseases preventable by vaccination.

•Computer terminals. For the past several years, people have speculated that women who work at computer terminals face an increased risk of miscarriage. In fact, miscarriage ends roughly 12%–15% of all recognized pregnancies, no matter what sort of work the mother does. There is no sound scientific evidence linking computer terminals to miscarriage.

•Dioxin. This synthetic chemical has been blamed for a host of ailments, including birth defects, miscarriage, and cancer.

Reality: While dioxin does cause tumors in guinea pigs, it is not especially toxic to other animals, including mice and frogs. Humans accidentally exposed to dioxin have suffered nothing worse than chloracne, a severe but temporary skin disorder. Nonetheless, millions and millions of dollars have been spent in a futile effort to remove all traces of dioxin from our air, soil, water and from consumer products …and at least two dioxin-tainted communities (Love Canal in New York and Times Beach in Missouri) were evacuated. Dioxin's threat to humans is minimal at worst.

•Agent Orange. Vietnam veterans blame their battlefield exposure to this dioxin-laced defoliant for health problems that range from miscarriage and birth defects to cancer. In fact, debate continues as to whether the chemical poses a health risk. As it turns out, cancer rates are no higher for Vietnam vets than for other Americans of the same age. And a recent study found that the blood of veterans exposed to Agent Orange contains no more dioxin than the blood of civilians who never went to Vietnam.

Bottom line:

Clearly, things aren't quite as dire as reports in the media would have us believe. If you'd like to protect yourself from needless alarm over the next health scare to come along— from reporters who use scare tactics to make a name for themselves, from scientists whose egos have clouded their objectivity and from environmental groups who feed upon the public fear—be more skeptical of what you read and hear…

•Realize that all humans are mortal. It's a fact so obvious that it's often overlooked—we'll all die of something.

Environmental alarmists often point out that cancer kills more people in the United States than in developing countries, blaming this fact on an environment overrun by toxic chemicals. But cancer is largely a disease of the elderly. It's not a big threat in developing countries because their citizens die younger, before cancer has time to strike. One out of every four Americans will develop cancer at some point in his/ her life, and one out of five will die of it. That means 20% of computer users, 20% of persons exposed to dioxin or Agent Orange, etc.

•Be skeptical of animal studies. Chemicals that cause tumors in mice or rats do not always cause tumors in humans—and vice versa. Animal studies are helpful in identifying potentially harmful chemicals, but they are no substitute for studies involving humans.

•Consider the source of the information. Newspapers, magazines, and TV news programs vary in the accuracy of their health coverage. Watch out for poorly researched and annotated books and reports. And, look for a hidden agenda behind alarmist reports. Representatives of some environmental groups are less concerned with scientific fact than with drumming up support for their organizations.

•Be wary of tragic stories. A mother who tearfully explains that her miscarriages were caused by a nearby toxic dump makes for good television viewing. That's all. Such anecdotal evidence proves no hard evidence about cause and effect, no matter how heartfelt her tears.

Before judging how alarmed you should be about a newly reported health threat, look for sound scientific studies conducted by reputable institutions. The substance found to cause cancer on Tuesday may be off the hook by Thursday. It makes much more sense to concentrate on the known causes of many cases of cancer and work to eliminate those risk factors from your life.

•Think logically about cause and effect. Many reporters and even some scientists who link disease to a certain chemical, drug or form of radiation are victims of a type of flawed logic known by the Latin phrase, *"post hoc, ergo, propter hoc"* (after this, therefore, because of this).

In the cellular phone scare, for instance, a user of the phones developed cancer, thereby "proving" that cellular phones cause cancer. But just because an illness develops after exposure to "something" does not prove a causal link between that "something" and the illness. Only a well-designed scientific study can establish cause and effect.

•Watch out for false experts. Just because someone is a doctor does not necessarily mean he/she is qualified to comment on the risk posed by a particular drug, chemical, environmental condition, etc. Carl Sagan, for example, widely quoted on environmental issues, is not a PhD in environmental science, but in astronomy.

To avoid being misled: Look for specific scientific degrees. Trust experts only when the topic under consideration lies within their field of expertise.

•Consider the risk in terms of potential rewards. To do so, you must answer three questions.

•First, what is the likelihood that something bad will happen?

•Second, how bad is this potential outcome?

•Third, what is the benefit for taking the risk?

If the reward is great and the risk small, it makes sense to take the risk.

Danger: Reporters and so-called "public interest" groups often exaggerate the risks posed by a particular product or chemical, etc., at the same time they're minimizing the possible benefit. To the extent that you're able to do so, perform your own reward-risk analysis.

Source: Michael Fumento, former AIDS analyst for the US Commission on Civil Rights, and science and economics reporter for *Investor's Business Daily*, the Los Angeles–based financial newspaper. He is the author of *Science Under Siege: Balancing Technology and the Environment*, William Morrow, 1350 Avenue of the Americas, New York 10019.

Blood Transfusion Self-Defense

Even if recent reports suggesting that a previously unknown virus might be causing an AIDS-like illness prove false, transfused blood is not now—and never will be—risk-free.

Risks: Despite rigorous screening methods now in place at blood banks across the US, one of every 250,000 units of blood contains HIV, the virus that causes AIDS...and one of every 2,500 units contains the viruses that cause hepatitis B and C, which can be just as deadly as AIDS.

Because of these risks, doctors and patients alike are increasingly wary of transfusions. When blood loss from surgery or trauma is especially severe, however, it's important to remember that receiving a transfusion is sometimes far less risky than *not* having one.

If you need a transfusion following a severe injury or emergency surgery, whether or not you receive tainted blood is essentially a matter of chance. But if you're scheduled for elective surgery, certain precautions can help lower your risk...

•Find a conscientious surgeon. While all good surgeons try to avoid giving transfusions, some try harder than others. The more conscientious your surgeon, the smaller your risk.

•Bank your own blood. Before you're scheduled for elective surgery, ask your surgeon about autologous blood donation. With this technique, you will receive blood not from an anonymous donor, but your own previously donated blood. Costs will vary, depending on what procedures are necessary.

Exception: Patients suffering from severe anemia and certain other conditions are *not* candidates for autologous transfusion.

•Insist on blood-saving surgical techniques. One way to reduce the need for transfusions during thoracic (chest), orthopedic (skeletal) and other forms of surgery where bleeding is often severe is to collect and then re-transfuse blood from the patient's surgical incision. The process—known as *cell-salvage*—uses sophisticated equipment not found in every operating room. Ask your surgeon beforehand if the hospital has the necessary equipment and if he/she is experienced in its use.

Source: Mark Feinberg, MD, PhD, assistant professor of medicine, microbiology and immunology, University of California at San Francisco.

Hospitalization Hazards For the Elderly

Hospitalization for a medical condition often leads to an elderly person's decline and drastic changes in quality of life—even if the condition is cured. *Common myths and ways to help keep the elderly vital…*

• *Myth:* High beds with rails are needed for the patient's safety. A high bed may actually be more dangerous than a low bed—elderly people tend to get injured climbing in and out of bed.

Helpful: Find out if the hospital has less dangerous, modified hospital beds.

• *Myth:* All hospitalized patients need an intravenous (IV) line. Many patients' needs could be met by placing fluids within reach and offering them regularly.

Helpful: Keep dentures nearby so the patient can eat normal food—rather than having a liquid diet or being fed through a tube.

• *Myth:* It's expected that the elderly become disoriented in the hospital. Reality: Orientation can be an important part of the patient's care.

Helpful: Proper room lighting, calendars, clocks, communal eating, dressing in personal clothing, etc. And—make sure you bring eyeglasses and hearing aids to the hospital.

• *Myth:* All elderly patients need bed rest. Bed rest weakens muscle strength and diminishes aerobic capacity—which can lead to falls …and greater dependency on others.

Helpful: Encouraging and assisting the elderly person to walk around, if possible.

Source: Morton C. Creditor, MD, the Center on Aging, University of Kansas Medical Center, Kansas City.

Permanent Damage

Dangerous: Home perm kits and other hair products containing caustic chemicals can cause serious burns to the face and/or throat if swallowed. *Beware:* Caustic hair products carry no warning labels…and those labeled "no lye" may be just as dangerous. *Bottom line:* Be careful with all hair and cosmetic products and keep them out of the reach of young children.

Source: Kerstin Stenson, MD, and Benjamin Gruber, MD, PhD, clinical professor, department of otolaryngology, University of Illinois.

Allergy/Cancer Link

People with severe allergies—bad enough to seek medical care—face greater risk of contracting prostate or breast cancer. In a study of 34,000 people with low cancer-risk factors but strong allergic reactions, men allergic to medication, for example, had a 33% increased risk of contracting any type of cancer—and a 34% higher risk of prostate cancer. Asthmatic women had a 19% greater risk for breast cancer, and women with hay fever were at 34% greater risk. *Self-defense:* Those with severe allergies should consider starting cancer-screening measures earlier in life.

Source: Paul K. Mills, PhD, who led the study at Loma Linda University, California, is now with the US Public Health Service in Cincinnati.

Cockroaches and Asthma

Cockroach allergens may be a common cause of asthma attacks. *Trigger:* Certain proteins secreted from cockroaches. *Recent finding:* Of 73 asthmatic children, 49% were allergic to cockroaches. An allergist can run a blood or skin test to determine if you are allergic to cockroaches. Then, a simple, $25 test* can determine if cockroach allergens are in your home at levels that can cause asthma or allergy problems. *Bad news:* Allergy medications and injections are not yet very effective against cockroaches. *Best defense:* Keep your home—especially the kitchen—impeccably clean.

*For information, write to Asthma & Allergy Center, Johns Hopkins University School of Medicine, Room 1A20, 5501 Hopkins Bayview Circle, Baltimore 21224.

Source: Robert G. Hamilton, PhD, is associate professor of medicine, Johns Hopkins University School of Medicine.

Prescription Drugs And Photosensitivity

Prescription drugs can cause extreme photosensitivity. Reactions—including augmented sunburn, painful swelling, hives, or blistering—can occur up to 72 hours after sun exposure. *Suggested:* Before using any medicine, ask your doctor or pharmacist if it could lead to photosensitivity. Other substances that can trigger photosensitivity include bergamot oil, found in some perfumes and soaps…coal tars, in medicated soaps and shampoos…even some foods, such as parsley, celery, limes and figs. *Self-defense:* Wear a sunscreen that protects against UV-A and UV-B rays, such as Photoplex or Shade UV-A Guard (most only absorb UV-B rays) or a sunblock containing titanium dioxide. *Danger:* UV-A light penetrates glass, so protection is needed even when indoors.

Source: Neal Schultz, MD, is a dermatologist in private practice in New York City.

Cavities Are Contagious

The bacteria most responsible for tooth decay originate in mothers' mouths and pass in saliva to their children after first molars come in—around age two. *Recommended:* Mothers of young children should be sure to maintain their own dental health.

Source: Study of children from birth to age five, led by Page Caufield, DDS, PhD, University of Alabama School of Dentistry in Birmingham.

Validity Of Heart-Disease Studies

Most heart-disease studies are of limited direct value to the public. *Trap:* They reflect limited statistical data rather than proven cause and effect relationships. *Examples:* It is unproven that wine or walnuts can prevent heart attacks—or that baldness is a risk factor. *The only established prevention factors:* Stop smoking, control high blood pressure, eat to lower cholesterol and avoid obesity, and exercise ap-

propriately. More research is needed to find the best way to prevent the nation's leading killer.

Source: Dr. James Muller, codirector, Institute for Prevention of Cardiovascular Disease at Deaconess Hospital, Boston.

Diseases Humans Get from Pets

The same household pets that raise our spirits can also transmit diseases—some serious and potentially deadly—to us. *The most common of these diseases are…*

• Cat-scratch fever. This usually mild infection—caused by a bacterium found on the claws of cats—produces swelling and inflammation in the area around the scratch. It usually goes away without treatment.

To avoid trouble: Clean cat scratches carefully. Your doctor will probably prescribe a course of antibiotics to clear up persistent symptoms.

• Lyme disease. This tick-borne bacterial infection can be carried by dogs, cats, horses, etc. and passed to their owners. It is easily cured with antibiotics—*if it's detected early.*

Late detection can result in severe—and permanent—neurological problems and arthritis.

To avoid trouble: Keep pet dogs and cats as tick-free as possible. Check your body for ticks after each venture into tick-infested areas. See a doctor immediately if you develop fever and a bull's-eye rash around a bite.

• Plague. Although this potentially deadly infection is rare, an Arizona man recently died of pneumonic plague. He caught it by breathing the same air of an infected cat that he pulled from a crawlspace.

There are actually three kinds of plague, depending on which part of the body is infected…*pneumonic plague* affects the lungs, *bubonic* the lymph nodes and *septicemic* the bloodstream. Bubonic plague and septicemic plague are usually spread by the bites of fleas from cats and rodents, but pneumonic plague is often spread through the air.

To avoid trouble: See a doctor at once if you develop a high and persistent fever in conjunction with badly swollen lymph glands—or with difficulties in breathing.

•Psittacosis. Caused by a bacterium found in the droppings of parrots, parakeets, pigeons, and turkeys, this illness produces coughing, shortness of breath, fever, and other pneumonia-like symptoms.

To avoid trouble: Bird owners who develop these symptoms should see a doctor. Persistent symptoms can usually be cleared up with a course of antibiotics.

•Rabies. The disease remains a real threat. Rabies is frequently transmitted to humans when pets, bitten by infected wild animals, bite their owners.

To avoid trouble: Make sure your pet is fully immunized, especially if rabid wild animals have been spotted in your area. Alert your local health department of any domestic or wild animal that behaves oddly, attacks without provocation, or foams at the mouth.

Helpful: If a person is bitten by an animal not known to have been immunized against rabies, the animal must be captured and tested for rabies. Otherwise, the bite victim must undergo the standard four-shot series of immunizations.

•Rocky Mountain Spotted Fever. Like Lyme disease, this ailment is tick-borne and is easily cured with antibiotics. But Rocky Mountain Spotted Fever is sometimes fatal.

To avoid trouble: Again, keep dogs and cats tick-free, and check yourself after venturing into the outdoors. See a doctor immediately if you develop a fever and body rash in conjunction with headaches and muscle pain.

•Toxoplasmosis. Spread by microscopic parasites found in cat feces, this relatively uncommon disease produces, in most cases, a mild flu-like illness that clears up without treatment.

Exception: Toxoplasmosis that develops during pregnancy. It can cause *spontaneous* miscarriage or serious health problems in the newborn, including jaundice, seizures, high fevers—even birth defects and mental retardation.

For a safe pregnancy: Wash your hands carefully after handling cat litter. If swollen glands or a fever develops, see your doctor and have your blood tested for toxoplasmosis.

Source: Evan Bell, MD, an infectious disease specialist in private practice in New York City, where he is affiliated with Lenox Hill Hospital.

Healthy Stress

Some stress actually keeps you healthy. *Positive stress* is produced by experiences that are challenging, exciting, arousing, or fun…or that give life purpose and meaning. Healthful stress is the body's way of adapting to the constant changes of life.

Source: Harriet Braiker, PhD, author of *Lethal Lovers and Poisonous People*, Pocket Books, 1230 Avenue of the Americas, New York 10020.

How to Protect Yourself From Hospitals

Not long ago, American hospitals were the envy of the world—proud institutions filled with high-tech equipment and staffed by dedicated and highly skilled workers.

But growing competition for a dwindling patient population, plus a decade of government-mandated cost-cutting measures, have transformed many once-outstanding facilities into dirty, dangerous places where care is haphazard—and overpriced, too. Until recently, there was no systematic method for comparing hospitals. Patients had to rely upon recommendations from friends and family members and from their doctors. Now, however, the federal government makes available detailed information concerning mortality rates at hospitals nationwide.

These statistics—known as Medicare mortality information—cover hospitals' overall mortality rates as well as their specific mortality for surgery performed. They give a good idea of the level of care the hospital offers. The higher the mortality rate, the lower the quality of care.

To be safe: Choose the hospital with the lowest mortality score.

If your doctor recommends a particular hospital, ask about its mortality statistics. If your doctor doesn't know, check with a medical library or with the local chapter of the American Association of Retired Persons. If you have trouble interpreting the data, take a copy to your doctor and ask for help.

Of course, even superb hospitals occasionally provide substandard care. *Some of the risks faced by patients—and how to guard against them…*

Incompetent surgeons:

While no one would dispute that the majority of surgeons are competent, some are so deficient in their skills as to be downright dangerous. Yet because even a bad doctor has specialized knowledge, it's hard for a patient to evaluate the level of care he/she is providing.

Self-defense: Before engaging a surgeon, make sure he has performed the procedure in question at *least* several dozen times. Ask what percentage of these operations succeeded and what percentage failed. Finally, check up on your prospective surgeon with the state medical board. Ask for all pertinent information, including the details of any disciplinary actions filed.

Missing anesthesiologists:

Patients scheduled for surgery know the importance of a skilled surgeon, yet few recognize the key role played by the person responsible for administering the anesthetic. *Result:* Patients fail to pay attention to one of the most important details concerning surgery—the administration of anesthesia.

Self-defense: If your operation calls for general anesthesia, you may want to confirm that the anesthetic be administered by an anesthesiologist.

Important: That the anesthesiologist be present for the entire operation. In some cases the anesthesiologist leaves the room once the operation is under way, leaving the patient in the care of an anesthetist—who might not be equipped to handle an emergency.

Inexperienced or incompetent operating room staff:

Successful surgery depends not just upon a skilled surgeon and anesthesiologist, but also upon a skilled and experienced operating room staff.

Self-defense: Never submit to surgery until you know that the hospital staffers have done the procedure at least several dozen times previously…and make sure that mortality rates for both surgeon and hospital staff are low. If the surgeon or hospital lacks significant experience, or if the mortality rates are high, have your surgery performed elsewhere.

Part-time nurses:

In an effort to cut payroll costs, many hospitals have slashed the number of full-time nursing staff, relying instead upon "temps" whenever patient ranks swell. *Problem:* Even when they hold proper credentials, temp nurses often lack the specialized skills of full-time nurses. Those who are equally skilled may lack familiarity with the hospital's particular way of doing things. *Result:* Needless mistakes in patient care.

Self-defense: Before hospitalization, inform your primary physician that you prefer to be treated only by full-time personnel. If full-time nurses are unavailable, consider hiring your own. Most hospitals do allow the practice. *Note:* Temps are especially common in resort areas—places with unstable or seasonal populations.

Medication mistakes:

Getting one drug when you are prescribed another doesn't happen often, thanks to repeated checks by pharmacists, doctors and nurses.

But mistakes do *sometimes* happen—often with catastrophic results.

Example: Two patients hospitalized for heart surgery died after receiving a glucose solution instead of the heart drug that doctors had prescribed.

Self-defense: Before allowing anyone to give you an injection or pill, ask the name of the medication, the reason it was ordered and whether it is absolutely necessary for your health. If the answers you receive fail to make sense to you, ask your primary physician for a clarification.

Fatigued personnel:

Hospital personnel must be clear-headed and well-rested if they are to give patients quality care. Unfortunately, hospital rules and personnel shortages often conspire to force doctors and nurses to work long shifts, sometimes on little or no sleep. One hospital facing a severe shortage of nurses "solved" its problem by having its nurses work *24-hour shifts.* Under such conditions, mistakes are extremely likely.

Self-defense: Whenever possible, schedule surgery and major diagnostic procedures for early in the day—and early in the week—when staff members are freshest.

Inflated or inaccurate bills:

American hospitals are notorious for charging excessive prices—but that's not the half of it. At least half of all hospital bills in this country are wildly inaccurate—and the errors invariably favor the hospital.

To avoid being taken: Do not pay your bill unless you are certain all charges are legitimate. If you discover you have been charged for an item or a service you did not receive, or if you do not understand the bill, contact the hospital and demand a complete explanation.

Unnecessary diagnostic tests:

Beware of any doctor who recommends an expensive diagnostic test and then refers you to a specific testing facility. *Reason:* The doctor may have a financial stake in that facility—and may have found a sneaky way to pad his wallet.

Self-defense: If this situation arises, ask the doctor point-blank if he has a financial stake in the testing facility. If so, or if the doctor declines to answer your question, get another doctor. Such a relationship is unethical—and in several states, at least, is now illegal.

Passive attitude:

People who question everything else in life often are all too willing to blindly accept treatments ordered by medical personnel. Questioning your caregivers is essential, even if you cannot understand the answers. *Reason:* The very fact that you ask questions demonstrates that you expect quality care. *Bonus:* In some cases, a seemingly naive question may provoke a doctor to reconsider a particular course of action, thereby saving money, time, discomfort or even a life.

Bottom line:

Ask any questions that occur to you. Do not worry about alienating your caregivers. Odds are they will not be annoyed. Even if they are,

you're still more likely to receive quality care than someone who silently accepts the hospital's course of action.

Source: Walt Bogdanich, a Pulitzer prize–winning reporter with *The Wall Street Journal.* Bogdanich is the author of *The Great White Lie: How America's Hospitals Betray Our Trust and Endanger Our Lives,* Touchstone, 1230 Avenue of the Americas, New York 10020.

Better Migraine Relief

Aerobic exercise significantly reduces the pain of migraines—while improving the cardiovascular fitness of migraine sufferers. *Possible:* Exercise may also help reduce the frequency, intensity and duration of migraines.

Source: Research led by Donna M. C. Lockett, department of psychology, Carleton University, Ottawa, Ontario, Canada, reported in *Headache,* Box 5136, San Clemente, California 92672.

Heart Attack Self-Defense

Before using CPR, call 911—if an adult is having a heart attack. Doctors used to recommend that trained rescuers give one minute of cardiopulmonary resuscitation before calling the emergency number. *New finding:* Survival and recovery rates are better if 911 is called first. *Important exception:* For children under age eight, a trained rescuer should use proper techniques *before* calling 911. All untrained rescuers should call 911 immediately.

Source: Emergency Cardiac Care Committee and subcommittee, American Heart Association, guidelines for cardiopulmonary resuscitation and emergency cardiac care, reported in *Journal of American Medical Association,* 515 N. State St., Chicago 60610.

How to Alleviate Allergies...Naturally

Drugs are often effective at controlling itching, sneezing, runny nose, and other allergic symptoms. But natural remedies sometimes do the trick *more* effectively. *Included:*

•Varied diet. The effects of food allergies are cumulative—the more you eat, the more you suffer. *Solution:* Eat a variety of foods, and rotate them in your diet to avoid taking them too often.

Example: Instead of having orange juice each morning, eat apples one day, grapefruit another, cereal another, etc.

Even if you are allergic to a particular food, you may be able to eat it and avoid allergic symptoms. *Key:* Eat the food in moderate quantities…and in rotation with other foods.

Note: Eating foods that you are allergic to, especially during the pollen season, can make hay fever worse and decrease the effectiveness of allergy medications.

Recommended: Fish, seeds, and fresh vegetables contain essential fatty acids, which help fight allergies.

•Dietary supplements. *Included:*

Vitamins. Considered nature's antihistamine, vitamin C is often highly effective at reducing allergic symptoms. It works only if taken in sufficient quantities. Consult your doctor for the dosage that's right for you. *Also helpful:* Vitamins B6, A, and E.

Minerals. Calcium and magnesium, selenium and zinc also help alleviate allergic symptoms. Consult your doctor for the proper dosage.

•Fresh air. Avoid airborne pollutants as much as possible—not just pollen, dust, molds, and animal dander. *Included:* Industrial chemicals, solvents, household cleaners, cigarette smoke, perfume, etc.

Source: Marshall Mandell, MD, an allergist and clinical ecologist in private practice in Norwalk, Connecticut. A former assistant professor of allergy at New York Medical College, he specializes in treating allergies by identifying their causes and contributing factors. Using this approach, Dr. Mandell can treat allergies with minimal use of medications.

Fingernails & Toenails— Barometers of Health

Changes in shape or color and other abnormalities in fingernails and toenails can reveal *serious* health problems. *What to watch for:*

•*Bluing of the nail bed and lunula (moon):* Caused by anemia or by silver poisoning. The latter is most common in Asian Indian populations. *Warning:* It can also be caused by some homeopathic medicines that contain silver.

•*Distal onycholysis:* The distal end of the nail (just before the overhang) lifts off the nail bed. Caused by systemic disease, particularly thyroid disease, psoriasis, or fungal infections.

•*Half-and-half nails:* The proximal half of the nail (nearest the body) is white and the distal half is pink. Associated with renal (kidney) trouble.

•*Longitudinal ridging and fragmentation:* Instead of the normal horizontal ridges, there are very thin longitudinal ridges. Fragmentation involves very brittle nails that separate to reveal layers. Both symptoms are caused by hypoparathyroidism (underactive parathyroid gland, which helps to maintain the proper level of calcium in the bloodstream). *Note:* These symptoms can also develop with age.

•*Melanoma:* Skin cancer, characterized by an *isolated* dark band (black, blue, dark brown, or tan) in the nail bed or plate. Especially of concern in light-skinned people. *Note:* Dark-skinned people often develop harmless dark bands in their skin as they age.

•*Muehrcke lines:* Two white, horizontal parallel bands that don't move out with the growth of the nail. Associated with hypoalbuminemia (lower than normal levels of albumin, a protein, in the blood).

•*Spoon-shaped nails:* The nail is concave (curves upward) instead of the normal convex (curves downward). Caused by anemia (lower-than-normal level of red blood cells).

•*Terry's nails:* The proximal part of the nail is white instead of the normal pink, while a narrow band on the distal end is pink. Most commonly associated with cirrhosis of the liver or hypoalbuminemia.

•*Watch glass deformity:* An abnormal curve of the nail that makes it look like a watch glass —the nail broadens towards the tip and curves downward from front to back as well as from side to side. And the tip of the nail and finger or toe become very broad and clubby. Associated with *very* severe lung damage, usually due to emphysema. May also be caused by extreme exposure to asbestos.

• *Yellow nails:* Caused by emphysema and lymphatic diseases associated with lung disease. *Other factors that affect nails:*

• *Acetone.* Used in nail-polish remover, this can leach lipids from the nail plate and make the plate brittle.

• *Age.* Nails become brittle with age. This can sometimes be treated with calcium supplements (in pill form) or increased calcium intake through diet.

• *High fever.* Can cause both ridges and white spots to temporarily grow in the nails.

• *Infection or yeast.* Either condition can cause inflammation of the paronychia (the area around the nail). Generally treated with antibiotics.

• *Injury.* Accidentally banging a finger with a hammer, for instance, can cause a temporary abnormality—blood in the nail bed, cracked or split nail, ridging, or complete removal of the nail. Injury to the matrix (where the nail plate develops) can cause permanent deformity.

• *Medication.* Tetracycline or anti-cancer medications, for instance, can cause nail changes, including bands and streaks of color. Nail growth returns to normal when medication is stopped.

• *Skin conditions.* Psoriasis, Darier's disease (mysterious scaling of the skin), alopecia areata (another mysterious condition that causes a person to shed patches of hair) and other skin disorders can cause changes in the nails such as pitting and ptygeria (when the cuticles grow out with the nail).

Source: Mary Ellen Brademas, MD, chief of dermatology at St. Vincent's Hospital, faculty member of New York University Medical Center and director of the sexually transmitted disease clinic at Bellevue Hospital, all in New York. Dr. Brademas is also in private practice in Manhattan.

Mail-Order Medication

The AARP pharmacy is open to all. You do not have to be a senior citizen to use the mail-order pharmacy of the American Association of Retired Persons. The pharmacy is a full-line

drugstore that carries both prescription medications and over-the-counter items. All orders are sent UPS or first-class mail. *Mailing fee:* One dollar per entire order. For more information or prescription price quotes: 800-456-2277.

Source: *Skinflint News,* 1460 Noell Blvd., Palm Harbor, Florida 34683.

Nasal Decongestant Danger

Older men—especially those with enlarged prostate glands—shouldn't use nasal decongestants or cold medicines containing pseudoephedrine, phenylpropanolamine, or ephedrine. Preparations with these drugs could increase urination problems. The ingredients, sometimes found in drugs prescribed for incontinence, cause contractions of the smooth muscles in the bladder sphincter, toning the muscles for better control. While this poses no problem for women, in males with enlarged prostates, those same muscle contractions can completely block an already impeded urinary tract. *Good news:* The problems stop when the use of the drug stops. Talk to your doctor about treatment if you have congestion.

Source: E. Douglas Whitehead, MD, is a urologist in private practice in New York City, and director of the Prostate Health Program of New York, 785 Park Ave., New York 10021.

Vitamin D vs. Bone Loss

Taking extra vitamin D during the winter months can help minimize bone loss. *Problem:* In the summer months, sunlight causes the skin to produce vitamin D. But from mid-fall to late-spring, the sunlight isn't strong enough for the skin to produce a sufficient amount of the vitamin. Postmenopausal women who take extra vitamin D during this period have significantly less spinal bone loss than women who don't. *Self-defense:* Consume more vitamin D-rich foods such as milk fortified with vitamin D... sardines...salmon...liver...or egg yolks. Or take vitamin D supplements of no more than 200 IU/day.

---

10 Common Health Problems

Many common diseases can be treated quite easily. Others take more effort. There are some *we* can't do anything about—but that go away by themselves. Even though doctors can't cure every disease, there's no harm in seeing a doctor when you aren't feeling right. At the very least, your physician can help you understand what's going on in your body, and advise you on relieving the discomforts.

Colds and flu:

These are caused by viruses, and nothing a doctor gives you will cure them. The infection will run its course by itself—usually within a few days though sometimes it takes several weeks.

Cold clues: If you have congestion, a cough and/or a sore throat, you probably have a cold.

Flu clues: If you have a fever and your muscles feel weak and tired, it's probably flu.

Antibiotics are completely ineffective against viral infections—though patients continue to demand them.

The best we can do is treat the symptoms. Aspirin, acetaminophen, or ibuprofen can relieve pain and fever. *For cough medicines, decongestants, and throat treatments:* Those containing dextromethorphan are most effective.

Bed rest will not make the cold go away any faster, but it might make you feel better in the meantime.

Bladder infections:

Bladder infections affect far more women than men. Because the urethra is shorter in women than in men, germs that live around the anus and vaginal area can travel up to the bladder fairly easily.

Antibiotics generally clear up most bladder infections within a week.

Some people believe baths encourage the spread of germs into the bladder. This has never been proven, but it can't hurt to take showers instead of baths until the infection clears up.

Cranberry juice is a popular folk remedy. It makes the urine more acidic—a hostile environment for germs. But, you have to drink a large amount of juice (a quart or two a day) for it to be effective.

It's hard to find pure cranberry juice—look for it in health food stores. The kind you buy at the supermarket is mostly water and sugar and won't do a thing.

Irritable bowel syndrome:

Irritable bowel syndrome (IBS) is considered the most common digestive complaint. When the intestinal muscles don't function as smoothly as they should, patients may experience constipation, diarrhea, cramps, and bloating, or some combination of the above.

No one really knows what causes IBS...and there's no sure cure. *Helpful:*

• Adding fiber to the diet can be beneficial. Eat lots of fruits and vegetables.

• If you know you're sensitive to certain foods—such as caffeine, other acidic foods, seeds—avoid them.

• Get plenty of exercise.

Also helpful: Low doses of antidepressants. We're not sure why—it may be that they alter nerves in the brain that regulate muscle function.

Lower back pain:

The back is very poorly designed for walking upright. The muscles are too small and weak to support the weight of the upper body, and the discs are easily injured. Ordinary wear-and-tear makes a certain amount of back pain almost inevitable with age.

If you experience acute pain, rest the back as you would any injured area. Applying heat and taking ibuprofen usually helps ease the pain. Most acute backaches subside within a few weeks.

If your problem is chronic, be aggressive. Most doctors don't know much about back pain, so look for one who specializes in backs—and who *doesn't* rush to recommend surgery. Minor complaints can often be helped by exercise programs and physical therapy to strengthen the back.

Psoriasis:

Psoriasis is a condition in which the skin grows more rapidly than normal, causing patches to turn red and flake off.

We don't know what causes psoriasis. Once the condition has erupted, however, any injury or irritation to the skin is likely to result in an outbreak. So psoriasis sufferers should avoid getting sunburned, and wear gloves when doing the dishes or if working with harsh chemicals.

Doctors commonly prescribe cortisone creams, which work by discouraging skin cells from multiplying. But long-term use of cortisone is a bad idea—it will make the skin thin and delicate.

Exposure to ultraviolet light is another fairly common treatment, but it increases the risk of skin cancer.

Best treatment: Tar, applied topically. Tar is a very old remedy. The current bottled solutions are not nearly as messy or smelly as the older kind of solutions. If the sufferer's doctor doesn't know about tar treatment, find a doctor who does.

Panic attacks:

It's very common for patients to complain of pounding heart, dry mouth, sweating, difficulty breathing, and feelings of intense anxiety or fright—for no obvious reason.

Some people are awakened in the night by these attacks—others may experience them in the middle of a meeting. They seem to be most common among young adults.

We don't understand much about panic attacks, except that they're usually harmless. Symptoms are caused by the release of adrenaline, and they subside when the body runs out of adrenaline...usually after 20 or 30 minutes. They're generally not a sign of heart disease. And they don't usually occur often. If the attacks are chronic and interfere with everyday functioning, several medications can help. Check with your doctor.

Impotence:

Not so long ago, impotence was thought to be a psychological problem, and patients were sent to psychiatrists for long, expensive treatments. Now we know that there are many physical causes as well—and that most cases respond to treatment fairly quickly.

Drugs are a common physical cause. Marijuana, alcohol, even smoking can interfere with sexual performance.

Impotence is also a frequent side effect of high blood pressure medication. If you take drugs for high blood pressure, ask your doctor about adjusting the dosage. There are so many different medications that you should be able to find one that doesn't cause this side effect.

Impotence is also associated with diabetes—but only as a long-term complication associated with damage to nerves or arteries.

Psychological causes include boredom, depression and anxiety.

It's rarely necessary to embark on a long, involved course of psychotherapy in order to cure impotence. Often, just understanding that these emotions can contribute to the condition—and that it's temporary—is enough to provide relief. For stubborn cases, sex therapy may be helpful.

Migraine headaches:

Unlike some other kinds of headaches, migraines are *vascular*. Blood vessels in the scalp become highly sensitive, and heartbeats stretch the arterial walls, creating a throbbing pain.

Migraine attacks tend to start during the teen years and decrease as a person gets older. They usually disappear by middle age.

Unless your symptoms are truly peculiar, don't invest a lot of time and money in tests—they probably won't show anything. Fortunately, migraines are treatable. Several drug families—including antidepressants and antihistamines—can be helpful.

Helpful: Standard pain medications, such as acetaminophen or Darvon, will relieve mild pain.

Better: Drugs that stiffen the arteries. Caffeine does this—a few cups of coffee for a minor attack may be effective.

For severe migraine, ergotamine is effective and prescribed by many doctors to be taken at the first sign of a migraine. It can be taken as a pill, suppository, or inhalant, and is sometimes combined with caffeine.

Nausea is a common side effect, so if the pill form makes you nauseous, ask your doctor about experimenting with the other forms.

Insomnia:

The best treatment for insomnia may be to put it in perspective. Very few insomniacs spend a lot of time feeling sleepy during the day. They may be sluggish in the morning, but once they get going they don't feel too bad.

Upsetting: Lying awake in the middle of the night, trying to sleep and feeling frustrated because you can't.

Sleeping pills don't cure insomnia—they just induce poor-quality sleep. And they can be addictive.

Try to view insomnia as simply irritating—not dangerous. If you can't sleep, don't drive yourself crazy about it. Turn on the light and read.

Note: Insomnia can be a symptom of depression. If that's the case, then the underlying problem should be addressed.

Warts:

Warts are viral and contagious—you can catch them from going barefoot in a public place, using someone else's comb or from scratching and spreading your own warts. However, they may not appear until up to a year after exposure.

Though unattractive, warts are not dangerous. They're more common in children than adults—it's possible that we build up resistance as we age.

The vast majority of warts go away by themselves within a year or two. Treatments include freezing with liquid nitrogen, corroding with acid, and burning or electrocoagulation. I prefer liquid nitrogen—it's simple, effective and not very painful.

Source: Family practitioner Michael Oppenheim, MD, who practices in Los Angeles. He is author of *A Doctor's Guide to the Best Medical Care* and *The Complete Book of Better Digestion*, both published by Rodale Press, 33 E. Minor St., Emmaus, Pennsylvania 18098.

Better Blood

Teenagers should be screened for anemia—upon the recommendation of the American Academy of Pediatrics. *Frequency:* Boys, at least once during adolescence...girls, every two or three years. Patients with known risk factors, such as heavy menstruation, poor diet or the heavy use of aspirin which can cause intestinal blood loss may require more frequent screenings. Of the adolescents studied, up to 10% may have iron deficiency anemia.

Recommended: Dietary counseling of all patients, a careful history and a good physical examination. If indicated, a laboratory screening is recommended.

Source: A review of anemia in adolescent athletes led by R. Austin Raunikar, MD, fellow in pediatric cardiology, and Hernan Sabio, MD, professor of pediatrics, at the Medical College of Georgia.

Back Protection

Ninety percent of Americans suffer an episode of severe, disabling back pain at some time in their lives. Of those, *80% recover*, with or without treatment, within a month.

Most of the remaining 20% can now be treated successfully without surgery. But the total cost of back pain in the US is still a staggering $20 billion a year. So it pays to take care of your back.

Good news: Most low back pain is *preventable.*

Back protection principles:

The basics are simple: Keep your back flat, not hunched...straight, not twisted...and supported. Flex and stretch frequently.

Caution: Your back may feel fine until you reach for a pencil you dropped, and—*youch!*

Reason: Back pain occurs when cumulative wear and tear damage from postural strains or improper movement make the back vulnerable to a sudden stressful or unguarded motion.

Most troublesome areas: Bending and reaching. *Solution:* Establish healthy habits of movement to preserve your back. *For best results:*

• Use foresight. Be conscious of your back as you plan each day's activities. Avoid strain and fatigue. Get help when you must move something heavy or awkward.

• Perform a pelvic tilt. To help maintain spinal alignment before initiating *any* movement, pinch the buttocks together, tighten the stomach muscles and rotate the pelvis forward.

•Avoid twisting. A torquing motion stresses the ligaments that hold the disks in place. *Better:* When bending, squatting, lifting, lowering, or reaching, position the feet forward and face the work *first*, then pivot with the feet, turning the entire body as a unit.

•Avoid reaching for overhead objects. When the arms are extended overhead, the back muscles are not able to stabilize the back. *Better:* Use a footstool, step ladder, or long-handled tool for overhead tasks.

•Support objects no higher than the shoulders—and no lower than the knees. Hold objects as close to the body as possible when lifting or lowering. Plan to use intermediate steps.

Examples: Lift a box from the floor to a chair, then to the desk. Rest groceries on the edge of the cart or car trunk before continuing.

•Use the hips, arms and legs to protect the back. When bending forward over a sink, counter or other low surface, bend from the hips, keeping the back straight. Support your body weight with your arms or elbows. Squat before lifting, keeping the back straight and using the powerful leg muscles to propel upward.

•Manage your stress. Emotional stress and psychological factors can contribute to back pain. Dealing with these stresses, therefore, may help control your back pain.

Source: Robert L. Swezey, MD, medical director of the Arthritis and Back Pain Center at the Swezey Institute in Santa Monica, California, and clinical professor of medicine at UCLA. Dr. Swezey's book, *Good News For Bad Backs*, is available by calling 800-350-2998.

Post-Operative Pain Relief

Plan post-operative pain relief with your doctor before surgery. Trap: Post-op pain could promote cancer-cell growth—by suppressing activity of natural killer cells in the immune system. Recent study: In rats injected with a fast-growing cancerous tumor after surgery, cell-killing ability was nearly halved in those not given post-operative painkillers. But those that received morphine showed virtually no difference in killer-cell activity from a control group that had no surgery. Because of immune-system similarities, this research applies to humans, too. Important: Let doctors know at once of any severe post-op pain.

Source: Gayle Page, DNSc, is a post-doctoral research fellow in the departments of psychology and psychiatry at the University of California, Los Angeles.

Free Help for Your Children's Health

If your child needs expensive medical care, the bills often can be handled without going into personal bankruptcy.

There are organizations that make billions of dollars available each year to families who need help with medical expenses. And you don't have to be impoverished to qualify.

Where the money is:

•Private foundations...the most accessible sources.

•Corporations...that often will offer programs to assist employees and their families. Ask your benefits representative or human-resources director if your company has such a program.

•Government agencies...federal, state, and regional awards. Grants often are not made directly to individuals, but are awarded through a nonprofit organization, such as a hospital.

•Associations that educate the public and work to combat specific diseases. Although associations don't usually give financial assistance to individuals, many offer in-kind donations—free services—such as transportation, counseling and medication.

How to apply:

Getting this money is neither quick nor easy. But it's well within the abilities of the average parent...who is willing to invest some time and effort. Steps that need to be taken...

•Research. Your library or local bookstore has guides to foundations, associations and government agencies.

•Make sure your child qualifies. Most common restrictions: Geographic and by disease.

Make a list of organizations where grant requirements fit your child.

•Get information and application materials. Don't call. Send a postcard to each organization on your list, requesting a grant application and guidelines. Be patient—it usually will take three to 10 weeks before you receive a reply.

•Fill out the application. This step may sound difficult, but it's no harder than filling out a college application. After you've put the first application together, you can quickly adapt it to others.

•Read the guidelines carefully. Type, don't hand-write, application materials. And keep a copy of everything you send, so you won't have to start from scratch if something is misplaced. *Typical application includes:*

•A letter or essay explaining why you need the money.

•Copies of recent tax returns. Don't worry— a high income won't necessarily disqualify you, and the information will be kept private.

•Statements from your child's physicians and/ or hospital. *Helpful:* Have your doctor send this statement to you—not directly to the organization you're applying to. That way you can put it all together efficiently…and effectively.

Source: Laurie Blum, cofounder of the Los Angeles–based fundraising firm Blum & O'Hara, and the nation's leading expert on "free money" for health, education, business, etc. She is the author of 16 books on the subject, including *Free Money for Children's Medical and Dental Care* and *Free Money for Childhood Behavioral and Genetic Disorders*, Fireside Books, 1230 Avenue of the Americas, New York 10020.

Most Commonly Asked Questions About Kids' Health Care

Despite the seemingly endless array of childhood ailments, concerned parents often find themselves seeking answers to the same basic questions about their children's health…

•How can I find a good doctor for my child? While a pediatrician is the most obvious choice, family practitioners and internists often make equally good doctors for children.

Interview different types of doctors, then pick one with a pleasant, caring attitude…a willingness to talk directly with your child as well as with you…a clean, orderly office… and a good system for fielding after-hours phone calls. Make sure your child gets along with the doctor and that the doctor accepts your health insurance plan.

Caution: If the doctor belongs to a group practice, ask that you be allowed to make appointments specifically with him/her.

Ask if the doctor can provide you and your child with videotapes, pamphlets, and other educational materials regarding specific health issues. They're a big help when illness strikes —or during puberty.

•Does my child need an X ray? In addition to being costly, X rays, CAT scans, magnetic resonance imaging and other diagnostic tests are typically frightening to children, risky and often unnecessary.

They should be administered only if their findings will have a direct bearing on your child's treatment. If your child has a cough, for example, a chest X ray is generally unnecessary—unless the doctor has reason to suspect a serious lung ailment. Before agreeing to any test, question the doctor thoroughly to make sure it is necessary. Key questions:

•What's the name of the test?

•Why is it necessary?

•What will it reveal that you don't already know?

•What will happen if the test is not performed?

•What are the possible side effects?

•Is a less-invasive test available?

•Are childhood immunizations safe? Most states require that all children be immunized against eight diseases—diphtheria, pertussis (whooping cough), tetanus, measles, mumps, rubella (German measles), poliomyelitis, and Haemophilus influenza type B (bacterial meningitis). These vaccinations, typically administered between the ages of two months and 16 years, are generally quite safe.

Exception: Pertussis. Half of all children who receive this five-dose vaccine develop fever, and one in 310,000 develops mental retardation or another permanent disability. Yet because pertussis is such a serious disease, it is still prudent to have your child immunized.

To minimize risk: Insist that your child receive the recently approved acellular pertussis vaccine. It's less likely to cause dangerous reactions than the old vaccine, which remains in use.

The pertussis vaccine should never be given to any child who is over age six, who has a fever or has already had pertussis. Any child who experiences fever, shock, persistent crying, convulsions, or neurological problems after the first pertussis shot should not receive any of the additional pertussis boosters.

• Is circumcision a good idea? While most doctors now agree that circumcision is not medically necessary, the procedure does seem to have certain benefits.

Compared with uncircumcised males, circumcised males experience fewer urinary-tract infections during infancy and reduced incidence of venereal diseases in adulthood. They also appear less likely to transmit the virus that causes cervical cancer to their female sex partners.

Like any surgical procedure, circumcision has drawbacks, including the possibility of infection, bleeding and—because anesthesia is rarely used—severe pain. Few insurance policies cover the procedure.

How to proceed: Discuss all options with your pediatrician, including the use of anesthesia if you do opt for circumcision…and the possibility of delaying the procedure until your son is older—but not more than one year old. Ultimately, the decision is a personal one.

• My child has recurrent throat infections. Should his/her tonsils be removed? Tonsillectomy is neither necessary nor particularly effective at curing recurrent ear or throat infections, even though doctors often urge surgery.

When it's appropriate: Only if the tonsils become so swollen that they interfere with the child's breathing, or if lab tests indicate the presence of abscesses behind the tonsils.

In all other cases, it's best to treat such infections with antibiotics.

• What about chronic ear infections? Ear infections (otitis media) are especially common among children of smokers. If you smoke—stop. New mothers should try to avoid bottle-feeding their children. Recent research suggests that breast-feeding helps prevent earaches. Beyond this, there's no real consensus on treatment.

The American Academy of Pediatrics recommends use of oral antibiotics (usually amoxicillin), although some of the most recent research casts doubt on their effectiveness. The surgical insertion of drainage tubes through the child's eardrums (tympanostomy) can cause serious complications, including severe infections and hearing loss.

Conservative approach—to discuss with your doctor: At the first sign of pain, give your child acetaminophen (Tylenol) or another non-aspirin painkiller. Every two hours, place two drops of warm (not hot) olive oil into each ear canal. Also helpful: A heating pad held against the ear.

• Do children's hospitals offer better pediatric care than general hospitals? Many parents seem to think so. In most cases, however, the standard of care in children's hospitals is no better than that in general hospitals with good pediatric sections. If your child requires inpatient surgery, pick a hospital that performs that surgery on a routine basis.

• My child's doctor refuses to give me details of my child's medical care. What can I do? Parents sometimes fail to realize that all doctor-patient relationships are private. When your child is very young, of course, you are by necessity intimately involved in all aspects of his/her medical care. As children approach puberty, however, they may wish to keep some aspects of their medical care private. Parents should respect that right.

Source: Charles B. Inlander, president of People's Medical Society, the nation's largest consumer health advocacy organization. He is the coauthor of several books on medical topics, including *Take This Book to the Pediatrician with You,* People's Medical Society, 462 Walnut St., Allentown, Pennsylvania 18102.

Frostbite Remedies

If you can't get indoors, breathe warm air onto the affected area or get it near warm skin. Example: Keep frostbitten hands under clothing and under the armpits. Important: Do not massage frostbitten skin. Rubbing can worsen skin damage even in mild cases of frostbite.

Source: *Johns Hopkins Health After 50,* 550 North Broadway, Suite 1100, Johns Hopkins, Baltimore, Maryland 21205.

Emotional Factors That May Make Some People More Vulnerable To Cancer

A rapidly growing body of research suggests that psychological factors play a role in physical disease. My own research, including studies of patients with malignant melanoma (a virulent and often deadly form of skin cancer), provides strong evidence that cancer is one of these diseases. Its development and progression—or the body's resistance to it—can be affected by emotions and behavior. I call this behavior pattern Type C.

The Type C pattern:

The core of the Type C pattern is a striking lack of emotional expressiveness—especially where anger is concerned. It seems that Type Cs do not express anger—or other emotions such as anxiety, fear, sadness, and even joy—and they are often unaware of even feeling these emotions.

Type Cs tend to be remarkably nice people. They are patient and cooperative. And they are highly focused on meeting other people's needs, while showing little or no concern for their own.

There's nothing wrong with being nice, cooperative, or considerate of others. These are admirable traits. But Type Cs carry this behavior to extremes.

Example I: Ask a Type C, "Will you help me move today?" and he/she will agree without thinking twice—even though he's exhausted and suffering from a sore back.

Example II: Most people would expect to be angry, sad, and/or fearful upon receiving a diagnosis of cancer. But when a Type C who's

newly diagnosed with melanoma is asked what is most upsetting about the situation, a typical response is: I'm not upset personally, but I'm very concerned about how my husband/wife/children will deal with this. I don't know what they will do without me.

For some people, a serene, unflappable approach is a healthy way of coping with the world. But for Type Cs, this unruffled exterior does not arise out of a sense of inner peace. It hides unacknowledged anger, anxiety…even despair.

The roots of Type C behavior:

These findings don't mean Type Cs make themselves sick. People with cancer did not want to get the disease…nor did they give it to themselves…nor do they allow it to happen by not thinking "positively enough." There are no data to support such misconceptions.

Like other human beings, Type Cs have developed their behavior patterns unconsciously, in order to deal with the environment as best they can.

Example: The passiveness of Type Cs is often an adaptive response to growing up in an abusive family. A child may hope to avoid harsh punishment by focusing on whatever the other person wants.

Even in non-abusive homes, many parents unwittingly encourage Type C patterns with messages such as, "Big boys don't cry." Good little girls don't get angry. Children learn from this that their natural responses are bad and should be disregarded or suppressed. Important: It's possible—and healthy—to draw the line at a child's destructive behavior, while still recognizing his right to feel what he feels.

Type C and the body:

Behavior patterns don't cause cancer. They are among the elements that may contribute—along with other factors over a period of time—to predisposing someone to an illness or pushing someone already at risk over the edge. Type C behavior appears to influence physical illness in two major ways…

• Stress. Type Cs tend to stay in stressful situations—such as a bad marriage or frustrating job—longer than other people. Because they don't recognize their emotions, they may not even know they're under stress. But the body knows—it produces stress hormones, including cortisol, which have been shown to suppress the immune system when chronically present in the body.

•Natural opiates. Part of the process of emotional suppression seems to involve production by the body of natural opiates (brain chemicals that have a pain-killing effect similar to artificial drugs like morphine). These opiates hook up with receptors on certain immune cells in the body, giving them the message to "turn off."

Plenty of healthful activities, including exercise, cause these natural opiates to be produced on a temporary basis. But in the case of emotional suppression, the opiates are chronically present...and continue to have a dampening effect on the immune system.

Self-defense:

Recognizing Type C behavior can be empowering. Studies have shown that people who work to reverse destructive behavior patterns can improve their resistance to disease.

I'm not saying that Type Cs should suddenly start going around yelling at everybody in order to become healthier. Behavior patterns can be seen as lying along a continuum. At one end is the Type A person, who is overexpressive of hostility...tense and aggressive... emotionally worked up much of the time. At the other extreme is the underexpressive Type C.

In the middle is a coping style we'll call Type B—relaxed but not passive...capable of meeting his/her own needs as well as responding to others' needs...able to express anger and other emotions appropriately—without lashing out indiscriminately. This flexible coping style seems to be the most health-promoting. If you notice aspects of the Type C pattern in yourself, here are some new options to explore...

•Become more aware of your emotions. They are giving you important information—respect them. You wouldn't run on a painful ankle—you know that would make it worse. Yet we often ignore similar emotional messages...and continue to act in ways that cause us emotional pain.

I strongly recommend therapy as a way for Type Cs to learn about their emotional lives and to cope more effectively. Group therapy can be especially useful—hearing other people talking about their experiences and feelings can help you recognize your own.

If your emotions are a complete blank to you, be alert for slight twinges of discomfort—a clenched jaw, a vague feeling that something isn't right, etc. Ask yourself: *"What happened just before I noticed this sensation?" What other sensations am I experiencing? What do I need right now? What are my options for dealing with this situation?*

•Say "no" more often—and ask for support when you need it. Challenge the belief that asserting yourself will lead to rejection—or that the consequences of rejection would be unbearable.

•Learn to express anger and other emotions in a constructive way. It's true that it isn't always in your best interest to express yourself—there are times when getting angry may cost you your job or cause you to be physically attacked.

But there are also situations in which anger can help you get what you want. Various kinds of assertiveness training can help you learn to stand up for your rights without blowing your top all the time. Have a range of responses available so that your automatic reaction is no longer, "What can I do for you?"

•Learn to relax. Regular practice of relaxation and body awareness techniques can strengthen immune response and enhance sensory awareness...helpful in learning to identify what you feel.

Source: Psychologist Lydia Temoshok, PhD, director of the US Military's Behavioral Medicine Research Program on HIV/AIDS. A former faculty member at the University of California School of Medicine, she is the coauthor of *The Type C Connection: The Behavioral Links to Cancer and Your Health,* Random House, Inc., 201 E. 50 St., New York 10022.

Genetic Predisposition To Heart Disease or Cancer

If there is a history of heart disease or cancer in your family, there's a straightforward way to cut your risk by up to 90%, no matter how strong your genetic predisposition to these killers.

Like many American families, my family was hard hit by heart disease.

My father was just 12 years old when his father died of a heart attack…and I was only 22 when the same fate befell my dad. By the time I reached my mid-30s, I too seemed headed for an early death. I was overweight, I had Type II diabetes and my cholesterol level was elevated. According to the statistics of the Framingham heart study, my risk of a heart attack was 175% of normal. ("Normal" in our society is a 75% chance of having a heart attack in one's lifetime.)

I decided to try to cut my disease risk by adopting the 30%-fat diet recommended by the American Heart Association. Problem: The diet had little effect on my excess weight, diabetes and cholesterol levels.

Reversing the inevitable:

At this point, I immersed myself in scientific literature and developed an alternative approach to this problem. I cut my fat intake all the way down to 10% of calories and adopted a program of regular exercise and stress control. In a few months I lost 45 pounds, my diabetes vanished and my cholesterol level fell so low that my risk of heart attack wasn't just normal, it was below that of someone with no family history of heart disease. My risk of heart disease fell 97%.

Bonus: I felt more relaxed and energetic than I had in years.

Here are the most common questions people ask me…

What exactly is involved with your "10% solution"? Several things. First, regular aerobic exercise. I recommend working out at least four times a week, for at least 45 minutes each time. Next, stress control. Learn to strike a balance between self, friends, family, and work. Stop smoking. Get plenty of sleep. Note: I don't mean to gloss over these nondietary recommendations because they're all-important. But the issue of fat intake is more critical—and more often misunderstood.

What's it like to eat a 10%-fat diet? Most people think it must be terribly Spartan. In fact,

while you will have to eliminate certain foods from your diet, you can continue to enjoy many of the foods you currently eat. The key is learning the subtle art of food substitution.

Illustration: A meal of broiled chicken, peas in a cream sauce, baked potato with sour cream and a dish of ice cream contains a whopping 55 grams of fat. But a similar meal of baked skinless chicken, steamed peas, baked potato with nonfat sour cream, and a dish of nonfat frozen yogurt contains only nine grams. Once you get used to low-fat eating, this meal is just as satisfying—and much more healthful.

But I love fatty foods. I don't think I have the willpower to eat as you recommend. What can I do? Oddly enough, while it's quite hard to eat a little less fat, it's actually quite easy to eat a lot less.

Reason: If you cut back only to, say, 20% or 30% fat, your appetite for rich, fatty foods never goes away. Consequently, every meal becomes a test of your willpower. But after five to six weeks on a 10%-fat diet, your taste buds actually begin to change. Fatty foods you once enjoyed will begin to taste too greasy while foods that once seemed impossibly bland will become tastier. Bonus: Because you'll be eating so little fat, you'll easily lose excess weight—while never feeling hungry or deprived.

Are any foods prohibited? I divide foods into three categories—those to eat as often as you like, those to eat occasionally and those to avoid.

Emphasize:

•Breads made without oils, butter or margarine and any other whole grains or grain products.

•Pasta made without oil or eggs.

•Cereals free of fat, salt, or sugar.

•Fruits, fruit juices, and vegetables (except avocados and olives, which are too fatty).

•Peas, beans, lentils, and other legumes.

•Nonfat dairy products.

•Tofu and other soy products.

•Egg whites.

•Lean meats, preferably fish or fowl. Up to 4 ounces daily of fish, clams, oysters or mussels or white meat of chicken or turkey (without skin). If you want red meat, choose round steak, flank steak, or other lean cuts.

Eat occasionally:

• Sugar, sucrose, molasses, and other sweeteners.

• Breads and cereals made with added fat.

• Pastas made with eggs.

• Low-sodium soy sauce.

• Low-fat dairy products (one-percent fat).

• Olive or canola oil…use very sparingly.

• Caffeinated drinks…no more than two cups daily.

• Lobster, crab, and shrimp. They contain too much cholesterol to be eaten regularly.

• Smoked or charbroiled foods. They contain a potent carcinogen.

Never eat:

• Fatty meats, including organs, cold cuts, and most cuts of beef and pork. Poultry skin is pure fat.

• Meat fat, butter, hydrogenated vegetable oils, lard, and margarine.

• Nondairy creamers and other sources of tropical oils like palm or coconut.

• Mayonnaise.

• Polyunsaturated fat, including corn oil and most vegetable oils.

• Whole dairy products, including cream, whole milk, and sour cream.

• Nuts (except chestnuts, which may be eaten regularly).

• Salt or salty foods.

• Egg yolks.

• Fried foods.

How can I tell how much fat I'm getting? At first you'll need to keep a food diary. Jot down the calorie and fat content of each food you eat. At the end of each day, calculate the all-important fat percentage.

Procedure: Multiply your total daily intake of fat (in grams) by nine (the number of calories in each fat gram), then divide this number by your total daily calories. If this number is above 10%, you must find ways to cut out more fat. After several weeks, you'll be able to judge your fat intake without using the diary.

How about polyunsaturated fats? Margarine, corn oil, and other sources of polyunsaturated fat have long been touted as safe alternatives to saturated fats. In fact, they are far less healthful than once thought—and may be more harmful than saturated fats.

Recent finding: Polyunsaturated fat not only raises levels of LDL (bad) cholesterol, but also reduces levels of HDL (good) cholesterol. And now it looks as if polyunsaturated fat promotes the growth of cancer cells.

Cancer rates in the US began to rise just about the time polyunsaturated fats began to replace saturated fats in the American diet. To be safe: Limit your intake of all fats—saturated and polyunsaturated fats in particular.

Are there any immediate benefits to eating less fat? Absolutely. Each time you eat a fatty meal, your red blood cells become "sticky." They clump together, moving slowly through the circulatory system and clogging up capillaries. This deprives your brain of oxygen, resulting in grogginess. But when you stop eating such meals, your red cells return to normal, and your capillaries open up. Result: You feel calmer and more energetic, you sleep better and your complexion improves. And at the same time a subtler but even more important change is taking place within your body. The fatty plaques inside your arteries shrink and your immune system grows stronger.

Doesn't a vegetable-rich diet raise your intake of pesticide residues? No. The pesticide content of fruits and vegetables is well below that of meat—which comes from animals raised on pesticide-sprayed crops. But to minimize your intake of potential toxins, buy organic produce.

Source: Raymond Kurzweil, chairman of Kurzweil Applied Intelligence, a Waltham, Massachusetts–based computer manufacturer. He is author of *The 10% Solution for a Healthy Life: How to Eliminate Virtually All Risk of Heart Disease and Cancer,* Crown Publishers, 201 E. 50 St., New York 10022.

Chiropractic Medicine Is Back

While recently, chiropractic medicine was lumped with such offbeat practices as crystal healing and shamanism—it has emerged as an effective medical therapy and has gained acceptance by mainstream physicians and the public. What it is…

Many perceptions of chiropractic medicine are tainted by images of mysterious bone manipulations and outrageous claims for cures of serious illnesses.

Its responsible practitioners, however, explain chiropractic medicine in less sensational terms. The chiropractic approach treats the whole person, rather than just a particular injury or illness. It relies on neither drugs nor surgery and seeks to take advantage of your body's self-healing processes and capacities for self-regulation.

Chiropractors also promote good body mechanics, nutrition, and healthy emotional relationships with others. These factors combined, they have found, play a major role in healing and keeping us well.

A typical visit:

Most people initially seek a chiropractor because of a musculoskeletal problem—back pain, chronic muscle ache, the proverbial "crick" in the neck. What to expect:

Chiropractors rely heavily on extensive patient histories. Your chiropractor will want to know about your work and exercise habits and how long you've had your particular problem. Then, he/she will examine you thoroughly, just as a typical physician would do.

You may also be X-rayed and have blood taken. A chiropractor emphasizes the importance of diagnosis. His first task is to determine the nature of your complaint and, if it's beyond the scope of his practice, to refer you immediately to an appropriate specialist.

Should the chiropractor decide to treat you, he may employ massage techniques designed to work on soft tissue and muscle.

He may use ice packs if there's swelling.

He may use ultrasound, a device that stimulates muscles and nerves through painless electronic vibration.

If your condition has impeded some movement, a chiropractor may manipulate nearby joints to restore the normal range of motion.

He will almost certainly advise you about exercise. If you incurred the problem working or during some other physical activity,

he'll have suggestions for less stressful ways of moving your body to prevent a recurrence.

It is, of course, spinal manipulation and adjustment for which chiropractic medicine is best known.

The "backbone" of chiropractic therapy stems from the theory that our spines are vitally integral to our health. Through manipulation, the spinal column can energize the nervous system and normalize body functions.

Spinal manipulation, however, is not always a necessity in chiropractic treatment. And before such treatment, a responsible chiropractor will explain some potential problems possible with spinal adjustment.

Finding a chiropractor:

The first step is to get a referral from someone you know. If you don't know anyone who has visited a chiropractor, call your local chiropractic society for suggestions. Most chiropractors are members of the American Chiropractic Association in Washington, DC.

Chiropractors are certified as chiropractic physicians in about half the states in the US. Being recognized as competent professionals in the medical community has been a longtime goal.

A good chiropractor should…

Do a health history and physical as part of your initial consultation.

Be trained to do spinal adjusting. You should ask before any treatment is given.

Be able to diagnose and, if necessary, refer you to the correct specialist.

Release you when you are well without pressuring you for follow-up treatment.

Like any area of health care, chiropractic medicine has its share of ambulance chasers and unscrupulous types. As a potential chiropractic patient, you should be wary of chiropractors who:

• Insist upon X rays, even if they don't seem to be indicated by your problem.

• Make "instant" diagnoses.

• Schedule weekly or monthly visits without a clear explanation about their necessity.

• Are reluctant or unwilling to refer you to other medical authorities or profess to be able to cure a suspiciously wide range of illnesses and injuries.

Source: James Winterstein, DC, chiropractic radiologist and president of The National College of Chiropractic, 200 E. Roosevelt Rd., Lombard, Illinois 60148. He is also president of the Council on Chiropractic Education in Des Moines.

The Hidden Enemy

Lead levels reported by your local water supplier may not accurately reflect the lead in the water in your home. To have your water —or soil or china—tested for lead, contact your state's certification office for a list of state-certified laboratories. To obtain a list of state certification offices, call the EPA Hotline (800-426-4791). Tests cost about $15.

Source: Environmental Protection Agency, 401 M St. SW, Washington, DC 20460.

Laundry Detergents Scare

Ultra-concentrated laundry detergents—liquid and powder—can burn the skin if used incorrectly, we hear from Dr. Jeffrey Weinstein. Danger: They may not wash out of fabrics completely. Perspiration can reactivate them, leading to chemical burns. Self-defense: Add detergent after the machine fills with water… and measure carefully. If a reaction occurs: Take a cool shower…apply cool compresses…call your doctor if it persists for more than a day.

Source: Jeffrey Weinstein, DO, is a general practitioner in Old Bridge, New Jersey.

Beware of Fluorosis

Too much fluoride causes fluorosis—a permanent discoloration in children's teeth. The biggest risk is for children who live in areas that have fluoride in the water and who ingest fluoride through vitamin supplements and fluoride toothpaste. Children under age two should not receive any fluoride supplements …most older children do not need fluoride supplements, nor should they use rinses unless otherwise directed by their dentists…monitor children's use of fluoride toothpaste—give only sparing amounts, and make sure they spit out the foam. Important: Have your tap water tested to determine its fluoride content…then discuss an appropriate fluoride strategy with your child's dentist.

Source: Steven Grossman, DDS, is co-chief of pediatric dentistry at New York's Lenox Hill Hospital and assistant professor of pediatric dentistry, New York University Dental School.

Prescription Trap

Standard drug doses are often higher than necessary, especially for older patients with chronic illnesses. Risks: Side effects…and excessive costs. Self-defense: When starting to take a new drug, ask your doctor if it would be prudent to begin with less than the usual dosage. This dosage can then be gradually increased, as necessary, without crossing into the toxic range.

Source: Marvin M. Lipman, MD, a clinical professor of medicine at New York Medical College, writing in *Consumer Reports on Health,* 101 Truman Ave., Yonkers, New York 10703.

What a Good Dermatologist Does

Dermatologic emergencies are rarer than other types of medical emergencies, but as anyone who's ever suffered a sudden rash or allergic reaction knows, they're not unheard of.

For this reason, a good dermatologist is accessible 24 hours a day, seven days a week— preferably via a professional answering service (answering machines are sometimes unreliable). Rule: After-hours calls should be returned within four hours.

Of course, accessibility isn't the only mark of a good dermatologist. Other considerations:

•Proper delegation of work. As a cost-cutting measure, some dermatologists are now leaving much of their routine office work to nurses or assistants. Problem: Assistants may lack the training to perform these procedures safely and effectively.

I believe nurses can safely take patient histories, check blood pressure, change dressings and perform the most basic procedures, such as opening pimples and administering ultraviolet treatments.

The bulk of work, however, including chemical peels and collagen injections, should be performed by the dermatologist. You're paying for a dermatologist's expertise…don't let yourself be exploited.

•Institutional affiliation. Besides being certified by the American Board of Dermatology, first-rate dermatologists are affiliated with a medical school or major hospital—or both. Such institutional affiliations confirm that the dermatologist is a skilled practitioner, up-to-date on the latest methods of diagnosis and treatment. It also indicates that he/she is in good standing within the medical community.

Bonus: If necessary, patients of a hospital-affiliated dermatologist can often get admitted to the hospital faster and with fewer headaches than patients of an unaffiliated practitioner.

•Medical philosophy. By the time certain forms of skin cancer are detected, it is often too late—they've spread and become fatal. Therefore, it's absolutely essential that dermatologists stress preventive care.

However, simply urging patients to wear sunscreen or avoid the sun is not enough. A top-notch dermatologist listens to patients' questions, then explains all aspects of prevention—how the sun damages the skin, for example, and how best to use protective clothing and sunscreen.

As an extra precaution, your dermatologist should offer a total surface examination of your skin. Such an exam, performed periodically, catches melanoma and other dangerous lesions in their earliest stages—when treatment is still effective.

Cost: $115 to $125 (often included in the price of a routine office visit). Note: Surface exams should be performed annually on adults with especially fair skin, every three years or so on those with darker skin. Your dermatologist should suggest what's most appropriate for you.

•Cost-consciousness. Like most doctors, dermatologists receive free drug samples from pharmaceutical salespeople. A thoughtful practitioner passes these samples along to patients, saving patients the needless expense and aggravation of filling their own prescriptions.

Source: Neal B. Schultz, MD, a dermatologist in private practice in New York City. Dr. Schultz is on staff at Mt. Sinai Hospital and Lenox Hill Hospital in New York City.

Food/Drug Interaction Dangers

Milk/tetracycline: Calcium in dairy products chemically binds to the antibiotic, inhibiting absorption. Avoid dairy foods one hour before and after taking the drug.

Broccoli/warfarin (sold as Coumadin and others): Foods rich in vitamin K (also lettuce, cabbage and spinach) neutralize the effectiveness of the anticoagulant. Consume these foods in moderation when taking the drug.

Cheese/MAO inhibitors (Marplan, Nardil, Parnate): Can cause high blood pressure, headaches, palpitations, nausea, and vomiting.

Source: *University of Texas Lifetime Health Letter,* 1100 Holcombe Blvd., Houston 77030.

Smoking: The Sobering Facts

By now, most Americans are well aware that smoking causes lung cancer.

But tobacco is a far bigger villain than most of us could ever imagine. Cigarettes, pipes, cigars, snuff, and chewing tobacco kill more than 434,000 Americans each year—accounting for almost one out of five premature deaths in this country.

Lung cancer is just the first in a long and harrowing litany of tobacco-related problems. *Other tobacco dangers:*

• Addictiveness. While some people have likened the addictive potential of nicotine to that of heroin, the good news is that tens of millions of people have been *trying to* quit smoking.

• Back pain. Smoking is probably a major risk factor in recovery from back pain (the leading cause of worker disability in the US) because poor oxygen levels of those who smoke prevent lumbar disks from being adequately oxygenated.

• Bladder cancer. Smoking causes 40% of all cases of bladder cancer, accounting for more than 4,000 new cases annually.

• Breast cancer. Women who smoke are 75% more likely to develop breast cancer than are nonsmoking women.

• Cervical cancer. Up to one-third of all cases of cervical cancer—7,000 new cases a year—are directly attributable to smoking. Women who smoke are four times more likely to develop the disease than are nonsmoking women.

• Childhood respiratory ailments. Youngsters exposed to parents' tobacco smoke have six times as many respiratory infections as kids of nonsmoking parents. Smokers' children also face an increased risk of cough, chronic bronchitis, and pneumonia.

• Diabetes. Smoking decreases the body's absorption of insulin. Also: Smoking exacerbates the damage of small blood vessels in the eyes, ears, and feet of diabetics.

• Drug interactions. Smokers need higher than normal dosages of certain drugs, including theophylline (asthma medication), heparin (used to prevent blood clotting), propranolol (used for angina and high blood pressure), and medications for depression and anxiety.

• Ear infections. Children of smokers face an increased risk of otitis media (middle ear infection).

• Emphysema. Smoking accounts for up to 85% of all deaths attributable to emphysema (chronic obstructive pulmonary disease).

• Esophageal cancer. Smoking accounts for 80% of all cases of esophageal cancer, which each year kills 15,000 Americans.

• Fires. Smoking is the leading cause of fires in homes, hotels and hospitals. The toll is astronomical in terms of suffering and of economic loss.

• Gastrointestinal cancer. Preliminary research indicates that smoking at least doubles the risk of cancer of the stomach and duodenum—the portion of the small intestine just downstream from the stomach.

• Heart disease. Smokers are up to four times more likely to develop cardiovascular disease than nonsmokers. Mechanism: Carbon monoxide and other poison gases in tobacco smoke replace oxygen on the blood cells, promote coronary spasm and cause accumulation of clot-producing platelets.

• Infertility. Couples in which at least one member smokes are more than three times more likely to have trouble conceiving than nonsmoking couples.

Explanation: Tobacco smoke interferes with the implantation of a fertilized egg within the uterus. It reduces the number and quality of sperm cells in a man's ejaculate and raises the number of abnormal sperm cells…and increases a man's risk of penile cancer. Women who smoke are more likely to miscarry or deliver prematurely than nonsmoking women. Some scientists now theorize that toxins in the bloodstream of pregnant smokers pass through the placenta to the fetus, sowing the seeds for future cancers.

• Kidney cancer. Smoking causes 40% of all cases of kidney cancer.

• Laryngeal cancer. Smokers who smoke more than 25 cigarettes a day are 25 to 30 times more likely to develop cancer of the larynx than nonsmokers.

• Leukemia. In addition to tobacco smoke condensate, better known as tar, tobacco smoke contains several powerful carcinogens, including the organic chemical benzene and a radioactive form of the element polonium, both of which are known to cause leukemia.

• Low birth weight. Women who smoke as few as five cigarettes daily during pregnancy face a significantly greater risk of giving birth to an unnaturally small, lightweight infant.

•Mouth cancer. Tobacco causes the vast majority of all cancers of the mouth, lips, cheek, tongue, salivary glands and even tonsils. Men who smoke, dip snuff or chew tobacco face a 27-fold risk of these cancers. Women smokers—because they have tended to use less tobacco—face a six-fold risk.

•Nutrition. People who smoke tend to have poorer nutrition than do nonsmokers. People who smoke also have lower levels of HDL (good cholesterol).

•Occupational lung cancer. Although a nonsmoker's risk of lung cancer increases six times due to prolonged occupational exposure to asbestos, that risk jumps to 92 times in an asbestos worker who smokes.

•Osteoporosis. Women who smoke experience menopause on an average of five to 10 years earlier than nonsmokers, causing a decline in estrogen production—and thinning bones—at an earlier age.

•Pharyngeal (throat) cancer. Last year cancer of the pharynx killed 3,650 Americans—and the vast majority of these deaths resulted directly from smoking.

•Premature aging. Constant exposure to tobacco smoke prematurely wrinkles the facial skin and yellows the teeth and fingernails.

•Recovery from injury or surgery. Smokers have delayed wound and bone healing. They also have a greater risk of complications from surgery, including pneumonia (due to weaker lungs) as well as a longer hospital stay.

•Stroke. Smoking doubles the risk of stroke among men and women. Special danger: In women who smoke and use oral contraceptives, the risk of stroke is ten-fold.

•Tooth loss. Use of snuff or chewing tobacco causes gum recession and tooth abrasion, two frequent contributors to tooth loss.

Source: Alan Blum, MD, family physician, department of family medicine, Baylor College of Medicine, Houston. Dr. Blum is the founder and president of Doctors Ought to Care (DOC), c/o department of family medicine, Baylor College of Medicine, 5510 Greenbriar, Houston 77005, an anti-smoking group long-recognized for its service to public health.

Asbestos Attack

Beware of loose fibers flaking from pipe insulation or ceiling tiles. It could be asbestos, a known cause of lung and bowel cancer—as well as noncancerous lung diseases. One step ahead: Place several fibers in water. If they do not dissolve, it could be asbestos. Have it examined and—if necessary—removed by a certified professional.

Source: *The Washington Post.*

Shorter People Seem To Live Longer

A larger body appears to put greater strains on the body's systems, according to preliminary studies by Dennis Miller, PhD, professor of economics, Baldwin-Wallace College in Berea, Ohio. Among Major League baseball players, the average life expectancy of those 6-foot-3 and taller was 66 years, while the average for players 5-foot-7 and shorter was 74. The average person lives 1.2 years less for each inch over 5-foot-3, based on a sampling of 1,600 people who died natural deaths. Surprising: Men and women of the same height have about the same life expectancy.

Natural Remedies For A Stuffy Nose

Chinese ephedra—Ephedra sinica—is an ancient medicinal herb used as a bronchodilator and a stimulant, we hear from Marvin Schweitzer, ND. The source of ephedrine—predecessor of pseudoephedrine, the active ingredient in Sudafed —this dried herb comes in pill form, or works well when you drink it as tea. Caution: No more than one cup every four hours. Also helpful: Bioflavonoids—available at vitamin and health-food stores. Take one or two capsules...stuffiness should clear up in about 20 minutes.

Important: Check with your doctor before using. Ephedra is not for use by those with hyperthyroidism or prostate disease.

Source: Marvin Schweitzer, ND, is a naturopath with the Center for Healing Arts, in Orange, Connecticut.

Painkillers Before Surgery

Painkillers before surgery cut postoperative pain in half—and lessen the need for medication during recovery.

Reason: Surgery sensitizes spinal-cord cells, which transmit pain impulses. Taking pain-killers before surgery prevents the sensitization of the cells—making post-surgical pain less intense.

Source: Eighteen-month study of surgical patients, led by Joel Katz, MD and Alan Sandler, MD, of the University of Toronto, reported in *The Medical Post*, 777 Bay St., Toronto, Ontario M5W 1A7.

Sudden Vision Loss

Sudden vision loss may occur when people with high blood pressure and a history of glaucoma or optic nerve strokes take hypertension medications at night.

Problem: Patients often take these drugs at bedtime to avoid dizziness...but doing so can cause a drop in blood pressure that can lead to gradual or sudden vision loss.

Safer: Ask your doctor about taking these medications in the morning or at midday.

Source: Sohan Singh Hayreh, MD, PhD, professor of ophthalmology and director of the Ocular Vascular Unit, University of Iowa, Iowa City.

2

The Smarter Traveler

Health Hazards of Flying

Although crashing is the most obvious and dramatic threat faced by airline passengers, the risk of going down is so small as to be almost negligible. *More realistic threats:*

•Dry/oxygen-deficient air. Air inside an airliner cabin contains only 2% to 20% of normal relative humidity—and about 25% less oxygen—than air on the ground. Cabin air is about as thin as the air atop a peak 6,000 to 8,000 feet high.

For most passengers, dry, oxygen-poor air presents no particular problems beyond dry skin and thirst. But for those afflicted with certain chronic cardiovascular and respiratory ailments—especially heart disease, asthma, and bronchitis—cabin air can be life-threatening. *To avoid trouble:*

•Drink at least one glass of bottled water for each hour you're aloft.

•Avoid alcohol, coffee, tea, colas, and other beverages with a diuretic effect.

•Sit with your legs elevated to prevent blood clots in your lower legs—a real possibility if flight-induced dehydration is severe enough to cause your blood to pool and thicken.

•If you begin to feel breathless or faint while flying, ask a flight attendant for oxygen. Federal law requires airliners to keep oxygen tanks on board for just such an emergency. If your breathing difficulty persists, ask if there's a doctor on board.

•Reduced air pressure. As an airliner climbs to its cruising altitude, air pressure inside the cabin falls. Most passengers recognize this phenomenon by the familiar "popping" effect that occurs when air that's inside the ears is squeezed out. Unfortunately, not all the effects of reduced air pressure are as benign. *Dangers:*

•Severe intestinal gas, toothache and—far worse—sudden hemorrhaging of stomach ulcers, ovarian cysts, or surgical incisions.

•Reduced air pressure can also cause the bends in scuba divers who fly too soon after diving. And, a boy wearing a plaster cast developed gangrene when air trapped beneath the cast expanded and cut off circulation in his arm.

To avoid trouble: Wear loose-fitting pants while flying, and avoid beans and other gas-producing foods for several hours before take-off. If you suspect you have any loose fillings, have them repaired before your departure. If you've been diagnosed with ulcers or ovarian cysts, or if you've recently had surgery, consult a doctor before flying.

Do not fly with a plaster cast. Never fly within 12 hours of scuba diving (24 hours if you've dived below 30 feet or have been diving for several days).

•Contaminated air. Long notorious for poor ventilation and stale air, airline cabins have gotten even stuffier in recent years.

In the interest of cost-cutting, cabin air on most flights is now being recirculated for 12 minutes at a time.

In the past, cabin air was recirculated for only three minutes at a time before fresh air was pumped in.

Result: Cabin air is depleted of oxygen and laden with disease-causing germs, carbon dioxide, carbon monoxide, and other contaminants—especially on flights where smoking is permitted.

Stale, contaminated air can cause coughing, shortness of breath and headaches, as well as eye infections, colds, the flu and even lung cancer.

To avoid trouble: Use a saline nasal spray to keep your nostrils clean and moist (the greater the moisture in your nostrils, the more effective they are at filtering contaminants from the air). On smoking flights, sit as far as possible from smokers.

•Radiation. Modern airliners fly in the upper reaches of the atmosphere, where cosmic and solar radiation is particularly intense. The longer and more frequent your flights, the greater your exposure. In most cases, this extra exposure causes no apparent problems. Under certain conditions, however, it can cause birth defects, infertility, and cancer.

To play it safe: Pregnant women should avoid flying during the first trimester, when rapidly dividing cells in the fetus are especially vulnerable to radiation.

Persons who spend more than 11 hours a week on an airplane should monitor their radiation exposure with a radiation film badge (dosimeter) worn at all times while aloft.

Frequent flyers should have regular check-ups by a doctor who specializes in aviation medicine.

For a list of flight doctors in your area, contact the Aerospace Medical Association at 703-739-2240 in Arlington, Virginia.

Source: Farrol S. Kahn, founder of the Aviation Health Institute in Oxford, England, and author of *Why Flying Endangers Your Health: Hidden Health Hazards of Air Travel*, Aurora Press, Box 573, Santa Fe, New Mexico 87504.

Better Car-Rental Rates

Quote the advertised discount directly from the company's ad when calling the reservation number. *Problem:* Reservation agents often will not volunteer the best available price up front. *Helpful:* Mention the promotion's discount code, usually listed in small print beneath the boldly displayed rate, or in the description of the terms and conditions of the rental.

Source: Ed Perkins, editor, *Consumer Reports Travel Letter*, 101 Truman Ave., Yonkers, New York 10703.

Airfare-Bargain Traps

Airfare "bargains" are often not what they seem. *Example:* One airline recently offered a discount on companion tickets, but the base fare rate was higher than normal. *Self-defense:* Find a smart travel agent with access to reservation computers that can track prices...and delay buying a ticket until 14 days before your flight, *except during holiday periods.* For holiday travel, book early to be sure of getting a seat. Insist that your travel agent continue to inform you about all deals that become available to your destination.

Source: Herbert J. Teison, editor, *Travel Smart*, 40 Beechdale Rd., Dobbs Ferry, New York 10522.

Best Places to See Animals in the US

•Alaska Zoo. The northernmost zoo in the world. Includes just about every species of animal that can survive Alaska's cold arctic climate…from the Glacier Blue Bear to the Bearded Musk Ox. The only species that aren't native to Alaska are an Asian and an African elephant—one paints pictures sold in the gift shop while the other is learning to play harmonica and drums.
Alaska Zoo, 4731 O'Malley Rd., Anchorage 99516. 907-346-3242.

•Audubon Park and Zoological Garden. Situated right along the Mississippi River. *Outstanding:* Louisiana Swamp Exhibit complete with boardwalks, docks, bridges, lush tropical gardens and the world's only known family of white alligators.
Audubon Park and Zoological Garden, 6500 Magazine St., New Orleans 70118. 504-861-2537.

•International Wildlife Park (also known as the Bronx Zoo). Situated on 265 acres bordering the Bronx River in New York City, it is the largest urban zoo in the United States. More than 4,000 animals are displayed here in both indoor and outdoor naturalistic habitats. *Highlights:* JungleWorld, Himalayan Highlands, Wild Asia and World of Birds.
The Bronx Zoo/International Wildlife Park, Fordham Rd. and Bronx River Pkwy., Bronx, New York 10460. 718-367-1010.

•Brookfield Zoo. Situated on 215 acres surrounding Indian Lake in a suburb of Chicago. Features more than 2,500 animals. *Highlights:* Tropic World, Aquatic Bird House, Seven Seas Panorama, Habitat Africa! and the Walkabout in Australia House.
Brookfield Zoo, 3300 Golf Rd., Brookfield, Illinois 60513. 708-485-0263.

•Busch Gardens. A zoo and amusement park in one. Last year it added The Myombe Reserve—The Great Ape Domain, the most state-of-the-art Gorilla exhibit in the world. The animals are fed right up next to the viewing window and the setting is a simulated rain forest complete with mist swirling around.
Busch Gardens, 3000 Busch Blvd., Tampa, Florida 33674. 813-987-5082.

•San Diego Zoo. Constructed on two levels —"mesas" and "canyons"—connected by moving sidewalks. *Highlights:* Australian koalas, wild Przewalski's horses from Mongolia, rare Sichuan takins from China, long-billed New Zealand kiwis, and the world's largest collection of parrots and parrot-like birds.
The San Diego Zoo, Zoo Place and Park Blvd., San Diego, California 92122. 619-234-3153.

Source: Tim O'Brien, author of *Where the Animals Are: A Guide to the Best Zoos, Aquariums and Wildlife Sanctuaries in North America*, The Globe Pequot Press, Box 833, Old Saybrook, Connecticut 06475.

Great Vacations That Won't Break the Family Budget

Family vacations can be more than just fun in the sun. Trips that combine adventure, learning, meeting new people, and experiencing new cultures are enriching in many ways. And vacations that bring all this together can be the most inexpensive.

Involve the whole family in vacation planning…particularly the kids. It helps them grow and learn. And people won't feel forced to go somewhere they'd rather not be.
Possibilities:*

•Nature hikes and bird watching. Most national parks and many state and local parks offer wildlife tours headed by experienced guides.

•Festivals and fairs. There's hardly a city in the country that doesn't have at least one annual celebration—from Mardi Gras in New Orleans to the Poteet Strawberry Festival in Poteet, Texas. Most feature music, local delicacies, and educational exhibits.

•Museum field trips.

•City walking tours. Sightsee at your own pace on self-guided tours that highlight architecturally significant buildings, historical sites and other points of interest.

•Cemetery tours. Historically educational as well as fascinating. Not just for the ghoulish.

•Factory tours. Many factories, both large and small, offer formal and informal tours.

Bonus: Many finish with free samples of the factory's product. Contact the company di-

*For more information on a particular vacation, contact the local state or city tourism bureau or the local chamber of commerce. Listings, including toll-free phone numbers, are available at most libraries.

rectly or call the local chamber of commerce for a listing of factories that run tours.

• Washington, DC. All government-run museums and monuments are admission-free, making the nation's capital a bargain traveler's paradise.

• Hostels. Now open to families, they offer hotel-style lodging at a fraction of the cost of a typical hotel.

• Budget hotels. Many hotel chains now cater to families. If you know where to look, you can stay at a wonderful hotel for very little money.

Source: Paige Palmer, author of 15 travel books, including *The Senior Citizen's Guide to Budget Travel in the United States and Canada*, Pilot Books, 103 Cooper St., Babylon, New York 11702.

Easier Travel With Children

Many hotels have begun catering to families with infants and children. Many will allow up to two children to stay free in their parents' room. Also: Rooms are childproofed and kits with toilet-lid locks, night lights, and door alarms are often available to parents…changing tables have been installed in all (men's and women's) public rest rooms…diaper pails, strollers, and cribs are usually available free of charge. Many hotels also run on-site "camps" with adult-supervised, age-appropriate activities for children. Note: Cost and availability vary by hotel.

Source: *Good Housekeeping,* 959 Eighth Ave., New York 10019.

Interesting Presidential Sites

President's Day sales save us money, but they don't tell us much about the history of the nation's chief executives. If you're traveling in the near future, here are some of our favorite presidential landmarks that are worth stopping off to see…

• Monticello/Charlottesville, Virginia. Thomas Jefferson inherited this 1,053-acre estate when his father died in 1757. He began construction of Monticello in 1769. Architecture being one of Jefferson's chief delights, the house was built and subsequently remodeled over a period of 40 years. It is considered to be one of America's foremost architectural masterpieces. 804-295-8181.

• Henry Ford Museum & Greenfield Village/ Dearborn, Michigan. Museum complex covers 93 acres and spans over 300 years of technological changes. It contains four presidential vehicles—including the 1902 Brougham used by Teddy Roosevelt and the 1961 Lincoln in which John F. Kennedy was assassinated. Other highlights include a folding camp bed used by George Washington during the American Revolution, the Victorian rocking chair Lincoln was sitting in when assassinated, and the courthouse used by Lincoln when he traveled the Illinois "mud circuit" as a young attorney. 313-271-1620.

• Springfield Plantation/Fayette, Mississippi. Andrew Jackson was married here to Rachel Donelson Robards who, it was later learned, had not yet been granted her divorce decree. The marriage issue was raised in the 1828 presidential election, with Jackson being called a "paramour husband" and Rachel accused of being a "convicted adulteress." This unusual event and the major architectural significance of the house make this site a notable landmark. 601-786-3802.

• Lincoln Birthplace National Historic Park/ Hodgenville, Kentucky. Impressive Greek Revival memorial structure stands here on the site of Lincoln's log cabin birthplace. Carved above the six granite columns at the memorial's entrance are Lincoln's famous words, "With malice toward none, with charity for all." The memorial has 56 steps, each representing a year in his life—and contains a replica of his log cabin birthplace. 502-358-3874.

• Franklin Delano Roosevelt National Historic Site/Hyde Park, New York. Roosevelt's birthplace home and library on a spectacular site overlooking the Hudson River. The home served as the summer White House during his presidency and was the scene of many historically significant conferences and events. Most furnishings date from the 1850s to the 1920s. Extensive displays on Roosevelt's life and career. 914-229-9115.

• Mount Rushmore National Memorial/ Keystone, South Dakota. Massive granite monument was originally intended to honor frontiersmen Jim Bridger, John Colter and Kit Carson. But when noted sculptor Gutzon Borglum was given the job, he decided the project should be of national significance. The presidents depicted—George Washington, Thomas Jefferson, Abraham Lincoln and Theodore Roosevelt—represent the first 150 years of American history. 605-574-2523.

• Mount Vernon/Mount Vernon, Virginia. George Washington's home from the time he was 22 up until his death in 1799. It overlooks the Potomac River and has been meticulously restored to its appearance at the time of his death. Also on site are more than 30 acres of gardens and wooded grounds, outbuildings where domestic activities took place, a museum with many of Washington's personal possessions, and the family tomb. 703-780-2000.

• Montpelier/Orange, Virginia. This was James Madison's home from shortly after his birth until his death in 1836. The central portion of the Georgian mansion—with its breathtaking view of the Blue Ridge Mountains—was built by his father around 1760. Madison inherited the home and part of the 2,700-acre estate in 1801. He retired there after his second presidential term. The estate includes the Madison graves, the 55-room mansion, and more than 100 other sights. 703-672-2728.

• Tuckahoe Plantation/Richmond, Virginia. The boyhood home of Thomas Jefferson from 1745 to 1752, this structure is considered by architectural historians to be the finest existing early 18th-century plantation in America. The home was constructed between 1712 and 1730 and stands in a virtually undisturbed setting on a bluff overlooking the James River Valley. 804-784-5736.

• The White House/Washington, DC. One of the most popular tourist attractions in America for obvious reasons, it is always exciting to visit. It has 132 rooms—but only a few are seen during public tours. These include the East Room (used for receptions, ceremonies and other events), the Green Room (which served as Jefferson's dining room), the Blue Room (considered the most beautiful) and the Red Room (a favorite of the First Ladies). 202-456-7041. Note: More extensive, Congressionally guided tours require special tickets available only by writing your Congressman or Congresswoman.

• Grant Cottage State Historic Site/Wilton, New York. Ulysses Grant and his family occupied this cabin during the last six weeks of his life. The year before he had learned he had throat cancer and that he faced financial ruin because a partner swindled him out of his investments. In an effort to leave his family financially secure, Grant rushed to complete his Civil War Memoirs. On July 16, 1885, he wrote a note to his doctor saying he was finished and now could rest. Six days later he died. His memoirs provided his family with half a million dollars. Seasonal. 518-587-8277.

• Richard Nixon Library and Birthplace/ Yorba Linda, California. The library's museum features several fascinating exhibits. Most notable are a re-creation of the White House's Lincoln Sitting Room and a display of bronze-tone, life-sized statues of 10 of the century's most notable leaders, including de Gaulle, Churchill, and Khrushchev. 714-993-3393.

Source: Louis Kruh and David Kruh, coauthors of *Presidential Landmarks,* Hippocrene Books, Inc., 171 Madison Ave., New York 10016. Louis Kruh is a New York attorney. His son David works in Boston.

Cheaper Travel

Ask about visitor transit-system passes. Many public transit systems in major cities sell passes that permit unlimited or extensive travel on buses, subways, trains and trolleys. Some are issued by the day, others cover multiple days or a week.

The price is more than one daily round-trip but can add up to significant savings—and you won't have to fumble for exact change each time you ride. For information, write, call, or visit the city tourist-information office.

Source: *Consumer Reports Travel Letter*, 101 Truman Ave., Yonkers, New York 10703.

Cut Costs in Las Vegas And Atlantic City

You don't have to be a high roller to enjoy free meals, rooms and drinks in Las Vegas or Atlantic City. Here's how:*

•Garage parking. Available to even non-gamblers. Have the parking ticket validated at the casino cage.

•Drinks. Served to anyone at a table or slot machine. Most hotels will also buy a round when you finish playing. Order from a casino waitress or ask the pit boss for a "chit" to be used at any hotel bar.

•Breakfast or coffee-shop lunch: Bet $5 to $10 per hand for one hour. Ask the dealer or pit boss for a "meal ticket."

See the pit boss for the following…

•Line pass: $5 to $10 per hand for an hour. Allows entrance to the casino show via the shorter VIP line.

•Free show pass: $50 to $200 per hand (depending on the performer) for four hours.

•Room discounts: $25 per hand for two hours. The "casino rate" is up to 50% off the regular room rate.

•Room, food, drinks and a show: $100 per hand for four hours per day, for three days.

•Airfare, mini-suite, food, drinks: $200 per hand, four hours per day, for three days.

•First-class airfare, suite, food, drinks: $500 to $1,000 per hand, at least four hours a day for three days.

Other ways to cut corners…

Join a casino slot club. Members earn points equal to about 1% of what they wager in the slot machines. Points can be redeemed for cash or room and food credits. Membership: Free.

Have your play "rated"—or tracked—by the

*For specific guidelines, contact the hotel's VIP Services Department by phone or in person.

casino. Up to 40% of what rated players are expected to lose (even if they don't) is rebated in room, food and beverage credits. Contact the pit boss.

Sit down at a game just before a table is scheduled to close, usually between 2:00 and 4:00 AM. The pit boss will be generous with comps to get you to leave.

Source: Max Rubin, who specializes in writing about complimentary casino services for the *Las Vegas Advisor*, 5280 S. Valley View Blvd., Suite B, Las Vegas 89118.

Have More Fun At Disney World

•Plan what you want to do before you go. The less time you spend waiting in lines and the more you are able to see, the more value you get for your money. Call in advance to see if any rides are closed for repair. Also…

•Get going early. The theme parks open about one-half hour earlier than the "official" opening time. The same four rides you can enjoy in one hour early in the day could take up to three hours after 11:30 AM. Recommended: Arrive 50 minutes before the official opening time, an hour and a half on major holidays.

•Avoid major holidays. Disney World is busiest from Christmas Day through New Year's Day, the week of Washington's Birthday and during spring break and Easter weeks.

Least busy times: After Thanksgiving weekend until Christmas, September until the weekend before Thanksgiving, January 4th through the first half of February, the week after Easter until early June.

Lightest days: Friday, Sunday.

•Buy tickets in advance by mail from Disney World or a Disney store. Do not buy tickets at non-Disney hotels, because you'll have to pay up to 10% more.

Admissions options: 1 Park/1 Day, about $36 for an adult. 4-Day/3 Parks Pass, about $125. 5-Day Super Duper Pass, about $172. Annual Passport, $190. Florida-resident Four-Season Pass, $95.

Best bets: For one- or two-day visits, one

day tickets. For longer visits, the 4- and 5-Day Passes.

Caution: The 5-Day Super Pass provides admission to Discovery Island, Pleasure Island, Typhoon Lagoon and River Country, for seven days only from the date of purchase. If you do not plan to visit the smaller attractions, don't pay for the Super Pass.

• Save the Magic Kingdom for last, especially if you are traveling with children who may not appreciate the more serious parks. Its rides and attractions are highly rewarding for kids and adults. Recommended: See EPCOT first, then MGM, then the Magic Kingdom. Allow a full day for each park.

• Consider a non-Disney World hotel. Some hotels near the Main Gate entrance on US 192 are closer to MGM and the Magic Kingdom than many on-site hotels. Staying off-site can cut your lodging costs by 40% to 60%. Savings on food off-site, especially breakfast and lunch, can be tremendous.

Trade-off: Luxury, convenience. The Disney hotels are much nicer than off-site hotels, and provide certain advantages.

Examples: Child-care options, preferential treatment at the theme parks, transportation independence for teenage children. Most of the expensive Disney hotels provide transportation to the various Disney parks. You do not need a car unless you want to visit attractions outside of Disney.

Best bets: Stay on-site during busy seasons. Join the Magic Kingdom Club ($49) for Disney hotel and admissions discounts. During the off-season, there is little impact on convenience staying off-site, and off-site may be more convenient if you plan to visit Universal Studios or other area attractions.

• Evaluate travel packages carefully. Choose a package with features you'll use. Compare package prices with what you would pay booking the trip yourself. If you don't intend to rent a car, choose a package that includes transportation from the airport. Cab fare to Disney World can run up to $42 one way.

• Limit on-site snacks. It is easy to spend $40 a day on popcorn, ice cream, etc. Helpful: Bring snacks, and set an itinerary before entering the park: We're going to go like crazy

until 11:30, have a snack break, then go to a show and then sit down and have lunch.

• Watch out for souvenir-madness. Even the most jaded visitors to Disney World find themselves wanting a Mickey T-shirt. Prepare your kids to stay within a budget and set limits for yourself, too.

• Remember that you will be in Florida. Bring sunscreen, sunglasses, hats, cool, comfortable shoes, aspirin, etc. Drink plenty of fluids. If you suffer from motion sickness, stay off the wilder rides.

Source: Bob Sehlinger, author of *The Unofficial Guide to Walt Disney World & EPCOT: 1993 Edition,* published by Prentice Hall Travel, 15 Columbus Circle, New York 10023.

Customs Alert

Seizures of undeclared goods from travelers returning to the United States from abroad amounted to nearly $3 million in the eight months ended May 31—at John F. Kennedy International Airport alone. *Customs focus:* Items worth $1,000 or more. *Most likely to be searched:* Travelers who don't declare much, but whose luggage and deportment suggest that they are big shoppers.

Source: US Customs Service, Kennedy International Airport, New York.

Secrets of a Much More Comfortable Flight

Airline travel may be fast, but it is not always comfortable. Too often, travelers, especially those seated in coach, are crammed into confining seats, fed factory-produced meals, and confronted with delays or lost luggage. Flights can be made more bearable, however, if you know how to work the system.

Getting a good seat:

Most travelers don't want to sit in the middle seat of a row. But if you're late checking in for a crowded flight, you're almost certain of getting one. Problem: Airlines automatically assign aisle and window seats first, even if the two passengers in a row are traveling together.

You can improve your chances of getting an end seat by asking the agent at the check-in counter to search the passenger list for two travelers with the same last name in the same row. Request the middle seat in that row. Chances are the other two passengers are related and will want to sit together, leaving you either the window or aisle seat.

Storing luggage:

Finding room for your carry-on luggage is always challenging. It is best, however, not to wait until you arrive at your seat to store your bags. Instead, put them in the first overhead compartment after you pass through the first-class cabin.

These compartments will likely be empty, since they are for the last passengers that board. In addition, you won't have to carry your bags to your seat as you enter or to the front as you exit the plane.

Better baggage handling:

Bags that have first-class or priority tags attached are usually first to come off the plane into the baggage claim area. Even if you're traveling in coach, you can benefit from this quick service by getting one of these tags.

Sometimes the airlines will give you a first-class tag if you ask for it. If not, try to find an old one from any airline. You can even make one up in advance by having a brightly colored card stamped with the word "priority" and laminated at a local printer. This will attract the attention of the baggage handlers.

Getting an upgrade:

Just because you have enough frequent-flier miles to qualify for a better seat doesn't always mean you'll get one, especially if the flight is crowded.

In fact, you may actually stand a better chance of getting one if the flight is over-booked. In this situation, airlines commonly offer free tickets to passengers turning in their tickets. If you hear this announced, immediately notify the check-in personnel that you're still interested in upgrading.

Reason: A surprising number of first-class travelers give up their seats for free tickets,

opening up space in the forward cabin.

A more comfortable flight:

Strong sunlight is a common problem that travelers face when flying during the day. It often forces you to travel with the shade down. To avoid the sunny side when traveling eastbound, request an A, B, or C seat. When traveling westbound, request a seat on the other side of the cabin.

Source: Randy Petersen, who travels up to 400,000 miles a year and is editor of *InsideFlier*, a magazine for frequent fliers, 4715-C Town Center Dr., Colorado Springs 80916. 800-333-5937.

Purchasing A European Car

Purchasing a European car in Europe saves big dollars, we hear from car expert Dré Brungardt. It can more than pay for your trip abroad to pick it up. *Examples:* A BMW 750IL has a US price of $80,900 vs. a European price of $71,200...Mercedes 300E (3.2L) $49,900 vs. $44,550. *Important:* The car must be *built for sale in America*. For more information, talk with your local car dealer.

Source: Dré Brungardt is editor of *Nutz & Boltz*®, Box 123, Butler, Maryland 21023. 800-888-0091.

Artificial Tans

Skin-coloring creams, lotions, and sprays are generally safe for people to use. But people who assume their artificial tans eliminate the need for sunscreens while outdoors risk getting skin cancer, we hear from dermatologist Perry Robins, MD. There are two main types of *topical* preparations—those applied to the skin: *Accelerators* supposedly work by darkening the skin's own melanin pigments—and speed up the process of tanning in the sun. *Coloring agents* are water-soluble dyes—they wash off in time.

Source: Perry Robins, MD, is associate clinical professor of dermatology at NYU Medical Center.

Thieves At Airport Parking Lots

Airport parking lots are a prime target for car thieves and vandals. *Self-defense:* Choose a spot not by how safe it looks when you arrive, but by how it will look when you return…park under a light or where there's a lot of nearby activity. *Example:* The cashier's gate or a shuttle bus stop. *Practical alternatives:* Public transportation, cab or limo service to the airport—or have someone drop you off.

Source: Advice from the National Safety Council, cited in *The New York Times.*

Credit Limit

Keep within your credit limit when traveling by using *two* credit cards and splitting expenses between them—for example, one for hotels, the other for car rentals and other expenses.

Source: Peter Savage, author of *The Safe Travel Book,* writing in *International Living,* 824 E. Baltimore St., Baltimore 21202.

Sunscreen For Sensitive Skin

Sunscreen for sensitive skin is free of PABA (para-aminobenzoic acid) and benzophenone, the two active ingredients used in most sunscreens that are also the major cause of allergic reactions, we hear from dermatologist Darrell Rigel, MD. Products containing titanium dioxide protect against the sun's damaging UV-A and UV-B rays by coating the skin with very small particles that deflect the sun's rays (other sunscreens are absorbed into the skin, and absorb the sun's rays). Drawback: Titanium dioxide sunscreens are neither waterproof nor water-resistant, so if you do not have sunscreen allergies, the other sunscreens are probably best.

Source: Darrell Rigel, MD, is associate professor of dermatology at New York University School of Medicine, and a dermatologist in private practice in New York City.

Back-to-Back Airline Ticket Basics

Travelers who fly on weekdays and can't take advantage of Saturday-night stay-over discounts can still save up to 40% off regular coach fares. *How:* Purchase two sets of discounted tickets, each with a Saturday-night stay-over, with one set originating in your home city, the other in your destination city. Use the first half of each pair to complete the round-trip. *Good news:* Although most airlines have long insisted this practice violated their rules—and have gone so far as to use computers to detect back-to-back ticketing—both Delta and American recently announced they no longer consider this a violation. Other carriers are expected to follow.

Source: Roundup of travel industry experts, quoted in *The Wall Street Journal.*

"Environmentally Clean" Hotel Rooms

"Environmentally clean" hotel rooms are not only smoke-free, many also contain filtration systems that remove odors, dust, and pollen from the air and impurities from the water. More than 200 hotels in North America and Europe offer these rooms at $5 to $10 above the standard room rate.

Source: Katryna Glettler, senior editor, *Travel Holiday,* 28 W. 23 St., New York 10010.

Developing Film

When having film developed, attach a label with your name and address to the container itself in case the envelope is lost.

Source: Professional photofinishers quoted in *The New York Times.*

Better, Healthier Eating On the Road

Use travel time as dieting time...drink lots of water and avoid alcohol...never use travel as an excuse to overeat...pay closer attention to what goes into your mouth...exercise regularly...don't try to eat exactly as you do at home—this will only lead to frustration and more overeating.

Source: *Healthy, Wealthy, & Wise: A Step-By-Step Plan for Success Through Healthful Living* by fitness consultant Krs Edstrom, MS. Prentice-Hall, Route 9W, Englewood Cliffs, New Jersey 07632.

Car-Rental Trap

The cheapest car-rental rates are usually for a subcompact car. Often, however, the desk agent will try to pressure you to upgrade to a larger, more expensive vehicle. Over the course of a week, that switch could add up to $100 or more to your bill. *Self-defense:* Consider the benefits of a larger car, but if it's a subcompact you want, stick to your decision.

Source: *Consumer Reports 1993 Travel Buying Guide: How to Get Big Discounts on Airfares, Hotels, Car Rentals, and More* by Ed Perkins and the editors of *Consumer Reports Travel Letter,* Consumer Reports Books, 101 Truman Ave., Yonkers, New York 10703.

Proof of Citizenship

Proof of citizenship requirements are becoming increasingly stringent in the Caribbean, Bahamas, and Mexico. A driver's license alone is no longer sufficient identification for an American tourist to enter some of those places. *Also:* While most islands will accept a birth certificate accompanied by a photo ID, they'll reject a voter's registration card. *Self-defense:* Consider "proof of citizenship" to mean that a passport is required.

Source: Travel adviser Arthur Frommer, writing in *Travel Holiday,* 28 W. 23 St., New York 10010.

"Marilyn Monroe's Los Angeles" Tour

"Marilyn Monroe's Los Angeles" tour visits more than 50 places that figured in the star's life—including "the bluff" above Santa Monica Beach where it's believed she used to meet JFK, "the pharmacy," her last home, etc. The tour lasts seven hours and is given daily beginning at 9 am. *Cost:* Adults, $46, under 12, $32. *Insider Tours:* 310-392-4435.

Avoiding the Last Flight

When booking an unaccompanied child on a connecting flight, avoid the last flight of the day. *Trap:* If the plane fails to take off, the child may spend the night alone in a strange city.

Source: *Travel Holiday,* 28 W. 23 St., New York 10010.

Discounts For Bereavement

Bereavement fares are discounted by 15% to 50% off full fares for passengers with a death in the family. *Most flexible:* TWA and Continental, which also offer discounts in cases of critical illness.

Source: *Condé Nast Traveler,* 360 Madison Ave., New York, 10017.

Jet Lag Smarts

To minimize jet lag, schedule important activities for when you will likely have the most energy. High-energy times: Evenings after jetting east...the next morning after jetting west.

Source: *Jet Smart* by Diana Fairechild, former flight attendant, Flyana Rhyme, Inc., Box 300, Makawao, Maui, Hawaii 96768.

Cutting Travel Costs

What companies are doing these days to keep a lid on air travel costs:
- 98% are paying something less than full coach fare—up from 82% just two years ago.
- One-third of all large firms have worked out special discounts with carriers.
- More firms now demand that their employees book early to get better deals.
- Nearly one out of five travel managers now use "hidden city" fares. With this approach, tickets are purchased to a distant, cheaper destination, and employees get off at an earlier stop.

Source: Surveys by Topaz Enterprises, a fare auditing system in Portland, Oregon, and *Corporate Travel* magazine, cited in *The Wall Street Journal*.

Cutting Costs When Traveling to Europe

The costs of traveling to Europe can be cut without sacrificing comfort. All it takes is a willingness to ask questions and a basic knowledge of how the travel industry works. Using this strategy, which for example might involve traveling off-season, can trim 25% to 50% off the price of hotels, airfares, and car rentals.

Airfares:

There are big advantages to going through a strong travel agent. Many have tremendous buying power that allows them to pass along

cut rates to their regular clients.

Or, consider a tour package. It is a great way to trim 25% or more off the cost of hotels and airfares.

Or, check for deals on airfares in your Sunday paper. Important: Don't bother calling on Monday. The deals are probably already booked up by then. Better: Call past fare promoters on Thursday before they send in their ads to the Sunday papers.

Hotels:
- Stay away from the center of town. Hotels away from the tourist centers are 15% to 40% cheaper than downtown hotels. Most major cities offer great public transportation so it isn't difficult to get around. Consider staying in small towns surrounding major cities. These usually have easy, inexpensive access to the more expensive tourist centers.
- Negotiate. Americans usually aren't comfortable bargaining about price. But it is a way of life in Europe. Most hotels, in fact, are willing to negotiate their rates, especially if you're planning to stay for at least three days. So long as there isn't a convention in town, you might get a break of 20% to 50%.
- Ask for the corporate rate. Virtually all hotels cut prices by at least 20% for business travelers.

Transportation:

Europe's special railway passes generally pay off if you're traveling far or at a fast pace. Buying individual tickets may be best for intercity or side trips.

Train travel may be best for a side trip. In most cases, purchase a second-class ticket. The cost is about a third less than first-class and the ride is still comfortable. Only in Italy, Spain, and Portugal, where second-class coaches get crowded, is it worth paying the premium.

Car rentals in Europe are always expensive. High local taxes is one reason. Some countries, however, traditionally offer lower rates. Good deals are usually found in Spain, Luxembourg, Ireland, and England. Also, check local rental companies. Sometimes they offer better rates than the big international firms. And always try to rent for a week on an unlimited mileage basis. The per-day charge is generally exorbitantly higher.

More money-savers:

•Entry fees for museums can be pretty high. Many major cities, such as Paris, sell museum cards that offer unlimited entry into its major museums for one low price. Some museums also set aside one day a week when admission is free.

•Tax refunds. European countries charge a value added tax of about 15% for most items. Visitors can get this back. The quickest way is to use a credit card. Ask for payment and VAT refund slips at the same time. If the store refuses, ask for specific details on VAT refunds for the country.

•Theater. In London, the discount ticket booth in Leicester Square sells tickets when available at half price. Many theater box offices also sell tickets at a discount that have been returned just before show time.

Source: John Whitman has logged more than two million miles exploring how to travel on a budget. He is the author of *The Best European Travel Tips*, published by Meadowbrook Press, available from the author, Box 202, Long Lake, Minnesota 55356.

Great Cooking School Vacations

You've heard of vacation destinations that rejuvenate body—and soul. There are palate rejuvenators too…

•A Taste of the Mountains Cooking School. Weekend and five-day courses are taught here at the historic Bernerhof Inn. Specialty: Healthful, creative cuisine. Also: Wine-tasting seminar and chocolate tempering demonstration—and skiing, hiking, golfing, racquet sports, horseback riding, canoeing, fishing, swimming, and bicycling available in the area. *Cost:* $375–$425/person (weekend program)…$950–$1,075/ person (five-day program).*

A Taste of the Mountains Cooking School, Box 240, Glen, New Hampshire 03838. 800-548-8007.

•Captiva Cooking School. The school itself is located at Captiva Island's 330-acre South

Seas Plantation Resort & Yacht Harbour and is taught by the resort's chef. The four-day cooking courses teach you how to buy, clean, cook, and sauce seafood, as well as how to decorate and present it. The resort is extremely private and offers golfing, boating, fishing, swimming, and tennis. Cost: $387–$595/person.

South Seas Plantation Resort & Yacht Harbour, Box 194, Captiva, Florida 33924. 800-237-3102.

•Channel Bass Inn. Three-day cooking classes. Specialties: Sauces, soufflés, vegetables, seafood, and desserts. Guests are housed in this 100-year-old, four-star inn's best rooms and can enjoy the beauty of the Delmarva Peninsula, the Chincoteague Wildlife Refuge, and the Assateague Seashore. *Cost:* $1,000/ couple or $850/person.

The Channel Bass Inn, Chincoteague Island, Virginia 23336. 804-336-6148.

•Cooking With Steven Raichlen. Four-day cook-and-ski program is held at the Snowvillage Inn in New Hampshire. Hands-on classes and demonstrations for preparing healthy country meals. Specialty: High flavor, low-fat international cuisine. Also available: Hiking and cross-country ski trails and ice skating on nearby Crystal Lake. Two lift tickets and cross-country ski instruction included. *Cost:* $475–$525/person.

Cooking With Steven Raichlen, Snowvillage Inn, Snowville, New Hampshire 03849. 603-447-2818.

•Jane Butel's Southwestern Cooking School. Five-day and three-session weekend classes are now offered year-round. Featured are the cooking techniques for authentic chile dishes, native breads, stews, appetizers, and desserts. Specialties: New Mexican and Southwestern cuisines. Afternoons and most evenings are open so that you can explore the area's cultural and recreational offerings. Shop in Old Town Albuquerque or in nearby Santa Fe.

Jane Butel Cooking School, 800 Rio Grande NW, Suite 14, Albuquerque 87104. 800-473-8226.

Source: Dorlene Kaplan, editor of *The Guide to Cooking Schools: Cooking Courses, Travel Programs, and Culinary Arts Schools Throughout the World,* ShawGuides, Inc., 625 Biltmore Way, Dept. 1406C, Coral Gables, Florida 33134. 305-446-8888.

*Prices are based on double occupancy and include all program activities, meals, and accommodations, except where noted.

3

Money Management For Tough Times

When You Need A Financial Planner... And When It's Best To Help Yourself

There are at least four reasons why most people turn to a financial planner for advice...

• We feel desperate because there's more money going out than coming in with no relief in sight.

• We feel frustrated because our financial goals are not being met fast enough and seem unattainable.

• We are so busy with other parts of our lives that we feel out of control.

• We face a near-term, specific decision.

While professional financial advice may be the solution, take your time finding help. The industry is largely unregulated and many salespeople masquerade as financial planners. Educational or professional credentials alone don't always ensure honesty and competence. *Questions to ask before you make your selection...*

• What experience do you have in budgeting, insurance, investments, taxes, retirement and estate planning? Don't assume that all planners cover all bases. Most are skilled in one, maybe two, areas. An honest planner will admit where he/she is weak—and will tell you what access he has to the expertise you may need. Look for a planner with a company that has on-staff specialists or good sources for specialized skills.

• How do you make your money? Planners are typically paid through fees, commissions, or a mix of the two. You want objective help. Someone who is paid a commission may not be acting in your best interest. It's not that you'll never get good advice from someone with a vested interest, but you will probably have to spend time researching whether the advice is sound or not. For this reason alone, a fee-only planner is usually the best bet.

• What's your approach to investing? Is it short-term (next year) or long-term (five to 10 years)? You want both. *Considerations:*

• *Investments.* Beware of advisers who suggest a few specific stocks and/or a couple of mutual funds before you have an overall strategy. You probably want a long-term allocation approach—so much to cash, fixed-income investments, stocks, hard assets such as gold and real estate. The proper asset allocation is probably the most important single consideration—more important than specific investment suggestions or timing—in long-term successful investing.

• *Insurance.* The planner should be able to advise you on all kinds: Health, life, disability. It's very important to be clear about your real needs before buying any policy.

• *Estate planning.* Can the planner and/or member of his team take it all the way from interviewing you on your intentions to suggesting various concepts and strategies? Legal documents may be a separate step.

• *Pre- and post-retirement planning.* What should I do now to build sufficient capital for a comfortable retirement? Given inflation, what will I really need? What should I do to stretch that capital in retirement?

• *Tax preparation and tax planning.* What should I do to be knowledgeable about regular taxes and the Alternative Minimum Tax, capital gains, gifting, etc.?

• *References.* Any planner will lead with his best-performing accounts. You should expect that. But you—and the planner—may be surprised at just how candid clients can be. So be sure to call and talk to references personally. Do it yourself:

Before you interview financial planners, think seriously about doing a lot of the work yourself. It's very expensive to go helplessly to a financial planner. At hourly rates ranging between $100 and $300, the bill mounts quickly. You can cut the cost from many thousands of dollars by following the five-step process that works well for most people:

• Organize yourself. No one else can do it for you. If you don't start with yourself you're seldom going to solve the problem. You can get a long way if you know how you handle money and bone up on areas of financial planning where you're weak.

• Set specific objectives. *Example:* You want to retire in 10 years and maintain your present standard of living.

• Formulate a strategy. How much will you need for retirement and what is the best way to realize your goal?

• Implement the plan. Don't proceed with this step until you've gone through the first three. Most people start with implementation, either on impulse or because a stock or insurance broker calls them with a suggestion. Essential: Measure every investment decision against your strategic framework.

• Review your progress regularly. Do this at least once a year.

Help when you need it:

Once you've made it through the first three steps, you may well be able to finish the job yourself. But if you need help, this is the time to reach for a good book, a computer financial-planning program, or an objective financial planner. Once you know where you are and where you want to go, you can interview planners more intelligently. And you're much more likely to be satisfied with the one you choose.

Source: George E. L. Barbee, executive director, Client Services, Price Waterhouse, 160 Federal St., Boston 02110. He is a contributor to the Price Waterhouse books on taxes, investments, and retirement.

How to Cut Credit Card Costs

The effective cost of carrying a credit card balance can hit 30% annually. While various charges are almost always disclosed in fine print, credit-card terms are now so complex that they're commonly confused.

Here's a plain-English summary and advice on how to cut costs...

• Interest on unpaid balance. This has come down in recent years, to an average annual rate of 18.5%, but most consumers are effectively paying more than 20%. Those who regularly carry a balance should shop around for the lowest rate.

• Interest calculations. Banks can use several different methods to calculate interest charges. The most common is the average daily balance method including new purchases: If you start the month with a $1,000 balance and make a payment of $990, you will be charged interest on $1,000—not the $10 you still owe. The cheapest method for calculating interest is the average daily balance method, excluding new purchases, which does not include new purchases when figuring your finance charge. Only a few banks use this method.

A few issuers use the two-cycle average daily balance method, which in certain cases calculates interest on last month's and this month's balances and adds them together. This method can be very expensive for consumers who sometimes pay in full and sometimes carry a balance.

Some banks now charge interest from the date an item is purchased, rather than the date a charge is posted to one's account. This adds several days' worth of interest per month.

•Grace period. With most cards, holders have 25 days to pay a bill before interest is assessed. However, for the roughly 70% of holders who make a partial payment, and thereby have an unpaid balance each month, the grace period doesn't apply. To cut costs, send your payment as soon as you get your bill. If you pay off your balance each month, look for a card offering a full grace period.

•Cash advances. Fees range from 2% to 2.5% of a cash advance. Usually there's a minimum fee such as $2 and a maximum fee as high as $20. Few credit cards extend grace periods to cash advances. Because of these terms, cash advances are often the most costly way for consumers to borrow money.

•Additional fees. When shopping around, don't overlook additional fees that can add to the effective interest charges. For instance, fees for exceeding one's credit limit commonly run about $11 per month. Late payments entail additional fees of around $8 per month.

•Minimum payments. Many banks have low minimum payments, encouraging more people to maintain larger balances. The result, of course, has been higher credit-card costs.

Example: If you owe $2,500 and make a minimum payment of 2% per month, it would take you more than 30 years to pay off the balance and would cost $6,500 in interest charges. Best: Pay off your balance as fast as you can. Even paying $25 per month beyond the required minimum will help make an appreciable dent in credit-card costs.

Source: Gerri Detweiler, director, BankCard Holders of America, Suite 120, Herndon, Virginia 22070.

How to Stay in Control Of Your Money...Now

What should individuals expect to be charged when they retain an adviser to help them make investment decisions?

The annual fee that a financial adviser charges should not be more than 1.5% of the value of your stock investments under management. For a bond portfolio, a fair annual fee is closer to 0.75%.

Annual fees should be on a sliding scale that declines as your investment assets increase. International investing is more complex, however, and it is the only category of investments for which a higher annual fee is justified.

In addition, most money managers charge a minimum fee of about $1,000 a year. That is warranted, in my view, since a substantial amount of time goes into setting up accounts, reviewing and reporting on performance, managing paperwork and counseling clients.

Most brokerage firms offer *wrap accounts*, which combine financial planning and trading services. The money-management and brokerage commissions are grouped into a flat, annual fee of about 3%. Over time, that can be pretty steep if you don't do much trading. I think those fees will eventually come down.

What services can clients expect for these money-management fees?

At the very least, you should receive a report each quarter on how your investments are doing. Each quarter, your adviser should also give you his/her opinion about what's going on in the economy and suggest changes in your investments—if applicable—based on that outlook.

49

When looking for a money manager, what information can an individual get on his/her past performance...or that of a brokerage firm's wrap account?

The performance of money managers, like that of mutual funds, is monitored by independent analysts. When you're considering a money manager for equity investments, ask to be shown his/her CDA performance rating* and review it on the basis of total return—*capital gains plus reinvested dividends.* Compare it to the total return of a market index, such as the S&P 500.

If you're considering a wrap account offered by a brokerage firm, you'll be able to choose a money manager based on your financial objectives from among a group that the firm selected.

Keep in mind that how well the manager has beaten the market in the past shouldn't necessarily be the primary reason for selecting him. Equally important might be how well the manager conserves capital in bear markets or the volatility of his performance.

After you've chosen a money manager, is it unusual for him to insist on managing only a cash deposit?

Not at all. A money manager is justified in thinking that he can perform better for you if you hand over a sum of cash to manage rather than a portfolio of stocks and bonds—from, say, an inheritance. In fact, some managers will take on a new account only if it's in cash.

Reason: Since money managers report their performance to independent analysts, they don't want their records hampered by investments in a portfolio that they would not have recommended.

This means you'll either have to liquidate some of your portfolio or authorize the manager to sell securities so that he has cash to invest for you.

If someone is paying a manager to monitor an account, should any of the money be in an index fund, whose portfolio matches that of a broad-based index such as the S&P 500?

I don't think so. You're already paying the money manager to do as well—and better—

*CDA Investment Technologies is the top independent analyst in the field.

than the market or an index over time.

Should investors be concerned if they don't receive a stock or bond certificate?

No. Money managers don't actually have custody of the certificates. The brokerage or bank with which they do business does.

In the near future, stock and bond certificates will probably be phased out and your holdings will increasingly appear only as computer entries. You'll just get a confirmation from the firm that handles the transaction, not a certificate.

Mutual funds do this now—sending you a regular statement showing how many shares you own, whether dividends or capital gains were reinvested, etc. Individual investors are resisting this trend, but it's inevitable.

How, then, is an investor protected when all he/she has is a statement from the broker to acknowledge what he owns?

Well, there's the brokerage industry's own insurance program, which covers up to $400,000 in securities and $100,000 in cash in each customer's account. Most firms buy additional insurance to protect their customers in case the company fails.

What kind of personal bookkeeping works best once you own a variety of investments rather than just a few bank CDs?

There are several computer software programs available that can help you keep track of your funds. I find, however, that the simplest, most effective system is a three-hole binder, loose-leaf paper, a set of tabbed dividers and a three-hole punch. You should use a tab divider for every investment account—brokerage account, trust fund, mutual funds, bank CDs, IRAs and so on.

Then, each time you receive paperwork in the mail—the original confirmation of a transaction, a dividend statement, notice of stock split, etc.—punch the holes if they aren't there already and slip it into the rings at the front of the specific section.

Mutual fund statements are cumulative, of course, so you can just take out the previous notice and put in the new one. The whole record will be right there when you do your taxes. Set it up right now for this year if you've had a lot of trouble getting your records together for last year.

Source: Alexandra Armstrong, chairman, Armstrong, Welch, MacIntyre, Inc., 1155 Connecticut Ave. NW, Washington, DC 20036.

Best Credit Cards For Different Situations

Too many Americans sign up for credit cards without comparison shopping or thinking about how they will use the card.

That's a mistake because everyone uses credit cards differently, and no two cards are exactly alike. If you choose a card that's inappropriate for your needs, you'll wind up paying more than you should. These are my current favorites...

If you pay your bill in full each month:

The new *General Motors MasterCard* (800-846-2273). It has no fee for life, offers a grace period and lets cardholders earn a 5% rebate on purchases of up to $500 per year for a total of $3,500 in seven years. This can be applied toward the purchase of a GM vehicle. The interest rate is currently 16.4%.

If you carry a monthly balance of more than $1,000:

First Consumer Bankcard (800-952-3388), which has a $29 annual fee and offers a variable interest rate that's currently 6.9%.

Trap: The rate goes up to 11.9% variable on April 1, 1994.

If you carry a balance of less than $1,000 from month to month:

Consumer National Bankcard (800-862-1616). It has no annual fee, a 25-day grace period and a variable interest rate of 9.9% currently, that will go up to a 12.9% variable rate on April 1, 1994.

If you sometimes carry a balance...and sometimes pay in full:

USAA Federal (800-922-9092) or AFBA Industrial Bank (800-776-2265). Both have no annual fee, offer a 25-day grace period, and carry a 12.5% variable interest rate. In addition, both are known for courteous customer service.

If you travel frequently on business:

American Express is still the king of corporate cards. A relatively new benefit, Membership Miles (800-297-6453), makes this the best corporate-card deal around. A $25 annual program fee buys membership in the program, which gives you one frequent-flier mile for every dollar charged.

After you've racked up 5,000 miles in a year, you can convert them to any of a number of frequent-flier programs. The $5,000 starting limit may be high for standard cardholders, but for business owners and travelers, it shouldn't be a problem.

If you plan to use your card for vacation travel:

AT&T Universal Visa or *MasterCard* (800-662-7759). AT&T offers 24-hour, 365-day customer service and will accept collect calls from overseas. These cards promise 24-hour emergency card replacement, plus enhancements such as purchase protection and free collision-damage waiver insurance—benefits usually reserved for gold cards. There is a 25-day grace period, and the current variable interest rate is 15.9%. The fee for a standard card is $20 a year, but there is a lifetime no-fee option if you transfer at least $1,000 balance from another credit card or cards.

For college students:

For parents who don't want to cosign the card or students who don't want to ask their parents to cosign, *First Chicago* offers a special Visa or MasterCard (800-368-4535) based on the student's own signature. It has no annual fee and a no-interest grace period of 20–25 days for bill payment. The current variable interest rate is 15.9%. *Credit limit:* $500 minimum—up to $1,000 if the student's credit history qualifies.

If you have damaged credit and can't get a card:

Signet Bank (800-955-7070) offers a secured credit card to people who have past credit problems. You deposit $300 or more in a bank account and you will get a Visa or MasterCard with a credit line equal to your deposit. Pay your bills on time and you will build a good credit rating with all three major credit bureaus.

Drawback: Not available in Delaware, Kansas, Maine, Missouri, New Mexico, North Carolina, Oregon, Vermont, and Wisconsin.

If you are a frequent flier:

Every major airline cosponsors a credit card that earns you frequent-flier miles as you spend, but this perk doesn't come cheap. Most cards have high annual fees (as much as $80) and high interest rates. USAir offers the most reasonable of the lot through NationsBank (800-759-6262). The annual fee of $35 is waived for the first six months, and the interest rate is 17.94%. You'll earn one frequent-flier mile for every dollar you charge on the card.

Trap: You must charge $20,000 on the card in order to earn a free round-trip domestic coach ticket, but if you already have USAir frequent-flier miles, you can use this program to "top them off."

Beware: You shouldn't use this card for revolving purchases because of the high interest rate. Use it only if you can pay the bill in full each month.

If you want to consolidate $2,000 or more in credit-card debt:

Wachovia (800-842-3262) offers a Visa or MasterCard that has an 8.9% variable interest rate, a $39 annual fee and a 25-day grace period. Wachovia makes it easy for you to transfer balances from other cards.

Source: Gerri Detweiler, executive director of Bank-Card Holders of America, 560 Herndon Pkwy., Herndon, Virginia 22070. She is the author of *The Ultimate Credit Handbook*, Plume Press, 375 Hudson St., New York 10014.

Ten of the Most Common Mistakes In Financial Planning

Mistake: Not knowing what is enough for your financial objectives. Too many investors are caught up in the cultural bias for *more...* more for more's sake. This is akin to putting the cart before the horse and then killing the horse. Too often, in investing, the push to make more requires overreaching—taking risks that can result, in the end, in *less* rather than more. Since more is by definition never

enough, financial planners are driven to accomplish the impossible. This creates anxiety for both you and your planner.

What I advocate in my professional planning practice is a radically different school of thought that I call *Enough*.

This approach puts the client into personal financial planning. It recognizes the essential truth that financial resources are only a means to achieve personal objectives. The goal is to look inward and identify your life goals and then align those goals with your personal resources.

If your retirement-income needs can be met, after adjusting for inflation and tax increases, with an investment that is safely earning 6%, why take a big risk to earn 20%?

When you have *enough* you can relax and be satisfied, or you can start a new fund. But you don't have to push for more.

Mistake: Abdicating responsibility. Too many people work for 40 years (that's about 80,000 hours of making money)—but don't spend the relatively few hours needed to protect their life's earnings.

You can't abdicate that responsibility. It's OK to let a planner help you row the boat, but *you* must steer.

Once you have determined your objectives, you can use a personal financial planner to provide technical advice. Avoid planners who are transaction-oriented, such as brokers and life insurance salespersons. They're working for themselves, not you. *Fee-only* planners are a better choice, *though they're not guaranteed to be competent.*

Beware: There are 250,000 people in the US who call themselves personal financial planners but have virtually no expertise and are subject to no industry or government regulations.

Mistake: Wanting results *now.* Remember, anything worth doing is worth doing slowly. This is particularly true of investments. Going for a quick kill is a sure way to get burned. Don't convey a sense of impatience to your planner. Be satisfied to make steady progress.

Mistake: Piecemeal planning. By doing piecemeal planning you may solve one problem, but you can create two others. Planners are now pushing what's called modular planning—e.g., how to finance your child's education. But you can't plan that in isolation. What if you need to put aside $10,000 a year and you become disabled? Comprehensive planning is the only answer.

Mistake: Concentrating on finances instead of on personal goals. Much too much financial planning is based strictly on managing assets instead of on aligning your personal finances with your personal goals. Life planning must come before financial planning, not the other way around. *Enough* is a very personal thing.

Mistake: Not asking what could go wrong. Before making any investment, you should know about the downside. What could go wrong? What would be the cause of trouble? What's the probability? The seriousness? How can you prevent or minimize risk? The best surprise is no surprise.

Mistake: Neglecting to ask to see the planner's own financial plan. This should not be a secret. If he/she is going to see your personal finances, you should be able to see his. If he doesn't have a plan or won't show you, go elsewhere. People who can't plan for their own lives certainly can't help you plan for yours.

Mistake: Not distinguishing the "closer" from the "doer." There are a lot of charming professionals out there who are very good at making the sale but don't actually do the work. It may be the partner of the CPA firm who signs you up, but your account is really handled by some clerk in a position that turns over every two years, meaning that you have to keep re-educating new people. Don't pay partner fees for a partner you never see. By the same token, an hour spent with a very good (but expensive) planner may be worth more than a month of someone else's time.

Mistake: Not getting an estimate of fees and commissions up front. Don't accept an answer of, *"We won't know until we see how your account works out."* Any professional planner knows how to qualify prospects. At the very least, the planner can tell you what other investors of your general description are paying in average fees and commissions.

Note: Although there are only about 1,000 fee-only planners, you may be able to negoti-

ate a fee-only relationship with a normally commissioned planner who's willing to strike a deal.

Mistake: Believing that the specific investment is more important than asset allocation. The term "financial planning" is used by insurance companies, brokers, investment companies, banks, partnership syndicators and others who are trying to put an independent-looking mask on what is really just a delivery system for the sale of a product. Fully 93% of portfolio value is based on investment classifications (how assets are allocated between different types of investments), *not* on the specific investment or the timing of the purchase. If you tell a planner you have, say, $100,000 to invest and the planner tells you where it should go *before* finding out about your plans, goals, other assets, etc., the planner has failed.

Source: James D. Schwartz, a fee-only personal financial planner and president of ENOUGH, Inc., Englewood, Colorado. He is the author of *ENOUGH, A Guide to Reclaiming Your American Dream*, Re/Max International, Inc., Creative Ad Fund, Box 3363, Englewood, Colorado 80155. 800-752-2987.

Financial Self-Defense For Women of All Ages… That Everyone Should Know About

Many women know far less about how to manage their family's finances than their husbands do.

Yet even younger women in their forties with careers are often surprisingly ignorant of the basics of finances—such as investing, tracking paperwork, handling debt, etc.

Danger: When their husbands die, these women are often completely in the dark. As a result, they frequently do nothing and let their investments languish…or they make impulsive decisions that are not in their best interest. This trend is particularly distressing, since widows make up about 11% of the adult female population in the US.

While most couples have read or heard the

standard advice about going over their finances at least once a year, the truth is that too few actually do it.

Example: Many widows are surprised to discover that a life-insurance policy they thought was in effect has actually lapsed. This can happen if the husband told his wife about the policy when he bought it 30 years ago but failed to tell her when he canceled it after the children were grown.

Is there anything that a woman can do to keep up with such information regularly? Frankly, this is one of the key advantages of using an outsider—a financial planner. The planner has to review the overall financial situation at least once a year, and probably does it every quarter. Most planners will encourage both husband and wife to be together as all three go over the family's financial picture and consider changes.

And a responsible financial planner will make sure all records and information are in good order and are promptly made available to a surviving spouse.

What's the most common mistake widows make about their finances? Making major decisions too quickly, especially decisions that are irrevocable, such as selling the home, moving to another part of the country, or making an investment that can't be changed.

One such example is a widow who uses the proceeds of her late husband's life-insurance policy to buy an annuity that pays out lifetime income. It's a logical, safe recommendation for the insurance company's salesperson to make.

Or the benefits consultant at the late husband's company might recommend that his pension benefits could be distributed to the widow as a guaranteed lifetime income or in a lump sum.

To a widow who has not yet looked at her whole financial picture, the promise of a regular monthly income sounds attractive. That's because the primary concern of most widows is whether there is sufficient income to pay the bills and cover immediate costs.

What's wrong with immediately choosing to receive a guaranteed monthly sum? It's a fixed income for the rest of her life. It doesn't

change. And with inflation, that could be a very bad choice in a few years.

Furthermore, putting your money into a deferred annuity is an irrevocable decision. You can't change it…it's done.

If the widow can get good financial advice before making that decision, she'd learn that it might make more sense to take the pension in a lump sum and take the insurance proceeds in cash, retaining the flexibility to invest the proceeds. At any rate, it's a decision that takes time to make—after all the information is in.

What can she do, then, immediately, with the proceeds of a life-insurance policy? Leave it with the insurance company so that it earns interest. Or simply take it as a check, and put it into a money-market fund while you gather information and figure out what you need to live on.

Just don't make any big decisions to commit large sums of money right after the death of a spouse. You need time.

Is there a temptation to make wrong spending decisions as well as wrong investment decisions? Yes, especially if a lot of money seems to be coming in from all directions—from life insurance, the company pension plan, Social Security, etc.

Example: The widow might try to pull the family together by arranging a lavish vacation with the children.

Usually such decisions are made impulsively because the widow feels out of control. Making a decision to commit a great deal of money is appealing. She feels like she's taking control.

But I remind clients who tell me about such plans that this money has to last them a lifetime. The reality is that they probably will not remarry and find someone who can support them.

There are no penalties for taking no action during this initial period following a spouse's death—but there are serious penalties for taking the wrong action. Make sure you gather all of the information and have discussed it with someone you trust.

How do you get everything organized? Many widows do not know where everything is that they need when their husbands die. There is going to be a mountain of paperwork during the initial month, so get ready for it.

Set aside an area of the house for this material—the dining room, for instance. Buy a file cabinet. In one file drawer put everything that relates to the estate…his assets, his Social Security information, his pension and profit-sharing information, etc. In a separate drawer, put all the material that relates to you—the bank account, current bills, etc.

Keep the estate-related files completely separate until all bills and taxes are paid and assets are distributed. As these obligations are settled, move the file from the estate drawer to your personal drawer.

Organize and pay bills. But if you have any doubts about paying a specific bill, get professional help to figure out what to do. If it's a substantial bill and you are concerned about when you will be able to pay it—or if you should pay it—write the company. Explain your situation and that you are getting matters under control and will get back to them shortly.

And—very important—begin immediately to keep a financial diary.

What's a financial diary? Buy a 5" x 7" spiral notebook and log in every conversation about the estate and any financial paperwork you have. Keep the notebook by the phone when you're at home and in your handbag when you go to any data-gathering or decision-making meeting.

You may think you are in full control of your mental faculties in the weeks following your spouse's death…that you are acting rationally. But many widows discover later that they didn't have their usual ability to recall conversations and decisions they made.

How do you wind up an estate? Leave it to the lawyer who drew up the will? You don't have to retain that same lawyer—unless the will makes that lawyer an executor of the estate. You can ask for help from another lawyer. Some widows even do it themselves—going down to probate court and finding out what they need to file and how to do it. They find the process therapeutic. But if you do it yourself you have to be careful to follow all the steps exactly.

Where might you make a misstep?

The first mistake is neglecting to appraise assets promptly after a spouse's death. An accountant will need that information to figure out whether you owe estate taxes or not. He/she will also need it to establish basis values, so you don't wind up paying unnecessary capital gains taxes years later when you might sell some of those assets.

How does that work, for instance, with a jointly owned house? Suppose you bought a house 20 years ago for $60,000. You have it appraised upon your spouse's death for $300,000. If you go to sell it in future years, your basis for figuring capital gains tax is your half of the original $60,000—which is $30,000—plus half the $300,000 value at the time of your spouse's death, which is $150,000. The basis cost is a total of $180,000 (plus capital improvements).

What about stocks and other securities you jointly own? It makes sense to file away the issue of *Barron's* the week your spouse dies—or the financial tables in the local newspaper on the day of death. This will provide you with a record of security prices at the time. Also keep the monthly statement of any brokerage and mutual fund account, showing the value at the time.

As a financial adviser, when I find out that a client or a client's spouse has died, I immediately appraise the client's portfolio. It's much easier to do the appraisal right away than to have to go back and collect all the data.

Source: Alexandra Armstrong, chairman, Armstrong, Welch & MacIntyre Inc., financial advisers, 1155 Connecticut Ave. NW, Suite 250, Washington, DC 20036. She is coauthor of *On Your Own: A Widow's Passage to Emotional and Financial Well-Being,* Dearborn Financial, 520 North Dearborn St., Chicago 60610.

Secrets of Saving

There are plenty of legitimate reasons why young adults and baby boomers find it hard to save—for a home…their children's college education…retirement—while their parents were able to do it quite easily.

One of the biggest reasons has to do with

taxes. In 1948, the median-income American family paid 2% of its income in taxes to the federal government.

In 1992, that same family paid 24% of its income to the federal government—plus as much as 9% in state and local income taxes. Here are a number of ways families and individuals can hold onto more of their income...
Face the facts:

The key to keeping more of what you earn is self-discipline—not self-denial. First, get a clear picture of your cash-spending and your cash-earning potential...

Sit down with your checkbook (or your bank statements and checks for the past couple of months). Draw a vertical line down the middle of a notebook page. List your income for the month on one side and your spending on the other. Add to your monthly spending a portion of the big outlays, such as auto insurance, that you might pay once or in a few installments.

When you get to the bottom of the page, the totals will tell the tale. Are you spending more each month than you earn? Are you financing the difference with debt? If your answers are yes, then it's time for you to take action.

Carefully think through the possibilities of adding to your income to fill the earning-spending gap. The easiest way to live on a modest salary is to supplement it with an additional income. Finding ways to earn a second income can be a lot less painful than many of the alternatives, such as cutting back on spending.

Possibilities: Set up a side business that you can do for profit in the evenings or on the weekend—such as word processing, tutoring students, keeping accounting books for small local businesses or managing household accounts for the elderly. Many people, including young executives, find second-income opportunities completely different from their full-time office work. Don't spend the extra money you're earning. Use it to pay off debts.
Discipline:

• Take all credit cards—except one for emergencies—out of your wallet. Cancel multiple Visas and MasterCards. Don't let them become a way to finance your daily living.

• Don't carry your checkbook around. Write yourself one allowance check every week...for lunches, newspapers and magazines, groceries, dry-cleaning and laundering, etc. Cash the check—and don't spend more than that for those expenses during the week. Become your own banker, and learn how to say "no."

• Make a list of your outstanding credit-card debts. Pay them off one at a time. Celebrate when you finish paying off the outstanding debt by cutting your card in half.
Concentrate on savings:

No matter how strapped for cash you feel you are, authorize automatic deductions from your salary for 401(k) savings or other company pension and profit-sharing programs.

Or set up your own automatic savings plan by arranging with a no-load mutual fund to make monthly transfers from your checking account into a mutual-fund investment account, preferably an IRA. When you get a raise, try putting all the extra money into automatic savings. Remember, up to $2,000 a year can go into an IRA. Even if you can't deduct your contributions, your investment will still grow tax-deferred.

Basic: If you don't see the money, you won't spend it, even though you're having a hard time living on your current income.

Set short-term savings goals—for a new car, for a new roof on the house, etc. Set up a money-market account separate from your long-term retirement account for this purpose. Make regular payments into it.
Resist home equity loans:

Don't try to solve your personal cash-flow problem by taking out a home-equity loan to pay off credit-card debts. Though ads for these loans point out that the interest expense is lower than credit-card rates and is tax-deductible, this is the most dangerous financing strategy left over from the 1980s.

The equity in your home is no longer growing as it once did. And, if you are in enough financial trouble to need a home-equity loan for this purpose, your tax bracket probably isn't high enough for the deduction to really matter.

Furthermore, many of these loans are structured so you pay interest only—with a big balloon payment of principal due down the road.

Putting your home on the line is a drastic step.

Added risk: Unless you totally give up your credit cards once you use the home-equity loan to bring the owed balances down to zero, the odds, unfortunately, are that you will start charging again and create new problems.
Young couples:

Even two very good incomes can be spent as easily as one modest salary—as we can see from all the two-income families that fall into terrible debt. The only way out of this trap is to deal with your finances openly and honestly. Set goals together and agree on a plan to meet these goals.

For many young couples, the most immediate goal is saving for a home. But be sure that you're not making yourself house-poor in the process of obtaining this goal. Before you buy a home, make sure that you have enough money for a down payment and a cash reserve for emergencies.

Trap: Most baby boomers have already bought their starter homes. Resale values are not likely to be very good. The costs of maintaining a condo, co-op, or house are rising much faster than rents right now. The so-called "American dream" of owning the most expensive home—with the largest mortgage—has turned into a nightmare for many families.

Showy competition about where you live and what you own is out now. Status these days is the increasing balance in your investment account. Build up your savings by living at home with your parents or sharing an apartment with friends longer than you (or they) might like. Grin and bear it, and save and invest money every month—it will pay in the long run.

Source: Terry Savage, syndicated personal-finance columnist for the *Chicago Sun Times*. She is the author of *Terry Savage's New Money Strategies for the 90s*, HarperBusiness, 10 E. 53 St., New York 10022.

The Secrets of Living On Just One Income

It's not only possible for an American family to live on a single income—in some cases, it may actually be better for the family. While some families are forced to live on one income, others make that choice to improve their family life.

In fact, many families that have adjusted to a single income report that they have come out ahead financially as well. Most families with two incomes spend huge amounts on child care and conveniences—housecleaning, laundry, lawn care, restaurants, take-out food, etc. Single-income families may take home only one salary, but they manage far better since they spend their money much more conservatively.
What's in it for you?

A second income can be desirable for a couple when both spouses enjoy their jobs and dislike domestic work. But many people work at jobs they hate—and they overestimate the value of the second income.

Example: It may really take you 60 hours a week to work at a 40-hour-per-week job for $15 an hour. If you factor in the time to ferry the kids to the babysitter, a lost lunch hour and commuting time, you're really making $10 an hour. Add taxes and costs for child care, your wardrobe and transportation, and you're down to $3.33 an hour, or less than $7,000 a year.

How to calculate: Figure out the taxes on the two incomes combined, then the taxes on the larger income alone. Subtract the difference from the smaller income.

Example: Given equal benefits, a couple with annual incomes of $25,000 and $15,000 pays $8,638 in taxes—or about 22%. On an income of $25,000, they would pay $4,516, or about 18%. The second income incurs $4,122 in additional taxes, reducing its value to $10,878.

Next, subtract the costs of child care, wardrobe and transportation from the second income to arrive at its ultimate value. Result: The net income of the second salary is often less than $5,000.

Alternative: Reduce family expenses by $5,000 and improve home life at the same time. Some ways to live comfortably—and well—on a single, modest income*...

*The income-earner can be either spouse or two part-timers.

• Reduce the family food bill. The average American family easily spends twice what it actually needs to on food.

Key: Comparison shop and keep track of prices. Eat at home more often. Pack school lunches. Prepare meals from scratch as often as possible. Also…

• Eliminate convenience foods—for example, single-serving sizes of "instant" soups, drinks and oatmeal, microwave meals or popcorn, soda (no nutritional value), even cold cereals (substitute homemade pancakes, waffles, muffins, oatmeal, and granola).

• Buy food on sale and in bulk. Structure the weekly menu and snacks around foods that are on sale.

• Buy generic brands.

• Make more soups, stews, and casseroles rather than meat-and-potato meals.

• Learn to make pizza from scratch, plant a garden, make jams and preserves.

Savings: Cut a $500 monthly food bill in half, or $3,000 a year.

• Economize on entertainment. The average kid receives 250 toys by the age of five—yet he/she is often bored. Better ways…

• Take kids to free events, borrow videotapes from the library, and stop spending so much on toys and games.

• Tolerate a period of complaining from your kids, then be amazed when they find imaginative things to do by themselves.

• Make kids responsible for buying their own extras. When they have to work for what they want, kids want much less.

Savings: $60 to $100 a month, or more.

• Buy secondhand clothing, especially for kids. Children's clothing is outgrown before it's outworn or out-of-style.

Urban and suburban areas offer great deals at yard sales and thrift stores. Buy clothes on sale—never pay full retail price for anything.

Example: Buy end-of-summer clothes for next summer.

Avoid fads…stick with the classics.

Annual savings: Several hundred dollars.

• Buy used furniture. Watch for classic furnishings that, when repaired, refinished or reupholstered, become "antiques." Savings: Hundreds to thousands a year.

• Practice small economies. Watch the pennies, and the dollars will take care of themselves. Make your own birthday and holiday decorations, Halloween costumes, valentines, wrapping paper, greeting cards.

• Change old habits. Use the library instead of buying new books. Give up bad, costly habits—particularly smoking and drinking. Be vigilant about turning off your heat, air conditioning and water heater when they are not in use. Buy generic prescription drugs. Water down your shampoo. Have a friend cut your hair. Savings: Hundreds to thousands of dollars a year.

More drastic measures:

• Drive cheaper cars. Buy a used car, or a new car you can maintain for 10 years.

• Move to a less-expensive neighborhood or region of the country.

• Instead of going on costly vacations, take day trips to local lakes, museums, state fairs, historic sites, or hiking trails.

Source: Amy Dacyczyn, author of *The Tightwad Gazette* (Villard Books), a book of cost-cutting strategies that have appeared in her newsletter of the same name, Rural Route 1, Box 3570, Leeds, Maine 04263. Monthly.

A Good Time For Low-Interest Loans To Family Members

Instead of giving money to a family member who needs it, consider making a low-interest loan. Both parties to the loan can benefit from the deal. Reasons to make family loans…

• To boost your investment income.

• To give a family member a favorable interest rate.

• To reduce estate taxes (a low-interest loan will be discounted for estate tax purposes).

• To shift income to low-bracket family members.

Bonus: Interest rates are exceedingly low today. Some believe that they are at their historic lows and can only go higher.

Caution: Low-interest loans can cause tax problems. In structuring the borrowing arrangements, be sure to avoid income-tax and gift-tax traps.

A parent as a mortgage holder:

Consider acting as "banker" for your child's purchase of a residence. Assume that you set the interest rate on a 30-year mortgage at 7%. This is a higher interest rate than you can get today on a long-term CD or Treasury bond, so your income will go up if you give the mortgage to your child.

On the other hand, the interest is lower than your child would pay for a commercial mortgage from a bank (currently about 7.5%). Thus, both parties benefit—you get more income than you could from other investments, while your child pays lower interest than he/she would otherwise have to pay.

Observe the formalities. In making a mortgage loan, consult an attorney. The debt must be secured by your child's principal residence and the mortgage filed with local authorities in order for the child to deduct the interest he/she pays on the loan.

"Imaginary" interest:

The federal government sets a minimum interest rate that must be charged on intra-family loans to avoid income-tax and gift-tax problems.

If you don't charge this minimum rate, the IRS can tax you on the difference between the federal rate and what you actually charged.

Example: If you give your child an interest-free loan, the IRS can say you should have charged 7% and tax you on the interest you should have received but didn't. This imaginary interest is called "imputed interest"—interest not actually received but treated as having been received.

Minimum interest rates are fixed monthly by the federal government according to the type and term of the loan.

• For demand loans and short-term loans (less than three years) made in July 1993, the federal rate was 3.95%.

• For mid-term loans (more than three but not over nine years), the rate was 5.54%.

• For long-term loans (more than nine years), the rate was 6.61%.

Exception I: The imputed interest rules do not apply to loans of up to $10,000 made to purchase non-income-producing property. Thus, for example, an individual could lend his brother $9,000 for the purchase of a car and not charge interest and not incur any imputed interest.

Exception II: For income-tax purposes, loans up to $100,000 escape the imputed interest rules if the borrower's net investment income (interest, dividends, or capital gains, all less related expenses) is under $1,000. For example, if a parent lends a daughter $100,000 to pay for medical school and the daughter does not have any investments that are producing income, interest need not be charged and the parent does not have any imputed income. If the daughter's net investment income is more than $1,000, imputed interest is limited to the amount of her net investment income.

Avoiding gift taxes:

For gift-tax purposes, below-market loans over $10,000 result in a deemed gift to the extent of the foregone interest, that is, interest below the federal rate. As a practical matter, no gift tax is generally owed, however, because gifts of $10,000 and under are not taxed.

Example: If an interest-free demand loan of $100,000 is made in July 1993 by a parent to a child, a deemed gift of $3,950 results when you apply the federal interest rate to the amount of the loan. This gift would not be taxable because it is more than offset by the $10,000 gift-tax exclusion.

Write it out: In making any intrafamily loan, be sure to put in writing the terms involved... stated interest rate, repayment schedule, and, if applicable, collateral. Failure to do so may result in a charge by the IRS that the entire loan is really a gift, not just the foregone interest.

Estate-planning loans:

The parent who believes that rates are bound to go higher in the future will realize estate-tax savings by making a long-term loan to a child.

Assume that the parent who made the 30-year mortgage loan at 7% in the example above dies 10 years after making the loan, when comparable rates are 10% or 11% (the rate in effect only a few years ago). The value of the remaining mortgage in the parent's estate will be discounted for estate-tax purposes to account for the low-interest rate it bears. Above-market loans:

Intrafamily loans can be used to shift income to family members on a tax-advantaged basis.

Example: A mother has $100,000 invested in CDs currently paying 3.5%, and her son plans to put an addition on his house. Instead of his getting a commercial home-improvement loan from a bank, his mother loans him the money at 8%. He avoids "points" and other closing costs, and his mother increases her annual income.

While the tax law specifies minimum interest rates, it does not mention maximums. However, the rate on intrafamily loans should be fixed according to the prevailing commercial rate because a higher rate could result in a "gift" from the child to his parent.

Source: Thomas J. Hakala, partner, personal financial planning practice, KPMG Peat Marwick, 599 Lexington Ave., New York 10022.

What Your Bank Won't Tell You About Your Bank Credit Card

Your bank is rarely on your side. Too often, it's trying to take more of your money than it actually deserves. It will seldom volunteer information that might save you time and money. Here are 10 secrets about your credit card that your bank probably has not told you…

•You risk being rejected for auto loans and home mortgages if you already have a walletful of credit cards. These days, less can be more when it comes to credit cards.

If you have 10 credit cards, five with significant outstanding balances, and apply for a loan, many lenders will be troubled by the amount of your outstanding debt. Some may also be put off by the amount of potential debt you could incur if you reached your limits on all your cards. It's always smart to get rid of excess plastic. Best: No more than two cards.

•You should say "no" when your bank in-creases your credit limit. Such increases may leave you feeling flattered but ultimately can leave you in worse financial shape. Reasons:

•A higher credit limit can bring increased temptation.

•Many lenders add up your credit limits rather than actual debts, so your new added borrowing power may cause you to be rejected for an important future loan.

You can say, thanks, but no thanks in writing or by phone. It's easy and painless.

•Merchants are not allowed to require minimum credit card purchases. While many merchants set minimum purchase amounts, they're forbidden to do so by MasterCard and Visa, and they violate at least the spirit of their agreement with American Express.

What can you do? Talk to the store manager and tell him/her that you know the rules. If he insists, the best way to retaliate is to report the action. Get as much information about the store as possible (address, phone number, etc.) and send it along with a letter to your credit card company.*

Exception: The Discover Card allows minimum purchase amounts.

•You can use your credit cards to earn 28% on your money. Let's say you put $100 in the bank and earned 28% (nice thought). In one year, you'd earn $28. If you were in the 31% tax bracket, that would leave you with an after-tax return of $18.48.

But what if you used that $100 to pay off a credit card debt charging you 18.5% interest? Since you are using after-tax dollars, you would save $18.48 in finance charges in the course of the year. That's a return of 18.48%— almost exactly the after-tax return on your 28% investment.

•You do not have to give personal information when paying by credit card. Merchants ask for this information to expand their databases, and many also sell their customer information lists to direct marketers.

No matter what a merchant says, you don't have to write any personal information on a credit card sales slip. Requiring such personal

*Complaints can be sent to: MasterCard, Public Relations, 888 Seventh Ave., New York 10106…or Visa, Consumer Relations, Box 8999, San Francisco 94128.

information as a condition of a sale is expressly prohibited by American Express, Master-Card, and Visa.

Furthermore, several states prohibit merchants from writing personal information on sales slips. Effective line: "It's against the credit card company's rules to require such information."

• You're entitled to free insurance when you rent a car. One great perk offered by gold MasterCard and Visa and green, gold and platinum American Express cards is free collision-damage-waiver (CDW) insurance when you rent a car. This benefit is particularly valuable for people who don't have their own auto insurance—and it can save you $10 to $15 a day when you rent a car.

• You can get a gold card credit limit on your regular card. If you're paying a high annual fee because you like your gold card's high credit limit, you may be wasting money. Reasons:

• You could get a no-fee gold card instead.

• Most bank card issuers want to keep you as a customer and will raise the credit limit on your standard card to $5,000 or sometimes even more. All you have to do is ask. There should be no additional charge.

• Never put your credit card number on your checks—even when paying your credit card bill. Do so and you're setting yourself up to be a potential fraud victim. Anyone who comes across such a check would have access to your name, address, telephone number and, of course, credit card number.

With this information—plus your Social Security number, which several states use as the sole identifying number on drivers' licenses—a thief would be able to request your credit report or, far worse, apply for credit in your name. Two common frauds today:

Mail-order fraud. A person uses your credit card number to order merchandise that will be sent to an address other than your own.

Application fraud. The crook temporarily "steals" your identity and applies for credit in your name.

You don't have to worry when you pay a credit card bill with a check and leave off your credit card number. Your account is credited as soon as the envelope is opened by the credit card issuer.

• Your ex-spouse can ruin your credit. Divorce does not dissolve the legal contracts you have with lenders. Credit card contracts, for example, can only be broken with the consent of one or both of the cardholders and the consent of the creditor. So if your ex keeps using an account that has your name on it and doesn't pay his/her debts, your credit rating could be decimated.

If you're facing a divorce now, contact lenders immediately to see what you should do to close your joint accounts permanently. Nothing your lawyer does—and nothing the divorce decree says—can release you from your obligations. Only the lender can do that.

• Your kids can kill your credit. Becoming a co-signer for your child's credit card or personal loan is a loving gesture—but it can turn into a disaster.

If he/she doesn't pay as expected, your credit rating could suffer. Remember, this includes late-payment problems as well as outright defaults. So, if you do co-sign for your child, make it clear that his financial irresponsibility could haunt you.

Co-signing can cause problems in another way, too. Co-sign for someone and that obligation will often be included in a tally of your total debts made by a creditor. As a result, you might have trouble getting a loan when you want one.

Source: Gerri Detweiler, executive director of Bankcard Holders of America, 560 Herndon Pkwy., Herndon, Virginia 22070. She is the author of *The Ultimate Credit Handbook*, Plume Press, 375 Hudson St., New York 10014.

How to Make the Most Of Coupon Clipping

By clipping coupons and mailing in hundreds of rebates, Sue Diffily has saved $3,700 on her supermarket bill during the past three years. Her cost-cutting, income-stretching secrets...

Setting aside time:

At my clipping peak five years ago, when

all of my three children were still at home and my food bill was $500 a month, I saved $75 every two weeks by using coupons and rebates. While today my food bill is lower, I still devote 17 hours each month to coupon clipping and rebates:

•Three hours for coupon clipping and sale hunting.

•Eight hours for filing the coupons.

•Four hours filling out paperwork on rebate offers.

•Two hours meeting with my coupon club, where I swap coupons and rebates.

This tally excludes the eight hours a month I spend shopping, since I would do that anyway.

Payoff: About $9 an hour in income, after taxes and expenses. It's a job for which I make my own hours and answer only to myself.

Rating the sources:

•Supermarket flyers are a great source of store coupons and company rebate forms. They are distributed through the mail or at the stores themselves. You can also find valuable rebates in the flyers of supermarkets at which you don't ordinarily shop. Many contain rebate offers from national companies—such as Pillsbury or General Mills—which are valid regardless of where you purchase the items.

•Daily newspapers—especially Wednesday and Sunday supplements—and women's and parenting magazines, such as *Parents, Good Housekeeping, McCall's, Ladies' Home Journal,* etc., often have coupon sections.

•Coupon club. Although it's not essential to join a club to profit from coupon clipping, it can't hurt. I joined one about 10 years ago by responding to an ad in my local supermarket. Today, six of us meet for two hours once a month to pool nearly 1,000 unwanted coupons and rebate offers. Anyone in the club is welcome to take as many coupons as he/she would like. But a simple rule applies to the rebate forms—which may be worth several dollars apiece or much more—when you take one, you replace it with another.

•Family and friends. They can be a great resource. If you put the word out, you'll be deluged with coupons they've clipped for you.

Organizing your files:

•Coupons. I keep my coupons in an ex-

pandable, accordion folder. Some people file them alphabetically by brand. This is great if you can keep track of every brand. However, I find this too difficult.

I prefer to organize my coupons by product category—breakfast products, meat and poultry, dairy and oils, beverages, desserts, cleaning products—which is how I shop.

Every two weeks, before I go shopping, I comb my file and pull out any coupons that are due to expire that month as well as any others I think I'll use. I also check the newspapers to see which products are on sale at my favorite supermarket. When I shop, I take along a shoe box filled with coupons.

•Rebates. Until recently, most rebate offers required that you mail a box top or side in with the rebate form. To save these items required a fair amount of space—for me, that meant three boxes, each of which were 1-foot-by-2-feet-by-1½-feet deep.

But lately, companies ask only for the product's bar code or proof-of-purchase seal, which is much less bulky. For every product I buy, I simply tear off the front of the product package, put it in a large resealable bag, and slip in the proofs-of-purchase and bar codes as I accumulate them. This helps me know immediately which products they're for, in case a rebate is offered.

To keep track of my rebates, I keep a notebook. I divide the pages into columns for the company, the particular item, the date I mailed the form, the amount of the offer, and the date I received the rebate. It usually takes between one and three months to receive a rebate.

In the event of a long delay, I call the company's 800-number. In most cases, the rebate check arrives soon after my call—often with some free coupons thrown in.

Some people spend their rebates as soon as they get them. To stay motivated, I have set up a separate bank account. Whenever I've collected $10, I make a deposit.

Saving more:

I don't clip every coupon—and I don't use every coupon I clip. I only purchase items that I know my family will use. If I overbought just to cash in my coupons, I'd be losing money on the deal. My other strategies...

•Watch for sales. By waiting until prices are marked down, you effectively increase the value of a coupon.

•Don't get locked into brand loyalty. I'll buy a store brand if the price is right and I have a good coupon. Often, one brand turns out to be just as good as any other brand, and if I don't like the store brand, I avoid it in the future.

•When you find a good deal, stock up. My family used to laugh when I'd come home with 20 bars of soap or a dozen bottles of cooking oil that I bought on sale with a coupon for each. But I knew we would use them eventually. In the long run, these big purchases make great financial sense.

•Look for "double plays" and "triple plays." These can save you two or three times what you would have saved with just a coupon.

Double play: This purchase involves a combination of a sale and a coupon or rebate.

Example: While I like a particular brand of lipstick, it normally costs about $6, which I feel is a bit steep. But when the company ran a "buy-one-get-one-free" sale, I got four for a total of $12. With a rebate form I obtained at my local beauty aids store, I got back $2.50 per stick. My net cost: 50 cents per stick.

Triple play: This is a purchase involving a sale, a coupon and a rebate. By capitalizing on all three, you could wind up paying virtually nothing for an item.

Example: My favorite detergent normally costs $3.99 for a 64-ounce box. I'll accumulate a number of $1 coupons for that brand—and then use them all when it goes on sale for $1.99. My net cost: 99 cents per box. But if I then use a typical rebate—$2 back for two proofs-of-purchase—I get the detergent free.

Triple plays and organization are the keys to couponing and refunding.

Source: Sue Diffily, a homemaker and former second-grade teacher who lives in Smithtown, New York. She lectures locally on coupon clipping.

Bank-Failure Loophole

If your bank fails and your deposits exceed $100,000 (the maximum amount insured by the FDIC), you can still use the uninsured portion to pay off any outstanding debt to the bank you may have. Request a "voluntary off-set" from the bank's claims agent. Example: Someone with $120,000 in deposits and a $50,000 bank loan can ask that the $20,000 not covered by the FDIC be used to pay down the loan. Rationale: You probably won't see the $20,000 for some time, and when you do, you aren't likely to receive the full amount. Meanwhile, your debt would be reduced by the amount offset, dollar for dollar.

Source: Cody Buck is a former senior executive of the FDIC's division of liquidation. He is author of *The ABCs of FDIC: How to Save Your Assets from Liquidation,* CoStarr Publications, Box 2052, Coppell, Texas 75019.

How to Protect Your Money from the People Who Protect the Places That Protect Your Money

Most of us who have accounts at banks or savings and loan institutions know little about Federal Deposit Insurance Corporation (FDIC) protection.

This lack of knowledge can be costly if your bank or savings and loan goes under—for part of your money may not be insured. Answers to the most common questions about FDIC coverage...

Are all banks and savings and loans protected by the FDIC? Most banks are protected, but some private banks are not. Be sure to look for the FDIC label on your bank's door or at the tellers' windows.

Are all individual accounts covered separately by the FDIC? Up to how much? Most people know that the FDIC covers individual accounts up to $100,000. What they don't know is that an individual account is determined by adding up each account held under a common name or Social Security number.

Example: If a person has a savings account with $50,000 in it and a certificate of deposit for $60,000 at the same bank, $10,000 is uninsured.

Accounts set up under the Uniform Gifts to

Minors Act are considered to be the child's account, even though the parent has control over it.

What about joint accounts? Are they fully protected? Joint accounts held by the same combination of persons at the same bank are only protected up to $100,000, regardless of whose Social Security number appears on them.

Example: A husband and wife with two joint accounts of $100,000 each are insured only up to $100,000, not $200,000.

Avoid this restriction by using both individual and joint accounts.

Example: If you have an individual savings account of $100,000 and a joint savings account with your spouse of $100,000 at the same bank, each account has full protection. Your spouse can have an individual savings account of $100,000 and receive full coverage on it as well.

Are all deposits covered by the FDIC? Mutual funds and other investments made through a bank are not protected. If you have any questions concerning FDIC insurance, call the FDIC at 800-934-3342.

Are trust accounts treated separately by the FDIC? Yes, but only if the trusts are for members of your immediate family—a spouse, child or grandchild. But, if you set up an account in trust for your father, for example, it is treated as part of your account.

Trust accounts for a spouse, child, or grandchild (including step and adopted children) enjoy separate coverage, even if you have both an individual and a joint account.

Example: If you have an individual account with $100,000, a joint account with your spouse of $100,000, and a trust account for your spouse of $100,000, the accounts are all fully insured.

Can an individual open accounts at several branches of the same bank and receive full protection for each? You cannot increase the limit of coverage by depositing funds in different branches of the same bank.

Self-defense: Diversify your funds among several banks.

Are IRAs and Keoghs fully protected? At the moment, each retirement account is treated separately from individual accounts and receives full coverage.

Example: If you have an individual account of $100,000, an IRA of $100,000 and a Keogh of $100,000 at the same bank, each account is fully insured.

Important: After December 19, 1993, IRA and Keogh accounts will be lumped together for purposes of coverage limits. But transitional rules afford some protection for existing accounts.

Self-defense: As IRA or Keogh CDs mature, roll over sufficient amounts to other institutions to maximize FDIC coverage.

Source: Cody Buck, a former executive of the FDIC and author of *The ABCs of FDIC: How to Save Your Assets From Liquidation.* CoStarr Publications, Box 2052, Coppell, Texas 75019. 800-925-3252.

ATM Self-Defense

Discarding your ATM receipt at the bank may help thieves loot your account, says bank expert Ed Mrkvicka. High-tech bandits are using video cameras to observe/record customers punching in ID numbers at teller machines. Then they match it to the account numbers on receipts left behind. Self-defense: Guard your PIN number…retain receipts to match up against monthly bank statements. If there's a withdrawal discrepancy, report it immediately to the bank.

Interest Rate Predictor

Though Clinton's plans for the economy are still unclear, keep an eye on the Commodity Research Bureau's Futures Index. It appears on the front page of the "Money & Investing" section of *The Wall Street Journal.* If the index goes above 205, interest rates will likely move higher. If it falls below 200, rates will drop.

Source: Roger Klein, PhD, is an economist and president of The Timing Strategies Corp., a money-management firm in Princeton, New Jersey.

Bank Junk Mail

Junk mail from banks shouldn't be considered junk. Carefully read all the enclosures with your monthly statements. Notices of potentially significant problems are crafted very carefully. Banks use them to announce policy changes, mergers and acquisitions...notify customers of new interest rates and fees... report earnings and compliance with federal regulations. If you don't understand a communication, call the bank and have an officer explain it.

Source: *Your Bank: How to Get Better Service* by Jeff Davidson and the editors of Consumer Reports Books, 101 Truman Ave., Yonkers, New York 10703.

The Credit Card Switch

Does it pay to switch credit cards every time you see a better deal on the annual fees? Does frequent switching affect your credit rating?

It pays to switch once—to a no-annual-fee card. There are many available, including some (like those from Texas-based USAA) that also offer low interest rates. Avoid cards that offer no fee for the first year only—after that, they have no advantages.

Officially, frequent switching does not hurt your credit rating, but why draw extra unwanted attention to your credit history with switches?

Important: Close accounts you no longer want by sending a certified letter to the issuer stating that you want the account closed—by customer request. This protects you against records saying your account was shut off. Accounts not formally closed may be carried in your credit history as still available for use, leading some issuers to reject you for new accounts because you have too much available credit already.

Source: Mary Beth Butler, Bankcard Holders of America, 560 Herndon Pkwy., Suite 120, Herndon, Virginia 22070.

Credit Cards Are Not All Alike to the IRS

The general rule is that you only get a tax deduction in the year you actually pay for a deductible expense. But there's an important exception when you pay with a credit card. For tax purposes, payment is considered made on the date of the transaction, not on the date you paid the credit card company. Expenditures charged at the end of this year can be deducted this year even though you don't pay for them until next year.

But if you charge a deductible expense on a credit card issued by the company supplying the deductible goods (or services), you can't take a deduction until the credit card bill is paid. Example: If you have a prescription filled at a department store pharmacy and charge it on a credit card issued by the store, you can't deduct the cost of that medication until you get the bill and pay it. But if you charge the same prescription on a credit card issued by a third party, such as MasterCard or Visa, you can deduct it right away.

Bank Credit Cards Are Not All Alike

Should you keep the bank credit card you have now, or apply for ones that offer greater advantages? One Visa card or MasterCard could be very different from another Visa or MasterCard.

The MasterCard and Visa organizations do not issue credit cards themselves. They provide a clearing system for charges and payments on the cards and license banks to use the Visa or MasterCard name. It is the issuing bank that determines the interest rates and fees.

A bank's name on a credit card does not necessarily mean that it is the bank actually issuing the card. Issuance of credit cards is a high-risk, low-profit business. Seldom does a small bank issue its own.

Generally, a small bank will act as an agent for an issuing bank. The agent bank puts its name on the card, but it is the issuing bank that actually extends any credit.

Aside from costs, this can be important if the cardholder encounters an error. The correction might have to be agreed upon, not by a friendly local banker, but by an unknown, larger institution, perhaps in a different state.

Visa, for example, has about 1,400 issuing banks in the U.S. and about 10,500 agent banks.

Choosing which card to take is becoming more difficult, because some of the nation's largest banks have begun active solicitation of customers throughout the U.S. Individuals must be especially careful about accepting any offer that might come in the mail.

A recently discovered quirk in the federal law allows federally chartered out-of-state banks to ignore state usury laws that limit the amount of interest or fees that the issuing bank may charge on its credit cards. In Arkansas, for example, state usury laws prevent local banks from charging more than 10% interest on credit card balances. But a federally chartered out-of-state bank, in lending to Arkansas residents, may charge whatever its home state allows. Even within individual states, the terms on credit cards can vary widely.

Aside from the actual rates and fees, individuals must carefully check the fine print of their contracts. Most banks, for example, do not charge interest on balances stemming from purchases until the customer is billed for such purchases. If the bill on which the charges first appear is paid in full by the stated due date, there is no interest charge to the holder. But some banks, those in Texas, for example, begin charging interest as soon as they receive the charge slip and make payments to the merchant. Thus, interest begins accumulating even before the cardholder receives the bill. These interest charges continue until the bank receives payment from the customer.

Source: Robert A. Bennett, banking correspondent, *The New York Times.*

Correcting a Bad Credit Report

What do you do if you are dissatisfied with a credit bureau's file and would like to contest the information contained in its credit report? Under the Fair Credit Reporting Act, you are allowed to dispute any item contained in your credit file. By law, the credit bureau is required to investigate and remove any information that is not correct.

What if you are still unhappy with the credit agency's resolution? Even if you can't change the actual information contained in the report, you always have the right to insert a statement of 100 words or less explaining why you feel the report is inaccurate.

Source: Thomas G. Collins, Jr., director of planning for one of the five major credit reporting companies in the US, The Credit Bureau, Inc., 1600 Peachtree St. NW, Atlanta, GA 30309. His responsibilities are business, marketing, and strategic planning for the firm.

4

Insurance Savvy

Why Buying Credit Life Or Disability Insurance From Your Bank Is A Rip-Off

When you apply for a car loan—or other installment loans, for that matter—most banks try to sell you credit life and disability insurance to cover the borrowed amount. Except in rare cases, banks are prohibited from requiring that you buy policies.

Many banks use high-pressure sales tactics because selling insurance is one of their most profitable sidelines.

Typically, a bank earns as much as 40% of an insurance policy's premium as commission.

How the banks get you:

The purpose of credit life and disability insurance is to repay the bank if you die or are seriously injured. Bank officers are often trained to sell these policies by painting a grim picture of a poor, grieving husband or wife struggling to pay off the loan after his/ her spouse is gone.

What some banks don't tell you, however, is that you don't have to buy it. It also doesn't tell those who want credit life insurance for protective purposes that they would be better off buying it directly from an independent agent.

An insurance agent can offer a whole life policy whereas credit life is a rapidly decreasing term policy. It would also be cheaper, and your survivors would be able to choose how they would deploy the proceeds. For example, they might need to use the cash some other way and would prefer to continue to make the monthly payments on the loan.

Bank's favorite scare tactics:

To put further pressure on you, banks often don't mention insurance until the closing, when all the papers have been drawn up. At this point, there's virtually no time left to think about it, and most people are afraid to jeopardize the loan by complaining. The best way to avoid this is by not waiting until the last minute to address it. Tell the bank in the early stages—but after receiving loan approval—that you're not interested in the policies.

Some banks also add policy premiums onto the principal of your loan and then calculate the finance charges on the total.

Example: Here's how such an error would work on a $10,000, 48-month car loan charging 10.25% in annual interest:

Without insurance

Loan amount	$10,000.00
Finance charge	2,231.36
Total	$12,231.36
Monthly payment	*$254.82*

With credit life insurance

Loan amount	$10,000.00
Credit life premium	250.76
Finance charge	2,287.32
Total	$12,538.08
Monthly payment	*$261.21*

With credit life and disability insurance

Loan amount	$10,000.00
Credit life premium	270.07
Disability premium	769.69
Finance charge	2,463.60
Total	$13,503.36
Monthly payment	*$281.32*

This means that you would be paying an additional hidden finance charge of $55.96 if you bought just the credit life insurance, and $232.24 if you bought both. That's because the high-priced premiums were included in the financing.

Finally, many banks often don't mention that you can pay these premiums in cash and avoid the added finance charges altogether.

Source: Edward F. Mrkvicka, Jr., author of *The Bank Book: How To Revoke Your Bank's License To Steal*, HarperCollins, 10 E. 53 St., New York 10022. He is also publisher of *Money Insider*, a financial newsletter for consumers, Reliance Enterprises, Inc., Box 413, Marengo, Illinois 60152.

Health Insurance Trap

Beware of opting out of your employer's health insurance plan because you're covered by your spouse's plan. While you may avoid paying premiums on a policy you think is unnecessary, there are risks. *Examples:* If your spouse loses his/her job you'll both be offered a COBRA plan, which only lasts 18 months. If your spouse's company goes under, both of you may have to pay higher fees for a conversion plan that may be more limited. And, if your spouse's employer downgrades its policy, you would be stuck with its coverage.

Source: Howard Klein is a partner with Klein, McGorry & Klein Ltd., an insurance broker and consultancy, 111 W. 57 St., New York 10019.

Life Insurance Trap

Life insurance policies bought just a few years ago probably are worth less, and will end up costing *more*, than policyholders were led to expect. *Problem:* Insurance agents use performance projections to illustrate expected value. But the projections aren't guaranteed—and performance figures are falling. Many insurers have cut dividends, and most will likely do so again this year. And some people with "vanishing-premium" policies (premium payments that are projected to stop at some point) are finding that insurers have either requested more premium payments…or are reducing the cash values of their policies. *Self-defense:* Review current insurance needs—and get current policy projections from insurers. If the reports are too complex to grasp, consider engaging a qualified insurance broker or financial planner to help you.

Source: Michael J. Chasnoff, CFP, is president of Advanced Capital Strategies, Cincinnati fee-only financial planners.

Doctors and Medicare

Doctors cannot charge *Medicare Part B* patients—those age 65 or older and on Social Security—more than 15% over maximum fees set by Medicare. Medicare pays 80% of these maximum fees, and the patient pays the other 20%. *Example:* On a Medicare-set fee of $250, a doctor can charge up to $287.50. The patient must pay 20% of $250 ($50)—plus the $37.50 difference. *Problem:* Medigap insurance covers a patient's 20% co-payment, but all policies may not pay the extra charge. Patients billed more than the legal 15% extra (as shown on their Explanation of Medicare Benefits forms) should show the form to their doctors—and request a refund.

Source: Elder-law attorney Barbara Weltman, Esq., is the author of *Your Parent's Financial Security,* John Wiley & Sons, Inc., 605 Third Ave., New York 10158.

Cheaper Term-Life Insurance

Switch underwriters every three to five years. *Reason:* Annually renewable term-policy premiums increase every year. But—a new insurance company will start your policy off at its low first-year rate. *Important:* This works only for those who are physically able to qualify for a new policy. If in doubt about health, stick to the old policy. *Caution:* Don't drop the old policy before the new one takes effect.

Source: Jonathan Pond, president of Financial Planning Information, Inc., in Watertown, Massachusetts, is the author of *The New Century Family Money Book,* Dell Publishing, 666 Fifth Ave., New York 10103.

How to Get the Lowest Rates on Auto Insurance

Finding affordable auto insurance need not be a headache. How to make sure you are paying the lowest premium for the coverage you need…

• Shop around. Prices for the same coverage can vary by hundreds of dollars. If you're looking for a new policy or considering switching policies, get quotes from several insurance agents and from at least one "direct writer," such as GEICO or Worldwide Insur-

ance. This will give you a good idea of the range of costs in your area.

Caution: Don't simply look for the best prices. The insurer you select should also offer excellent service. Ask friends and business associates whether their insurers pay claims quickly, and for the ones with which they've had a bad experience.

Once you've narrowed the list, check the financial stability of the insurers you're considering at the public library in such publications as A.M. Best, Standard & Poor's and back issues of *Consumer Reports.*

• Take the highest deductible you can afford. Ultimately it saves money on your premium. That's because the higher your deductible, the lower your insurance premium. Since the odds of your having an accident are slim, your annual savings will be considerable. *Prudent:* Invest some of this savings in a fund for use in case you get into an accident and have to meet the high deductible.

• Buy a low-profile car. Your rates will be higher if your car is flashy and therefore more likely to attract thieves. When buying a new car, find out which models are the most and least frequently stolen.*

• Buy a safe car. Cars that best withstand crashes and are least expensive to repair qualify for discounted rates, while cars that are costly to fix or easily damaged are charged higher premiums.

Safest: Large, four-door models, station wagons, passenger vans, etc. The Highway Loss Data Institute also issues information on injury and collision rates by automobile make and model.

• Buy a good used car. New cars lose much of their value the moment they are driven off the lot, which means the amount you can recoup if the car is totaled is immediately less than the amount you paid for it. A good-quality used car may be worth less than a new one, but it costs less to insure. The April 1993 issue of *Consumer Reports* is devoted to car-buying information and includes a list of used cars to consider and which ones to avoid.**

Contact: Highway Loss Data Institute, 1005 N. Glebe Rd., Arlington, Virginia 22201.
**Consumer Reports*, Box 51166, Boulder, Colorado 80321. 800-234-1645.

•Drop collision or comprehensive coverage on older vehicles. Collision coverage is limited to the value of your car at the time of an accident. Comprehensive coverage reimburses you for the value of possessions in the car if it is stolen or damaged by a calamity other than an accident—earthquake, flood, etc.

These two types of coverage can account for as much as 45% of your total premium. If your car is worth less than $1,000, your deductible and premiums probably exceed the amount of any claim you might file.

•Eliminate duplicate medical coverage. In some states the medical section of auto-insurance policies covering hospital and doctor expenses if you or your family is injured in an auto accident is optional. You should opt out if the insurance duplicates coverage already provided in your standard health-insurance policy.

•Take advantage of special programs. If you are older than age 50, the American Association of Retired Persons (AARP) offers low-cost insurance coverage. Current or former military officers can get low rates from the USAA (800-531-8080). Several states have companies that accept customers who fit low-risk profiles.

Examples: New Jersey Manufacturers, 20th Century Insurers in California.

•If you are considering moving, check rates in the surrounding area. Auto-insurance rates vary not only by state but by city—*and neighborhood*. If you live in a low-crime area or in an area in which few accidents have occurred, your rates will be lower than most.

Source: Jeanne M. Salvatore, manager of consumer affairs at the Insurance Information Institute, 110 William St., New York 10038. The Institute is a nonprofit organization that encourages public understanding of the property- and casualty-insurance industries. For additional information on auto insurance, call the National Insurance Consumer Helpline: 800-942-4242.

How to Protect Yourself from Your Health Insurer

Millions of Americans have no problems with their health insurance. They file the necessary forms…their claims are paid…and all parties are satisfied.

But thousands of Americans do have serious complaints regarding health claims. Frequently, policyholders are abandoned by their insurers when they most need the coverage. *Problem:* The higher the ultimate amount of your claim, the more likely you are to encounter a violation of your insurance contract by your insurer.

Due to the complexity of the laws governing insurance, what insurers can—and what they can't—do is often unclear. Here are some of the most common questions policyholders must face…

Can my insurer change or reduce my coverage? Unfortunately, yes. *Key:* The insurer must give policyholders early notice of the changes. *Recommended:* Read all mail from your insurer—*carefully*. Often, such notices are buried in communications that appear to be junk mail.

Self-defense: If the reduction in coverage is made before you have a health problem, complain to your employer or union or switch policies.

What if the coverage is reduced after I have filed a claim? It is unclear if insurers can legally reduce coverage once a policyholder is "on claim" for a particular accident or disease. However, insurance companies have recently been getting away with it in court.

Reason: Every state has consumer protection rules that limit an insurer's ability to change coverage in midstream. But for individuals insured through their employers, state laws are preempted by a federal law, ERISA (the Employee Retirement Income Security Act). ERISA makes *no* provisions for arbitrary reductions or changes in coverage.

Some courts are sympathetic to insurers rather than individual policyholders in the belief that premiums will rise if insurers are forced to pay all of the claims they have contracted to pay.

Example: Recently, a man who was insured under his employer's self-insurance plan had the $1 million AIDS coverage his policy promised reduced to a mere $5,000—*after* he became ill. The court allowed the reduced benefit to stand.

In this controversial area, trial attorneys take the position that this is a vesting issue… that once a person is "on claim," it is illegal to reduce benefits.

Self-defense: Seek legal advice if your benefits are reduced after you are on claim.

Can I be dropped from a group, or can my health insurance be cancelled? Generally, no. If you are insured as a member of a group, the insurer would have to cancel the entire group. It is illegal to single out just one person.

Exception: If you are insured through your employer and become so seriously injured or ill that you cannot work, your insurer may try to claim that your employment relationship has ended. Thus you are no longer part of the group—and can be cancelled in mid-claim.

Again, this is a gray area. Many states prohibit this type of cancellation, but the state laws are negated under ERISA. Trial attorneys say that a person is vested if he/she becomes injured or ill while employed. Case law precedent holds that the insurer must continue to cover claims resulting from that particular illness or injury. However, some courts have held otherwise.

Self-defense: Check your insurance contract for conditions under which you can be dropped. They are usually headed "Termination of Coverage." Don't automatically accept a cancellation if it occurs. This area of law is technical and esoteric. Insurance companies are making up the rules, generally to their advantage and policyholders' disadvantage, and thereby forcing policyholders to challenge them in court. Seek an attorney who is experienced in this area.

There are cases in which an insurer has dropped an entire group of policyholders, claiming it's discontinuing its group health coverage business. State laws that once required insurers to provide alternate coverage for such policyholders have been negated under ERISA, leaving large numbers of people uninsured, and uninsurable, in mid-claim.

When can my insurer decide that my *new* claim was a preexisting condition? This is an area where policyholders frequently fail to get the coverage they believe they are paying for.

Carefully check your policy for conditions that are excluded for either a certain amount of time, or altogether.

General rule: For an insurer to deem a condition "preexisting," you must have seen a doctor for the condition, and had a symptom the doctor could diagnose as indicating that condition, previous to your insurance policy taking effect.

Everyone may have the symptomless beginnings of an undetected health problem. But some insurers stretch their definition of "preexisting."

Example: A man is denied coverage for his heart attack because his doctor told him he had high cholesterol three years earlier and recommended that he watch his diet.

Self-defense: Challenge the denial. Your condition must have been diagnosable to be considered preexisting. If it wasn't diagnosed, you have a strong case for coverage. Even if it was diagnosed, you may be able to prove it wasn't preexisting.

Can insurers apply exclusions in unfair or illegitimate ways? They can, and they do. Coverage exclusions are legal, and common for entire categories of treatment, such as alcoholism, drug dependence, and psychiatric care.

Caution: Insurers may try to "weasel out" of coverage *related* to these exclusions. *Example:* An insurer may deny coverage for a liver ailment, claiming it was a result of alcoholism and is therefore excluded.

Self-defense: Challenge the denial. It's the liver that's being treated, not the alcoholism.

Insurers also tend to deny coverage based on broad interpretation of legitimate exclusions.

Examples: Experimental treatment…medical versus "custodial" care…treatment or hospital days that are "not medically necessary."

Danger area: Policies that pay for accidents but not sickness. *Catch:* You file a claim for injuries resulting from a fall, the insurer says the fall was caused by dizziness resulting from a disease, so the fall was not accidental.

Can the insurance company's doctor's opinion overrule my doctor's judgment? Usually, yes. A number of insurance policies even state that the insurer reserves the right to have its own "medical director" make a final determination when benefits are being disputed.

Problem: As an employee of the insurer, this medical director almost always rules against the policyholder.

Self-defense: The best insurance contracts state that the deciding opinion in a claim will be by the policyholder's treating physician.

Reality: Most insurers will not put this issue in writing, and most insurance policies say *nothing* about who decides in the event of a dispute.

Exception: A union or large corporation may be able to negotiate an appropriate clause in its contract.

What can I do to protect myself? It's impossible to be totally secure, no matter what your insurance contract says. But there are ways to minimize risk. *Suggestions:*

• If your employer offers a choice of insurers, investigate the claims records of each company.

Best source: Whoever handles claims for your employer. Inquire about each insurer's history of paying claims, delays versus timeliness, invoking exclusions and preexisting conditions, etc. *Reason:* There is no way to access an insurer's records on how well it pays claims. Your state department of insurance may keep records of complaints filed, but many don't keep records.

• To ensure more clout when contesting a claim, consider buying additional group insurance that is not provided through an employer and thus does not fall under the jurisdiction of ERISA. Such policies are regulated by state insurance law and are therefore easier to take recourse on if problems arise.

Examples: Plans offered through professional associations, organizations such as AARP, NOW, and many others.

Source: William M. Shernoff, a specialist in consumer claims against insurance companies, and author of *How to Make Insurance Companies Pay Your Claims*, Hastings House, 141 Halstead Ave., Mamaroneck, New York 10543. His Claremont, California law firm, Shernoff, Bidart & Darras, has a staff of insurance analysts who will answer questions regarding insurance coverage, disputes and ERISA. Policyholders can call 714-621-4935.

How to Protect Your Health Insurance Rights

In 1988, Jack McGann filed a claim for medical expenses related to his treatment for AIDS. After reviewing the claim, his employer altered its health plan, capping payments for AIDS treatment at $5,000. The company argued that this was necessary to avoid jeopardizing benefits paid to the rest of its employees.

Mr. McGann sued, claiming that the company had no right to reduce his benefits retroactively.

McGann lost in court. And he lost in the US Court of Appeals. So far, the US Supreme Court has declined to hear the case.

Significance of this case for other employees: No one who is insured through an employer-sponsored plan is protected from having those benefits capped or reduced.

That's because employer-sponsored insurance plans are governed by a federal law, the *Employee Retirement Income Security Act (ERISA) of 1974*. Although the law was enacted to protect the rights of employees, a 1987 Supreme Court ruling held that ERISA is legally allowed to supersede state laws.

Although most states have "bad-faith" laws regulating insurance practices that would prevent an employer or insurer from changing the terms of an insurance contract *after* a policyholder files a claim, ERISA preempts these laws.

The problem is that ERISA does not contain insurance consumer-protection clauses to make up for the laws it eclipses. In fact, it grants insurance companies complete immunity from punitive damage suits.

Under ERISA, policyholders are allowed to sue insurers only for benefits they believe are due. They can't sue for the financial damages they suffer when they believe payment of medical bills is wrongfully withheld.

And ERISA allows employers enormous leeway in how they choose to provide coverage. *What this means:*

If you have group health insurance through your employer and must file a costly medical claim, even though you have a contract with the insurer and have paid your premiums in full and on time, the insurer is legally permitted to reduce the benefits promised in the policy *after* you become ill.

Catch: The insurer must make the same change for everyone in the group. The larger the group, the less likely this will happen, since insurers don't want to risk losing customers.

The risk is greatest, however, for those who need coverage the most. Those are the victims of catastrophic illness or accidents, who are subsequently fired from their jobs and lose their benefits because the carrier takes the position that they're no longer part of the group.

Are your benefits safe?

Safest: Any insurance plan that is ERISA-*exempt*, including those sponsored by public schools, churches, and government agencies. Also exempt is nonemployer-sponsored group plans and coverage taken out by individuals.

Relatively safe: Group plans with a large number of members. Union-negotiated plans. Companies that have an aggressive employee-benefits negotiator.

Risky: Small group plans. Self-insured companies.

Self-defense: If you fall into the "risky" category, look for group medical coverage through an organization or association other than your employer.

Hopeful: Several bills now before Congress address this problem. A recent bill drafted by Rep. William Hughes (D, NJ) would bar insurers from retroactively cutting policyholders' benefits. Another bill, H.R. 1602, amends ERISA to close the loophole that causes it to override state consumer-protection laws.

Source: William M. Shernoff, a specialist in consumer claims against insurance companies. His Claremont, California law firm, Shernoff, Bidart & Darras, has a staff of insurance analysts who will answer questions regarding insurance coverage, disputes and ERISA, 714-621-4935.

What Should We Know About Life Insurance... Now???

Most people don't understand life insurance and don't want to understand it—and that's dangerous.

Here is useful information about the major categories of life insurance policies that will help you ask better insurance questions—and help you do what's best for you and your family.

Get an agent:

With almost 2,000 companies selling life insurance, choosing the best policy can be confusing. Your insurance agent is the key. Seek out someone with whom you feel comfortable, who has excellent credentials and who wants to have a long-term relationship with you.

The basics:

There are two basic classifications of life insurance—term and permanent. The most common types of permanent insurance are whole life...universal life...and variable life. For a first-time buyer, each classification has its own strengths and weaknesses to consider in light of your family and financial situations.

Let's look at each of these categories, their drawbacks and ideal candidates...

Term insurance:

A term insurance policy gives you protection for a specified time—usually up until age 70. The insurance premium is used to purchase risk coverage, after expenses are deducted from the premium.

Although premiums generally increase at stated intervals over time, the annual premium for term insurance has a much lower out-of-pocket cost initially than the premium for comparable whole life insurance purchased at the same age.

Term drawback I: Some term policies have reentry provisions, whereby you have to requalify medically every four, five or 10 years to keep your premiums at the lower term levels.

Term drawback II: Term insurance premiums increase periodically as you become older.

Term drawback III: Once you are over age 55, it can be quite expensive to acquire this kind of insurance.

Ideal candidates: People who require protection for specific purposes, such as mortgage payments or college tuition, and can't afford whole life insurance.

Whole life insurance:

A typical whole life, or ordinary life, policy covers you for your entire life and offers a guaranteed death benefit—a fixed sum payable to your heirs when you die. Some whole life policies pay dividends, which can:

• Reduce your premiums.

• Buy paid-up additions to your life insurance policy to increase your death benefit.

• Be returned to you in cash.

• Be deposited with the insurance company, where it will earn interest and serve as an additional savings account.

When you purchase a whole life policy, part of the premium pays the actual cost of the insurance risk, part pays the insurer's expenses and part goes into a reserve fund known as cash value.

This cash value, which allows the premiums to remain level during your lifetime, builds up annually and grows in value on a tax-deferred basis. Insurance companies are not obligated to tell you how your premium dollar is divided.

Because of the conservative nature of life insurance, various state regulations and the desire of insurers to fulfill their obligations, these guarantees are very low. But your actual cash available is usually higher than that which is guaranteed in the policy, if your dividends are used to purchase more insurance or are left in savings accounts with the company.

The most widely used whole life contract insures one life and pays a death benefit to the beneficiary upon his/her death. A newer variation is called second-to-die insurance, which insures two lives and pays the death benefit when the second person dies. The cost of a second-to-die policy is lower than that of two individual policies.

Whole Life drawback I: The premiums for a whole life policy are higher than those for a term policy because some of the money goes toward cash value.

Whole Life drawback II: Not all whole life policies pay dividends. And even when dividends are paid, they are not guaranteed...but rather reflect the insurance company's earnings, net of expenses.

Ideal candidates: Individuals with estates of more than $600,000, or couples with a combined estate of more than $1.2 million, who will be hit with estate taxes upon the death of the surviving spouse.

Universal life insurance:

Universal life insurance is a variation of whole life insurance. However, in a universal life plan, the cash value and actual insurance cost are unbundled.

Thus, the premium is used first to pay for insurance protection and expenses. Any excess amount is held by the insurance company at an annually predetermined rate of interest. The minimum rate—about 4% now—is guaranteed by the contract, but it is the current rate that is actually credited to your account.

Universal Life drawback I: Watch out for interest rates, since the investment return on your cash value is tied to them. When rates are high—as they were in the 1980s—universal life insurance looks more attractive than whole life insurance. When rates are low—as they are now—whole life insurance looks more attractive. This difference is most apparent in the first 10 years of the policy.

Universal Life drawback II: Unless you have a lot of self-discipline, you may not put aside enough each year in premium payments, which could mean that your death benefit won't be as high as you'd like it to be—or you have to come up with larger and larger premium payments to make up the difference and keep the same death benefit.

Ideal candidates: The same people who might buy whole life insurance but want premium flexibility and the ability to see how their premiums are used.

Variable life insurance:

Variable life insurance is also a modification of the traditional whole life insurance concept. However, the rate of return on the cash value portion is not determined by the insurance company. Instead, it's dependent on earnings of "mutual funds" within the contract selected by the insured.

Companies selling variable life policies generally give you a choice of several such funds, ranging from the most conservative to the most aggressive.

Variable Life drawback: While there are fixed premium payments and a guaranteed death benefit, there is no minimum guaranteed cash value. That's because with variable life insurance, you assume the investment risk yourself and therefore could wind up with little or no cash value if the stock market declines.

Ideal candidates: People who are risk-oriented and willing to participate in the sometimes fast-moving securities markets.

The cost of conversion:

Many term insurance policies can be converted to other types of insurance, regardless of your health at the time. But before you even consider a conversion, consider the following…

• The cost of a permanent contract is always greater than a term policy issued at the same age.

• You usually cannot convert a permanent policy to a term policy without a medical examination or questionnaire. On the other hand, the conversion from term to whole life insurance is normally guaranteed contractually without any medical requirements.

• The conversion to a permanent life insurance policy by the same company that issued the term policy may actually be more expensive than simply purchasing a new policy from a different company.

• Be sure that the new policy is in place before dropping coverage on the old one.

When it pays to convert:

You should think about converting a term policy to a permanent one under two scenarios…

I. When you can afford a tax-sheltered savings account. Ask for a realistic comparison illustration for the new policy showing the current interest rate and one that is two percentage points less. This will help show what your return might be starting at that moment.

II. When you have a number of small policies. Exchanging them for a single large policy with equal or greater total death benefits may be financially advantageous—if you're in good physical condition.

Bottom line:

Life insurance planning and purchasing should relate to your objectives at different points in your life cycle. That's why it is so important to deal with a professional insurance agent or financial adviser for guidance and advice.

Source: Virginia Applegarth, president of Applegarth Advisory Group Inc., a Boston-based fee-only financial insurance advisory firm. She is author of *How to Protect Your Family with Insurance,* Lee Simmons Associates, Inc., 40 Richards Rd., Port Washington, New York 11050.

How to Protect Yourself From Your Insurance Company

What is this world coming to? Institutions that we were taught to trust implicitly have broken their solemn promises and squandered our hard-earned money.

So far, six major life insurance companies have failed, and in most cases customers with annuities or whole-life policies have been unable to withdraw the full value of their policies.

Even when a failed insurer is on the mend, as in the case of Executive Life of California and Mutual Benefit Life, policyholders have few rights.

Though both companies are currently in rehabilitation and are meeting the majority of their contractual obligations, the courts have prohibited customers from transferring money to stronger companies, or taking out policy loans or cashing in policies until further notice.

Both are expected to agree in principal to pay about 55 cents on the dollar to policyholders who want their money now. Settlements on the full amount, however, are not final and there is no firm date yet for distribution. The new challenge: Know what happens if your insurer fails—and what you can do now—to protect yourself.

Not at risk:

• Variable annuities and variable life policies. Policyholders with these investments at any insurer are never denied access to annuities or the full benefits of their polices as promised, even if the insurer fails.

Reason: Your money is never commingled

with the general account of the life insurance company. Instead, it is invested in separate accounts, which are not available to the insurer's creditors.

•Death benefits. It is the avowed intention of the insurer and/or its regulators and rehabilitators to pay death benefits in full.

What is at risk, however, is your access to and the eventual return of the full cash value of your policy while you're still alive.
What about state guarantee funds?

These are funds set up by the states to protect policyholders when life insurers fail.

In the case of Mutual Benefit Life and Executive Life, most state guarantee funds are taking the position that they are not obligated to make up the principal losses of policyholders who accept the early settlement offers.

Example I: Colorado will pay nothing to policyholders of these insurance companies because it says they were in trouble before the state established its guarantee association in 1991.

Example II: In Minnesota, the state guarantee association agreed to make up the shortfall but won't pay out, however, until the insurance companies' final settlement, which could come in five to seven years or more.
What you can do:

If your insurer fails, consult with your insurance agent, accountant, lawyer, and/or financial planner to fully understand your options and determine the following…

•If you have taken out loans against the policy over the years, how much cash value is left in the policy?

•Will you be able to qualify for a new life-insurance policy?

•Do you still need the full insurance-policy coverage or do you need even more?

Do not pay the insurer any new money. Instead, take out an automatic premium loan from the company against the cash value of your policy. Use it to pay the interest or principal payments on policy loans and/or premium payments. In most cases it won't significantly erode your death benefits.

Executive Life or Mutual Benefit Life Policyholders: Be wary of an offer of a cash discount for cash payments. It's unlikely to be worth it. Remember, you'll only get about 55 cents on the dollar now, while it may take years before you get the full value of your policy. You are dealing with insurers that have failed to keep their promises and are financially impaired. Treat them suspiciously.
If you are insurable elsewhere:

If you qualify, apply for a hardship withdrawal from the failed insurer. You may qualify if…

•You can prove the money is needed for college tuition bills.

•You are permanently disabled or have a terminal illness.

•You have medical bills but no health insurance.

•If you are being evicted from a hospital or nursing home.

That way you will get 100 cents on the dollar rather than 55 cents on the dollar for the amount you withdraw. If you win a hardship agreement, you'll receive up to $30,000 at Executive Life, and up to $50,000 at Mutual Benefit Life.

Though the criteria are extremely demanding, especially at Executive Life, thousands of hardship cases have been granted.

Call the companies for details on their policies on hardship withdrawals. Mutual Benefit Life/800-821-7887, Executive Life of California/800-444-3542.

If you are denied a hardship withdrawal, take the early-settlement deal, file a claim with the state guarantee fund, hope you don't have to sue to get paid, and get on with your life.
The next step:

When you buy new insurance, investigate no-load and low-load insurance policies—as well as full-loaded insurance for the best buy. And be choosy. Buy new insurance only from strong companies rated C+ or above by Weiss Research.*

It's also important to diversify. Don't put all your eggs in what may very well turn out to be one surprisingly fragile basket. Where practical, spread your total insurance needs among a few strong companies.
If you are uninsurable:
*800-289-9222, $15 per rating.

Review your current needs for life insurance. If they are less than they were originally, you may want to reduce the size of your insurance benefits so the money you have already paid will cover the policy.

Important: If you don't have enough cash value, do not stop making payments, which would cause your policy to lapse. While you may not have immediate access to the cash value at 100 cents on the dollar, you are still insured. Remember why you bought the policy in the first place.

Source: William E. Donoghue, publisher of *Donoghue's MONEYLETTER* and the new audiocassette service *MoneyTalk,* 800-982-2455.

Who Needs Life Insurance

In the strictest sense, it is not you—but your beneficiaries—who need life insurance. If you're young and have no dependents, you may not need it at all. But anyone who has assets to protect or who will need to provide cash to family members in the event of his or her death does need life insurance.

Reasons to buy insurance:

The most common reasons for buying insurance...

•Protecting a business. If you have a family business, it's essential to have life insurance on key people in order to preserve the family assets and income stream. Insurance proceeds can be used to buy out partners if the business is to be reorganized on the death of a key person. And it can cushion the financial blow to the business that will result from the loss of a key manager.

•Paying taxes. Insurance proceeds can be used to pay estate taxes. Trap: A family that owns valuable assets that aren't readily convertible into cash (such as real estate or shares in a family business) may be forced to sell off assets to pay a large estate tax bill. A properly designed insurance arrangement can help avoid this problem.

•Securing income. If your family depends

on your salary or other income that you generate, life insurance can meet their future income needs in the event of your death. Estimate how much income your family would need for how long, then buy a policy with a benefit sufficient, when invested, to meet those needs through interest and principal.

•Pay off debts. You may owe amounts on mortgages or other loan arrangements that couldn't be paid off if you died, leaving your family with debts. Life insurance can secure these amounts.

Who doesn't need insurance:

Persons who have no assets or dependents that need protection (the house is paid off, the children are grown and earning good incomes for themselves, and your spouse has ample income of his/her own). Also, generally, there's no need to insure people who don't contribute to the financial support of the family. So you probably wouldn't insure the lives of minor children.

Choosing the right policy:

With some 1,600 insurance companies offering a total of about 40,000 life insurance choices, it's naive to think one can find the policy that best fits without expert assistance.

Don't try to make the choice by yourself, and don't be overwhelmed by a high-pressure salesperson. Find a broker you trust. Feel free to seek a second opinion.

What not to buy:

Don't buy policies pushed by credit card companies or banks. The rates on these policies are often higher because they're based on the companies' experience with high-risk policyholders. Also avoid trip life insurance, which is very expensive. You may pay nearly as much for a two-hour flight as around-the-clock protection for a year would cost.

Term vs. whole life:

Term insurance is least expensive because it is pure life insurance. You are left with nothing when the policy expires.

Whole life insurance, in contrast, accumulates cash value which you can borrow against, and pays dividends that can be applied against future premiums.

Some financial planners advise buying only term insurance, investing your premium savings elsewhere to earn more than the 6% or so that life insurance typically pays. There's truth to this idea—and traps…

•Term insurance gets much more expensive as you advance in age. If you don't have the discipline to set aside and invest premium savings during early years, you may face much higher premiums later, without having available funds to pay them. (Premiums on a whole life policy are calculated to be level over the policy's life.)

•Investments that are more aggressive than life insurance (such as the stock market or real estate) may earn more in some years, but can also go down in value. If you make a poor investment you may lose the premium savings earned from term insurance. Earnings on a whole life policy, in contrast, are conservative, but very secure.

If you do buy term insurance, be sure the policy is renewable and convertible into whole life later on.

Problem cases:

If you're getting on in age or have any health problems, it's even more vital to put yourself in the hands of a good insurance broker. A good broker will know which companies are underwriting aggressively at any given time. Right now, for example, I'm aware of three companies that are underwriting coronary conditions that they would not have accepted two years ago. There are windows of opportunity when companies are willing to accept more risk to increase their business.

Caution: Always tell the truth about your condition. If you don't divulge your history, the insurance company can later claim fraud and refuse to pay off on the policy. Companies that don't investigate thoroughly when writing a policy are much more likely to before paying a benefit.

Terminal illness benefits:

Recently, one of the US's largest insurers announced a new plan to let the terminally ill collect life insurance benefits before they die. This is a very progressive idea intended to help patients who face the terrible costs of long-term care.

Catch: At present, many states forbid such accelerated death benefits on the basis that consumers may confuse life insurance and health insurance and that survivors may be left destitute. But the industry seems to be moving in this direction, and this may be one more benefit to purchasing whole life insurance.

Source: Arthur Schechner is chairman of Schechner Lifson Ackerman Chodorcoff Inc., 225 Millburn Ave., Millburn, New Jersey 07041.

5

Tax Savvy

The Secrets of IRS Problem-Avoidance... Without Paying Too Much in Taxes

A mistake in your tax paperwork need not lead to an encounter with the IRS—which could escalate into an audit, tax assessment and costly court fight.

Preparation can help head off most paperwork problems with the IRS. Understanding how the bureaucracy works will enable you to efficiently resolve those problems that do arise.

Prevention:

Begin by minimizing those risk factors that can lead to unwanted inquiries from the IRS in the first place. *Advice:*

•File all required forms and answer all questions on the tax return—even if they don't seem to apply to you.

Examples: Answer the question about whe-

ther you have a foreign bank account. If you made a noncash gift to charity, file Form 8283. Work through the Alternative Minimum Tax computation on Form 1040, even if it shows you do not owe the tax.

•Avoid claiming large refunds. A return requesting a large refund is likely to draw extra scrutiny from the IRS. Also, a request that a refund be applied to the next year's taxes gives the IRS a chance to misapply the refund.

Best: Adjust wage withholding and estimated tax payments to balance out your final tax liability for the year, so you neither owe tax nor get a large refund. Remember, being entitled to a large tax refund simply means that you've made an interest-free loan to the government.

•Report all income. Check all the 1099 returns issued to you by payers of income during the past year. Be sure they are accurate and that you include all of them on your return. Copies of these forms have been supplied to the IRS, and any discrepancy will likely draw a query from the agency.

• Act on inaccuracies. If you find that a 1099 is inaccurate, ask the issuer to send a new, corrected one.

• Report rollovers. If you received a Form 1099-R reporting a rollover of retirement-plan proceeds into an IRA, remember that you *do* have to report the amount shown on your tax return even though the rollover is tax-free. These amounts and the taxable portions are reported on lines 16 and 17 of Form 1040.

Remember that any IRS inquiry about your return will likely occur 18 months to two years after you file. Make sure that you keep your tax files in good order so you can quickly respond to any question that arises at a later date, and provide necessary documentation.

Solution:

An IRS notice concerning a filing or payment problem will most likely be sent to you from the IRS Service Center where you filed your tax return. Service Centers are not well-equipped to handle telephone inquiries. *Best:* Resolve the problem by mail.

While a notice from the Service Center may provide a telephone contact number, the agent who answers the phone will not have your file in front of him/her, so you'll have to handle the matter through follow-up correspondence anyway.

When corresponding with the IRS, make it *easy* for the agent who opens your letter to handle your problem. That agent initially is unlikely to know anything about the matter except what you relate, so try to present him with the letter. Include copies of canceled checks, tax forms, and any other documents that relate to the matter. Remember, if the agent finds it necessary to go back through the IRS's own files to find any documents, it will only delay your case.

Do not send originals of important documents to the IRS—only copies. Correspond with the IRS by certified mail with a return receipt requested. Your mailing receipt proves that your letter was sent before any applicable deadline, and the delivery receipt proves the IRS actually received it.

After you mail your explanation to the IRS, you are likely to continue receiving computer-generated notices concerning the problem. This may be because the computer simply hasn't been updated—but don't assume it. Never ignore an IRS notice. Answer it with a letter referring to your previous reply, and include a copy of your earlier response.

If the notices keep coming, make contact by phone with an individual in the branch of the agency that sends the notices—for example, the collection division if you are receiving collection notices.

Phone numbers for IRS offices can be found among the government listings in the phone book, and a detailed IRS phone directory may be available in the office of your tax adviser, or among the tax reference services in the public library.

Although it can be difficult to find an individual within the IRS who is willing to take responsibility for handling your file—including the documentation you have already provided to them—doing so can be the key to solving a recalcitrant problem.

Again, keep full records concerning all phone conversations with IRS personnel, including the name and title of any agent you talk to.

Inside help:

If in spite of all your efforts you find yourself with a problem that just won't go away, you can contact the IRS's *Problem Resolution Office (PRO)*. The PRO is the taxpayer's advocate *within* the IRS.

Generally, you must be able to show that you have made at least two attempts to solve your problem on your own before turning to the PRO—an important reason to keep good records of all contacts with the agency.

Also, the PRO handles only administrative problems. It won't get involved in a dispute involving interpretation of the tax law, such as whether or not a deduction is proper. However, the PRO *will* handle such matters as lost refunds, miscredited tax payments, unexplained tax bills or penalties, the loss of documents from IRS files, or the refusal of an IRS office to answer taxpayer queries or provide tax account information.

There is a PRO in every IRS Service Center and District Office. The phone number for the PRO can be found in the phone book under

United States Government Offices/Treasury Department.

Specific conditions must be met before you can get help from the PRO concerning these common problems:

•Missing refunds. You must have made at least two inquiries about the refund, the last one being made at least 90 days after the refund claim was filed.

•Notices. After responding to two IRS notices, you can go to the PRO if you receive a third notice on the same issue that does not acknowledge your earlier replies.

•Questions. After asking the IRS a question, you must wait at least 45 days for a response before you ask again. You can go to the PRO if you receive no reply to the second inquiry or if you fail to receive an answer promised by a specific date.

While you can contact the PRO by phone, you may have to follow up with correspondence containing a detailed explanation of your problem, copies of relevant tax forms and documents, and a record of the previous attempts you have made to resolve the problem.

Cases accepted by the PRO are assigned to individual case officers, so you'll no longer be dealing with the nameless IRS bureaucracy. And you should at least receive an explanation of the status of your problem fairly quickly, even if the resolution of the problem takes longer.

Emergency help:

In an *emergency* situation—if you're informed of a levy or property seizure and you received no prior notice—the PRO can provide *immediate* help. File IRS Form 911, *Taxpayer Assistance Order*, with the PRO. Mail the form to the Internal Revenue Service Problem Resolution Office in the IRS district where you live. These requests get top priority.

To get a copy: Call the IRS at 800-829-3676. It's a good idea to have a 911 form handy in case you're ever stymied by IRS bureaucracy, especially since it may take a week or two to get the form. *Alternative:* The PRO will fill out a Form 911 for you over the phone.

Source: Paul W. Eldridge, partner, KPMG Peat Marwick, 599 Lexington Ave., New York 10022.

Three Ways to Avoid The 20% Withholding Trap

If you take your retirement money with you when leaving a job, you're going to see only 80% of it. The IRS gets the rest.

This applies to funds in 401(k) plans, 403(b) annuities, pension plans, employee stock ownership plans (ESOPs) and profit-sharing plans. *Ways to avoid the withholding tax…*

•Don't touch the money. In general, you can leave your money in your present plan until you reach retirement age—even if you leave the company. If you're happy with the investments offered and have no other immediate option, this may be your best move. Don't let the company push you out.

•Have the company transfer the money directly to a *rollover* IRA. If you plan to roll the money over into another company's retirement plan once you're eligible, you must have it placed in a separate rollover IRA for the time being. The funds can't be commingled with any of your existing IRA accounts.

The company can do this directly…or you can have the check sent to you, provided it's made out to the trustee of the new retirement plan. The notation "direct rollover" must appear on the check.

Once the money has been rolled over into this IRA, you can withdraw it without penalty, providing you return it within 60 days.

•Take your distribution in stock. The 20% withholding tax doesn't apply to stock.

Alternative: Sell the stock and put the proceeds into an IRA account within 60 days to defer taxes and avoid an early-withdrawal penalty.

Source: Stephen Pennacchio, tax partner, KPMG Peat Marwick, 345 Park Ave., New York 10154.

What to Do If You're Audited

Fear of being audited by the IRS is one of the biggest fears people have. But audits are very straightforward and nothing to be afraid of. *Specifics:*

Correspondence audits:

Correspondence audits are conducted by mail. The IRS has information about something that should have been on your income tax return but wasn't. The IRS writes you, saying it is going to adjust your return unless you can prove otherwise.

• *Loophole:* Respond immediately. If you don't, the proposal will become an assessment and you'll owe the IRS extra tax plus penalties and interest. If you made an inadvertent error on your return, you may be able to avoid penalties by responding to the notice promptly and explaining the circumstances of the error. If the mistake was reasonably beyond your control, the IRS may excuse any penalties it has charged.

Office audits:

Office audits are conducted at IRS offices. They are initiated by a letter from the IRS that usually tells the taxpayer the items on his/her return that are being questioned.

• *Loophole:* Try to resolve the issue by mail. You may be able to wrap up an audit without ever setting foot in an IRS office. Write to the IRS explaining that you can't attend in person but you are enclosing copies of all your substantiation for the deductions it has questioned. Time the letter so it arrives at the IRS at least two weeks before your appointment date. Give a telephone number where you can be contacted during the day. It has been my experience that the IRS accepts this method of proving deductions. If your proof is sufficient, you'll get a letter back from the agent telling you that your return has been accepted as filed—examination closed.

• *Loophole:* Limit your exposure. Take only the information the IRS asked to see to the audit. While office audits don't generally go beyond the items checked off on the audit notification letter, the IRS isn't precluded from digging into other areas on your return. If you take only the information requested, the agent will have to go to the trouble of scheduling another appointment to dig deeper into your return.

Caution: Don't volunteer information. Answer only the questions that are asked by the agent.

• *Loophole:* If you're missing some proof for your deductions…prepare a detailed schedule for the audit showing how you arrived at the figure shown on your return. Be as detailed as possible. The IRS is not obliged to accept this, but the agent will usually go along with some or all of it if your explanation makes sense and is reasonable.

Trap: Don't ignore the IRS's request for an office audit. This can get you in very deep trouble with the service. The IRS will disallow every single item on your return, not just the items it says it is auditing, and send you a bill. Then you will have to substantiate everything on your return.

Field audits:

Field audits are conducted on the taxpayer's premises, usually his/her place of business.

• *Loophole:* Avoid having the audit at your home. Have it at your accountant's office instead. If you allow the agent to come to your home, he/she may very well form opinions about your standard of living. This could lead to questions about unreported income. Another reason to avoid having the audit at your home is that people tend to be more relaxed when audits are held in familiar surroundings. They may very well let down their guard and say something they shouldn't to the agent.

Reminder: You can never tell the auditor too little.

Business audits:

The best place to have the audit of a business is at your accountant's office—it's neutral ground. The agent, however, may try to have the audit at your place of business. Don't go along with this. The agent may form opinions about the company's deductions if the audit is held at the business. He may overhear damaging conversations about the company.

Self-defense: Insist that the audit be held at the agent's office at the IRS. You have a right to have the audit there.

If the audit does not take place at your business, the agent will still want to see the premises. Arrange this for a time when you, the owner, are not present. Having the agent meet you there can't help your case. The agent may get ideas about your life style if he meets you at your place of business. He may feel jealous. He may decide that your deductions are extravagant.

Appeals within the IRS:

If you don't agree with an auditor's findings, you can take your case to the appeals division of the IRS. The purpose of the appeals division is to settle cases without going to court.

•*Loophole:* You get a fair hearing at an appeals conference. It's not a kangaroo court. An appeals officer will be more inclined than an auditor to settle a case that appears to be reasonable.

•*Loophole:* Appeals officers can take into account the hazards of litigation in deciding whether to settle. The hazards of litigation are the chances the government might lose the case if it goes to court. If the appeals officer thinks the IRS has only a 50% chance of winning in court, he may settle for half of the disputed amount.

Tax Court:

If all else fails, you can take your case to Tax Court. You can go either to regular Tax Court...or to the small case division if the amount of tax in dispute is less than $10,000—whichever is appropriate.

•*Loophole:* You have a second chance to settle the case in discussions with an IRS attorney before it is set for court. Like the appeals officer, the attorney will take into account the hazards of litigation, *but these carry more weight here.* You may have a better chance of settling the case with an IRS lawyer than with an appeals officer.

Avoiding an audit:

•*Loophole:* File your returns on time. There's a high audit rate among individuals who have not filed returns for many years. Eventually these people are picked out by the IRS and made to file their delinquent returns.

•*Loophole:* Attach detailed proof of items for which you're filing an amended return. Amended returns for large refunds are more likely to be audited than original returns. You can reduce the audit risk by attaching complete, detailed proof of the items that prompted the amendment.

•*Loophole:* Avoid repetitive audits. The *Internal Revenue Manual* says that taxpayers shall not be subjected to needless and repetitive examinations. If you've been audited in either of the past two years on a particular issue, and the audit resulted in no change in your tax bill, you can request not to be audited on that same issue again.

Procedure: As soon as you receive your audit notice, write to the IRS to claim an exemption under the Repetitive Audit Program. Enclose a copy of your previous audit notice and report. *Important:* You must request the procedure before your first appointment with the agent.

Important:

Good records. If you can document your deductions with the proof the IRS requires, you'll have no trouble at an audit.

Source: Edward Mendlowitz, partner, Mendlowitz Weitsen, CPAs, Two Pennsylvania Plaza, New York 10121. He is the author of *New Tax Traps, New Opportunities*, Boardroom Special Reports, Box 736, Springfield, New Jersey 07081.

IRS Loses/ Business Gains

Use these latest business tax victories over the IRS to help guide your company's own tax-planning strategies...

Best winners:

•Currency loss deductible. A company operating retail stores abroad deducted a loss on holdings of foreign currency that resulted from a shift in exchange rates. The IRS disallowed the deduction saying the loss wasn't real because it didn't affect the business conducted within the foreign stores. *Court of Appeals:* A loss on currency holdings is a real financial loss, so the deduction was allowed. *Plus:* The IRS had to reimburse the company for $90,000 in legal fees it incurred as a result of the IRS's meritless position.
Sam Ellis Stores, CA-9, No. 91-55969.

•Probationary workers aren't employees. A telemarketing firm's new hires had a very high turnover rate, so it treated their first weeks on

the job as a probation period. During this period, it also treated the new hires as contract workers rather than employees, and did not withhold employment taxes. But the IRS ruled that the workers were employees and assessed back employment taxes. *Court:* There was a reasonable basis for the company's practice, other firms in its industry followed the same practice, and all workers were treated consistently. Thus, the company's treatment of the workers was upheld and no taxes were due.
World Mart, Inc., D. Ariz., No CIV 90-1596-PHX-EHC.

• Late payment penalty avoided. A company with cash-flow problems properly paid over Social Security taxes that had been withheld from employee pay, but delayed paying its own half of the Social Security tax bill. *Mistake:* The company didn't designate how its partial payment was to be applied. The IRS applied it to the company's half of the taxes, then imposed personal liability on the company's officers for the withheld taxes it said had not been paid over. *Court:* Personal liability results only when a failure to pay withheld taxes is willful. The nonpayment here was not willful, so the officers weren't liable.
Orran D. Oakey, IV, W.D. Va., No. 91-0397-R.

• Cash reserves not taxed. The IRS imposed an $11 million accumulated earnings penalty tax on a company that kept large amounts of cash on hand. *Court:* The penalty tax is imposed on profits owners keep in a business to avoid the tax that would be due on them if paid out as dividends. But this company's cash balances were not retained profits—they were amounts that shareholders had paid for their shares, and that the company kept as cash to maintain flexibility. Thus, the company did not owe the tax. Because the IRS's position would defy common sense by taxing contributions to capital, it had to pay the legal costs it had forced the company to incur.
Network Systems Corp., D. Minn., No. 4-91-CV-869.

• Corporation beats ex-officer. A company bought out a top officer to settle a management dispute. He treated payments he received as a capital gain on the sale of his company shares. He did this even though the terms of his agreement with the company said the payments were made in settlement of his

contract and for his entering a noncompete agreement. That made them deductible by the company and taxable to him as ordinary income. The officer protested that the agreement had been changed without his knowledge and that he wouldn't have signed it had he known. *Court:* The officer was responsible for reading what he had signed. The agreement's terms were to be followed.
Ronald D. Taylor, TC Memo 1992-664.

• Taxes paid with stolen funds returned. A company employee embezzled a large amount of money and transferred it to an investment partnership of his own—and he used it to pay taxes. The company found out and sued the IRS to get the money back. The IRS said it could keep the money because it had been received in proper payment of a tax bill. *Court:* The IRS is required to *return* stolen property in its possession—even when the property is money received in the form of a legitimate cash payment. So the company gets the money back.
Pershing v. Timothy A. Sirmer, N.D. Ill., No. 89 C 2239.

• Wrongdoer's defense deductible. A company that was accused of illegally dumping pollutants incurred expensive legal defense bills. *IRS ruling:* The defense costs are deductible as a business expense even if they result from the company's own wrongdoing.
IRS Letter Ruling 9315004.

• Deposit not a payment. A change of accountants kept a business owner from estimating his tax bill, so he filed a return extension with a $25,000 check. Years later, the IRS determined the taxes had been overpaid but it refused to allow a refund of the excess because the time limit for requesting a refund of an excess tax payment had passed. *Tax Court:* The $25,000 had been not a payment, but a deposit. *Key:* A payment is made against an existing tax liability while a deposit is made against a potential but uncertain tax liability, which was the case here. Because the $25,000 was a deposit, the IRS had to return any amount not needed to pay the owner's taxes.
Robert B. Risman, 100 TC No. 13.

• No discrimination. A company that laid off workers during a business slump refused to rehire the same workers when business improved because it did not want to incur the cost of their unvested pension benefits which would vest with further service. The workers protested that they were being discriminated against. *Court of Appeals:* The former employees had no grounds to sue because they were no longer plan participants. Their case was dismissed.

Joan A. Shawley et al v. Bethlehem Steel, CA-3, No. 92-3149.

•Not employees. A company used a large number of contract workers who were hired as needed and were paid by the job. It let them hire their own helpers and did not supervise their work. All the workers properly paid self-employment taxes. Nevertheless, the IRS ruled that they were employees and assessed back employment taxes. The company protested and an arbitrator ruled in its favor, but the IRS insisted on a trial. In court, though, the IRS quickly conceded. *Court:* The IRS's effort to pressure the company into an unfavorable settlement was a "perversion" of the legal process since the facts "unequivocally" supported contractor status. The IRS had to pay the legal costs it had forced the company to incur to defend itself.

Apollo Drywall, W.D. Mich., No. 591 CV 16.

•Liquidation revoked. A company's charter was revoked after it accidently failed to pay an annual franchise fee to the state, and the IRS taxed its shareholders as if the company's assets had been distributed to them in a corporate liquidation. The company then filed reinstatement papers with the state. *Court:* Under state law, a company that has had its charter revoked in this manner can file correcting papers and reinstate itself as if the revocation never occurred. Thus, the liquidation was revoked retroactively, and the IRS could not collect the tax.

Puckett's Creek Coal Company, Inc., Bankr. E.D. Ky., Adv. No. 92-6002.

•Too late for new issues. The IRS could not assert new tax liabilities against a business partnership on the first day of the trial of a tax dispute that had been pending for years. It was "grossly unfair" to make new claims at such a late date, so the claims were disallowed.

Joyce Elms, Bankr. E.D. La., No. 91-1301B.

•Deduction not reduced. A city offered a property-tax discount to companies that prepaid their taxes. One company prepaid its tax and took the discount, then deducted the full undiscounted amount of the tax on its federal tax return. The IRS objected that the company could not deduct the full tax. The company argued that it had paid the full tax and that the discount was actually interest paid to it by the city on the prepayment. The IRS replied that in that case the interest was taxable income to the company. *Court:* For the company. The prepayment was a loan of funds to the city, and the interest paid by the city on the loan was tax-exempt.

Consolidated Edison of New York, S.D.N.Y., No. 88 CV 5985 (KMW).

How to Get the Most After-Tax Income

The big increase in the top tax rates imposed by the Clinton tax program makes it more important than ever for you to maximize your after-tax income.

In fact, many valuable opportunities to earn tax-favored income continue to exist under the new tax program. These can save taxes even for those whose taxable incomes are below the threshold level at which the new higher tax rates apply—$115,000 on a single return, $140,000 on a joint return.

Important: Plan to maximize your personal wealth. Manage and minimize your tax liability under the new law.

Basics:

First, examine your tax position and cash-flow needs in light of the tax-law changes. *Important:* Remember that tax-rate hikes are retroactive to the beginning of 1993.

If necessary, adjust your wage withholding by filing a new W-4 form with your employer to balance the year's withheld taxes with your projected year-end tax liability. This should prevent you from underpaying your taxes and owing a large tax bill...or overpaying and making an interest-free loan to the government.

Similarly, make appropriate estimated tax payments on nonsalary income. Keep in mind that the government will let you pay the portion of your 1993 tax that is caused by the Clinton tax hikes in three equal installments payable with your 1993, 1994, and 1995 returns. There will be no interest or penalties imposed on the installments.

After setting aside funds to pay your taxes, consider your personal cash-flow needs. Determine the amount you have available for investments and the amount you will have to earn from these investments to maintain your standard of living now and in the future. Overall, your investments must beat the rate of inflation for you to build wealth.

With these factors in mind, you can plan the best use of the tax-favored investment opportunities under the new tax program.

Favored investments:

• Capital gains. The new tax law reestablishes a significant tax break for long-term capital gains (investments held for a year or more). While the top personal tax rate increases to 39.6%, long-term capital gains are taxed under the new law at a maximum rate of only 28%. Moreover, tax on the appreciation of a capital asset isn't owed until the asset is sold, so taxes on appreciation are deferred even though you are adding to your wealth.

Consider making investments that produce capital-gain income, such as growth stocks, growth-oriented mutual funds, real estate, and other appreciating assets.

Strategy: If you rely on your investments to produce income, consider investing in a growth-and-income mutual fund. In today's market, the average dividend yield on stocks is about 3%—the same return obtained from money funds or CDs. But a mutual fund also provides the opportunity to build your future wealth through the appreciation of fund assets.

Special break: As an investment incentive, the new tax law provides a maximum tax rate of only 14% on gains earned by initial investors in certain small businesses—when the stocks are held for more than five years. A broker or banker may be able to direct you to such an investment.

Caution: Don't let this very attractive tax rate blind you to the risks involved in investments in start-up companies.

• Municipal bonds. With tax rates going up,

the tax exemption that's available for interest paid on municipal bonds becomes even more valuable than before.

Important: Don't buy municipal bonds blindly. Always consider the risk posed by the creditworthiness of the issuer, which can vary widely. There are two basic types of municipal bonds…

• General-obligation bonds are backed by the taxing power of the issuing locality.

• Specific-use bonds, or private-activity bonds, are backed by the revenue generated from a specific project—such as a housing agency—or by a business that will use the bond proceeds.

General-obligation bonds are generally safer. They pay a lower rate of interest because a municipality can use revenue from any source to pay them off.

Specific-use bonds are riskier and pay a higher rate of interest because the anticipated revenue stream that is earmarked to pay off the bonds may prove insufficient.

Examine the specifics of the issuer's creditworthiness. Some specific-use bonds are very safe, while some general-obligation bonds are relatively risky.

One way to reduce risk is to invest through a mutual fund that buys a diversified portfolio of bonds. But pay attention to the riskiness of the fund's investments as indicated in its prospectus and related information provided to you.

Insurance:

Investment-oriented insurance products emerge from the new law virtually unscathed. These products offer investors tax-deferred investment returns.

Example: The growth in cash value of these products—whole life, universal life or variable life insurance—increases with no current income-tax liability.

Even better, you can access cash value from the insurance policy at no current tax cost by borrowing against the policy. And you may never have to pay back the loan, since outstanding borrowings can be subtracted from the benefit paid by the insurance policy when you die. Keep in mind that you will owe interest on the amounts borrowed.

While you will owe interest on any loan taken against an insurance policy, the interest may be deductible depending on how you use loan proceeds.

Wealth can also be built, tax-deferred, from an investment in an annuity contract. Returns earned on the investment are tax-deferred until they are paid out.

Caution: Certain withdrawals from a tax-deferred annuity taken before age 59½ may be subject to a 10% early-withdrawal penalty. If you withdraw the full amount within the first five to seven years after the purchase of an annuity, you may be subject to surrender charges imposed by the issuer. Ask about these terms before investing.

Qualified retirement plans:

With tax rates increasing, retirement plans are more valuable means of investing because of the exclusions from taxation that are available for contributions and the tax-deferrals that are obtained for investment earnings that accrue within plan accounts.

Example: A contribution to an employer-sponsored 401(k) savings plan eliminates the contributed amount from your taxable income. And it enables you to postpone paying tax on both the contribution and earnings that build up on the contributed amount until you withdraw it. The compounding of tax-favored investment returns over several years can add to wealth in your retirement years. Additional benefits will result when your employer matches your contributions.

Similar benefits are available from Keogh plans for the self-employed, simplified employee pension plans, and IRAs, so make full use of them.

Source: Jeff J. Saccacio, director of personal tax services, Southern California, and John D. Barrett, partner-in-charge, taxes, Southern California, Coopers & Lybrand, 350 S. Grand Ave., Los Angeles 90071.

Check For SS Errors

Self-employed women who are married and have kept their maiden names should regularly check for errors in their Social Secu-

rity records. *Reason:* In the past, the IRS routinely reported self-employment taxes paid with joint returns under the husband's last name. If the name on the return didn't match the wife's Social Security number, the account would not be credited properly, possibly resulting in reduced retirement benefits.

Source: *Kiplinger's 12 Steps to a Worry-Free Retirement* by Daniel Kehrer, editor of Los Angeles-based *IB: America's Small Business Magazine,* Kiplinger's Books, 1729 H St. NW, Washington, DC 20006.

Medical Deductions For Nursing-Home Expenses

Deductions for nursing-home care fall into a gray area of the tax law. The types of expenses that can be taken as medical deductions depend on the reasons for being in the nursing home. *Guidelines:*

• Fully deductible. The entire cost for nursing-home care—including meals and lodging—is deductible if a principal reason for being in the home is to receive continual medical services.

• Partly deductible. In situations where medical need is not a principal reason for being in a nursing home, expenses attributable only to medical care can be deducted.

Example: If your grandmother were in a nursing home because she was too frail to care for herself, she would not be able to deduct the cost of meals and lodging at the home. However, she could deduct the cost of any medical services received while in the home. Ask the nursing-home operator to break the bills down into medical and non-medical care.

• Lump-sum payments. In some cases, a lump-sum fee is paid for lifetime care in a nursing home. The home should be able to provide you with a statement detailing the portion of the fee that will be required for the patient's future medical care, based on the nursing home's past experience. This amount is generally deductible in the year it is paid—

even though it is for future medical care.

•Dependents' medical expenses. You may deduct medical expenses that you pay for your spouse or a qualifying dependent. Your parents or other relatives generally qualify as your dependents if you could claim a personal exemption for them on your tax return.

Note: The gross income test, which says that a dependent must earn less than $2,350, does not apply when claiming a dependent's medical expenses. The person must be your dependent either at the time care was received or when the expenses were paid.

•Nature of services. Whether or not an expense is deductible is determined by the nature of the services provided, not by the qualifications or experience of the provider.

Example: Assume you broke your hip and hired domestic help. If that person also helped with your in-home physical therapy, you could claim as a medical expense the charges for the time spent on your exercises. It wouldn't matter if the provider were not a qualified medical professional, as long as the physical therapy program was for legitimate medical reasons and was prescribed by a doctor. However, the cost of having the same person do housework would not be deductible. The fact that your injury made you unable to do the housework yourself is irrelevant.

Reminder: Medical expenses are only deductible to the extent that they have not been reimbursed by insurance and exceed 7.5% of your Adjusted Gross Income.

Source: William G. Brennan, partner, Ernst & Young, CPAs, 1225 Connecticut Ave. NW, Washington, DC 20036. Mr. Brennan is the editor of the *Ernst & Young Financial Planning Reporter*.

Inside the IRS

Forcing the IRS to take action. Taxpayers often complain that when they have an IRS problem, IRS personnel don't want to be bothered. IRS collection personnel, for instance, only want to collect the amount of money the computer says is owed, even if the taxpayer claims the computer has made a mistake.

Solution: File IRS Form 911, Request for Taxpayer Assistance Order, with the Problem Resolution Office (PRO). It will compel the IRS to take the corrective action required. Although the prevailing use of Form 911 is to stop the IRS from taking an action that will result in a financial hardship, it can also be used to force the IRS to take the action it is required to take under the law.

Divorce and the IRS. It is not unusual for spouses undergoing a divorce to transfer property to one another as part of a marital settlement. What if one spouse owes the IRS unpaid taxes and a federal tax lien has been filed against his/her property? The effect of one spouse taking title to the other spouse's property, which is subject to a federal tax lien, is that eventually the unpaid tax plus interest and penalties will be deducted by the IRS from the sale proceeds. *Advice:* Before you agree to a property settlement, have your attorney order a federal tax lien search to determine whether your spouse owes the IRS money.

IRS mistakes. When the IRS claims that penalties are owed because of late payment of estimated taxes, it is very important to double-check their calculations. Many times the IRS ignores Form 2210, Underpayment of Estimated Tax by Individuals and Fiduciaries, which should be submitted with your tax return, to compute the underpayment penalty. In fact, Form 2210 provides for different methods of calculating the penalty, including exceptions to avoid the penalty. When the IRS sends a tax bill, many times it is wrong. Double-check all penalty calculations.

Innocent spouse. What if your spouse has been caught cheating the IRS? Can the IRS come after you for the extra tax, interest, and penalties simply because you filed a joint tax return? Usually the answer is "yes." A jointly filed tax return subjects each spouse to "joint and several liability," which means that each of you owes the entire amount even if one spouse had no income at all. Loophole: If an IRS audit produces an extra tax bill, you may be able to escape liability if you qualify as an "innocent spouse." Internal Revenue Code Section 6013 gives the rules that qualify one spouse as an innocent spouse. Key: You must be able to prove that, based on all the facts and circumstances, it would be inequitable to hold you, the innocent spouse, liable for the additional tax.

When the IRS says your sideline business is a hobby. Revenue agents examining a sideline business that shows a loss may be inclined to reclassify the business loss into a nondeductible hobby loss. Prime targets are losses from any business that the revenue agent feels has an element of personal enjoyment. For instance, a business engaged in horse racing, car racing, yacht charter, or anything related to collectibles, such as antiques or stamps, is especially vulnerable to attack.

Counterattack: Remind the revenue agent that there is no law that says a business must actually show a profit. The law says only that you must intend to generate a profit. Be prepared to show the IRS how you tried to make your business profitable.

Source: Ms. X is a former IRS agent still well-connected.

Business Deduction

If you fly for business and take advantage of a bargain fare by extending your trip over a Saturday, you can deduct the cost of meals and lodging for the extra travel day even if no business is conducted on it. The IRS recently said a deduction can be claimed for such costs when the airfare savings that result from extending the trip exceed the other costs of extending the stay.

Source: Randy Blaustein, partner, Blaustein, Greenberg & Co., 155 E. 31 St., New York 10016.

Charitable Deductions

How do I prove out-of-pocket charitable contributions for which I don't have receipts?

The IRS requires some sort of written record to support any deduction for a charitable

contribution. In the case of small cash contributions—such as contributions to church collections, or out-of-pocket expenses paid to a charity, for which no receipt is expected—the IRS instructions say it accepts as reasonable documentation a reliable, written record recorded at or near the time when the contribution was made.

Source: David S. Rhine, partner, BDO Seidman, 15 Columbus Circle, New York 10023.

College-Aid Tax Strategy

Deductible retirement-plan contributions made by parents can increase the amount of college financial aid offered to their children. How: The amount of aid offered to a child depends in part upon the value of the parent's assets. For financial aid purposes, however, the amount of money accumulated in retirement plans—such as IRAs, Keoghs, and 401(k)s—is not considered an asset in determining eligibility for assistance. Therefore, by putting assets in retirement accounts before a child goes to college, and by making plan contributions while the child is in college, you may increase aid significantly.

Source: Kalman A. Chany, president, Campus Consultants Inc., 338 E. 67 St., New York 10021. Mr. Chany is author of *The Princeton Review/The Student Access Guide to Paying for College*, Villard Books, 201 E. 50 St., New York 10022.

Frequent Flier Tax Trap

The IRS has long said that frequent flier miles that are paid for by a company but used by an employee for personal travel should be considered taxable income to the employee. It has never acted to enforce this position, but that may now be changing. One IRS district has begun auditing frequent fliers and imposing income tax on those individuals who are found to have sold their mileage credits—a common practice even though it is prohibited under frequent flier programs. The IRS says the district is acting on its own, but this could be a precursor of tougher enforcement efforts to come.

Secrets of Paying Less Taxes…When Taxes Are Rising

Higher taxes are definitely coming, even though no one is quite sure at the time this publication goes to press when or what shape the new tax laws will take.

But there are many ways to save taxes in 1993.

The following strategies will give you a head start on preparing for stiff tax rates down the road…

•Accelerate income into 1993. It appears that the 1994 income tax rate will be higher than the 1993 rate. Further, in the Clinton administration's bill, the 1.45% Medicare tax won't apply to all taxable wages until 1994. This year the tax is levied on up to $135,000 of wages.

Opportunity: Accelerating $100,000 of income into 1993 saves you $1,450 in Medicare taxes. How to do it:

•Avoid deferred compensation arrangements this year. Take the income in 1993.

•If you're self-employed, send out bills early enough so you receive the income in 1993.

•Check your withholding to avoid stiff underpayment penalties. Because mortgage rates dropped, many people refinanced their higher-rate mortgages, reducing their monthly payments—and their mortgage interest deduction. Forgetting to factor the smaller deduction into your withholding or estimated tax payments in 1993 could subject you to steep underpayment penalties.

Rule: In general, you must pay in 90% of this year's tax or 100% of last year's tax to avoid the underpayment penalty. High-income taxpayers whose income increases must pay 90% of the current year's tax.

•Contribute the legal maximum to retire- ment plans. As tax rates rise, retirement plans become more valuable. You get two bene- fits…a current deduction for the contribution, reducing this year's taxes…plus tax-deferred growth of the money until retirement.

•Shift from income investments to capital gains investments. Bond funds and other investments that produce taxable income are worth less when taxes rise because more of the investment earnings are lost to taxes.

Alternative: Look for investments that aim for capital gains instead of current ordinary income. By owning stocks or stock funds with capital gains appreciation potential, you defer current taxes on the income.

Bonus: Capital gains rates are capped at 28% under the Clinton proposals, which could be 10 percentage points less than the regular in- come tax rates in 1994. So converting income to capital gains makes more sense than ever.

•Consider tax-free investments. People who need current income should consider shifting from taxable bonds to municipal bonds or muni bond funds. Income is free from federal taxes—and may be free of state and local taxes, too.

To compute your after-tax return: Divide the fund's yield by one minus your tax bracket.

Example: An investor in the 31% bracket is considering a tax-free investment that yields 5%. The taxable equivalent yield is 7.2%, that is, $5 \div [1 - .31$ (your tax bracket)].

•Consider a charitable remainder trust to shelter gain on appreciated assets. One of the few benefits of the Clinton tax plan is a pro- posal to eliminate the Alternative Minimum Tax when appreciated property is donated to charity.

How a charitable remainder trust works: You donate stocks or other appreciated prop- erty to a trust, retaining an income interest for your lifetime. The charity gets the balance of the assets at your death. You take a deduction for the remainder value of the property donated. Because neither you nor the trust pays capital gains tax on the appreciation, you deduct the entire amount of the property donated, not just its after-tax value. Caution: The property must be placed in trust before the sale is negotiated.

•Use a seller-financed mortgage if you sell your residence and don't plan to reinvest the entire proceeds in a new residence. Your gain from the sale is taxed. But if you finance the buyer's mortgage, you get favorable installment-sale treatment on the monthly payments you receive.

Example: You sell property for $200,000 with a tax basis of $100,000, taking $20,000 down plus a note for $180,000 at 7% interest. Instead of owing $40,000 in taxes (taxable gain of $100,000 taxed at 40%), you owe only $8,000 ($20,000 x .40) using the installment method. Further, you are investing $192,000 ($200,000 – $8,000) at 7% instead of $160,000 ($200,000 – $40,000). At 7%, this generates an additional $2,240 per year of income.

•Borrow from your 401(k) retirement plan. If you need a loan, borrow from your 401(k) plan, not your local bank. Most plans have provisions for short-term loans. The interest rate will be comparable to what your bank would charge. But instead of paying nondeductible interest to the bank, you repay interest to your own account—where it builds up tax-free until you retire.

•Begin a lifetime gift program. There has been talk in Washington about lowering the one-time estate and gift tax exclusion from $600,000 to $200,000.

Other proposals to limit estate tax breaks:

•Impose a capital gains tax on appreciated assets transferred at death.

•Force heirs to take the basis of the donor instead of a market value basis in the property.

Strategy: Start giving gifts to your heirs sooner rather than later. Gifts of up to $10,000 per recipient per year are tax-free ($20,000 per recipient if your spouse joins you in making the gifts).

•Don't overpay your Social Security taxes. If you took a new job in 1993, watch out for Social Security tax overpayments. Your new employer will begin withholding Social Security taxes from your paycheck as if you had paid nothing at all. Unless you claim the overpayment on your tax return, you lose it.

•Open a bank account in your child's name. Money held by children younger than 14 years old can earn up to $600 in interest

tax-free. The second $600 is taxed at their own low rates, usually 15%.

•Helping support elderly parents—or other family members. When you pay more than one half of your parents' support and they earn less than $2,350, excluding Social Security or tax-free income, you can claim them as dependents on your tax return.

Variation: When you and your siblings all chip in but no one contributes more than 50% of your parents' support, one of you may claim the exemption if you and your siblings complete IRS Form 2120 and you attach it to your tax return.

Source: Donald A. Blackwell, partner, Ernst & Young, 501 W. Broadway, San Diego, California 92101.

Hide Assets From The IRS—Legally

Many people keep assets in a safe-deposit box thinking that no one will ever find out about it. But the name of the renter of a safe-deposit box isn't kept secret. It doesn't help to rent a box in your own name; there's an organization that, for less than $100, will run a search of every bank in the country to see if you are a safe-deposit box customer. And the IRS, if it's looking for assets of yours, will do a bank search for safe-deposit boxes held in your name. (It's especially easy for the IRS to track down boxes that you pay for with a personal check...it simply goes through your canceled checks.)

To conceal the existence of a safe-deposit box:

•Ask your lawyer to set up a nominee corporation—a corporation that has no other function but to stand in your place for the purposes you designate, such as to rent a safe-deposit box.

•Rent a box in the name of the corporation and pay for it in cash. Your name and signature will be on the bank signature card, but the corporation, not you, will be listed as the box's owner on the bank's records. And because you paid cash, there will be nothing in your records to connect the box with you.

• You can, if you wish, name another person as signatory in addition to yourself. Then, if something happens to you, that person will be able to get into the box.

Additional protection: Having a safe-deposit box in a corporation's name permits the box to be opened by your survivors without the state or the bank being notified of your death and having the box sealed. Otherwise, the survivor must get to the box before the funeral to look for a will and to find whatever else may be there.

Source: Edward Mendlowitz, partner, Mendlowitz Weitsen, CPAs, New York 10121.

Homeowners' Tax Breaks

For the alert taxpayer, the family home can be a major source of tax savings. Federal tax law is studded with provisions that encourage and enhance home ownership, as opposed to other forms of investment.

Breaks when you buy:

Mortgage points. For borrowers other than homeowners, mortgage points (a prepayment of interest represented by a percentage of the loan) have to be capitalized and deducted over the life of the loan. But points charged on money borrowed to buy a principal residence are fully deductible by homeowners in the year they're paid.

Deductions for interest paid on personal debts have been eliminated. But interest paid on mortgages on your primary residence and on one second residence are fully deductible up to a total of $1 million in acquisition debt (to acquire, construct, or improve a residence) plus $100,000 in home-equity loans (for any purpose). Note: The dollar limits don't apply to mortgages taken out before October 14, 1987.

Source: Ivan Faggen, tax partner with Arthur Andersen & Co. in charge of the Tax Division for the South Florida offices, 1 Biscayne Tower, Suite 2100, Miami 33131. Mr. Faggen is coauthor of *Federal Taxes Affecting Real Estate*, Matthew Bender, 235 E. 45 St., New York 10017.

6

Success In The Office

Prepare to Become Your Own Employer

The main workplace issues over the next year or two will be further downsizing and greater use of contingent workers and independent contractors. More and more people will have to learn how to become their own employer, to work for more than one company, and to position themselves as a business.

Don't do this as an interim measure in the hope that the economy will turn around again.

Think of it as the rest of your life. People who have full-time jobs now should thank their lucky stars, but also prepare for the day when they may not. Instead of worrying about the next step up in a company hierarchy, judge how each new assignment will add to your overall competency and skills. That's more important than how much a job pays.

Sometimes what seems to be a demotion on paper will provide you with more salable skills three years out.

If you're a vice president of human resources, for example, and are offered a chance to become the manager of a line operation, grab it. Although the title is not so important, the line experience will be invaluable.

Most of us are not true entrepreneurs in the sense of being willing to assume a lot of risk. If we have to, we call something a business—and print up stationery and business cards, but often we are still sending out résumés and we would jump at the chance to go back to a company job.

Problem: Even if you get a job today, there's no guarantee that you'll be kept on for more than a year. It's still smart to think of yourself as an independent contractor, ready to move on at the next opportunity that presents itself.

Instead of thinking about the job you just had or what you think you're qualified to do based on your résumé, start to reinvent yourself.

Retread your whole system and prepare to be self-sufficient in terms of plotting your next career move, arranging your own insurance, and saving for your retirement. Make a serious analysis of your interests, skills, and talents and how you want to package those going forward for the next five years. Get used to the idea of selling yourself and becoming your own boss.

The company's dilemma:

While companies will be continuing to downsize, because they must downsize to stay globally competitive, that means ever lower morale among employees, a reduced feeling of loyalty on both sides, and lessened competitive excellence because when people are afraid of losing their jobs, they are afraid to challenge the status quo. That, in turn, means that a company won't change with the times.

In a period when intellectual property—inventions, copyrights, patents—and customer relations have never been more critical to companies, increased turnover of people risks losses in both areas. There is a very real danger that competitors can then effectively wipe a company out.

Given these problems, we can expect that companies will pay much closer attention to the drafting of restrictive covenant or non-compete agreements in the next year or two, even though these don't always hold up in court and are under active attack in some states, e.g., California.

New emphasis on office environment:

In the next year or two, there's going to be a lot more attention paid to the biological environment of the office. Questions of the ergonomics of white-collar equipment, lighting, the quality of the air, and workplace stress will be addressed. This is because more and more companies are recognizing that problems in the office environment are raising their health care costs, reducing productivity, and causing stress that often carries over to workers' lives outside of the workplace.

More strategic alliances:

Companies will be entering more and more into strategic alliances. They're going to be outsourcing a lot of their work. People who are self-employed or in smaller businesses will find that the future belongs to those who create good strategic alliances with other kinds of companies. This is the time to start building alliances—saying to another business or other

professionals, "I can do this for you if you will do that for me"…"or together we can provide this product or service for others."

Source: Edith Weiner is president of Weiner, Edrich, Brown, Inc., futurists and strategic planning consultants, 200 E. 33 St., New York 10016.

Meeting Mistake

Don't feel obligated to say something in a meeting because silence will be interpreted as ignorance. *Better:* Choose statements very carefully at the first few meetings. If what you say is well thought out and insightful, you will carry far more weight at future meetings. *Caution:* Do not use meetings to say uncomplimentary things about subordinates. This can undermine the department—and you, as its manager.

Source: *The First-Time Manager* by Loren Belker, a management trainer based in Escondido, California. Amacom, 135 W. 50 St., New York 10020.

Career Booster

Volunteer to serve at a charity fund-raiser. It's the quickest way to get to know the movers and shakers in your community.

Source: *The Sir Winston Method: The Five Secrets of Speaking the Language of Leadership* by communications consultant James C. Humes, William Morrow & Co., 1350 Avenue of the Americas, New York 10019.

The Best Managers Don't Manage

The best managers lead, sponsor, and facilitate. Old-style autocratic management is increasingly frowned on—and has proven to be ineffective. *Much better:* Team building…willingness to bypass formal corporate structure to get the job done…participatory decision-making…willingness to change the organization's structure as its market changes…

sharing rather than hoarding information…a focus on results—not on long hours.

Source: Consensus of managers and management consultants, reported in *Fortune*, Rockefeller Center, New York 10020.

Work and Self-Esteem

The "who/where/what we do" connection has created difficult problems for a growing number of people today who feel trapped in unsatisfying jobs. These people are afraid they won't be able to find another one…or they can't afford to lose seniority and pension rights…or they can't face the difficulty of relocating their families.

Problem: If you feel unappreciated or taken for granted or inadequately rewarded at work, it has an adverse effect on your work, your relationships with your boss and colleagues… and your own psychological and emotional well-being.

The unresolved anger that you feel in your job may spill over into your private life, with family and friends its innocent victims as you scream at the kids, kick the dog, knock down two fast martinis, etc.

Getting back on track:

Doing nothing only adds to feelings of anger, frustration, and exploitation, and victimization will probably continue.

Helpful: Realize that because you have control over yourself, you have control over the situation. Then figure out what you can do to improve the situation. *Questions to ask…*

• *Am I appreciated?* The very fact that you have a job is an important sign that you are valued by your employer. If you're being paid more than people doing similar work elsewhere, that's another good sign.

• *Should I be appreciated?* If your work is marginal or if your achievement level is lower than colleagues in your unit, then it's not realistic to expect compliments and reassurances about the quality of your work.

Try to appraise your real contributions to your employer…and look for ways to bring those to management's attention.

In addition to self-appraisal, it's imperative to get frequent feedback from your boss. If your company doesn't have formal evaluations, request a meeting to discuss your job effectiveness. Work review sessions—in one form or another—should happen much more than once or twice a year, for they give you a good sense of whether you're on the right track.

Try to communicate with your boss about signs of appreciation. If he/she seems to be piling work on you or always giving you the tough tasks, you might interpret it as punishment, while your boss meant to show confidence in your ability. *It helps to talk these things out.*

Also ask colleagues what they think of your work. Assure them that you're not fishing for a compliment, but that you really need an objective appraisal. You may find that you are far more respected than you realize—perhaps for talents or skills you didn't know you had. Team support is a two-way street. Remember to thank and congratulate co-workers when they have done something well, too.

Customers can also be a valuable source of recognition and job satisfaction. When they thank you for your promptness or effectiveness or thoughtfulness, accept the compliments graciously and tell them how much you appreciate the kind words.

But if someone *withholds* praise that you believe you deserve, do not let it cause you to lose confidence in yourself. There's nothing wrong with giving yourself a pat on the back—or a special reward.

Boredom—the bane of self-esteem:

We read frequently about the financial costs of smoking or substance abuse in the workplace, but we rarely hear about the costs of boredom.

Some of boredom's many manifestations: Indifference, anger, disillusionment, procrastination, gossiping, tardiness, absenteeism, and physical aches and pains like headaches.

Bored individuals are not stimulated to go to work, to get there on time, to do the job promptly or well, or to remain loyal to the company. People who are bored because they feel their skills or talents aren't being adequately used often become resentful toward their employers.

Boredom is also a classic cause of stress. It is stressful to spend an eight-hour day in an un-stimulating environment. It is stressful not to have the opportunity to work on challenging problems. And, it is stressful to realize that you are not growing or developing or reaching the goals you set for yourself. We become spirit-less, listless zombies whose minds are on hold. *Solutions to job boredom:*

First admit that job boredom does exist and then take personal responsibility for overcom-ing your boredom. *Some suggestions:*

•Create a log. Chart the activities that you find stimulating and those that are deadly dull. Include contextual information that might help identify whether you're truly bored or simply tired or depressed.

•Analyze your activities and look for pat-terns. After several weeks of keeping a log, analyze the data to see what patterns emerge. If meetings bore you but you feel stimulated while preparing for and delivering a sales pre-sentation, it may be that you need to perform, to persuade, to be creative. Ask yourself how you can do more of this in your job.

•Reenergize your job. Balance routine, repetitive tasks with work that you find more stimulating. Wherever possible, shuffle the order, break boring patterns, and change loca-tions. If you have a morning full of mind-dead-ening tasks, reward yourself by going out to lunch instead of brown-bagging it. Question whether all routine tasks are really necessary. Take occasional work breaks. Try to rotate jobs or swap responsibilities with a colleague to vary the monotony.

•Stretch—reach beyond your grasp. If you have mastered your job so that it no longer uses your full talents and abilities, ask for a new assignment or see if your job description could be broadened. *Alternative:* Transfer to a different job in another department.

•Welcome positive problems at work. Con-fronting and solving problems adds spice to a job. Finding solutions keeps us emotionally and intellectually alive.

•Shake it up—avoid complacency. If you've become too comfortable in your job, take a new look at it. Look for ways to improve coop-eration. Set additional goals. *Bonus:* The fresh excitement new accomplishments generate.

•Do something new. Read new relevant books. Attend a seminar, a workshop, a pro-fessional meeting, or an educational course. Create or design a new product, a new pro-duction process, a new marketing strategy, or a new information system and then try to "sell" it to management. Study Continuous Quality Improvement (CQI) to stimulate your-self by planning to do all that you do better—each time you do it.

•Develop a life outside of your job. Thoughts of how you will spend your free time away from the job can provide a mental escape from work that is boring. Pleasurable activities in private life can also provide the excitement and fulfillment that may be miss-ing in your career—and maybe even add to it.

Coaching, reading, working on a political campaign, listening to music, volunteer work, sports, and hobbies give balance and verve to your life and put you in control of your emo-tional well-being. Spend time with people who are energetic and enthusiastic, vital and vibrant…and thoughtful about their life and work. *Learn from them.*

If it's impossible to eliminate boredom and reenergize your enthusiasm for the job, face the fact that it's time to move on. You've grown and changed and are now ready for new chal-lenges…new beginnings…new dreams.

Source: John Sena, PhD, professor of English, and Stephen Strasser, PhD, associate professor, division of hospital and health services administration, both at Ohio State University. They are authors of *Work Is Not a Four Letter Word*, Business One Irwin, 1818 Ridge Rd., Home-wood, Illinois 60430.

How to Make Networking Work for You

Networking is not just for executives who have fallen off the success track and need powerful contacts to help them find new jobs, assist in closing deals, etc.

Aside from helping in a career crisis, networking—continuously building contacts with people with information, expertise, and ideas from a wide spectrum of business, politics, and philosophy—is invaluable for day-to-day productivity, efficiency, and achievement.

Executives from unrelated companies face many common concerns. Sharing experiences—good and bad—on questions of compensation, incentives, labor negotiations, regulatory and legislative activities, and other topics is very helpful.

A peer outside the company may provide new information, suggest a consultant or expert, or provide an entirely fresh way for you to evaluate recommendations from your own corporate staff.

Organizing your network:

Important networking rule: Make a continuous investment of time in assessing the strengths of your own network—to identify where you are already strong and where you need to build. You can't delegate this task... you're the only one who can do it.

Tools for managing your network: A three-ring binder with loose-leaf, lined paper. *It should contain:*

- Address book.
- Business card file.
- Professional directories.
- Alumni associations and class reunion publications.
- Christmas card list.
- Membership rosters of organizations you belong to and contribute to—including groups such as the Little League, health and recreation club members.

Some people prefer to use a computer and personal organization software instead of paper and binder. There are many such programs available.

Identify your base of contacts:

Take several sheets of loose-leaf paper and give each sheet a heading from the following list:

- People in position to influence.
- People who know others.
- Coworkers and former coworkers.
- Clients and former clients.
- Suppliers.

- Colleagues and competitors.
- Family.
- Ex-family.
- Extended family.
- Neighbors/former neighbors.
- Classmates and alumni.
- Associates from organizations, charities, religious affiliations.
- Special interest groups (health, sports, bridge, etc.).

List names, addresses, and phone/fax numbers from your input sources under each category. Continue to add names and numbers as you build your network.

Once you've organized your contacts, identify gaps...and ways to fill them. Identify areas where the network can be significantly strengthened. *Key questions to ask yourself:*

- What kind of advice or information is most difficult to get?
- What group could I join that might help?
- Do I know enough senior executives in my own industry...among suppliers to my industry...in related businesses...in other areas?

Using the network:

Some of the best networkers find it difficult to use their contacts when they most need them. They're never reluctant to call a person if they have a useful piece of information or a new contact to offer. But it's hard for many successful executives to ask for help from network contacts when they really need the help and have nothing to offer in return.

It's important to remember that if you have been a giver in the past, people will respond when you need them. Call in your chips... that's part of the value of strong networks.

Example: A successful real-estate developer fell on hard times when commercial real-estate values collapsed in the late 1980s. When times were good, he had been very generous with his help to others. Now he was about to declare personal bankruptcy—and for the first time in years was looking for a job. He confided his situation to a colleague and asked him to keep his ears open for any openings. Before the day was over, the business friend's son called, explaining that his father-in-law was in a business that might be able to use the man's skills. He invited the developer to his child's christening party that weekend so that the two of them could meet. It worked. The developer was able to join the father-in-law's firm and stave off financial disaster.

Reciprocity is the glue that keeps networks together. And it's not only a career-building skill...it can be a career-saving skill. Giving without expectation works. In fact, giving is what builds your standing with a network.

Not giving back usually backfires. The network has a way of knowing when you owe too much.

Caution: A critical but frequently overlooked part of giving involves simply acknowledging advice, time, referrals, leads, or gifts from others. Gestures of appreciation are a powerful tool in the networking game.

Source: Susan RoAne, The RoAne Group, 14 Wilder St., San Francisco 94131. She is the author of the best-selling *How to Work a Room* and *The Secrets of Savvy Networking.* Both books are published by Warner Books, 1271 Ave. of the Americas, New York 10020.

How to Overcome Teamwork Blues

Teams and teamwork have become terms of worship in American business. Amazingly, though, neither works very well in most US companies. In fact, only 17% of managers and team members surveyed by Wilson Learning in 1992* said that teamwork was working well for their companies. The rest of the respondents said teamwork was mostly talk and little substance.

Probing further, Wilson Learning discovered what the companies that have succeeded in team-building have in common...

•They evaluate individuals on their effectiveness as team members. The vast majority of company performance appraisal systems still concentrate entirely on individual accomplishments—with no measures of team performance.

•They compensate managers and team

*Conclusions based on interviews and data collected by Wilson Learning Corp. from 25,000 team members in 4,500 teams in over 500 organizations.

members for their performance as members of teams—and for meeting defined goals.

•They reduce barriers to the free flow of important business information across functional lines in the company. Getting people to give up their urge to withhold information to bolster their status within the firm is a key factor in getting teams to function efficiently.

•They give teams clear goals and ensure that team members understand and are focused on those goals. *Too typical:* Management responds to pressure from consultants or managers who read about teams or go to seminars explaining how teams work by asserting how important it is for the company to adopt teamwork. But they fail to realize that teams are not an end in themselves. The most important factor in generating a team's effectiveness is the clarity of its objective and focus.

Mechanics of effective collaboration:

Once the company has clarified a team's goals, the team's effectiveness in meeting those goals depends on how well members work together.

Trap: Managers often stall team performance by getting too involved in working out team processes and techniques of team leadership. Instead, right from the start, management should focus on coaching team members to...

•Support themselves as individuals. This means encouraging them to advocate their own ideas and training them in ways to persuade others of their points of view. Too often, emphasis on not making waves and cooperating inhibits this essential training.

•Support others in the team. Valuing other people's styles for solving problems is essential to working well on a team. *Managing* conflict does not mean *reducing* conflict. On a team, efficiency often requires creating tension while at the same time effectively resolving conflict. Politeness alone won't suffice. Team members must learn how to air differences, tell hard truths, and ask hard questions of one another. When a team is not facing the core issues that prevent it from reaching its goal, its work will not move forward and creative solutions will not unfold.

•Support the team. Keep the goal in focus. Commit team members' energy to getting the team to work. Discourage those who try to undermine the team—or who simply refuse to "buy in" to the team spirit.

Bottom line:

Teams represent a valuable way for organizations to structure work processes. However, the key to success is getting people to work together toward common goals. Creating this collaborative environment is the challenge businesses face.

Source: Michael Leimbach, PhD, research director, Wilson Learning Corporation, developer and implementer of business training in management, quality, customer service, and sales for companies around the world, 7500 Flying Cloud Dr., Eden Prairie, Minnesota 55344.

For Your Eyes Only

Destroy quantities of confidential papers by soaking them overnight in a bucket of laundry bleach. Repeat if necessary until images disappear.

Source: *Complete Trash: The Best Way to Get Rid of Practically Everything Around the House* by Norm Crampton, secretary, Institute for Solid Wastes of the American Public Works Association, M. Evans and Co., 216 E. 49 St., New York 10017.

How to Protect Yourself From a Package Bomb

Package bombs and letter bombs often have clues to alert recipients to possible trouble.

Danger signs:
- Excessive weight for the size.
- Too much postage.
- No return address.
- Mailed from a foreign country, or via airmail or special delivery.
- A rigid or lopsided envelope.
- Common words are misspelled.
- Restrictive markings, such as "Confidential" or "Personal."
- Incorrect title for the addressee, or a title without a person's name.
- Handwritten or poorly typed address.
- Protruding wires or tinfoil.
- Excessive securing material, such as tape or string.
- Oily stains or discoloration on the outside of the package.

If you're suspicious: Don't touch the package—not even to move it out of the way... immediately call your local FBI office, or police or fire department...or call the FBI's Bomb Data Center at 202-FBI-BOMB.

Source: William Carter is with the Federal Bureau of Investigation at their headquarters in Washington, DC.

The Alertness/Effectiveness Connection

In today's 24-hour world, workers are given extensive training, equipped with very reliable automated machinery, and provided with comfortable surroundings. But that doesn't guarantee effective performance around the clock.

Bizarre example: In the cockpit of a Boeing 707 en route to Los Angeles, the entire crew fell asleep while the autopilot continued to fly the plane westward...far over the Pacific Ocean. When air traffic controllers on the ground noticed the wayward plane, their verbal inquiries went unanswered. The desperate controllers averted disaster when they managed to wake up the crew by triggering loud chimes in the cockpit.

Alertness is key to effective performance:

That near-disaster was caused by the failure of one critical human factor—*alertness*. Like so many systems today, the airplane was designed to perform so well automatically that it was hard for the pilots to remain alert.

But alertness is vital for people to perform effectively. Only in that state are people fully aware of their surroundings...able to think clearly...consider all options...make sensible decisions.

Physiological basis:

To physiologists, alertness represents a desirable state of balance between two human nervous systems.

One of these nervous systems—*the sympathetic nervous system*—automatically triggers the fight-or-flight response…heart pounding…blood pressure rising…pupils dilating…hair standing on end.

It represents a peak of alertness vital for dealing with emergency situations…but it usually can't be sustained for too long.

Minimum alertness occurs when the body is highly relaxed…under control of the *parasympathetic nervous system.* Consider someone dozing by the fire after a heavy meal… heart beating slowly…blood pressure dropping… pupils constricting. It is essential for the body and mind to rest sometimes…but a state of total relaxation is bad news if you're supposed to be working…studying…even observing.

In a state of alertness, the brain is engaged and ready to react appropriately to evolving situations. But we're often not alert when we need to be because our external environment or our internal state—or a combination of both—work to disengage our brain.

Nine switches of alertness:

Research into the physiology of alertness has shown there are nine switches that control alertness. We can improve our alertness by learning what they are and how to switch them on or off. *They are:*

1. Sense of danger, interest, or opportunity. Nothing switches us faster from drowsiness to alertness than awareness of imminent danger. The brain can also be awakened in a less extreme way by other forms of stimulation.

Helpful: If you're in a meeting about a subject that's not too exciting and feel yourself dozing off, try to stimulate yourself. Ask questions…make comments…take notes…bring others into the discussion.

2. Muscular activity. Vigorous exercise can improve alertness for an hour or more. Many people performing tasks where alertness is vital cannot move around—pilots, drivers, nuclear-plant operators. But they can find other types of muscular activity to help keep them alert.

Helpful: Stretch in place…chew gum…take periodic breaks to walk around.

3. Time of day on the biological clock. Humans have their own biological clock that tells when it's time to wake and to sleep. If you're on shift work or traveling between different time zones, it's not easy to adjust your built-in clock to match the environment.

Helpful: If you're running a meeting with people from all over the country or the world, be aware of their biological clocks. Try to schedule a compromise time that helps as many as possible stay awake. Remember that people feel drowsy after lunch and are most alert when their body tells them it's mid-morning or late afternoon.

4. Sleep bank balance. Alertness depends on how long it is since we last slept. It is possible to restore the balance in our sleep bank by a good single night's sleep or by a number of brief naps at strategic intervals.

Interesting: A short nap of 10–15 minutes provides more benefit than one of 30–40 minutes, which leaves you drowsy. Research has shown that people can work 22 hours a day for extended periods if they get a 20-minute nap every four hours.

5. Ingested nutrients and chemicals. Stimulation by food, drink, or chemicals can improve our alertness. In moderation, it may be sensible, but it's often a poor way to cope. Two or three cups of coffee are fine to help you stay awake, but any more than that stays in the system and makes it hard to sleep after work, and it makes you more tired the next day. Similarly, people who pop too many stay-awake pills develop insomnia and then become dependent on sleeping pills.

Helpful: A 10-minute coffee break. But if you have the choice, a 10-minute nap is better.

6. Environmental light. Bright light keeps people alert, but to be truly effective, it must be about the level of natural light at dawn—about the level of a hospital operating room, which is twice as bright as a well-lit office. This level of light doesn't just help you see well, it stimulates the brain. Today, exploiting light for alertness is on the technological frontier.

7. Environmental temperature and humidity. We all know that a cold shower wakes us up… a warm bath puts us to sleep…and that when driving on a boring highway, one of the best ways to wake up is to open the window and get a blast of cold air.

8. Environmental sound. The rolling surf at the beach or the smooth rushing of a mountain stream can lull us to sleep. These are examples of "white noise" that is also generated by machines that people use to help them go to sleep...and resembles the background noise produced by much equipment found in industrial control rooms where operators are expected to stay awake at night.

Helpful: In control rooms, try to use irregular sources of sound that vary in pitch and intensity...allow workers to listen to stimulating radio programs when possible.

9. Environmental aroma. Although this switch has not been scientifically investigated as much as the other eight switches, there are intriguing reports that aromas like peppermint may help alertness.

With an awareness of how these nine switches work, you can improve your own alertness. By learning to put them in the "off" position, you can learn how to relax better, as well.

Source: Martin Moore-Ede, MD, PhD, associate professor of physiology at Harvard Medical School, director of the Institute for Circadian Physiology. He is the founder and CEO of Circadian Technologies, consultants to industry worldwide on enhancing alertness in the workplace and author of *The Twenty-Four-Hour Society: Understanding Human Limits in a World that Never Stops*, Addison-Wesley, Jacob Way, Reading, Massachusetts 01867.

Many Hiring Mistakes Can Be Avoided

Nearly 40% of all new hires fall short of expectations. Within a few months, these new recruits must either be heavily trained to meet the company's standards...moved to another position in the company...or terminated.

To avoid hiring mistakes: Write performance-based job descriptions before beginning the hiring process.

Conventional job descriptions don't work. They are mere lists of skills, personality attributes, experience, and educational requirements.

Such descriptions rarely have anything to do with successful performance. Skills and experience should never be the primary factors to define company goals for a job.

While specific skills and experience may be a prerequisite for many positions, the employee's character traits—such as creativity, optimism, determination, and attention to detail—are what determine whether expectations of the employer will be met. *Key:* Make the company's objectives and goals define the kinds of people needed to achieve those results.

To write performance-based job descriptions: List measurable results that are expected of the person being hired for the job—based on the company's goals. *Examples of viable results to list in a job description:*

• Increase sales by 10% in consumer market channels within six months.

• Develop a network of international sales representatives by the end of the year so that the company is in a position to increase market share in specified overseas markets.

• Learn the company's special chart of accounts and general ledger system within 30 days.

• Reduce operating costs in the department by 10% within 12 months and develop a plan to implement that goal within 90 days.

The next step in the process is to convert these expected results in the job description into the questions that will be asked in evaluating candidates.

Examples: How would you go about achieving a 10% cost reduction in the department within 12 months? What would you do to be able to implement the plan within 90 days?

Evaluate candidates on the basis of the aptitude they demonstrate for solving problems...achieving improvements...progressing toward the company's goals.

Caution:

Verbally gifted candidates may have a significant advantage in such interviews. Be alert to that—especially when interviewing candidates for sales, marketing, or creative jobs.

Helpful: Set several objectives for each job—to get a wide variety of responses to evaluate. Have more than one person interview the candidate using this method.

Follow-up:

Once an individual is hired and begins working toward the goals set out in the job description, make sure to meet with the person regularly—at least quarterly—to adjust priorities and goals.

There's nothing wrong with setting high goals at the outset and then adjusting them downward later—as long as improvement continues.

Source: Lou Adler, president and founder, CJA Associates, Inc., executive search and organizational consulting firm, 17852 17 St., Tustin, California 92680.

How to Get Your Paper Flow Under Control

Though many office workers don't agree that it's necessary to have a clean desk, few would dispute the importance of being able to quickly put their hands on information when they need it.

My principle: If you don't know you have it—or you can't find it—it's of no value to you.

Clients often tell me sob stories of missing important meetings because they misplaced the notice. Others bemoan their failure to meet loan payments or other deadlines. One entrepreneur even lost out on a promising business opportunity because he couldn't locate his passport.

Reality: Even with computers playing a bigger part in everyone's lives, there will always be plenty of paper to manage. The same principles that guide this paper management system can be applied to computers.

First—centralize:

Offices are dedicated to handling a flow of paper. But everyone needs a similar central location at home. If possible, this should be a permanent spot, available to you at all times. Avoid desks that look pretty but aren't functional.

Effective: A large butcher block top or a piece of plywood placed across two good-quality file cabinets. Since filing is a major factor in managing paper, it's ideal to have the filing system located close by.

Install adequate lighting and a comfortable chair. You want to make doing paperwork as pleasant as possible.

Key supplies: A "To Sort" tray (better to think of it this way than as an "In Box"), a large wastebasket, a nearby telephone, a rotary telephone file, and a calendar.

Where to start:

Paper clutter indicates a pattern of postponed decisions. You've let those papers pile up because you failed to make an immediate decision about what to do with them. Begin now by putting today's mail, or whatever pile of papers you wish to organize, into your "To Sort" tray.

Use this spot consistently, bringing papers from everywhere to this base location. But think of it as only a temporary stopover. For most people, the goal of handling a piece of paper just once is too ambitious. But you should decide on its final resting place when it comes out of the "To Sort" tray. Sort out the tray on a regular basis.

The duty to discard:

Learning to throw out unneeded paper is the next step toward effective paper management.

People never use 80% of the paper they collect.

Your stress level will decrease as your use of the large wastebasket increases. Before the wastebasket, however, think about how to avoid even *seeing* unnecessary paper. *Examples:*

• *Get rid of 40% of your promotional mail* by writing to Mail Preference Service, Direct Marketing Association, 11 W. 42 St., Box 3861, New York 10036, and asking them to remove your name from direct mail lists. Every chance you get, instruct companies not to sell or rent your name and address.

• *Don't send for magazines you won't read.* Uncontrolled information is not a resource—*it's a burden.* Piles of old magazines or clippings—no matter how interesting or informative they may be—soon turn into dust collectors that depress you and make you feel guilty.

Better: Play a game with yourself to see how much you can throw away or recycle. *Questions to ask yourself:*

• Did I request this?

• Is this the only place this information is available?

• Is it recent enough to be useful?

• When, exactly, might I need this information? "Just in case" is not an acceptable answer.

• Are there any tax or legal reasons to keep it?

• What's the worst possible thing that could happen if I threw this away? (Most things can be reordered, found at the library, etc.)

Keep a calendar:

Using a calendar can eliminate lots of paper from your desks (home and office), dressers, mirrors, bulletin boards, and wallets.

Key: Get into the habit of extrapolating the needed information, entering it on your calendar, and then throwing away the paper—or filing it if you really must.

The most effective paper managers I know keep a master calendar that records all business and personal commitments for every member of the family. You can keep it either at home (the refrigerator door is accessible to everyone) or the office. Or, you can carry it with you.

In addition, you may need separate calendars for specific functions—a travel schedule, a meeting schedule, etc. But don't fall into the trap of having too many calendars. Coordination is an ongoing problem, especially when dates are changed. Keep key players informed.

The calendar is a tool that helps you to be realistic about time management. People who are most successful in accomplishing their goals make appointments with themselves to complete specific tasks by a certain date or to at least check on things.

I've developed some abbreviated symbols that remind me what I need to do: C (call), D (discuss), H (hold in file), LM (left message), WC (they will call me).

Note: I keep a corresponding WC file near the phone so that when people do call back I'll remember what I wanted to talk about.

If you're comfortable with a computer, you may want to use one of the many software scheduling programs now on the market. They're especially helpful when more than one person schedules your time.

Names and numbers:

Many of the little scraps of paper floating around our homes and offices contain important telephone numbers or ones that we think might become important.

Solution: Think of the one word that would prompt you to call this person—such as Atlanta…or kitchen…or speechwriter.

Then record or file the information that way and throw away the paper. I use my rotary phone file for all kinds of names and numbers, even for listing family Social Security numbers and the numbers of combination locks. Rotary phone-file cards now come in a variety of colors that you can use to flag different categories.

Action vs. reference files:

After you've eliminated as much paper as possible by using your wastebasket, calendar, a daily "To Do" list, and telephone listing, what remains will go into action files or reference files.

Action files: For papers that need immediate attention.

Reference files: For papers you know you will need at some point in the future.

Reference files can become action files or vice versa.

Example: A reference file on Europe can become an action file if you're planning a trip to Paris.

You can also have reference files and action files with the same or nearly the same heading—*Community Association* and *Community Association–1993 Dues Campaign.*

Potential action categories: Based on the next action needed, here are some of the action file categories I find useful…

• Call	• Photocopy
• Computer entry	• Read
• Discuss	• Sign
• File	• Take to office/home
• Pay	• Write

The key to reference files is not only to put papers away but to be able to find them again. File information according to *how you will use it*, not where you got it.

Ask yourself: Under what circumstances would I want this information? What word would first enter my mind?

Example: If you will need the information when you sell your house, then set up a *House-Main Street* file.

Put all papers in their most general category first—such as *Warranties and Instructions.* If that file becomes too bulky, you can break it down into *Warranties and Instructions–Kitchen Appliances, Warranties and Instructions–Autos.*

Organize your files logically—such as *Medical–Anne, Medical–John.* Group like files together.

Example: Instead of filing *Biking* under B and *Skiing* under S, you could have files named *Recreation–Biking* and *Recreation–Skiing.*

The very important master file: To remind yourself of how you filed information, keep an alphabetical master file index, with cross-references to related files. Keep the master file index right up front so when you file something, you can tell whether to put it under *Auto, Car, Chrysler,* or *Vehicle,* and you won't end up with all four.

If there's a particular piece of paper you're afraid of losing, you can list it in the index— *"Divorce decree,* see *Legal Information."*

Source: Barbara Hemphill, Hemphill & Associates, Inc., 1464 Garner Station Blvd., Raleigh, North Carolina 27603. She is president of the National Association for Professional Organizers and author of *Taming the Paper Tiger,* Kiplinger Books, 1729 H St. NW, Washington, DC 20006.

How to Increase Your Productivity

At an almost breathtaking pace, medical science is discovering new insights into human biology.

Used the right way, much of this new knowledge can help managers heighten workers' job satisfaction and increase their own productivity. *Major discoveries...*

Light and color secrets:

Researchers have found that light has a profound effect on our bodies. Though not completely understood, the reason is probably linked to the effect light has on two vital areas of the brain—the hypothalamus and the pineal gland.

Our moods, even those of color-blind people, are affected by the intensity and color of the light around us.

Examples: People brainstorm better when surrounded by bright colors. Subdued shades are usually best for negotiating. Red cars command higher prices.

Helpful: Use a consultant to help you decorate your office...and choose your wardrobe. The right color and lighting can raise output and make work more enjoyable. Wearing the right colors can also boost a sales rep's closing rate.

Where to find an expert: Most large management consulting firms can make recommendations. For color, try the Pantone Color Institute, 201-935-5501.

Also, bring more natural light into the workplace. Tests show that it has a positive impact on performance. There are lights available now that simulate natural light. For advice, consult a lighting engineer.

Sound secrets:

Women are far more sensitive to sound than men. They can also hear higher-pitch sounds. Some research suggests that women may even be subliminally sensitive to sounds beyond the conscious hearing range.

Example: Some scientists believe high-frequency tones given off by computer terminals can cause stress in women who use them. Harm may occur even though users aren't actually aware of the sound.

If your company has complaints from VDT users, consider hiring an acoustical engineer. The problem may be with the sound, not the light source.

Other research has discovered how we screen background noise from conversation that we want to hear.

Helpful: If you want someone's attention, don't talk more loudly, just move closer. Halving the distance quadruples the sound.

Smell secrets:

This may be the most exciting area of research. Science has discovered that odors have a profound effect on our moods and performance.

Examples: Exposure to apple-cinnamon may improve editing skills...fruit scents may induce women to make certain purchases...clove has a calming effect...and peppermint elevates mood and may relieve headaches.

Try scenting your office with various fragrances to find the ones that have the effect you want.

Helpful: Contact the Fragrance Foundation (212-725-2755). This organization tracks the latest research in the field and can put companies in touch with consultants.

Biorhythm secrets:

Each individual has a natural rhythm to his/her activities, but in a typical business environment we're all expected to arrive, work, and eat at more or less the same times.

Helpful: Give yourself (and employees) more schedule flexibility. Experiment with having several snacks instead of one long meal. Take a midday nap if it helps rejuvenate you in the afternoon.

As far as possible within the demands of the business world, tell employees you're more interested in results than in when they're achieved.

Biorhythms are also affected by sunlight. If you must start work before sunup, take an outdoor break as early in the day as possible. It can boost your mood and productivity.

Keep a chart of your own cycles of high and low energy levels. Try to schedule meetings and other tasks accordingly.

Gender secrets:

The latest tests confirm again that women are biologically equipped to process a wider range of sensory information than men.

Women are less obsessed with beating out rivals and getting super-rich than men are. They want to succeed for the sake of personal emotional fulfillment.

Men are more prone to tunnel vision—aiming at destroying their enemies quickly. Women, by contrast, see the broader picture and strategize better for long-term success.

Despite these differences between the sexes, managers don't have to plan one set of tasks for women and another for men. Instead, be attuned to using the assets of each to the best advantage.

Example: When assembling a project team, try to include a balance of men and women. If you don't, chances are greater that the team will overlook an important strategy, side-effect, market, or other opportunity.

Age secrets:

As people grow older, their gender-hormone levels decline. In women, declining estrogen during menopause can bring on irritability and forgetfulness. In men, declining testosterone levels can cause low energy levels and loss of concentration.

If you manage people who show these symptoms, help them find support. And do the same for yourself if you're nearing 50.

Helpful: To increase productivity and job satisfaction among older workers, offer to redesign offices for them—provide softer colors, comfortably built chairs, equipment with large enough displays to be seen by someone with less than great vision.

Brain secrets:

Science is rapidly discovering that while the brain has many similarities to a computer—which stores and processes information—the *brain* also *interprets* information.

Not appreciating this difference has led many companies to rely too heavily on computers.

The brain works in a way that usually makes it easier to remember what we read in a book than what we see on computer screens.

Example: You probably have a good idea of where in this issue of *Bottom Line Yearbook 1994* the chapter entitled "Very, Very Personal" appears. But you would have much less of an idea if you had scrolled through the chapters on a computer.

Recommended: Ask for advice from a neuropsychologist or neurobiologist at a local university whenever the company is developing or revising training programs. Their expertise about how people learn can be valuable in making training techniques much more effective.

Source: Edith Weiner, president, Weiner, Edrich, Brown, Inc., futurists and strategic planning consultants, 200 E. 33 St., New York 10016. She is also co-author of the very useful and insightful new book, *Office Biology,* MasterMedia Ltd., 17 E. 89 St., New York 10128.

Priorities

The classic crisis between work and home life for busy people with children is the school play or recital or Little League game that conflicts with an important business meeting.

Trap: Making spur-of-the-moment decisions about priorities when these conflicts arise. That almost always results in hurt feelings, poor productivity, or your own disappointment in having accomplished too little.

Solution: Longer-term time management. Budget specific amounts of time each day for certain activities—and consistently hold to the schedule you set. *Examples:*

• No business calls after 7 PM.

• Four hours of take-home work over the weekend, and no more.

• An hour or half-hour alone with your spouse when you both get in from work—no interruptions from children, work, or neighbors.

Make those times inviolate—something that others can count on.

Helpful: Make a public announcement to family and key coworkers of the times you've scheduled. That helps "trap" you into keeping to the plan.

When you establish a record of setting and sticking to priorities, the occasional missed Little League game or dinner out won't be seen as such a catastrophe—either for family members or for yourself.

First: Choose the right priorities.

For most families, life is too full of opportunities and responsibilities to be able to do everything. To accomplish as much as possible, some low-priority activities must be eliminated. *Challenge:* Choosing *which* activities to drop. Start by asking yourself: "What must I accomplish this week...or this day, this month, this year...even if I accomplish nothing else?"

Example: For daily priorities, set aside a time each evening to list what you must do the next day. Review that list in your head in the morning as you get ready to start the new day.

Key question: "What must I absolutely get done today?" If it's a phone call or a meeting with someone that you know will be difficult but which must be done that day—don't make excuses for not following through.

Caution: Don't fall into the trap of dutifully making a long "To Do" list every day—only to end up completing less than half of it each day. "To Do" lists are useless unless you score at least a B grade every day—getting at least seven out of 10 tasks accomplished. C—five out of 10 tasks—isn't good enough. And, three out of 10 is an F.

Important: Don't get so caught up in daily schedules that your weekly, monthly and yearly priorities go unattended.

For longer-term priorities, keep a file for updating your progress weekly or monthly. *More than just getting it done...*

Even a good record of task completion, however, doesn't mean you're setting priorities most effectively. For that, you must track the quality of your progress.

Key: Take time at the end of the day to analyze whether you devoted significant attention to each project you handled. Are you sure that the time and effort you spent on each task succeeded in moving it closer to completion?

General rule: To improve the quality of your work, tackle the complicated tasks first. It's too easy to persuade yourself that it makes sense to get rid of the least demanding tasks to free yourself to take on the big jobs. But it rarely works that way. This is simply a classic delaying tactic. Avoidance takes more energy than it's really worth—energy that you can direct better elsewhere.

Executives have another set of priority traps...

• Spending more and more time on big strategic decisions that are removed from the day-to-day realities of keeping the business running smoothly.

• Avoiding big decisions by spending more time on minutiae.

There's no magical way to achieve the proper balance. The most successful managers, though, are constantly aware that they are in danger of veering toward one side or the other.

They keep developing a kind of dual vision that allows them to set the short-term, day-to-day priorities that keep the company moving and improving...and to continually set longer-range, strategic priorities that steer the company toward important goals.

As you struggle to work out these priorities, explain to your staff what the priorities are and why you have set them that way.

Encourage discussion. The more those who work with you buy into your goals for improvement and positive change, the more cohesively they work and the more productive the results of their efforts.

Source: Mortimer R. Feinberg, PhD, chairman, BFS Psychological Associates, Inc., 666 Fifth Ave., New York 10103.

Modesty Traps

Being overly modest is as bad as unabashed bragging. In either case, the people who should be aware of your accomplishments either won't learn about them (if you're too modest) or won't believe you (if you brag). *Best:* Share your accomplishments matter-of-factly, in casual conversation. For example, tell how a customer was satisfied, a crisis averted, or a problem solved. And when someone compliments you, express your appreciation.

Source: Ted Pollack, management consultant, Old Tappan, New Jersey, writing in *Production*, 6600 Clough Pike, Cincinnati 45224.

How to Be A Better Manager

While guiding a work team to excellence does not require physical prowess, many of the principles used by great sports coaches in leading their teams to victory are applicable for workplace coaches as well.

Skilled manager-coaches instill in workers...
- A sense of loyalty.
- Pride in their work.
- Willingness to help others toward a common goal.
- Self-discipline.

- Reliability.
- Honesty.

Mistake: Thinking that all winning coaches must be hard-nosed taskmasters like Vince Lombardi or Leo Durocher.

Reality: Some athletes respond to this style, while others perform better under coaches who are low-key and restrained—like UCLA's John Wooden.

The same is true for coaches in the workplace. Effective ones can be abrasive, diffident, or anywhere in between. The very best know how to adjust their style according to the individual "athlete" they're dealing with.

Coaches' key talents:

To maximize the benefit of coaching, a company should develop the coaching skills that managers already have, and look for these abilities in new hires. *Characteristics of outstanding coach-managers:*

- Supportiveness. Effective coaches derive satisfaction from helping others learn and succeed. Without this trait, managers will have a difficult time getting the best performance from their employees.

Example: When a subordinate makes an error in an important project, an unsupportive manager might simply resort to tough discipline. A nurturing manager immediately lets the worker know he'll be helped to develop skills so that similar mistakes can be avoided in the future. Coworkers will be encouraged to help in the effort.

- Empathy. This is the ability to see a problem through the eyes of others. Among other advantages, empathy helps a manager sense team members' needs as well as their problems *before* they become serious.

Training and hiring:

The traits that make effective coaches are probably not inborn. They often can be learned.

But, such traits are acquired early in life. By the time a person becomes a manager, these personality characteristics are largely fixed.

Result: Training programs aimed at restructuring managers' personalities are of limited value. Some management-training organizations try to force personality changes, but the cost is usually high and lasting benefits are few.

Much more effective: Help develop manager-coaches by restructuring operations around work teams. Even managers without great personality characteristics can be highly effective in teams.

Management-training firms that specialize in teamwork can help managers make the transition from traditional hierarchical operations to a team-based approach. Most major human-resource consultants offer seminars and workshops in teamwork. *Look for courses that teach managers to...*

• Build their workers' self-esteem.

• Focus on problems instead of personalities.

• Encourage mutual respect among the workers they supervise.

• Use positive reinforcement to shape behavior.

• Set reasonable goals that are clearly communicated.

Even if a company doesn't offer formal courses to its managers, it can encourage them through rewards and evaluations aimed at getting them to practice and improve the techniques to become effective coaches. The five objectives just mentioned should be among the criteria in performance evaluations.

Important: To help in hiring managers with coaching ability, consider rewriting the job description for most managers to include the functions of coaching.

Too often, businesses seek out managers with flawless credentials or a track record of monetary success. These may be desirable, but if managers are expected to lead a team, coaching skills should also be included.

Helpful: Screen for applicants with a history of coaching in their previous jobs. In interviews, ask questions that reveal how empathic the manager is and whether he/she derives satisfaction from encouraging others to do an outstanding job.

And after the hiring decision:

To improve the odds that manager-coaches will succeed in boosting the performance of their employees, follow the lead of successful sports teams...

• Give them clear goals. In sports, the goal is winning or, perhaps for some teams, re-

building and improving. In business, a group of workers supervised by a coach must have similarly clear objectives.

Example: Not merely to improve production, but to improve it by a specific amount... or not simply to raise quality, but to raise it by reducing the percentage of defects to a specific number.

• Reward successful coaches and their team members. Rewards can be money, recognition, or a mix of the two, depending on the company's culture. Bonuses are usually effective since they reward team effort but don't lock the company into a higher salary structure, either for the coach or the coach's employees.

Important: Instruct managers to alert their supervisors as soon as a team shows signs of not being able to meet its goals. That gives the company time to adjust the goals, get another coach, or add some heavy hitters to the team.

Source: Dr. Brian Kleiner, professor of management, California State University, 800 N. State College Blvd., Fullerton, CA 92634.

Business/Career Resolutions... Just in Time

Today, knowing the right way to behave in business is more than polite. It's a vital strategy for keeping clients and customers and for getting ahead.

Based on interviews with top executives, as well as an analysis of 108 surveys by human-resource professionals, here are 12 fundamental business protocol rules you should follow in 1994, if you're not doing so already...

1. Cultivate new business...and maintain contact with old clients/customers...and fulfill current work assignments. Keep up with your customers throughout the year—and remember them during the holidays. Interest in others goes a long way to promote business success.

• Stanley Heilbronn, first vice president at Merrill Lynch, makes it his business to keep in touch with his clients: "If there's an article in a magazine or newspaper that I think would be of interest to them, I scribble a note right on the top—and keep the information flow to clients constant."

2. Be courteous, positive, and upbeat regardless of how you or your company is doing. Especially in these challenging economic times, customers and associates want to be around those who work even harder because times are tough. They avoid pessimists and complainers. For similar reasons, if things are going well, be humble—don't brag.

3. Accept criticism graciously. Give it carefully, preceding and following it with something positive.

• J. Douglas Phillips, senior director of corporate planning at Merck & Co.: "Look for the positive within the negative situation."

4. Sexist/racist/ethnic slurs/jokes and actions are unacceptable.

5. Say "thank you." Drop a note or send flowers, fruit, or another appropriate gift to someone who sends business your way.

• Nella Barkley, president of Crystal-Barkley Corporation, a career-consulting firm: "Make thank-yous timely and very appropriate to the occasion and the person—never pro forma. A warm, personal note or follow-up phone call with news about what happened as a result of a referral will mean much more to the recipient than a standard gift ordered by your secretary."

6. Be discreet about company business or secrets—and the intimate details of your personal life.

• Mitchell P. Davis, editor at Broadcast Interview Source, an information publisher: "People don't want to hear about your problems. They want to hear about opportunities. That's why they're in business."

7. Cultivate friendships at work and with customers. It helps to create a very pleasant workplace. It also enhances productivity, since work friends provide emotional support and comradery and network with each other. But exercise discretion in work-based friendships.

• Marsha Londe, director of corporate accounts, Shadco Advertising Specialities: "You don't have to spill your guts to make a friend."

8. Dress appropriately. Even at companies with new "dress down" codes of more casual dress, it's still important to dress to impress.

• Irene Cohen, chairman, Corporate Staffing Alternatives, Inc., a human-resource management company: "If you're in a business where letting down your guard in terms of dress code for even one day, for one hour, could make a difference with a customer, client, or applicant, don't do it. Business is too important in this economy to take this kind of risk."

9. Use proper written and spoken language. Scrutinize your memos, proposals, reports, and letters. Are you proud of the way your correspondence and written communications look and read? Are your letters too long? Show concern for others, who are also very busy, and keep written communications as brief and clear as possible. While it's usually harder to write a short, lucid letter, it's easier on the person receiving it. For the same reasons, keep your phone conversations succinct. However, include enough appropriate "chit chat" so you continue to build your business relationships. Most importantly, avoid foul language.

10. Be on time. Arriving at work on time in the morning, or turning in a report when it's due, shows you're a good time manager, a necessary trait in today's competitive workplace. It also shows you put others before yourself—another attribute of the successful businessperson—since lateness usually involves inconveniencing others.

• Lucy Hedrick, time-management consultant: "By being on time, you're saying that the person you have an appointment with is important to you."

Return phone calls within 24 hours, if possible. Try to answer letters immediately, but definitely within a week.

11. Start planning now, so next year's holiday cards, gifts, and parties are extra special.

• Mary Kent, photographer, likes to design a holiday card that can serve as a mailing piece throughout the year: "In these hard economic times, we have to think in those terms."

• Nona Aguilar, director of a money-management service for women, has figured out a special gift for her clients with substantial net worth: "They receive a letter saying that I'm paying to send an inner-city kid to the country for two weeks in their names."

12. Be concerned with others. Concern for others should include customers, coworkers, superiors, and subordinates.

•Dorothy Paleologos, director, strategic planning for information technology for Aetna Insurance: "What we are selling are promises and the trust relationship that underlies those promises, and that the company is going to look after a client's best interest when it makes good on those commitments."

Source: Jan Yager, PhD, is a Stamford, Connecticut-based business-protocol and executive-communication consultant and speaker. She is the author of 10 books, most recently *Business Protocol: How to Survive & Succeed in Business,* John Wiley & Sons, 605 Third Ave., New York 10158.

How to Start a Business Without Quitting Your Job

The least risky way to start a new business is to do it on the side—while still holding your regular job.

Learn at your own pace, without undue financial pressures.

If your new business takes off—great. If your satisfaction on your regular job grows, you can just phase out the sideline business.

It's key, however, to avoid potential conflicts of interest. That could jeopardize your job. Conflicts of interest are most likely to arise when a sideline business is labor-intensive, when it operates during normal business hours, involves 24-hour responsibility, or requires travel.

Conflicts of interest are least likely when you specialize in a single product, develop a proprietary product, start a family business (other people to handle work), or do direct marketing (perform tasks at your place, on your time).

Where do you find good business ideas? Look around. *Examples:*

•What have you gained from your career that you would enjoy making into a business?

•Do you have a hobby that can become a moonlight business?

•Do you have any specific know-how that you would enjoy doing on the side as a business?

•What would your family enjoy doing together?

•What could you do as a moonlighter that would give you a great deal of fun and satisfaction?

•Is there a product or service missing in your life that others would buy?

Note that for every trend, there's a potential countertrend.

Example: Commercial real estate is generally depressed, but this is a great time for informed buyers of distressed property.

Beware of financial risks that commonly sink businesses. *Examples:* Personal-loan guarantees, a long-term lease, excessive inventory, uninsured losses, slow-paying customers, personal liability for business-related lawsuits. Take advantage of opportunities to limit these risks. *Helpful:* Do business as a corporation, raise as much equity capital as possible (and minimize borrowed money), sign short-term leases with clearly defined sublease rights, strictly limit extension of credit.

Additional ways to limit risks:

•Do everything you can to become an expert before starting up, so you won't waste time on an idea that other people already do better or cheaper.

•Determine the likelihood that you might face formidable competition from overseas.

•Work for someone else in your contemplated field before starting your own business.

•Test your product before spending money in a big way.

•Don't start your sideline business unless you can handle anticipated cash flow needs for at least a year.

•Minimize your operating costs and increase prospects for success by paying people as much as possible on performance, such as commissions—rather than salary.

As a part-timer, it's difficult to compete with full-time businesses unless you concentrate your limited time only on tasks that you alone can do—and subcontract as much work as possible. You might design a new product, for example, but have others do actual production. *Advantages of subcontracting:*

•No initial investment in factory, equipment, and operating costs.

•You can get a fix on manufacturing costs.

•You use the expertise and technology of others, and let someone else handle hassles with labor.

•You can start much faster than if you tried to do everything yourself.

•You can start on a short-term basis and bail out if things don't work as expected.

The potential disadvantages of subcontracting:

•Less control over quality.

•Competition from your supplier.

•Problems can arise because design and production are done by entirely different organizations.

•Less control over supply.

What to do about disadvantages:

•Carefully anticipate how a design might involve production problems and modify it accordingly.

•Provide your subcontractor with clear, unambiguous specifications.

•Establish adequate quality-control procedures.

•Develop back-up subcontractors.

Caution: Never subcontract work unless you understand completely what the costs will be. It's amazing how development costs can add up, even for a simple product. And don't give your on-the-spot approval to the terms of any contract until you have carefully reviewed the issues.

Source: Philip Holland, founder of the Yum Yum Donuts chain and author of *How to Start a Business without Quitting Your Job,* Ten Speed Press, Box 7123, Berkeley, California 94707.

Everyday, Low-Level Tension Can Kill Us

Psychological stress means much more than just sweaty palms, headaches, and a queasy stomach. Stress can contribute to all sorts of serious health problems, including insomnia, chronic diarrhea and constipation, high blood pressure, stroke, heart disease, and depression.

A decade ago, scientists believed that the most harmful form of stress was the result of major life crises—the death of a spouse, the loss of a job, divorce, etc. Now it's clear that while stress associated with these events is often severe, it is usually short-lived. Consequently it has little time to cause damage to our bodies.

Far worse, scientists now theorize, is the everyday stress to which all of us are routinely subjected—being late for work, arguing with a loved one, etc. Each little frustration that occurs throughout the day speeds the heart rate, dilates the pupils, and floods the bloodstream with powerful hormones, setting the stage for stress-related problems.

The best way to fight stress is by adopting a more relaxed attitude about everything...a state of mind that can be achieved by taking advantage of the many relaxation techniques now available.

Benefits: Increased happiness, reduced vulnerability to illness, and increased creativity and productivity at work.

The causes of stress:

Don't blame stress on your environment. Stress has less to do with your immediate surroundings than with your psychological makeup.

It is not eliminated through a better job, a more supportive spouse, or fewer money problems.

Example: Some people experience a great deal of stress even in the calmest environment, while others remain stress-free—even when things are collapsing around them.

Clearly stress is not something external but a product of the mind—and therefore something that each of us can control. *Here's how...*

•Avoid stress-promoting forms of thought and speech. If someone cuts you off in traffic, you can become enraged...or you can accept the fact that you have no direct control over the actions of others. Most of us explode rather than catch ourselves before being consumed by stress. This occurs not out of any character flaw but because we're victims of stress-promoting ways of thought and speech.

•Avoid catastrophic thinking. This occurs when you describe unpleasant situations with words like "awful," "terrible," or "horrendous." Such extreme labels usually overstate the reality of the situation and needlessly create stress.

Remedy: Avoid these words. In their place, use less dire descriptions.

•Avoid absolutist thinking. This is marked by the use of "must," "should," "ought," and other words that set up standards of behavior. Typically these codes are difficult, if not impossible, to live up to. Absolutist thinking encourages us to expect too much of ourselves and those around us...and leads to undue frustration and stress.

Remedy: Cut those words from your vocabulary. Accord yourself and those around you greater compassion and understanding.

Self defense:

Make daily use of relaxation techniques. These techniques range from biofeedback and sensory deprivation to meditation. Some methods, such as biofeedback, require equipment. Others require little more than a quiet room.

Recommendation: Experiment with several techniques before settling on one or more. Be sure to use them every day, not just when you're feeling particularly frazzled.

Of all the relaxation techniques, three are especially powerful...

•Progressive relaxation. The most common form of relaxation, this method involves alternate tensing and relaxing of each of the body's 16 major muscle groups. It can be done with or without the supervision of a therapist.

Procedure: Sit or lie with your eyes closed in a dimly lit room. Adopt a relaxed, passive attitude. Clench the muscles of your right hand and forearm as tightly as possible. Hold this tension for seven seconds, then relax your hand and arm for about 45 seconds. Do this several times until your muscles feel warm and relaxed. Then move on to your right biceps, your left hand and forearm, left biceps, forehead, middle portion of your face, lower portion of your face, your neck, upper back, chest and abdomen, right upper leg, right calf, right ankle and shin, left thigh, left calf, left ankle and shin.

Once you've completed all the muscle groups, your entire body should feel relaxed and warm. If any areas of tension remain,

repeat the appropriate tensing/relaxing exercise until it disappears.

•Meditation. This family of techniques includes yoga and transcendental meditation. It offers a systematic method for eliciting a profound state of relaxation.

Procedure: Sit or lie in a quiet, soothing environment. As you breathe slowly and rhythmically, softly recite "peace," "calm," "om," or some other word of your choosing. Adopt a passive attitude. As you focus on this word and your respiration, troubling thoughts will gradually subside. For maximum relief from stress, meditate twice daily for 10 to 20 minutes at a time.

•Autogenic training. This technique, used with or without a therapist's supervision, involves adopting a passive, relaxed attitude and focusing on a set of six different relaxation themes—heaviness, warmth, regular heartbeat, regular breathing, abdominal warmth, and cooling of the forehead.

Procedure: Sit or lie in a quiet, dimly lit room. Close your eyes and envision yourself in a comfortable, relaxing environment—stretching out on a sandy beach, for instance, or sitting in a warm, sunny meadow. Repeat to yourself, "I am at peace." Chant this phrase softly again and again, until you really do begin to feel at peace. Next, repeat the following line: "My arms and legs are heavy and warm." Do the same for the following phrases: "My breathing is calm"..."My abdomen is warm"..."My forehead is cool." Repeat these phrases for 20 to 30 minutes. Try not to let your mind wander, but don't be bothered if it does. Again, a passive attitude is essential.

Also helpful:

•Hold your breath. The effects of meditation and other formal stress-reduction techniques are very powerful—but can be time-consuming and the results short-lived.

For an effective and convenient "touch-up" during the course of the day, try controlled breath-holding. It not only distracts you from the source of your annoyance but also temporarily boosts bloodstream levels of carbon dioxide, which has a calming effect on the brain.

The technique can be practiced anywhere, anytime, whether you're alone or in a crowd

—whenever you feel yourself growing angry or frazzled.

What to do: Inhale deeply, hold it for a few seconds, then exhale slowly. If you prefer, say "relax," "calm"…or another soothing word or syllable as you exhale. This may be said aloud or silently. Inhale and exhale slowly four more times. Your tension will ebb.

•Take regular vacations. A long, uninterrupted run of routine activities eventually saps your ability to cope with stress. One way to boost your "coping" behavior is to take regular breaks from the daily routine. *Good news:* These vacations need not be long or costly. A weekend in the country is often enough.

•Take good care of your body. Some people quickly fall prey to the deleterious effects of stress—developing headaches, ulcers, or other stress-related ailments.

Others seem immune to such problems no matter how stressful the environment. Similarly, individuals capable of coping well with stress at one time of the day succumb at another time.

While heredity plays a key role in determining your ability to avoid and to withstand stress, it's by no means the only factor.

Important: Good nutrition, regular exercise, and proper sleep patterns. You're far more vulnerable to stress when you're tired, hungry, and lethargic than when you're in tip-top shape. Don't allow yourself to become run down.

Source: Kenneth L. Lichstein, PhD, professor of psychology and former director of clinical training, department of psychology, Memphis State University, Memphis. He is the author of *Clinical Relaxation Strategies,* John Wiley & Sons, 605 Third Ave., New York 10158.

How to Increase Your Creativity

You don't have to be an artist or writer to be creative. Creativity involves your ability to use your brain to change, renew, and recombine aspects of your life. Creativity means sensing the world with vigor and making new use of what you have perceived.

Frederic Flach, MD, a New York psychiatrist who has made a specialty of studying the creative process, believes that the source of a creative idea is the *preconscious.* According to Dr. Flach and other psychoanalysts…

•The preconscious includes all ideas, thoughts, past experiences, and other memory impressions that, with effort, can be consciously recalled.

•To be conscious means to be aware and to have a perception of oneself, one's acts and one's surroundings.

•The subconscious is a state in which mental processes take place without conscious perception.

When we are conscious, we are aware of our surroundings, Dr. Flach explains—but we are limited by our sense of reality and the restrictions of conscious language. In our subconscious, our feelings are so buried they are inaccessible. Our painful past experiences and emotions are locked up.

In our preconscious, however, things are close to the surface. It's our computer data center, where we put things together—memories, fantasies, and the vibrations we pick up from other people. It's where we are in touch with ourselves.

How to tap into your preconscious and increase your creativity…

•Talk about yourself and your past. It is a process that's similar to psychotherapy. You can uncover new facts or new relationships among new and old data and rid yourself of inhibitions caused by people and circumstances you faced in the past—the teacher who told you that you were inadequate or your teasing sibling.

•Don't be a character actor. If you select a defined role, such as button-down executive or superwoman, you may be unable to do things another way.

•Think like a child. Youngsters are filled with wonder, curiosity, playfulness, and imagination. Pursue activities that you have always wondered about. Play a new game. Daydream. As famous psychologist L. S. Vygotsky observed, "Imagination is the internalization of children's play."

•Verbalize or write down all your ideas for a particular project or problem. Don't judge as the ideas are flowing, no matter how far out or silly your conscious side may be telling you they are.

•Write or tape your frustrations. If you are having trouble coming up with ideas, record what is bothering you. It can help free up the creative flow.

•Change your environment. If you are still having difficulty starting the flow of ideas—change the room in which you are working—or change your clothes. Take a "mental excursion" by thinking about a place you'd like to go.

•Review and analyze. Once you have un-clogged your creative idea flow, you can eval-uate whether any of your ideas are workable.

•Don't be afraid to make mistakes. If you fail, learn what doesn't work. Try a new ap-proach. If you are not failing, you are not being very creative, because new trails are un-marked and full of pitfalls. Many mistakes, though, can be eliminated by a higher round of creativity. Write out your ideas—in precise detail. Look for the flaws. Then, through more creative thinking, you can develop new solu-tions.

•Don't make excuses. Age, infirmity, and lack of time are frequent reasons given for not being able to create. They are rarely valid. Picasso, at 91, kept art supplies by his bed in case he awoke during the night and had an idea. George Bernard Shaw wrote *The Mil-lionairess* in his eighties. William Carlos Williams, the physician-poet, suffered his first stroke at age 68. In spite of paralysis and a transient inability to speak, he published three books of verse before his death at age 79.

•Associate with encouragers, not discour-agers. Many a wet blanket has smothered ano-ther person's creativity. Choose associates who will support your efforts.

Source: Arthur Winter, MD, director, New Jersey Neuro-logical Institute's Memory Enhancement Clinic. Dr. Win-ter is coauthor with his wife, Ruth Winter, of *Build Your Brain Power*, St. Martin's Press, 175 Fifth Ave., New York 10010.

Small-Business Ideas for Kids

Kids are always thinking about ways to earn money. Daryl Bernstein, author of *Better Than a Lemonade Stand!*, suggests these money-making opportunities…

•Wake-up caller. Call customers at a pre-arranged time to wake them up. Greet them pleasantly, give them the weather forecast and top news stories of the day. You'll need to rise early, scan the newspaper and weather report, and make your calls. Each call should last no longer than a minute.

What to charge: $10 a month. Offer one free call, and ask customers to pay in advance for each month.

•Price-shopper/product-researcher. Many people want to buy a computer, microwave, VCR, or other costly product, but don't have the time to call stores for the best prices and equipment for their needs. To prepare, get on the mailing lists of major mail-order company catalogues. Plan to spend 15 minutes with each customer, then up to two hours to find the lowest price. Research can take longer.

What to charge: $10 for the lowest price… plus $20 to $30 for research.

•Elderly helper. Aid the elderly by running errands, doing light cooking, cleaning, repairs, and chores, reading aloud, writing letters, walking with them. Find clients by calling or posting flyers at churches, organizations such as the Elks Club, etc.

What to charge: $3 per hour. Many elderly people can't afford more, unless you work out a deal with their adult children.

•Recycler. Ask neighbors, businesses, and schools to save newspapers and cans and put them on a curbside once a week for you to pick up and take to the local recycler. You'll need a cart or wagon to do the pickups, a stor-age area, and an adult to drive you to the recy-cling center.

What to charge: The recycling center will pay you by the pound for the recyclables.

•Flyer distributor. Circulate advertisement flyers in your neighborhood for local busi-nesses. You'll need a backpack and a bike. It takes about two hours to distribute 100 flyers.

Best time to distribute flyers: Before holidays. Call back customers every six months, and always remember to ask customers for referrals.

What to charge: $10 to $15 per 100 flyers, depending on how far apart the homes are in your area.

•Cake baker. Baking and decorating a cake takes about 2½ hours. You'll need access to a kitchen, baking supplies, and cake boxes, which can be bought from a bakery-supply company. You can learn good recipes and techniques from popular cookbooks.

Find customers by placing a small classified ad or posting flyers at party-supply stores and supermarkets.

What to charge: $15 to $30, depending on the size of the cake.

•Disc jockey. You can either provide the stereo equipment and tapes, records, or CDs yourself or rent a sound system and borrow the tapes and CDs from friends. Find jobs with ads and flyers. Plan to work on weekend nights.

What to charge: $15 per hour. Parties generally last about four hours. Offer to help clean up afterward for an additional $5 or so.

•Sheet-and-towel washer. Visit customers' homes once a week, strip the beds, wash the sheets and towels, and replace them with fresh ones. It takes about two hours to wash and dry several machine-loads of sheets and towels.

Helpful: Get several customers who live close together, so you can go from house to house while you're waiting for the wash cycles to finish.

What to charge: $20 a month.

•Silver polisher. You'll need dishcloths, silver polish, and rubber gloves.

What to charge: $7 per hour, or $1 per dish or cup, 50 cents per utensil. Charge more for large bowls, trays, serving pieces.

Source: Daryl Bernstein, a high school student in Scottsdale, Arizona, and owner of a successful graphic-design firm. He is the author of *Better Than a Lemonade Stand! Small Business Ideas For Kids,* Beyond Words Publishing, 13950 NW Pumpkin Ridge Rd., Hillsboro, Oregon 97123.

First Person Interviewed Rarely Gets the Job

It shouldn't make any difference in hiring whether the candidate was interviewed first or last. But it does.

One of the major reasons that the first person interviewed is frequently not hired is that after many interviews, the interviewer tends to forget the first person. *How to avoid this trap…*

•Pay attention to your choice of interview options. You may be offered an interview on Monday, Tuesday, or Wednesday. Pick Wednesday. Or, you may be offered a choice of 9 AM, 10 AM, 11 AM or 4 PM. If possible, opt for the last appointment.

•Don't make the mistake of deferring any interview too long. By the time you're ready to pick a mutually convenient time, the job may be filled.

•Follow up the interview by calling the hiring executive to thank him/her for his time, and if possible, add something that was not discussed at the interview.

Example: It didn't come across in our interview that I have excellent writing ability.

•Then, in a few days, mail a letter to the interviewer to serve as another reminder. It would be nice to include a newspaper or magazine clipping that you think the executive would appreciate. Polite persistence pays off.

Source: Robert Half is founder of Robert Half International, Menlo Park, California 94025, and author of *How to Get a Better Job in this Crazy World,* Plume, 375 Hudson St., New York 10014.

How to Turn a Big Idea Into Big Money

Many people who think they have a million-dollar idea for a new product spend—and often lose—a small fortune trying to market their invention. In fact, it's easy to run through $50,000 to $150,000 before learning that your product just won't sell.

But spending this kind of money is often unnecessary. A new product can be brought to market in a professional manner for less than $5,000. And, after such a comparatively small investment, you'll know if your idea has a real chance for success, or if it should be scrapped or dramatically altered. *Steps to take...*

1. Document your idea. Buy a bound notebook, preferably with numbered pages, and keep a running dated "diary" about your invention at each stage. This log will come in handy later if you need to show the US Patent Office or a court that you had the idea first.

To further document your idea, file your concept with the US Patent Office's Document Disclosure Program.* Telling potential investors and associates that you have done this can boost your credibility.

What to do: Send a $10 check, two copies of a written description of your invention or product idea, and two copies of a drawing (or two photographs) of the product to Document Disclosure Program, US Patent and Trademark Office, Washington, DC 20231.

You should also file for a copyright, which is appropriate for products with a distinctive look, such as a game board, a T-shirt design, etc.

What to do: Request *Copyright Basics* and *Publications on Copyrights*, free information booklets from the Registrar of Copyrights, Copyright Office, Library of Congress, Washington, DC 20559.

Cost to document: No more than $50.

2. Determine whether your idea can make money. Find out what other businesses charge for similar products. Your price should be competitive. In addition, this information will help you establish costs to manufacture the product. To make money, your product should not cost more than 15% to 25% of the retail price of the product. Use business contacts and trade magazines to locate a manufacturer that will make it for the right price.

3. Do preliminary market research. Before

*The Patent Office will accept invention documents and keep them on file for two years in the Document Disclosure Program. When you file, you will receive a file number and a date of acceptance. This is not a patent or patent search. It only gives you evidence of when you filed an idea.

you begin your research, you'll need a product prototype.

Opportunity: Hire a student at a design school...and/or attend a model car or railroad trade show where you'll meet people who are excellent at assembling prototypes.

Once the model is built, ask 15 to 20 people you trust to rate its features and benefits. Have them compare it with five or six similar products. Would they buy it? Why not? What changes do they suggest?

Cost: $250 to $1,000 for the design and manufacture of a prototype.

4. Develop the final product design. Find industry insiders who can give you advice about product design and marketing. Show them what you have. Keep in mind that these people may become your investors later. Do they think people will pay as much as you hope to charge?

Warning: Many new-product developers overvalue secrecy and undervalue constructive input. The key is actually telling as many people as possible about the product. However, avoid sharing information with big companies and their employees unless you get a statement of confidentiality from them.

Cost: About $250 for phone calls and business lunches.

5. Produce a small quantity of products to test market. Since you probably will want to attract investors, you must be able to show them that the product can sell in the real world.

Make 50 to 200 units of your product to sell in three stores. Approach the store managers and offer the product on a consignment basis.

Warning: Many inventors waste money by producing too many products at this stage, while others don't produce enough. Ask insiders what the best number is for your product.

Cost: $500 to $1,500 for limited product production.

6. Conduct the test. Run a few small ads to pull people into the stores...or offer the stores co-op advertising support. If nothing you do helps the product to sell fast enough and encourages the stores to reorder, you may have to kill the idea. Or you may have to repeat this step. Or repeat steps 3, 4, 5, and 6.

Test marketing is absolutely crucial and an important reality check. *What it tells you:* Will enough people pay real money for your product to justify continuing to pursue your dream?

Cost: About $500 for the ad, production and placement.

7. Transition to much broader distribution. Print a flier describing the results of your successful test. Have someone with desktop-publishing equipment produce a three-color, one-page flier with photos. Write the flier copy yourself—or put together a first draft and hire a professional to edit and smooth it out.

Show the flier to key contacts and industry insiders as you seek backing for a broader product rollout. Secure financing by approaching those experts who have already helped you along.

Cost: About $1,000 for printing of a flier.

8. Make and sell the product during this transitional phase. Often, you'll have to invest a little more of your money to show good faith at this stage. As sales pick up, begin to broaden product distribution. Once your markets are solid, think about going national.

Cost: About $1,000 to boost your equity in the product.

Source: Don Debelak, president of DSD Associates, 888 Country Rd., D #104, St. Paul 55112, a loan inventor-assistance firm in Minneapolis. He is author of *How to Bring a Product to Market for Less Than $5,000,* John Wiley & Sons, Inc., 605 Third Ave., New York 10158.

Businesses You Can Start for Under $500

Starting a business is not as hard as you think. You don't even need a great deal of money to launch one. Here are seven businesses that you can run out of your home with an investment of $500 or less…

• Credit-repair service. Customers usually seek this service after being rejected for a home or car loan. You would resolve their credit disputes, set up payment schedules with credit-card companies, etc.

Key: Screen potential clients. You want those you can actually help. To be eligible for your services, problem accounts must have been paid off for at least one year, preferably three or four. Guarantee clients an overall improvement in their credit.

Cost: $500 for office expenses, placement of ads in area newspapers, research of credit record-keeping and reporting laws. *Earning potential:* $100,000 a year.

• Drop shipper. You publicize, take orders for, and accept payment in full for a small manufacturer that produces consumer products such as books, garden tools, gourmet foods, etc. In effect, you are acting as a middleman.

First you negotiate a reduced price for the product with the manufacturer. When the orders come in, you forward them to the company along with half the negotiated price plus postage. The company then ships the orders with your mailing labels. You pay the balance of what you owe the company after your customers pay up.

Don't compete with established direct-mail businesses. Find a niche and work with specialized manufacturers.

Cost: $50 to $250 to publicize a product, process orders, and print labels. *Earning potential:* $3,000+ a year, part-time.

• Estate sales. Visit estate sales and study the business before soliciting clients of your own. You will need to learn how to price antiques and how to draw up a contract with clients.

Key: Letting clients know that you will take care of everything.

Cost: $200 to $300 to advertise your service in daily and shoppers' newspapers. The clients pay to advertise sales. *Earning potential:* 25% of sales.

• Mapmaker. Create colorful, informal community maps featuring advertisements for local businesses. Market each as a "community promotional piece."

Calculate costs of hiring an artist and printing. Charge businesses to appear on the map, plus $35–$40 in production costs. When the maps are printed, deliver 35 to 40 maps to each business, which they can sell for $1, recouping this cost.

Cost: $500 or less to solicit businesses. *Earning potential:* $11,000 or more per project.

•Meeting planner. Put together events, meetings, and conventions for clients.

Key: Pay attention to details. Thoroughly research hotels, restaurants, meeting facilities, and travel arrangements you make for clients. Your business will grow through word-of-mouth referrals.

Cost: $500 for office expenses, yellow pages ad. *Earning potential:* $30,000+ a year.

•Self-publisher of booklets. Research, write, and have printed—either at a copy shop or on a desktop system—informative booklets on specialty topics.

Your writing must be accurate, authoritative, and clear. *Most popular:* "How-to" booklets on money, self-help, self-improvement, special skills.

Cost: $200 to $500 for first printing, classified ads. *Earning potential:* $5,000+ a year.

•Tradespeoples' referral agency. Screen and schedule top-notch painters, carpenters, plumbers, and electricians to do everything from small repairs to major remodeling. Solicit tradespeople to list with you for free. Take 10% of the jobs you book.

Key: Familiarity with construction basics, reliability, commitment to quality.

Cost: $500 for a phone line, answering service, classified ads, flyers. *Earning potential:* $65,000 to $100,000 a year.

Source: Stephen Wagner, associate publisher and editor of *Income Opportunities* magazine and author of *Mind Your Own Business: The Best Businesses You Can Start Today for Under $500,* Bob Adams, Inc., 260 Center St., Holbrook, Massachusetts 02343.

How to Safeguard Your Job

When employees read about the millions of Americans who have lost their jobs in the current economy, they wonder how secure their own positions are.

They're right to wonder. If a company is concerned about financial survival, the first area to be cut is jobs.

While I believe that the worst of the employment crisis is over—that we're headed for a positive turnaround within one to two years—large and mid-sized companies are still spooked...and still trying to cut back to "fighting weight" after the wild expansion of the 1980s.

In this climate, your job becomes more than the duties you were hired to do. It's now imperative to safeguard your job.

Even though you may be operating with smaller support staff and be busier than ever, you must take the steps now that will make you invaluable to your company—someone it can't afford to let go.

Warning signs:

When jobs in your company are in danger, you can see it...if you look. Many people close their eyes to the signals and deny reality. But denial is not a good survival skill. *Signals that your job may be on the line:*

•You or your department has been losing accounts...you're now just holding steady—rather than gaining back lost business.

•You're being left out of the communications loop. Your supervisors may have stopped including you in meetings. Or you may sense that you no longer have access to the grapevine...that informal sources of information are drying up.

•An outsider is called in—someone who looks grim and doesn't socialize. Since no company likes to fire its own people, a large organization is likely to turn over the dirty work to a consultant from outside the company...or someone from the head office, if the company is a subsidiary.

The best time to put survival strategies in place is before your job is in imminent danger. By the time you notice the warning signs, the decision to fire may already have been made.

No matter how late you develop them, the following strategies will help you build alliances with others in the industry. And if you should lose your job, these skills will help you get—and keep—a new one.

Guiding principles for job survival:

•Strengthen your relationship with your boss...and your boss's boss. Imagine that the fate of the company depends on your activities during the next few months. What would you do? Do those things now.

•Think creatively about ways to generate business. Examine past successes and build on them. Look for old projects that you can expand on or old clients you can call.

•Actively gather information. Read journal articles and conference reports. Discuss developments with others in your company—and industry. Brainstorm. Share what you're doing with your superiors.

Example: "I'd like to look into projects we've done in the last few years and see how we can piggyback on them." Or, "Here's what I've been thinking. We could have a focus group with our suppliers…We could continue with the project, part two…We could talk about a different kind of extended credit."

Bonus: If you do fall victim to "downsizing," your research will keep you up to date on where the opportunities are in your industry.

•Analyze the past. Examine projects that lost money, and find out where errors occurred. Look for ways to protect the company next time.

•Build morale. If you're naturally sociable, capitalize on that by organizing low-cost celebrations to boost your department's spirits.

Examples: A Labor Day picnic…a free concert in the park…a trip to a ball game to celebrate the end of a project.

•Treat your boss like a human being. For fear of appearing too eager or desperate, some employees practically ignore their bosses, except to follow orders. But at work, as in every other situation, people are your best resource. You should put as much energy into developing work relationships as you put into the technical aspects of your job.

Bosses, like everyone else, need to be appreciated. When your boss handles something difficult in a way you admire, say so. Bosses also need to be heard. So develop your listening skills.

Example: Look for an opportunity to say, "As you look ahead to the next few months, what do you see?" Ask how you can help your boss get there. Then let him/her talk for 10 minutes or so—without telling your own story or offering advice.

•Expand your network. Make sure your boss is not the only superior with whom you have a relationship. Pay attention to company reports and newsletters to find out who's doing what. Riding in the elevator or passing someone in the hall can be an opportunity to discuss what's going on.

•Improve yourself. What do you need to know in order to do your job even better? Don't wait—learn it now. If your company is exploring overseas markets, take a course in one of those country's languages. If your public speaking needs work, join Toastmasters or give presentations for your professional association. If you're dissatisfied with your appearance, get someone to go shopping with you…or use an image consultant.

•Enrich your personal life. The more stressful your job, the more you need nonprofessional, creative outlets—to lift your mood, give you a feeling of achievement, and keep your job in perspective.

Examples: Start a woodworking project… sew a quilt…join a community choir.
If the job is lost:
It's not the end of the world. Many, many people find that once they get past the initial shock, a job loss leads to opportunities they never imagined.

Make the most of the contacts and information you have been gathering. Even if every company in your industry is laying off people in your type of position, employers must still get these skills somewhere—you may be valuable to them as a consultant.

This may also be your chance to evaluate whether you'd like to change careers—or make a renewed commitment to your current career.

Source: Adele Scheele, PhD, career consultant, 225 W. 83 St., New York 10024. She is author of *Skills for Success,* Ballantine Books, 201 E. 50 St., New York 10022.

Working the Room

The more people you know, the greater your chances for career advancement.

When you go to trade-association meetings, alumni get-togethers, or social occasions, try to have a little conversation with a number of people—mostly those you don't know.

•Introduce yourself…start with a bit of idle chatter: "This is a nice party. How long have you known the host?"

•Drop a hint about what you do: "I'm with one of the Big Six CPA firms." Then add, "What do you do?"

•If you consider it appropriate, give the person your business card. You might very well get one in exchange. If you had an interesting conversation, offer to send him/her something such as a clipping of a news item that you had just discussed. Now you have an address and perhaps a phone number, too.

Do's and don'ts:

•Don't be a leech. As soon as it appears the person you're talking to is getting restless, excuse yourself and move on.

•If you suspect that someone may be a good contact but you don't think it is appropriate to ask for an address and phone number, write down his/her full name—but not until after you walk away. You can get other information from the host.

•Don't give a sales pitch while working the room. That may be offensive to your host…and others.

•A good way to start off is with social talk. Talk about family, friends—or play the geography game: "Oh, you're from Detroit. Do you know Charlie Smith? I think he's with one of your competitors."

•If you have unusual credentials, casually and quickly let them be known.

•Discuss interesting things—even humorous ones—that happened at work.

•If you have unusual education and business qualifications, let them be known—but keep it short.

A long time ago, I met a lawyer at a small gathering in London. We exchanged business cards. His practice was in Louisville, Kentucky, and at least once a year for 10 years, I received announcements of partnership changes, etc., from him. I thought that he was wasting his time since I would never need a lawyer in Louisville—and I was right.

But…a friend of mine, who knew our company had offices almost everywhere, asked me if I knew a lawyer in Kentucky. Guess what?

Source: Robert Half, founder of Robert Half International Inc. and Accountemps Worldwide, 2884 Sand Hill Rd., Menlo Park, California 94250.

Ingredients for The Perfect Business Partner

Business partnerships are like marriages—intense, intimate relationships that involve a great deal of compromise.

But, like a marriage, a business partnership can sour, leading to bitter recriminations and nasty legal disputes. Because of these potential traps, entrepreneurs should choose their partners carefully.

Fundamental question:

Do you really need a partner? If you're looking simply for companionship or a "clone" of yourself to share the workload, the answer is probably no. In such cases, it's better to hire someone to work for you. That way you retain absolute control over your business.

But if you lack important skills needed to make a go of your new venture or if you have the skills but lack the funding, the answer is…maybe.

Strategy: Write down everything you bring to your new venture (skills, contacts, financing, etc.) and everything you think will be needed. Consider them carefully. If you can get by without a partner, do so.

If you're convinced that you need a partner, however, proceed with great caution.

Here's how to find one…

•Personal contacts. Tell everyone you know that you're looking for a partner—friends, family, business contacts, etc. Surprisingly, the owners of similar businesses are often good sources of information—even though you'll be competitors once your venture gets off the ground. If you need a partner to help you launch a new magazine, for instance, call an editor listed on a magazine masthead. If he/she proves unhelpful, pick another name. Don't be afraid of rejection.

• Professional associations. Ask someone in the association's personnel department to give you a few names. If you don't know of a relevant professional association, consult the *Encyclopedia of Associations*, available at local libraries.

• Advertisements. Scan the "jobs wanted" section in newsletters, newspapers, professional journals, and business periodicals. If you don't find what you need, place your own ad. *Important:* Be specific when listing skills, business contacts, and financial resources you require.

• Consultants. If you're having trouble finding a partner on your own, a professional headhunter can do the work for you. Check the yellow pages under "Employment Agencies" or "Financing Consultants."

• Outplacement firms. Workers newly laid off by large employers often make good business partners. Check the yellow pages under "Outplacement."

• Venture capital groups. These investors' groups are eager to bankroll and otherwise nurture promising start-ups. To find a group in your area, check the yellow pages under "Financial Services."

Extra steps:

Once you find a half dozen or so prospective partners, schedule face-to-face interviews with each candidate. Conduct the initial meeting as if it were a job interview. Check the résumé. Get references. Find out what specific skills, contacts, etc., the candidate would bring to the partnership. Finally, examine the candidate's background for a pattern of success, especially if he/she has been involved in prior start-ups.

If there's any question of the candidate's veracity, have a detective conduct a background check. Let the candidate know you're planning the check, and express your willingness for him to check on you.

A single formal interview is too brief to give you an accurate sense of a candidate. *Better:* Arrange several different meetings in a variety of settings—in your office, over lunch or dinner, in your home, etc. If possible, schedule a get-acquainted dinner for both families.

Remember: Being smart and personable aren't enough.

Source: C. D. (Pete) Peterson, a business consultant based in Brookfield, Connecticut. He is author of *Staying in Demand: How to Make Job Offers Come to You,* McGraw-Hill Inc., 1221 Avenue of the Americas, New York 10020.

There Is a Way To Delegate Effectively

How well you succeed at work today depends largely on how well you delegate.

Corporate downsizing has widened the responsibilities of fewer executives, and the more senior your position, the more time you should spend planning strategy, rather than working on tasks.

To accomplish what needs to be done on time, you must be able to turn work over to others—and know when to do so.

A manager's primary responsibility is to develop his/her staff members, and a primary purpose of delegation is to teach or empower the people you supervise—not just to off-load menial tasks.

Yet most managers are not comfortable delegating. *The most common excuses...*

• "I can do it better myself." Maybe so. But can a subordinate do it well enough? If you hang on to it, no one else has an opportunity to learn. Teach them.

• "I don't have time to teach them." It is true that effective delegation takes time. You must plan, train the assigned employee, and follow up periodically. Therefore, you must weigh whether you will save time in the future.

Do you spend one day every month on this task? If so, it is worth a day to train someone to do it for the rest of the year.

• "I lack confidence in my staff." If you don't trust your employees, you must examine your reasons closely. Identify specific reasons: "Harold submitted two inaccurate reports," not "Harold is sloppy." Watch for any unsubstantiated assumptions you might have: "Cheryl doesn't have the math skills." Are you sure?

Solution: Delegate tasks that build skills—research for Harold, math for Cheryl.

•"I'll lose my power or control"…and/or "I won't get credit." A pang at the loss of ego gratification is normal but does not need to be crippling. This is seldom a problem for managers with healthy self-esteem. Effective managers focus on what they can accomplish through their employees, not how much they can control them.

If you feel threatened by your subordinates' accomplishments, work on developing confidence in your own abilities.

•"But I like to do it." Some managers are reluctant to delegate the tasks they enjoy the most. *Example:* The manager who loves to toy with the computer even though his assistant can accomplish those tech tasks faster.

Solution: Keep one or two "occupational hobbies" if you must. But let employees grow by finding the discipline to let go of tasks that prevent you from growing.

•"I can't figure out what to delegate and what not to delegate." *Delegate:* Tasks that are routine and necessary…that are development opportunities for your staff…that staff members excel at—that's why you hired them, remember?

Don't delegate: Confidential or personnel matters…policy-making tasks…development of those reporting directly to you…assignments your boss asked you to handle personally—ask whether you should delegate them if you aren't sure. Never delegate crises. Bring in help if needed, but shoulder the responsibility yourself. Never delegate unnecessary tasks.

Better: Identify activities that don't contribute to the company's goals and eliminate them. *Example:* Status reports no one reads.

How to delegate:

Delegation can be formal or informal, but it's always important to be clear about your goals and expectations. *For best results:*

•Review your purpose. You must decide what must be done, who should do it, and when it should be done. Does your boss agree with your assessment of the priorities?

•Know your people. You can't decide who's best for which tasks unless you learn about your subordinates' strengths and weaknesses,

and their goals and desires. Ask for input so you can create opportunities for growth.

Key: The "right" person is not always the "best" person. Sometimes you'll have a gut feeling that someone can't handle the responsibility. Try giving that person another task. Delegate even to employees who resist new assignments.

•Hold a delegation conference. Explain how the task relates to the company's overall goals. State the results you desire before listing the required tasks. Say, "We'll need," rather than "You'll have to." Ask for input from your staff members.

•Establish deadlines, allowing the person to set his/her own deadlines within reason. Make sure the priority of the task is clear.

•Establish a reporting procedure. Schedule regular reviews.

•Grant the necessary authority so the person can be effective. Inform other coworkers that Susan will be handling project X. Always delegate an entire task to avoid confusion.

•Follow up. Compose a memo, or ask the staff member to do so, summarizing the delegated project. This provides an opportunity for you to stress the person's responsibility for the task and for the person to commit to it.

Compliment the employee throughout the task, but review work only at regularly scheduled times. Don't meddle. The purpose of review sessions is to protect against failure and advise without reducing accountability. Your aim is development, not perfection. Give feedback and constructive criticism. Always give the person credit for success, but take the blame for any failure yourself.

Source: Frank F. Huppe, PhD, retired director of the engineering physics laboratory for the duPont Company and author of *Delegate: Multiply Your Impact,* National Press Publications, 6901 W. 63 St., Shawnee Mission, Kansas 66201.

Avoid Sabotaging Your Own Success…Or Else

Why do some seemingly sensible people act in ways that harm their own interests?

They set out to succeed but somewhere along the way they either misjudge how to achieve their goals...do not want to face criticism and failure...or defeat themselves with the intention of hurting someone else. The most common types of self-defeating behavior and how to avoid them...

Deliberate miscalculation:

Most of us go through life trying to overcome the hurdles set in our way. We avoid doing things that slow us down or increase the odds of failure. Those who exhibit self-defeating behavior choose strategies that will backfire.

Poor decisions are made either because of overconfidence or because the desire for a short-term gain is stronger than the appeal of a long-term goal.

Example I: Jane wanted to study clinical psychology in graduate school. After her initial application was rejected, she decided to show the school she was really a desirable prospect by taking a few courses as a nondegree student at her own expense...a good strategy if carried out correctly. But instead of demonstrating her prowess by taking subjects in which she could easily get A's, she took the hardest courses she could find and scored only C's...dooming her graduate school hopes.

Jane miscalculated because she was overconfident. Had she estimated her strengths and weaknesses more realistically, her chance of success would have been much greater.

Example II: Gary was happily married and prosperous. For many years, he indulged his hearty appetite for eating, drinking, and smoking but avoided exercise. Not surprisingly, he suffered a heart attack while only in his early 50s. When the doctor told him he had to change his lifestyle, he did so...for a time.

But after just three months, Gary decided he couldn't do without his vices. Two years later, he had another heart attack...this one fatal.

While it doesn't always lead to such unfortunate results, the same kind of poor trade-off between present benefits and future costs is found in many kinds of self-destructive behaviors—drug addiction...excessive sun exposure...overdependence on credit cards...even procrastination.

To avoid miscalculation mistakes: Evaluate your strengths and weaknesses and the long-term costs and benefits of your actions as realistically as you possibly can...and try to consider all the alternatives.

Trying to avoid the truth:

Many forms of self-defeating behavior occur because people don't want to admit their limitations. They sabotage their own success in ways like these:

•Self-handicapping. This occurs when successful people deliberately construct obstacles for themselves so they will have an excuse for failure.

Example: Whenever French chess champion Deschapelles played, he insisted on giving his opponent the advantage of removing one of Deschapelles' pawns and taking the first move.

Result: Deschapelles increased his chance of losing...but always had a good excuse if he lost.

•Substance abuse. Alcohol and/or drug abuse serves two purposes for self-destructive people. It helps them blot out their own faults and inadequacies...and gives them an external excuse for failure.

Example: Violinist Eugene Fodor was a national hero at age 24 after he won the Tchaikovsky Violin Competition in Moscow. But within a few years, his reputation sank as he turned to drugs and was eventually arrested after breaking into a hotel room.

Reason: Great fame at an early age creates great expectations in audiences...and great stress in performers. Drugs eased the stress Fodor felt and provided an excuse for his failure to perform adequately—but allowed him to believe in his musical ability.

To face the truth: Develop a sense of perspective on yourself, recognize your imperfections, and learn to accept criticism.

The quest for revenge:

Sometimes self-defeating behavior is a misguided attempt to redress emotional wounds inflicted in childhood.

Example: Despite obvious talent, Stuart, aged 36, would break rules...steal...drink on the job...in an obvious manner that was sure to be detected. Then his supervisor would reprimand him and threaten his job.

This replicated a pattern from Stuart's childhood, when his father would beat him. After the beating, while Stuart was sobbing, his alarmed mother would scream at his father until his father withdrew into a state of depression. Thus Stuart would enjoy the sweet taste of victory over his father...even though he was in physical agony himself.

I call this self-defeating strategy "Pyrrhic revenge," after the famous "victory" of the Greek king Pyrrhus, who won a battle against the Romans but almost wiped out his whole army in the process.

Pyrrhic revenge is typically found in marriages in which one spouse suffered abuse as a child...often from an alcoholic parent. He seeks out a partner who has the same problem his parent had. He tries to correct the problem and, in doing so, cure his own childhood wounds. This usually doesn't work, so instead he ends up venting the long-repressed anger against the parent...and doesn't mind destroying himself as long as his spouse goes down, too.

To avoid self-destruction via revenge: Realize your own interests...judge whether you are acting to help yourself or to hurt someone else.

Choking under pressure:

Choking is a self-defeating behavior that occurs when people under pressure, striving to do their best, fail because they try too hard to succeed and do not perform as well as they can.

Example: Beth, an outstanding student, had to recite a speech from Shakespeare in front of her high-school class. After memorizing it perfectly, she stood up to speak...and nothing came out.

Reason: Smoothly speaking memorized lines is an automatic process. Beth wanted so intensely to succeed that her self-consciousness prevented her memory from working naturally.

The same phenomenon causes sports champions to falter in important matches and winning teams to lose championship games.

To avoid choking under pressure: Develop perspective. Remind yourself that success in life doesn't depend on just one event.

Example: If it's the last minutes of an important event or presentation, and victory or defeat depends on your next move, remember that just being there shows that you already are a success.

Source: Steven Berglas, PhD, clinical psychologist and management consultant, Harvard Medical School, Boston. He is coauthor with Roy F. Baumeister, PhD, of *Your Own Worst Enemy: Understanding the Paradox of Self-Defeating Behavior,* Basic Books, 10 E. 53 St., New York 10022.

How to Help Your Child Find a Job

As young people reach their late teens and early 20s today and especially as they finish college, they—and their parents—are preoccupied with one big question: Where are they going to get a job?

Most parents are anxious to assist in their children's job search.

Trap: The traditional parent-child relationship is ill-suited for this project. Parents of young adults tend to be judgmental, authoritative, protective...or, at the other extreme, indifferent. None of these qualities inspires an open, productive collaboration.

To help a child find a job—and, more important, a fulfilling work life—parents must first change their relationship with the child.

•Become a coach and adviser, and treat your child like a client. This dramatically alters the parent-child dynamic because:

•A client is automatically "elevated" to the parent's level and therefore treated with respect.

•A client maintains control of the job-hunting process.

•A client must be pleased with the results of the job search.

•While a coach may be expert in certain areas, the client decides whether to accept or reject any particular advice. *Result:* A coach will place more emphasis on effective presentation, since a client cannot be forced or coerced.

•A coach won't try to "fix things" that clients should handle themselves.

•A coach will offer steady doses of positive feedback to build a client's self-esteem.

In most cases, one parent—whoever is less judgmental—should assume the coaching role. When both parents participate, at the dinner table for example, they must be careful not to gang up on the child. *Words to abolish:* "Can't" and "shouldn't."

•Learn to listen. Parents tend to preempt conversations with their children, even when their children are middle-aged. They offer a solution before they hear the child's concept of the problem.

Everyone has skills that could be applied to the job market. What many young people lack is a sense of direction.

Example: When pressed to define his goals, he might say, "I need to make money."

A parent/coach can help provide direction by broadening the inquiry. *Good question:* "How do you want to live your life—and what sort of work will enable you to do that?"

Some people need the formal trappings and structured interactions of an office setting. Others, who would shrivel up if forced to punch a clock and wear a suit, might thrive working from home. There is room for both types in today's job market.

•Be patient. It's easy for both the child and the parent to panic when the child is unemployed. There is tremendous pressure to "get this settled" and snap up the first decent job offer that comes along.

Remember: There are no quick fixes in finding one's path in life. The "easy" solution can cause great pain later on. I see people in their 50s who now ask, with terrible regret, "Why did I ever become a lawyer (or a salesman or a manager)?"

Myth: A job that pays well makes you happy. *Reality:* When people do what they love, they are happier and tend to make more money.

•Beware of family tradition. Despite the fact that the last three generations have worked as accountants or cooks, it is a mistake to shepherd a child into the family business—even if he/she seems eager to join. *Better:* Guide the child to explore other interests or a nonfamily employer first, and *then*—if he's still determined—he can return to the original interest. Children who take this course will...

•Feel better equipped to risk mistakes and thereby gain confidence.

•Earn self-respect for accomplishing something on their own.

•Gain their parents' respect by making independent judgments—the foundation for a successful working relationship.

•Don't rely solely on a résumé. In today's difficult job market, the race goes to the unorthodox—to those applicants who constructively set themselves apart. Each year, hordes of college graduates comb the classified ads and storm the personnel departments...and many come up empty.

Their most common failings: They haven't defined the lifestyle they want, the skills they wish to use, or the needs of a particular job market.

Alternative: Rather than join the thousands of conventional job-seekers, young people should set aside a block of time—whether one month or six prior to or after graduation—to conduct a systematic survey of their chosen fields. This time should be scheduled around two activities—researching the specific ideas they would like to implement and meeting with the people who are active in their field to get their counsel.

Advantage: By talking to people who are working in the field, young people gain new insights about given careers—and make contacts. As the late John Crystal, my partner and the pioneer in my field, once said, "Every job is a need wanting to be met. For people to present themselves successfully for jobs, they must understand the needs."

To be effective, these initial meetings can't be job interviews in disguise. Even if the "surveyor" is offered a job, he must have the confidence to delay any decision until the survey runs its full course.

Sample response: "I would be happy to come back when I have completed my research if I determine that I can be of use to you."

The surveyor remains in control of the process…and the prospective employer sees the young person with new and appreciative eyes.

Source: Nella Barkley, cofounder of the Crystal-Barkley Corporation, 152 Madison Ave., New York 10016. She is author of *How to Help Your Child Land the Right Job* (*Without Being a Pain in the Neck*), Workman Publishing, 708 Broadway, New York 10003.

Personal File Power

All companies keep a file on each employee. It contains the employee's résumé, application form, memos for doing things above and beyond the call of duty—and memos on what the employee may have done wrong.

You should keep a personal personnel file to keep a record of your achievements—little ones and big ones—along with a copy of your latest résumé. Every time you accomplish something worthwhile, scribble a note on a piece of paper, date it, and insert it into your file. *Why this is valuable:*

•If you want to ask your boss for a raise or promotion: The best way to get the raise you want is to remind your supervisor of your achievements. If you don't write them down, you'll forget them. And if you forget, you can be sure your boss will, too.

•If you need to work up an effective résumé in a hurry: Take your old résumé and plug in your current data and significant achievements.

Source: Robert Half is the founder of Robert Half International Inc., and Accountemps Worldwide, 2884 Sand Hill Rd., Menlo Park, California 94250.

Testosterone And Your Job

The job you choose may be determined by the amount of testosterone in your body. Highest levels of this hormone—linked to aggression, sensation-seeking, and antisocial behavior—were found in actors and lawyers…

lower levels in nurses and teachers…lowest in ministers.

Source: Study by the Georgia State University psychology department, reported in *Health*, 3 Park Ave., New York 10016.

How to Win At Telephone Tag

Telephone tag, the seemingly endless cycle of calls and returned calls that are missed, is one of the more time-consuming frustrations of executive life. Beat the frustration by organizing your telephone tactics.

If the person you want to talk with isn't in, and you do want him to call you back:

•Leave a detailed message of the subject of the call.

•Note a time span when you'll definitely be available.

•Make a phone appointment—a specific time when the party can reach you.

•Tell the secretary that no reply will be an assumed consent or agreement.

If you don't want the other party to call back:

•Ask for a specific time when he/she will be available, so you can try again.

•Find out if the person can be paged.

•Request that the secretary relay the information to your secretary, keeping the bosses out of the phone process.

Source: *Execu-Time,* Box 631, Lake Forest, IL 60045.

Simple Ways To Reduce Job Stress

Job-related psychological stress takes an enormous toll on Americans. It affects one of every five workers in this country…and costs our economy billions and billions of dollars a year in absenteeism, lost productivity, and medical expenses—including expenses caused by accidents and alcoholism, both of which often originate in stress. Stress produces a remarkable variety of emotional and psychological symptoms.

Typical: Rapid heart rate and/or breathing… stammering…a sense of isolation from colleagues…headaches, stomach aches and chest pain…reduced sex drive…stomach upset, diarrhea, and other gastrointestinal problems …chronic fatigue and insomnia…sweating… proneness to accidents…ulcers…and even drug addiction.

If you suffer from one or more of these symptoms—or if a co-worker or family member remarks that you seem irritable or ill—it's time to evaluate the stress in your work life… and, if necessary, take steps to alleviate it.

The costs of chronic stress:

Untreated chronic stress leads not only to burnout, but also to heart attack, stroke, and other deadly health problems.

Workers often try to control their job stress via nonpsychological approaches—exercise, hobbies, vitamin pills, special diets, vacations, etc. While these approaches are healthful and might afford temporary relief, they eventually fail. In fact, such approaches often wind up increasing stress levels.

Example: A man who jogs every day to reduce stress feels even more anxious than usual if for some reason he must forgo jogging even for a day.

Bottom line: Stress is a psychological problem, and it can be fully controlled only by a psychological approach. I believe that the best way to do this is to recognize the 12 types of myths that cause job stress…and to systematically replace these myths with attitudes that are healthy and more realistic.

Stress-causing myths:

Myth 1. Something awful will happen if I make a mistake. *Reality:* Mistakes in the workplace may be a source of embarrassment and frustration, but rarely do they lead to anything more dire than a reprimand. The lesson sounds trite, but it's wise—don't fear mistakes, learn from them.

Myth 2. There's a right way and a wrong way to do everything. *Reality:* What's right for one person or situation is often not right for another. Mistakes are common in business, and they seldom result in tragedy. In fact, many excellent business decisions appear at first blush to be enormous blunders.

Myth 3. Being criticized is awful. *Reality:* Criticism—of oneself and of others—is central to personal growth. Being criticized is not tantamount to failing, and the process should never be viewed as something to be endured. Instead, workers should welcome criticism as a learning opportunity. *Note:* Do not accept criticism that is abusive or disrespectful.

Myth 4. I need approval from those around me. *Reality:* While you might welcome praise for a job well done, you don't really need "positive strokes" to be an effective, fulfilled worker. Expecting praise in a work environment where it is rarely forthcoming can lead to disappointment and frustration.

Myth 5. I must always be viewed as competent. *Reality:* No one is good at everything. Even if you were perfect, there is no guarantee that your coworkers would admire you. How others view you lies entirely within their control. Worrying about your image only sets the stage for anxiety and more frustration.

Myth 6. People in authority must not be challenged. *Reality:* Most superiors are willing to listen to their subordinates' complaints and criticisms—if these are presented fairly and constructively. In fact, many bosses welcome complaints because they suggest better ways to do things. If you're inclined to confront your superior, do so. Even if you don't get all you want, the act of speaking out releases emotions that might otherwise lead to anger and resentment.

Myth 7. The workplace is essentially fair and just. *Reality:* Hoping for total fairness at work is not only unrealistic, it's not even desirable. Some of the best and most productive business solutions result from controversy and argumentation, which may seem unfair at the time.

Myth 8. I must always be in control. *Reality:* The notion that you can easily meet every deadline and fill every quota is appealing, but it only sets you up for frustration and stress. Even the best routines and systems break down occasionally. Rather than worrying about control, focus upon what you're doing …and what you want out of life.

Myth 9. I must anticipate everything. *Reality:* Surprises are inevitable on the job as in other parts of life. Sensing things before they happen and gauging colleagues' "vibrations" certainly make good sense—but remember, you are dealing with probabilities, not foregone conclusions.

Myth 10. I must have my way. *Reality:* Good salaries, beautiful offices, and prestigious positions don't come easily—in fact, they may never come. No doubt there will be setbacks along the way. Effective workers do their work conscientiously without insisting upon immediate realization of their goals. Certainly you can strive toward such goals. Just don't demand them as conditions of continued employment.

Myth 11. Workers who make mistakes must be punished. *Reality:* An effective workplace calls for effective teamwork…and teamwork is impossible when employees are continually trying to assign or escape blame.

Essential for workers: Acceptance, tolerance, patience, allowance for imperfections—in yourself as well as in others.

Myth 12. I need a shoulder to cry on. *Reality:* A compassionate coworker is often helpful in difficult times—but not essential. Workers who resent not having one only cultivate their own self-pity and dampen the morale of themselves and of people around them.

Source: Samuel H. Klarreich, PhD, vice president of Mainstream Access Corp., a Toronto-based consulting firm. He is the author of several books on stress, including *Work Without Stress: A Practical Guide to Emotional and Physical Well-Being on the Job*, Brunner Mazel Inc., 19 Union Square West, New York 10003.

7
Retirement Planning

The Most Common Retirement Traps

Retirement should be thought of as the beginning of a new phase of living, not just the end of your working career.

Because Americans are living longer—and are more active than ever before—much more planning is required these days to achieve a comfortable level of financial security in your retirement years. *The most common traps retirees should avoid...*

• *Trap:* Relying solely on income-oriented assets. A major error made by many retirees is sticking with only low-risk investments, such as municipal or Treasury bonds, bank certificates of deposit, and similar low-yield investments. However, this apparently conservative strategy is far riskier than you might imagine when you factor in the effects of inflation.

It makes more sense to diversify your assets and consider including some equities, mutual funds, mortgage-backed securities, or international holdings in your portfolio. Over and over again, studies have shown that the key to reducing risk over the long run is diversification. Your goal should be for your money to outlive you, rather than you outliving your money.

• *Trap:* Investing a lump sum all at once. A typical pattern at retirement is that you receive a big gain on the sale of a house or business, a large lump-sum pension or insurance distribution, or other windfall. All too frequently, this money is invested immediately and with little diversification.

You would probably do better financially—and certainly sleep better—by carefully considering your options. Structure an investment ladder of different types, maturities, and issuers. Invest, say, 20% of your lump sum every three months or so. Your income-oriented investments should be spread out so they mature in different years. This way, you're "dollar-cost averaging."

By creating such flexibility, you can determine the best alternatives as each of these investments mature.

•*Trap:* Engaging in investment clutter. Most of my clients of retirement age have entirely too many different investments. Holding 40 or more separate stocks or bonds in your safe-deposit box can be extremely dangerous, since it is likely to become harder and harder to keep track of them—and certainly difficult to manage them well—with each passing year.

Ask yourself: If you were the person named as the agent under a durable power of attorney to take care of a person's finances when he/she was disabled, would you have the time and patience to deal with all of those securities?

If the answer is no, consolidate your holdings to a number you can manage. And think about placing your portfolio in an asset-management account at a brokerage firm, so that both safekeeping and recordkeeping will be handled professionally, and you will get a single monthly statement.

•*Trap:* Falling prey to a "snake oil" salesperson. As soon as you retire, shady salespeople peddling investment, insurance, and real-estate products target you.

When a person with experience meets a person with money, the one with experience gets the money and the one with money gets the experience.

Most important: Retain your common sense and probe beneath the surface when so-called "one-time-only" deals are offered to you. What are said to be money-making investments might seem different if you insist on reading the prospectus or talking to former clients. There is no such thing as a free lunch.

•*Trap:* Neglecting proper insurance coverage. People who have given a lot of attention to accumulating a considerable estate during their working years—and have been diligent in purchasing sufficient life insurance for their heirs—can lose everything after retiring due to inadequate property and casualty insurance.

Yet a simple solution exists...buying an umbrella liability policy to supplement your homeowners and automobile insurance coverage.

Misconception: Long-term-care insurance to pay for nursing homes and home health services is an unnecessary luxury.

Since two out of every five people over age 65 will at some point enter a nursing home,

and Medicare or Medicaid will not pay for everything, your long-term-care cost could be enormous if you are not properly insured.

Good policies, especially those with inflation riders, will ease the financial problem while you cope with the medical and emotional problems of long-term care.

•*Trap:* Thinking that estate planning is no more than a will. It's not unusual for recent retirees to ask me to draw up a will or review a will that was written years ago.

But when I tell them that even well-drawn wills do not address some of their critical estate, financial and personal planning needs, more often than not they are quite surprised.

A will does not take effect until death...and does absolutely nothing to protect you and your family while you are alive.

At the very least, two other documents should be prepared even before you retire. One is a durable power of attorney, which provides for the management of assets in the event of temporary or permanent disability. The other is a living will or health-care proxy, which provides for health-care and medical decision-making when you are unable to do so.

A revocable living trust can also be an extremely effective tool. But while it can minimize many problems, it does not avoid them completely. This is why other documents and planning are necessary.

Whichever of these documents are right for you—and it may very well be all of them—don't procrastinate in gathering the essential material and consulting an adviser for implementation.

Source: Martin M. Shenkman, an estate attorney practicing in New York City and Teaneck, New Jersey. He is author of *The Complete Book of Trusts,* John Wiley & Sons, Inc., 605 Third Ave., New York 10158.

How I Dealt With My First Year Of Retirement

No matter how active you plan to be after you stop working, retirement always takes some getting used to.

While most people say that they look forward to the day when they'll no longer have to work, they are unprepared for the emotional turmoil.

For about 30 years, I worked at CBS Network Television, where I wrote scripts for Walter Cronkite and Dan Rather. In 1991, I retired. *Here are the retirement issues that most people face and how I handled them...*

•No longer having a job that identifies you. Anyone whose sense of self springs from his/her job is destined to have an unhappy retirement. The people who are most at risk are those who don't like weekends and who hunger for the return to battle every Monday morning.

Solution: Figure out who you really are before you retire, and then learn to enjoy your time off. (Put that on your to-do list.)

Most late-middle-aged people have interests and passions that define who they are much more than their job descriptions do—if only they'd realize it.

Besides, no one ever really liked you because you were the senior vice president. And if someone did, what does that say about that person?

To those who worry that when they stop contributing, they'll just roll over and die—I have two things to say...

•You've contributed enough already.

•You don't have to stop contributing just because you're retired. You just don't have to give at the office.

•The changing relationship with your spouse. For some years, my wife has been teaching children with learning disabilities in our New York apartment while I was at work. Now we're together all the time, which I regard as a joy.

First, I try hard to respect her space and not get in her way. And I've adjusted some of my daily routines to fit her schedule. Every morning, I read three newspapers and go through our mail while she teaches.

When I have lunch with my wife each day—the old line, "For better or for worse, but not for lunch," doesn't apply here—I find that we invariably have a great deal to talk about, even if "nothing has happened" that day.

This type of conversation tends to get lost when you're still working. When you have a demanding job, the stuff that happens in the early morning seems very remote by the time you sit down to dinner—unfortunately.

•Having no set schedule and creating one. I've never been a great planner. I think I tolerate a lack of structure better than most people. Still, some scheduling helps keep you focused.

One of the great luxuries of retirement is that you get to try out different schedules to see which one really works for you. You can develop a routine and then quickly change it the moment it gets stale.

Or you can do something every day, but not always at the same time. Lunch with my wife is a given, as is working on my new book and reading Shakespeare—I've done that every day for 30 years and have no plans to stop.

But I don't read Shakespeare at the same time every day, nor do I have a rigid routine for writing.

I regularly take long walks—my favorite form of exercise—but not at any particular hour. I want to feel active, but I also want to feel retired—free to come and go as I please.

•Living on less money. My retirement would be less pleasant if I didn't have a good pension, health benefits, and savings to last for as long as I'm going to last. But I know some people who use their fear of living on less to delay their retirements.

The good news is that when you retire, you save money in ways great and small. Your taxes drop. You save a fortune on clothes because you don't have to get dressed up every day. And you pay half-fares on public transportation and reduced prices for movies, museums, and concerts.

Nonetheless, sticking to a budget is essential when you're retired. That doesn't keep me from pursuing my passions, but it does mean I often do so "on the cheap." My wife and I love the theater, and we go often—and almost always pay half-price.

•Learning the joy of keeping your options open. Do what you want to do. If you're in the middle of something and get bored, drop it—perhaps permanently.

Spend your time on your true passions—mine are writing, reading, theater, opera, and pro football—but always consider adding new things to the mix.

Learn to keep fresh: Remember that education is a lifelong proposition. Take courses in art, cooking, crafts, literature—or whatever. Remember why, when you were 30 or so, the idea of retirement looked so delicious and appealing. It really is.

Shake things up. There's something absolutely wonderful—and almost illicit—about taking your wife to a movie on a Tuesday afternoon. Try it.

Sometimes it pays to remind yourself what you're missing. The only thing in life that I've ever found consistently boring is a corporate meeting. But I don't have meetings anymore.

• Facing projects you've put off for years. The wrong approach is to spend your time on what you think you should be doing or to figure that being retired means your bluff has been called, that you no longer have the world's easiest excuse—too little time—to justify project avoidance.

Either thought can make you miserable. This is your retirement. This is your life. You've worked hard for this.

A project isn't worth pursuing simply because it's been hanging over your head for years. It's always worth a fresh look. Does it make sense today? Is this the best use of your time? Should you pay someone to do it for you?

In my case, I've always talked about writing a novel (I've published three nonfiction books), and I'm not going to pay someone to do it for me. So I've started my novel. I hope to finish it, and I hope it will be good. But if it's never finished or isn't any good, I'm not going to regard my life or my retirement as a failure.

I care about my novel passionately, but I'm not taking it that seriously. I call it the Manhattan Project—because it's secret and it may turn out to be a bomb.

• Relating to people who still have jobs. This hasn't been a problem for me, but I understand that some retirees find it a little intimidating to talk to people who are still employed. They seem so busy, so focused, so sure of their roles.

Sometimes they aren't entirely comfortable with my new circumstances. You'll feel better if you assume that it's their envy and uncertainty that's causing the problem.

You're as important and interesting as you ever were. In fact, if you keep active and continue to explore new things, you're probably much more interesting than you were before.

Leaving your job is a big deal, but it's not as if you've retired from life.

You haven't retired from life at all.

Source: John Mosedale, author of *The First Year: A Retirement Journal,* Crown Publishers, Inc., 201 E. 50 St., New York 10022.

Getting the Most Out Of Your 401(k) Plan

If you want to know who is managing your 401(k) plan, look in the mirror. In an effort to give employees more say in their financial future, companies are increasingly giving them more control over where their individual retirement contributions are invested.

With freedom, however, comes greater room for error. Many employees make the wrong investment decision—or are too conservative with money they won't need for another 30 years or more.

Here are my 10 golden rules of 401(k) investing...

• Participate to the max. Your 401(k) plan is your best bet for retirement savings. You get a tax deduction going in—since your contributions are deducted out of pretax dollars...and your money grows tax-deferred until it's withdrawn.

Even if your contributions to an Individual Retirement Account (IRA) are tax-deductible, it's usually better to favor your 401(k) plan. For those with lower incomes, your 401(k) contributions will lower your annual Social Security taxes. More important, your company may be one of the many that match part or all of your contributions.

•Avoid Guaranteed Investment Contracts (GICs). Study after study shows that the majority of investors choose to put the lion's share of their 401(k) money into GICs. People think "guaranteed" means guaranteed by the government. In fact, GICs are a sort of souped-up money-market fund sold to corporate pension plans by insurance companies. They aren't risk-free, and so far their long-run returns have proven to be lower than those generated by stocks and bonds.

•Buy stock. For most plan participants it makes sense to have at least half of their 401(k) money in stocks. Younger investors may want to have a higher amount...and older investors somewhat less.

If you're planning your retirement carefully, you probably won't be touching this money until you're in your 70s. A 50-year-old would therefore have 20 years. Over that time, stocks are expected to significantly outperform bonds.

•Keep your portfolio's investment ratio consistent. Suppose you allocate your money, 60/40, between stocks and bonds. Periodically, you should check the ratio between these investments, since stock and bond values rise and fall. Shift money to get your portfolio back into the 60/40 balance. Rebalancing can force you to sell stocks when they're high and buy when they're low.

You shouldn't rebalance more than twice a year, unless stocks move more than 10%...or interest rates change 1% or more. If that happens, rebalance your portfolio immediately.

•Understand the choices. If you're going to properly diversify, you have to figure out what investment style is used by each of your plan's investment options.

For your stock-market money, put 20% in a growth fund, 40% in a growth-and-income fund, 20% in small-company stocks, and 20% in an international fund. On the bond side, split your money equally among Treasuries, corporate bonds, and Ginnie Maes.

•Coordinate your 401(k) with your other investments. Keep careful records of everything you own, both in your 401(k) and in other accounts. Check to make sure you're well diversified.

You might, for instance, own a lot of municipal bonds in your personal account. If that's the case, consider having all or most of your 401(k) money in stocks.

Most people should own some small-company stocks and foreign stocks. But your 401(k) plan may not offer these investment options, so you might want to purchase foreign stocks and small-cap stocks outside of your 401(k).

•Never own your company's stock in your 401(k) plan—no matter how strong your company's prospects are. Every day, major companies are getting slaughtered on Wall Street. If you put your 401(k) money in your company's stock, you could be the next victim of a Wall Street bloodbath. With your 401(k), what you want is diversification—and you can't get that with a single stock.

Exception: If your company offers an employee stock-purchase plan. With a stock purchase plan, you can often buy company stock for 85 cents on the dollar—and then consider selling part or all of it to reinvest elsewhere.

•Avoid market-timing. In many plans, employees are allowed to make unlimited switches among their 401(k) investments. A large percentage of people use this privilege to shift actively between stocks and bonds, hoping to own stocks when they're moving up and then switching into bonds in time to avoid stock-market declines.

But market-timing doesn't work. The professionals with their computers and years of Wall Street experience can't predict the market, so it's foolhardy for amateur investors to think they can.

•Monitor performance. Many plans offer both actively managed funds and index funds, which simply buy and hold the securities that make up a market index such as the Standard & Poor's 500 stock index.

Look at how the actively managed funds perform compared with similar funds. To do that, you'll have to go to the library and look at research services, such as *Morningstar Mutual Funds* and *CDA/Wiesenberger's Mutual Funds Update.*

Skip the funds that don't perform well compared with other funds in their category. If none of the actively managed funds are any good, use the index fund. And if all the funds in your 401(k) plan are lousy, then go to your company's management and fight to get better investment options. It's worth the effort. For many employees, their 401(k) money will become the biggest asset they have.

•Park your 401(k) in a rollover IRA if you switch jobs. Imagine a 30-year-old who receives $10,000 from his 401(k) when he changes jobs. There is a great temptation to spend the money rather than roll it into an IRA...and that would be a big mistake. By spending that $10,000 now, the 30-year-old gives up the chance to have $200,000 when he's 65, presuming a 9% rate of return.

If you're parking the money in a rollover IRA, you have to set up a so-called trustee-to-trustee account, or the government will hit you with a 20% tax.

Contact the mutual-fund company or brokerage that you'd like to handle the money and ask them to arrange the transfer. Don't take possession of the money, or you'll get hit with the 20% withholding tax.

Important: If you're faced with a choice between putting your 401(k) money into a rollover IRA or parking it in your new employer's 401(k) until you're eligible to make contributions, go with the IRA. You'll have more flexibility when picking investments.

Source: Jonathan D. Pond, president, Financial Planning Information Inc., and author of *The New Century Family Money Book*, Dell Publishing, 1540 Broadway, New York 10036.

Better 401(k) Investing

It pays to know your options for investing your 401(k). Most company plans offer three to five choices. *Examples:* Company stock, equity mutual funds, money-market funds, and/or guaranteed investment contracts issued by insurance companies. *Helpful:* Request a prospectus from each company that

manages one of these investment options and read it very carefully—with your accountant, if necessary. Contact your employer's retirement-plan manager for the name and address of each of these companies.

Source: Legg Mason, president, Legg Mason Wood Walker, Inc., investment advisers and stockbrokers, 99 Summer St., Box 1, Boston 02101.

How to Pass Your IRA On to Your Children And Grandchildren

Most people leave their Individual Retirement Accounts (IRAs) to their spouse. But if your spouse is adequately provided for, you may want to leave some or all of your IRA money to your children or grandchildren. You get the greatest mileage from an IRA that you leave to your grandchildren or other beneficiaries who are much younger than you. *Benefits of leaving an IRA to a grandchild...*

•The IRA will continue for a long period of time—50, 60, or even 70 years, depending on the grandchild's age and the payout method selected.

•IRA earnings will accumulate on a tax-deferred basis for that period of time. This can add hundreds of thousands of dollars to an IRA.

•There's a substantial income-tax saving in leaving money to a low-bracket grandchild rather than to a spouse. A spouse will pay income tax on IRA payouts at the 31% rate or more. But once a grandchild reaches age 14, income is taxed at his/her rate, not the parent's. A child is in the 15% tax bracket for the first $22,100 of income in 1993.

•There's an estate-tax saving. The IRA assets and their growth over the years will not be included in your spouse's estate.

•The IRA assets avoid probate.

Caution: The most you can give to your grandchildren is $1 million. After that, gifts to grandchildren are subject to the generation-skipping tax, which is a 55% tax on gifts that pass over a generation of heirs—usually the parents' generation.

Problem: Few professionals know how to keep an IRA alive for a person's grandchildren. Some consultants may advise non-spouse beneficiaries to take all the money and pay tax on it the year after the account holder dies.

Solution: Understand how IRA distribution rules work. Do the paperwork now to keep the IRA alive long after you are gone.

Distribution rules:

IRA owners are required to begin taking money out of their account by April 1 of the year after they reach age 70½. But the distribution rules for beneficiaries are different.

• If you die before reaching your required beginning date, which is April 1 after the calendar year in which you attain age 70½, and you've named a grandchild as beneficiary, your grandchild has two options...

• Option 1: Take all the money in the account by the end of the year following the fifth anniversary of your death, or

• Option 2: Begin taking annual distributions based on his/her life expectancy in the year following your death. *Example:* A grandchild who was 20 at this time would have a life expectancy of 61 years. To satisfy the minimum distribution rules for IRAs, he/she would have to take only ⅟₆₁ out of the IRA in the first year. If there was $200,000 in the IRA at the end of the year in which you died, the required distribution would be $3,278.69 (⅟₆₁ of $200,000). The IRA would continue for another 60 years.

To use the life expectancy method (option 2), your grandchild or his trustee will have to file a written election with the IRA institution by no later than December 31 of the year after the year you die, saying the IRA money is to be paid out over the grandchild's life expectancy—61 years in the above example. Payments from the IRA must commence no later than December 31 of the year after you die.

If these requirements aren't met, your grandchild will default into option 1, and all the money in the IRA will have to be paid out to your grandchild five years after your death.

• If you reach your required beginning date, the rules are different. You must begin taking money from the IRA by April 1 of the year following the year you reach 70½ The amount you withdraw each year can be based on the joint life expectancy of you and your beneficiary.

If your beneficiary is your grandchild and he is more than 10 years younger than you, the withdrawals must be based on what is called the Minimum Distribution Incidental Benefit (MDIB) table that is found in IRS *publication 590, Individual Retirement Arrangements*, in Appendix E. The table calculates the withdrawals as if your beneficiary were only 10 years younger than you. This is required by the tax law.

Example: You are 71 and your grandchild, your beneficiary, is 12 in the year you attain age 70½. (If you are born in the first half of the year, you are 70 instead of 71.) Your joint life expectancy is 69.8 years. But the MDIB tables say you must use 25.3 years and take out ⅟₂₅.₃ as your first withdrawal. Each year thereafter, the period is adjusted based upon the MDIB table.

Surprising: When you die, your beneficiary can pick up the original joint life expectancy—69.8 years in the above example minus the number of annual withdrawals that have been made—to calculate future annual withdrawals. The MDIB tables have to be used only while you're alive.

Example: You die at 74 after taking out four annual payments. Your grandchild would be able to withdraw the remaining money over 65.8 years, starting the next year (your joint life expectancy of 69.8 years, minus the four years you've taken money out).

Letter to your IRA custodian: To make this all perfectly clear, you should write a letter to your IRA custodian spelling out the distribution methods you're using...

"I hereby elect to take the money out of my IRA based on my life expectancy and my grandchild's life expectancy determined in the year I attained age 70½. [69.8 years in the above example.] However, while I'm alive, the MDIB rule is operative and that table shall be used. Upon my death, payouts shall be based on the original joint life expectancy of me and my grandchild, reduced by all years that have passed since I was 70½."

Trust required:

If your grandchild is a minor, you'll need an irrevocable trust for the benefit of your grandchild to handle the money being paid from the IRA. You can name a family member as trustee.

Bank accounts: On the death of the grandparent, the trustee would open up a bank account in the name of the trust. He/she would also open a custodial account for the grandchild at a bank or brokerage firm.

The trust says that money goes from the IRA to the trust, and then from the trust to the custodial account, until the grandchild reaches the age of majority—18 or 21, depending on state law. After your grandchild turns 21, the money goes directly to him. Under appropriate circumstances, the custodian could use the money to pay your grandchild's college expenses.

There's no tax to the trust because the money is going right out—the trust is just a conduit. The money is taxed to the grandchild, but at the grandchild's tax rates.

One of the advantages of having a trust is that the assets will be protected from the child's creditors, should the child have an accident or become involved in other legal problems—such as bankruptcy, divorce, etc.

Note: The fact that the trust is irrevocable doesn't mean that you can't change beneficiaries if circumstances dictate a change. You can make beneficiary substitutions until you die.

Best: A separate trust for each grandchild to whom you leave IRA money. *Cost:* $3,500 to set up the trust (or multiple trusts for a number of grandchildren) and an annual fee of $200 or $300 to prepare and file tax returns for the trust after you die.

Practical use: This is a good way to develop a college fund for a grandchild at low tax cost.

Source: Seymour Goldberg, professor of law and taxation at Long Island University and senior partner in the law firm of Goldberg & Ingber, 666 Old Country Rd., Garden City, New York 11530. Mr. Goldberg is the author of *A Professional's Guide to the IRS Distribution Rules,* Field Services, New York State Society of Certified Public Accountants, 200 Park Ave., New York 10166.

Build Retirement Wealth In 10 Years With A Defined-Benefit Keogh Plan

Anyone with self-employment income from personal services, including sideline business income, consultant's fees, freelance income, and director's fees, can have a Keogh plan. Keogh plans are retirement plans for self-employed taxpayers.

They're approved by the IRS and their tax benefits weren't cut back by tax reform. *Main benefits...*

• Contributions to the plan are tax-deductible.

• Earnings on contributions are not taxed while in the plan.

• Taxes are deferred until retirement, when you are likely to be in a lower tax bracket than you are now.

Problem: Defined-contribution Keogh plans—the most common kind of Keogh—won't work for someone who is 50-plus because the most you can put away each year is 13.04% of self-employment income, up to $30,000. This is enough for people who have many years to save before retiring, but not for people who are closer to retirement.

Solution: A defined-benefit Keogh plan. With defined-benefit Keoghs you can put away a much bigger percentage of your income. That's because you are funding an account that is designed to pay you a fixed monthly amount when you retire. So the older you are, the more you can contribute to the plan each year.

They're perfect for someone who has 10 to 15 years to go before retirement.

Opportunity: Because contributions are deducted on your tax return each year, you can shelter large amounts of income during your peak earning years. Money in the account builds up tax-free until withdrawals begin.

How defined-benefit Keogh plans work: The size of your annual retirement payment is based on a percentage of your salary and the number of years that you have remaining to work before retirement. Next, actuarial tables are used to calculate how much money must be contributed to the defined-benefit plan every year.

In 1993 you can set aside enough money in a defined-benefit plan to pay you as much as $115,641 a year when you retire. The limit is indexed annually for inflation.

Example: A self-employed 55-year-old sets up a defined-benefit plan to provide annual payments of $115,641, the legal maximum, starting at age 65. The first year's contribution is $51,893. That rises each year, to $95,403 by year 10. Assuming the investment earns 7% a year, the account would be worth $954,038 at retirement.

Caution: The $115,641 annual limit is reduced if you retire before the Social Security retirement age, from 65 years old to 67 years old depending on the year you were born. Also, the benefit cannot exceed 100% of your average compensation for your highest three consecutive years' earnings.

Drawback: Tax rules are much stricter for defined-benefit plans than for defined contribution plans. You must make minimum contributions every year or face a 10% underfunding penalty.

Cost: The defined-benefit plan must be custom-made for you by a pension specialist. Expect to pay between $1,000 and $2,000 a year to administer the plan.

Source: Richard A. Imperato, principal, KPMG Peat Marwick, 345 Park Ave., New York 10154.

Pension Knowledge

How can I tell if my pension is in trouble? Ask your pension-plan administrator—often in the employee-benefits office—for a copy of your plan's annual report (Form 5500) or an abbreviated version, called the Summary Annual Report.

To see if your future benefits are fully funded, look for any "unfunded-benefit liability." If there is a dollar figure shown, your pension plan is not fully funded. Next, look for the plan's "funding ratio," which is expressed as a percentage of a plan's assets to a plan's liabilities. Any ratio below 100% means the plan is not fully funded. The lower the percentage, the more seriously underfunded the plan is.

What should I do if my plan is underfunded? First of all, don't panic. It may be a temporary blip, caused by falling interest rates coupled with increases in pension benefits. Second, let your employer (and your union, if it is a collectively bargained retirement plan) know that you are concerned that its promises of income in the future may not be kept.

Your company may respond that if it is forced to make larger contributions in order to fully fund its pension plan, it may also be forced to resort to layoffs...and your job may be among those eliminated. You might have to make a trade-off between having a job today or a pension tomorrow. So, you might also want to start looking for a job with another employer, or in another industry with a rosier economic future.

Social Security Card Secret

Few people know it, but the first three digits of a Social Security number are a code for the state in which the card was issued. This code, which can be used to confirm a place of birth or an employment history, is not public knowledge. However, many private detectives have the key to the code and will crack the Social Security number for a fee.

Source: Milo Speriglio, director and chief of Nick Harris Detectives, Inc. (Van Nuys, CA), the second-oldest private detective agency in the US, and administrator of Nick Harris' Detective Academy. Speriglio, now in his thirtieth year as a private eye, is the author of *The Marilyn Conspiracy* (Simon & Schuster), a book about the mysterious circumstances surrounding the death of Marilyn Monroe, and its soon-to-be released sequel, *Crypt 33: The Final Chapter.*

8

Estate Planning

What Everyone Should Know About Estate Planning Now

Most people think that by drawing up a will, they have done all that is necessary to get their estate and financial affairs in order.

Nothing could be further from the truth.

In reality, using a will to pass along property is one of the most expensive—and most vulnerable—ways to set up an estate. There are other, more advantageous and tax-effective ways to transfer property to your heirs. What to consider when planning an estate…

Don't confuse probate with estate taxes:

Probate is the legal process by which property in a deceased person's name can pass to his/her heirs or beneficiaries after debts and expenses of the estate are paid.

Probate property includes anything that is in the deceased's name alone at the time of death. It does not include jointly held prop-

erty, assets that are payable to a named beneficiary at death, or assets in a living trust.

By itself, the probate process does not generate any revenue to the state or federal government in the form of taxes. But probate is a necessary process, and there are legal fees and expenses involved.

Estate taxes, on the other hand, are based on who had ownership and control of the property, regardless of whether that property had to go through probate. If there are estate taxes due, the probate court will not allow the beneficiaries to collect what is left of an estate until the taxes are paid.

Include a "no contest" clause:

One way to discourage challenge to your will is to include an "anti-contest" provision. This provision states that anyone who contests the will automatically forfeits any bequest made to him/her. It does not mean that all contests are legally prohibited. It merely means that challengers will lose their share of your estate if they attempt to interfere with your wishes.

Of course, to make this clause work, you must leave potential challengers a meaningful amount…enough so that they will think twice before they rush to their lawyers and start running up legal fees.

Prepare a durable power of attorney:

This allows someone else to act for you in the event of your disability or incapacity. A regular power of attorney gives someone else the authority to act for you, but that authority automatically ceases if you become incompetent. In such cases, it is necessary to start probate proceedings in order to appoint a personal representative for you.

A durable power of attorney avoids the need to go to probate court because it survives your disability or legal incompetence. By naming someone to act as your "attorney in fact," that person is authorized to sign checks, enter contracts, buy or sell real estate, enter safe-deposit boxes, run your business, make transfers to your trust, and in some cases make health-care decisions on your behalf. Since this gives that person tremendous power, be careful about whom you select.

Consider a "living trust":

This is a trust you set up during your lifetime that can provide for your living expenses and other benefits while you are alive. Upon your death, it allows for the transfer of whatever property is left to your surviving spouse or other beneficiaries you may name.

Since there is a lifetime transfer of the property to the trust and the trust specifies what is to be done with that property upon your death, the probate court does not get involved.

With most living trusts, you have the right to change or revoke the arrangement at any time. While this power to change the terms of the trust means you do not get any immediate income-tax benefits, it also means that the property placed in the trust avoids the costs, delays, and publicity of probate, and it can save estate taxes in the future.

A trust is very flexible and allows you to do just about anything, as long as it is not illegal. It can, for instance, run a business, provide for minors or elderly persons, pay medical bills, create a scholarship fund, and provide for retirement, education, marriage, even di-vorce. A trust can hold real estate, cash, securities, or any other type of property.

For the trust to become effective, you must actually "fund"—or transfer property to—the trust. All too often, people do not change the title on their existing holdings, so the trust has no substance.

If property is held in joint names, for example, those assets pass to the joint survivor. If property is held in your name alone, it must go through probate, and will go to the trust only if that is what your will provides.

Although some attorneys disagree, I think it is advisable for you to name yourself as trustee of a trust that you establish. This allows you to maintain full control over your property for as long as you wish and are able. You can also name a successor trustee to take over if you are ill or die.

Picking the right executor:

An executor's job is to collect and preserve all estate assets, pay all appropriate debts, expenses, and taxes, and distribute what's left according to the terms of your will. You are free to choose anyone you want to act as executor, and usually the probate court is obliged to follow your wishes.

But one other approval is essential to your selection of executor—that of the executor himself. So it is a good idea to discuss the matter with the person you choose, to be sure he/she will accept. After all, it is not an easy job, and if the person wishes, he can decline the appointment after your death.

Important: To guard against this occurrence or the possibility that your executor may die before you, make sure you name at least one successor executor in your will.

It is essential that you not name as executor someone who may be hostile to your heirs or beneficiaries. The problem is that, while the family may fume over such an appointment, there's usually very little they can do to overturn it after you die.

Picking the right attorney:

Fashioning a plan to distribute your property after your death involves interrelated components, and a will is just one of them.

To find an attorney experienced in this field, see if there's an "estate-planning council" in your area. This is made up of professionals who specialize in this field. Request the names of two or three attorneys to interview. *Alternative:* Ask the trust department of a local bank for its best referrals.

Inform the people you call that you are interviewing attorneys to help you make your estate plan. *Some questions to ask...*

• What are your feelings about avoiding probate?

• What are your recommendations about choosing an executor?

• Do you recommend that I act as trustee of my own living trust?

• Can you tell me how to transfer assets to my living trust?

Source: Alexander A. Bove, Jr., a Boston estate lawyer and author of six books on estate and tax planning. His latest book is *The Complete Book of Wills and Estates,* Henry Holt and Company, 115 W. 18 St., New York 10011.

About Being an Executor

Many people name a spouse or adult child as executor for their estate, expecting that the person can handle all of the details involved.

However, while a family member can surely be trusted, they're typically ill-prepared for the burdens. Those estate burdens can be overwhelming. And if they fail to seek outside legal and accounting assistance at the outset, it can cost your estate plenty, from missed deadlines or overlooked liabilities.

Be prepared:

Despite the numerous technical responsibilities of an executor, naming an attorney or bank as executor of your will is usually not a good idea.

They're almost impossible to get rid of, even if there's a serious problem—including poor management of funds. But there are steps you can take to make things easier on the relative you name to execute your will...

• Empower your executor to hire the professionals necessary to perform the complex tasks of settling your estate. State in your letter of instructions that you recognize your estate isn't so simple. Accordingly, you expect that

your executor will appoint proper counsel to act as agent, enabling things to be settled quickly with minimum demands on the executor's time.

Such language should discourage relatives from carping about money spent on outside assistance. (A letter of instructions is an informal document that gives your survivors information concerning important financial and personal matters.)

When the time comes, your executor can determine the scope of professional services needed and can then retain the appropriate professionals—attorney, accountant, bank, investment adviser. By hiring them to perform specific tasks, your executor has more control over fees, making it possible to lower the costs of settling the estate.

• Establish compensation for the executor. Even though hired professionals are helping out, the executor still has a lot to do, and deserves compensation. A family member who serves as executor, only to get an even split of assets, is likely to feel resentful. *Helpful:* Your family's financial advisers can advise about ways to minimize income taxes on executor's compensation.

• Put your financial affairs in order, even though you expect to live a long time. This means gathering together—in one easily accessible, agreed-upon place—information on each of these crucial items:

• Your will.
• Marriage certificate.
• Naturalization papers.
• Safe-deposit-box key.
• Income-tax records.
• Debts owed to the estate.
• Life insurance.
• Real-estate records.
• Automobiles.
• Credit cards.
• Birth certificate.
• Military records.
• Divorce papers.
• Post-office box and key.
• Loans outstanding.
• Social Security.
• Investments.
• Household contents.

- Bank accounts.
- List of expected death benefits.

The better organized you are, the quicker the estate settlement process, and the more money that will go to your beneficiaries rather than to payment of unnecessary professional fees.

Source: Jonathan Pond, president of Financial Planning Information Inc., 9 Galen St., Watertown, Massachusetts 02172, and author of *1001 Ways to Cut Your Expenses*, Dell Publishing, 666 Fifth Ave., New York 10103.

Using Disclaimers To Save Estate Taxes

Despite the way it seems in the movies, the instructions in a person's will are not necessarily the last word on how assets are distributed.

After death, those named in the will can alter a decedent's estate plans—and save taxes—by filing what is known as a *disclaimer*.

A disclaimer is a legal document in which a person refuses to accept some or all of the benefits that result from a decedent's death.

The heir making the disclaimer cannot say who will inherit in his/her place. Under the terms of the will, the property passes as if that heir had died before the decedent.

Example: A decedent's will leaves $1 million to his adult child who is already wealthy and planning his/her own estate. The adult child does not wish to add to his estate by these additional funds, so he executes a disclaimer refusing to accept the bequest. The disclaimed amount passes, as if the child had predeceased his father, to the grandchildren or other beneficiaries named in the father's will. If the disclaimer is properly executed, there will be no additional gift or estate tax.

Trap: A disclaimer must be signed within nine months after a decedent's death. Failure to act promptly can mean that the person disclaiming will be treated as making a gift, subject to gift tax, to the person who inherits as a result of the disclaimer.

Caution: Before signing a disclaimer, check to see who will inherit under the terms of the will as a result of the disclaimer. Make sure the property does not pass to someone who might not benefit from the disclaimer, such as a relative in a nursing home who is on Medicaid and can't own any property.

A disclaimer is an important after-death estate-planning tool since it is, in effect, a second chance to rework a decedent's will. This does not necessarily mean that the will is faulty. It can simply mean that since making the will, tax laws or family economic circumstances have changed.

There are certain key situations in which to consider using a disclaimer:

- To save taxes. Suppose a will provides that all property is to go directly to a surviving spouse. There will be no tax in the first estate because of the unlimited marital deduction. But the survivor's estate will be taxable. Tax in the survivor's estate could have been reduced had the decedent left $600,000 worth of property to persons other than the survivor. The survivor can, in effect, create this tax break by disclaiming up to $600,000 worth of benefits provided under the will. This $600,000 will then pass to other beneficiaries. It will be tax-exempt because of the $600,000 exemption every estate is entitled to. *Impact:* Less tax on the death of the surviving spouse.

- To bring a pre-1981 will up to date. Some married couples may not have redone their wills since the laws on the marital deduction where changed in 1981 to allow an unlimited amount of property to pass to a spouse tax-free.

Their wills may still specify that only 50% of the estate go to the surviving spouse, with the balance in trust. That trust may provide for other beneficiaries besides the surviving spouse and would not be eligible for the marital deduction. If those other beneficiaries disclaim, it may be possible to have the trust qualify for the marital deduction. *Impact:* Less tax on the death of the first spouse.

The use of disclaimers is not necessarily limited to property passing under a will. Disclaimers can be applied to assets that pass automatically as a result of the decedent's death. For example, an individual can disclaim the inheritance of an IRA or other pension benefits.

When making a will, keep in mind the possibility of an heir disclaiming. Check that the "fall-back position," the terms that apply if the named beneficiaries are out of the picture, are conducive to disclaiming.

Example: A grandfather with successful children may not want to disinherit them. But the grandfather should be mindful of the fact that the children may choose to disclaim in order to avoid additions to their own estates. If the grandfather's will provides that bequests to minors will be distributed outright at age 18 or even 21, the children may be reluctant to disclaim for fear that their children will dissipate the property. On the other hand, if the grandfather's will provides an extensive trust arrangement for minors with distributions spread out to age 35 or 40, the children can disclaim without worry.

How To Give More To Charity…And Leave More For Heirs

It is possible for you to have your cake and eat it, too. By planning carefully, you can increase the amount of money your heirs will receive on your death, benefit your favorite charity, and retain a lifetime income for you and your spouse.

Bob is 64 years of age and his wife, Rhonda, is 62. They reside in California and have four adult children who are essentially on their own. Bob's investment assets include a portfolio of tax-exempt municipal bonds. Both Bob and Rhonda want to benefit Charity X substantially, but they do not want to see their children's inheritance diminished by the gift to Charity X.

Solution:

Step one. In February 1994, Bob's lawyer prepares a charitable remainder annuity trust, the assets of which will flow to Charity X at the death of the survivor of Bob and Rhonda. The trust is set up with $250,000 worth of Bob's tax-exempt municipal bonds.

Bob and Rhonda are named income beneficiaries of the trust, receiving a six percent per annum annuity ($15,000) through the life of the survivor, to be distributed in a single payment annually.

Bob's charitable deduction for his contribution to Charity X is equal to $250,000, minus the present value of the life incomes that Bob and Rhonda will receive, or $107,022. The charitable deduction produces a cash tax benefit of $44,219. (These calculations are based on the applicable federal discount rate for December 1991—9%—since Bob has the right to elect the rate for the month the trust is funded or either of the two immediately preceding months. Further, it is assumed that the approximate maximum income tax rate for California residents is 41.25%.)

The trust retains the $250,000 of tax-exempt bonds with an average annual return of 6.5%, so that the $15,000 annuity, payable to Bob and Rhonda in satisfaction of the trust's 6% payout requirement, is well covered.

Step two. Bob and Rhonda give the sum of $44,219 to the trustee of another newly created trust for the benefit of their four children (The transfer is handled in a way that avoids both gift-tax liability and the use of any lifetime gift-or estate-tax exemption). This constitutes the full amount of the tax saving resulting from the transfer of $250,000 to the charitable remainder annuity trust.

The money is used to purchase a universal survivorship ("second-to-die") insurance policy on the lives of Bob and Rhonda.

This policy is issued under a "one pay" plan designed to provide for the children a death benefit substantially greater than the loss to them of the net after-estate-tax value of the $250,000 transferred to the charitable trust.

The approximate amounts of the income-tax deduction, the tax savings, and the death benefit under the policy to be acquired with the tax saving, for individuals aged 64 and 62, respectively, were determined as follows…

Charitable Deduction	Tax Saving at the 41.25% Tax Rate	Life Insurance Death Benefit
$107,022	$44,147	$358,419

Summary:

As a consequence of these steps, Bob and Rhonda have made a major gift to Charity X but also have retained a flow of annual income for their lifetimes.

Had they done nothing, the $250,000 would have been subject to federal and state estate taxes and consequently would have been diminished to only about $112,500 when received by their children.

Now, however, their children will receive, upon the death of the survivor of Bob and Rhonda, life-insurance proceeds (from a policy fully paid for by tax-refund dollars) in the amount of approximately $358,419.

The children's net inheritance has been increased from $112,500 to more than three times that sum as a result of this transaction. In this case, everyone ends up winning.

Source: Stanley S. Weithorn, Esq., a tax attorney at 40 W. 57 St., New York 10019. Mr. Weithorn specializes in charitable tax planning and sophisticated estate planning.

Revocable Living Trusts

Revocable living trusts' value depends on probate costs in your state. The trusts bypass probate—which can be simple and low-cost, or eat up 2% to 5% of an estate and take more than a year. The trusts can be altered or ended anytime. You can name yourself trustee* and select beneficiaries and successor trustees to distribute assets quickly after you die. *Cost factor:* An estate plan that includes living trusts can cost up to $5,000...a simple will that does not bypass probate, as little as $500. *Other considerations:* Trusts keep settlement of your estate private, probate is public... trusts require regular maintenance, a simple will requires only periodic review. *Best:* Talk through your options with an estate-planning specialist to determine the right arrangement for you.

*Except in New York.

Source: Alexander Bove, Jr., a Boston lawyer, is author of *The Complete Book of Wills and Estates*, Henry Holt & Co., 115 W. 18 St., New York, 10011.

Beware of the Many Nontax Considerations In Estate Planning

Estate planning to ensure your family's future financial well-being involves considering more than just taxes.

The most sophisticated estate plan devised by the most expensive accountants and lawyers can be undone by the failure to take common sense steps to preserve your family's wealth...

Investments:

•Beware of inflation's impact. A common retirement strategy is to live off the interest earned on savings while keeping the principal intact. That way, the principal remains available to meet emergencies and can be passed on to the next generation.

Trap: This strategy neglects the fact that even low inflation rates annually reduce the real value of your retirement account balance.

Example: Inflation of only 4% reduces the value of $1 by half in 18 years.

In today's world of earlier retirements and longer life spans, retirees can easily live to see even low inflation reduce the value of their life savings by 50%, 75%, or more if inflation picks up. Of course, the real value of income earned on savings diminishes at the same rate.

Helpful: Plan the size of account withdrawals so that they don't reduce the value of your nest egg. Over a long retirement, the principal in your retirement account must grow by the rate of inflation just to stay even. Design an investment portfolio that combines security with the opportunity to grow and offset inflation.

•Check the security of investments. The wisest savings strategy won't pay off if the bank, insurance company, or other investment holder can't pay you when it is time to collect. Several independent firms rank the fiscal status of banks, insurance companies, and other financial institutions. Check your library for ratings by companies that specialize in this service. A.M. Best, for example, rates insurance companies.

These rankings are published in the financial press, and you should be able to get them for any institution in which you wish to invest. An institution with a solid rating will be glad to brag about it—so ask.

There are other rating services, for insurance companies and banks, that sell ratings of specific companies to interested parties. Some individuals prefer to buy these ratings and explanations because they may be more objective since all the revenues of the rating company are from sources other than the financial institutions being rated.

In addition, pay close attention to account guarantees.

Example: Make sure bank accounts are guaranteed by the Federal Deposit Insurance Corporation (FDIC)—not all banks are—and keep account balances under the guarantee limit, currently $100,000.

•Pay attention to the credit rating of the state or municipality that issues the bonds owned by the fund. Consider investing in insured bonds to secure your investment—the cost to you is a slight drop in yield.

Insurance:

Use insurance to protect yourself thoroughly from any unexpected contingency that could deplete your wealth.

Insurance strategy: The proper role of insurance is to protect against unexpected disaster, not against foreseeable expenses such as fender benders and minor house repairs.

Insurers retain a large portion of every premium dollar for their own expenses and profits—so don't pay for coverage of costs that you can afford to pay yourself.

In most cases, you can significantly cut premium costs by taking the largest deductibles you can afford on auto, casualty, health, and disability coverage. Protect yourself by reinvesting the premium savings in "umbrella" liability coverage and high-dollar limits on other types of insurance that will protect your family against calamity.

•Liability insurance. Be sure you are adequately insured against liability for injuries that may occur in your home, car, place of business, or elsewhere. You may well be underinsured and unwittingly place your assets at risk.

Trap: The typical auto-insurance policy provides liability coverage of $300,000 per accident and $100,000 per individual plaintiff, which is just not enough in these days of spiraling health-care costs and skyrocketing court damage awards.

Fortunately, there's a simple solution to this problem. All liability insurers offer excess liability or "umbrella" insurance in $1 million increments, which applies on top of regular auto and household coverage. The cost is very low, and it may pay off better than any other investment you ever make.

Example: About $200 per year for the first $1 million in high-cost New York.

Trap: If you serve on the board of directors of a business, co-operative housing association or even a nonprofit organization, you could be legally liable for the organization's actions. Be sure it provides you with directors' liability insurance.

•Property insurance. Protect your home and other valuable properties from disasters—storms, fires, and floods.

Keys:

•Valuation. A home or vacation home may be worth much more than you originally paid for it. Be sure the insurance you have is based not on the acquisition cost, but on its real current value and replacement cost.

Similarly, make sure that household items—televisions, computers, etc.—are insured at replacement costs rather than their market values as "used" goods.

•Inventory. Have the records you will need to make an insurance claim if you have to—there's no point in paying for insurance protection if you can't use it. Keep an inventory of possessions, and retain receipts showing their costs. It's a good idea to make a videotape of your household possessions to prove their existence and condition.

Store these records in a safe place away from your home, such as in a safe-deposit box, so they won't be lost in the same calamity that gives rise to the claim.

•Disability insurance. Although most people often don't realize it, they are more likely to become disabled in a given year than they are to die—yet people who carefully arrange life-insurance protection for their families often neglect to protect their family income with disability insurance.

If you are self-employed, be sure to obtain adequate disability coverage to compensate for lost earnings if you become ill or injured. If you are employed, check the disability coverage, if any, provided by your employer. You may wish to obtain supplemental coverage.

•Long-term health insurance. Illness that results in the need for long-term medical care can devour a family's life savings. Investigate long-term-care insurance policies that can protect you. This is still a developing area, so shop around and get expert advice.

Get a policy that covers home care as well as institutional care and that does not require you to be hospitalized before becoming eligible for benefits.

•Life insurance. Explore innovative new life-insurance products that can help preserve your family wealth:

•Second-to-die life insurance can be used to provide funds necessary to pay estate taxes due on the estate of a surviving spouse. Since the policy cost is spread over two life expectancies, premiums are lower than with conventional coverage.

•First-to-die life insurance pays off upon the death of the first spouse. This is useful for protecting the finances of a family in which both spouses work. The policy compensates the family for lost income upon the death of either spouse, making a second policy unnecessary.

Common sense:

•Don't take on other people's debts. Don't be an easy touch for friends, business associates, and family members who ask you to guarantee their debts—whether to keep a business going or to buy a car or a house.

There's a reason someone can't get credit on his/her own. By guaranteeing another person's debt, you take on a risk without a corresponding opportunity for gain.

Of course, you may wish to guarantee a debt for a child or other family member. But before doing so, ask yourself if you would want that amount to pass to that family member anyway—as it will if the guarantee is collected upon.

•Watch your health. Exercising and maintaining healthy weight and blood pressure is not normally considered part of estate planning. But good health will not only let you live a longer and happier life—it may enable you to avoid the huge financial drain of health-care costs that could dissipate your family's income.

•Don't wait. It is always later than you think. Get extra casualty and liability insurance before the unexpected happens…lock in low life- and health-insurance rates while you are still young and a good insurance risk…make gifts to the next generation while you still can—for tax purposes, the IRS will ignore certain gifts made within three years of your death.

Don't put off taking actions upon which your family's future may depend.

Source: Robert S. Holtzman, PhD, professor emeritus of taxation, New York University. He is the author of *Encyclopedia of Estate Planning*, Boardroom Classics, Box 736, Springfield, New Jersey 07081.

All About Living Trusts/ Avoiding Probate

While many seminars, books, and articles are now touting the benefits of using living trusts to avoid probate—and the message has its merits—there are other important points to consider.

Challenge: Living trusts do not solve all estate-planning problem.

For smaller estates, there are easier alternatives than living trusts.

For anyone considering setting up a living trust, it is important to weigh the positives against the negatives.

Basics of living trusts:

Living trusts are set up while you are still alive.

The most common is a *revocable living trust*, which can be changed, amended, or revoked at any time.

A *testamentary trust,* in contrast, is established by your will and comes into existence after your death.

For tax purposes, the property in a trust remains the property of the grantor. If the grantor receives income from the trust assets until death, as is usually the case, he/she reports the income from the trust directly on his/her individual income-tax return.

For purposes of ownership under state law, however, the trust and not the grantor becomes the owner of the property. Title to the property is transferred from the grantor to the trustee (the person—or institution—who manages the trust), and the trustee holds the property for the benefit of beneficiaries named by the grantor.

You can name an institution as trustee, but you probably wouldn't want to because of the cost and possible loss of control over investments (although many institutions will allow the grantor to direct investments).

Avoiding probate:

Probate, the court-supervised process of gathering assets, paying debts and taxes, and distributing property after a person's death, applies only to those assets titled in an individual's name.

Living trusts avoid probate simply by having title to property in the trustee's name rather than the grantor's. *There are good reasons for avoiding probate…*
- Probate can be very costly.
- Probate can be very time-consuming…
- Probate is a matter of public record. This may not be a major consideration for most individuals, but those in smaller towns may prefer to keep such matters private. Living trusts are private.
- Probate entails legal fees and court filing fees. In some cases court procedures can be lengthy. A living trust avoids all this. It provides a greater measure of certainty than probate about how assets will be distributed. This is because it is more difficult, legally, to overturn a trust than to contest the validity of a will.

What living trusts won't do:

Despite the great hype being given to living trusts, there are important limitations to be aware of. Individuals with minor children still require a will and probate to appoint a guardian. While the trust can be used to oversee property for minor children, this does not obviate the need for a guardian to care for them. A court must appoint a guardian for any minor.

There are certain assets that are difficult, if not impossible, to place within a living trust…
- Title to jewelry is problematic.
- Title to a car presents trouble because an insurance company may be reluctant to give insurance to the trust.
- Probate is required if there is any litigation in the works, either pending at the time of death or as a result of death (e.g., wrongful-death action usually due to a third party's negligence).
- Probate cannot be avoided if there is a tax audit under way. Only the court can give the authority to someone, through the appointment of an executor, to handle the affairs of a decedent—including an audit.

Living trusts may not necessarily solve all the problems of probate. Legal fees, administrative costs of distributing assets, and delays associated with probate can apply with equal force to living trusts. Privacy secured by a living trust can be lost if there are wills that "pour over," that is, transfer assets from the estate to trusts, since judges may require such trusts to become part of the public record.

Most importantly, there are virtually the same costs of administration with living trusts as with probate. With or without living trusts.
- Someone must arrange for the payment of income tax earned up to the time of death and after death but before the distribution of property.
- Someone must file an estate-tax return if assets exceed the filing threshold ($600,000 for federal estate-tax purposes…different thresholds at the state level).

Important: Living trusts do not save income taxes, and they do not save estate taxes.

When to use living trusts:

Balancing the positives against the negatives, there are certain special situations in which living trusts are advisable.
- Anyone owning real estate in more than one state should consider a living trust. This

will avoid ancillary probate—the judicial process that results when the person who dies owns real estate in a state other than the one in which he/she lived.

Ancillary probate greatly increases the cost, time, and complexity of distributing assets to heirs.

•Living trusts can also be useful in avoiding family disputes. If there are less traditional family arrangements—for example, multiple marriages with children from each—living trusts can provide for whomever the grantor wants with less likelihood of successful challenge by disgruntled relatives.

Alternatives to living trusts:

Living trusts generally are not advisable for those with small estates, simply because there are easier and less costly alternatives. Small estates are generally those with assets under $60,000, but the term really depends on the type of assets in the estate.

Jointly owned property can accomplish much the same goals as living trusts. Property that is jointly owned will pass outside of probate directly to the surviving joint owner. Joint ownership is created by putting property in the names of two people, specifying rights of survivorship. By using joint ownership, the cost of setting up a trust is avoided while both are alive.

Other assets may already be probate-proof. Retirement benefits, annuities, IRAs, and life-insurance proceeds need not be placed in a living trust since they already pass to the named beneficiary outside of probate.

Source: Stanley Hagendorf, Esq., 6170 Central Ave., St. Petersburg, Florida 33707 and 575 Fifth Ave., New York 10111. Mr. Hagendorf, who specializes in estate planning, is a former professor of law at the University of Miami Law School and a member of Commerce Clearing House's advisory board for financial and estate planning.

Keep a Diary

An estate-planning diary helps to document your assets...and provides a roadmap for your heirs. *Important:* Buy the right one. An estate diary, or organizer, serves as a one-stop aid for your heirs, who will need to quickly find vital information—funeral arrangements, location of safe-deposit boxes, list of investments, medical records, life-insurance policies, etc. *Trap:* Some organizers are more complex than they need to be. Others aren't complex enough. It all depends on what your needs are. *Self-defense:* Examine before you buy.

Source: David Rhine, CPA, partner in the accounting firm of BDO Seidman, 15 Columbus Circle, New York 10023.

Estate Taxes

Estate taxes hit life insurance when parents buy the policy—and children are beneficiaries. Insurance proceeds are income-tax-free—but not estate-tax-free. *Alternative:* The children take out the policy and own it, so it is not part of the parents' estate. Parents can give children up to $10,000 per year for premium payments using the annual $10,000 gift tax exclusion. *Problem:* As owners, children have total control—they can cancel the policy, borrow against it, or change beneficiaries. *Better:* An irrevocable life-insurance trust. This removes the insurance from the taxable estate while making sure a trustee follows parents' wishes.

Source: Alan Nadolna, ChFC, is president of Associates in Financial Planning, Chicago.

9

Investment Savvy

Secrets of Picking The Next Hot Stocks

Lee Kopp, who manages a small investment-management firm outside Minneapolis, has amassed an incredible performance record. For that, he has been called the next Peter Lynch—the legendary stock picker who recently rejoined Fidelity as a consultant.

Kopp's firm concentrates on small- and mid-cap companies. For 1991, Kopp Investment Advisors' first full year in business, the firm produced a total return of 101% for its average account. In 1992, that number was 32.5%. Below are some of Lee Kopp's suggestions on how individual investors can choose the next top stock performers.

•Get informed—and stay informed. Become a regular reader of your local paper's business section, read *The Wall Street Journal,* and, if you're analytically oriented, subscribe to specialized investment publications. If you have a full-service stockbroker, make maximum use

of his/her research reports.

•Look for stocks that are being ignored by Wall Street. My firm concentrates on small- and mid-cap companies that are under-followed by professional analysts. I think they are the most fertile area to find hot growth stocks—those whose prices will double within a three-year period and whose earnings are growing at a rate of at least 25% a year. Don't be afraid to look where others have not. It pays to be early.

•Check what's going on in your own back-yard. This way, you're in a unique position to get in at the start of a big run-up in a relatively unknown company and can closely follow developments in its fortunes.

•Attend annual meetings of nearby companies. This will give you a chance to study the organization's players in action. Are they enthusiastic about new products in the pipeline? Overly optimistic about where the company stands in terms of meeting its objectives?

•Scrutinize the company's balance sheet. Look for such things as research-and-development spending and available cash. For technology stocks, my rule of thumb is that companies should be spending at least 10% to 15% of revenues on research and development to prepare for the future. If a high-tech company is skimping here, find out why. Sometimes a company can be criticized for sitting on too much cash, but the flip side is that a cash hoard can be a good tool for future acquisitions.

•There's no such thing as a buy-and-forget investment. We live in a rapidly changing world, and product obsolescence occurs more quickly than ever. It's vital to keep tabs on industry developments to make sure continued holdings are warranted, especially in the technology sector.

•Keep portfolio turnover to a minimum. My firm's portfolio turnover (annual changes in portfolio holdings) is about 30%. It's about 100% for the typical growth mutual fund. By being selective about our purchases in the first place and holding tight during the inevitable business cycle bumps, we not only keep transaction costs to a minimum but also save taxes for clients with taxable accounts.

•Don't overdiversify. I think you can get adequate diversification with between 15 and 20 holdings. That way, if you hit two or three major home runs, they can really have a big impact on your performance. But if you have a portfolio with between 100 and 200 holdings, it is very hard not to diversify into mediocrity.

•Don't expect immediate gratification. I am basically a buy-and-hold investor. My firm's holding period for most stocks is generally three to five years. But some investors want a stock to move two or three points in just a few months. Then they start looking for the next hot performer. That's simply not realistic. Really, really good new ideas simply don't come along that often.

Source: Lee Kopp, head of Kopp Investment Advisors, an investment-management firm in Edina, Minnesota. 800-333-9128. Total annual return for the typical emerging growth account averaged 48% for the three years ended June 30, 1993. That's more than four times the return of the S&P 500...and three times that of small-company stocks. The firm's initial minimum required investment is $500,000.

Be Wary of Bank Mutual Funds

Despite all the criticism of banks—that they charge too much for credit cards and checking privileges, that they make it difficult for individuals to borrow money—large numbers of consumers are being attracted to their wide range of financial services.

One category that is rapidly growing in popularity is the mutual-fund business, where banks currently account for about 160 funds with over $160 billion in assets—or about 8% of the nearly $2 trillion dollars now invested in mutual funds.

Banks are hoping to trade on their "reputations" for service and safety, which, quite frankly, are much more stellar in the minds of the bankers than in their customers' minds.

Trap: Very few bank funds have long-term track records. Even if a bank is registered to offer a no-load growth, international, or junk-bond fund in your state, how do you evaluate the fund's track record if the bank just started it?

The SEC standards on track-record presentation are neither well-known nor uniformly followed in the banking industry, and the SEC is reluctant to assert its authority to audit banks. *Further risks of a bank fund:*

Managing mutual funds is quite different from selling Certificates of Deposit (CDs), checking accounts, and ATM services.

Banks must face rules and regulations that are different from those that apply to banking. *Traps:*

•There are no promised yields or federal insurance to guarantee your principal.

•Mutual funds require full disclosure, licensing of sales personnel, and a minimum level of investment knowledge, something banks are not accustomed to doing. Remember, banks have long ignored consumers' investment concerns and have themselves invested badly.

•This inexperience and questionable commitment by banks, given their other financial responsibilities, raises a number of safety questions...

• What will happen to a bank-managed fund if it proves unable to grow fast enough to break even?

• Will it be merged quietly into the bank's other funds?

• What will happen if interest rates rise, market values fall, and the bank's marketing staff loses interest in mutual-fund marketing?

• Will fund services be relegated to the least competent employees or be understaffed?

Before going forward:

Investing in a bank-managed fund may not be as risk-free as you think. *Ask the bank the following questions…*

• Is the fund insured by the FDIC? This is a trick question. If the salesperson says "yes"—or does not know—hang up. No fund is FDIC-insured. Your banker should know this.

• How much is the sales charge? If he/she says it's a no-load, ask how much it will cost to take your money out of the fund. If there is a redemption charge (called a contingent deferred sales charge)—forget it. There are plenty of terrific—and safe—no-load funds available.

• Is the salesperson a bank employee? If not, find out why not. If you're buying a mutual fund from your bank, you probably want to do business with the bank. Why, then, are you dealing with someone who isn't affiliated with the institution?

• Is the bank's fund listed in the newspaper tables? Only a small number from major banks, such as Citibank and Bank of America, are listed. If the fund isn't listed, how will you know how it's doing?

• Ask for the bank's financial statements and its FDIC rating. Both can be obtained from the bank. If it doesn't know or is unwilling to give it to you, you probably shouldn't be doing business there.

After you receive the material, call the bank's controller to make sure the FDIC rating that you've been given is the most up-to-date and accurate data. If the bank cannot manage its own investments well, why should you entrust it with yours?

• Compare the bank fund's performance with that of a few no-load mutual funds. Ask for the one-year performance record of all funds you're considering for comparison.

Source: William E. Donoghue is publisher of *Donoghue's MONEYLETTER* and the new audiocassette service *MoneyTalk,* 800-642-4276.

The 10 Worst Mistakes A Mutual-Fund Investor Can Make

Though mutual funds have made it easy for individuals to invest in the stock and bond markets, there are plenty of ways to lose money in mutual funds. *Ten of the most common mistakes and how to avoid them…*

• *Mistake:* Market-timing. This is a favorite strategy of mutual-fund investors—but one that doesn't work. The thinking here is to own stock funds when the market is going up, and then switch to bond and money-market funds in time to sidestep market drops.

In practice, few investors have managed to make the needed astute switches in and out of stocks. And even if they did, the additional gains wouldn't be that great. Over the last 50 years, the stock market has returned 12.9% a year. During that period, if you had dodged the worst 10 calendar years, your annual return would have climbed modestly, to 15.4%.

While the rewards of market-timing are small, the dangers are great. There's a chance your money will be languishing in a bond fund when the stock market is roaring ahead.

Over the past 50 years, if you missed the best 10 years for the stock market, your annual return would have plunged, from 12.9% to 6.2%.

• *Mistake:* Trading sector funds, or switching among these narrowly focused funds, hoping to catch the market sectors that are moving up. The pros can't win at it, so it's folly to think you can. You may want to own some sector funds, but only as a long-term holder.

• *Mistake:* Owning too many funds. People tend to become mutual-fund junkies. They read about one fund, so they buy it. Then they read about another fund, so they buy that fund as well. Soon, they own a dozen or more funds. For most stock-fund investors, five to seven funds is plenty. Consider owning a couple of small-company stock funds, a couple of large-company stock funds, and a couple of international funds.

• *Mistake:* Ignoring the asset-allocation decision. Investors often jump into fund investing without first deciding how to allocate their portfolio among stocks, bonds, and money-market funds.

But studies show that this asset-allocation decision is the biggest determinant of your investment returns. Even if you pick the best stock fund possible, you're still not going to make a lot of money if you have 90% of your portfolio in bond and money-market funds.

• *Mistake:* Not being aggressive enough. Mutual-fund investors have too much money in bond and money-market funds. Stock funds account for roughly 30 cents of every $1 invested in mutual funds.

That's really low, especially when you consider that stock funds outperform bond and money funds by far over most five-year time periods.

• *Mistake:* Selling during a market decline. If the market is going down, that's usually when the best bargains can be found in stocks. You should hang onto your stock funds—*and even consider buying more.*

If the idea of a sharp stock-market decline worries you, consider buying conservative no-load stock funds such as…Lindner Fund (314-727-5305)…and T. Rowe Price Equity-Income Fund (800-638-5660), which shouldn't get hit so hard in bear markets.

• *Mistake:* Setting your expectations too high. Investors say, "I want to earn 20% on my money." But the average annual return for stocks is more like 10% or 12%. If you shoot for returns that are too high, you'll end up taking much too much risk, and you'll probably earn rotten returns in the long term.

• *Mistake:* Investing blindly in hyped funds. Investors frequently rush to buy funds that have been mentioned in the press or that were the top performers for the past quarter or the past year. Oftentimes, these people have no idea what they're buying.

If anything, you should steer clear of funds that are in the limelight. Right now, I would avoid fast-growing funds.

• *Mistake:* Paying Uncle Sam too much. Imagine that you invest $10,000 and a decade later sell your shares for $35,000—pocketing a $25,000 gain. A lot of people think they have to pay taxes on the full $25,000.

What these people forget is that, over the prior 10 years, they received regular income and capital-gains distributions from the fund, which they already paid taxes on each year.

If those distributions were reinvested in additional fund shares, then they should be added to the $10,000 initial investment when figuring out your cost basis for tax purposes. Once you do that, you'll find that your taxable gain is probably a lot less than $25,000.

• *Mistake:* Chasing yield. When interest rates fall, many investors scramble to buy higher-yielding funds. But higher-yielding funds are typically riskier funds.

Right now, I'd avoid high-yield municipal-bond funds. Interest rates are probably near bottom. The next rate move is likely to be up, which will cause bond-fund share prices to fall. If that happens, holders of high-yield muni funds could get badly hurt.

One bond fund I like is the Benham Treasury Note Fund (800-472-3389). It owns bonds with very short maturities, and it's entirely invested in Treasury securities. As a result, the fund is taking very little interest rate risk and no credit risk. That's great, especially if interest rates head higher, as we expect.

Source: Gerald Perritt, editor of the *Mutual Fund Letter*, Investment Information Services, 680 N. Lake Shore Dr., Tower Office #2038, Chicago 60611.

How to Look For Good-Quality Stock

1. A price/earnings ratio that's lower than the market average. I'm buying stocks with p/e's of no more than 14—and preferably no more than 12. When their p/e's rise to market levels, it's usually time to sell.

2. A solid track record. The growth of its earnings and dividends over the past five to 10 years should have outpaced the S&P 500.

3. Above-average return on equity compared with the S&P 500 for the past five to 10 years. This shows that the company really knows how to use capital intelligently to create higher profits.

4. A strong balance sheet. A good company can have long-term debt, but it should not exceed the company's equity. In recent years we've seen far too many companies struggling to get out from under debt that has prevented them from growing and prospering as they otherwise would have done.

Source: David Dreman, chairman, Dreman Value Management, which manages $2.7 billion in stocks, bonds, and mutual funds for individual and institutional clients, 10 Exchange Place, Jersey City, New Jersey 07302.

When...And When Not To Redeem Your Savings Bonds

On March 1, 1993 the federal government lowered the guaranteed interest rate on US savings bonds from 6% to 4%. Where does this leave investors? Are savings bonds still worth buying? And should people who own them sell?

If your low-risk options are CDs, money markets, and savings accounts, then 4% on newly purchased savings bonds is still attractive. As for selling bonds you now hold, it depends on what they're currently worth and at what rate they're collecting interest. *Most common mistakes investors with savings bonds are likely to make...*

• *Mistake:* Not knowing what interest rate your bonds are earning. Savings bonds bought today cost half of their face value, and, as of March 1, are guaranteed to reach face value in 18 years. If the bonds are redeemed after six months, investors are guaranteed at least a 4% annual return on their purchase price, not the face value.

Most people do not realize, however, that not all savings bonds are paying the same interest rate. The interest rate for each bond depends on the purchase date.

Example: A bond purchased in September 1969 might be earning as much as 7.5% per year, while one purchased within the last six months could be earning as little as 4%.

If you know what your bonds are earning, you'll be able to compare them with other investments. This will help you decide whether or not to redeem them.

• *Mistake:* Selling before your bond's semiannual increase. Savings bonds that are purchased before March 1 and held at least 30 months will increase in value twice a year. The dates on which the value of your bonds increases depends on when they were purchased.

Trap: Redeeming your bonds shortly before an increase. This will cause you to forfeit up to six months of interest.

Example: You could forfeit up to $375 for every $10,000 of bonds owned if you redeem your bonds just before an increase is due on them.

• *Mistake:* Automatically selling because the bond has reached face value. Even though all EE bonds purchased from November 1986 through February 1993 are guaranteed to reach face value in 12 years, they continue to earn interest for *30 years from the date of purchase.* This means that by continuing to hold onto an EE bond, you can earn two to four times its face value. And you also have the opportunity to continue earning tax-deferred interest as long as you hold the bond.

• *Mistake:* Not knowing the value of your bonds. A bond can be worth as little as half its face value...or as much as six times its face value, depending on when it was purchased. This means that if you have savings bonds with a face value of $20,000, their actual redemption value can be as high as $120,000 (if they are E bonds purchased in the early 1950s) or as low as $10,000 (if purchased in 1992).

Bottom line: Correctly timing your redemptions will make all the difference in how much you wind up with in your pocket. In addition, any E bonds purchased before May 1953 are no longer earning interest. If the bonds are less than 41 years old, they can be exchanged for

HH bonds, which currently pay 4% and can be held for up to 20 years.

Source: Dan Pederson, former director of the savings bond division of the Detroit branch of the Federal Reserve Bank of Chicago. He is the president of the *Savings Bond Informer*, a service that provides reports on the value of savings bonds for a fee. Box 09249, Detroit 48209. 800-927-1901.

How to Protect Yourself From Investment Frauds

As more and more people move out of relatively simple investments, such as bank CDs and money-market accounts, and into higher yielding and more complex securities, the opportunities for misunderstanding increase. And so do the opportunities for securities fraud and deception.

When they do you wrong:

Review the record of your investment to identify any evidence of…

•Unsuitable recommendations. Securities laws require brokers and salespeople to make only those recommendations that are in line with your experience as an investor and other securities that you own.

Example: If you were looking to invest money from a maturing CD and typically invested only in CDs or money-market funds, the salesperson probably should not have encouraged you to speculate on commodities or options. And the adviser should have exercised caution in having you consider a complex tax shelter or mortgage-backed security.

•Churning. Your account should not show an excessive number of securities purchases and sales—and heavy commissions. Excessive means that the size or frequency of the transactions is out of line with the depth of your financial resources and the character of your investments.

•Unauthorized trades. There should not be any purchases or sales of securities appearing on your account statement that you do not recall personally authorizing. You have only 30 days in which to make any corrections to your account.

Misstatements and omissions:

Deception can be far more subtle and indirect, however. *This includes…*

•Important information left unsaid and never put down in written form.

•Guarantees implied.

•Risks not made clear.

If you feel sure that misstatements or material omissions of fact were what led you to make the unfortunate investment, you still have protection under securities law.

Many investors who have put money in unfamiliar fixed-income securities in the past few years, for instance, feel they have been misled about yields. The problem is that most individuals purchase bonds on the basis of a phone conversation and, as a result, tend to ask few questions.

Key questions to ask yourself about an investment in bonds…

•Were you informed that the attractive, high-yielding bond you bought with a maturity date years away was subject to a call? Were you unpleasantly surprised when the bond issuer called the bond—paying you off at face value and cutting off your income stream long before you expected anything like that could happen?

•Was the yield information made clear in the phone conversation? You want to know the yield-to-call as well as the yield-to-maturity on the bond.

•Did you purchase a municipal bond with a surprisingly high yield only to discover that it was not "rated?" Always ask your broker if the bond is rated and what the rating is.

•Does the broker have information about anything that could affect the bond's rating?

Fighting back:

The statute of limitations for securities fraud is three years from the date of the transaction or one year from the date you can prove was the first time you could have detected the fraud, whichever is later. It's in your interest to bring up possible problems promptly.

•If you believe you spot an error, request in writing that the branch manager provide an explanation. Do not rely on a phone call to your broker to get action. Brokers are often reluctant to admit errors. If the branch manager's explanation doesn't satisfy you, write directly to the firm's office of supervisory jurisdiction. Send your letter by registered mail and get a receipt. Keep a copy of both.

•If you are not immediately satisfied by the response, make it very clear that you mean business. On any call you make after it becomes clear there is going to be a problem, tell the person that you are recording the call. (Telling them you are recording the call is really a signal that you are moving toward legal action. If you record without informing the other person, the tape cannot be used as evidence.) Most answering machines allow you to record calls. If brokerage executives won't talk with you under such circumstances, conduct everything by registered mail.

•Get the name and address of your state's securities commissioner. Call the secretary of state's office in your state capital for exact information. Get the official state securities complaint form. Fill it out and send it to the broker dealer as well as to the state authorities. Request restitution and an immediate response.

What to expect: Brokers are generally willing to settle small claims promptly to avoid further problems. The smaller the sum, the easier it is to recover.

Chances are that you agreed to arbitrate disputes when you opened your brokerage account. This can be an economical and effective way to handle disputes that involve $35,000 or less. For larger sums, you probably will need to engage a good securities lawyer.

Establish the claim:

If you are unable to recoup your losses from your broker or dealer, then, to establish a loss, you must sell the investment to prove how much less it was worth than your original investment. At a minimum, you can take a tax loss and collect 31 cents on the dollar as a deduction, or use the tax loss to offset capital gains elsewhere. If there are no capital gains, then the tax loss is subject to an annual $3,000 limit.

When you begin a suit to recover a loss, you and your lawyer will seek out the "deepest pockets" among the firms or individuals who can be considered liable for misrepresenting the investment.

The Civil Liabilities section of the 1934 Securities Act states that anybody mentioned in the

transaction is liable, including lawyers, accountants, bankers, investment bankers, management, even real estate appraisers or public relations firms involved in the deal.

Source: N. Richard Fox, Jr., a former senior manager of a national brokerage firm, and Vernon K. Jacobs, CPA, former vice president and controller of a major life-insurance firm. They are two of the founders of Heartland Management Co., a fee-only investment advisory firm, 6804 W. 107 St., Overland Park, Kansas 66212. Heartland also has an audiotape on how to get out of a bad investment.

Lessons From One Of America's Most Successful Investment Clubs

The Beardstown Ladies Investment Club in Illinois has averaged a 23.4% annual return since 1983…and is the only club that has made the National Association of Investors Corp.'s All-Star team for six consecutive years. Charter member, Shirley Gross shares the investing secrets of these 16 women, many of whom are in their sixties…

Our strategies:

•Buy stocks that have had steady, predictable growth. We choose companies with sales and earnings that have grown at 15% per year over a five- or 10-year period. We also make sure that this rate is projected to continue for the next five years. Investors can do this by consulting the *Value Line Investment Survey*, which is available at most libraries. It ranks more than 1,700 stocks on a 1-through-5 basis …1 being the best in terms of performance over the next 12 months.

We avoid stocks with earnings that have grown well annually—while sales have grown much more slowly. Companies that fit this profile aren't real growth stocks.

•Stalk a stock before buying it. This strategy helps us avoid paying more for a stock than we should. Track a stock's price/earnings ratio for the preceding five years. We use the *National Association of Investors Corp.'s Stock Selection Guide*. It is an excellent tool to use when studying stocks to buy. The *SSG* is available through the NAIC or its regional councils.

Formula: Determine the stock's high p/e for each of the past five years. Add them up. Do the same for the stock's low p/e. Divide each sum by five to get the average high and low. Next, add these two figures and divide by two to get the average p/e for the last five years. Avoid the stock if its current p/e is higher than its average p/e.

•Ignore most broker tips, but rely on research with proven value. Don't listen to the so-called experts. Our club has an account at A. G. Edwards, a full-service brokerage firm. By going through a full-service broker, we're able to avoid having to get the signatures of 16 members every time we buy or sell. But we seldom look to the broker for advice. Instead, we swear by *Value Line*, relying on its research and rankings to lead us to potentially attractive stocks.

We almost always buy companies with *Value Line* timeliness rankings of 1 or 2, and never those with a 4 or 5. We also use *Value Line's* industry rankings as a sector screen, typically choosing companies in an industry in the top 25 (out of 98).

•Avoid companies with substantial debt or unresolved problems. Stocks in companies with comparatively low levels of debt traditionally do not drop dramatically in price. For almost all stocks purchased, the company's debt should not account for more than one-third of its capitalization. This information is also available through *Value Line* or the company's annual report.

•Get paid for the risks you take. Growth-stock investors can get clobbered if the company doesn't prosper, so make sure you invest in companies where the upside will be big.

Use the *Stock Selection Guide* and the data from *Value Line* to establish an upside/downside ratio for any stock being considered. It is the ratio used to evaluate the relative odds of potential gain versus our risk of loss for a given price per share. Look for ratios of at least 3 to 1.

Example: Determine the projected high price ($40). Subtract the present cost ($15). This leaves you with $25. Take the present cost ($15) and subtract the projected low ($10). This leaves you with $5. Divide the $25 by $5. This gives you a ratio of 5:1, a good buy.

•Know when to sell. When we buy a stock, we have a price in mind that we expect it to reach within five years. When it hits that price, we reevaluate the stock. If it's still strong, we hold onto it. If it's weak, we sell. If the stock price remains flat or drops, we also reevaluate. If the fundamentals are weak, we sell and take a loss.

•Avoid any stock with a beta over 1.05. A beta is the measure of a stock's volatility. A stock with a beta over 1.0 is more volatile than the market. Since our club meets only monthly, we prefer steadier stocks.

Source: Shirley Gross, charter member of The Beardstown Ladies Investment Club. A video on the club's methods, *Cookin' Up Profits on Wall Street,* is available from Central Picture, 2222 W. Diversey St. #310, Chicago 60647, 800-359-3276.

How to Know When To Sell Your Stocks

Often, the difference between being a Wall Street winner and a Wall Street loser isn't knowing when to buy…it's knowing when to sell. *Seriously consider selling when…*

•The reason you originally purchased the stock is no longer valid.

Example I: You bought because of rumors of an impending takeover. Six months later, the rumors are a memory and the stock is going nowhere.

Example II: During a recession, you buy in the belief that the company will soar when the economy turns around. But when the economy improves, the stock is left behind. Don't wait for a run-up that might never come—sell now.

•The stock's rate of gain exceeds expectations. Take profits when they become unreasonable.

Example: Sell when a classic 15% long-term grower (Coca-Cola, McDonald's) rallies 20% in a month. *Reason:* You've realized a year's profit in only a couple of weeks. Don't wait for the stock to cool down—take the money and run now.

• You wouldn't buy the stock today. The world has changed. Holding is really recommitting money to the stock for one more day, commission-free.

• The stock reaches your original target price…even if you now expect it to go higher. When buying a stock, put in a stop order to sell once the stock reaches a specified price. This relieves you of having to make the difficult decision to sell.

• The stock runs up on good news that's not truly important. Strategic news is significant. Quarterly earnings surprises or a routine dividend are not significant—certainly not in the long run.

Examples of strategic news: The sale of a money-losing division…a change in top management…the securing of a critical patent.

• The company's industry gets widespread bullish coverage in the popular press. That's a sure sign "everybody" knows the story and there's no one left to buy anymore—and it can't go anywhere but down. *Recent media darlings:* The gold and casino industries.

• The Dow rises six or seven days in a row. *Reason:* This happens only once or twice a year and signals a crest that will probably be followed by reduced bullishness.

• All your holdings have increased at the same time. Take some of your profits and go home.

Source: Donald L. Cassidy, analyst with Lipper Analytical Services and author of *It's Not What Stocks You Buy, It's When You Sell That Counts: Understanding and Overcoming Your Self-Imposed Barriers to Investment Success,* Probus Publishing Co., 1925 N. Clybourn St., Chicago 60614.

Investing in a World In Radical Change

Sir John Templeton knows a bargain when he sees one. As an early pioneer of global investing, his Templeton Funds have been among the best performers, primarily because he purchased undervalued stocks.

Though he sold his mutual-fund company recently to Franklin Resources, a major fund group, Sir John continues to aggressively monitor global economic trends. To explain where yield-hungry investors can find the best global bargains, he answered some pertinent questions…

Where is the world economy headed? The powerful trend is for worldwide progress to continue. This trend will be driven by increased scientific research, better management, and an explosion in international trade. It has often taken 1,000 years for the standard of living to double in the most advanced countries, yet it may double for the world as a whole in just the next 20 years.

I also expect production to double, resulting in improved corporate sales, profits, dividends, and share prices. There will be substantial opportunities for investors.

Unfortunately, the downside to all of this will be the persistence of inflation. In fact, I can think of no currency on earth that is gaining purchasing power, which is because democracies are especially prone to excesses that eventually overheat their economies.

Voters, in turn, don't like economic depressions and ask their governments to take steps to prevent them. These steps include increased government spending, which results in inflation.

Unfortunately, I don't expect any major shifts in spending attitudes by either governments or individuals. During the next 10 years, global inflation may run from 1% to 15% annually and average about 6% to 7%. It will probably never drop below zero. That means the cost of living may double every 12 years.

What can investors do to prosper in this environment? The first principle is to diversify. Continuing inflation pretty much makes the case for getting out of cash, which will lose value dramatically over time.

To protect against inflation, you can invest in equities and participate in the rapid increase in total worldwide production. Safety is achieved by diversification. Everyone should own assets in more than one corporation, industry, or nation.

The second principle is to buy where you get the most value for your money. Look for investments with remarkably low prices in relation to true value. Buy equities where other people are selling.

Should investors be heavily committed abroad? Only about one-third of all common stocks in the world are in the US. Two-thirds are abroad. So common sense suggests that's how a portfolio should be allocated. And studies show that in the long run, a globally diversified portfolio yields higher returns with less volatility than a diversified, single-nation portfolio.

But it's unusual for an American to be even marginally diversified abroad. Investors could prudently go to 40%.

What's the best way to invest abroad? Through global mutual funds managed by people with worldwide experience. It's hard to find the very best values on your own, given the barriers to entry, difficulties in obtaining information, different trading systems and accounting methods. No individual can keep track of this on his/her own.

Where in the world today can an investor find bargains? You will not find bargain stocks where investors are optimistic since share prices are already high. The key is to buy shares where investors are discouraged, usually for a temporary reason.

Numerous nations have had severe bear markets, in which shares have lost 50% of their value—Argentina, Austria, Brazil, Indonesia, Italy, Korea, Portugal, Spain, Taiwan, and Turkey. In Greece and New Zealand, share prices have dropped by as much as 70% from previous peaks.

You were one of the first to see the huge potential in Japanese stocks. Should one invest in them now? Even though share prices in Japan are down 50% from their peak, they're still high. When we first started investing there 28 years ago, Japanese shares were selling for only four times earnings. They hit a peak of 75 times earnings on the last day of 1989, and even now they are selling at 60 times earnings, versus 16 times 1993 earnings for the average US stock. So there are few big bargains in Japan—yet.

Japanese shares are four times more expensive than American stocks. Compare dividend yield. You get an average dividend of 3.2% on US shares—four times the dividend yield of 0.8% for Japanese shares.

Is the Hong Kong market too risky now that China is slated to take over in 1997? Share prices in Hong Kong today are about as high as they have ever been—double what they were three years ago. But they are not too high.

Many people don't realize that Hong Kong will actually keep many important rights for 50 years after it becomes part of the People's Republic of China. These rights include electing a government, maintaining the legal system, and negotiating international accords. It will have much autonomy in economic, financial, and monetary areas. Therefore, it is likely to remain one of the world's leading financial centers.

Where do you see the greatest potential? In the rapidly developing countries of the Pacific Rim—China, Hong Kong, Indonesia, Singapore, South Korea, Taiwan, and Thailand.

Although Europe will be a great economic power, the Asian countries will probably be the linchpins to substantial growth in the next few decades.

The reason is that the Pacific Rim region is twice the size of Europe and the US, and it contains half the world's population. That figure is likely to jump to two-thirds by the end of the decade. In a growing economy, that's an enormous number of consumers with money to spend—a $3 trillion market growing at the rate of $3 billion a week. US trade with Asia may well be twice that with Europe within 10 years.

Is the US market a good bet now? The bull market here is nearly three years old, so the opportunities are not as good as before. Prices are not high or low but reasonably normal—at 16 times expected earnings for 1993.

But if you're trying to find the best values, you're more likely to find them in nations that have already had their bear markets. If shares are down 50%, they're not likely to go down another 50%. The short-term investor would be wise to put his money there and not worry about investing where he thinks there may be a bear market.

What is your best piece of advice for investors? Don't try to outguess the market, and don't move in and out of the market often.

Over the years, the average holding period for stocks in the Templeton Funds has been about five years. That's not because we decided on that time span, but because the stocks didn't go up immediately.

It takes patience. If you are diversified and hold shares of well-managed, established companies, the rewards will be there.

Source: Sir John Templeton, chairman emeritus of the Templeton Mutual Funds Group and the donor of the Templeton Prize for Progress in Religion, one of the world's largest monetary prizes for achievement. The author of several books, he is the editor of *Looking Forward: The Next Forty Years,* HarperCollins, 10 E. 53 St., New York 10022.

The Bulletproof Portfolio

Prepare for all possibilities—including the worst—when planning your financial future. While the worst is unlikely to happen, it's important to protect your assets now.

Only then will you be able to take advantage of opportunities, seeking out investments that yield excellent rates of return.

Getting rid of the waste:

The first step in making sense of your finances is to stop wasting money. Assuring your financial future is not simply a matter of generating a lot of income. You must not waste the money that you earn.

Minimize your insurance bills. Insure only when the cost of a loss would be devastating. If the probability of loss is high, insurance would be prohibitively high.

Example: Few of us suffer fire losses, but it certainly makes sense to have insurance.

To stop wasting money on insurance:

Set aside $3,000 or so to cover small losses (damage to your home or auto, theft, small medical bills, etc.) and raise the deductibles on your policies. This tactic alone may give you the equivalent of the highest rate of return on any investment.

Reduce your taxes. Give primary attention to investing in tax-deductible and/or tax-deferred ways—which means building up your retirement accounts—IRAs, Keoghs, SEPs, 401(k)s, etc.

Because the money you invest through these accounts is tax-deductible, the federal government—in effect—contributes about one-third of the funds. And your account builds up faster, because income taxes are not extracted each year. You pay tax only when you finally withdraw the funds—usually after retirement. This, too, is a superb investment deal.

Next to consider: Variable annuities for mutual-fund investments that are not in retirement accounts. Shop around for variable annuities with good performance records and modest fees. In my opinion, about 70% of mutual-fund investors can probably benefit from the tax-deferred feature of variable annuities.

Don't rely on your attorney, accountant, stockbroker, real-estate broker, or any "experts" for financial advice. If you want to use a financial planner make sure that he/she:

•Has at least five years of full-time experience.

•Doesn't sell the financial products of only one company.

•Understands and respects your goals.

•Gives you Form ADV—that's an SEC form financial advisers are required to give prospective clients. It spells out how the financial planner will be compensated for his advice.

•Has many clients in financial circumstances similar to yours.

Protect yourself:

The next step to bulletproofing your financial future is to protect yourself against calamity. This is what liability insurance is for.

Be sure to have an umbrella liability policy that covers you for at least $1 million—$2 million in particularly litigious states such as California and New York—over and above the usual $300,000 liability on your homeowner and auto liability policies. *Typical cost for such peace of mind:* $100 to $150 a year, in most states.

If you own rental properties—an apartment house, a condominium, or a second home that you lease out—be sure to get a commercial liability policy (also for $1 million) for the rental property. Your personal liability umbrella won't cover you if someone is injured or killed on the property

Don't panic:

As you systematically plug up the holes through which your cash is draining away and shield yourself against a catastrophe, give thought to the panic buttons that drive your investment decisions.

For some older investors, the greatest fear is an economic depression—because they remember living through one.

For many in their 30s, 40s, and 50s, the most difficult economic situation they lived through —the one that most colors their current investment decisions—is the inflation of the late 1970s and early 1980s.

Here's how to build protection for yourself against both these economic calamities…

•Depression protection. In a typical depression, hard assets—particularly real estate—can go down 30% to 70%, prices may drop 30%, and interest rates hover around 1%. Bonds bought before the depression that pay higher rates of interest will go up in value—if the interest payment is secure.

So, put enough Treasury bonds in your portfolio to assure that you won't lose purchasing power relative to what you have today. If prices decline 35% and interest rates fall to 1% —as they did in the Depression of the 1930s— every dollar you invest in a Treasury bond today will buy you more than $4.25 worth of goods and services during a severe depression.

If you put $23,500 of a $100,000 portfolio in long-term Treasury bonds and a depression hits, the purchasing power of these bonds will be $100,000 ($4.25 times $23,500). You'll hold your own in purchasing power.

•Inflation protection. The value of certain investments, such as commercial real estate, go up at an increasing rate as inflation builds up steam—up 30%, for instance, at a 20% overall inflation rate and up as much as 200% when the inflation rate hits 100%. As inflation surges, those with money in securities are unable to keep pace. They bail out and rush to buy hard assets—real estate, gold, etc.

Devote about 30% of your total assets to inflation protection—about 20% to fully paid (not leveraged) real estate and 10% to one-

ounce gold bullion coins (Eagles, Krugerands, Maple Leafs, Pandas) bought at no more than 15%—and preferably at 5%—above the current price of bullion.

Rules by which to invest:

Now, with your protection in place, you are ready to look for the best investment opportunities. *Simple rules to follow:*

•Keep a rainy-day fund—at least three months' worth of expenses—in a money-market account.

•If investing in stocks and bonds keeps you awake at night, get out of the market. It's too easy to panic at the wrong time if these investments just feel too risky for you.

•Buy and hold your securities investments. Don't try to time the market. Don't panic during downturns if you've done your homework on your investment choices.

•Don't look over the shoulder of the next guy for investment ideas. He's no more likely to be right than you are. And like fishermen telling tales, other investors are far more likely to tell you of their successes than of their failures.

•If you find a good idea, make it your own. Originality is not necessary for success.

•Diversify your holdings to reduce risk.

•Have realistic goals. Don't expect extraordinary wealth.

•Start saving early to unleash the power of compounding interest. Encourage your children to save early, too.

Source: Bruce A. Lefavi, MBA, CFP, and head of Lefavi Financial Center, a financial planning group, 1245 E. Brickyard Rd., Suite 550, Salt Lake City 84106. He is author of *Bulletproof Your Financial Future,* Pocket Books, 1230 Avenue of the Americas, New York 10020.

Series-EE-Savings-Bonds Trap

Series EE savings bonds purchased in the early 1980s may be earning less than you think. *Trap:* While bonds issued between November 1982 and October 1986 have been earning a guaranteed annual rate of 7.5%, this guarantee expires as the bonds reach face value—after 10 years. The new rate is only 4%.

Important: Before deciding to cash in the bonds, determine each one's variable rate. It could add a point or two.

Source: Dan Pederson is president of the *Savings Bond Informer*, a Detroit-based service that provides reports on the value of savings bonds. 800-927-1901.

Investment Lessons

There's no shortage of financial advice on Wall Street. The problem is that much of this financial advice is conflicting and leaves individuals confused or stuck in bad investments. So what's an investor to do?

To help individuals make better decisions, financial experts George Stasen and Robert Metz give us their basic lessons of investing...
Decisions/decisions:

•"Buy low and sell high" is sound financial advice—but there are actually four decisions to make. Stock-market experts like to say that timing is everything, and most investors strive to sell at the top of a market and buy at the bottom.

This strategy is also known as the "contrary opinion"—doing the opposite of what most other investors are doing at a given time.

But moving successfully against the crowd is very difficult.

Trap: Market cycles contain many small, deceptive movements—so the buy-sell phases aren't always clear. *Here are six decisions a contrarian investor must make...*

•When the market is approaching the bottom of a cycle, sellers no longer have the stomach to buy. This creates an opportunity for bargain hunters. To determine when the market has reached this point, you can evaluate stocks using historically low valuations of revenues, earnings, and dividends. Or you can wait for an uptrend before buying.

•After you buy, don't sell immediately after the bull trend becomes obvious to everyone. Let the crowd join you as the movement upward progresses.

•When serious overvaluation is reached, go against the majority and sell. Determine this moment by setting a price objective beforehand. Or base your timing on the heat of the market. Wait for the first sign of market weakness.

•As the downward cycle advances, resist the temptation to buy back your stock at a lower price. Wait until the market approaches the bottom again before buying.

•Don't confuse portfolio activity with progress toward investment goals. A common mistake made by many investors is rapid portfolio activity. They regard time as the enemy and believe that if they wait too long, that is an invitation for something to go wrong.

It's unrealistic, however, to expect that instant profits are easy to grab. When too much attention is focused on achieving short-term goals, the real opportunity—which is long-term—is forgotten. Think of time as an ally, not as an enemy.

•Beware of the company that offers creative excuses for underachievement. Some companies have a talent for making excuses for problems. Be especially wary of companies that wrap bad news in good news. *Danger signs:*

•When shortfalls and disappointments come with good-news announcements, such as the introduction of a new product or overhead-reduction programs.

•When you find your mailbox jammed with "We love you, shareholder" letters from the company.

•When bad news is accompanied by an announcement of a management shake-up. Did the company also say what took so long for them to clean up the problem? If not, incompetents may still be in charge.

Once credibility has been destroyed, it takes a long time for a company to win it back. When management repeatedly says, "Things will be better next year," it's time to sell.

•Focus on essentials...skip the merely interesting. Experienced investors are humble. They've learned that they can't possibly know everything. Less seasoned investors, on the other hand, may feel that if they had only a few more hours to do research, their investment returns would be considerably better. Usually this is hogwash.

Save time by not seeking out the opinions of yet another expert. Formulating intelligent questions that you then go out and seek to answer is much more valuable than collecting opinions.

Focus on an industry's prospects, the strength and track record of a company, and the long-term implications of a new development.

• Good corporate news can lead to a dangerous sense of euphoria. When there's good news, companies can't wait to circulate it. Many ladle it out in advance, tipping off key stock-market analysts. The result is that these stocks often rise before the news hits the media and afterward rise only slightly—or even fall.

Reasons: Many pros "sell on the news"—or take profits as the news becomes widely known and the price rises—and companies often use good news as an opportunity to seek more equity financing.

Similarly, beware of remarkably upbeat presentations at investment conferences. Instead, wait a few weeks or a month, and you'll almost always be able to buy the stock cheaper. *Opportunity:* Look at the volume in the weeks before an "announcement." If it's high, this tells you that you may be late in getting the word.

• Study the composition of a company's board of directors. The role of a company's board of directors is to represent the interests of all stockholders. One way to determine whether the directors are representing your interests is to look at the people who make up the board. *How to tell a good board from a bad one...*

• Determine how many directors come from the company and how many are from the outside. If most are from the inside, the board may not be independent enough to resist undue pressure from top management.

• Examine the credentials of the outsiders. If they are not particularly distinguished, they may have been chosen as "good buddies."

• If the board is small—fewer than five members—it's likely that outside directors were chosen for their cooperative attitude toward management preferences.

On the other hand, a large board—more than 10—is probably too unwieldy to support much independence on the part of outside directors.

• The company's proxy statement will reveal the extent of each director's stock ownership and options and interest in the future of the company. Token holdings are danger signs.

• Learn to distinguish the truly underappreciated stock from the real losers. *Key questions:* Is the stock misunderstood by Wall Street or is it more likely that management misunderstands what's happened to its market?

Don't be fooled by a company's aura or unduly impressed by its past glories. "What have you done for me lately?" is a legitimate question to ask. "What do you plan to do tomorrow?" is an even better one.

Don't jettison a stock simply because it's the biggest loser in your portfolio. That's a short-term balm that usually turns into a long-term mistake.

Source: George Stasen, a venture-capital expert and chief operating officer of Supra Medical Corp., and Robert Metz, a financial journalist. They are coauthors of *It's a Sure Thing: A Wry Look at Investing, Investors, and the World of Wall Street,* McGraw-Hill, 1221 Avenue of the Americas, New York 10020.

How to Avoid The Tricks & Traps In Making Choices

Many investors make the mistake of thinking that all money-market mutual funds are the same. But there can be significant differences in yield, services offered, fees, and—of special concern today—safety.

To date, money-market mutual funds have a good track record for safety. In the few instances where there have been defaults on securities in fund portfolios, the parent companies of the funds have absorbed the loss, so investors have not lost money. But fund sponsors are not under any legal obligation to make the fund whole. They're doing it because they want to maintain investor confidence and keep those dollars flowing in.

In fact, money-market funds have been putting about half of their assets in commercial paper—the unsecured IOUs issued by corporations. If defaults should ever become widespread, sponsors might not be able to make up the losses. Money-market mutual funds are not federally insured the way bank deposits are.

Protection: Read the prospectus to see how much of a fund's assets are invested in commercial paper and European certificates of deposit. The more a fund has invested in these —and the less it has invested in US Treasuries —the greater its risk.

• The safest funds invest only in US Treasury securities. They have a slightly lower yield.

• Next-safest funds invest only in Treasuries and government-agency securities.

If the fund invests in commercial paper, question its buying standards. Look for a fund that restricts its holdings to companies with the very highest credit ratings—A-1 by Standard & Poor's or P-1 by Moody's Investors Service.* Avoid funds that invest in A-2 and P-2 rated securities, which are definitely lower in quality.

The Securities & Exchange Commission is currently proposing a new rule (2a-7). It would limit money-market funds to no more than 5% of their assets in A-2 or P-2 rated securities.

Trap: Since most money-market funds offer check-writing privileges, investors come to think of them as checking accounts. Technically, they're not, and you should be aware that there have been two cases where the SEC suspended fund redemptions for a period of time. This meant that any checks written against the fund did not clear during that period, through no fault of the individual investor. Even if no loss eventually results from this suspension, investors will suffer an embarrassment and an inconvenience.

Yield and fees:

Money-market mutual funds typically yield at least 1% more than do bank money-market funds, which helps to explain their popularity. And their great record for safety indicates that you're not taking on much risk to earn that extra point.

When you choose among money funds, however, be careful not to assume extra risk for the sake of an additional quarter or half point of yield.

*A fund's prospectus usually makes a statement about the quality of the investments. Ask for the annual report, which must include a balance sheet of the fund's investments with ratings of each security.

Yield is a function of…

• Quality of securities in the portfolio (the riskiest investments pay the most).

• Average maturity of the portfolio (longer maturities yield more when rates are falling but shorter maturities allow quicker reinvestment when rates are rising).

• Fees charged by fund managers.

Strategy: If the fund meets your needs for quality and service, choose a fund that is waiving fees. That's like buying at a discount price. Recognize, too, that the fund can decide to stop waiving fees at any time. If that happens, shop around. Too many investors pick a money-market fund and stay with it no matter what. In some cases, you may find that fees for writing checks or other special charges significantly cut into your yield.

In terms of average maturity, it's best to stay with a fund that's close to the average for all taxable funds, currently a fairly long 46 days. These are short-term investments, after all.

Money-market guru Bill Donoghue advises going out no more than 50 to 60 days. The SEC's proposed new rule would prevent funds from having average maturities of more than 90 days.

General guidelines:

Larger funds usually have lower expense ratios because costs are spread over more investors. They also have the deep pockets to absorb losses if any of the fund's securities default. And if the fund is part of a large family that allows telephone switching, you'll have the greatest possible flexibility for managing your money during difficult times.

Source: Dr. John Markese is director of research for the American Association of Individual Investors, 625 N. Michigan Ave., Chicago 60611.

Tax-Exempt Municipal Bonds

If I buy a tax-exempt municipal bond for less than face value, then hold it to maturity and redeem it at full face value, is my gain tax-free?

If you bought the bond at original issue for less than face value, then the gradual gain in its value until maturity is considered part of the interest paid on it and is tax-free.

Much more common, however, is the case where a previously issued bond, issued at face value, is purchased in the market at less than face value because it now pays a below-market rate of interest. In this case, any gain on the sale or redemption of the bond is a capital gain that is taxable. Any loss is a deductible capital loss, subject to the limitation on deductions for capital losses.

Source: Richard Shapiro, partner and director of taxes, financial services industry, Grant Thornton, 7 World Trade Center, New York 10048.

Municipal-Bond Trap

Bond prices have risen sharply due to the recent dramatic drop in interest rates. But when considering whether to take profits on bonds you own, remember that only the interest paid on tax-exempt bonds is tax-free. A profit earned from an increase in a bond's value is a taxable capital gain when the increase in value results from a change in market conditions—such as a decline in interest rates.

The Dumb Mistakes

• *Mistake:* Following every trend put forth by the press. Sure, serious investors are supposed to know better since they deal with financial matters daily. But big investors are just as insecure as small ones, and they often give in to the many opinions of the financial press. The problem is that the press and the pundits are wrong just as often as they are right.

Don't be distracted by what you read in the papers. Keep yourself focused on your personal financial goals, and don't join every prominent economist and fund manager in second-guessing the economy and companies that momentarily falter.

• *Mistake:* Taking high-rate-of-return risks. If a broker shows you an investment returning 15% a year when comparable investments are paying 3%, there's a reason for the difference. Be suspicious if an investment seems too good to be true. Even sophisticated folks' greed occasionally overtakes their common sense—and they wind up losing money.

• *Mistake:* Not protecting the assets you already have. This often occurs when you're holding a stock whose price has declined precipitously. Say you bought at $10 a share and it has fallen to $5 a share. A common reaction is to say you'll sell when the price recovers. What you're really saying is that you expect this stock, which has fallen by 50%, to rise by 100%.

If you are so convinced that the stock is a good prospect, you should invest more in the stock. When the rationale for holding onto the stock is expressed in these terms, most people back off. The point is, be realistic. When an investment fails, sell it, forget about it…and go on to better things.

• *Mistake:* Trying to time the market—predicting each upturn and downturn, and constantly shifting from one asset class to another, such as stocks to bonds, growth companies to value companies, and so on. Even the pros are unable to do this consistently.

The only person who gets rich with market timing is your broker—by raking in commissions. Successful investors use time and patience. They set their goals and stick with them —overrunning temporary market fluctuations.

• *Mistake:* Not monitoring your holdings. You may not be doing as well as you think. Once every six months, tally up your net worth—not counting your house. Over time, that number should be rising.

You should set a specific target for how much you expect your assets to grow over the next three years and the next five years. I aim for at least 10% average growth a year. At that rate, your assets will double every seven years.

• *Mistake:* Neglecting your greatest asset… you. The rate of return on your own labor is far greater than you can get on any other investment. Think of how much income you produced between last January 1 and the end of the year. Regardless of whether you made $20,000 or $200,000, you went from no earnings at all to your total annual salary or business income. Be sure to take good care of yourself. You want to safeguard your most valuable money-making machine—you.

It's also important to invest in yourself. If your company doesn't provide a car phone, but you know it can help you conduct business, buy one yourself. If your 10-year-old knows more about computers than you do, increase your knowledge by taking a course at night school. Continuously strive for excellence...it will pay off financially.

• *Mistake:* Being afraid to invade your principal. Only the super-wealthy can afford to live on their income alone. Sure, it's great to save for a comfortable retirement, but once you've stopped working, don't forget to use some of the money you've accumulated to improve your quality of life.

Example: A 60-year-old woman with a $10 million portfolio worries about the cost of nursing-home care—until she's told that, with her assets, she could afford to hire a staff of 50 for 24-hour care for the rest of her life.

If you are worried about outliving your principal, make sure your portfolio is not 100% in fixed-income investments. Historically, they have had a low rate of return. *Better:* Fashion a diversified portfolio of stocks and bonds, which will produce a higher rate of return. That way, you can systematically withdraw some of the "growth" by selling stocks.

Your real goal should be to accumulate enough money to support you and your life partner for the rest of your lives, not to make your kids wealthy after you die.

• *Mistake:* Being embarrassed to invest small amounts of money. What's important is to establish the habit of savings, even if you're investing only $5 or $10 a month. There are several mutual-fund families that have a low minimum initial-investment requirement, and no minimum-investment requirement after that.

They know that people who get hooked on the savings habit tend to be very loyal customers. So don't be embarrassed to earmark modest sums for your portfolio. And when

larger sums become available—because of a tax refund or a bonus at work, for example—siphon off at least some of that money for investments.

• *Mistake:* Being too busy making money to become financially successful. Regardless of whether you make $50,000, $100,000, or $200,000, it's important to keep track of your spending. There's no doubt that spending all you make can give you the sensation of being wealthy. Yet it's not how much you spend but how much you save that matters. The old adage, "Pay yourself first" works only if you adopt a good method for paying yourself.

Solution: Once a month, when you write a check for your rent or mortgage, get in the habit of writing another check—say, for $50 or $100—for your investments.

Once you get in the saving habit, you won't even notice a dent in your spendable income.

Source: Lawrence A. Krause, chairman of Lawrence A. Krause & Associates, Inc., a San Francisco financial-planning firm. He is the author of *The Money-Go-Round: How You Got On and How to Get Off,* Simon & Schuster, 1230 Avenue of the Americas, New York 10020.

Money-Market Funds Are Not All Alike

Americans have more than $380 billion invested in money-market mutual funds.* And, contrary to popular opinion, they're not all alike. With literally hundreds of funds available these days, how can investors select the best?

Questions to ask:

• What is the quality of the fund's assets? Read the fund's prospectus to find out what specific investments the fund is permitted to make. From this you will be able to determine how risky an investment would be.

The safest and most conservative funds limit their portfolios to the safest investments—Treasury securities. *Drawback:* You'll get a lower

*Mutual funds that invest their portfolios in very short-term, interest-producing securities and bank deposits, and generally offer check-writing privileges.

yield than with more aggressive funds that are allowed to buy bank CDs, commercial bonds, and other investments.

If a fund is allowed to invest in less stable investments—including second- or third-grade commercial bonds, or even unrated bonds—it will be stated in the prospectus.

• Will the fund disclose its current portfolio? Don't rely on the financial information in a fund's annual or six-month reports. It can be months old by the time you receive it, and only represents a snapshot of the fund's holdings at a particular moment. *Warning:* The portfolio may have been window-dressed for positive impact for mailings to shareholders…and can be adjusted after the mailings are sent.

A fund should be willing to disclose its current portfolio on request. And in our rating system, we downgrade funds that refuse to provide this information.

• How diversified is the fund's portfolio? The more issuers a fund has in its portfolio—regardless of what types of securities it holds—the less likely it is to have trouble if one of those issuers runs into a repayment problem.

A fund should have a minimum of 50 issuers. And no more than 5% of its assets should be with any single issuer.

Again, this information can be gleaned from a fund's current portfolio, and should be available upon request. If a fund balks, keep on looking.

• What is the fund's average maturity? Most funds don't have average maturities of more than 100 days. If interest rates soar, funds with longer maturities would find it difficult to quickly adjust their portfolios, and their rates would lag behind more nimble funds with shorter maturities.

Example: The only time investors ever lost money in a money-market fund was in the case of a fund that had an average maturity of more than 400 days. The fund had bet interest rates would fall…and, when they rose instead, shareholders lost eight cents on the dollar.

• What is the size of the financial organization that sponsors the fund? This is especially important today.

Example: Several major funds were invested in one real-estate investment trust that recently

went bankrupt. Although it originally appeared that the funds' shareholders would lose money, their parent companies stepped in and covered losses.

Given the uncertain economy, and concerns about certain segments of it, the safest strategy is to stick with funds that are backed by substantial parents with deep pockets—a publicly traded company or a subsidiary of a publicly traded company, for instance.

• What are the fund's management fees? Because there are actually few differences among money-market funds within different investment categories, the size of a particular fund's fees in relation to its total assets has a major impact on that fund's yield to investors. The lower the fees, the greater the earnings that flow into the shareholders' pockets.

Example: On $10,000 invested over just 12 months, a one-point difference in yield would amount to $100.

Best buys now:

Right now, investors can profit from a battle over fund expenses that is being waged by the giants of the money-market mutual fund industry—Dreyfus, Fidelity, and Vanguard.

In addition to yield, there are important differences among the funds' minimum-investment requirements and fee schedules that should be taken into consideration. *Details:*

• Dreyfus Worldwide Dollar Fund currently has the highest-yielding portfolio, earning a compounded annualized rate of 8.9% for the year ended May 31. And no management fees have been subtracted from this yield since the fund sponsor offered to subsidize all of the fund's management fees until June 15 of this year, or until the fund reached $7.5 billion.

Because Dreyfus has already extended this offer 12 times, it is likely to continue to pick up 100% of the fund's expenses even after this deadline.

• Fidelity Spartan Money-Market Fund is earning a bit less than Dreyfus Worldwide. And it has a similar, although not identical, fee guarantee.

Fidelity has extended until the end of 1995 its guarantee that expenses will not exceed a cap of .45%. But the actual cost to investors is far less, since the company is currently absorbing all but 0.15% of the fund's annual expenses. *Result:* Fidelity Spartan has a current net yield of 8.6%.

•Vanguard Money-Market Reserve Prime, although not absorbing expenses, has a modest expense ratio of 0.3% of assets. After subtracting its expense charge, the fund's net yield to investors is a respectable 8.4%.

Note: The company has complained to the SEC that Dreyfus is guilty of misleading advertising, since Dreyfus could stop absorbing fund expenses at any time, and thus lower its net yield to investors.

Strategy:

For now, the best strategy for investors who seek the highest possible money-market yield is to put money into Dreyfus Worldwide and keep it there as long as the fund's expenses are fully subsidized.

But when Dreyfus's management fee kicks in, it will be time to consider a shift to Fidelity Spartan or Vanguard Prime.

Source: Norman Fosback, editor, *Income & Safety*, which provides safety ratings, yield forecasts, and buy-sell-hold recommendations for a variety of investments, including money-market funds, Institute for Econometric Research, 3471 N. Federal Highway, Fort Lauderdale 33306.

When to Drop A Mutual Fund

Major change in organization...turnover among key professionals...change in its investment philosophy...significant change in fund size—if it grows too much, it likely will not perform as well in the future...five to 10 years of underperformance compared with similar funds.

Source: *Get Rich Slowly* by William Spitz, treasurer, Vanderbilt University, Macmillan, 866 Third Ave., New York 10022.

10

Successful Living

How to Avoid the Most Common Obstacles To Success…Love… Happiness

Life is often difficult enough without us standing in our own way, blocking our path to career success, satisfying relationships, and the attainment of our personal goals. Yet many of us exhibit particular behaviors and cling to particular beliefs that keep us from getting precisely what we want out of life. *Seven most common obstacles…*

1. Poor time management.

The ineffective time manager doesn't know how to prioritize his/her time. He will often come late for meetings or personal appointments and will hand in things past their deadlines. That's not because he's a procrastinator but because he just doesn't have a realistic feel for how much time things take.

Other possibilities: Job dissatisfaction…or

passive-aggressive behavior, which in this case means trying to control events by showing up late and holding up progress. *Solutions…*

- Plan activities the night before so you can prepare for what needs to be done.
- Get a time-and-project organizer to help you anticipate and plan for future activities.
- Look at your watch frequently so you can begin to gauge where your time-management skills are off.
- Build in down time to unwind as well as help you plan future work time better.

2. Disorganization.

People who have a disorganization problem don't know how to control the paper on their desks and can't distinguish between important material and junk.

They feel an irrational discomfort about getting rid of things and have an irrational need to read and know everything. They are forever promising themselves that someday they'll get to those newspapers and magazines, but they never do…and the mess accumulates and swallows them up.

Solution: Stop being a collector. Start prioritizing and acting on everything that comes across your desk or into your home. Toss out all unnecessary papers, and file those you need. The key is to act *immediately.*

3. Unassertiveness.

Unassertive people have trouble saying no to requests...and they don't express annoyance because they fear negative evaluations or being disliked. If they're angry at someone, rather than express their anger directly they will engage in passive-aggressive behavior, such as moodiness or lateness, which is particularly destructive on the job.

Solutions...

•Examine the values with which you were raised. *Example:* Did you grow up believing that being assertive meant being impolite...or that it's wrong to express anger?

•Learn the necessary social and career skills. Do you know the best ways to start a conversation...state your opinions...negotiate a deal?

•Learn to overcome your fear of criticism or rejection. *Helpful:* With a friend, rehearse a difficult situation and deliberately respond differently from the way you naturally would. See how it feels to ask for that raise—while maintaining eye contact and without being apologetic. If a friend isn't available, use a tape recorder and replay your replies.

4. Awfulizing.

The awfulizer has a fertile catastrophic imagination and always assumes the worst will happen. These anxious, fearful people constantly ask themselves "what if" questions: "What if I don't get the job?"..."What if he/she notices that I'm balding?"

Solutions...

•Shift the degree of intolerability in your mind and recognize that while there may be things in life that are uncomfortable, there's very little that people can't endure.

•Examine the probabilities. In any given situation, ask yourself, "What are the actual chances that the worst will occur?" If you begin to do this regularly, you'll realize the unlikelihood of the horrible outcome you're anticipating.

•Actively challenge your beliefs. If you catch yourself engaging in "what if?" thinking, write down any evidence you have that you won't be able to handle the upcoming situation. This will help you see how silly your fears are.

•Recall past successes. Remind yourself that whatever is coming up is simply a variation on something you've already done.

5. Perfectionism.

Perfectionists can't stand being viewed as wrong or inadequate in any way. And because the perfectionist believes he must do everything perfectly, it can lead to procrastination out of fear of doing an imperfect job.

Solutions...

•Accept the reality that all humans are fallible. We're constantly making mistakes—it's part of our nature.

•Deliberately do some things imperfectly... to prove to yourself that you'll survive.

Example: I have one client who's a perfectionist when it comes to her dressing—she wastes a tremendous amount of time changing clothes, matching accessories, and running home from wherever she is if she spots a run in her pantyhose. As an exercise, I've had her deliberately go to work with a run in her pantyhose or with mismatched shoes and purse.

Until you've actually risked being imperfect, you won't make those fundamental philosophical changes crucial to overcoming the problem.

6. Demandingness.

This is the irrational belief that you always deserve to be treated right. Every problem in life is blamed on unfair people or an unfair world. These men and women feel that they're special somehow and entitled to a break because they've always been a good spouse, parent, child, or employee.

Solutions...

•Understand that, in reality, the world operates quite independently from what you want or demand.

Example: A woman discovers that her husband has been philandering. She's devastated because she feels she was such a good, self-sacrificing wife for years. How could he do this to me? she asks. That question presupposes that being a good wife will guarantee protection from anything hurtful a husband can do...but the reality is quite different.

• Look at the big picture. The economy is bad and that's why nobody in your office—not even you—got a raise last year.

• Eliminate the words *should, ought,* and *must* from your vocabulary. These are words that set up absolutist thinking. You'll be a lot happier once you start "desiring" and "preferring" things rather than "demanding" and "requiring" them.

7. Discomfort anxiety.

These people just can't bear hassles. Anything that disrupts the smooth running of their day is perceived as insurmountable. They can't stand to hear bad news or confront somebody on a difficult issue. So they regularly practice "discomfort dodging"—palming off unpleasant tasks onto others or avoiding the problems altogether in the hope they'll just go away.

Example: An executive flips through her stack of phone messages when she gets to work in the morning and routinely gives all the unpleasant ones to her secretary to handle...or stashes them permanently at the bottom of the pile.

Solution: Try systematic desensitization, the treatment of choice for people who suffer from discomfort anxiety. First, practice relaxing using any common relaxation skill you feel comfortable with—tensing and relaxing the muscles, etc.

Then, while you're completely relaxed, practice "seeing" yourself doing whatever unpleasant activities you regularly avoid. If done often enough, the relaxation will neutralize the anxiety, and in time you should be able to carry out the task in real life.

Source: Psychologist Barry Lubetkin, PhD, director of the Institute for Behavior Therapy in New York. His most recent book is *Why Do I Need You to Love Me in Order to Like Myself?*, Longmeadow Press, 201 High Ridge Rd., Stamford, Connecticut 06904.

Music Can Help Heal the Brain

A prescription for music therapy is becoming more common as scientists prove how combinations of sounds affect brain and body.

Humans have long used the rhythm and tempo of music to make repetitive tasks easier. Stanford University experimenters recorded electrical patterns from the elbows of women 18 to 35 years old performing tasks. They found music really did improve synchronization of nerves and muscle signals.

Music is being studied intensively today for its physiological effects. It has been shown to be beneficial for muscular development, physical coordination, a sense of timing, mental concentration, memory skills, visual and hearing development, and stress control. The cerebellum, at the base of the brain, is devoted to the regulation of the sort of movement we use when playing an instrument or dancing to music. Current research suggests one of the cerebellum's fundamental functions may be to help us learn and remember movements.

Dr. Jon Eisenson, a Stanford University Medical Center professor emeritus of hearing and speech science, has long advocated music for stroke and brain-trauma patients unable to speak.

Many beneficial physical effects can be derived from listening and moving to music. In fact, merely listening to music has been found to lower blood pressure and reduce sweating and respiratory rates.

Music can also change moods. Just think of how rock concert patrons behave—or how you feel when you hear a song associated with a past love.

Source: Arthur Winter, MD, FICS, director of The New Jersey Neurological Institute. He is coauthor, with his wife, Ruth Winter, of *Build Your Brain Power*, St. Martin's Press, 175 Fifth Ave., New York 10010.

How to Find Anyone... Anywhere

There are two keys to tracking down an old acquaintance, Army buddy, or some other long-lost friend or relative—perseverance... and knowing exactly where to turn for help. *Best sources of information:*

• National telephone directory. One of the best places to start your search. Consisting of two CD-ROM discs, "PhoneDisc USA-Residential" contains 80 million names—the equivalent of over 80% of the nation's white pages in a single file.

How it's used: Type in a name, and you get a listing of all US residents with that name, along with their addresses and phone numbers. *Purchase price:* $113. The directory is also available free of charge at many libraries and for a per-use fee from private investigators.

More information: PhoneDisc USA, 70 Atlantic Ave., Box 648, Marblehead, Massachusetts 01945. 617-639-2900.

•Public library. Another great source, especially if you can find a helpful librarian. Several helpful references should be on file.

Best bets: "City" and "crisscross" directories, in which local residents are cross-referenced according to name and address. The missing person's current address may be listed. Or, if you find a former address, someone still living in the neighborhood may know the person's current address.

•Post office. If you know the missing person's former address, the US Postal Service can provide you with the new address—if a change-of-address form was filed within the last 18 months.

Procedure: Fill out a "Freedom of Information" request form (available from your local post office). The new address will be mailed to you. *Fee:* $3. *Special case:* If the missing person used to live in a small town, the local postmaster may know his/her current whereabouts.

•City hall and county courthouse. Deeds, car-registration records, marriage licenses, voter-registration rolls, professional licenses, tax records, trial records, etc., are all on file here and available to the public. They often reveal not only addresses but also Social Security numbers (see below). This information is usually best obtained in person or by mail.

•Phone company. Local phone companies often make available to their customers old and out-of-town phone directories. In addition, operators can search an entire area code for the missing person, so call directory assistance even if you're unsure of the missing person's place of residence.

Note: If the missing person has an unlisted number and it's urgent that you reach him, ask the operator to call the person for you and relay your message. This service is not available in all areas.

•Motor-vehicle department. In most states the names and addresses of licensed drivers are part of the public record. To obtain an address, you must supply the name and date of birth of the missing person (no date of birth is required for unique names). *Note:* Some motor-vehicle departments require a written request. *Typical fee:* $5.

•Social Security Administration. It will forward a letter to any person listed in its files—so long as there's a strong humanitarian reason for doing so.

Acceptable reasons: An immediate relative of the missing person has died or is gravely ill...a parent wishes to locate a missing child...an accused felon is looking for a witness, etc.

Procedure: Send the letter to your local Social Security office in an unsealed, stamped envelope. Include a check for $3, along with a note specifying the missing person's name and Social Security number, the last time seen, your reason for wanting to contact him, and a history of your efforts to contact the person using other means. If you don't know the number, give the person's date and place of birth, his parents' names, and the name and address of the person's last known employer and period of employment.

More information: Social Security Administration, OCRO–Division of Certification and Coverage, 300 N. Green St., Baltimore 21201.

•Colleges and universities. Federal law allows schools to release certain information on current and former students, including address, phone number, major, date and place of birth, and dates of attendance. Schools unwilling to release this information may be willing to forward a letter.

Best contacts: The school library or its alumni association.

•Veterans Administration. Any regional VA office will forward a letter free of charge to a veteran at his last known address. If the person is deceased, the letter will be returned to you.

•Federal Aviation Administration. It will provide the address of any certified pilot, provided you can supply either the date of birth or Social Security number of the missing person. (No additional information required if the missing person has a unique name.)

More information: DOT-FAA Airmen Certification Branch, AVN-460, Box 25082, Oklahoma City 73125.

• Salvation Army. If the missing person is a member of your immediate family, the Salvation Army will conduct a search through its nationwide missing person network. *Fee:* $10.

More information: Contact your local Salvation Army office.

Source: Lt. Col. Richard S. Johnson, one of the nation's foremost authorities on locating missing persons, especially those with a connection to the US armed forces. Johnson, who served 28 years in the US Army, is the author of *How to Locate Anyone Who Is or Has Been in the Military*, MIE Publishing, Box 5143, Burlington, North Carolina 27216. 800-937-2133.

Healing and the Mind

Bill Moyers' ground-breaking PBS-TV series and book, *Healing and the Mind*, explored new findings about the mind-body relationship and how the medical community—from teaching hospitals to individual practitioners—is incorporating this knowledge into methods of healing. Moyers talks about what the series taught him, and what we all can learn from these methods...

How did the experience of researching Healing and the Mind *affect the way you view health and illness?*

First, it confirmed what folk wisdom has always told us. I remember my parents talking about Widow Brown down the street, who "died of a broken heart"—she'd never been sick a day in her life until her husband died. That was a folk way of saying that her emotions were involved somehow in her physical well-being.

Now science, too, is telling us that there is, in fact, a relationship between our emotions and our bodies—that emotions can have adverse or positive effects on our immune system, for example.

Second, it made me realize the importance of managing stress. I always intuitively be-

lieved that my headaches and back tension were connected to the deadline pressures related to my job. But this research confirmed what my own body was telling me: *You have got to find a better way to meet deadlines and handle stress. Tension mustn't become an anvil against which to pound your own well-being.*

Third, I discovered that caring is good medicine. The best physician isn't just an expert—he/she has to be a companion, a friend, a counselor. It isn't enough for the doctor to know what's wrong. The patient must also understand what's wrong. Of course, part of the trouble with modern American medicine is that it's economically time-driven, so that even when doctors know the technical essence of a disease, few take the time to help the patient understand it through sympathetic, consoling, and encouraging communication.

How can patients find doctors who express compassion as well as technical knowledge? People need to be more frank with doctors. They need to say, *"You and I aren't connecting"..."I don't understand"..."I need to know more."* If they don't find satisfaction through that kind of communication, they should seek another opinion. Your doctor may be terrifically well-informed, but if he/she is not caring, you may need another doctor.

You also have to work at informing yourself. Health is not something you can take for granted or that comes easily. Just as being a good citizen requires hard work, so does being a healthy person.

You say the physician needs to be a counselor and companion. What do you mean by this? In the West, we traditionally think of the body as a machine. If a part is out of order, you call the doctor, who lifts up the hood, locates the broken part, and adjusts or replaces it.

In traditional Chinese medicine, the doctor's role is to help you learn how to take care of yourself. Teaching the patient is as important in the long run as prescribing an herb or a drug.

In China, the physician is also thought of as a gardener. The human body is considered a garden where each species is connected to every other. The physician's task is to tend that garden the way you tend to roses—to cultivate and nourish. The physician should teach the patient to be a gardener, too, and help the patient understand how to summon the healing faculties of our own bodies for recovery.

How did working on this project change your own approach to health? I now practice a form of meditation every day, using the techniques Herbert Benson of Harvard Medical School described in *The Relaxation Response* or what Jon Kabat-Zinn wrote about in a book called *Full Catastrophe Living*. When I'm traveling, I meditate on the plane.

At the office, in the afternoon, I try to find a quiet place—the editing room is a good one—and concentrate on my breathing for 25 minutes. It's amazing to experience the recuperative and restorative powers of meditation on muscles that have grown tense and tired.

Also, though I've always walked a lot, I now try to build it into my schedule every day so that it's not ad hoc or serendipitous. I've learned that healthy practices like exercise, good nutrition, and meditation are not grand designs we have to follow. They can be built into our regular routines…if we just consider them as important as we do watching an hour of TV, reading the newspaper, or just fiddling around.

What were some of the most significant insights you gained while researching the series? One of the high points I experienced occurred in China, while we were filming a tai chi class taught by a grand master in his nineties. A group of 100 or so elderly Chinese comes every day for two hours of physical and mental instruction from this great teacher.

As I looked through the camera at this activity, I suddenly remembered an interview I saw many years ago with Charles de Gaulle, who was known for his fearlessness. The interviewer asked him, "Is there nothing you fear?" and de Gaulle replied, "There is one thing I fear—the shipwreck of old age."

I fear that, too—most of us do. But as I watched that marvelous rhythmic squadron of people—in their seventies, eighties, and nineties—moving in harmony with each other, I could see through the lens the sense of joy and peace and camaraderie they were feeling.

For the first time I realized that old age doesn't have to be a shipwreck. Certainly we can't avoid death or the ultimate effects of age. But we can make of old age something like what these people had.

I'm 59, and though I hopefully have many years of professional activity ahead, I know the day will come when I will be superfluous to society as a professional. But I don't have to be superfluous to life.

In a sense, *Healing and the Mind* is not about medicine but about an attitude toward living and caring for ourselves and for each other…and that is a philosophical quest, not just a scientific quest.

How do we begin to develop that attitude? One doesn't have to become a fanatic in order to reap the rewards of good health. People don't have to sacrifice the pleasure in their lives for it. But they may have to sacrifice some of the super-busyness of life in order to substitute a different kind of purpose for some of the frantic and wasteful activities that we all go through every day. We've let the increasing busyness of modern life crowd out the thoughtfulness that can make being busy more fruitful. We need to recover what Kabat-Zinn calls *mindfulness*.

People ask me, "Are you saying we should all practice Chinese medicine?" That's not what this is about. We don't have to give up the best of what Western medical science has to offer. But just as the Chinese physicians admire our form of medicine, we should also covet deeply their philosophical understanding of health—so as to have the best of a scientific and philosophic approach to what life is about.

Source: Bill Moyers, award-winning broadcast journalist, founder of the independent production company Public Affairs Television and author of numerous books, including *Healing and the Mind* (companion to the PBS-TV series), Doubleday, 666 Fifth Ave., New York 10103.

All About Selficide

Many people do not find satisfaction in today's world. They find life to be a flat, unreal experience. They cannot enjoy intimate relationships with others. They are not in touch with their own selves. I use the word *selficide* to describe this state of being unable to learn and grow from life's experiences.

As we age, we increasingly need to understand who we are and how to behave as responsible, caring adults. Important questions to ask yourself to see if you are on the right track...or on the road to *selficide*...

•Do you control your own behavior...or are your actions governed by a need to rebel or comply with other's rules? My patient Denise was anorexic. She ate sensibly—but whenever she reached a healthy weight, she stopped eating and lost weight again.

Her eating problem was the symptom of an internal struggle between her perception of the voice of her parents, which told her she must eat to be loved, and her desire to be herself.

She was able to solve her problem when, with encouragement, she disciplined herself not to control her eating habits. Instead she focused on doing something that she really *wanted* to do...*not* what she felt she *should* do.

•Are your thoughts, feelings and actions consistent with each other? We all know the old joke about the Boy Scout who took an hour to help an old lady across the street... because she didn't want to go. His behavior was inconsistent with his goal—to do good.

•Do you truly play a meaningful part in your own activities and dealings with others...or are you often just there physically? Some people are so involved in regret over the past that they can't think about what they should be doing now. Others are so busy daydreaming about the future that they aren't acting now to make their dreams possible.

•Do you willingly surrender yourself to reality...or do you begrudge it? Can you ever leave a discussion without having the last word?

•Are you able to give and take...or do you insist on only one direction? Do you feel like a martyr...and let everyone know it?

•Do you accept others as they are...or do you always feel the need to judge them?

•Do you act naturally, without pretension... or are you dishonest or phony?

•Do you take joy in your experiences...not just look at life as a series of tasks to accomplish?

Example: Ned, a patient of mine, wondered why his business was always outperformed by a small rival company, so he went to check on it. He noticed that the owner of the company was an exceedingly enthusiastic individual. When Ned asked him, "You really enjoy what you do, don't you?" he replied, "Yeah, it sure beats the hell out of working!"

•Do you have an inner aesthetic sense of morality that makes it seem repellent to you to do something wrong?

•Are you willing to take risks—to try something new to satisfy your real inner desires... or are you afraid of doing anything that people don't expect of you?

•Do you exercise your creativity—the willingness to dismiss old ways or experience to be free to grow in new directions...or are you afraid to lose the security provided by always repeating the same pattern—even when you find it to be unsatisfactory?

How to avoid selficide:

People who cannot give positive answers to any of the questions are well on their way to selficide. But selficide is not the same as suicide...life always contains the possibility of growth.

If you are willing to look into yourself as you confront the issues of everyday living and examine your inner feelings, you can find new responses that better satisfy your needs and those of the people close to you.

Those new responses will develop as you embrace new experiences and adopt less fearful ways of dealing with the world. That joyful approach is not really alien to anyone's nature, because it represents a return to the way everybody starts out life.

Babies explore the world fearlessly and joyfully...they accept bumps and falls as the price of growth. They learn to walk and talk at their own pace...nobody else can make it happen faster or slower. Before babies learn to walk, they crawl...but when they learn to walk they stop crawling.

As long as they are able to act naturally, children continue to learn and grow because they are *open to new experiences*...willing to *ack-*

nowledge their true feelings...able to *react in new ways*.

Many adults have forgotten those natural instincts.

As analyst Erich Fromm said, "We listen to every voice and to everybody but not ourselves. We are constantly exposed to the noise of opinions and ideas hammering at us from everywhere...motion pictures, newspapers, radio, idle chatter. If we had planned intentionally to prevent ourselves from ever listening to ourselves, we could have done no better."

But if we pause as we go about our daily activities and look carefully at the world around us...at the people we are with...and most of all deep into ourselves...we can find what we want from life and we can achieve it.

Source: Patrick Thomas Malone, MD, medical director of Mental Health Services at Northside Hospital in Atlanta, and a psychotherapist at the Atlanta Psychiatric Clinic. With his father, Thomas Patrick Malone, MD, PhD, he wrote *The Windows of Experience: Moving Beyond Recovery to Wholeness*, Simon & Schuster, 1230 Avenue of the Americas, New York 10020.

The Power Of Positive Relationships

People who build constructive relationships with their personal friends and family members gain important benefits...

- They are healthier.
- They live longer.
- They succeed in most of their activities.

A Duke University study of 1,300 patients who had suffered coronary attacks showed that those patients who were socially isolated ...unmarried, with no confidants...had a death rate three times as high as those with stronger social ties. *How positive relationships help...*

- Sociable people take better care of themselves. People who value their friendships with others are more likely to stop smoking...continue to take required medications...go to the doctor more often when they're ill. That's because even when they are tempted to let things slide, their friends get after them.

Example: In a support group for women with breast cancer observed by Dr. David Spiegel of Stanford University, when one woman mentioned new pains, the other women in the group convinced her to report it immediately to the doctor even though she was inclined to wait until her next appointment.

- Sociable people are physically healthier. Researchers have found that social ties have physiological effects that make people healthier. Sociable people feel less depressed... notice fewer aches and pains...have lower levels of stress-related hormones.

Psychologist James Pennebaker found that when people discussed stressful events with others, even with strangers, their blood pressure declined.

Building better relationships:

Obviously, it's in everyone's self-interest to build good relationships with others...and fortunately it's a skill that can be learned even if it doesn't come naturally.

If you want to form more positive relationships but have always found it difficult because of your personality, your best strategy is to begin by changing your behavior, not your attitudes. *Strategies that can help you improve your relationships...*

- Practice listening. At least once a day, when someone is talking to you, force yourself to let that person finish what he/she is saying. Even if you find it hard to pay attention, don't interrupt or disconnect...at least look attentive.

It may be difficult at first, but gradually you will learn that other people may have something worthwhile to say, you can learn something from them...and when you show them that you recognize that, you'll get through to them better, as well.

You will gradually come to appreciate where other people are coming from, become more tolerant, and find relationships with others easier to make and more enjoyable.

- Get involved with community affairs or volunteer work. If you don't already have satisfying personal relationships, one good way to make connections is to participate in community-service activities. Research studies have found that men who volunteered had greater longevity and reported better health than their non-volunteer counterparts.

Volunteering to help other individuals or groups is not only an excellent way to learn specific caring behaviors, it also enlarges your capacity for empathy with others and helps reduce your social isolation.

Helpful:

Seek out opportunities for about two hours a week of one-on-one helping…try to help strangers…look for problem areas where you can feel empathy with those you are helping…look for a supportive formal organization so you can feel part of a team…find a service that uses a skill you possess…and when you are volunteering, forget about the benefits you are giving or receiving—concentrate on enjoying the feeling of closeness with the person you're helping.

•Have a confidant. The best source of personal support is an intimate relationship with at least one person. A spouse or best friend with whom you share your inner life can help you carry out your duties…act as a sounding board to help you make important decisions…and comfort you when you are feeling down.

If you already have a confidant, cultivate the relationship to forge even closer ties. If you don't, try to find someone suitable.

•Get a pet. If you're initially uncomfortable with people…or live in socially isolated circumstances…positive relationships with animals can produce dramatic health benefits. A University of Maryland study of coronary patients showed that only 6% of the pet owners died within a year…compared with 28% of those without pets.

Source: Redford Williams, MD, director of behavioral research at Duke University. He is coauthor of *Anger Kills: Seventeen Strategies for Controlling the Hostility that Can Harm Your Health,* Times Books, 20 E. 50 St., New York 10022.

New and Healthier Way Of Looking at Life

Heart disease, cancer, AIDS, and other life-threatening illnesses bring pain and suffering, to be sure. But they can also serve as a "wake-up" call, bringing a new and healthier way of looking at life…of distinguishing that which truly matters in life from mere distractions.

Of course, it's best to learn these invaluable lessons before you're diagnosed with a life-threatening illness…

•Don't be afraid to show your vulnerabilities. Almost all of us were raised to be strong in the face of adversity, to put on a "brave front" no matter what. *Problem:* Acting one way when we're feeling another way saps our vitality, leaving us vulnerable to depression and illness and resentful of the world. We wind up with few friends and little support to help us through life's inevitable crises.

Better way: Admit your frailties. If you feel you need help, ask for it—and be willing to help others.

Exercise: Next time someone asks how you're doing, admit your true feelings. If you feel fine, say so. But if you feel lousy, admit it. Being honest might be hard at first, but it paves the way to honest, caring communication. That's essential for good health and happiness.

•Relinquish your need to be in control. As a young doctor, I thought the key to life was to get things done. My daily routine involved jotting down and then ticking off entries on "to-do" lists. When I failed to get everything done, I got nervous and frustrated.

As I grew older and got in closer touch with my feelings, I came to realize that life is inherently disorderly. Now I know that living well means forgetting about rigid schedules. It means learning to find happiness, fulfillment, and tranquility in the face of disorder.

Lesson: Stop trying to control all situations. Don't be a slave to your intellect. Make plans, but don't be upset by redirection. Something good may come of this redirection.

•Learn how to say "no." Our parents and teachers taught us that it's rude to say "no" to others. So when people ask for favors or tell us how to behave, we give in to their wishes.

Danger: Saying "yes" when you'd rather say "no" may be good manners, but it's destructive to our health. Doing so keeps us in unfulfilling jobs and makes us bitter. It leads us to do things we detest, and it distracts us from the things we cherish. We wind up resentful and possibly ill.

Better way: Stand up for yourself. If you don't want to mow the lawn, pursue a particular career, etc.—don't do it. I'm not asking you to be selfish or needlessly rude. I'm merely asking you to have enough self-esteem to stand up for yourself, to pursue life on your own terms, to realize that you can say "no" when someone asks you to change your plans.

• Confront your fears. People in crisis often seek peace of mind by burying or denying their fears. But real peace of mind comes only when we confront our fears head-on.

What to do: First, define exactly what it is you're afraid of. Don't say, "I'm afraid of dying." Be specific.

• Are you afraid of pain?

• Or what a medical treatment might do to you?

• Or that no one will take care of you?

Once you've pinned down your exact fear, find a metaphor for it. I tell patients to imagine their fear as a tiny baby crying in a crib. I tell them to pick up the baby, caress him/her, and see what happens. This exercise shows people that they're distinct from their fears and suggests that they, and not their fears, are in control. Learning to control fear is very reassuring.

• Live in the moment. If you spend all your time ruing the past or fearing the future, you'll have a hard time deriving any pleasure from the present. To fight this tendency, remind yourself that death could come at any moment. Don't let that thought frighten you. Just try to assimilate it into your psyche. Once you do, you'll be freer to enjoy a blue sky or a poem or the presence of a loved one. *Ultimate goal:* To approach life with a childlike sense of awe and wonder.

• Identify your true feelings. Ask a child what he wants to do, and you'll get 40 answers.

Ask an adult, and the response will likely be, "I don't know." What do you want to do? Adults have a hard time knowing what to do—for an afternoon or a lifetime—because they're so out of touch with their feelings that they've lost track of what really matters to them.

People without emotions live almost like automatons. Helen Keller used to ask, "If you had three days to see, what would you choose to see in those days? Your answer to this ques-

tion will teach you about what you truly love in your life."

• Define pain and suffering in positive terms. When I ask my lecture audiences if they think life is fair, they usually answer with a resounding, "No!" But I believe that life is fair. All of us experience difficulties, problems, pain, and losses. But while some people give in to self-pity, others retain their vitality and optimism—even in the face of terminal illness.

Lesson: We should not only avoid suffering, we should respond to it in a constructive manner.

Strategy: Redefine whatever pain you're feeling as labor pains. Just as the anticipation and joy of bringing a new baby into the world can help to ease a mother's suffering during childbirth, other types of pain will seem less awful if you view them as integral to the process of birth you're undergoing.

Examples: The pain of chemotherapy leads to the birth of a person who is cancer-free... the pain of divorce leads to the birth of a happy single person.

• Refuse to be a victim. To some extent, we're all prisoners. Some of us are prisoners in the literal sense. Others, suffering from some debilitating ailment, are prisoners of our own bodies. Still others are imprisoned by emotional scars from a difficult childhood or a violent crime. No matter what form your prison takes, you don't have to feel or behave like a victim.

Example: Franklin Roosevelt could have pitied himself after polio left him wheelchair-bound. Instead, he became president of the United States.

Bottom line: No matter what befalls you, retain the ability to choose what sort of life to lead.

Source: Bernard S. Siegel, MD, a noted lecturer on healing and the founder of Exceptional Cancer Patients (ECaP), a nonprofit support group for people with cancer, AIDS, or other life-threatening illnesses. A retired surgeon formerly on the staff of Yale University School of Medicine, Dr. Siegel is the author of three books, including the just-published *How to Live Between Office Visits: A Guide to Life, Love, and Health,* HarperCollins, 10 E. 53 St., New York 10022.

All About Civility

The great lack of civility in America is the major factor behind the breakdown in family life, unethical practices in business, selfishness, and dishonesty in politics.

Civility means much more than politeness. Civility is all-embracing—a general awareness by people that personal well-being cannot be separated from the well-being of the groups to which we belong...our families, our businesses, and our nation.

Lack of civility is tied to unreasonable expectations in recent decades of constant happiness and constant comfort. When real life presents us with painful experiences... when something hurts us...when we feel unfulfilled —we feel cheated. And too many of us—too often—reach for instant happiness by illegitimate means that disregard the interests of other people.

Consciousness and civility:

The route to improved civility begins with greater awareness of our shortcomings and our tendencies to manipulate others.

Greater awareness leads to a willingness to accept pain in the short term, recognizing that it is an unavoidable part of any growth process, leading to significant personal growth. Learning how to handle pain realistically is a prerequisite for warmer, more meaningful relationships over the long term. Civility does not happen automatically. You have to train yourself to be aware of your true motives, to be honest with yourself and others, and to judge yourself first.

Civility in the family:

The first training ground for civility is the family. Children learn how they are expected to behave by observing their parents' behavior, not just by listening to their words. So if you want your children to demonstrate civility now and later in life, you have to practice it yourself.

Example: Your two kids are having a disagreement and your six-year-old son slugs his little sister. Then you tell him, "Don't ever hit your sister!" and hit him.

That will deliver quite a different message than you want to give: "It's OK to hit someone else...but don't hit your sister when your mother or father is around."

With that kind of discrepancy prevalent between parental educational words and actions, it's not surprising that so many people grow up with an internal moral code that tells them, "You can do whatever you want as long as you don't get caught doing it."

Civility in business:

Successful businesses are built on cooperation. Businesses have a right to both demand and expect cooperation from their employees, because the main purpose of any business is to make a profit. But companies also have a responsibility to treat their workers fairly and honestly in the process.

Example: Some companies that vest workers with pension benefits only after a long period of employment save money by laying the workers off only a short time before they become vested.

This is uncivil. It is obviously unfair to the workers and may also hurt the company by encouraging the best employees to leave.

Better way: Set up a system that recognizes both the company's interest in dedicated, hardworking employees and the employees' interest in security and fair compensation. This will only work when both sides honestly keep their parts of the bargain.

Honest communication:

Companies, families, and all types of organizations become more civil when they encourage honest, two-way communication—straight talk and listening. That is not easy, but it can be done if you follow these principles:

• Don't expect perfection...just do your best and learn from your mistakes.

• Set aside time for communication.

• Clear your mind and listen to the other person.

• Be honest...with yourself and others.

• Judge yourself first. Look into your real motives.

• Take time to respond and think. Don't be afraid of silence.

• Be willing to be hurt—and to risk hurting others by speaking honestly. If someone is too fragile to respect your point of view, he/she cannot be a part of your community.

•Try to be as gentle as possible. Don't make any unnecessarily painful statements... yet don't be so subtle that the point is completely missed.

•Speak personally and specifically. Don't talk about "the system" or some impersonal authority. Don't generalize. Document what you say.

•Don't analyze other people's motives. Don't play psychologist.

•Speak when you are moved to speak. Don't cop out.

Bottom line: It takes hard work to get an organization to operate in a mode of civility. But those who have made the transition do not want to go back.

Source: M. Scott Peck, MD, a founder of the Foundation for Community Encouragement. He is author of *The Road Less Traveled* and, most recently, *A World Waiting to be Born*, Bantam Books, 1540 Broadway, New York 10036.

What Ever Happened To Loyalty

Loyalty is out of fashion these days. People would sooner switch than fight...not only in the marketplace, where customers rapidly switch to suppliers who offer better deals...but also in their personal, social, and political lives.

As soon as they think they might do better elsewhere, baseball players change teams... professors leave their colleges...voters desert their parties...husbands abandon their wives, and vice versa.

Rather than trying to build better relationships where they are, people abandon their old associations and enter into new ones... which are likely to be temporary, too.

What happened to loyalty?

The breakdown of loyalty is not only a result of selfishness—it also has ideological roots.

For the past 200 years, giants of philosophy, particularly Immanuel Kant and Jeremy Bentham, have argued that people should not make decisions based on what is best for themselves but instead based on an imper-

sonal calculation of what would be best for the entire society.

These ideas have had a powerful effect on the way many educated people think, but they certainly have not produced a society in which people act better...or even feel better. That is because the world is too complicated for people—even philosophers—to figure out what is best for humanity at large.

Result: Many people reject the old-fashioned belief that we owe loyalty to those who are close to us and helped to make us what we are. They also do not believe we owe loyalty to the nation whose benefits we enjoy. In the short run, this disregard of loyalty hurts some people. In the long run, this attitude hurts everyone.

Advantages of loyalty:

Loyalty in marriage, family life, social interactions, and politics strengthens bonds between people. It assumes that the relationships we are born into—or choose voluntarily— should continue. It encourages us to accept the other party's good faith and so includes a willingness to accept mistakes.

Under these conditions, with time to correct mistakes and a healthy degree of flexibility, relationships can become stronger. Each partner is willing to allow the other to change previous patterns of behavior without fear of immediate abandonment, so each can help the other to grow.

A one-sided, individualistic approach to life may work as long as things are going well, but it is likely to fail when problems arise. Loyalty builds strong, long-lasting mutual relationships that can help overcome temporary setbacks...it leaves both sides better off in the long term.

Loyalty in families:

Successful families are built on a web of loyalty between father, mother, and children. Today's emphasis on personal happiness over loyalty to others is a major cause of family breakdown.

The same emphasis on self that leads to divorce also corrodes the relationship between parents and children.

Example: A huge number of divorced fathers who have remarried simply abandon the children from their first marriage...therefore, a new generation fails to learn how to practice loyalty and enjoy the satisfaction it provides.

How to build loyalty:

Loyalty stands us in good stead when times are tough...but it should be established when things are still going well. *Five steps to loyalty:*

•Affirmation. Think about the good things others are doing for you. Show them how much you appreciate them...in both word and deed.

•Confrontation. Show that the relationship is important to you by pointing out how it can be improved. When you disapprove of your partner's behavior, don't be afraid to say so... but always constructively.

•Complicity. I use this term, which is translated from the French, to mean the sense that you and your partner(s) are separate from the rest of the world. You possess something nobody else has. Feel very happy about it.

•Ritual. Find ways to do things for the special people in your circle.

Example: When loved ones are coming to visit, meet them at the airport.

•Privacy. Keep the details of your shared relationship away from outsiders. How you make decisions is nobody else's business. Never complain to outsiders about your partner.

The tendency today is to think of intimate relationships in political terms. Both men and women are excessively concerned about whether their private conduct meets the standards of behavior set by their friends. Traditional men are concerned about whether they look like they are "wearing the pants in the family." Liberated women worry about whether their sisters would approve of their cooking and washing dishes. This manner of looking over one's shoulder reflects a conflict of loyalties. Loyalty to one's spouse comes into tension with loyalties to those outside the relationship. This conflict undermines trust and destroys intimacy.

Conclusion: Be loyal to your spouse and forget how your private way of doing things may look to outsiders.

The toughest challenge of personal loyalty is to stand by another when the going gets tough. Loyalty becomes important only when we are tempted to "jump ship." Fair-weather loyalty is but convenience. The next time you are tempted to leave, think, "This is the time to show my loyalty."

Source: George P. Fletcher, Beekman Professor of Law at Columbia University and author of *Loyalty: An Essay on the Morality of Relationships,* Oxford University Press, 200 Madison Ave., New York 10016. 800-451-7556.

Secrets Of Appreciating Life

Despite the ever-growing amount of information we have about human nature, the soul is still impossible to define in pragmatic terms and still remains an enigma.

Unlike the brain, the soul has no physical or material reality. Yet it governs our values, relatedness, and personal substance. Lose touch with your soul and the effects can be debilitating...even devastating.

For example, many people who are in perfect physical health and have attained wealth and fame feel a deep sense of unease when they neglect their souls.

Not knowing how to care for your soul leaves you at a serious disadvantage, since painful experiences are unavoidable. Confronting them and learning from them are the ways to nurture the soul.

Most of us recognize that some of the more simple aspects of life are particularly satisfying. That is why we refer to them as "food for the soul" and "music that is good for the soul."

But every aspect of life—family, love, work...even dark aspects like jealousy, depression, and illness—can provide spiritual food for the soul if we approach them in a receptive way.

Family and the soul:

Many people today who regard themselves as self-sufficient have lost the important truth, which was taught by traditional societies, that we must honor our families.

Honoring the family helps the soul because the family is a source of religious awareness.

A family forces you to realize that you did not create yourself...that you have a unique place in the world. Within your family, you can be who you really are and learn to appreciate the individuality of others.

To help family appreciation: Don't expect too much from your family. Try to appreciate each member's unique qualities. If you are miserable and feel it's because of the way you were treated by your family when you were young, try a different perspective. Ask yourself, "Where did my good qualities come from?" It's highly likely that your family had a great deal to do with them.

Love and the soul:

Many people have unrealistic expectations of love—within the family, with spouses, with friends. Love isn't perfect and eternal. It passes through different stages...and often ends.

To satisfy your soul, a loving relationship must honor the other person's soul as well. That means recognizing who the other person really is...and allowing that person to change. You must pay attention and allow the relationship to develop.

For soul-satisfying relationships: Spend time together...write letters to each other... visit friends together. When you talk to each other, don't just talk about work—talk about what's in your heart.

Work and the soul:

Work is a major part of life. Few things satisfy the soul more than a fulfilling vocation. But if the work you do conflicts with your soul—because of your sense of ethics or aesthetics—it may make you very unhappy, no matter how much you earn.

If you are in that position, look into a career change. If a change isn't immediately feasible, don't despair. Look around...for years, if necessary. And meanwhile, even though you are unhappy in your current work situation, practice other ways to care for your soul.

To help your soul if you are unhappy at work: First, acknowledge your situation. Then, make the best of it by putting more effort into areas that do satisfy your soul...family, friendships, hobbies, sports, travel, etc.

Soul and the darker side of life:

Anyone who thinks that life's only goal is happiness will be troubled. The less-pleasant parts of life cannot be avoided.

If you reflect on your unhappy experiences, you will find that they offer their own gifts... and contribute to the development of your soul. *These experiences include...*

•Jealousy, which comes with intense relationships. It teaches that relationships are demanding...and deepens your understanding of both the self and the relationship.

•Depression, which deepens the personality, leaving you better able to cope with future problems. People who have only seen the sunny side of life may be overwhelmed when something bad happens...those who have gone through depression look at the world in a more realistic, accepting way.

•Illness, which forces you to reflect on your own mortality and teaches that you are not as strong or as independent as you thought.

To benefit from troubles: When you suffer physical, social or economic setbacks, see what you can learn from the experiences. Acknowledge your human frailties...don't be afraid to ask others for help. You will gain a richer perspective on friendship and the meaning of life.

The art of life:

Modern society pursues functionality and efficiency at all costs, but the human soul craves beauty. Much of the unhappiness in today's world comes from a neglect of the beauty of life in favor of acquiring things and getting results quickly.

Since schools don't often teach the arts, your soul is starved of the imaginative diet it needs. You can make up this deficiency by striving to bring beauty into your life.

To feed your soul in everyday life: Even if you don't consider yourself artistic, you can use your imagination to enrich the way you live.

When you decorate your home, for example, don't settle for someone else's taste... even if it's advice from a high-priced interior decorator. Your home should express your feelings and imagination. Think about the location, the furnishings, and the decorations, so they satisfy you emotionally and express your soul's individuality.

By living in a way that cares for your soul faithfully every day, you can let your individual genius emerge and discover in full measure who you really are.

Source: Psychotherapist Thomas Moore, PhD, a former monk with academic degrees in theology, music, and philosophy, and author of the best-seller *Care of the Soul: A Guide for Cultivating Depth and Sacredness in Everyday Life,* HarperCollins, 10 E. 53 St., New York 10022.

Top 10 Etiquette Points For Adults

•Return calls and answer letters promptly. Calls should be returned within 48 hours and letters within two weeks. If you cannot respond yourself within that time, have someone else do it for you.

Telephone etiquette: When you call someone and your call-waiting signals, ignore it. You made the call, so you should give it priority. Be respectful of a person's schedule and obligations when choosing a time to call.

•RSVP within one week to all invitations. Go to an event when you have accepted...call ahead if you can't make it. If you accept an invitation and then fail to attend, call or write to apologize.

•Introduce people properly and in a flattering way. State the person's name clearly and correctly, as well as his/her title, occupation, and city of residence if somewhere other than where you are. Also give their hobbies or interests, especially when they are similar to those of the person to whom you're making the introduction. And always introduce the less important or younger person to the more important or older.

•Take care to use people's titles properly. Doctors, judges, people of military rank, and elected officials should always be addressed with their titles or "the honorable." Too few of us are doing this today, and it's very bad manners.

•Be sensitive to the culture, religious laws, and diet of international friends and colleagues. Brief yourself on their country before you see them. Know their country's leading politicians, the names of their country's great museums, their universities, and what types of foods they can and cannot eat.

•Watch your table manners. This can never be stressed enough. Don't stuff food in your mouth or talk while eating. Do not leave your dirty napkin on the table when you excuse yourself during a meal. Leave it on your chair instead. Wipe your mouth frequently. When finished, move your fork and knife to the right-hand rim of the plate—and sit up straight. Ignoring these things makes you appear rather uncouth.

•Don't monopolize the guest of honor. Give equal time to every guest, regardless of how important or unimportant his/her position. This is an act of kindness as well as good manners.

•Teach your children to respect their elders. Have them stand up when your friends enter the room...say, "How do you do?"...and shake hands. Parents seem to be failing in this, perhaps because they are not around their children as much these days. But making the effort will make your children's lives much easier as adults.

•Know how and when to apologize. Always make your apology as soon as possible after the event. Some acts require only a spoken apology, others require a spoken and written apology...and some require much more.

Example: About 10 years ago, I accepted an invitation to be the guest of honor at a dinner party, and then completely forgot about it. I called several times to apologize, wrote two letters of apology, and finally sent a dozen roses. To this day, I am still apologizing for that incident.

•Write thank-you notes for gifts, favors, meals, or any act of kindness. Also write notes to encourage, congratulate, and commiserate.

Source: Letitia Baldrige, renowned expert on manners and author of 14 books, including the new *Letitia Baldrige's New Complete Guide to Executive Manners,* Rawson Associates, 866 Third Ave., New York 10022. The book draws upon her experiences in the business world, diplomatic life, and the Kennedy White House.

How to Complain... Successfully

Complaining is a normal part of human life, especially among people who live together.

Without complaining, our resentments fester into permanent barriers to communication. But even though they are essential, complaints have two strikes against them...

• They convey that there is something wrong with the other person's behavior, which no one likes to hear.

• They contain a command or a request—which is an indirect command—that the other person's behavior be changed.

Most adults have knee-jerk negative reactions to commands from other adults. *Result:* Rather than considering the content of the complaint, they respond with denials, defensiveness, and counteraccusations.

To complain more effectively, it's important to define the goal of your complaint. If you're simply venting your anger, it doesn't matter what you say. But if you want the other person to change his/her behavior, you should use a different technique.

The three-part message:

I use a verbal tool for complaining that works so well it seems almost magical. I call it the "three-part message": When you X...I feel Y... because Z.

The point of the three-part message is to avoid triggering the listener's resentment. It succeeds by targeting a specific, verifiable behavior and then linking that behavior to the speaker's feelings and a real-world consequence.

Example I: "When you forget to water the tomato plants, I feel angry, because the plants die."

Example II: "When you overdraw our checking account, I feel embarrassed, because our checks bounce."

Example III: "When you bring the car home with no gas, I feel anxious, because I might run out on the way to work the next morning."

The three-part message works only when you absolutely stick to the pattern. *Ground rules...*

• Part One/When you X: Cite one—and only one—specific behavior, which must be verifiable and beyond dispute. *Useful:* "When you yell at the children...." *Not useful:* "When you act like some tyrant...."

• Part Two/I feel Y: The emotion should be stated simply and without any exaggeration. *Useful:* "I feel distressed...." *Not useful:* "I feel like a second-class citizen...."

Pitfall: Drawing conclusions about your partner's feelings. *Not useful:* "I feel as if you don't respect me...."

• Part Three/because Z: Complainers must prove their right to complain...by describing a nondebatable consequence that reasonable people would want to avoid. *Useful:* "When you leave all the lights on, I feel frustrated, because our utility bills get so high." *Not useful:* "...because it means you don't care about how hard I work for my money."

The three-part message is not suited for intimate or complex issues. But if you use this to-the-point tool for your everyday problems, your partner may become more receptive to longer discussions as the need arises.

Source: Suzette Haden Elgin, PhD, founder of the Ozark Center for Language Studies in Forum, Arkansas (501-559-2273). She is the author of 23 books. Her latest book is *Genderspeak: Men, Women, and the Gentle Art of Verbal Self-Defense,* John Wiley & Sons, 605 Third Ave., New York 10158.

The Great Alan Lakein On Time Management... 20 Years Later

Those who achieve the most in this world are not those with the highest IQs...the greatest natural skills...the hardest workers...but those who make the best use of their time.

The search for better ways to use your time every day is not a recent phenomenon. Americans were grappling with the same issue back in 1973, when Alan Lakein, a leading expert on personal time management, wrote *How to Get Control of Your Time and Your Life.* This book is still a rich resource when you're looking for ways to create more time and make better use of the time you have...when you want help in deciding what you really want to do and making time for it. His advice today...
Time planning:

The key to using your time wisely has not changed during the past 20 years—learn how to improve your efficiency and effectiveness.

Doing things as quickly as possible—mechanical efficiency—is certainly valuable. Choosing the best task to do—and doing it the right way—that's effectiveness.

Since I wrote my book, technology has helped us boost our efficiency, but I haven't noticed a comparable improvement in effectiveness.

The mechanics of time planning have improved, thanks to a proliferation of planning books and forms that are now available from every office-supply house.

Using these aids and, more recently, computer scheduling software, we are able to account for nearly every free minute and coordinate our schedules with those of other people so that mutually acceptable meetings can be arranged.

We have become more efficient at using our time…but not necessarily more effective at doing the right thing. That depends on how you set priorities.

Setting priorities:

Setting priorities requires determination and clear thinking. To do it right, you need to make firm decisions about what you want to achieve in your lifetime as well as during the next few years, months, days…and, ultimately, right now.

As I explain in my book, only when you have a firm grasp on your priorities can you classify the tasks facing you as As, Bs and Cs. Then you have to discipline yourself to tackle the most important first—the As…and only after they are accomplished should you turn to the Bs and the Cs.

Setting priorities is more critical and more difficult than ever. In today's harried environment, you probably don't even have enough time to complete all your As.

Time management and groups:

Back in 1973, I emphasized the importance of setting your own individual priorities…making private time for yourself…avoiding pointless meetings, etc. Your personal needs are still important, but if I were writing the book for today's more complex world, I would pay more attention to the importance of teamwork.

Today, businesses—and families—realize that success depends on groups working together. The watchwords of current management philosophy are total quality management and reengineering continuous improvement. These concepts can be implemented only by group commitment to common goals and priorities.

The whole group will be able to follow priorities successfully—and the priorities will be realistic—only if they are set in a way that allows and encourages every member to participate.

That same principle is necessary to make everyone agree on the priorities shared by the whole group and the individual members.

Complexity and time pressure:

Everywhere we turn today, growing complexity is increasing the pressure on our time. Businesses are faced with new complexities… increased competition…workforce diversity. Working husbands and wives must juggle their work, homes, and families.

How can you choose priorities when you are faced with so many alternatives and they all seem to be As?

There is no simple solution. You just have to work at it. Think it through from all sides…listen to different opinions…and make a decision.

Example: You are a successful advertising copywriter who has always dreamed of writing a book. Thanks to your spouse's income, you might be able to take off some time to work on it…but your spouse wants to start working part-time in order to spend more time at home with your young child.

The only way you can arrive at a reasonable set of priorities is to discuss all sides of the question…how the decision will affect you, your spouse, and your child…and your respective employers.

Important aspects: What is most important to each of the parties…economic well-being, personal fulfillment, parental attention? How is the situation likely to change in a year or two…or five or 10?

You are likely to come up with the best solution if everyone gives it his best try. While you are unlikely to come up with a completely consistent and mutually satisfactory set of priorities right away, don't be afraid to try out whatever seems reasonable.

If it doesn't work, you can try something else. With your hard-earned knowledge of what didn't work for you—and some thinking about why it didn't work—your next approach should do better.

Bottom line:

Setting priorities with others is more important today than ever. Investing time and effort on common As today is the key to saving time further down the road.

Source: Alan Lakein, author of the classic time-management book, *How to Get Control of Your Time and Your Life*—more than 3,000,000 copies sold. Signet, 375 Hudson St., New York 10014.

Since Almost Everything in Life Is a Negotiation

Too often we walk into a negotiation unprepared—and consequently uncertain. Whether we are going to be talking about a raise, a job, a house, the rent, summer plans, or where the kids go to school, it's unrealistic to expect to get everything we want.

That's because each person involved in a negotiation has different interests. Being well-prepared will help you understand the different interests. There is always the prospect that each side would do better by working out an agreement. The basic question is how to pursue that possibility—as a form of warfare or as joint problem solving.

Traditional haggling, in which each side argues a position and either makes concessions to reach a compromise or refuses to budge, is not the most efficient and amicable way to reach a wise agreement.

Better: Principled negotiation, or negotiation based on the merits of what's at stake, which is a straightforward negotiation method that can be used under almost any circumstances.

Checklist for principled negotiations:

Separate the people from the substantive problem. Think of preserving the relationship.

Attack the problem, not the person. If the other side attacks you, as often happens, call him/her on it and ask him to return to the problem.

Focus on interests, not positions. Negotiating positions often obscure what people really want. Try to determine the true interests on both sides—usually you can find some common ground.

Generate a range of options before deciding upon one. Having a lot at stake inhibits creativity. Do not try to determine a single, correct solution. Instead, think of a wide range of possibilities that could please both sides. Look for a solution that benefits everybody.

Insist on using some legitimate standard of fairness. By choosing some objective standard—market value, the going rate, expert opinion, precedent, what a court would decide—neither party loses face by conceding. He is merely deferring to relevant standards. Never yield to pressure, only to principle.

Develop your best alternative to a negotiated agreement. If you haven't thought through what you will do if you fail to reach an agreement, you are negotiating with your eyes closed. You may be too optimistic about your other options—other houses for sale, buyers for your used car, plumbers, jobs, etc.

The reality is that if you fail to reach an agreement, you will probably have to choose just one option.

An even greater danger lies in being too anxious to reach an agreement because you haven't considered your other options. It may be better to walk away.

Consider what kind of commitment you want. It's a mistake to think that every meeting has to result in a final decision. It's much smarter to view a meeting as an exploratory session. You can draw out what interests motivate the other side and draft promises without nailing anything down. This gives you a chance to sleep on the alternatives or consult others. If the other side comes back with new demands, you have the right to renegotiate as well.

Communicate. Without communication, there is no negotiation. But whatever you say, expect the other side to hear something different.

Solutions: Listen actively, paying close attention and occasionally interrupting to make sure you understand what is meant. Ask that ideas be repeated if there is any ambiguity or uncertainty. It's very important to understand perceptions, needs, and negotiating constraints.

Understanding is not agreeing. You can understand the other side's position—and still disagree with it. But the better you understand the other side's position, the more persuasively you can refute it.

Negotiating strategies:

•Marital roles. Learn to disagree without being disagreeable. You can disapprove of someone's behavior but still love that person. Discuss problems in a caring way. Make a joint list of issues that need to be addressed. Be firm but reasonable. Don't try to decide right away …mull things over for a few days.

•Requesting a raise. As with all negotiations, prepare beforehand. Find out what others at your level are earning, both inside and outside your company. Be ready to explain why you deserve more—you've been coming in every Saturday to help with the workload…you've been training newcomers…you're dealing with the company's toughest customers…or you've been offered more elsewhere. Your boss needs a rationale that he can use with his boss or other employees who also want raises.

•Buying a house. Often, by exploring various options and payment schedules, an agreement can be reached that provides maximum tax advantage and financial satisfaction for both the buyer and the seller.

Example: If you want to move in before the current owners want to move out, you might allow them to store their furniture in the garage. Flexibility might be enough to make your offer more acceptable than a higher one from someone else.

•Divorce negotiation. Suppose you are a wife who doesn't trust your husband to make his agreed child-support payments. Fearing that you will have to keep going back to court to get payment, you ask your lawyer to negotiate for equity in the house instead. Your husband's lawyer says that's ridiculous. He's certain that your husband will meet his obligations. "OK," says your lawyer, "then the husband won't object to signing a contingent agreement—if he misses two payments for any reason, his ex-wife will automatically get the equity in the house and he will be off the hook for future child-support payments."

•Resisting early retirement. Your company is having financial difficulties and has to lay off thousands of people. Early retirement packages are being offered, but you really can't afford to retire yet. Instead, see what you can negotiate—offer to take part of your pay in promissory notes…if you don't need the medical coverage, offer to give it up…if health benefits kick in at 20 hours per week, offer to work only 19 hours…become a freelance contract worker.

If you can dodge the bullet for six months or a year, the company may be on track again.

Source: Roger Fisher, director of The Harvard Negotiation Project and Williston Professor of Law Emeritus, Harvard Law School, 1563 Massachusetts Ave., Cambridge 02138. He is coauthor of *Getting to Yes,* Viking Penguin, 375 Hudson St., New York 10014.

For Those Who Simply Can't Stop Smoking

Given the evidence for the ill effects of cigarette smoking on health and appearance, and a social climate that all but ostracizes smokers, it is difficult for nonsmokers to understand why anyone continues to smoke.

But cigarettes still have a stranglehold on about 46 million Americans, many of whom think they cannot quit or have no desire to try.

For many smokers, tobacco is more than a pleasure and more than a drug addiction. It is an antidepressant that helps people concentrate, remember, and think more quickly, and for such immediate benefits they are willing to put their health, even their lives, on the line.

Should society simply give up on die-hard smokers or should they be advised on how they might at least partly protect their health from the daily ravages of nicotine, tars, carbon monoxide, and other noxious gases?

And what about the nonsmokers who are endangered by involuntary exposure to the toxic substances in tobacco smoke at home, at work, and now increasingly in the street? Short of wearing a gas mask all day, can they reduce the now well-established risks of passive smoking?

Clearly, there is no substitute for quitting smoking and banishing it from the air Americans breathe. But as evidence continues to accumulate for the protective value of a nutrient-rich diet and regular exercise, there is reason to believe that active and passive smokers can to some degree counter the ill effects of tobacco.

Although it may be questionable whether smokers willing to risk their health on tobacco would bother to pursue other habits that foster good health, they and especially those exposed to other people's smoke should at least know how to reduce their risks.

Protective nutrients:

Much of the harm caused by tobacco smoke can be traced to what biochemists call *oxidative damage*—an attack by highly reactive oxygen on cell membranes, serum cholesterol, and chemicals that can be converted into carcinogens, among other materials, in the body.

To counter such damage, recent studies strongly suggest, the diet should be rich in a group of nutrients known as *antioxidants.* These can help prevent, for example, the conversion of serum cholesterol to a form that readily attaches to coronary arteries and can fortify cells against cancer-causing assaults.

The major dietary antioxidants are vitamins C and E, beta-carotene and other carotenoids and, to some extent, the trace element selenium. Vitamin C and beta-carotene (a "previtamin" that the body converts to vitamin A) are prominent in many fruits and vegetables.

Smoking seriously depletes the body's supply of vitamin C. Good dietary sources of vitamin C include broccoli, turnip greens, citrus fruits and juices, tomatoes, strawberries, melon, green peppers, and potatoes (especially in fall and winter). Smokers might also consider a daily supplement of up to 500 milligrams of vitamin C as an addition to, not a replacement for, vitamin-rich foods.

Beta-carotene is also readily available in many ordinary foods, including dark-green leafy vegetables, such as broccoli and spinach, and many deep yellow and orange vegetables and fruits

like carrots, sweet potatoes, cantaloupe, and mangos. Again, a daily 25-milligram supplement may give added protection, according to a continuing study of thousands of doctors.

Selenium, a trace element, is needed in only tiny amounts. An excess much beyond 150 micrograms a day can be toxic. It is found in seafood, whole grains, pasta, garlic, and milk.

Selenium works hand in glove with vitamin E, whose antioxidant properties have been well documented both in laboratory animals and in people. But vitamin E is hard to come by in an otherwise wholesome diet, for it is most prominent in vegetable oils and margarine, which should be cautiously consumed in a low-fat diet. Other sources include wheat germ and, to a lesser extent, whole-grain breads and cereals, liver, dried beans, and green leafy vegetables.

To raise vitamin E intake to effective antioxidant levels, a daily supplement is necessary. Accordingly, many experts now recommend a capsule of 400 International Units once or twice a day for everyone—and especially for those who smoke.

Fish, especially species like mackerel, salmon, bluefish, and sardines, that are rich in omega-3 fatty acids, are another good source of protective nutrients.

Diets rich in omega-3 fatty acids are associated with a low risk of developing coronary heart disease and suffering heart attacks. Other sources of these protective oils are flaxseed and purslane, which are hardly commonplace in American diets. Ordinary people are now being advised to eat fish at least twice a week. For smokers, double that amount might be wiser.

Other foods that should be prominent in a diet intended to ward off heart disease and cancer are garlic and onions, fiber-rich whole (unrefined) grains and whole-grain breads and cereals, and cabbage-family vegetables like broccoli, cauliflower, Brussels sprouts, kale, bok choy, watercress, mustard greens, and all manner of cabbages.

In addition, calcium-rich foods like nonfat and low-fat dairy products, collard greens, and canned sardines and salmon with the bones may be important to counter the raised risk of osteoporosis among smokers.

Most important of all is to stick to a low-fat diet, since dietary fat seems to encourage the growth of cancer and development of coronary heart disease.

Exercise:

The cardiovascular benefits of regular aerobic exercise like brisk walking, cycling, and swimming laps are well-known, but few people are aware of the role that exercise seems to play in preventing cancer. Indeed, according to a study of more than 13,000 men and women, when compared with the fittest individuals, those who were least fit had cancer death rates that were four times as great among men and 16 times as great among women. Various studies have indicated that physically active people are less likely than sedentary people to develop cancers of the colon, breast, and prostate.

Exercise also helps to maintain strong bones and may even increase the mineral content of bones. And its antidepressant—some would say euphoric—effects may even help smokers cut back on cigarettes for the emotional lift many smokers seem to need.

Smoking damages the collagen in skin and can result in heavy facial wrinkling in midlife. To keep from wrinkling further, avoid unnecessary exposure to the sun and always use a good sunscreen, with a sun protection factor of 15 or higher.

Source: *The New York Times.* Reprinted by permission.

How to Tell When Someone Is Lying

Detecting a lie isn't easy...even for experienced law-enforcement professionals. They spend many hours studying videotapes to understand the psychology of liars as well as the physical and emotional signs that give them away.

My research, however, has uncovered a variety of telltale clues that often can help you determine when someone is trying to deceive you.

What is a lie?

It's important to remember that not every untrue statement is necessarily a lie. Some are innocent mistakes, some are attempts to be polite...and some are purposeful and to be expected.

Example: At a magic show, the audience knows the magician is trying to fool them. The magician knows that they know it, so his/her untrue statements are not lies.

When I use the word "lie," I mean a deliberate attempt to mislead someone without making that person aware of it. Lies are also usually at the other person's expense. They may be outright false statements...or a concealment of something the liar is obligated to tell.

Example: A job applicant who omits information that he is required to disclose, such as a previous job.

Why we believe lies:

Sometimes people deliberately overlook obvious lies because they want to believe what they're being told. This is especially true when the misinformation confirms the listener's way of doing things.

Straining to accept a lie may be a short-term way to avoid admitting that you have been fooled, but you may not be able to avoid the truth in the long term. So it is important to know when you're being told a lie—and how to overcome the psychological factors that cause you to accept the misinformation.

How to spot a liar:

A person who is lying is likely to give himself away through a variety of clues related to one or more of the emotional effects that lying produces.

• Fear of being caught. A liar who is afraid of being caught may signal that fear verbally and/or physically. Watch out for words that are evasive, indirect and halting—and a voice that is strained and/or higher pitched than normal.

These signs are not definite proof of lying. They are best when you can compare the "suspicious" indicator with what is normal behavior for the suspected liar.

• Unconscious gestures. Psychologists recognize three kinds of gestures that change in different ways when someone is nervous...as a liar often is. But detecting them is not easy. I have found that it takes at least eight solid hours of training exercises with videotapes for the average person to acquire the necessary sensitivity. The basic clues...

•Emblems. These are deliberate gestures whose meanings everyone understands, such as shrugging your shoulders to show you don't know. Someone telling a lie may give it away by unconsciously signaling via an incomplete emblem...like shrugging only one shoulder. Not everyone makes these slips. They are subtle—therefore, hard to notice.

•Illustrators are body movements that accompany speech...like the way people move their hands when asked to describe a spiral staircase.

Lies are likely to be accompanied by fewer than normal illustrators because the liar has to think more about his invented story than someone who is telling the truth.

•Manipulators are fidgeting gestures—like scratching or twisting hair—that become more common when someone is nervous. But everyone is aware of the stereotype that guilty people look nervous, so any liar with normal intelligence will try not to fidget. Therefore, fidgeting is usually not a very good indicator of lying.

•Facial clues. A lie-catcher needs to become sensitive to the two messages sent by the face—the false expression that the person wants to give...and the true expression that he cannot hide.

•Squelched impressions, when his concealed emotion starts to emerge and he quickly covers it with a false smile

•Micro-expressions, when the true feeling flashes on his/her face for an instant. While micro-expressions are easy to miss, you can train yourself to catch them.

•Inability to control muscles. This occurs when certain facial muscles used in natural expressions of emotion cannot be controlled because the emotion is not felt. That is why a genuine smile, not a fake one, crinkles the eyes.

Caution: Truly skilled liars—or those who have come to believe their own lies—may not give any of these clues because, like actors, they are able to truly feel the emotion they are trying to express to you.

Bottom line:

There is no infallible way to detect lies, because all liars are different.

Source: Paul Ekman, PhD, professor of psychology at the University of California, San Francisco. He is author of *Telling Lies: Clues to Deceit in the Marketplace, Politics and Marriage.* W. W. Norton and Company, 500 Fifth Ave., New York 10110.

11

Your Family, Your Home

Mistakes Parents Make Can Be Avoided

The most common problem for many parents is being afraid to be definite with their children. Parents are hesitant in expressing their wishes or their demands.

Example: Charlotte is eight years old. Her mother says, "Charlotte, it's half an hour after your bedtime." Charlotte immediately replies, "All my friends go to bed at 8:30. Besides, last week you let me stay up until 9:30."

Instead of repeating her request for Charlotte to go to bed or helping her along by offering to read her a story, run her a bath, etc., the mother is nonplussed by Charlotte's vigorous objections. She wonders whether she's trying to send her child to bed too soon. She doesn't want to be thought of as a mean, old, crabby mother.

So instead of showing Charlotte that she means it, she gives in—and Charlotte goes back to watching television, having defeated her mother for the time being.

This cycle gets repeated until it's so late that the mother is absolutely sure that Charlotte should be in bed. That overcomes her hesitancy and her guilty feelings, and this time Charlotte does go to bed.

Being hesitant with your children doesn't cause delinquency or any serious problems. But the child is encouraged to argue about every single thing that the parent asks the child to do. The parent is worn out from arguing with the child—and being defeated.

Solution: The parent has to decide what the right bedtime is and stick to it. You don't have to be disagreeable about it. All you have to do is to get a reputation with the child of meaning what you say.

This may sound easy to say and hard to do—but children sense immediately what their parents really want and whether their parents mean it or not. It's up to you not to be hesitant.
Scolding:

Many parents feel that the only way to get children to behave is to scold them.

How do you get children to do what you want without scolding? By having a good relationship with them on a non-scolding basis.

Example: A respected friend is visiting you. After dinner, she sits down to watch a program on television that she is particularly interested in. You're left washing the dishes.

You don't say to that friend, "Turn off that television and come and help me with the dishes!" You say, "Harriet, I am terribly tired tonight. Would you mind coming and helping me do the dishes?"

I think that children are just as reasonable in most respects as adults. If that kind of polite, friendly attitude has been developed since early childhood, children love to be helpful as part of being grown up.

Not asking your children to help:

Another problem in our society is that children aren't asked to be cooperative nearly as much as they should be. I've known couples to say, "Oh, they are only young once, let them have a good time."

It's fine for children to have a good time. But that doesn't mean not having any duties, especially when children are very proud of being asked to help if the request is presented nicely.

Encouraging excessive competitiveness:

In the excessive competitiveness of our society, too many American children are brought up with the main ideal of *getting ahead*.

Example: I remember during the Vietnam War period, a young man of college age was becoming very concerned about the war and what he would do if he were drafted. I heard one father say to his son, "Never mind about politics. Your job in life is to get ahead as an individual."

I think that has been the lesson that so many business organizations have taught: "Don't worry about the other people, you get ahead of them." I believe that some of our mounting social problems are a result of children's absorbing this attitude.

I often hear people say that America is a child-centered society. It's child-centered in the sense that we give our children music lessons, dancing lessons, athletic lessons. We get their teeth straightened, which is a relatively expensive job.

As parents we take care of our own—we want them to have every so-called advantage. But as a society we are way behind Scandinavian countries for instance, or most European countries, in providing in general for our children.

We don't feel a strong obligation everywhere, at all times, to provide the best schooling. The result is that the children in deprived cities and towns have the poorest schooling, because schooling is paid for by local real-estate taxes. It shouldn't be that way.

There are other examples of this. We read a lot about juvenile justice in the newspapers, but in most parts of this country we don't actually do much to protect children from abuse or to help rehabilitate children whose behavior has become antisocial and violent. Whereas in Scandinavian countries, they are very serious and logical about protecting children and recovering those who have gone astray.

Example: Lack of medical care for millions of American children who never see a doctor from the day they are born until the day they die. There's no excuse for that whatsoever, except that Americans don't naturally think that the society as a whole has an obligation to the children, as a whole.

Not enjoying your children:

If there were one thing I could say to parents, it would be—*try to enjoy your children*. That is a somewhat theoretical piece of advice, because at the deepest level you tend to do what your parents did, and if you are going to do things differently it is a constant effort to squelch the past. You have to feel very strongly about it.

In my own case, throughout my two sons' childhoods—they were 11 years apart—I didn't enjoy them nearly as much as I now wish I had. I only realized how little I enjoyed them when I would be away on a trip and would write a letter home, or something else made me think of my sons. I would think, "Gee, my sons are marvelous. Why don't I ever act as if they are marvelous?" I think the easiest way to explain it is that my mother never enjoyed her children nearly as much as she should have.

That is partly the difference between parenting and grandparenting. So many grandparents have said to me, "I wish I could have enjoyed my children the way that I enjoy my grandchildren." I think it's true that most grandparents do enjoy their grandchildren more.

Example: We have some friends who do a little babysitting for their grandchildren and enjoy them enormously. They are impressed by their grandchildren's wisdom, the original way that they present things, and how obviously the children enjoy this kind of treatment.

Grandparents know that they can turn responsibility over to the child's parents, and so feel less pressured in caring for the child. I think the most basic reason for this is that parents are meant to feel responsible for their child. This is part of the instinctive makeup of the human being.

Most important:

Most parents do the best they can. We know much more than we think we do, and we have to learn to trust ourselves as parents. If your child knows that you love him/her, and if the parents' communication is good with each other, then regardless of what any expert says, things will probably turn out just fine.

Source: Benjamin Spock, MD, coauthor, with Dr. Michael Rothenberg, of *Baby and Child Care*, Pocket Books, 1230 Avenue of the Americas, New York 10020. Dr. Spock is also a columnist for *Parenting* magazine.

Words That Get Parents into Trouble With Their Kids

Even though our intentions are good, it's easy for parents to use words or phrases with children that are insensitive at best—hurtful at worst—and that actually work against the results we want.

This is especially true when we're annoyed, frustrated, tired, or stressed. We react automatically and don't even think about what we're saying.

One of the quickest and best ways to change this pattern is to watch out for red flag words. These are usually short, simple words that almost always escalate any conflict with a child

—or a spouse or anyone with whom we have a close relationship.

By becoming aware of these words, we can substitute expressions that are more likely to result in cooperation and understanding. Words to avoid:

Most red flag words occur at or near the beginning of a sentence.

"If"—usually followed by "you"—when used as a threat.

• If you do that again, you'll be sorry.

• If you don't get in that bathtub, there will be no story tonight.

• If you keep leaving your clothes all over the floor, I won't buy you any more this year.

Many children perceive a threat as a challenge and may repeat the offense just to see what the parent will do.

These threats are often impossible to carry out. We make them when we're least rational—and often when we've lost control of the situation. And, if we don't follow through on the threat, the child stops taking us seriously—we lose the ability to be authoritative.

In addition, a threat that is irrational or out of proportion relative to the offense doesn't teach the child anything about the realistic consequences of his/her behavior.

Better: "As soon as" or "when." These phrases are more positive and less punitive. They encourage you to stay rational—and make a statement that can be followed through.

• As soon as you've taken your bath, we'll have a story.

• When you've hung up your jacket, we can play a game.

"Who started it?" Obviously, this question applies to an argument or fight between two or more children. But think about it: Have you ever heard any child answer "I did?"

This question implies that we are looking for somebody to blame rather than trying to resolve the problem effectively. The result is likely to be even more fighting or finger-pointing.

Better: Take a neutral, problem-solving approach.

• You two have a problem. There's only one book here, and you both want it at the same time. What can you do about that?

Instead of looking for a bad guy, you're helping the children work out a solution to the problem.

"Why"—especially when followed by "don't you," "can't you" or "won't you."

• Why don't you pick up your things?

• Why can't you keep your hands to yourself?

• Why won't you listen?

These questions are unanswerable. In fact, we're not even asking why because we want a rational answer. Instead, we are really just blaming or making a critical statement. Children are not likely to cooperate when they feel they are being accused.

Another common use of the word "why" is "Why did you"...as in, "Why did you hit your sister?"

Children don't usually know why they do things. They're basically impulsive—and don't think before they act. You're likely to get a useless response such as, "I don't know, I felt like it," or, "Because she's a dork."

Better: Leave out the why and change the question to a clear, firm, nonaccusatory statement.

• There will be no hitting.

• Those toys need to be picked up.

• I would appreciate your hanging up your jacket without my reminding you.

"Never," "ever," and "always."

• You never think about anybody else.

• When will you ever learn?

• You're always such a slob.

These words can become self-fulfilling prophecies. They hurt a child's self-esteem and discourage him from trying to change. What they really say to the child is, "You're a disappointment...you're hopeless."

Better: Be concrete—describe your expectations clearly and specifically.

• Instead of "You never do anything I ask," try, "It's your job to take out the garbage, and that needs to be done this afternoon."

• Instead of "You never pick up after yourself," try, "I expect the blocks to be put in the toy box."

"You"...plus a negative adjective, noun, or phrase.

• You're impossible.

• You're selfish.

• You're spoiled.

• You're a clod.

• You're acting like a baby.

At worst, these are global statements about a child's character, which he can't change, as opposed to statements about his behavior, which he does have some control over. Even when they address his behavior, the statements are perceived as accusatory and negative. Accusations put people—children and adults alike—on the defensive, and a defensive person isn't likely to be reasonable.

"You" statements can be destructive to a child's self-esteem. Like "always" and "never," they can be self-fulfilling prophecies and are not likely to encourage your child to cooperate.

Better: Instead of telling your child what's wrong with him, talk about yourself, and keep it short. Try "I'm mad," which is much more effective than "You're bad." An "I" statement encourages the child to take your feelings seriously—and respect them.

Beware: "I think you're bad" does not qualify as an "I" statement—it's still a "you" statement that happens to start with "I."

Another alternative is a brief, impersonal reminder about house rules, such as, "The rule is no TV until you've finished your homework."

Source: Nancy Samalin, founder and director of Parent Guidance Workshops in New York. She is consulting editor and columnist for *Parents* and author of *Loving Your Child Is Not Enough: Positive Discipline That Works* and *Love and Anger: The Parental Dilemma,* Penguin Books, 375 Hudson St., New York 10014.

The Most Common Mistakes That Parents Make with Teens...And How Not to Make Them

One of the most effective ways to help your children become happy, successful adults is to create a warm, supportive environment in your home during their teenage years. You'll also get along much better under the same roof. The most common mistakes parents make with their teenage children...

•Mistake: Indiscriminate threats. Parents often make threats when they're angry. Then once the heat of the moment passes, they don't bother following through on them. *Result:* Your word will mean little, and your teen will believe that he/she need not pay attention to you—or any other authority figure. Promise disciplinary action only if you really mean it.

•Mistake: Setting unrealistic goals. Teens whose parents expect too much of them eventually become discouraged, and chronic discouragement sets many teenagers on a path toward personal crises. *Better:* Encourage them and don't expect perfection.

Be careful with praise, which celebrates the results of your child's efforts. Encouragement celebrates your child's effort—regardless of outcome. Effort is what you should reinforce.

•Mistake: Nagging about trivial issues. If you disapprove of your teen's views or behavior, it's acceptable to say so. But don't let essentially trivial issues—hair length, matters of style, for instance—drive a wedge between you and your teen. Adolescents dress, talk, and behave in ways distasteful to their parents just to see if their parents will continue to love and respect them. Your teens will grow up to be fine, well-adjusted adults despite dozens of wrong choices.

•Mistake: Interrupting while your teen is talking. Make a conscious effort to listen. Don't be judgmental. Listening is one of the best ways of showing your love.

When talking with them, remember that simple questions deserve simple answers. Teenagers quickly "tune out" parents who talk to excess—especially those who utter too many sentences beginning with "When I was your age..."

•Mistake: Hiding your feelings. If your teen asks your opinion, be open and direct—but not controlling.

Example: If your teenage daughter asks how she looks, and you think her skirt is too tight, tell her so. She might wear the dress anyway, but she'll at least respect your candor.

Call things as you see them, but don't think you can say anything you please just because you're the head of the household. That's unfair—and also counterproductive. *Better:* If you've been inconsiderate of your teen, apologize, and when appropriate, ask for forgiveness.

•Mistake: Invading your teen's privacy. If your teen seems to use your home only as a place to eat and sleep and catch up on phone messages—congratulations—you have a normal child.

Rather than pry into your teen's affairs, help him cultivate a sense of independence. Unless you suspect a major problem, don't read his notes or go through his drawers or closets. And never listen in on phone conversations.

•Mistake: Overlooking irresponsible behavior. Don't let your teen get away with shirking responsibility. If he says something hurtful and then asks for a lift to soccer practice, for instance, say that you can't do it. Odds are, he will quickly sense that something is wrong and apologize for his behavior. Or, you arrive home and find that your teens have failed to get dinner started, as you had asked. Don't yell. Instead, say, "Goodbye, kids. I'm going out for dinner with your father/mother."

But don't overreact. A youngster who spills a glass of milk needs a rag to wipe it up, not a lecture on clumsiness. The same holds true for teens. Don't blow up over insignificant things. Don't berate your teen for every minor transgression.

•Mistake: Ducking tough issues. Discuss problems well before they crop up. This will give your teen time to prepare to confront them rationally.

Example: If you have a 13-year-old daughter, now is the right time for the two of you to discuss problems that might arise when she turns 16.

Traditionally, mothers have discussed sexuality with their daughters, fathers with their sons. This is not always the best approach. *Reason:* An adolescent girl knows how she feels about love and sex. Her father can give her a sense of how adolescent boys feel. Likewise, a teenage boy needs to hear his mother's perspective about girls and dating. In fact, both of you may want to have this discussion with her/him.

• Mistake: Acting like your teen. Parents often try to behave like teenagers in a misguided attempt to fit in with their kids' lives and experiences. In fact, teens want and expect parents to behave like parents. They're uncomfortable around parents who act like they do.

• Mistake: Making teens do things your way. Be willing to let them fail when they make the wrong choice.

Example: Consider giving your teen the choice of mowing the lawn or using his allowance to hire someone else. A teen who opts for the latter quickly realizes that he has less money for compact discs, movies, etc. Occasional failure helps the person understand the importance of personal responsibility.

• Mistake: Making their lives hassle-free. Occasionally helping your teen with homework is okay—as long as your help is requested. But offering help when none is needed encourages your child to be overly dependent upon you. Intervene on your child's behalf at school and elsewhere only when absolutely necessary. This will help your teen develop problem-solving strategies and learn to anticipate them before they occur.

• Mistake: Spoiling their fun. If your teen asks to go dancing or camping, don't carry on about how worried you'll be.

Bottom line: If you've decided it's okay for your teen to do something or go somewhere, outline potential problems to prepare him for issues he might not have anticipated.

• Mistake: Putting your teen on the spot. Never ask your teen to perform for friends or relatives without first asking permission. Certainly, avoid disciplining your teenager in front of friends. Wait until the two of you are alone.

Adolescence is a time of low self-esteem. The pressures of high school, dating, schoolwork, and competitiveness may be greater than your teen lets on. Odds are your teen is well aware of his flaws without your pointing them out.

Source: Kevin Leman, PhD, a Tucson, Arizona-based psychologist, author of *Smart Kids, Stupid Choices: A Survival Guide for Parents of Teens,* Dell Publishing, 1540 Broadway, New York 10036.

All About The Oppositional Child

The oppositional child is a source of frustration and bewilderment to parents.

The oppositional child is consistently aggressive, argumentative, uncooperative, and in conflict with others—especially parents, teachers, and other authority figures…

• Yelling doesn't help.

• Reasoning doesn't help.

• Threats of punishment are ignored.

• Actual punishment doesn't seem to bother the child.

Parents may wind up feeling as though nothing they do will make a difference.

The oppositional child's point of view:

The key to dealing with the oppositional child is to see the world the way the child sees it.

People of any age want to have control over their lives. Control helps us feel that our lives are ordered, predictable, and secure.

While children feel that they have very little control in a world run by adults—some of them seize control aggressively…others by being overly dependent.

Oppositional children go after control assertively and forcefully, by manipulating the emotions of others.

They may not be able to take away their parents' car keys or send them to their rooms—but they can enrage and frustrate them. That's why angry confrontation makes the problem worse—the child has won by causing parents to focus their emotional energy on him.

Parents, too, want to be in control:

Parents tend to try to control children by force—overpowering them, out-arguing them—or trying to reason them into seeing things the parent's way.

But using force with an oppositional child actually reinforces his/her behavior. You wind up with a noisy turf battle—and the child continues to control the emotional atmosphere of the home.

Trying to reason with the child is equally ineffective. Kids are smart—they can see when the parent is emotionally invested in bringing them around to the parent's point of view. This only reinforces the child's sense of control.

Handling the oppositional child:

Paradoxically, we can actually have much more control by recognizing the child's need for control. When the child feels understood, he's more likely to come over to our side.

This does not mean stepping aside and letting kids "do their own thing." Children are inexperienced in the ways of the world and need our guidance.

By virtue of age, wisdom, and experience, parents are the natural leaders in the home. But leadership is demonstrated more effectively through communication than force. A wise leader solicits and takes into account the needs and desires of each family member... then makes the final decision.

Understanding is not the same as agreement. You don't have to approve of what your child is doing...but if you understand what motivates his behavior, you'll be less likely to act in ways that encourage it.

Tactics that don't work:

• Making threats that won't be carried out.
• Shouting to make a point.
• Making sweeping generalizations such as "You always"..."You never"...etc.
• Trying to reason with the child.
• Interrupting.
• Withholding affection.
• Trying to convince the child to agree with you.

What parents can do:

• Control their own emotions. The parent needs to develop a sense of detachment from the child's difficult behavior. That doesn't mean hiding your emotions—that would be impossible. It does mean allowing your child the room to make his own mistakes.

Trap: When a child does something we don't approve of, we tend not to stop at the behavior—we try to change the child's emotions and opinions as well.

The child's problem then becomes our problem...and he's once again in control.

Detachment isn't easy. Instead of thinking, "Well, 12-year-olds do that kind of thing," parents tend to think, "No 12-year-old girl is going to control me." But adults, too, are capable of maturing throughout life. We must be honest with ourselves and continually strive to develop insight into our thoughts and actions.

• Set clear, consistent boundaries. Rather than guiding by giving orders, offer choices that indicate the limits of behavior. Let the child know ahead of time which behaviors will result in punishment—and what those consequences will be. Avoid excessively harsh or aggressive punishment, particularly spanking. And don't ever punish when you're not in control of your emotions. Call a time-out first.

Example: Missing curfew results in loss of use of the car for a week. If the child exceeds the boundaries, impose the consequences—without lecturing or getting emotional about it. Parents don't have trouble getting the first part right. A teenager comes in at 3 AM and the parent says, "You know that you're supposed to be home by midnight. It's 3 AM—no more car this week."

The problem arises when the parent then starts to lecture or harangue the child: "I told you to be in by midnight! I tried to be fair! Now you've broken the rules again—I can't believe it! How do you expect me to trust you?"

Children may test the boundaries for a while to find out whether parents are serious. This is when it's especially important not to get emotional—just keep enforcing the rules.

• Read between the lines. Kids aren't skilled in verbal communication. It's often difficult for them to put what they feel into words. Often, it's through their behavior that they express what's going on inside.

With practice, parents can learn to cut through the offensive behavior and respond to the emotion beneath.

Example: A child who shouts "I hate you!" may mean, "I hate being told I can't do something!" or "I have no power in this family, and it's not fair!"

A parent's usual tendency is to tell the child why he shouldn't feel that way. A more effective response might be, "It feels pretty bad when I tell you what to do. I know you hate that." This allows the child a right to his feelings.

A nonopinionated, nonjudgmental response will encourage the child to reveal more layers of emotion until he feels understood...and once he feels understood, he's more apt to cooperate.

This response is difficult for parents. The parents who haven't mastered detachment fear that they are telling the child, "Go right ahead and hate us—we're rotten people." But when the child knows his feelings are accepted, the feelings will pass much more quickly.

•Don't give advice unless the child asks for it. You may have useful insights, but the child won't benefit from them unless he's interested. He can usually work out his own solutions if you listen in a nonjudgmental way.

•Work on building a positive relationship with your children. The oppositional child is crying out for attention, so make sure he's getting enough of the positive kind.

Recommended...

Spend time playing games and talking with your children.

Be generous with physical affection for your child.

Note: This is easier with pre-adolescents than with teenagers. Older children—who look to their peers, not their family, for support—may resist your attempts to enter their world. But it's important to show your willingness to build rapport.

Invite your child on outings—or to a one-on-one dinner. Don't give him a hard time if he turns you down. Even if he says no, continue to invite him to other activities in a no-big-deal way.

Or try a chat before bedtime. A child who's winding down at the end of the day may be more receptive to building rapport.

Source: Wm. Lee Carter, EdD, a psychologist at Child Psychiatry Associates in Waco, Texas, and author of *Kidthink*, Word Publishing, Inc., East Tower–Williams Square, 5221 North O'Connor, Suite 100, Irving, Texas 75039.

Your Children... School And Other Transitions

Some children are naturally adventurous—they jump into any new activity or environment with relish. Others, however, are much more cautious and pessimistic about change.

While edgy behavior about the unknown is perfectly normal, there are ways for parents to help make dramatic transitions less stressful for their kids.

Empathic listening:

Most important—take your child's feelings seriously. Don't minimize his/her concerns by saying, There's nothing to worry about." That just tells him that he has no right to his feelings. It may also convince him that there is something wrong with him for feeling that way.

More helpful: Acknowledge those feelings and say, "I can see that this might be scary for you." Then, follow up with an encouraging comment, showing him that you have confidence in his ability.

You also shouldn't assume your child is worry-free just because he hasn't told you that he's anxious. Often, it's hard or embarrassing for kids to articulate what they're afraid of.

Instead of waiting for your child to bring up the subject, do so yourself. If you can help your youngster find the words to talk about his fears, you'll be better able to address his questions and concerns as well as let him know you're available to listen.

Providing structure:

These are two techniques that will help you provide the structure and familiarity that kids need to feel more at ease with transitions.

•Preparation. Help your child retain his sense of control by including him in the planning stages. Rehearse potentially difficult situations so that he can practice acting appropriately.

•Ritual. Having special rituals is reassuring to a child—it gives him something familiar to fall back on. Rituals don't have to be elaborate, but they do need to have a certain regularity. They can be as simple as reading a story aloud at bedtime or talking over problems while sitting in a favorite chair.

Common transitions and ways to handle them...

•First day at a new school:

Preparation: Visit the school with your child before classes begin. Show him where the bathroom and lunchroom are. Have him meet the teacher, if possible. If he will be walking to school, walk there with him a few times beforehand...if he'll be taking the school bus, go with him to the bus stop for a dry run.

If an older relative, neighbor, or friend attends the same school, arrange to have him show your child around the first day.

If your child is worried about his ability to talk to kids he doesn't know, try some role-playing.

Example: You could say: "Let's pretend we've just gone to the lunchroom and somebody sits down next to you. You could ignore him, or you could say, 'Hi, I'm Paul—what's your name?' Pretend I'm this new person and let's practice."

Rituals: You might help your child pick out the next day's clothes and lay them out the night before...send him off with a special wave...serve a favorite snack each day when your child comes home from school.

•When a friend moves away:

Preparation: Remind your child that he can stay in touch with his friend, even if they live miles apart. Find the friend's new town on a map. Explore the feasibility of exchanging visits. Go shopping for farewell cards. Help your child plan a going-away party for his friend.

If you have a going-away party, take Polaroid pictures of the friend with each of the guests...and make sure everyone goes home with a photograph.

Rituals: Consider allowing your child to call his friend long-distance on special occasions, such as birthdays and holidays. In addition to letters, it might be possible to exchange a monthly fax. Ask your child to think of other ways to stay in touch.

•Moving to a new city:

Preparation: Reassure your child that even though he'll be far from his friends, they won't forget him.

Take him with you to the post office to buy change-of-address cards and help him fill them out to send to his friends.

Let him know what to expect on moving day...will a moving van arrive? Will you drive to the new house, or take a plane or train? Suggest that he draw pictures of the old and new houses.

Rituals: Have a farewell open house for the friends your child will be leaving.

Caution: In your attempt to pack light, don't just throw out toys your child has outgrown. Let him choose which ones he wants to take along. Once he gets used to the new house, he may decide he's ready to give some of them away.

•When parents go out of town:

Preparation: Talk to your child about the person who will be looking after him while you're away, and about your expectations.

Example: "Aunt Ella will be staying with you. I'll tell her about your favorite book. She knows you're supposed to be in bed by 8:00—no later."

If a new babysitter will be staying in your home, make sure your child meets that person a day or two before your departure.

To avoid misunderstandings, go over house rules with the caregiver—in the child's presence. If your child will be staying at a relative's home, explain that this person's rules may not be the same as yours. Be as specific as you can: "Grandma only wants you to eat at the table—not in front of the TV. And once dinner's over, the kitchen is closed."

Arrange to phone your child at a certain time each day.

Rituals: Make sure the caregiver understands the daily rituals that are important to your child, and encourage him to maintain them as consistently as possible.

Example: Preparing for bedtime might involve reading a storybook aloud, then a hug and a bedtime chant ("Good night, sleep tight...").

•When a parent returns to work:

Preparation: Before you start a new job, show your child around your office. This will help him have a vivid mental picture of you when you're at work—one of the ways kids cope with separation.

Give him a transitional object—something he can associate with you, such as a stuffed bear from your own childhood or a handkerchief doused with your perfume. Ask him to make a painting or drawing that you can hang in your office. This is particularly helpful for pre-schoolers.

Rituals: If time permits, some families enjoy sitting down to breakfast together. Have a snack ready in the refrigerator so your child can help himself when he gets home from school. Set up a daily phone call from the office.

When you get home from work, spend a little low-key time with your child before you plunge into dinner or housekeeping chores. You might want to play a game on the living-room floor or hold him on your lap while you sit in a rocking chair.

Remember, it takes time to adjust to any new situation, but adjustments will become less stressful as situations become more familiar.

Source: Nancy Samalin, founder of Parent Guidance Workshops in New York and consulting editor and columnist for *Parents* magazine. She is author of *Loving Your Child Is Not Enough: Positive Discipline That Works* and *Love and Anger: The Parental Dilemma,* Penguin Books, 375 Hudson St., New York 10014.

How to Help Your Child with Schoolwork

Many intelligent parents know surprisingly little about how best to help their children with their schoolwork. Prodded by guilt and ambition, these parents compensate for their limited time at home by putting enormous pressure on their kids to excel in school—and in extracurricular activities.

This maximum-involvement approach can be just as destructive as not helping your children at all. Symptoms of maximum involvement...

•Physically hovering over your child throughout the homework session.

•Chronically providing answers or dictating sentences.

•Thinking in terms of "my homework" or "my grade"...as if the teacher is evaluating you as well as your child.

Drawbacks:

While maximum involvement may indeed produce higher grades, it is quickly counterproductive. A hovering parent creates an anxious, dependent child—one who is ill-equipped to cope in a class where many other children are vying for the teacher's attention.

Parents who keep children from making mistakes also prevent them from learning from those mistakes...and confuse teachers as to what the children actually know.

Worst of all, these parents are sending a negative message to their children: "I don't think you're capable."

Better way:

Fortunately, there is another way for busy parents to deal with homework...what I call *moderate involvement.*

The ultimate goal of homework is to help children develop the skills they need to be successful. Moderate involvement helps achieve that goal. It saves time, reduces guilt, and keeps the responsibility of homework and learning where it should be—with the child.

Moderate involvement with homework can be boiled down to two words: Monitor and review. What a moderately involved parent should do...

•Establish a quiet, positive homework environment...a set time and place out of range of television.

•Find a convenient time to help the child. If you're feeling rushed or preoccupied, you'll only get frustrated.

•Confirm that the child can follow written directions.

•Avoid hovering...especially with a child who feels dependent or indifferent about homework. After seeing the session off to a good start, say, "I'll be back in a while." Then back off for a fair amount of time before checking in again. Trap: Parents who stay in close proximity are tempted to give their children the answer...rather than letting them hunt for it.

• Review the assignment after it is completed. This lends added significance to the child's work.

Strategies for specific subjects:

While moderate involvement keeps parents in touch with their children's studies, it also allows children to think for themselves…to develop responsibility and self-discipline…to reach their potential. This approach can be applied successfully to all subject areas. In each case, ask yourself: "What is the teacher trying to accomplish?"

• Writing. To encourage your child to express his/her own ideas—without being paralyzed by a blank page—start the session with some informal brainstorming. Toss around a few ideas with your child until he/she finds one that is attractive. Then help with the toughest sentence in any story or report—the first one.

If your child is capable of carrying on from there, assure him that you'll return…and retreat to another room.

After the report is finished, read it carefully. For beginning writers—first- or second-graders—it is inappropriate to harp on every error in spelling or punctuation. (This is especially true if your child is being taught with a "whole-language" approach, which stresses a free flow of ideas over perfect spelling.)

For all age groups, balance corrections with praise for whatever is positive in the work.

• Math. Monitor your child through the first one or two problems to make sure the correct process is in place. For the dallying student, set a 15-minute timer and announce, "I hope you'll be done with number 12 by the time I get back."

• Science. No homework is more prone to excessive parental involvement than science-fair projects. To avoid this trap, divorce yourself from the attitude that your child needs to win a blue ribbon. A science project should be a learning experience for the student—no more and no less.

To set the right tone, guide your child toward choosing a project that isn't too advanced or complicated for his age group.

If your school's science fair is already out of hand, with parents who are obviously doing much of the work, you might approach your child's teacher or principal, or the PTA. Propose a change in the fair's format—at least for the lower grades—to a less competitive "invention convention." This can relieve pressure on parents to compete…and return the projects themselves to their rightful owners… the students.

Source: Nancy Haug, MS, a former elementary and junior high school teacher and the mother of five young children. She is the coauthor of *Erasing the Guilt: Play an Active Role in Your Child's Education—No Matter How Busy You Are*, Career Press, 180 Fifth Ave., Box 34, Hawthorne, New Jersey 07507. 800-CAREER-1.

Better College Application Essays

If you can choose your own topic, avoid academic ones unless you really know the material. Stay away from religion…and sex. Be careful of very personal topics or explanations of why you want to go to college. Key: Admissions people look for writing ability—not existing knowledge. Write clear, crisp prose. Avoid humor if there is any chance it could be misinterpreted. Recommended: Have your essay reviewed by someone who can write.

Source: *College After 30: It's Never Too Late to Get the Degree You Need!* by college counselor Sunny Baker, Bob Adams, Inc., 260 Center St., Holbrook, Massachusetts 02343.

College-Aid Tax Strategy

Deductible retirement-plan contributions made by parents can increase the amount of college financial aid offered to their children. How: The amount of aid offered to a child depends in part upon the value of the parents' assets. For financial aid purposes, however, the amount of money accumulated in retirement plans—such as IRAs, Keoghs, and 401(k)s—is not considered an asset in determining eligibility for assistance. Therefore, by putting assets in retirement accounts before a child goes to college, and by making plan contributions while the child is in college, you may increase aid significantly.

Source: Kalman A. Chany, president, Campus Consultants Inc., 338 E. 67 St., New York 10021. Mr. Chany is author of *The Princeton Review/The Student Access Guide to Paying for College*, Villard Books, 201 E. 50 St., New York 10022.

Protect Your Child From Sports Injuries

More than twenty million children are active in some form of organized sports in this country. In the coming year, one in three—close to seven million—will suffer an injury requiring the attention of a parent...or doctor...or both.

High school athletes alone will suffer one million sports-related injuries, including 20,000 that will require surgery.

Many of these injuries can be prevented. Actively involved parents can help minimize problems. Key safety guidelines...

•Beware of the injury-prone child. Not all children are suited for all sports. If a child has had multiple injuries—concussions, fractures, severe sprains, etc.—over the course of two seasons, it's time to consider switching him/her to a different activity.

Typical adjustment: From a physical team sport to an individual sport, where the chances for injury are less.

Example: A young person may lack the strong foot control to perform safely in soccer...but may have great hand-eye coordination for tennis.

•Watch out for overuse or stress injuries. Stress injuries have become epidemic over the last 10 years...even among the under-12 set.

Reason: Children are competing harder—and during more months out of the year—than ever before.

Solution: Take six months off from all sports. Then choose just one to resume the following year.

•See to it that your child is adequately conditioned. Good conditioning can enable a child to safely absorb a fall or collision. Pre-activity warm-ups are vital, but teenagers also need physical preparation months before their season starts.

Examples: Swimming, biking or running, for endurance...weight-training for strength...stretching for flexibility.

Caution: Overstretching can lead to back and sciatic nerve injuries.

•Make sure that your child isn't over-matched by much larger athletes. A 12-year-old pitcher who stands 5-foot-6-inches tall and weighs 130 pounds can terrify a smallish 10-year-old batter.

Injury prevention: Ask the coach to outfit all batters with a plastic face mask...switch your child to a league that uses the new, softer baseballs.

•Check out the coach's priorities. A win-at-all-costs syndrome leads to many unnecessary injuries.

Danger signs: A track coach who pushes tired runners on when they are obviously unfit to continue...a football coach who keeps a player in a big game despite a significant injury that could get worse.

•Watch the weather. Whenever the temperature is over 85 degrees and the humidity exceeds 70%, coaches and parents should be on the lookout for heat illness.

Symptoms: Abnormal movements and bizarre actions. In some severe conditions, practice should be suspended.

Hot-weather precautions: Urge coaches to schedule practice sessions for early morning or evening...require loose white clothing...provide rest in the shade between sessions...make water available at all times and see that it is consumed.

•Insist that your child use appropriate safety equipment. This applies to practices as well as games. Children tend to neglect safety because they think they are indestructible. It's up to parents and coaches to see that safety headgear, mouthguards, and running shoes fit properly and are not worn out.

Source: John F. Duff, MD, a practicing orthopedic surgeon and director of the North Shore Sports Medical Center in Danvers, Massachusetts. He is author of *Youth Sports Injuries: A Medical Handbook For Parents and Coaches*, Collier Books, 866 Third Ave., New York 10022.

Kids' Teeth

Kids' knocked-out teeth can be reimplanted if children are brought to a dentist quickly enough, says Geraldine Morrow, DDS. Key: Treatment within 30 minutes after a permanent tooth is knocked out—if possible—but definitely within two hours. Reimplantation success rate for treatment within 30 minutes: 90%. Rinse the dislodged tooth gently to remove dirt—but don't scrub. Gently replace it in its socket for the trip to the dentist—or carry it in a cup of milk or cool water.

Source: Geraldine Morrow, DDS, is immediate past-president of the American Dental Association, and a practicing dentist in Anchorage, Alaska.

All About Healthy Pregnancies...And Healthier Babies

Many women know that if they're pregnant, they should watch what they eat and drink, stop smoking, see their doctors—and read up on pregnancy, labor, and child-rearing. All this is good.

But to wait until the pregnancy test is positive before making these changes is not good.

That's like preparing a meal by dumping all the ingredients in a bowl, and reading the recipe afterward. The time to read the recipe is before you mix the ingredients together. And the time to prepare for pregnancy is before you conceive.

The fetus is most vulnerable very early in pregnancy—including the weeks before you know you're pregnant. Most organ systems are formed within eight to 12 weeks of conception—and most birth defects occur during that period.

I suggest to my patients that they view pregnancy as a 12-month process that begins when they first think about becoming pregnant.
Nutrition:

An undernourished mother—and that could include a seemingly healthy woman who's dieting to keep her weight down—is more likely to have a baby whose growth is retarded. Growth retardation is associated with disorders such as cerebral palsy, mental retardation, and metabolic problems.

Being overweight causes more problems for the mother than for the baby. A woman who eats heavily and gains too much weight during pregnancy may have a bigger baby that's harder to deliver. And heavy mothers have a higher incidence of diabetes, toxemia (pregnancy-induced hypertension), and phlebitis.

Before you stop using birth control, have your doctor assess your eating habits, and compare your weight and height against commonly available data for ideal weight. If you're significantly underweight, you should improve your nutritional status and approach your ideal body weight before trying to conceive.

If you need to lose weight, do it before, not during, pregnancy.

There's nothing mysterious about eating properly during pregnancy. You don't have to weigh or measure your food. Eat a balanced diet, with a variety of foods from the major food groups. Pay particular attention to protein, calcium, fruits, vegetables, and fiber. Your doctor can give you more specific guidelines.

Taking a vitamin and mineral supplement can't substitute for a balanced diet, but it can help to ensure that you're getting the minimum requirements for yourself and your baby.

Especially important: Iron, folic acid, calcium.

Excess alcohol during pregnancy is known to be harmful to the fetus...but we don't know at what quantity it presents a problem.

An occasional alcoholic drink may not be dangerous, but to be on the safe side, I recommend that my patients avoid alcohol completely during pregnancy—and do the same while they're trying to conceive.
Exercise:

Exercise is an important part of a healthy life, and a woman who works out regularly can continue to exercise throughout her pregnancy. While there's no evidence that exercising will make the fetus any healthier—exercise does benefit the mother.

As the mother gains weight over the nine-month period, being in good shape will make her daily activities easier. A physically fit mother may also be better able to tolerate the strenuous physical demands of labor. But there's no evidence that fitness can shorten the duration of labor or lower the risk of complications.

If you're a couch potato, don't suddenly take up exercise when you learn you're pregnant—you'll put your body under stress. It's better to start an exercise program before you try to conceive.

Beware: Exercising strenuously, especially in hot weather, can raise your core body temperature, increasing the risk of birth defects. If you work out, make these modifications in your exercise program as soon as you stop using birth control...

• Don't wear warm clothes while exercising.

• Don't exercise in a warm environment.

• Reduce the length of your workouts to between 15 and 30 minutes.

• Reduce the intensity of your workout. Don't push yourself until you're huffing and puffing—you should have enough breath left to talk. Keep your heart rate under 140 beats per minute.

• Avoid saunas and hot tubs.

Environmental risks:

As soon as you consider becoming pregnant, evaluate your exposure to chemicals, radiation, and other hazards at home and at work.

Examples: Pesticides, weed killers, household cleansers, formaldehyde in carpets and pressed-wood products, X-rays.

We have very little information about the effects on pregnancy of chemical and other environmental hazards.

Rule of thumb: If you're not sure about the safety of a substance, and you can realistically avoid it, do so.

You don't need to be paranoid or live in a sterile environment, but if there are modifications you want to make, you should make them now—before you become pregnant.

What about the VDT controversy? Studies suggesting that women who work at video display terminals have a higher incidence of miscarriage have not held up to proper scrutiny—too many variables were involved in these studies. If you are concerned about VDT radiation, you should pay attention to the workstations near you more than your own—more radiation is emitted from the back and sides of a computer than from the front.

Smoking is a reproductive poison. Women who smoke have a higher incidence of infertility, miscarriage, and babies with birth defects...as well as serious complications during pregnancy. If you haven't stopped smoking, stop when you discontinue your form of birth control. (If you're already pregnant and still smoke, stop—the hazard continues throughout pregnancy.)

Recreational drugs are also dangerous to the fetus. The time to stop taking these drugs is before conception.

Medical problems:

If you have a condition such as diabetes, high blood pressure, or lupus, it's important to have a reproductive checkup before you try to conceive.

You and your doctor will want to be sure the disease is under control, and that any medications you're taking are appropriate to continue during pregnancy.

You should also make a point to discuss with your doctor ahead of time how pregnancy will affect the disease—and vice versa. Don't wait until you're pregnant to find out.

Even if you're not aware of any chronic medical condition, it's a good idea to have a pre-conception checkup. Make sure your tests—such as a Pap smear—are up to date. A medical problem identified after you're pregnant generally is more difficult to diagnose and treat.

Example: If you discover a breast lump while you're pregnant, you may be reluctant to have the X-ray that would aid in diagnosis...or the surgery and/or chemotherapy that might be part of the recommended treatment if you weren't pregnant.

You should also find out whether you're immune to rubella, also called German measles, which is known to be associated with birth defects. About 15% of the population is not immune. If you're among them, get immunized at least three months before you try to conceive.

Source: Barry Herman, MD, assistant clinical professor of obstetrics and gynecology at UCLA and coauthor of *The Twelve-Month Pregnancy*, Lowell House, 2029 Century Park East, Suite 3290, Los Angeles 90067.

How Some Miscarriages Can Be Avoided

Of all the medical problems that can befall a pregnant woman, few are more common—or more devastating—than miscarriage. Doctors now estimate that miscarriage ends 50% to 60% of first pregnancies—and more than 30% of all pregnancies.

The major risk factors associated with miscarriages and how to protect against them...

•Inadequate medical care. Waiting to see an obstetrician until after conception is simply not sufficient, especially for older women and those with chronic medical problems. By then it's often too late to take the steps necessary to maximize your chances of delivering a healthy baby.

Examples: The dosages of antidepressants, steroids or other drugs that can cause problems during pregnancy need to be reduced before conception. So, too, with medication to control high blood pressure, diabetes, lupus, and other ailments that are linked to miscarriage...or diagnosing and treating chlamydia and other infections.

To avoid trouble: See a doctor before trying to conceive. After conception, see the doctor once a month for the first 32 weeks, twice monthly through week 36, then once a week until delivery. Depending upon your age and possible risk factors, your doctor may recommend ultrasound, amniocentesis, or additional diagnostic tests.

•Age. The older a woman, the greater her risk of miscarriage. *Especially vulnerable:* Women over age 35. They're two to three times more likely to miscarry than younger women. The father's age has less bearing upon miscarriage risk, although women whose partners are over 50 seem slightly more likely to miscarry.

•Anatomical problems. Repeated gynecologic procedures (especially dilation and curettage associated with abortion) weaken a woman's cervix...and the weaker the cervix, the greater the risk of miscarriage. Miscarriage can also result from a misshapen uterus. Both conditions are easily diagnosed.

To avoid trouble: Make scrupulous use of contraceptives until you're ready to become pregnant. If your cervix is weak or your uterus is misshapen, ask your doctor about treatments, including bed rest, stitching the cervix, and corrective surgery.

•Poor nutrition. For best health, discuss your diet with your doctor.

Ideal: A gradual weight gain of 25 to 30 pounds. Avoid raw meat and raw fish. Have no more than three cups of coffee a day. Take a multivitamin. It should contain at least one milligram of folic acid, which helps prevent spinal-cord defects.

•Tobacco. Women who smoke tobacco or marijuana or who are around smokers face an increased risk of miscarriage.

To avoid trouble: Don't smoke during pregnancy. Don't breathe smoky air.

•Alcohol. An occasional beer or glass of wine during pregnancy is thought to be harmless, but excessive drinking can cause birth defects and miscarriage.

To minimize risk: Avoid alcohol.

•Electromagnetic fields. The apparent link between miscarriage and the invisible fields generated by computer terminals, microwave ovens, electric blankets, and other appliances remains unconfirmed—but it's scary nonetheless.

To minimize exposure: Stay at least 28 inches away from any microwave oven or computer terminal.

Caution: The fields emanating from the sides, backs, and tops of terminals are even stronger than those from the screens.

•Environmental toxins. Chronic exposure to certain chemicals, including industrial solvents and anesthetics, boosts a woman's risk of miscarriage. If your work brings you in contact with chemicals, consult your doctor. It might be prudent to seek other work during pregnancy—or at least find some way to limit your exposure.

•Body heat. Recent studies link miscarriage to activities that raise body temperature for an extended period of time.

To be safe: During the first trimester, avoid saunas, steam baths, and whirlpools. Exercise vigorously for no more than 30 minutes at a time.

•Stress. Scientists now suspect that stress and fatigue play a role in miscarriage.

Self-defense: Any pregnant woman who is chronically exhausted or "stressed" should relax—via bed rest, vacations, relaxation exercises, etc.

Source: Jonathan Scher, MD, an assistant clinical professor of obstetrics and gynecology at Mount Sinai Medical School and an obstetrician in private practice in New York City. He is coauthor of *Preventing Miscarriage: The Good News,* HarperPerennial, 10 E. 53 St., New York 10022.

Watch the Age

As a man ages, there may be a greater risk that a child he fathers will have a serious birth defect.* Because of this, sperm banks have recently been advised to no longer accept sperm from donors older than 40. But this does not mean a younger man planning to postpone fatherhood until his forties should freeze his sperm. Freezing sperm is expensive—about $1,000 to freeze the sperm and $500/yr. to maintain it, and hundreds of dollars more for artificial insemination. Also, there is a decreased chance of actually conceiving a child when the sperm is not fresh.

*The American Fertility Society and the American Association of Tissue Banks found that, at age 20, the risk is 20 per 1,000 births. At paternal age 50, the risk is 30% higher.

Source: Edwin Peterson, MD, clinical associate professor at the University of Michigan, and a fertility specialist in private practice in Ann Arbor.

Alzheimer's or Not?

Alzheimer's disease is a progressive disease of the brain in later life* that is accompanied by dementia—decline in memory, reasoning, and other intellectual functions.

An older person whose mental abilities are impaired does not necessarily have Alzheimer's disease. There are many other causes of dementia—and many of them are treatable. *Included:*

•Effects of prescription drugs—or combinations of drugs.

•Depression—especially if memory and concentration problems are accompanied by sleep disturbance, weight loss, or diminished interest in daily activities.

•Diseases of the body's other organ systems, such as heart, kidney, lungs, or blood.

•Tick-borne Lyme disease.

•Vitamin deficiencies.

•Alcohol abuse.

•Disorders of the thyroid, pituitary, or adrenal glands.

To avoid misdiagnosis: Make sure the patient is evaluated by a medical professional who has special training and experience in diagnosis and treatment of diseases of the brain and aging. *Also helpful:* Seek a second opinion after any diagnosis.

*Although there are some cases with victims younger than 65.

Source: Robert Friedland, MD, clinical director of the Alzheimer's Center at University Hospitals of Cleveland, Case Western Reserve University, Cleveland 44106.

What Never To Ask Your Spouse

Many couples use questions to assert power ...put down their partner...express anger covertly...or to test the emotional waters.

Many questions try to force your spouse to feel or act the same way you do. *Reality:* Everyone is an individual...and you're rarely going to get your spouse to significantly change his/her behavior—he must do that himself. *What never to ask:*

- Why do you always act that way?
- Whose side are you on, anyway?
- Why must you always embarrass me?
- Why don't you think logically?

Some questions provoke answers that will either feed your insecurities or be the basis for an argument. *What never to ask:*

- Are you angry again?
- Do you think I'm getting old…fat…bald?
- Do you still feel the same way about me as you did when we met?
- Do you think I'm stubborn…bossy…sloppy?
- Are you having an affair?
- Do you think so-and-so is attractive?
- Are you sure that it's okay for my mother to visit?

Many women are frustrated and angry about their husband's unwillingness to talk about their feelings. Their questions often mask criticism. *What never to ask:*

- Why don't we talk anymore?
- Why don't you ever tell me how you feel?
- Why don't you ever ask me what I want?

Some questions are attempts to assert power and authority over the spouse. They undermine the concept of equal partnership on which a marriage should be based. *What never to ask:*

- Who taught you to do that?
- Why are you acting just like your mother?
- Isn't it your turn to take out the garbage?
- Why can't you learn to balance a checkbook…be more responsible?
- Why can't you do anything right?

Asking such questions is often a way to avoid making a statement. *Better:* Statements that start with the word "I" and express how you feel.

Source: Psychologist Edward P. Monte, PhD, administrative coordinator, senior staff therapist, supervisor, and clinical director of the South Jersey office of the Marriage Council of Philadelphia, department of psychiatry, University of Pennsylvania School of Medicine, 4025 Chestnut St., Philadelphia 19104.

Too Many Dangerous Chemicals Are in Too Many of Our Homes

According to the Environmental Protection Agency's estimates, the average household contains between three and 10 gallons of hazardous chemicals—and many of them are organic compounds that vaporize at room temperature.

In the effort to save money by sealing our homes to reduce heating and air-conditioning bills, and by becoming do-it-yourselfers for many tasks once left to professionals, we expose ourselves and our families to high levels of these toxic substances.

Read the label:

"We are all guilty of not thoroughly reading labels," according to Charles Jacobson, compliance officer, US Consumer Products Safety Commission.

If vapors may be harmful, it doesn't do much good to read the label after you have used the product and inhaled the vapors.

Important: Read the labels before buying a product to select the safest in a category. If you find any of the 11 ingredients listed below on a container, avoid buying it. If you must buy it, use extreme caution when working with…

Dangerous chemicals:

1. Methylene chloride. A widely used solvent, it is in pesticide aerosols, refrigeration and air-conditioning equipment, cleansing creams, and in paint and varnish removers. Some paint strippers are 80% methylene chloride. Its toxic effects include damage to liver, kidneys, and central nervous system. It increases the carbon-monoxide level in the blood, and people with angina (chest pains) are extremely sensitive to the chemical. Methylene chloride has been linked to heart attacks and cancer.

2. Dichlorvos (DDVP). An investigation by the National Toxicology Program of the Department of Health and Human Services revealed a significant leukemia hazard from this common household pesticide. It's been widely used in pet, house, and yard aerosol prod-

ucts since the 1950s. The EPA has had DDVP in special review since February 1988 and it has been considering banning it from food packaging.

3. 2,4-D. A weed killer related to Agent Orange—which allegedly caused health problems in exposed Vietnam veterans, 2,4-D is widely used by home gardeners and farmers. It does not cause acute toxicity, but its long-term effects are scary—much higher incidence of cancer and non-Hodgkin's lymphoma has been associated with its use among farmers. The National Cancer Institute also reports that dogs whose owners use 2,4-D on their lawns have an increased rate of a type of cancer closely related to human non-Hodgkin's lymphoma.

4. Perchlorethylene. The main solvent employed in the dry-cleaning process, metal degreasing, and in some adhesives, aerosols, paints, and coatings, it can be absorbed through your lungs or your skin. The most common effects of overexposure are irritation of the eyes, nose, throat, or skin. Effects on the nervous system include dizziness, headache, nausea, fatigue, confusion, and loss of balance. At very high exposure it can cause death.

5. Formaldehyde. An inexpensive and effective preservative used in more than 3,000 household products. They include disinfectants, cosmetics, fungicides, preservatives, and adhesives. It is also used in pressed-wood products—wall paneling, fiberboard, furniture, and in some papers. There are serious questions about its safety. It is estimated that 4% to 8% of the population is sensitive to it. Vapors are intensely irritating to mucous membranes and can cause nasal, lung, and eye problems.

6. Benzene. Among the top five organic chemicals produced in the United States, this petroleum derivative's use in consumer products has, in recent years, been greatly reduced. However, it is still employed as a solvent for waxes, resins, and oils and is in varnish and lacquer. It is also an "antiknock" additive in gasoline—thus, make sure your house is well ventilated and insulated from vapors that arise from an attached garage.

Benzene is highly flammable, poisonous when ingested, and irritating to mucous membranes. Amounts that are harmful may be absorbed through the skin. Possible results: Blood, brain, and nerve damage.

7. Cyanide. One of the most rapid poisons known, it is used to kill fungus, insects, and rats. It is in metal polishes (especially silver), art materials, and photographic solutions.

8. Naphthalene. Derived from coal, it is used in solvents, fungicides, toilet bowl deodorizers, and as a moth repellent. It can be absorbed through the skin and eyes as well as through the lungs. It may damage the eyes, liver, kidneys, skin, red blood cells, and the central nervous system. It has reportedly caused anemia in infants exposed to clothing and blankets stored in naphthalene mothballs. This chemical can cause allergic skin rashes in adults and children.

9. Paradichlorobenzene (PDB). Made from chlorine and benzene, it is in metal polishes, moth repellents, general insecticides, germicides, spray deodorants, and fumigants. PDB is also commonly found in room deodorizers. Vapors may cause irritation to the skin, throat, and eyes. Prolonged exposure to high concentrations may cause weakness, dizziness, loss of weight, and liver damage. A well-known animal cancer-causing agent, the chemical can linger in the home for months or even years.

10. Trichloroethylene (TCE). A solvent used in waxes, paint thinners, fumigants, metal polishes, shoe polish, and rug cleaners. Tests conducted by the National Cancer Institute showed TCE caused cancer of the liver. A combination of alcohol ingestion with exposure to trichloroethylene can cause flushing of the skin, nausea, and vomiting.

11. Hydroxides/lye products. These include automatic dishwasher detergents, toilet bowl cleaners, fire proofing, paint remover, and drain cleaners. Ingestion causes vomiting, prostration, and collapse. Inhalation causes lung damage. Prolonged contact with dilute solutions can have a destructive effect upon tissue, leading to skin irritations and eruptions.

Sources: Karen Carroll, MD, departments of pathology and infectious diseases and Paul Summers, MD, department of obstetrics and gynecology, both at the University of Utah Medical Center in Salt Lake City.

What to Do if There's A Burglar in the House

Outdoor lighting, alarm systems, timers that automatically turn on and off household lights, and other precautions all help protect your home from burglary.

Just as important as taking steps to keep burglars outside is planning what to do if someone makes it inside. *Most important:*

•Create a "safe haven." Inside every home should be a specially equipped room where occupants can retreat in case of an attack or intrusion. This room—ideally a bathroom or bedroom—should have a window or some other means of escape...a solid-core door with a one-inch deadbolt that latches from the inside...a telephone...and a list of emergency phone numbers. If your home is equipped with an alarm system, install a panic button inside your safe room.

•Develop an escape plan. Know the fastest way out of your house from every room. Periodically rehearse your escape. Make sure windows, doors, and other escape routes can quickly be opened from the inside.

•Don't go to investigate. Confronting a burglar face-to-face can turn a simple burglary into an assault or even murder.

More prudent: Leave the investigation to the police. If you arrive home and find evidence of a break-in, *don't go inside.* The intruder might still be there. Leave the premises immediately and call the police.

If the burglary takes place while you're inside, lock a door between yourself and the intruder—ideally that of your safe haven—and telephone the police. If you cannot reach a phone, open a window and yell for help.

If it's possible to escape without risking an encounter with the burglar, then do so. Call the police from a neighbor's house.

•Remain calm. If you come face-to-face with an intruder inside your home, try not to panic. The more level-headed you are, the more likely you'll be able to think of a way to defuse the situation...and the less threatening you'll appear to the burglar.

If you don't provoke him, odds are he/she won't harm you. Most burglars just want to get out of the house once they've been detected. Don't attack or attempt to hold him until the police arrive. Just give him a wide berth so he can escape.

Most important: Fight only if attacked. Then use any weapon at hand—a knife, scissors, a heavy object, a canister of irritating chemical spray, etc. A gun is useful only if you know how—and are willing—to fire it at the intruder. If you wield a gun tentatively, he might take it away and use it against *you.*

Source: Richard L. Bloom, founder of the Crime Deterrent Institute, Houston. A frequent lecturer on crime prevention and victims' rights, Bloom is the author of *Victims: A Survival Guide for the Age of Crime*, Guardian Press, 10924 Grant Rd. #225, Houston 77070. 800-771-8191.

Cutting Utility Costs at Home

Most of us turn out the lights when we want to save energy, but there are even smarter ways to reduce your bills this winter....
Refrigerators:

The refrigerator represents about 30% of most electric bills. To find out how well yours operates, open the door and place a dollar bill against the seal. Then close the door. If you can remove the bill easily, the seal needs replacing. Vacuuming the coils behind or below the unit can improve efficiency as well, but be sure to first unplug the refrigerator.
Insulation:

Up to 40% of home heating escapes outdoors unnecessarily because of inadequate insulation. A free energy audit by your local power company will show you how to improve insulation. *Opportunities:* Install more insulation under the roof and behind walls, and weather strip the windows or replace them entirely.
Lighting:

Compact fluorescent bulbs last at least 10 times longer than regular bulbs and use one-fourth of the electricity while producing the same amount of light. Unlike the long fluorescent bulbs found in offices, these screw into ordinary sockets. Some utilities offer compact fluorescents at a discount. Some even give them away.

Water:

Once all leaks are fixed, the largest water-waster is the toilet. At about six gallons per flush, a lot of good water—and dollars—go down the drain. Low-flush toilets only use about 1.6 gallons, but there are other ways to save water without replacing the fixture. *Simple way:* Fill two or three slim plastic bottles with dirt or gravel and place them in the toilet's water tank. This will displace the tank water so that less is used with each flush. Flow-restricters for shower heads save water too.

Source: Susan Jaffe is a writer who has been specializing in environmental issues for well over a decade.

Environmentally Friendly Household Cleansers

Your favorite household cleansers may do a great job, but their contents are often toxic to breathe, hard on the hands and surfaces—and hazardous to the environment. In addition to being expensive, the containers in which they're sold add up to mountains of waste.

How to make environmentally friendly versions that are just as effective, but cost much less...

• Air freshener. Place a few slices of lemon, orange, or grapefruit in a pot of water. Let simmer gently for an hour or more. Your house will be filled with a citrus scent.

• All-purpose liquid cleanser. Cuts grease and cleans countertops, baseboards, refrigerators, and other appliances.

Combine in a plastic spray bottle: One teaspoon borax, one-half teaspoon washing soda (a stronger form of baking soda—available in supermarkets), two tablespoons white vinegar or lemon juice, one-half teaspoon vegetable-based detergent (i.e., Murphy's Oil Soap), two cups very hot water.

• Floor cleaner. Use on wood, tile, or linoleum for a long-lasting shine.

Mix one-eighth cup vegetable-based detergent, one-half cup white vinegar, and two gallons warm water in a plastic pail.

• Oven cleaner. Sprinkle water on the grimy spots, then cover with baking soda. Repeat the process, and let sit overnight. The grease will wipe off the next day. Use liquid soap and water to sponge away any residue.

• Overnight toilet-bowl cleaner. Pour one cup borax into the toilet bowl. Let sit overnight. Flush in the morning. Stains and rings are lifted away.

• Nonabrasive cleanser. Scours sinks and bathtubs, and leaves no gritty residue.

Combine one-quarter cup baking soda and enough vegetable-based detergent to make a creamy paste.

• Window cleaner. Combine in a plastic spray bottle...one-half teaspoon vegetable-based detergent, three tablespoons white vinegar, two cups water.

• Wood-furniture dusting and cleaning cloth. Mix one-half teaspoon olive oil and one-quarter cup white vinegar or lemon juice in a bowl. Apply to a cotton cloth. Reapply as needed.

Source: Annie Berthold-Bond, editor of *Green Alternatives,* a magazine on environmentally friendly products and services, 38 Montgomery St., Rhinebeck, New York 12572. She is author of *Clean and Green: The Complete Guide to Nontoxic and Environmentally Safe Housekeeping,* Ceres Press, Box 87, Woodstock, New York 12498.

Beware of the Brass

Brass faucets can leach lead into water, especially when new. *Prevention:* Always run water for one minute before drinking.

Source: *University of California Berkeley Wellness Letter,* Box 412, Prince St. Station, New York 10012.

Renovations: A Big Plus

Renovations add more to home value than changes that increase the house's size or modernize it. *Most important:* Plumbing, electrical, heating, and cooling systems...roof, windows, and doors. *Key:* Renovations must improve comfort and convenience. *Big-ticket items that cost more than they add to value:* Swimming pools, hot tubs, outdoor spas, tennis courts, customized or built-in furnishings, deluxe wall and floor coverings.

Source: *The Big Fix-Up: How to Renovate Your Home Without Losing Your Shirt* by Stephen M. Pollan, financial consultant and personal finance commentator for CNBC, Fireside, 1230 Avenue of Americas, New York 10020.

Smoke Detector Disposal Challenge

Most smoke detectors contain radioactive material that could, if the unit become damaged, be dangerous. *Helpful:* Pick the smoke detector up with your hand in a plastic bag. Then turn the bag inside out around the unit and seal the bag. Don't throw the detector in the trash. Don't take it to a hazardous-waste collection site—they don't accept radioactive materials. *Best:* Return the unit to the manufacturer or retailer.

Source: *Complete Trash: The Best Way to Get Rid of Practically Everything Around the House* by Norm Crampton, secretary, Institute for Solid Wastes of the American Public Works Association, M. Evans and Co., 216 E. 49 St., New York 10017.

Dogproof

If you want a dog to help guard the house, get one that's nervous and loud. Fox terriers are ideal. They'll deter burglars much more effectively than a quiet, 200-lb. mastiff. Forget beware-of-dog signs if you don't have a dog. While burglars usually aren't too bright—a sign still won't fool them. The same is true for phony burglar-alarm signs.

Pest Controls Poison-Free

There are many alternatives to the dangerous chemical pesticides sold to control household pests.

Your first line of defense against indoor insects is to make your home as pest-tight as possible. *What to do:*

•Caulk, paint, and patch all holes.

•Screen necessary openings—attic air grilles, chimney caps, etc.

•Cut back shrubs and plants that hug outside walls.

•Install an 18-inch-wide strip of sand circling the foundation to barricade against crawlers—cockroaches, earwigs, beetles.

Next, starve any indoor insects by keeping your home as clean and dry as possible. *What to do:*

•Vacuum carpets, furniture, draperies, and shelves frequently.

•Clean spills immediately.

•Store dry foods in tightly closed metal, glass, or plastic containers.

Take specific steps to eliminate specific pests. *How to get rid of...*

•Cockroaches. There are many non-toxic ways to get rid of roaches. *Included:*

•Fill a half-pint jar halfway with a beer, a piece of banana peel, and some anise. Wrap the entire outside of the jar with masking tape to give the roaches footing and spread a thin layer of petroleum jelly along the inner upper inch of the jar so they cannot escape. Leave the jar out overnight where roaches have been seen. They will crawl in and die.

•Freeze them out. Roaches die at 23°F. If the weather permits, leave your windows open all day to wipe out roaches. This works for silverfish and clothes moths, too.

Warning: Take steps to make sure your pipes don't freeze and burst.

•Use technical boric acid. A least-toxic pesticide is good for bad infestations. Apply a light layer in out-of-the-way areas—under the stove and refrigerator, behind the bathroom vanity, etc.

Warning: Boric acid is toxic. Do not use it where children and pets can get at it. And do not use it where food is stored.

•Ants. Mix three cups of water with one cup of sugar and four teaspoons of boric acid. Pour half a cup of the mixture into three or four empty jam jars wrapped with masking tape and loosely packed half-full with absorbent cotton. Smear the bait along the outside of the jar and set along ant trail. The ants will swarm into the jar. Some will carry the mixture back to the colony, where it will kill other ants.

Warning: If you have small children or pets, screw the lids onto the jars, poke several small holes through the lid and smear some of the bait on the outside of the jar.

•Mosquitoes. Make your yard as dry as possible. *Suggested:*

•Drain all standing water.

•Change the water in birdbaths and wading pools every three days.

•Store wheelbarrows, plant tubs and other items so they can't catch water.

•Stock ornamental pools with mosquito fish—a type of minnow that eats mosquito larvae.

•Rats and mice. Repair cracks and holes in your foundation. Fit pipes and wires that enter the building with metal guards.

Don't use poison to kill rodents. Poisoned animals can crawl away and die in an inaccessible place. *Result:* Dead-rodent odors. *Better:*

•Use snap traps—make sure the trap is the right size for the rodent you are trying to catch.

•Use glue traps—open-ended boxes with glue on the bottom of the inside. Rodents can get in…but not out. Best for mice.

•Garden pests.

Many successful gardeners control pests without poisons. Techniques:

•Pick off pests by hand. Best for small gardens. Put the insects into a glass jar with some water and let them drown and decompose. If the same species appears again, set the open jar under the plant they're invading—the smell will act as a repellent.

•Try natural controls. *Suggested:*

•Rotate crops so plant-specific pests will not have a chance to build up.

•Plant onions and garlic throughout the garden to repel insects.

•Make your own bug spray. Spray your plants with a mixture of one or two tablespoons of liquid soap (Ivory works well) dissolved in one gallon of water. These dislodge or smother mites, aphids, and thrips—tiny insects that destroy buds and blossoms. *Caution:* Rinse your plants with clear water after several hours to avoid leaf burn.

Source: Bernice Lifton, author of *Bug Busters: Poison-Free Pest Controls for Your House and Garden*, Avery Publishing Group, 120 Old Broadway, Garden City Park, New York 11040.

Golden Opportunity Now For Home Refinancing

Mortgage interest rates keep dropping. Should I investigate refinancing the mortgage on our home—or are still lower rates in sight?

Following the temptation to put off taking action until they were certain the bottom of the market had arrived, a lot of people put off investing in stocks all through 1991 because they kept waiting for the market to drop. They wound up missing a great bull market. Don't try to predict interest rates. Mortgage rates have already come way down. This is a golden opportunity to lock in a low fixed rate mortgage. Almost everyone with an 11% or so mortgage should be looking to refinance.

What are the rules for judging if it makes sense to refinance?

The basic rule has been that refinancing makes financial sense if you can cut the rate by two percentage points or more.

Once you're sure that mortgages are being offered in your area at rates low enough to make refinancing attractive, start comparing the number of "points" lenders are charging to write those lower rate mortgages. Points are a form of prepaid interest.

• One point is 1% of the amount of your mortgage paid up front.

• Two points is 2%...etc.

What's important about the points in a refinancing?

How long you expect to stay in the home you're refinancing is a factor in figuring out what to do about points.

Some lenders are now offering no-point mortgages—but at a slightly higher mortgage rate than if the borrower pays points.

Example: You must choose between paying no points on a 9¼%, 30-year fixed rate mortgage, or one point on an 8⅞%, 30-year fixed rate mortgage.

On a $100,000 mortgage, the monthly payments on an 8⅞% mortgage would be $796. On a 9¼% mortgage, they would be $823 a month. If you wind up paying the mortgage for more than three years, you would be better off paying the points to get the lower rate.

Work it out. Paying the points for a lower rate may even be in your interest if you're simply planning to hold on to the property through the current real-estate slump and sell—you hope—for a higher price in three or four years. But if you're pretty sure that you're likely to move or want to sell in a couple of years, you might want to opt for zero points in a refinancing and pay the higher interest rate.

Are the points you pay up front tax-deductible?

This is something that confuses a lot of people when they refinance a mortgage. When you buy a home as your primary residence, you can deduct the amount you pay as points in the year you take out the mortgage.

But points paid to refinance a mortgage—regardless of how you arrange to pay them—are not deductible in full in the year you pay them.

If you refinance a $100,000, 11%, 30-year mortgage and get a $100,000, 9%, 30-year mortgage, the amount paid up front as points can only be deducted over the 30-year term of the mortgage. So it takes several years to recapture that expense in tax deductions.

The only exception to this IRS rule on refinancing is if you refinance to obtain cash for home improvements. For that kind of refinancing, you can deduct the points you pay in connection with the improvements from that year's taxes.

But points aren't the only expense to consider when making a decision to refinance.

What other expenses might you have to pay up front?

In some areas there's a local tax on a new mortgage. In many areas, there are expenses for a credit check and appraisal. And there's always an attorney's fee for closing the mortgage.

Figure on about $500 for the appraisal and credit check. And about $1,400 for a lawyer with experience in real-estate settlements. Don't try to cut corners on the legal expense by using your friendly family lawyer or the lawyer in your financial planner's office. Pay for the specialist.

How's the market for refinancing?

There's plenty of money available for residential mortgages for people who qualify. But the mortgage brokers and lenders are deluged with applications.

Homeowners are shopping around at various sources, but many keep putting off the decision to refinance while they decide whether rates have bottomed. So, some of the brokers and lenders now ask people to pay for the privilege of keeping their places in line.

They ask for the fees for the credit check and appraisal up front with the application, along with a half point—one half percent of the value of the refinanced mortgage. If you do eventually refinance with them, they'll credit the up-front charge toward your loan.

With the economy and real estate in the doldrums and so many banks in trouble, how tough are the lenders on who qualifies for a mortgage?

The big difference borrowers have to be aware of from previous years is a much more rigorous credit check. That credit check used to be pretty perfunctory. But now most lenders verify everything. So be very accurate in the information you give on the application about credit cards, liens, and other indebtedness.

Do self-employed people have any special problems qualifying?

Lenders basically look for a healthy trend in self-employed earnings. A person who made $100,000 two years ago and $50,000 last year —an average of $75,000 for the two years—is a much less attractive prospect to a lender than a person who made $50,000 two years ago and $100,000 last year—the same $75,000 average.

How about the size of a mortgage in relation to the value of the property?

Restrictions aren't any tighter than they have been. Especially if you don't plan to take any cash out—you just refinance one $200,000 mortgage with another one for the same amount.

The best deals, of course, are for what lenders call conforming loans—mortgages up to $202,300 on homes with four or fewer dwelling units. These are the mortgages lenders can sell off to the federal agencies, such as Fannie Mae (Federal National Mortgage Association). A qualified borrower can expect to get a mortgage for up to 90% of the appraised value of a house or condo with a conforming loan.

Does that ratio change if you want to take some cash out?

Well, then you can expect to get a mortgage for up to 75% of appraised value in a refinancing. There's a bigger restriction on the size of the loan relative to the value of the property.

How does my outstanding debt affect the size of a mortgage I qualify for?

The formulas haven't changed. For conforming loans, if you have no other long-term debt, you'll qualify for a mortgage as long as no more than 28% of your income goes to pay principal, interest, hazard and mortgage insurance, and property tax. If you have other long-term debt, say for a second home, the limit for these expenses on both homes is 36% of your income.

If you refinance with a nonconforming loan—usually that means a jumbo loan over $202,300—the limit of such expenses is 33% of income when you have no other long-term debt...and 38% of income when you do.

Does refinancing affect the deductibility of mortgage interest?

If you refinance simply to replace your high-interest mortgage with a mortgage of the same amount at a lower interest rate, the interest is all deductible. The mortgage interest is also fully deductible if you refinance for any amount over the balance of your existing mortgage on your primary residence as long as the funds are used to improve that primary residence.

Remember: You can deduct the interest only on $100,000 over the existing balance on your mortgage if you use the funds from a refinancing for some other purpose—say, college tuition or paying credit bills.

Of course, some people believe that Congress may eat away at some of the mortgage-interest deductions currently in the Revenue Code as the government gets hungrier for revenue. You can use a refinancing to protect yourself somewhat against changes in the future.

How can a refinancing now protect the borrower against a tax law change further down the line?

There has been speculation, for instance, that Congress might sometime drop the mortgage deduction on second homes. If you're paying a relatively high interest rate on a mortgage on a second home, refinancing could save you money and also reduce your vulnerability to that risk. You could refinance your primary house with a lower rate fixed mortgage and pay off the second home mortgage with the proceeds.

You seem to favor going for a fixed rate mortgage. But some of the adjustable rate mortgages (ARMs) are offering rates as low as 5½ plus points for the first year. Would you ignore them?

I'm not a subscriber to going for those low initial rates. Some of those ARMs, it's true, have a cap, which means the worst that could happen is that you wind up paying 12% or so in a few years. I'd much rather lock in the 9% rate now. Also, beware of additional costs associated with ARMs that do not exist with fixed rate mortgages. As I said, I see this as a golden opportunity.

Source: Alexandra Armstrong, CFP, chairman, Armstrong, Welch & MacIntyre, Inc., financial advisors, 1155 Connecticut Ave. NW, Washington, DC 20036.

Pet Danger

Cancer risk from pets: Lung cancer risk doubles in people exposed to pet birds for up to 10 years…and triples in those exposed for more than 10 years. *Theory:* Airborne bacteria from bird waste or bird-feather particles, cause lung irritation that eventually develops into cancer. *Self-defense:* Keep bird cages clean and air out rooms frequently.

Source: From a study of 239 lung cancer patients at Berlin's national institute of health led by Lenore Kohlmeier, MSC, PhD, professor of epidemiology and nutrition, University of North Carolina, Chapel Hill.

Dust Allergy Self-Defense

House dust is the most common irritant for allergy sufferers and asthmatics. *Self-defense:**

• Dust and vacuum your home at least twice a week. Conventional vacuum cleaners can blow dust back into the room. Use a vacuum fitted with a HEPA (High-Efficiency Particulate Actuation) filter, such as Nilfisk Model GS90. *Note:* The allergic person shouldn't perform these tasks. If no one else can do the cleaning, the allergic person should wear a face mask while doing the work.

• Keep floors bare. Dust mites, the main allergen in dust, thrive in carpets.

*Although these suggestions are aimed at the bedroom —where we spend a third of our lives—many can be used throughout the home.

• Cover pillows, mattresses, box springs, and furniture with plastic encasings. Mites breed in furniture and bedding, but can't get through plastic encasings. The plastic should be vacuumed once a week when the linens are changed.

• Wash linens in hot water. Warm or cold water doesn't kill mites.

• Keep the windows in your house shut. This helps to keep outdoor allergens outside. *Note:* Many trees pollinate between 2 am and 4 am, so keep windows closed at night.

• Don't use a humidifier. It increases the mold content in the air. Use a dehumidifier for damp spaces.

• Avoid heaters that release irritating particles, such as wood-burning stoves, fireplaces.

• Use the air conditioner in warm weather. It filters out a lot of troublesome particles from the air. Clean or change the filter once a week.

• Get an air filter. Use it when it's too cool for the air conditioner. *Best:* A HEPA filter, which can remove particles that other filters can't. *Important:* When the filter is on, keep room doors and windows closed. *Cost:* About $150 and up.

• Ask your allergist about injections.

Source: Gerald L. Klein, MD, Allergy and Immunology Medical Group, 2067 W. Vista Way, Vista, California 92083. Dr. Klein is an associate clinical professor at the University of California and a member of the Board of Regents of the American College of Allergy and Immunology.

12

Nutrition, Fitness, And Exercise

Food Oddities/ Food Realities

While there's little doubt that a diet that's high in fat and cholesterol is linked to heart disease, such a diet is by no means the sole culprit. In fact, it's quite clear that the primary causes of heart disease are your genes, obesity, smoking, uncontrolled high blood pressure or diabetes, and a sedentary life-style.

Yet many Americans are now adopting extreme diets in a misguided attempt to protect their health. Extreme diets not only fail to eliminate risk, but in some cases they can raise the risk—of heart disease and of several other ailments. *Here's why...*

Case study #1:

A middle-aged man's triglyceride and cholesterol levels remained high even though he had been on a radical low-fat/low-cholesterol diet for eight years.

He was worried—and rightly so—that unless his levels were brought under control, he would eventually suffer a fatal heart attack, just like several other members of his family.

A battery of tests revealed that this man's ultra-low-fat diet had thrown his metabolism completely out of whack. In fact, he was eating so little fat that his body was behaving as if it were starving. *Result:* His liver was producing more, rather than less, bad cholesterol, and his triglycerides were out of control.

To reverse the problem, I recommended that this man—who had been living mostly on steamed vegetables and skinless chicken—eat more fat. He did so reluctantly, but eventually it brought the fat in his diet from roughly 10% of his total calories to 25%.

His triglyceride and bad-cholesterol levels fell to a much safer level. His risk of heart disease is now dramatically reduced—all as a result of raising his fat intake.

While adding fat to the diet is not the answer for everyone, it can help those whose fat intake is dangerously low.

Case study #2:

A woman in her thirties was experiencing

many vague, troubling symptoms, including anxiety, dizziness and a feeling of pressure inside her chest. Her previous doctor had prescribed nitroglycerine for her chest pressure, and—believing her other symptoms to be psychosomatic—had given her sedatives. He also had recommended psychiatric care.

That doctor's diagnosis was incorrect. I traced this woman's emotional problems to a bad case of hypoglycemia, caused by a poor diet, and to multiple allergies, including severe reactions to mold, pollen and certain foods. Once these allergies were treated, her symptoms disappeared. She is now full of energy, anxiety-free, and the chest pressure has vanished and she no longer feels the need to carry nitroglycerine pills.

Allergies can produce all sorts of symptoms beyond a runny nose, itching, hives, etc. Mysterious symptoms call for thorough allergy testing by an experienced allergist.

Case study #3:

A middle-aged business executive came in to see me after his boss told him he needed help controlling his extreme emotional volatility.

Even though he had a history of severe allergies, he did not suspect that allergies were to blame for his emotional problems. He thought he might need to see a psychotherapist. Yet, as it turned out, he was allergic to food additives and to a mold found in certain foods.

Once he changed his diet and began regular allergy treatments, his emotional explosions disappeared.

He got a promotion, his marriage improved …and he stopped coming to see me. Two years later he called to say that he was again having emotional problems. When I asked how his allergy treatments were going, he confessed that he had stopped them. He resumed treatment, and his symptoms again disappeared.

Case study #4:

A nine-year-old boy was suffering from severe Attention Deficit Disorder (ADD), plus some apparently unrelated symptoms including a skin rash and indigestion.

His ADD was so severe that he was scheduled to be transferred from his regular class to a special-education class—and his parents were distraught at the prospect. I discovered that his "mental" problem was actually the result of a hypersensitivity to sugar. Once sugar was eliminated from his diet, he calmed down immediately. Not only was he able to stay in his regular class, but he is also now an outstanding student.

Self-defense:

Though the specifics of these cases vary widely, I recommend for all my patients the same basic medical advice for preventing illness. *Key points:*

• Maintain your total fat intake to roughly 25% of calories. That's leaner than the traditional American diet, which is roughly 40% fat, but more fatty than the 10%-to-15%-fat diet recommended by many health gurus. Avoid fried foods and fatty cuts of meat—hamburger, sausage, etc. Limit your intake of both saturated fats (butter, tallow, lard and tropical oils) and polyunsaturated fats (corn oil, safflower oil, margarine, etc.). Concentrate on monounsaturated fats such as olive oil and canola (rapeseed) oil. They're far less likely to act as oxidants in the body, and thus are less likely to promote formation of atherosclerosis and heart disease.

• Exercise regularly. Twenty to 30 minutes at least three times a week is ideal.

Caution: Working out at extremely high intensity promotes formation of free radicals, substances that promote oxidation in the body and thus lead to premature aging and heart disease.

• Don't smoke. Period.

• Drink alcohol sparingly, *if at all.* Consume at least six eight-ounce glasses of water a day.

• Take supplemental vitamins and minerals. For maximum protection against oxidants, take vitamin E (400 international units a day), vitamin C (1,000 milligrams, twice daily) and beta-carotene (25,000 international units daily)…but check with your doctor first.

• Consume 1,500 mg. of calcium a day to help ward off osteoporosis and colon cancer. A cup of low-fat yogurt contains roughly 400 mg…a cup of whole milk/291 mg…a cup of skim milk/302 mg.

Source: Thomas Brunoski, MD, a physician in private practice in Westport, Connecticut. Dr. Brunoski specializes in the treatment of medical problems with nutritional and allergy therapy rather than medication.

Good News For Lobster Lovers

Based on the results of new analytic techniques, North Atlantic lobster is no longer considered to be a high-cholesterol food. *Bonus:* Lobster is very low in fat.

Source: Ann M. Williams, health and science editor for The American Heart Association, writing in *Modern Maturity*, 3200 E. Carson St., Lakewood, California 90712.

The Minerals In Our Food

Thanks to everything we've read and heard lately about fat, fiber and food additives, we've all become much smarter about what we're eating—and that's great.

However—a surprising number of myths remain concerning the minerals we take in, both in our daily diets and in the form of supplements. And that misinformation can be dangerous…even deadly.

What we do know for certain is that minerals are essential for life. To a large extent, the body is composed of minerals. For example, our blood carries significant amounts of sodium, potassium and chloride. And our bones and teeth are rich in calcium, phosphorous and magnesium.

The news about minerals is generally good: If you eat a healthy, varied diet—including adequate amounts of milk, fruits and vegetables—your body should get all the minerals it requires. Special needs do arise, however.

Example: As people age, calcium is less well utilized, and extra amounts are recommended, especially for women. Prolonged gastrointestinal illness, and certain drugs, may also change requirements.

Minerals are an often-misunderstood category of nutrients, and you may do well to let go of some of the myths:

• *Myth:* A salty taste is a reliable indicator of salt content.

Truth: Food-content labels must be read very carefully—some items that you would never suspect to be high in sodium are. For example, ounce for ounce, certain dry cereals contain more salt than potato chips.

As most of us now know, too much salt in the diet can promote high blood pressure—and possibly strokes in susceptible individuals. We require only a tiny amount of salt to maintain good health: Just 500 milligrams daily, or the equivalent of a quarter-teaspoon. Chances are you're getting more than that amount naturally from the foods you eat each day—you need never go near a salt shaker. In fact, the average American consumes closer to 4,000 to 5,000 milligrams per day—10 times what's needed, and in some ethnic groups, it can be twice that amount.

If you're a salt-lover, you'd be wise to wean yourself off it. Our taste for salt (or any other flavor) is acquired and thus can be unlearned at any age.

To keep your kids from getting hooked on salt, don't serve them salty food or snacks.

• *Myth:* Calcium deficiency is really only of concern to women approaching menopause.

Truth: Women are never too young to step up their calcium intake to help ward off future osteoporosis. Even teenage girls should start taking calcium supplements to build bone strength, especially if they don't drink milk. Bones that are strong at an early age are less likely to leach out calcium, a process that leads to fractures and other problems later on.

Between the ages of 19 and 24, women (and men) should be sure to get 1,200 milligrams of calcium per day—the amount provided by approximately a quart of milk. If you know you're not taking in sufficient quantities of calcium from your food—and most people's diets are imperfect—by all means take a calcium supplement.

• *Myth:* "Health" foods are better sources of minerals than ordinary foods.

Truth: Some so-called "health" or "natural" foods can in fact be harmful.

Example: Health-food fans will often buy "natural" calcium supplements. These supplements are generally produced from limestone and are rich in calcium and magnesium, but they can also contain dangerous impurities,

219

including lead.

In general, it's unwise to buy foods that haven't been carefully inspected and analyzed by government agencies. *Problem:* Many products found in health-food stores have not undergone rigorous inspection. If you choose a food or a supplement that hasn't been government-approved, you run the risk of ingesting impurities. While some of them are harmless, others are not.

• *Myth:* Minerals lost through sweat during strenuous exercise should be replaced via a mineral-rich drink such as Gatorade or by taking salt tablets.

Truth: Gatorade, a dilute solution of some of the minerals found in the body, is a perfectly fine product, but you rarely need it. Your body will restore its lost minerals on its own.

It's far more important to replenish the water your body has lost in sweat.

As for salt tablets, athletes used to rely on them, but nowadays we know that these tablets can do more harm than good. Again, it's best to stick to plain water after your workout, unless the salt loss was truly excessive.

Exception: Pedialyte is a solution that pediatricians may give to children who've become dehydrated from excessive vomiting or diarrhea. That's because youngsters have a much more delicate constitution than adults, and so their water and mineral levels must be restored quickly and completely.

Minimum daily requirements:

• Sodium. 500 mg. (¼ teaspoon of table salt). *Sodium-rich foods:* Those that have been pickled, canned, smoked or cured…soy sauce…luncheon meats…salted snack foods.

• Potassium. 2,000 mg. *Some potassium-rich foods include:* Bananas (four)…orange juice (four 8-ounce glasses)…carrots (six).

• Chloride. 750 mg. (or ¼ teaspoon of table salt). *Chloride-rich foods:* Most processed foods.

• Calcium. 1,200 mg. (ages 19 to 24)…800 mg. (age 25 and over). *Some calcium-rich foods:* Milk (three 8-ounce glasses)…plain yogurt (three 8-ounce cups)…cheddar cheese (6 ounces).

• Phosphorus. 1,200 mg. (ages 19 to 24)…800 mg. (age 25 and over). *Phosphorus-rich foods:* Same as those rich in calcium.

• Magnesium. 350 mg. (men), 280 mg. (women). *Some magnesium-rich foods:* Green beans (five cups)…Brazil nuts (12).

• Sulfur. A daily requirement has not been established. *Sulfur-rich foods:* Cheese, eggs, milk, meat, nuts, vegetables.

Some essential trace elements—needed by the body in miniscule amounts…

• Iron. *Daily requirement:* 10 mg. (men)…15 mg. (women ages 19 to 50)…10 mg. (women 51 and over). *Some iron-rich foods:* Liver (4 ounces)…breakfast cereal, such as Cheerios or Raisin Bran (2 ounces).

• Selenium. *Daily requirement:* 70 micrograms (men)…55 micrograms (women). *Some selenium-rich foods:* Canned tuna (2½ ounces)…molasses (2 ounces).

• Iodine. *Daily requirement:* 150 micrograms. *Some iodine-rich foods:* Iodized salt…haddock (4 ounces)…milk (8 ounces)…plain yogurt (two 8-ounce cups).

Source: Mia Parsonnet, MD, a member of the clinical faculty of the New Jersey College of Medicine and Dentistry. She is author of *What's Really in Our Food? Fact and Fiction about Fat and Fiber, Vitamins and Minerals, Nutrients and Contaminants*, Shapolsky Publishers, Inc., 136 W. 22 St., New York 10011.

Cholesterol Testing

Cholesterol testing can usually wait until men reach age 35 and women age 45. Adults found to have elevated cholesterol at younger ages will obtain almost all the benefits of cholesterol-lowering therapy by waiting until middle age to start treatment.

Earlier treatment could actually do harm if dietary control did not succeed and patients started lifelong regimens of medications that could have side effects.

Source: Research led by Stephen Hulley, MD, MPH, epidemiologist, University of California at San Francisco.

Caffeine Withdrawal

Fatigue…or headaches…or nausea? These could be symptoms of sudden caffeine withdrawal. New studies show that even people who routinely drink just two cups of coffee each day can experience fatigue, headaches, or nausea after only two days without caffeine. Motor skills are impaired too, making driving dangerous. When you cut down, taper off slowly. If you have to stop for a short term (such as in preparation for an operation), discuss it with your doctor.

Source: Roland R. Griffiths, PhD, psychiatry and neuroscience, quoted in *Hopkins Medical News*, 550 N. Broadway, Baltimore 21205.

Food Danger

The bacteria that cause food poisoning are frequently tasteless, colorless, and odorless. *Self-defense:* Keep refrigerator temperature at 40°F and freezer at 0°F. *Also:* Don't eat foods you feel might be unsafe. Refrigerator life for raw fish is at most two days...fruit/one week...leftovers/three to four days...raw meat and poultry/two to three days.

Source: *American Institute for Cancer Research Newsletter,* 1759 R St. NW, Washington, DC 20069. Four issues/yr. Free.

Breakfast Cereal Trap

Most people buy dry cereal because it's convenient...but prices keep going up and a large family can finish a $4 box in one sitting. *Better:* Buy only if the price is less than eight cents per ounce (it can run as high as 20 cents per ounce—that's 40 cents per serving). Low-cost options (five to eight cents per serving): Cooked oatmeal...cornmeal mush...cooked rice (serve like oatmeal—with milk and sugar)...homemade pancakes, waffles, granola, muffins...eggs and toast.

Source: Amy Dacyczyn is editor of *The Tightwad Gazette,* RR 1, Box 3570, Leeds, Maine 04263.

How to Protect Yourself When Buying Seafood/ When Eating Seafood

Seafood and fish are an excellent protein source that is low in saturated fat, light on calories, and high in vitamins, minerals, and the omega-3 fatty acids that help reduce the risk of heart disease.

But there *are* risks. More than 80% of the seafood eaten in the US has not been inspected for chemical or microbial contaminants. Fortunately, there are things that you can do to enjoy maximum health and minimum risk...

•Avoid chemical contaminants. When you buy fish, choose younger, smaller ones, since they've accumulated fewer contaminants. Low-fat, offshore species like cod, haddock, and pollack are especially good choices. Always trim the skin, belly flap, and dark meat along the top or center, especially when it comes to fatty fish such as bluefish. Don't use the fatty parts to make sauce. Don't eat the green "tomalley" in lobsters or the "mustard" in crabs.

•Avoid natural toxins. When traveling in tropical climates, avoid reef fish such as amberjack, grouper, goatfish, or barracuda, which are more likely to be contaminated. Buy only seafood that has been kept continuously chilled, especially mahi-mahi, tuna, and bluefish, which produce an odorless toxin when they spoil.

•Avoid disease-causing microbes. Bite for bite, raw or undercooked shellfish is the *riskiest* food you can eat.

Self-defense: Don't eat shellfish whose shells remain closed after cooking. Do not eat raw fish or shellfish if you are over 60, HIV-positive, pregnant, have cancer or liver disease, or are vulnerable to infection. Cook all fish and shellfish thoroughly. Raw clams, oysters, and mussels should be steamed for six minutes.

•Don't buy fresh fish that has dull, sunken eyes, or fish that smells "fishy." Do not buy ready-to-eat seafood that is displayed too close to raw seafood.

Source: Lisa Y. Lefferts, an environmental health consultant in Hyattsville, Maryland, who specializes in food-safety, environmental policy and risk-assessment.

Safer Water

Boiling drinking water before use will not make the water safe. *Problem:* Boiling only kills off *bacteria*—it won't remove many heavy metals and other toxic chemicals such as lead, asbestos, copper and trihalomethanes (carcinogenic by-products of chlorination). *Result:* Even water labeled "distilled" could still be contaminated.

Worse: Boiling actually *concentrates* harmful substances in the water left after evaporation. *Self-defense:* Run tap water for several minutes before use to remove lead...buy a quality home water filter to remove other substances—even from commercial bottled waters, which could possibly have the same contaminants.

Source: Robban Sica-Cohen, MD, is a physician with the Center for Healing Arts, in Orange, Connecticut.

Nutritional Supplements

Over-the-counter nutritional supplements—popular among bodybuilders and fitness buffs—often contain ingredients whose effects on the human body are poorly understood...and they may be toxic. *Particularly suspect:* Supplements containing ingredients derived from the testicles, hypothalamus glands, adrenal glands or pituitary glands of animals. However, because different supplement manufacturers use different names for the same ingredient, and because Food and Drug Administration regulations allow supplements to contain untested ingredients, it's often hard to tell what's safe and what's potentially dangerous. *Generally safe in moderation—with*

doctor's OK: Conventional vitamin and mineral tablets.

Source: Rossanne M. Philen, MD, is a medical epidemiologist at the Centers for Disease Control and Prevention in Atlanta.

Coffee and Nicotine Gum

The acid in coffee prevents absorption of nicotine from the gum for up to half an hour. *Other blockers:* Cola...many juices...acidic foods. *Recommended:* Avoid eating or drinking anything except water for at least 15 minutes before chewing nicotine gum.

Source: Thomas Cooper, DDS, professor of oral health sciences, University of Kentucky College of Dentistry in Lexington, reported in *American Health,* 28 W. 23 St., New York 10010.

Red Wine

Cabernet sauvignon contains a higher level of *resveratrol*—a natural cholesterol fighter—than most other red wines. Consumers should be aware, however, that for resveratrol to be effective, two to three glasses of the wine must be consumed *daily,* not just on the weekends or at parties. *Important:* The wine should be accompanied by food, which slows the alcohol's absorption into the blood stream. French Bordeaux also contains 80% of the resveratrol-rich cabernet grape.

Source: Leroy Creasy, PhD, professor of pomology, New York State College of Agriculture and Life Sciences at Cornell University, Ithaca, New York 14853, who originally identified resveratrol as the cholesterol-lowering substance in wine in 1991.

Calcium Supplement Warning

Natural-source products using bone and oyster shell sometimes contain unacceptably high levels of lead. This can be dangerous to pregnant women and children. *Better:* Synthetic compounds, such as calcium carbonate, or USP-type tablets…which are refined from the natural sources.

Source: Research in the US and Canada led by Alfred Quattore, California Department of Health Services, Sacramento.

Margarine Health Risks

Women who eat the equivalent of four or more teaspoons a day have a 50% increased risk of developing heart disease. And women eating other forms of solid and semisolid vegetable fat—equal to six or more spoons of margarine daily—have a 70% increased risk. These types of vegetable fats are found in cookies, cakes and fried fast-foods.

Source: Eight-year study of more than 88,000 women, aged 34 to 59, led by Walter Willett, DrPH, professor and chairman, department of nutrition, Harvard School of Public Health, Boston.

Antacid Warning

Eating too many calcium-containing antacid tablets can damage the brain and the heart. A 53-year-old man with mild kidney trouble who consumed 20 to 25 antacid tablets a day suffered both a stroke and a heart attack. *Cause:* Too much calcium in his blood from the antacids. *Self-defense:* Get dosage instructions from your doctor before taking antacid tablets.

Source: Jeffrey Frank, MD, director of neuromedical/neurosurgical intensive care, The Cleveland Clinic Foundation.

Odor and Weight Loss

Sniffing your favorite food odors helps weight loss. In a recent study, dieting patients inhaled a common food additive that smells like corn chips whenever they felt hungry. They had 10 times the weight-loss of those who didn't. *Reason:* The olfactory bulb, the part of the brain that processes aromas, is linked directly to the part of the brain that controls hunger. Strong odors of any favored food may diminish hunger. *Dieting strategy:* Sniff food deeply before eating…eat hot food (smells are enhanced by heat)…chew thoroughly to get more aroma molecules to the olfactory bulb.

Source: Alan R. Hirsch, MD, is neurological director for the Smell and Taste Treatment and Research Foundation, Chicago. 800-458-2783.

How Men Can Lose 10 To 75 Pounds…For Good

From everything we read and hear, it may seem as though weight were primarily a woman's problem.

In fact, there are more overweight men than overweight women. There are now approximately 25 million men in the United States who are considered clinically obese (more than 20% above their ideal weight).

And there are another 10 to 15 million men who are heavier than they would like to be. For men, weight-gain frequently accompanies middle age and a higher-than-average socio-economic status.

Four basic steps:

•Control stress-eating. Uncontrolled, unplanned nibbling tends to involve high-fat, snack-type foods.

If you find yourself eating from stress or other emotions, such as anger or frustration, seek out enjoyable alternatives, which can include reading a mystery or going out to a movie.

If you're at your job, try to leave the building for a 10-minute walk or do some deep breathing while sitting at your desk.

•Avoid alcohol. Alcohol is high in calories and impairs judgment. In addition, it tends to work against your self-restraint when you're eating out.

Example: Drinking a glass or two of wine before ordering an entrée can lower your guard when the waiter shows up. Alcohol improves the chances that you'll switch from the plain green salad and broiled fish you intended to order to prime rib and salad drenched in bleu-cheese dressing. Further, alcohol in the system slows down the body's fat-burning process.

•Decrease the amount of fat you consume. This one basic nutritional change can make a big difference in your weight.

Reduce dietary fat, found in red meat, fried and greasy foods, cheese, chips and ice cream, to name but a few. You'll lose weight even if you eat the same quantity of food as before. That's because eliminating high-fat items automatically means replacing them with low-fat, low-calorie carbohydrates (fruits and vegetables, breads and grains) and protein (fish, poultry, beans and low-fat milk products).

•Increase exercise. Exercise reduces stress, helps burn more calories and produces a "post-exercise burn"—so that your metabolic rate remains at a higher-than-normal level, even hours after your workout.

Exercise also raises the levels of endorphins, resulting in a nice, drug-free "high." Sustained weight loss is virtually impossible without an ongoing exercise program. If you don't continue to exercise, any weight that is lost will almost certainly return.

Start slowly. Unlike out-of-shape women, out-of-shape men tend to plunge right into a new fitness program, attempting to accomplish too much too soon.

First, get your doctor's OK. Then, begin a brisk-walking program five to six days a week, 20 to 25 minutes a day.

If necessary, break up your exercise into two sessions—morning and afternoon. Increase your time by five minutes per week until you're up to 45 minutes a day. You may want to eventually graduate to slow jogging or a stationary bicycle.

Smart food choices:

After 15 years of working with both male and female dieters, I've discovered that smart men are nutritionally ignorant—they just don't know what's in the food they're eating and why it can be harmful.

Example: A chef's salad and a diet soft drink is many men's idea of a healthy, low-calorie lunch…but they couldn't be more wrong. A chef's salad is a 750- to 1,000-calorie, high-fat meal, usually containing cheese and luncheon meat (each approximately 100 calories per ounce) and about 80% to 90% fat—all smothered in two or three ladles of dressing (200 to 250 calories).

A man will wash down his chef's salad with a diet drink—and feel virtuous because the soda has no calories. But, in fact, he may have just consumed more than half his caloric and fat limits for the entire day.

Healthy, long-term weight control means making smart choices. Some simple food substitutions that will produce weight-loss without a feeling of deprivation:

Instead of…	Have…
Half a pepperoni pizza	2 regular slices and a green salad
A bran or corn muffin	Bagel or English muffin
A handful of cashews	2 handfuls of popcorn
Chicken nuggets	Broiled chicken sandwich
Fettuccini Alfredo	Pasta with vegetables in tomato sauce
16 ounces of red meat	6 ounces of red meat with a baked potato and tossed green salad

Important: Don't let yourself feel deprived. While you will have to give up the notion that you can eat whatever you want whenever you want it, there is no reason you can't eat the foods you like and still slim down and improve your health. You should try to stick to the rules you have set, but you don't have to be perfect.

Source: Clinical psychologist Morton H. Shaevitz, PhD, director of the behavioral health programs at the Scripps Clinic and Research Foundation in La Jolla, California. He is the author of *Lean & Mean: The No Hassle, Life-Extending Weight Loss Program for Men*, G. P. Putnam's Sons, 200 Madison Ave., New York 10016.

Fat Facts

Some poultry is fattier than others—and some parts are fattier than some cuts of beef. If you are on a low-fat diet, you should know…

•Chicken has 1½ times the fat of turkey.

•Skinless chicken thighs have almost twice

the fat of skinless drumsticks.

•A 4-oz. skinless chicken thigh has more saturated fat than 4 oz. of thoroughly trimmed, select-grade round steak, sirloin—or even pork tenderloin.

•Chicken wings are fattier than drumsticks —backs are even fattier than thighs.

Self-defense: Stick to breast (white) meat… eat ground chicken and turkey only if made from breast meat—with no skin. Beware the "other white meat"—pork. Typical trimmed cuts of pork are one-third fattier than skinless chicken—and twice as fatty as skinless turkey.

Source: Bonnie Liebman, director of nutrition, Center for Science in the Public Interest, 1875 Connecticut Ave. NW, Washington, DC 20009.

Nutrition…And Common Ailments

By now, the rules for healthful eating are familiar to most Americans—if not always properly heeded…

•Eat lots of fruits, vegetables, and whole grains. For maximum nutritional benefits, fruits and vegetables should be fresh or frozen. Canned vegetables are lower in several nutrients and higher in salt.

•Eat a variety of foods. Doing so will help ensure that you get all the nutrients you need to fight disease.

•Limit your intake of dietary fat. It should account for no more than 30% of your daily calories.

Saturated fat—like that found in meat and dairy products—should account for no more than 10% of calories. Monounsaturated and polyunsaturated fats (found in nuts, seeds, and olives) should account for roughly the same percentage each.

•Limit your intake of cholesterol. Eat no more than 300 milligrams (mg) daily. If you eat a typical American diet, you'll have to cut back by about one-third. One egg has 272 mg of cholesterol…an ounce of cheddar cheese about 30 mg.

•Restrict your intake of sugar—and salt,

salt-cured, salt-pickled, smoked, and charcoal-broiled foods.

•Drink in moderation—*or not at all. Maximum:* Two drinks a day. There is some evidence that a small amount of red wine daily may be beneficial for heart disease sufferers.

•Don't overeat. Eat only enough to maintain your proper body weight.

•Limit consumption of meat. *Maximum:* No more than four ounces of red meat, fish, or fowl a day, although fish or skinless fowl are preferable. If you eat beef, try to get as lean a cut as possible—avoid prime and higher grades of meat, which tend to be especially fatty.

Less well-known:

Certain foods and nutritional supplements may help many common ailments, although these remedies are less well-proven…

•Carpal tunnel syndrome. Though usually blamed on improper or repeated use of the arms or hands, this disorder may be caused by a nutritional deficiency. *Helpful:*

•Vitamin B6: 40 mg daily.

•Magnesium: 400 mg daily.

•Vitamin B2: 50 mg daily.

Essential: Check with your doctor before taking nutritional supplements—some could give you worrisome side effects.

These and other supplements are widely available at drug and health-food stores.

•Common cold. To reduce congestion, drink at least eight eight-ounce glasses of water daily.

Also, eat lots of chicken soup or other hot soups—they help "thin" the mucus in the nose. Spicy soups are especially helpful.

Contrary to popular belief, vitamin C does not help prevent colds. However, it does seem to reduce both their duration and severity. Take 500 mg four times daily. *Also helpful:*

Zinc: Suck on one 180-mg lozenge for at least 10 minutes every two hours.

•Constipation. Increased intake of grains, fruits, and vegetables, and other fiber-rich foods helps in most cases. *Also helpful:*

Pantothenic acid: 250 to 500 mg daily. Good food sources of pantothenic acid are organ meats, eggs, whole grains, and many vegetables.

Increased consumption of cantaloupe,

oranges, spinach, cabbage, broccoli, salmon, and other foods rich in folic acid.

•Fatigue. Although caffeine gives a short-term energy boost, regular use of this drug impairs the ability of the muscles to contract properly. *Result:* Increased fatigue. Sufferers of chronic fatigue should reduce their intake of coffee, tea, and soft drinks. *Also helpful:*

Vitamin B$_{12}$: Injections every one to four weeks.

Vitamin C: 1,000 mg daily.

Zinc: 100 mg daily.

Aspartic acid: 1,000 mg twice daily.

If these steps fail to provide relief, have your doctor test your blood levels of iron, magnesium, and potassium. If you have a mineral deficiency, your doctor may recommend nutritional supplements.

Caution: Some research suggests that iron supplements promote heart disease in persons who don't have an iron deficiency.

•Heartburn. Drink plenty of water and avoid big, stomach-distending meals. Also, avoid foods known to cause trouble—alcohol, chocolate, coffee, fatty or spicy foods, milk, orange juice, peppermint, spearmint, sugar, tea, and tomato juice.

Finally, avoid obesity. Excessive body fat presses in on the abdomen, forcing the contents of the stomach into the esophagus.

•Infections. Sugar impairs the body's immune system. Avoiding it will boost your resistance to infections. *Also helpful:*

Vitamin A: 20,000 international units (IU) daily to prevent infections, 200,000 IU daily for a few days to treat an existing infection—in either case only under a doctor's supervision. (Pregnant women should take no more than 8,000 IU daily.)

Vitamin C: 1,000 mg twice daily.

Vitamin E: 400 IU daily.

Zinc: 50 mg daily.

Bromelain (an enzyme derived from the pineapple plant): Various dosages, depending upon the preparation.

Echinacea (an herb): Various dosages. Read product labels.

Garlic: A few cloves or a deodorized garlic preparation daily.

•Insomnia. Avoid all sources of caffeine and alcohol, especially in the afternoon and evening. *Also helpful:*

Vitamin B$_3$: 1,000 mg 30 minutes before bedtime.

Valerian (an herb): 150 to 300 mg of standardized aqueous extract 30 to 45 minutes before bedtime.

•Muscle cramps. Many forms of cramping seem to be caused by low blood sugar (hypoglycemia), a condition that can often be prevented by eating a sugar-free, high-fiber diet with frequent snacking throughout the day. *Also helpful:*

Vitamin E: 300 to 600 IU daily.

Magnesium: 400 mg daily.

For severe leg cramps associated with pregnancy...

Calcium citrate: 1,000 mg twice daily, morning and evening.

•Osteoarthritis. Many arthritis sufferers find pain relief simply by eliminating foods of the nightshade family—tomato, white potato, and all forms of pepper except black pepper—from their diet. *Also helpful:*

Vitamin C: 1,000 mg twice daily.

Vitamin E: 400 IU one or two times a day.

Devil's claw (a medicinal herb): 1.5 grams daily.

Vitamin B$_3$: Dosage depends on severity of symptoms. Consult your physician for more information.

Glucosamine sulfate: 500 mg three times daily.

Extract of the New Zealand green-lipped mussel: 1,050 mg daily.

S-adenosyl-methionine (related to an amino acid): 1,200 mg daily.

Shark cartilage extract: Four 740-mg capsules four times daily.

Superoxide dismutase: Six to 12 400-mg tablets daily, one hour before the first meal of the day.

•Osteoporosis. Cut your intake of sugar, salt, alcohol, caffeine, fatty foods, and meat—all promote loss of calcium from the body. Focus your diet instead on fruits (except cranberries and plums), vegetables (except corn and lentils), and dairy products (except for cheese). *Also helpful:*

Vitamin C: 500 mg daily.

Calcium citrate: 500 mg daily…1,000 mg daily for menopausal women.

Magnesium: 500 mg daily.

•Periodontal disease. Minimize sugar intake, of course, and be sure to brush and floss after eating. Folate mouthwash also seems to help keep gums healthy. Rinse your mouth with one tablespoon of 0.1% solution twice daily. *Also helpful:*

Vitamin C: 1,000 mg twice daily.

Calcium citrate: 750 mg daily.

Coenzyme Q: 25 mg twice daily.

Sanguinaria (bloodroot) mouthwash or toothpaste.

If the bone beneath your gums is being resorbed, ask your dentist about supplements.

•Ulcer. Contrary to popular belief, milk does not help cure ulcers.

Helpful: Avoid late dinners. An early dinner will release less stomach acid than a late dinner. Avoid tea, coffee, soft drinks, and other sources of caffeine. *Also helpful:*

Vitamin A: 100,000 IU daily (but only under medical supervision).

Vitamin C: 500 mg before meals and at bedtime.

Vitamin E: 400 to 800 IU daily.

Magnesium hydroxide antacid: 15 to 30 milliliters four times daily.

Zinc: 50 mg three times daily, taken with meals. When taking zinc, be sure also to take copper: 2 mg daily.

Deglycyrrhizinated licorice: 760 mg three times daily, between meals.

Raw cabbage juice: One quart daily. This is a good source of the potent anti-ulcer compound S-methylmethionine.

Source: Melvyn Werbach, MD, assistant clinical professor of psychiatry at the School of Medicine, University of California at Los Angeles. He is the author of several books on nutrition, including the newly released *Healing through Nutrition: A Natural Approach to Treating 50 Common Illnesses with Diet and Nutrients*, Harper-Collins, 10 E. 53 St., New York 10022.

Apple Cider Danger

Fresh-pressed unpasteurized cider—the kind sold by many rural roadside vendors—can harbor the potentially deadly E. coli 0157 bacterium. *Danger signs:* Abdominal cramps and diarrhea, which is often bloody. *Safe:* Any pasteurized apple drink.

Source: Patricia Griffin, MD, Centers for Disease Control and Prevention, Atlanta.

Lower Cholesterol Danger

Lower cholesterol may lead to increased aggression. Analysis of the cholesterol levels of 50 men admitted to a forensic hospital for crimes of violence showed that the 21 most violent men had lower cholesterol levels than the 29 who were less violent. Although preliminary, the present findings are consistent with large-scale studies that have shown that reducing cholesterol levels reduces heart-related mortality but increases mortality from suicide, murder, and accidental death.

Source: Study by Marc Hillbrand, PhD, Whiting Forensic Institute, Box 70, Middletown, Connecticut 06475.

Moderate Drinking May Not Be Safe Anymore

A recent report warning heavy drinkers against taking supplements of beta-carotene prompted several queries from perplexed readers. One man asked whether having two or three drinks over a weekend constituted "heavy drinking." Another wanted to know if half a bottle of wine a day, which he described as "light drinking" compared with his friends, was heavy drinking in my view.

The confusion is common, according to experts at the National Institute on Alcohol Abuse and Alcoholism. As the Institute pointed out in a recent health alert: "Moderate drinking is difficult to define because it means different things to different people. The term is often confused with 'social drinking,' which refers to drinking patterns that are accepted by the society in which they occur."

If you travel in a bar-hopping crowd, you are likely to consume far more alcohol "socially" than, say, a person who drinks only on special occasions or at parties now and then. You may also drink more than someone who downs a cocktail each night before dinner and a glass of wine with the meal. And all of you may consider your drinking habits to be "moderate." But are they?

Meaning of "moderate":

There is, in fact, a definition of moderate drinking that is generally accepted by scientists and other experts concerned with the health effects of alcohol. The definition is based on the daily amount of alcohol that can be consumed by an average healthy adult without untoward effects. According to guidelines issued by public health officials, moderate drinking means no more than two drinks a day for most men and no more than one drink a day for most women.

That does not mean that if you forgo alcohol on one or more days, you can make up for lost time the next time you drink. Having two drinks a day for seven days is not the same as downing 14 drinks over the weekend. Nor does "a drink" mean whatever amount happens to be in your glass.

A standard drink is defined as supplying half an ounce (12 grams) of absolute alcohol. That is approximately the amount found in each of the following: 12 ounces of regular lager beer (4% alcohol), 8 ounces of stout (6% alcohol), 5 ounces of wine that is 10% alcohol or 4 ounces of wine that is 12.5% alcohol, 3 ounces of sherry (16.5% alcohol), 1¼ ounces of 80-proof distilled spirits (what most people call "hard liquor," including brandy, cognac, liqueurs, and cordials, 40% alcohol), or 1 ounce of 100-proof distilled spirits (50% alcohol).

So if you really want to know whether you are drinking moderately, you must measure your drinks or consume them from a premeasured container. You might want to measure your glasses to find out how much they hold because one person's wine glass is another's water goblet.

Sex, age, etc.:

The different definitions of moderate drinking for men and women are based on physiological differences. It is not a myth that women typically get drunk faster than men do when they both drink the same amount. There are several reasons for this.

First, women generally weigh less than men do, so the same amount of alcohol is concentrated in a smaller body mass.

Second, women typically have a higher percentage of body fat and less body water than men do. Since alcohol dissolves much more readily in water than in fat, the difference in body composition means that when alcohol enters a woman's body, it becomes more concentrated, and therefore has a more potent effect, than the same amount of alcohol would in a man's body.

Third, there is an enzyme in the stomach that metabolizes alcohol before it gets into the bloodstream, and that enzyme is about four times as active in men as in women. So even if a man and a woman weigh the same, have the same proportion of body fat and drink the same amount, more pure alcohol is likely to reach a woman's blood and brain than a man's.

It is also true that alcohol tends to have a more potent effect on older people. That is largely due to the increases in body fat that accompany aging. Thus, an elderly man is like a young woman with respect to his ability to handle alcohol. Accordingly, experts at the National Institute recommend that the elderly limit their alcohol intake to one drink a day.

Health risks:

Some people should not drink at all. Among them are women who are pregnant or trying to become pregnant. Heavy drinking during pregnancy can cause serious birth defects and mental retardation…lesser amounts of alcohol (two or three drinks a day) have been linked to diminished size, minor physical abnormalities, and lower scores on intelligence tests among the resulting offspring. Since it is not possible to say how much alcohol a pregnant woman can safely consume, the general advice is not to drink at all until after the baby is born.

Other adults who should steer clear of alcohol include people with peptic ulcers and other health problems that might be aggravated by alcohol—people taking medications like sleeping pills, antidepressant or antianxiety drugs, or certain painkillers that are known to interact with alcohol—and people with a history of alcohol addiction or problem drinking, and perhaps even those with a family history of alcoholism.

Of course, alcohol should not be consumed by those who will soon be operating a motorized vehicle or other machinery that requires attentiveness, manual dexterity, and quick reaction time.

Even in moderate amounts, alcohol may increase the risk of certain health problems. Although the evidence is controversial, there are some suggestions that moderate drinking may slightly increase the risk of developing breast cancer and colon cancer. Alcohol may also increase the risk of developing a hemorrhagic stroke, the relatively rare but most devastating type of stroke, which results from a ruptured blood vessel in the brain.

Finally, alcohol does contain calories: Seven per gram, or 84 calories in "a drink," not counting the calories in the rest of the drink, such as in mixers like tonic or cola. If you have a weight problem, alcohol can add to it, especially if its uninhibiting effect prompts you to eat more than you might otherwise.
Possible benefits:

Why, you may wonder, should you drink at all? Dr. Enoch Gordis, director of the National Institute, points out that "there are trade-offs involved in each decision about drinking."

Most people drink because they like the effects of alcohol on their emotional state and sociability. Alcohol diminishes stress, anxiety and self-consciousness and induces feelings of relaxation and conviviality. Someone who has trouble becoming acquainted with strangers at a party may find it much easier to converse under the influence of a drink or two.

As for health benefits, researchers at the University of Pittsburgh found that moderate drinking by postmenopausal women raises their estrogen levels, which may in turn reduce their risk of developing heart disease and osteoporosis. And nearly a dozen major studies in several countries and among various ethnic groups have linked moderate drinking to a decreased risk of suffering a heart attack or a stroke caused by a blood clot. These cardiovascular benefits have been noted in both men and women.
Source: Jane E. Brody.

Vitamins and Workouts

Supplements of vitamins C and E significantly reduce muscle damage that can occur during heavy physical training.

Result: Athletes taking vitamin supplements can potentially train longer and harder—and recover faster—than athletes who do not use the supplements. *Unexpected bonus:* The vitamin supplements also helped keep male athletes' testosterone levels—and sex drives—at normal levels.
Source: Research led by Ian Gilliam, lecturer, Phillip Institute of Technology, Canberra, Australia, reported in *The Medical Post*, 777 Bay St., Toronto, Ontario M5W 1A7.

Headphone And Jogging Danger

Noise triggers a release of adrenaline, which constricts the blood supply to the ears and diverts it to the arms, legs, and heart. Aerobic exercise also diverts blood from the ears to those muscles. *Result:* The one-two punch of loud music and less blood destroys cilia in the ear canal…doubling risk of hearing loss.
Source: Audiologist Richard Navarro, PhD, quoted in *Men's Health Advisor 1992*, edited by Michael Lafavore, editor, *Men's Health* magazine, 33 E. Minor St., Emmaus, Pennsylvania 18098.

Walking Vs. Running

Running and walking are equally effective forms of exercise. Both improve your muscle tone and cardiovascular system…and help you burn calories. *Advantages of walking:* Easier on joints…better for those starting a fitness program—especially older or overweight people.

Advantage of running: Provides a better cardiovascular workout for those already fit.

Caution: If you have a family history of heart disease or have been inactive, ask your doctor before starting to run.

Source: Mark Anderson, PhD, PT, ATC, professor of physical therapy at the University of Oklahoma Health Sciences Center.

Benefit Of Exercise

Once-a-week exercise lowers the risk of adult-onset (type II) diabetes by as much as 23%. *Furthermore:* Vigorous exercise from two to four times a week reduces a person's risk of developing diabetes by 38%…at five times or more per week, the risk is cut by 42%.

Danger of inactivity: Lack of exercise contributes to as many as one of four cases of type II diabetes.

Source: Study of more than 21,000 male physicians, aged 40 to 84, reported in *The Johns Hopkins Medical Letter*, Health After 50, 5 Water Oak, Fernandina Beach, Florida 32034.

Better Jogging

Rest one or two days a week for a balanced training program. The body must have time to replenish the *glycogen* (blood sugar) lost during training. Weak muscles—drained of energy—are more prone to injuries. If trained hard without resting, the body cannot regenerate the muscle filaments, which can cause damage in the long term.

Source: David L. Costill, PhD, director, Human Performance Laboratory, Ball State University, Muncie, Indiana, writing in *Runner's World*, 33 E. Minor St., Emmaus, Pennsylvania 18098.

Healthy Walking

Brisk walks strengthen your immune system—but too-strenuous workouts can lower immunity to colds and flu, we hear from David Nieman, Doctor of Public Health. Exercising near your maximum capacity for just 45 minutes—or more—produces a six-hour "window" of vulnerability afterward. *Better:* Exercise at a moderate level—the equivalent of a brisk walk—if not training for competition.

Source: David Nieman, DrPH, is professor of health, department of health and exercise science, Appalachian State University, Boone, North Carolina.

13

Your Car

Used-Car Trap

Totaled vehicles are being sold—after being restored—to unsuspecting buyers. While selling a fixed-up wreck is not against the law, it is illegal for the owner—or dealer—not to inform the buyer of its history.

Self-defense:

Do not buy a used vehicle if it has had more than one owner. Get the name and number of its previous owner and ask him/her thorough questions. If the story does not ring true, walk away from the sale.

Additional protection: In 13 Midwestern states, Carfax (314-874-0834) will provide a partial history of the car if you have its vehicle identification number, found on a small plate just below the windshield on the driver's side. *Fee:* $20 per request.

Source: Bernard Brown is an attorney specializing in consumer-plaintiff car fraud, the Law Office of Bernard E. Brown, 9250 Glenwood, Overland Park, Kansas 66212.

What to Look for When You Test-Drive a Car

Before you buy a new car, take full advantage of your test drive. Make sure the dealer lets you drive the vehicle where you can give it a thorough workout...on bumpy roads...in stop-and-go traffic...and on highways, especially the entrance and exit ramps. Pay special attention to how the car matches up to your expectations for comfort, drivability, interior layout and *power*.

Comfort:

Engineers call the science of fitting the car to the person *ergonomics*. You'll soon see how well they did when you climb in behind the driver's seat.

You probably won't be the only one driving the new car regularly. Don't forget that the "feel" of the car should suit your co-drivers and frequent passengers.

Clearance: Can you get in and out without hitting your head?

Headroom: Your hair shouldn't touch the ceiling. If it does, and you love the vehicle, consider ordering it with a sunroof. This will give you another inch or two.

Seat height: Does it give you good road visibility?

Headrest: Will your head, neck and back be comfortable after driving for a while?

Leg room: Does the seat move far enough forward and back not only for you but for all drivers?

Drivability:

Test-drive the car at night to make sure that the headlights are powerful enough for your comfort.

Power: Does the car run smoothly and accelerate adequately? *Hint:* Make sure the car you test has the engine size, transmission type or gear ratios that you want.

Rear visibility: Can you see adequately with the exterior rear-view mirrors? If they're too small, be aware that replacements don't exist.

Noise: Does engine exhaust or wind noise bother you?

Fuel type: Does the car need expensive high-test gas? High-performance, multi-valve, super- and turbo-charged models all do.

Interior:

Instrumentation: Can you read the gauges easily?

Controls: Do you hit the wiper switch and put the radio on?

Door handles: Can you find them in the dark?

Bottom line:

If you're satisfied with your test drive, don't assume the car that the dealer delivers to you will be as good.

Check out the finish of the car you want to buy to make sure you haven't been sold a vehicle that already has been driven…or damaged in transit. Look for tell-tale signs of re-painting…like paint traces on the rubber stripping or trim, mismatched colors and misfit panels. And take a good look at the undercoating. It should look slightly weathered— not sparkling clean and still soft.

Insist on a test drive of your new car before you accept delivery. *Also:* Never take delivery at night. You want to examine your car carefully in broad daylight. You may also want to

have the car looked over by a good mechanic.

Source: Dré Brungardt, editor of *Nutz & Boltz®,* Box 123, Butler, Maryland 21023.

Dealer Logo Decal Removal

Remove a dealer logo decal from a car by heating it a bit with a hand-held hair dryer set to *low*. This should soften the glue enough for the decal to be gently peeled off. *Better:* When buying a car, get the dealer to agree—in writing—that the car will not have any dealer identification when you take delivery.

Source: *Used Cars: Finding the Best Buy* by *Chicago Tribune* auto editor Jim Mateja. Bonus Books, Inc., 160 E. Illinois St., Chicago 60611.

How to Make Your Car Last Twice as Long

The best way to save money on a new car is to put off buying one for as long as possible. Motorists can easily double or even triple the life span of their present cars simply by performing proper maintenance, practicing good driving habits and avoiding the kinds of mistakes that send most cars to the junkyard.

Most common mistakes:

•*Mistake:* Failing to observe the "break-in" period. Drive gently during a new car's first 50 miles—and be sure to vary your speed for the first 1,000 miles of the car's life. Failing to do so results in improper seating of the piston rings, which leads to increased oil consumption for the life of the car. Also, change the oil promptly after the first 1,500 miles to eliminate bits of metal and grit found in a new engine.

•*Mistake:* Making sudden starts and stops. Accelerating aggressively only to slam on the brakes at the next traffic light does little to save time—but does cause needless wear to your engine, transmission, suspension and brakes—and wastes gas. *Better:* Anticipate traffic patterns to keep your speed as constant as possible. Emulate good truck drivers—they tend to be very gentle on their vehicles.

•*Mistake:* Downshifting needlessly. In the early days of automobiles, brakes were so unreliable that prudent drivers always shifted into a lower gear when descending hills or approaching busy intersections. Today, brakes are very reliable…and far less costly to repair than engine and transmission components. *Rule:* Use "engine braking" only when descending a long, steep grade. At all other times, use your brakes.

•*Mistake:* Driving with a cold engine. Engine wear occurs most swiftly not during high-speed driving but in the first moments after a car has been started, when the cylinders are starved for oil. *To avoid trouble:* Before driving off, let your engine idle with your foot *off* the accelerator pedal for one minute—*no more and no less*. Once you're under way, drive slowly and avoid using your heater, wipers and other power-hungry accessories until the engine reaches its proper operating temperature—usually about three minutes.

Special danger: Accelerating briskly with a cold engine causes head gaskets to fail. Premature use of accessories speeds wear of engine bearings.

•*Mistake:* Shifting gears haphazardly. Manual transmissions cost less and are cheaper to maintain than automatics—if you learn proper shifting techniques. Picking too high a gear for a given speed "lugs" your engine. Picking an excessively low gear causes it to "over-rev." Both practices waste fuel and damage your engine bearings. *Better:* Shift so your engine speed remains between 2,000 and 3,000 revolutions per minute (RPM). Use overdrive settings only for speeds greater than 45 miles an hour.

Common problem: With many manual transmissions, shifting from neutral to first gear causes an audible grinding of the transmission's synchronizer rings.

Remedy: Avoid shifting directly from neutral to first. Instead, move the shift lever briefly into second, then shift into first gear. And—never rest your hand on the shift lever or rest your foot on the clutch pedal. Use your right foot for both accelerator and brake. Use your left foot for the clutch.

•*Mistake:* Driving with dirty and/or worn-out oil. To many motorists, oil maintenance means simply adding the occasional quart of 10W40. In fact, 10W30 offers far more protection against engine wear. And by the time you're a quart low, it's time for another oil change.

Change conventional motor oil once every three months or 3,000 miles, whichever comes first. Better: Switch to synthetic oil.* It costs a few dollars more but offers superior protection for up to 12,000 miles.

To keep oil clean between changes, select the biggest oil filter that will fit under the hood. (Most cars accept either a "tall" or "short" filter. The tall one always provides better filtration.) If you live in a dusty environment, bolting on a bypass oil-filtration system provides an extra measure of protection without voiding your car's warranty. *Cost:* About $80, plus labor.

Avoid oil additives: Despite manufacturer's claims, they neither reduce engine wear nor boost performance.

Switch from a disposable pleated-paper air filter to a more effective—and reusable—wetted-foam filter. *Cost:* $20 to $40. To help lock out dirt, apply a thin layer of grease to the seal between the filter and the filter housing.

•*Mistake:* Driving with dirty fuel. Although owners' manuals often give it short shrift, clean fuel is essential for long engine life. Replace your fuel filter every 10,000 miles or two years, whichever comes *last*. *Cost:* $12 to $50.

In either case, stick to the recommended fuel. Using regular in a car designed to run on premium causes "knocking," which can quickly destroy an engine. Using premium gas in a car designed to run on regular wastes gas, money and causes drivability problems.

If your car has fuel-injection, never let your tank drop below one-quarter full. Cornering on an almost-empty tank can momentarily disrupt the flow of fuel to the fuel pump, thus damaging or destroying it.

•*Mistake:* Failing to guard against weather damage. To reduce exposure to sunlight and other environmental threats, keep your car

*Several synthetic oils are now available. *My favorite:* Redline. For information on where to obtain it, call 800-624-7958.

garaged or at least covered. If your car must remain outdoors without a cover, put a dashboard-protecting sunscreen in your windshield and park so that it faces a different direction each day. (This helps "spread out" sun-induced damage.) To preserve weather-stripping and other rubber surfaces, use silicone spray. Wash your car by hand or in a "dancing chamois" car wash. Avoid car washes that use rotating brushes.

•*Mistake:* Ignoring your antifreeze. Antifreeze not only keeps your car working in cold weather but also helps prevent rust and corrosion. For optimal protection, use a 50-50 antifreeze-water mix. *Important:* Use distilled water, not tap water. Change annually.

•*Mistake:* Cleaning your engine. While an under-hood cleaning might make your engine look better, it can severely damage sensitive electronic sensors and connectors located there. Better to leave your engine dirty. If you insist on a clean engine, hire an experienced professional to do the job.

•*Mistake:* Leaving your car in gear while parked. Automatic transmission cars should be put into "Park" while parked. Cars with manual transmissions should be left in neutral while parked. A parked car left in gear may sustain a chipped transmission gear tooth if it's bumped by another car.

Applying the parking brake not only keeps a parked car from rolling away, but also helps to keep the brake itself from "freezing up" or falling out of adjustment.

•*Mistake:* Over-tightening your lug nuts. Though it sounds trivial, improperly tightened lug nuts or bolts represent a big source of trouble for car owners.

Too much lug-nut torque, and your brake rotors will warp and cause your brake pedal to pulsate. Too loose, and your wheels will not be securely attached.

Problem: Many mechanics tighten lug nuts with air wrenches, which are notorious for over-tightening.

To avoid trouble: Get your own torque wrench. *Cost:* $15. Each time your wheels are removed for maintenance, use the wrench to check the torque readings on your lug nuts against your owner's manual.

•*Mistake:* Failing to perform "hidden" maintenance tasks. While owners' manuals usually specify how and when to perform the most crucial maintenance tasks, they often provide incomplete information about other key tasks.

Example: Manuals typically say nothing about brake fluid, which should be changed once every two years or 24,000 miles. Anti-lock systems' brake fluid should be changed annually.

Power steering fluid should be changed every three years or 30,000 miles, whichever comes first. Timing belts should be replaced every 60,000 miles, timing chains every 100,000 miles.

Note: Without regular use, certain systems quickly fall out of adjustment. *To avoid trouble:* Run your air conditioner and defroster at least once every two weeks. Release and re-apply the parking brake daily.

•*Mistake:* Failing to recharge or replace an old or weak battery. Besides increasing the risk of leaving you stranded, a weak battery causes needless wear of both the alternator and the starter. Both need a good power source to operate properly.

To avoid trouble: Choose the biggest, most powerful battery that will fit under your hood.

•*Mistake:* Rustproofing your car. After-market or dealer-applied rustproofing treatment is not only costly, in many cases, it can void your car's rust warranty.

Source: Dré Brungardt, editor, *Nutz & Boltz*®, Box 123, Butler, Maryland 21023.

Seat Belt Danger

Seat belts in a used vehicle should be carefully examined before the deal is closed. They're unsafe if... the stitching is unraveling or the webbing is frayed or torn...the buckle doesn't function properly or has been tampered with. *Ideal:* Have the seller replace them before you put money down. *Cost:* $150–$200 per seat. *Important:* Seat belts should be replaced if the vehicle has been in an accident. They have been stressed and are no longer safe.

Source: Dré Brungardt, editor, *Nutz & Boltz*®, Box 123, Butler, Maryland 21023.

Safest Car Colors

Greenish-yellow is best...then cream, yellow and white. *Least-safe colors:* Red and black. *General rule:* Light-colored, single-tone cars are safer. They have significantly fewer accidents than dark cars because it is easier for other drivers to distinguish them from the surroundings.

Source: *Lemon Book: Auto Rights for New & Used Cars* by Ralph Nader and Clarence Ditlow, Moyer Bell, Ltd., Colonial Hill, Mt. Kisco, New York 10549.

Traffic Tickets

1. Keep talking. The longer an officer chats with you before writing a ticket, the better your chances of getting off with only a warning. To buy yourself as much time as possible, pull your car off the shoulder as far as you can so the officer can talk to you without fear of becoming roadkill.

2. Know his place. Using a policeman's correct rank will make it seem that you're somehow involved with law enforcement or the military. Check his sleeve; if it has three or more stripes, call him "Sergeant" or "Sarge." If it has one or two stripes, call him "Corporal." If you see no stripes and he's a state cop, call him "Trooper." If he has no stripes and he's driving a county sheriff car, call him "Deputy." If you're not sure, call him "Officer."

3. Don't make a scene. The less an officer remembers about you and the stop, the better your lawyer's chances of getting you off the hook. Most tickets get reduced, or won by the defendant in court, because the cop doesn't remember the specifics of the stop.

Source: Sgt. James M. Eagan, retired New York State Trooper, author, *A Speeder's Guide to Avoiding Tickets.*

Safety Tests Are Misleading

Car-crash safety tests by the government give misleading results. *Why:* All cars are run into a wall at 35 mph. Lighter cars hit the wall with less momentum than heavy cars, so less damage results. But in real life, heavier cars have better safety records, especially in collisions with lighter vehicles. *Examples:* Although government tests panned the Ford Taurus, insurance records show it to be among the safest vehicles. And the Ford Escort scored well in tests, but has a poor record with insurers.

Source: *The Wall Street Journal.*

Car Engine Death Trap

Teflon engine oil additives—advertised as engine protection agents—can actually *destroy* your engine. Depending on driving conditions, these additives can either cause engine oil pressure to drop to zero, cause the engine to freeze—or have no effect at all. Safest strategy is to stay away from the Teflon products altogether.

Source: Dré Brungardt, editor, *Nutz & Boltz®*, Box 123, Butler, Maryland 21023.

Gasoline Cancer Trap

Gas and gas fumes contain toxic chemicals that can cause cancer. *Unsettling:* Gas-station attendants have a significantly elevated risk of death from leukemia. *Consumer self-defense:* Carry old gloves in the car—wear them when you fill up at a self-service station to keep gasoline off your skin.

Keep windows closed so fumes won't accumulate in the car. Be sure to stand upwind from the pump. Choose stations equipped with vapor-recovery lines. These accordion-like bellows on the nozzles return gas vapors to an underground tank.

Source: Peter Infante, Occupational Safety and Health Administration, quoted in *Good Housekeeping*, 959 Eighth Ave., New York 10019.

Tinted-Windshield Danger

Fully tinted windshields (not those with just a tinted band along the top edge) drastically reduce dusk and night vision. In combination with the usual 60-degree tilt, tinting cuts incoming light by 35%, and makes pedestrians and obstacles hard to see. *Worst yet:* It cuts red light—important to the partially color-blind—by about 50%. *Self-defense:* New cars can usually be ordered with clear glass windows.

Source: *Lemon Book* by Ralph Nader, Moyer Bell Limited, Colonial Hill, Mt. Kisco, New York 10549.

How to Protect Yourself From the New Auto Terrorism

Last fall, a car theft in a Washington suburb resulted in the death of the driver, a mother taking her child in a BMW to preschool. As two men commandeered the woman's auto at an intersection, they shoved her out, but one of her arms became entangled in the seat belt. She was dragged a mile and a half, and died. The child was found unharmed alongside the road in her safety seat.

The grisly crime focused headlines on carjacking, the theft of a car from a driver, often at gunpoint or knife point. Auto-safety experts cite various causes for what appears to be an upsurge in this crime, including the copycat effect, but they point mainly to the increasing sophistication of antitheft devices and alarms, which make it easier to seize a car from a driver than cross wires to start an empty vehicle in a parking lot.

There are many painful accounts of this kind of crime and experts agree it is spreading, but most resist calling the development a trend. For example, carjackings are being reported in Los Angeles, Detroit, Chicago, Miami and New York as well as their suburbs. But an official for a big insurer in the Los Angeles area does not consider the number of carjackings large enough to be assigned a separate category of claims.

The official, Mike Brink, is the division manager of specialized claims for the Auto Club of Southern California, which insures 550,000 club members, making it the fourth-largest auto insurer in Southern California. Mr. Brink estimated that carjackings accounted for 1% or less of the company's auto theft claims.

Emanuel Ross, the statistician for the police in Washington, said there were 147 carjackings there in 1991 out of 8,132 reported car thefts, a rate of 1.8%. In 1992, the rate may have been higher. By the end of August of last year, he said, there had been 190 carjackings.

John Maes, a spokesman for the National Crime Insurance Bureau in Illinois, which is supported by 650 insurance companies, said carjackings could be listed under auto theft, armed robbery, assault and battery or homicide. "We have been watching it for about a year," Mr. Maes said. "There has been a spurt of cases lately, but we are not sure that is a long-term trend."

Words to the wise:

Whatever the statistical incidence of this crime, reports about it are bound to worry people traveling to another city and renting a shining new car at the airport. Getting lost is easy, and anxieties about breakdowns on deserted state roads hover in most travelers' minds.

The American Automobile Association (AAA) and other safety-insurance groups have put together advice for drivers on avoiding trouble, and what to do if it develops. The following suggestions may be rudimentary, but they could thwart some crimes...

•Know how to get where you are going. Study your route ahead of time and make notes if need be. Looking at a map is hard when you are driving.

•Lock all car doors, and keep windows up in unfamiliar areas. Parents with children probably do this already, but other drivers should, too. If it is hot and there is no air conditioning, open a window a crack at the top, not enough for an arm to get in.

•Keep your purse or wallet hidden. Put it under your seat or, if it is large, in the trunk.

Don't leave it on the seat behind you or in your lap or clothes.

•Park in well-lit areas. If you want to buy gas or use a pay phone, pull in where the station attendant or motorists can see you. Buying gas at a station where someone pumps it for you is less hazardous than getting out to pump and pay. Safety experts say that theft at remote self-serve stations has become a danger. Pay telephones built for use from the driver's seat offer some protection if they are not in deserted spots.

•Don't be tricked into getting out of your car. If you are bumped from the rear and are uneasy about getting out to exchange insurance information, motion the other driver to follow you to a police station, a fire station or a 24-hour store.

•Don't stop for flashing white or blue lights. Law-enforcement vehicles normally use only red flashers, not blue and white ones.

•Drive in the middle lane if you don't like the area. Try not to get in a position where you can be cut off. If a car blocks you intentionally, honk repeatedly for help, but do not get out.

If your fears materialize, remember the prime rule: Give up your car, your wallet or your jewelry rather than your life.

Breakdown ABC's:

A standard anxiety for car renters is a fear of a breakdown or a flat on the road because their vulnerability multiplies if they get out of the car. The Automobile Association recommends following these steps...

•Signal and pull off the road onto the shoulder.

•Turn on the emergency flashers.

•If you feel safe opening the window, tie a cloth onto the driver's door handle or antenna, or use some other object to signal for help. Remember, in a rental car, you are not going to have a windshield shade with "call the police" printed on the other side. Anyway, I have my doubts about the value of these things because I only see them in empty cars at malls.

•Keep doors locked, windows up.

•If someone other than a police officer stops, roll down the window only enough to ask that a call be placed to the police, the auto club or a service station.

The AAA says a citizen's band radio or a car phone is a good investment if you drive alone frequently, and either can be used to summon help in the event of an emergency.

One evidence of the value of this advice is that the car-rental companies are increasingly offering cellular phones as extras with their rentals. The charge for portables is usually about $5 a day. Built-in phones come with the car at no extra charge. In either case, there is a fee of around $1.50 or more for a minute of calling time. All provide free 911 calls.

Hertz offers car phones in 40 of the 60 major cities it serves, including Miami, Atlanta, Los Angeles, Chicago, New York and Detroit. Some of the phones are built into Hertz's mid-size to luxury autos. "It's growing," Joe Russo, a spokesman, said. "By the end of the year we will have 20,000 cellular phones in the fleet, and our contract with GTE calls for a total of 50,000."

Budget Rent a Car offers car phones at 29 airports, including those at Los Angeles, Chicago, Houston and Miami. According to Tim Hermeling, a spokesman, the franchise holder for the downtown Los Angeles sites also offers installed phones.

Avis has built-in cellular phones in its cars at airports in the San Francisco Bay area as well as at O'Hare in Chicago and the Los Angeles area airports. In addition, portable phones are being tested at airports in Seattle, Portland, Oregon, and Denver.

National offers phones at four airports: Dallas, Los Angeles, San Francisco and John Wayne in Orange County, California.

Two years ago, armed thefts from rental cars, and of the cars themselves, created such a problem in Miami that Dade County required rental companies to remove all promotional stickers. This year the Florida legislature eliminated license plates identifying rental cars, and these plates are disappearing as they expire.

Source: Betsy Wade has written "The Practical Traveler" column in *The New York Times* for many years.

Airbag Self-Defense

Airbags in cars have their own safety risks. Cars equipped with airbags require different driving techniques. Don't drape your hand or arm inside the steering wheel—you could get a broken wrist or arm if the airbag fires and traps your hand.

Airbag units are meant to be most effective for drivers sitting with their arms extended—any closer and you could suffer facial abrasions if the airbag is activated.

If you frequently rent cars with airbags, be sure you know where the horn button is on any model you drive—they're all in different locations.

Added risk for smokers: It is dangerous to have a lit cigar or cigarette in your mouth when the airbag goes off. *Important:* Even if the car you drive is airbag-equipped, always buckle up.

Source: Dré Brungardt, editor, *Nutz & Boltz®*, Box 123, Butler, Maryland 21023.

Get More For Your Old Car

Get 25% more for your old car—on average—by selling it yourself. But beware of keeping your old car after you buy a new one—even if the dealer will not give you what you think it is worth. *Reason:* It is usually more important to lower the amount borrowed on the new car than to get the most possible for the old one. Use the trade-in value—or cash—to reduce the new-car loan.

Source: *Life After Debt: How to Repair Your Credit and Get Out of Debt Once and For All* by Bob Hammond, credit consultant based in Redlands, California. Career Press, 180 Fifth Ave., Hawthorne, New Jersey 07507.

14

Very, Very Personal

Your Personal Life... Steering Through Many, Many Changes

The personal lives of many Americans will undergo profound changes in the coming years because of a new phenomenon—constant transitioning.

How constant transitioning works:

Twenty years ago, we began undergoing many more transitions in our lives—marriage, divorce, remarriage, career changes, early retirement, return to work, leaving school, returning to school.

Now, the transitions aren't just frequent but constant. Americans must be prepared to cope with less and less knowledge about where they're going to be in a few years, professionally, geographically, financially and personally.

Yesterday, we could reasonably expect to achieve our traditional middle-class goals—stable employment, stable family relationships, affordable education, good retirement.

In the coming years, constant transitioning means that these expectations will become less and less realistic.

Succeeding in the new world:

Threading your way through a more volatile and demanding environment may require a new personal strategy...

•Reevaluate what you mean by success. We used to think that people who were fired were no longer successful. Today we can't afford that notion since we may be those people.

And we used to think that a person who decided to make less money doing something he/she liked wasn't a success. But in today's world of constant transitions, these are the people we're beginning to admire.

•Learn new skills that will lead to more competencies. Yesterday, we were told that skills would bring success. In the next few years, we'll see more clearly that skills aren't enough...that we'll need competence.

Important in the years ahead—competency in technology, motivation and the ability to learn. Helpful: Suspending your own judgment so you can listen and understand the rush of new ideas in the world.

The more competencies you have, the more likely you'll be to succeed. Reason: In the environment of constant transition, adaptability—not skills—will bring success.

•Develop your networks. People with special competence or authority will be essential in helping you make important transitions—professionally, economically and socially.

Networks will become even more important as our personal and business lives continue to blend. If there's a crisis in one of them, we'll need a strong support system to pull through successfully.

•Be prepared for a greater chance of suffering from stress. It may be a result of coming to grips with what success is actually achievable, or it may come from just having to cope with a world of constant transition. If you suffer from stress, get medical help, but also consider relaxation techniques (laughter does lower stress levels) or sincere religious involvement.

•Consider volunteer work. Apart from compensating for any lack of satisfaction with work, volunteerism can help build your network and expand skills and competencies.

•Change your expectations for your children. In the past, we've wanted to see our kids set their mind on a single goal. Tomorrow, a kid who dabbles in several fields may ultimately achieve the adaptability that brings success.

We used to disparage a middle-class child who wanted to become a plumber. Today, we have to recognize that the child may have picked a career that will bring him satisfaction and a livable income.

Review your retirement plans:

If you're like most Americans, your retirement income isn't likely to go as far as your parents'. That puts a burden on you to review finances regularly with an adviser who knows both you and the country's social trends.

Americans have always been impulsive in the sense that we've thought we could always afford our impulses. In the near future, what we impulsively want may be far out of reach.

Source: Edith Weiner is president of Weiner, Edrich, Brown, Inc., futurists and strategic planning consultants, 200 E. 33 St., New York 10016.

PID Danger

Bacterial vaginosis (BV), which affects up to one in four women, raises a woman's risk for pelvic inflammatory disease and infertility. *Problem:* BV is frequently misdiagnosed as yeast infection—and the two conditions require different treatments. *BV symptoms:* A foul or "fishy" vaginal odor and a milky discharge that can stain undergarments. Your doctor can administer a vaginal pH test and a microscopic examination for "clue" cells.

Source: James McGregor, MD, professor of obstetrics and gynecology at the University of Colorado.

Surprising Cause Of Impotence

Impotence is caused in 10% to 15% of all cases by injury during intercourse. Weight-induced pressure or abnormal bending of the erection can cause chronic impotence by damaging the lining of the erection chamber. The most common situation in which such injuries occur is when the female is on top.

Source: Research led by Irwin Goldstein, MD, Boston University Medical Center.

Annual Mammograms

Annual mammograms for women age 40 to 49 *can* benefit those with a family history of breast cancer. But, there are fears that these x-rays may *cause* breast cancer. Radiation creates free radicals—molecules in the body that damage cells. *Self-defense:* Check with your doctor about taking *antioxidants*—supplements that neutralize free radicals before they attack cells the day before, the day of…and the day after a mammogram—or any x-ray.

Source: Robban Sica-Cohen, MD, Center for the Healing Arts, 325 Post Rd., Orange, Connecticut 06477.

Fertility Drugs And Cancer

Taking fertility drugs increases a woman's risk of developing ovarian cancers though the risk is higher if she does *not* become pregnant. *Self-defense:* Women who have used fertility drugs in the past should have regular gynecologic exams—and consider a yearly pelvic ultrasound. Others considering taking fertility drugs should discuss their cancer risk with their doctor before deciding whether to take them.

Source: Harold E. Fox, MD, MSc, professor of clinical obstetrics, gynecology, and pediatrics at the Sloane Hospital for Women of the Columbia Presbyterian Medical Center in New York City.

Prostate Problems Self-Defense

The good news about prostate cancer is that the disease is almost 100% curable—if it's caught early.

The bad news: Because most men fail to get regular checkups, and because they often ignore the telltale symptoms—chiefly frequent urination, especially at night, and a weak urine stream—most cases of prostate cancer are spotted far too late for successful treatment. *Result:* Prostate cancer now kills more men than all other forms of cancer except lung cancer.

Prostate cancer strikes men of all ages, but it is remarkably common among men in their fifties and sixties. Recent statistics suggest that roughly one of every 20 men aged 50 or older has prostate cancer, even though few are aware of the problem. *At special risk:* African-Americans and those with a family history of prostate cancer.

•Having one primary relative (father, brother, or son) with prostate cancer doubles your risk of having the disease.

•Having two increases your risk to three to four times.

•Having three raises your risk by a factor of eight to 10.

Recent reports which suggest that having a vasectomy promotes prostate cancer are inconclusive. Men who have had vasectomies do seem to have a higher incidence of prostate cancer. But it's simply not yet clear whether this additional risk stems from the vasectomy itself or merely from the fact that men who get vasectomies tend to see a urologist more frequently than men who do not. In any case, this apparent increase in risk is extremely slight.

Bottom line: Men who have already undergone a vasectomy need not take any special precautions—beyond regular checkups.

To prevent prostate trouble:

•Eat less fat. As with heart disease and many other forms of cancer, prostate cancer is more common among men who eat a fatty diet than among those who don't. *Especially dangerous:* Saturated fat, found primarily in meat and dairy products. It seems to be particularly effective at promoting tumor growth. To protect yourself, eat less meat and dairy products. Increase your intake of fruits, vegetables, grains, and non-fat dairy products.

•Don't smoke. Recent studies show clearly that men who smoke face an increased risk of prostate cancer. While this additional risk is small, it's best not to smoke at all—especially if you're elderly, African-American, or have a family history of prostate cancer. Try also to avoid exposure to second-hand smoke.

•Have regular checkups. All men should have an annual prostate exam starting at age 50—age 40 for men at risk. This exam should be conduced by a board-certified urologist or radiologist. It should include not only the familiar digital rectal exam, in which the doctor inserts a gloved finger into the rectum to feel for prostate tumors, but also the recently developed blood test for prostate specific antigen (PSA).

An elevated PSA level does not necessarily mean prostate cancer.

Other possibilities: Enlargement of the prostate (benign prostatic hypertrophy or hyperplasia) or prostate inflammation (prostatitis). Like prostate cancer, these conditions raise PSA levels. And they cause the same symptoms. Yet unlike prostate cancer, these conditions are generally benign. They can often be controlled through the use of drug therapy.

To pinpoint the cause of an elevated PSA level, the doctor must conduct an ultrasound examination of the prostate. In this procedure, performed without anesthesia on an outpatient basis, the doctor inserts a needle-tipped fiber-optic probe into the rectum. If any suspicious areas are found, the doctor uses this same probe to take tiny tissue samples. These samples are then biopsied.

If the biopsy confirms the presence of cancer, your doctor will likely recommend surgical removal of the prostate or radiation therapy. The best treatment for advanced prostate cancer is hormone therapy. Chemotherapy is usually ineffective against prostate cancer.

Source: William J. Catalona, MD, chief of urologic surgery, Washington University Medical Center, St. Louis. He is also urologist-in-chief at Barnes and Allied hospitals in St. Louis. Ninety-five percent of Dr. Catalona's practice is devoted to the treatment of prostate cancer.

Unreliable Birth Control

Breast-feeding is unreliable as a means of birth control, even though the ovaries do remain unresponsive to fertility-stimulating hormones for some time after the birth of a child, says Susan K. Schulman, MD, a pediatrician in private practice in New York City, and Audrey Rosner, CPNP, co-authors of a report on postpartum fertility. *Recent finding:* Nursing mothers do take longer to resume normal ovulation after childbirth than do mothers who bottle-feed, but the effectiveness and duration of this contraceptive effect vary greatly. Some women become fertile again in as little as 90 days after childbirth, while others remain infertile for as long as a year. *Rule of thumb:* The effect lasts longest when a nursing mother continues to nurse her baby at night as well as during the day…and when she delays the introduction of solid foods in her baby's diet. But because of the risk of unwanted pregnancy, it's safer to rely on other methods of birth control. *Flip side:* Breast-feeding mothers who do want to conceive may experience problems doing so.

"No-Scalpel Vasectomies"

I've heard about a vasectomy that doesn't require the patient to go under the knife. Is that possible?

"No-scalpel vasectomies," which have been performed safely on 11 million men in China, and 10,000 men in the US, use special instruments to clasp the vas deferens and seal it through a small puncture hole—instead of a wide incision used in conventional vasectomies. Advantages: Less pain, less bleeding, fewer infections, no incisions or stitches, and takes only seven minutes to perform.

Source: Marc Goldstein, MD, director of the male reproduction and microsurgery unit, New York Hospital–Cornell Medical Center, New York City.

All About the Virtues Of Being Open…Very Open

True intimacy is the key to personal, emotional, and physical health and interpersonal fulfillment.

True intimacy is achieved when two people travel beyond conventional romance and explore each other's emotions, experiencing the deepest level of trust, openness, and sharing. They feel a flame in their spirits, a celebration of self and each other, a movement toward wholeness, and a lust for life.

Genetic predisposition and cultural norms do play a role in how close we allow ourselves to get to others. It starts at the beginning of life, in the bond that unites mother and child and serves as a model of giving and receiving care.

Everyone can experience true intimacy—if they're able to overcome the barriers that prevent them from freely expressing themselves. *The basics of intimacy:*

True intimacy is a two-way street. It requires that two people be able to express the following:

• Trust. You must be able to rely on the other person to live up to his/her word so you can be open without the fear of being betrayed.

•Empathy. This requires putting yourself in someone else's shoes, to know and anticipate what the other person is feeling.

•Enthusiasm and courage. Both are needed to shatter illusions, strip defenses, break through stereotypes, confront fears, and explore emotional boundaries together until our insides "touch."

•Sharing each other's worlds. You must be able to maintain a solid sense of self. While you are fully engaged with the other person, you do not give up your separate life.

Sex and intimacy:

The spiritual connectedness and awakenings triggered by true intimacy can be achieved in a relationship without sex—between friends and family members. But sex within an intimate relationship can unite mind, spirit, and body to an explosive energy release. When no limits are placed on the physical interactions, touch and nonverbal communication can express deep levels of pleasure and intimacy.

The goal is to be with someone who expresses an equal interest and commitment to the journey toward true intimacy. Most people, however, are not so fortunate. Types of people who fight true intimacy…

•The macho but insecure man who tells a woman he loves her in order to seduce her into a sexual relationship.

•The workaholic who says he/she wants to be in love but constantly breaks dates to work.

•The martyr who appears to fall madly in love but constantly with "the wrong people." People who profess they want but cannot find anyone capable of true intimacy have an intimacy problem themselves.

•The avoiders, or those who engage in transitory relationships or make superficial commitments. They do not seek or encourage strong emotional ties. These include loners, control freaks, abusers, misanthropes, self-absorbed narcissists, and romanticists endlessly seeking the perfect romance.

•Intimacy junkies, who are so concerned about being emotionally close to others that it interferes with their ability to accomplish responsibilities. When deprived of the "rush" of such closeness, they get depressed and are further unable to function.

This problem can lead to an endless cycle of starting and ending relationships, an inability to make commitments, chronic infidelity, and destructively inappropriate choices of partners.

Fears…and realities:

The goal to achieving true intimacy is to acknowledge your fears…and analyze your misperceptions. See your fears as repressed excitement, and mobilize this energy to be intimate. Make an effort to get over the most common fears…

•Fear of being judged.

•Fear of abandonment, rejection, or loss.

•Fear of conflict.

•Fear of being hurt.

At the same time, you must also move beyond the common misperceptions about intimacy…

•*Misperception:* A long-term relationship with true intimacy gets boring. *Truth:* It is quite the opposite. There is no limit to learning about oneself and each other. Face guilt, shame, laziness, and other feelings underlying boredom. Keep digging deeper into each other's archeology of self. See boredom as an opportunity into which risk, engagement, action, and communion can enter.

•*Misperception:* Intimacy is a loss of freedom. *Truth:* Fear of intimacy is a prison of the self where no one can touch you. More intense intimacy frees you to discover yourself.

•*Misperception:* People who resist intimacy are tough. *Truth:* These people are missing joy and deep down can be very lonely, disengaged, and alienated.

Overcoming the hurdles:

•Explore and self-analyze your feelings. The deeper you know and feel for yourself, the deeper you are able to enter the lives of others. Understand the past that defines present patterns of intimacy.

Example: The woman who witnessed her father's constant betrayal of her mother grows up mistrusting all men.

•Be open and honest. Disappointment over past relationships and other issues cause you to close up emotionally.

Example: A 40-year-old man in danger of losing his job and being unable to send his child to college becomes fearful of sharing his concerns with his wife, so he shuts her out.

•Develop self-esteem and independence. In order to feel confident about sharing oneself, and prevent being either suffocating or suffocated in a relationship, one must develop a secure sense of self. Repeat affirmations and focus on successes.

•Unfreeze your emotions. The deeper you feel, the more you can enter another's life.

Exercise: Imagine lying on a rug before a fire with your partner. He/she whispers "I love you" in your ear. Feel the tenderness flowing.

•Recover your "personal mythology." Identify the negative stereotypes that you grew up with...and recognize the truth about who you are and what relationships and life are all about. Identify these stories so that you can recognize the difference between living a lie and experiencing a more honest and fulfilling relationship.

Limits to intimacy:

It's important to remember that in real life, the perfect balance needed for true intimacy is difficult to achieve—or sustain. Each person can be rocked anywhere along the way by insecurities, illness, distractions, stress, etc. In addition, people can naturally have different goals, careers, or levels of sophistication, maturity, or commitment. Frequently, there is discouragement or depression over these barriers to true intimacy.

Solution: Appreciate and adjust to differences as best as possible, but expect fluctuations in intimacy levels. Work toward the greatest potential of sharing, but allow for supplemental relationships with friends.

Source: Sam Keen, PhD, author and philosopher who practices in northern California. Keen is the author of several books, including the best-selling *Fire in the Belly and Inward Bound: Exploring the Geography of Your Emotions*, Bantam Books, 1540 Broadway, New York 10036.

How to Make the Most Of Our Midlife Years

Many of us are raised to believe that once we are "grown up," we are finished growing...

that adulthood is a long, long seamless period that separates adolescence from old age.

And then we are surprised—even frightened —by the inner struggle we experience on entering the second half of our lives.

Some people call this the "midlife crisis." I prefer "midlife quest," the time we begin questioning—from the Latin *quaerere*, "to search" —the lives we have created so far.

•Why does my job seem meaningless?
•Why am I so alarmed at my body's aging?
•Why do I feel so empty?
•Is my marriage dying?
•I thought only teenagers felt like this. Why am I so confused?
•Who am I, anyway?

Each person's quest is different. But our purpose in the second half is the same...we seek wholeness.

The search for wholeness:

As we are building our lives during our twenties and early thirties, we tend to favor certain parts of ourselves at the expense of others.

In midlife, the parts of ourselves we have neglected or suppressed—what Jungians call "the shadow"—start to agitate for recognition.

•A single-minded career-builder begins to crave intimacy or leisure.
•A rootless free-spirit wants a place to call home.
•A laid-back, nurturing parent begins to feel ambition and drive.

In short, we yearn to live our unlived lives.

Problem: Before we can find new direction, balance, and deeper meaning, we must often face denial, confusion, and resistance to change.

How to win the midlife quest:

•Listen to your body. Our midlife bodies can speak to us in ways our twenty-year-old bodies could not. And most of us are aware of ways we misuse our bodies. *Key:* Listen to your body's signals. Consider the purpose of your physical regimens. If you are training for a marathon, you may need endurance. But most of us at midlife seek energy.

We find we want to eat more simply, and eat less...we exercise for flexibility and strength rather than bulk...we practice stillness rather than hyperactivity.

• Seek loving relationships. Many people find themselves dissatisfied with their marriages at midlife. Divorce, separations, and affairs are common. Once, our partner could do no wrong. Now, the person we married has become a stranger.

Similarly, people who have remained comfortably single often find themselves searching for a mate at midlife. Something is missing.

Problem: Our culture tends to view long-term marriage as boring. But there is no journey more exciting—sexually or otherwise— than the wondrous adventure of a lifelong love.

Regardless of the circumstances, changes in relationships at midlife are often a source of deep pain.

At midlife, we must allow our shadow selves to unfold, and risk revealing the parts of ourselves that might threaten, trouble, or upset our long-unspoken domestic agreements. For some, the process may create pressure—or growth—that the relationship is unable to bear. But for those willing to seek the spiritual dimension of marriage with patience and love, the result can be a marriage that is incomparably deeper, more authentic, and more meaningful than was possible before.

• Find your calling. The midlife quest almost always involves a desire to make a deeper match between who we are and what we do.

We begin to hear our inner voice, our vocation—from the Latin *vocare*, "to call."

We look for ways to express this mature "calling" in our work. For many, midlife leads to a career change.

Risk: "Grass is greener elsewhere" thinking can result in an impulsive move that may come at a high price. So…examine yourself before you jump ship. What is it that is not being expressed? An internal change in the same company or a shift in the same field may satisfy you—or you may want to make a dramatic change. Finding one's calling can be a lonely and secretive process.

Helpful: Find an ally who will give you support and comfort as you plan your move.

• Seek meaning in aging. It is a common view in our culture that aging is bad, and our goal is to stop it.

Problem: Hating aging is ultimately self-hatred. We are obsessed with what we lose as we age, and ignorant about what we gain. Every season has its beauties. Who would want to live only in the morning?

Reality: We grow older. Our aim must be not to age slowly, but to age deeply…to come to a greater appreciation of the whole. And…we must begin our preparation for death. And in so doing, most of us find joy, freedom, and comfort in the contributions we make to life that will remain after we are gone. People find meaning in many ways… through service, artwork, teaching, volunteering, caring.

• Honor the seven generations. Wholeness requires participation in an authentic, multigenerational community. We must recognize that we are connected to all generations…our parents and children, grandparents and grandchildren, great-grandparents and great-grandchildren.

We must avoid isolating groups by their age. We must ensure that our young are cared for, educated, and initiated by adults…that those at midlife are supported as they carry out their responsibilities…that our elders are respected, and their skills and wisdom utilized.

• Cherish the planet. Our quest for wholeness also leads to a deep, personal understanding of our connection to our world and our political beliefs. We are entrusted with the future of all generations. Never has caring for our planet been more important than it is today, and never has the wisdom of elders been more needed.

• Increase spiritual awareness. In all these dimensions—our relationships with our bodies, our loved ones, our work, our communities and planet—our quest is ultimately a spiritual one. At midlife, we receive our wake-up call— it is time to start listening to our inner life.

Helpful: Attend to the dreams that strike you as being significant. Practice meditation. Schedule quiet time for spiritual retreat. Re-connect.

A final word on wholeness:

All parts of our quest for wholeness are deeply connected.

Example: If you are frustrated in a boring job, it affects your marriage and your health. Growth in any area enriches all areas. Even given the enormity of the problems facing us now, we are not without hope. *Reason:* Any small change affects the whole. And making small changes gives us the courage to make bigger ones.

Source: Mark Gerzon, author of *Coming into Our Own: Understanding the Adult Metamorphosis*, Delacorte Press, 666 Fifth Ave., New York 10103. Gerzon was trained in psychology and family therapy at Harvard University and runs workshops on the subject.

Are You a Target Of Unrequited Love?

Targets of "unrequited love" often feel as much pain rejecting would-be suitors as their admirers feel in being turned down. Rejecters feel bewilderment, guilt, and anger at pursuers …and dislike hurting them by turning them down flat. *Trap:* Conciliatory words are often misinterpreted, and the rejecter continues to be pursued.

Source: Research on more than 150 men and women—the first study ever to look at both sides of unrequited love, the would-be lover and the rejecter—led by psychologist Roy Baumeister, PhD, Case Western Reserve University.

Intimacy Danger

While sharing one's innermost thoughts with a loved one helps bring couples closer together, spouses who betray your trust by teasing or throwing the secret back at you create bigger problems in the relationship.

Source: *He Says, She Says: Closing the Communication Gap Between the Sexes* by Beverly Hills communications expert Lillian Glass, PhD, G.P. Putnam's Sons, 200 Madison Ave., New York 10016.

Laughter—A Great Strengthener

Making each other laugh strengthens a relationship. Anyplace filled with laughter is a haven from stress where people want to spend time. *Significant:* Early in relationships, partners often try to generate laughter—by being entertaining or funny, or sending humorous cards or notes. Over time, the efforts frequently disappear…along with laughter itself. *Recommended:* Build more fun into your relationship to enliven it at any stage.

Source: *Lethal Lovers and Poisonous People* by Los Angeles psychologist Harriet Braiker, PhD, Pocket Books, 1230 Avenue of the Americas, New York 10020.

Lessons in Love And Marriage

The nature of love is one of the great mysteries of life. But after 10 years of researching what anthropologists know about the way men and women fall in and out of love in societies around the world, I am beginning to understand some of the many facets of love and marriage in America today.

Stages of love:

When a couple first falls in love during a courtship phase that establishes their mutual interest, they show the classic signs of infatuation…euphoria when together and constant thoughts about each other when apart.

But infatuation usually lasts no more than two or three years between adult lovers who see each other regularly. At that point, passion often gives way to attachment…a comfortable, secure feeling. That attachment is strong enough to keep many couples—half of all Americans, for example—married to each other for life.

But—for many married couples, attachment leads to boredom…and boredom leads to straying or divorce.

This same pattern occurs all over the world, with divorce occurring most often about four years after marriage. This "four-year itch" seems to be a part of human nature. We can explain it with the basic principles of biology.

Human nature vs. monogamy:

A basic drive of every living creature is to perpetuate itself…and humans are no exception. The most successful mating strategies of our long-forgotten ancestors are in the genes of every person alive today.

These biological drives urge men and women to pair off and stay together for three or four years…just long enough for them to cooperate in raising their infants until these children begin to join play groups and no longer need constant care.

Then these biological drives encourage both men and women to seek new partners with qualities that their first mates lack. That way of life probably suited an ancient hunter-gatherer society, but it conflicts with modern values.

Lesson: If you want to stay married, try to understand your needs and desires. They may cause destructive feelings that you have to anticipate and redirect.

Hidden biological forces:

•Chemical basis of love. Scientists have found that when a person falls in love, his/her brain produces large amounts of a natural amphetamine called *phenylethylamine*—or PEA—which causes the euphoric "high" of infatuation.

The brain eventually reacts to this overstimulation by producing *endorphins*—morphine-like drugs that produce the quiet, satisfied feeling of attachment. Sometimes, years later, the brain primes itself for a new round of excitement, spelling potential trouble for the relationship.

Lesson: If you want a long-term marriage, be prepared to provide the stimulation your partner needs…and work on avoiding your own "burnout" by appreciating what he/she is giving you.

•Male-female differences. Despite feminist rhetoric, men and women seem designed to play different roles and view the world in different ways. Men's genetic makeup—reflected in their hormones—prepares them to be strong protectors, while women excel as nurturers. Men are hunters by nature and often prefer to work side by side, with less verbal interaction. Women are mothers by nature and often like face-to-face contact, with more talk.

Lesson: To stay together, men and women must acknowledge their differences and appreciate the value of these differences. For exam-

ple, men should try to talk more intimately and directly to their wives, while women should try more side-by-side activities with their husbands …leisurely drives, fishing, skating.

Social factors that lead to divorce:

•Economic equality. When men and women both work and are relatively economically independent, partners feel free to cut marital bonds.

•Nomadism. I use this term to describe people who have left their birthplaces and families and all the networking that often keeps spouses together. These people face fewer barriers to divorce. If they live apart, in a commuter marriage, divorce is even more likely.

•Urbanism. Away from the intimacies and social pressures of a small town, it's easier for couples to split up.

•Secularism. With less belief in religious objections to divorce, it becomes more prevalent.

Solid factors that discourage divorce:

•Age. As couples age, they are less inclined to divorce. And if they are older when they marry, they are also more likely to stay married.

•Children. Childless couples divorce most frequently, and the rate decreases as the number of children increase—with three children, the rate drops to 7%…and then gets even lower.

How to improve your marriage:

Armed with this knowledge of how biology, psychology, and society affect marriage, you can take some concrete steps to improve yours.

•Avoid boredom. Wives should try to stay as attractive as possible to their husbands… husbands should listen carefully and talk often with their wives.

•Don't drive your partner away with threats of divorce…and say no to adultery.

•Increase commitment by responding to each other's interests. That includes work and play…a shared sense of humor can be a great incentive to stay together through life's challenges.

Source: Helen E. Fisher, PhD, research associate in the department of anthropology at the American Museum of Natural History in New York. Dr. Fisher has received the Distinguished Service Award of the American Anthropological Association and is the author of *Anatomy of Love: The Natural History of Monogamy, Adultery and Divorce,* W.W. Norton and Co., 500 Fifth Ave., New York 10110.

The Most Romantic Videos

Although love is what is supposed to make the world and movies go round and round, remarkably few memorable love stories have materialized on the screen. Somehow we never lose our childhood giggles or embarrassment when the kissing scenes come on the screen.

Hence, despite the omnipresence of "sex appeal" and "love interest" in the casting, writing, and directing of motion pictures, most movies pretend to be about something else.

Significantly, the two most famous love films, *Gone With the Wind* (1939) and *Casablanca* (1942) profess to be concerned with Great Wars rather than the chemistry between Vivien Leigh's Scarlett and Clark Gable's Rhett in the former, and Ingrid Bergman's Ilsa and Humphrey Bogart's Rick in the latter. In neither romance do the lovers live happily ever after. But that is consistent with most of the great love stories of literature and music.

Most of my favorite love stories on film are somewhat more optimistic, though true love doesn't run smoothly in any of them, least of all in my all-time favorite, *That Hamilton Woman* (1941), in which Vivien Leigh's Emma Hamilton and Laurence Olivier's Horatio Nelson bring more passion and feeling to their ill-fated adulterous love affair than the historical originals ever did.

On a happier note, Wendy Hiller and Roger Livesey brought civilized grace and humor to a wartime romance in the Scottish Isles in the haunting *I Know Where I'm Going* (1945).

The great male lover of the 1930s and 1940s in Hollywood was, fittingly enough, a Frenchman, Charles Boyer. Three of his most charismatic partners in passion were Irene Dunne in *Love Affair* (1939), Margaret Sullavan in *Back Street* (1941), and Jean Arthur in *History Is Made at Night* (1937), one of the most adventurously romantic titles in the history of the cinema.

The lost art of letter-writing to one's beloved is preserved in the epistolary eloquence of *Shop Around the Corner* (1940) in which Margaret Sullavan and James Stewart carry on an anonymous romance by mail after placing ads in the personals columns...and *Love Letters* (1945) in which Jennifer Jones becomes victimized through a Cyrano-like imposture by which the Right Man writes love letters for the Wrong Man. A murder must intervene before a twentieth-century Roxanne finds happiness with Joseph Cotten's handsome Cyrano.

Life imitated art in *Woman of the Year* (1942) in which Katharine Hepburn and Spencer Tracy began their enduring love affair off-screen as they were making love on-screen in a movie ahead of its time in celebrating the emotional electricity generated by two highly competitive career people of opposite sexes. The picture was marred by a studio-tacked-on ending in which Ms. Hepburn gets her comeuppance in a disastrous kitchen sequence. For the most part, however, Hepburn's and Tracy's characters bickered in the exhilarating manner of Beatrice and Benedict in Shakespeare's *Much Ado About Nothing*.

Billy Wilder has given us two magical romances in two very different decades with *The Major and the Minor* (1942) in which Ginger Rogers plays a faux Lolita to Ray Milland's chivalrously susceptible Major Kirby—and *Love in the Afternoon* (1957) in which Audrey Hepburn as an impressionable virgin chooses as her first lover Gary Cooper's much older and disreputably promiscuous playboy-businessman. In one of the great endings in film history, the first love of her life almost miraculously becomes the last love of his.

You may have noticed that most of my favorites date back to the 1930s and 1940s, the most tightly censored period in Hollywood's history. There were no nude scenes back then, no rollicking between the bed sheets, but instead an eroticism of the heart.

Source: Andrew Sarris, the noted film critic for the *New York Observer*, is professor of film at Columbia University and the author of 10 books on film, including *The American Cinema, Confessions of a Cultist* and the forthcoming *The American Sound Film*.

Is it Possible for Men To Get Breast Cancer?

Men can get breast cancer—although the disease is far more common in women. About one out of nine women develop breast cancer, compared with about one out of 1,000 men. *At highest risk:* Men who have male or female blood relatives with the disease.

Source: A study led by Karin Rosenblatt, University of Washington School of Public Health and Community Medicine, Seattle.

Frequently Misdiagnosed: Vaginal Infections

Most women being treated for chronic yeast infections—either by their internists or by themselves with over-the-counter preparations—actually have a different condition. *Other causes of symptoms:* Bacterial vaginosis or herpes infections, which require different treatments than that for yeast infections. *Caution:* Never diagnose yourself. Over-the-counter treatments could make your symptoms worse. If you think you have a vaginal infection, ask your doctor to perform a complete physical examination and comprehensive medical history.

Source: Karen Carroll, MD, departments of pathology and infectious diseases, and Paul Summers, MD, department of obstetrics and gynecology, both at the University of Utah Medical Center in Salt Lake City.

Breast Cancer...If Only I Had Known...

I was 46 when I was first diagnosed with breast cancer. My tumor was 1.5 centimeters in diameter and had spread to the lymph nodes. I underwent a lumpectomy, radiation and six months of chemotherapy. Only a few weeks ago, I passed my five-year checkup with a clean bill of health.

My story has a happy ending. Looking back, though, I would have been greatly helped and comforted had I received certain information, not just from physicians but also from women who had undergone the same experience...

•Having cancer is not your fault. No one knows exactly why women develop breast cancer, but it's certainly not because they have a "cancer personality." That idea is a lot of bunk. I've seen happy, optimistic cancer patients die very quickly after their diagnosis...and I've seen negative, hostile people live long after they "should" have been dead.

Lesson: Never view cancer as your own fault. I once overheard two therapists talking about a woman whose cancer was not responding to therapy. One said, "If she could only visualize better, she could cure this." What a ridiculous notion!

There's nothing wrong with trying alternative methods of healing, such as visualization, if they make you feel happier or more in control. But no one should ever blame you for your cancer.

•You have more time than you think you do to make decisions about treatment. Like most women newly diagnosed with breast cancer, I felt I had to decide immediately about whether I'd have a mastectomy (removal of the breast), a lumpectomy (removal of just the tumor), radiation, etc. I was afraid that if I delayed treatment, my cancer would spread like wildfire.

Truth: In most cases, it's safe to take a couple of weeks to consider your options—and come to terms with your diagnosis.

Waiting also gives you the opportunity to get a second opinion—and that could help you avoid making a big mistake. Some old-school surgeons, for example, continue to recommend mastectomy even though in many cases it's just as effective—and far less emotionally wrenching—to have a lumpectomy followed by radiation.

•You'll find yourself resenting the doctor who diagnosed your cancer. Being diagnosed with breast cancer is so unnerving that women often find themselves resenting the doctor who made the diagnosis...and many find a new doctor. It's the old shoot-the-messenger feeling. You want the floor to open up and swallow him/her. But if the doctor is compassionate and competent, changing doctors at this stage is often a mistake.

•Coping with your fear is the hardest part of having breast cancer—but the fear doesn't last forever. At first, the fear that the cancer will spread and that you will die is almost overpowering. It affects everything you say, feel or do.

Eventually, the fear subsides. Although you might occasionally lapse back into fearful thinking, you get on with your life.

•Breast cancer surgery isn't painful. I was afraid my operation would cause a great deal of pain. As it turned out, neither the surgery nor the recovery period was particularly painful physically—although the drainage tube inserted in my armpit for a week or so following surgery did cause a little discomfort. I was also weepy, depressed and maybe even a little irrational after surgery…but that quickly passed.

•The timing of breast cancer surgery affects your chances of survival. Recent studies have shown that premenopausal women survive longer when tumors are removed during the second half of their menstrual cycles. Although this finding remains a matter of debate among cancer specialists, ask your doctor about scheduling surgery during the second half of your cycle, after ovulation.

•Chemotherapy affects your memory. During the months I was undergoing chemo, I experienced several memory lapses. I'd be trying to write and suddenly find myself unable to remember what it was I wanted to say next. At first I thought I had a brain tumor. I was terrified. Only later did I learn that temporary memory problems were a common side effect of chemotherapy. When they stop pouring the poison into your body, your memory returns to normal.

•Breast radiation is generally not very debilitating. Compared to chemotherapy, it's a piece of cake. It leaves you feeling a little tired, but not sick.

•Support groups are a tremendous source of emotional comfort during your recovery.

Having cancer is a lonely, isolating experience. After my diagnosis, one or two longtime friends suddenly stopped calling and visiting. If your friends abandon you, realize that it's because of their fears—not because of something you did.

Even if your friends don't abandon you, they may be uncertain of how to behave in your presence. This can cause a lot of awkwardness. You may feel, for example, that you have to crack jokes or tell funny stories just to lighten the mood. After a while, these kinds of feelings become an enormous burden.

Joining a group of other women with breast cancer can lift this burden. When you're among peers, you don't have to take care of anyone else. You're free to laugh or cry—just be yourself.

•It's important to be kind to yourself. Guilt is a constant companion when you have cancer. If you eat too much fatty cheese or don't exercise one day, you feel you're contributing to your demise. But that's just not true.

Bottom line: Chemotherapy is hard on your body and will make you feel tired and cranky. If watching the soaps and eating popcorn will make you feel better, then do it. There is no need to feel guilty.

•You don't feel like celebrating at the end of treatment. I thought that when I eventually finished my chemotherapy treatment I would be ecstatic. But when that day finally came, I found myself pleased—but also sad to say good-bye to all the doctors, nurses and technicians who had been my "teammates" for so long. Suddenly, I was alone with my enemy and no longer doing anything to fight it. Fortunately, I had a great support group to make me feel less vulnerable.

•Life after cancer can be more satisfying than it was before. Although I would never have wished cancer upon myself, I must admit that having the disease has helped me understand my real priorities in life. I no longer worry about rejection, nor am I driven to spend time trying to gain prestige and status in the business world. I want to be with my 15-year-old daughter, Anna, and make my writing as strong and beautiful as it can be.

Cancer has also made me tougher and

more gutsy. After all, what can hurt me after I've had cancer? But I'm also a much nicer person now. I'm more apt to send a sympathy card or visit someone in the hospital because I know how much such gestures mean to someone who is sick and frightened.

Source: Juliet Wittman, an award-winning reporter for the *Boulder Daily Camera*, Boulder, Colorado. She is the author of *Breast Cancer Journal*, Fulcrum Publishing, 350 Indiana St., Golden, Colorado 80401. 800-992-2908.

Old Condom Danger

Old condoms rupture far more frequently than new ones. Study: 262 couples were asked to test about 5,000 condoms over a four-month period. Result: Less than 5% of brand-new condoms ruptured during intercourse. But condoms a year or two old broke about 10% of the time...and seven-year-old condoms broke about 19% of the time.

Source: Research by Markus Steiner, BA, contraceptive use and epidemiology division, Family Health International, Research Triangle Park, North Carolina.

College Students' Hepatitis B Problem

Incidence of this sexually transmitted disease has increased 77% in the past 10 years among college-aged adults. It is 100 times more contagious than the human immunodeficiency virus (HIV), which causes AIDS. Symptoms range from mild nausea and vomiting...to more dangerous liver disease and death. Important: Hepatitis B vaccinations for all college students—especially those who have had more than one sex partner in six months...engage in unprotected sex...or have had other sexually transmitted diseases.

Source: MarJeanne Collins, MD, chair, American College Health Association's Vaccine Preventable Diseases Task Force, Baltimore.

The Importance Of Solitude

Many Americans admire the rugged individualists in novels and films who take on the system or overcome adversity single-handedly.

Yet, we don't feel comfortable with those who keep to themselves. We tend to distrust contemplation and view solitary people and pursuits with suspicion.

Opportunity: We would be better off if we engaged in positive solitude—time alone that is used thoughtfully to benefit mind and soul. Positive solitude is an important element of self-discovery and growth.

Solitude provides the opportunity to identify your most cherished goals and develop ways of achieving them. Regular reflection contributes to a sense of inner peace...and makes you feel more in control of your life.
The problems of being alone:

Positive solitude takes conscious effort, whether you live with others or alone.

• People who live with others are often so caught up in the demands of family life that they don't take time for self-reflection. Time alone feels like an expendable luxury to them. Thus, they're in danger of defining themselves through others.

These people need to make private time a priority and be creative about ways of finding it.

Examples: Evaluate work and community responsibilities, and determine which are essential—and which can be cut back. Join a babysitting co-op so someone else can look after your children one or two days a week. Plan a solitary retreat to a quiet place for a few days to reflect on what's really important to you.

People who live alone may feel left out in a world of couples and families. They may fight solitude by compulsively seeking company, filling their days with "busy-ness" that isn't very satisfying...and missing a wonderful opportunity for self-discovery and growth.

They need to challenge the belief that having a family is the only way to be happy...look for ways to nurture themselves instead of waiting for a partner to make life satisfying...and take advantage of the chance to learn more about their own values and perceptions.

I believe that living alone doesn't have to be lonely—nor should it be viewed as a way station on the path to "coupledom." Living alone can be a deeply rewarding life style in its own right.

Positive solitude actually enhances relationships when people do come together. People who are not afraid of solitude can meet as strong wholes instead of incomplete halves that are desperate for fulfillment.

Turn off the TV:

One of the biggest threats to positive solitude is television. It's the easiest, but possibly least-satisfying, way to fill up your time.

Watching television does not put you in contact with other people or yourself. Instead, it bombards you with the agenda and values of the TV programmers and advertisers.

Spending a lot of time in front of the TV feeds loneliness. It encourages us to let someone else decide what's interesting, discourages us from looking inward and takes up time that could be spent developing original ideas or actively challenging or supporting the ideas of others.

Ways to use private time:

In solitude, we can explore what's most meaningful to us—free from other people's expectations. We can begin to develop a personal philosophy or life plan.

This isn't an easy task, but it's an exciting one. Key: Ask yourself the kinds of questions that don't have simple answers...and be prepared to return to them again and again. Examples...

What contribution do I want to make to the world? Focus on what's significant to you—not to your parents, spouse or boss. Possibilities: Create a new variety of rose...raise healthy, loving children...comfort people in distress...make music...gather and analyze information about nature or politics.

What are the gaps in my life? Are there things you'd like to understand better or have more control over? Goals you've abandoned out of fear—but still wonder about? What are some ways to address these gaps?

Tools that can help in your exploration include a journal...walking...meditation... quiet time in a natural environment. Exercises:

•Write for 15 minutes about a topic of your choice, without stopping or censoring yourself. You'll be surprised at the ideas that come up.

•Write about a dream you had recently, the emotions it stirred and the messages it might have. Dreams often introduce important themes we haven't yet faced consciously.

Moving outward:

Quietly thinking and writing aren't the only ways to discover meaning. In fact, planning and taking part in challenging activities can be an outgrowth of positive solitude. We can try activities that reveal new aspects of ourselves—physical, intellectual and spiritual. The key is to identify and follow those pursuits that engage you—not to please friends or family or because you've always done them. Exercises:

•Write down 10 or 20 activities that you used to love but haven't done for a long time. What did you most enjoy as a child or adolescent? Try some of these activities again.

•Make a list of activities you always wanted to try but never got around to. Pick one—and do it.

Planning is essential for this stage. If we don't plan, then the easiest things will happen, not the most fulfilling. We'll come home and switch on the TV instead of going to a concert or arranging a kayaking trip.

Make activity dates for yourself...pencil them into your calendar...and make sure you keep them.

Be patient:

Don't be surprised if this self-analysis feels uncomfortable at first—or if you don't make dramatic discoveries right away.

Getting to know yourself takes some time. Challenging and reexamining your assumptions do not happen in a day. But the effort will bring satisfying rewards...including a deeper understanding of your values and needs...increased confidence in your capabilities...a richer enjoyment of life...and a greater receptivity to others.

Source: Rae André, PhD, associate professor of management psychology at Northeastern University. A consultant, lecturer and workshop leader, she is the author of *Positive Solitude: A Practical Program for Mastering Loneliness and Achieving Self-Fulfillment.* Harper-Collins, 10 E. 53 St., New York 10022.

Key To Self-Confidence

No one is born competent. We develop competence through repeated exposure, study and practice. This requires willingness to take some risks without knowing what the outcome will be. Also important: Accepting the possibility of failure. Ironically, fear of failure actually creates failure. If you do not test your dreams or try to do something important to you, you are sure to fail.

Source: *On Target: Enhance Your Life and Ensure Your Success* by Jeri Sedlar, president, Sedlar Communications, New York marketing and productivity consultants. MasterMedia Limited, 17 E. 89 St., New York 10128.

To Break A Bad Habit

Make a 21-day agreement with yourself to change your behavior. It takes 21 days to form a new habit or break an old one. If you come up with excuses to break your 21-day deal with yourself, remind yourself that you only have less than 21 days to go. Key: If you skip one day, the whole 21-day cycle starts over again.

Source: *Choose to Live Peacefully* by Susan Smith Jones, PhD, founder, Health Unlimited, Los Angeles human potential consultants. Celestial Arts, Box 7327, Berkeley, California 94707.

Male Myth

Myth: Penises shrink as men age. Fact: As a man gets older he tends to gain weight until the base of the penis is hidden by two or more inches of prepubic fat. Younger, chubby men are similarly affected. But the penis itself remains the same size.

Source: *Superpotency: How to Get It, Use It, and Maintain It for a Lifetime* by Dudley Seth Danoff, MD, FACS, senior attending urologic surgeon at Cedars-Sinai Medical Center. Los Angeles, California. Warner Books, 1271 Avenue of the Americas, New York 10020.

Flexibility Self-Test

It is natural to become set in our ways as we age and gain experience. But periodic self-examination can help guard against rigidity. Ask yourself: When was the last time I changed, or considered changing, a firmly held position in light of new information? How often do I accept a subordinate's revised proposal after previously rejecting it? How often do I ask for alternative approaches to my own or others' proposals? If your answers for the last six months are "rarely" or "never," you are probably more rigid than is healthy for you or your company.

Source: Ted Pollack, management consultant, Old Tappan, New Jersey, writing in *Production*, 6600 Cough Pike, Cincinnati 45224.

Positive Reappraisal

Reformulate negative thoughts through positive reappraisal. If you find yourself thinking, "I can't do this," change it to, "This will be a challenge, but I'll go at it—one step at a time." Instead of a negative self-message, this gives you one of being innovative and capable. Instead of "I don't want to get out of bed," say, "I'll feel better after a warm shower." The self-message is that you can help yourself. Key: Recognizing negative thoughts so you can rethink them.

Source: *Living with Rheumatoid Arthritis*, by Tammi Shlotzhauer, MD, clinical associate professor of medicine, Rochester Medical Center, Rochester, New York. The Johns Hopkins University Press, 2715 N. Charles St., Baltimore 21218.

15

Self-Defense

How to Avoid Becoming a Victim Of a Violent Crime

From purse-snatching and car-jacking to assaults, rapes, and kidnappings, violent crime has become a frightening fact of everyday life. While there's little you can do to control the rise of these crimes, there are ways to limit your chances of becoming a victim.

In your car:

•Car-jacking self-defense. Unlike professional car thieves, who have no wish to encounter car owners, car-jackers are out for a thrill—and violence for them is thrilling. Tell yourself *now* that if someone tries to pull you from your car or demands your keys, you will behave passively and give them the car. When the event occurs, you should instinctively give up the vehicle rather than panic and fight back.

•Keep doors locked while driving. Close windows in slow traffic and at red lights. When

coming to a stop, leave enough room between you and the car in front. This will allow you to maneuver around the vehicle if necessary.

•Pay attention to your surroundings. Car-jackers almost always approach on foot. Avoid self-absorbed distractions, such as combing your hair, fumbling with cassette tapes, etc.

•Park under a street light or as close as possible to the mall or well-lit buildings and stores. Avoid parking next to potential hiding places, such as dumpsters, woods, etc.

•Scan parking lots before approaching your car. Try to walk with other people, or ask a doorman or security guard for an escort.

•Have your key ready in your hand as you approach your vehicle. Look inside the car and around the outside before getting in. *Caution:* On some new cars, all doors will unlock when the driver's door is unlocked—a dangerous feature if someone is hiding outside the passenger door. If you do sense danger, retreat to a place of safety and call the police immediately. Do not confront an intruder.

On the street:

• Carry purses and briefcases close to the body—but be able to release them if necessary. *Avoid:* Shoulder straps across the body, straps wrapped around the wrist. People have been dragged by the straps and injured in purse-snatchings. If someone tries to take your wallet or purse, let it go. *Useful:* "Fanny pack" belts and pouches seem to be an unattractive target for street thieves.

• On the bus or subway, do not sit next to an exit door or place briefcases or purchases on an empty seat. Robbers tend to grab valuables as they are leaving and while doors are closing.

• If you are held up, do not resist. Most armed robbers only want your money. *Problem:* Many will turn to violence if they are alarmed or disobeyed. Surrender your valuables quickly.

At home:

• Keep doors and windows locked, especially after you turn in for the night. Keep curtains drawn after dark. Most home intruders are opportunists.

• Install deadbolt locks with reinforced strike plates on front and back doors. A few dollars will purchase a reinforced strike plate that secures the door frame to the first wall stud. Locks like these are also deterrents.

• Secure sliding glass doors by placing a broomstick or piece of wood along the interior track and by blocking the dead space in the upper channel that allows the door to be lifted off the track.

• Consider installing an alarm system. Ground-floor windows can be equipped with an alarmed jamming stick for $30 to $40.

• Never confront a burglar. If you come home to a door that's ajar or has been tampered with, leave the scene immediately and call the police. If you wake up to find an intruder in your bedroom, pretend to be asleep until he leaves.

• Don't depend on your dog to alert you. Most people command their dogs to *stop* barking when a stranger arrives. Many a dog has slept through a burglary or been seduced by a doggie treat.

• Do not open the door to strangers. If you have to hire an unfamiliar repairman, ask someone to be with you at home or plan to be on the phone when he arrives…or pretend there is someone else at home. If a repairman or stranger arrives at your door unannounced, do not let him/her in. Lock the door and call his office for verification.

• If you think you hear a prowler, call the police. Don't assume it's just the wind, that the police are too busy, or that they might get mad if no one is there. It is always better to feel foolish than to be a victim.

• Unless you are well-trained, do not keep a gun in the house. People who are untrained with firearms are more likely to have them stolen or taken away from them by intruders, who may have arrived unarmed. If you do keep a gun in the house, the gun and ammunition should be stored separately.

Caution: According to law, in order to shoot an intruder on your property, you must be "in fear for your life." This does not mean in fear of losing your TV and jewelry.

• Know your neighbors. Neighborhood watch programs and "telephone trees" to alert neighbors of strangers in the area are very effective.

At work:

• Know your neighbors. Set up a building-wide security policy to identify visitors. "Business watch" programs for merchants in shopping areas are highly effective, too.

• Team up in pairs to use public rest rooms or locked rest rooms located in public hallways. Avoid using remote stairwells alone.

• Keep the office's doors locked when working late, on weekends, or early in the morning.

• Do not get on an elevator with someone who makes you feel uncomfortable or unsafe.

• When traveling on business, ask a bellhop to accompany you to your hotel room and to check it before you enter. Avoid ground-floor rooms. Make sure that the phone is working and that security numbers are provided. Never open the door to someone you're not expecting. If someone knocks unannounced, call the lobby for verification.

At play:

• Exercise with a partner, or take along a dog or stick while jogging. Avoid isolated parks and paths. Wear glasses if you normally need them, and do not use a stereo headset. Avoid loose clothes that are easy to grab.

• At parks, beaches, or other recreation areas, know where the ranger or lifeguard stations are located. Leave expensive cameras, jewelry, and credit cards at home or locked in the trunk of the car. Do not use recreation areas after hours.

In all situations:

• Make direct eye contact with people around you. This sends a message of confidence, an effective deterrent to violent crime. Criminals seek passive, distracted victims, who make easy targets.

• Trust your instincts. Humans are extremely instinctive. *Important:* Tune into the messages. Some of the most common statements police officers hear following a crime are, "I had a feeling I shouldn't have walked to my car" "The guy gave me the creeps, but…"

Bottom line: If a situation makes you nervous, avoid it. Learn to respect your instincts and act on them.

Source: Patricia Harman, a crime-prevention officer with the Prince William County, Virginia, police force. Harman, who conducts lectures nationally on personal safety, is the author of *The Danger Zone: How You Can Protect Yourself from Rape, Robbery, and Assault,* Parkside Publishing, 205 W. Touhy Ave., Park Ridge, Illinois 60068. 800-221-6364.

The Most Commonly Asked Legal Questions

Sooner or later, you'll probably need the advice of a lawyer. What are you most likely to ask about and how can these legal problems be resolved? Here are the top eight…

When and how can I use small claims court? This is a quick, inexpensive way to solve minor legal problems (typically around $1,000). You don't even need a lawyer.

Step 1: Look in your local telephone directory under "Courts," "City of…" for Small Claims Court, Justice Court, Magistrates Court, or Court of Common Appeals. You must sue in the county where the defendant lives or conducts business. Check the county clerk to make sure it's the right court, and to get the proper legal name for the company you're suing.

Step 2: When you arrive at court for the first time, a clerk will give you a complaint form to fill out. *Cost:* Between $2 and $10. It asks for your name and address, the defendant's name and address, a brief description of why you're suing and the damages claimed. *Note:* Small claims courts only award money. They cannot order actions.

Step 3: The clerk will assign you a hearing date (usually in about two weeks) and notify the defendant by mail. Often the sessions are held in the early evening.

Step 4: Before your hearing, gather evidence—contracts, photographs, accident reports, witnesses—and organize how you will present your case. A written outline helps. Be sure to get to court on time.

Step 5: If the judge is overloaded, you may be asked to submit your dispute to arbitration—to an impartial third party…often an attorney. That may make sense, but you should know that an arbitrator's decision is final. You won't be able to appeal it to a judge or a higher court. If the defendant fails to appear, you will be sent before an arbitrator who will listen to your testimony and award you appropriate damages (usually including repayment of your filing fee and interest). If the defendant, after being notified by mail, fails to pay up, call the court clerk and ask how to use law-enforcement personnel to collect your judgment.

Is there a statute of limitations on medical malpractice? Yes. As with other causes of action, claims of medical malpractice must be initiated within a given period of time, which differs from state to state. In New York, in the absence of qualifying circumstances, a medical malpractice suit must be initiated within 30 months of the act. However, New York and most other states grant children under age 18 who are the victims of malpractice an extension of time within which to sue. Ask your local bar association for the name of an attorney who can tell you exactly what the law is in your state given your particular circumstances.

What can I do if my landlord refuses to make repairs...or paint? A lease is a contract entitling the landlord to receive rent if he/she provides you with certain guarantees, including a "warranty of habitability" that the place is safe and livable. This means the plumbing should work, etc. Repairs must be made within a "reasonable" period of time, which, of course, varies depending on whether it's a dangerous gas leak or merely a broken dishwasher.

Recourse: Most towns have special housing courts where tenants can file complaints without a lawyer. You could also send the landlord a letter by certified mail warning him that if repairs are not made immediately you will hire a contractor yourself and deduct the cost from your monthly rent.

Under very damning circumstances—if, for example, he has a policy of refusing repairs in order to drive tenants out—you could withhold rent. However, this carries with it the risk of eviction. Don't do it without first consulting a lawyer.

The terms for painting are usually specified in the lease. If the landlord stalls, you can go to the special housing court or to small claims court to have your rent reduced or to get the money needed to hire a painter yourself.

Do I need a lawyer when I'm buying a house? Yes. Buying a house is an extremely complex undertaking and you should be represented by counsel who will look out for your best interests. Is the title good? Does the seller have a faulty deed? Are there any outstanding claims against the property? Does the house satisfy zoning ordinances? Many of these questions are matters of subtle legal interpretation, and you will want written guarantees that fully protect you.

What happens if my credit card or ATM card is stolen? Under the Consumer Credit Protection Act consumers are liable for only $50 if a credit card is stolen, and even that may be waived under some circumstances. However, a different standard applies to automated teller machine cards. Under the federal Electronic Fund Transfer Act, your liability is limited to $50 if you notify the bank within two business days. Thereafter, your liability jumps to $500.

If an unauthorized transfer appears on your bank statement and you don't report it within 60 days of the mailing date you risk losing everything in your account plus any credit line. Report any lost or stolen card to the bank immediately by phone and in writing.

Protection: Don't carry your ATM password in your wallet, and avoid obvious numbers like your birth date and the first four digits of your Social Security number.

Am I legally entitled to see my personnel file at work? You might be, depending on the kind of job you have and the state in which you work. Virtually all employees of the federal government have access, and union contracts provide this same privilege to many workers in the private sector.

Otherwise, your rights depend on the laws of the state where you work. California's Labor Code mandates access to all records "which are used or have been used to determine that employee's qualifications for employment, promotion, additional compensation, termination, or other disciplinary action." Letters of reference and records relating to the investigation of possible criminal offenses are exempt.

Many states have similar statutes, and Oregon requires employers to keep personnel records available to employees for at least 60 days after termination of employment. Contact your State Department of Labor to find out what the law allows.

What can I do about a noisy neighbor? Depending on the specific complaint, your neighbor's actions may constitute a violation of civil or criminal law. Playing loud music late at night amounts to disorderly conduct, for which you can call the police. Civil steps can also be taken under the "nuisance" law, which provides that people have the right to reasonable comfort in their homes. Acts that might be perfectly proper under some circumstances become unlawful if they interfere with your enjoyment of this right.

Example: Your neighbor can use a chain saw, but not at midnight. He has the right to mow his lawn, but maybe not at 6 am on a Sunday morning since he could do it at another time that wouldn't interfere with others' one day to sleep in late.

Do I have a case when I wait for a delivery person who never comes? Yes. This is a breach of contract. If you take a half day off work, for example, and the couch isn't delivered as promised, the store has violated its part of the contract. Call and ask for a new delivery time at your convenience. Most stores can deliver at night, for example, although they don't advertise that. Failing satisfaction, demand that the cost of additional time off from work be deducted from your bill. If all else fails, take the case to small claims court.

Source: Thomas Hauser, lawyer and author of *The Family Legal Companion,* Allworth Press, 10 E. 23 St., New York 10010.

Crime Victims

Crime victims who remain calm stay safer, says self-defense instructor Arnold Howard. If you are calm, an enraged assailant is more likely to calm down too, and you can prevent any undue harm. *To keep yourself calm:* Breathe slowly and deeply...say the word "relax" over and over in your head...view the mugger as a person instead of an evil criminal—this image is much less intimidating. *To keep the assailant calm:* Be respectful—listen closely to what he says...never argue...give up any possessions he asks for.

Source: Arnold Howard, a black belt in karate in Mesquite, Texas, teaches self-defense nationwide. 214-288-7557.

Police-Cruiser Self-Defense

The color of the flashing lights atop police cars are not standardized across the United States. While red flashers are common, many police forces use combinations on their vehicles, such as blue-and-red and blue-and-white. Other police forces use just blue lights. *Self-defense:* To protect yourself from criminals impersonating highway police—without violating the law—turn on emergency flashers when an unmarked vehicle signals you from behind...stay on the road...slow down...then stop at the first well-lighted, populated area, such as a gas station.

Source: Phil Lynn is manager, National Law Enforcement Policy Center, International Association of Chiefs of Police, Alexandria, Virginia.

Fabric Danger

Formaldehyde resin used to keep no-iron linens, permanent-press clothing, and polyester/cotton fabrics wrinkle-free emits formaldehyde fumes for the life of the fabric—which could be years. *Symptoms of formaldehyde vapor inhalation:* Tiredness, headaches, coughing, watery eyes, respiratory problems. *Self-defense:* Buy only natural fibers, which are generally not treated with formaldehyde. *Also:* Avoid fabrics with labels reading "easy care 100% cotton" or "no-iron cotton," which could mean formaldehyde finishes.

Source: *The Nontoxic Home and Office: Protecting Yourself and Your Family from Everyday Toxics and Health Hazards* by consumer advocate Debra Lynn Dadd, Jeremy P. Tarcher, Inc., 5858 Wilshire Blvd., Los Angeles 90036.

Beware of Telemarketers

Beware of telemarketers who ask for your checking account number rather than your credit card number, warns bankcard specialist Gerri Detweiler. With a checking account number, they can print a "demand draft," which permits them to withdraw your money. Your bank probably won't notice that your signature is missing because drafts look like checks and are processed quickly.

Source: Gerri Detweiler is executive director of Bankcard Holders of America, 560 Herndon Pkwy., Suite 120, Herndon, Virginia 22070.

How to Get Rid Of Nightmares

A nightmare, technically, is a frightening dream that wakes you up. If you don't wake up, it's a bad dream.* Nightmares' contents are no different than the contents of normal dreams, according to my research. *What is different:* How you react to your dreams.

How we respond to our dreams is affected in great part by how we feel both physically and emotionally. You can get rid of your nightmares by getting rid of things that can cause you to react badly to your dreams. *These include:*

• *Medications.* Certain drugs can increase the incidence of nightmares. Beta blockers (for hypertension and irregular heartbeat), tricyclic antidepressants, sleeping pills, nasal sprays.

Solution: Ask your doctor about changing prescribed medications.

• *Stress.* Feeling on edge increases your susceptibility to nightmares.

Solution: Use stress-reduction and relaxation techniques…and exercise.

• *Illnesses.* Any illness can make you feel bad. And feeling bad can cause nightmares. Sometimes, a nightmare can warn you of a medical problem that hasn't even been diagnosed yet.

Solution: For minor illnesses, the nightmares will go away as you get better. If other nightmare-causing factors are ruled out, see your doctor for evaluation.

• *Miscellaneous problems.* For many, nightmares have no obvious cause.

Solution: Figure out what's causing the nightmares by making a connection between the nightmare and real life. *To make the connection:* Think metaphorically.

Example: A nightmare about being assaulted may be a metaphor for feeling threatened or intimidated by your boss, or a friend or relative.

*Nightmares should not be confused with night terrors, which are most common in children. The child wakens from a deep sleep screaming, crying, frightened, and perspiring, with a very rapid heartbeat and rapid breathing…but no memory of what scared him. This physiological response is not related to dreaming.

Alternate solution: Confront a recurrent nightmare by imagining how you want it resolved before you go to sleep.

Examples: A person who dreams that he's being followed by a stranger can imagine that the person is simply a friend who wants to say hello…a child who dreams that a monster is chasing him can imagine turning to the monster and saying, "You can't scare me anymore. Go away."

Source: Milton Kramer, MD, director, Sleep Disorder Center, Bethesda Oak Hospital, Cincinnati.

Lead Poisoning From Pewter

Eating or drinking from pewter can cause lead poisoning. Even though pewter sold in the United States is supposed to be safe, don't bet your life on it, says Richard Wedeen, MD, nephrologist and author of *Poison in the Pot: The Legacy of Lead.*

Although the US has regulated lead content in pewter manufacturing since 1867, it is difficult to establish an item's age or country of origin.

And pewter products that contain no lead may be soldered with it. *Bottom line:* Any pewter should remain suspect until it has been tested for lead leaching. *Home test:* The Frandon Red Alert Kit, 800-332-7723.

Appliances: Repair or Replace?

Appliance repair people are becoming scarcer by the year, and the cost of service calls has gone through the roof. Consumers face a difficult decision over whether to repair appliances or opt for new ones. A survey of appliance marketers and repair people disclosed what life expectancy appliances have and how to determine whether they are worth fixing.

• Televisions. The big, old American sets (like Zenith and RCA) frequently lasted ten years. Today, most sets last from five to eight years.

After that, the set will start needing a new high-voltage transformer, a new picture tube, and a new tuner. It's best to replace the television at that point.

Television repair. It costs from $250 to $300 to repair or replace the picture tube of a color television (including parts and labor). It costs more to replace the tube of a 13-inch or 19-inch color television than of a 23-inch set.

Reason: Most color replacement tubes are rebuilt from old tubes. And there are more 23-inch tubes around to salvage because that size used to be more popular.

The most expensive television set to repair is the Sony. Repair people find it the most difficult to work on, and its parts are hard to get. Picture tube replacement can cost $400.

• Air conditioners. They should have a life expectancy of ten to twelve years.

Two problems may arise at that time: The compressor fails or the Freon leaks. If Freon leaks, don't expect a repair person to fix it permanently.

• Refrigerators. They have the same time span and problems as air conditioners.

• Dishwashers and washing machines. They last ten to twelve years.

Longest-lasting items: Stoves, vacuum cleaners.

Rule of thumb:

When repairs cost 50% of the price of a replacement, it's time to get rid of the appliance.

If you are going to repair:

Try to deal with authorized service centers. They have a better knowledge of individual brands. Furthermore, you can be sure with an authorized service center that you are getting the right parts.

When buying a new unit:

The best buys on appliances can usually be had at discount appliance stores or through buying co-ops. The discount stores advertise loss leaders to get you into the store. Go with the advertised special.

Alternative:

Rebuilt appliances. They come with complete warranties and are generally below the discount house's prices.

What's Going On With the Weather?

We've all noticed how bizarre our weather patterns have been. The extremes of flood and drought are making the old saying *When it rains it pours* a reality. Dr. Paul Handler, the eminent climate consultant and weather expert, tells us exactly what is happening—and what we can expect in the months ahead.

Is the weird weather we've been having indeed weird? We are seeing weather extremes that are breaking records nationwide. We've just had the most devastating floods ever recorded in the Mississippi region.

The March 1993 blizzard that hit the East Coast from Pennsylvania to North Carolina was the worst recorded.

Hurricane Andrew, one of the most damaging storms in decades, struck Florida in September 1992.

Northern California had one of the wettest years ever in 1992/1993, breaking a six-year drought.

The winter of 1991/1992 was the warmest recorded. The summer of 1992 was the coldest in the corn belt since 1915.

And the El Niño (warmer-than-normal waters in the eastern tropical Pacific Ocean) has been one of the longest ever.

Is this happening by chance, or is there a cause? It's no coincidence. We are seeing the aftereffects of the violent volcanic eruption of Mount Pinatubo in the Philippines in June 1991.

This was the most powerful tropical eruption the planet has seen since Krakatau, located near Java, erupted in 1883. Following that eruption, we experienced five years of storms and disturbances. For more than 10 years, I have predicted the same effect if a similar eruption occurred.

What effect did Mount Pinatubo's eruption have? The eruption spewed sulfur dioxide gas 10 to 15 miles into the stratosphere. There, it condensed into sulfuric acid aerosol and formed a haze that reflects earth-bound sunlight back into outer space. During the two years after the eruption, we lost 1% to 3% of the sun's radiation.

That doesn't sound like much. Few understand how sensitive our global climate is. A small change in radiation can cause drastic consequences.

Mount Pinatubo erupted for 24 hours, with a force equivalent to detonating one atom bomb per second...or launching one million space shuttles. The volcanic aerosol was distributed around the globe. The consequence has been global oscillation of climate. Variability has gone up, so we are seeing more extremes of weather. After Mount Pinatubo's eruption, South Africa had the worst drought in 100 years...the Mideast had its coldest winter in 50 years...rains and flooding devastated Bangladesh, northern India, Japan, Korea and Nepal.

What should we expect in the near future? We'll continue to see extremes in the form of storms and droughts. I would expect Lake Michigan to rise again. It may reach a peak level close to the record high of 1986, when wind-driven waves eroded the bluffs and shoreline ...and house foundations were undermined.

The Great Salt Lake will probably also rise to near-record levels.

Last year we had fewer tropical storms and hurricanes, but Hurricane Andrew was certainly destructive. We'll have fewer storms again this year, but I can't predict now how destructive each may be.

We'll have a colder-than-normal winter in the East.

It will get cold early in the West.

We'll see more snow than last year, but probably not beyond the normal range.

The summer of 1994 will be drier than normal in the corn belt.

Is there anything we can do to be better prepared? Stay informed about the extremes of weather in your region. I believe that I was the only person to predict under what circumstan-

ces the five-year California drought would end. I said in April 1990 that it would rain heavily after the next major tropical volcanic eruption.

In areas subject to flooding, community action is necessary. For example, dams should be discharged so water levels can accommodate extreme storms. We're likely to experience weather extremes at least through 1996.

Source: Paul Handler, PhD, a private crop and climate consultant. He is the editor of *Atlas Forecasts*, a monthly newsletter for businesses that depend on long-range weather trends. 706 W. Oregon St., Urbana, Illinois 61801.

Secrets of Launching New Products In Tough Times

The sluggish economy doesn't have to be a barrier to new-product introductions. By relying less on advertising—and more on creative ways to reach customers—companies can introduce new products and cut costs.

Not fully understood by all companies: For many consumers, advertising has lost its punch.

In the past, a company could flood the market with ads that would create enough demand for a successful product introduction. Today, markets are fragmented, and consumers are bombarded with so many ads that they've begun to take their buying cues from other sources...

...from celebrities, from free samples and, increasingly, from retailers. *Benetton* and *Conran's*, for instance, are as much in the marketing business as they are in retailing.

Lesson: New-product introductions must be designed with this new, complicated customer psychology in mind.

It's not enough to bring a fabulous new product to market and expect to be an instant winner. Success depends as much or more on marketing the product in a way that makes the consumer view it as unique. We refer to this strategy as gaining proprietary consumer access. *What we find effective today:*

• *Shrewder free sample campaigns.* Free samples are such an old way to introduce new products that few businesses appreciate how effective they can be. For the price of a full-page newspaper ad in most cities, a company can usually put thousands of samples directly into the hands of prospective customers. In addition, if a sampling promotion is supervised by professional marketers, it can result in invaluable feedback from customers.

Key to success: Combine the campaign with retail participation so that customers who want to try the product again can easily find it on the shelf. Too often, sampling is done before retailers are stocked, leaving frustrated customers with a negative image of the product.

Sampling works best for inexpensive products that are often bought on impulse by definable market segments.

Example: All Sport, a nutrient-rich beverage Pepsi is introducing to compete with Gatorade. Pepsi's free-sample campaign targets sporting events with many competitors, such as marathon races and beach volleyball tournaments.

• *Shrewder distribution.* Many upscale retailers are trend-setters. The mere fact that they sell it is some of the best advertising a new product could have.

Examples: Instead of advertising a new hair-care product, the manufacturer might get more effective exposure by distributing it through upscale salons. Several makers of new alcoholic beverages have taken the route of introducing their products through upscale bars and restaurants.

Even if the company must offer some financial inducement to the distributor— and this is normal—it will be minimal compared with the cost of advertising.

Building up demand in this way may take longer than it would through print or broadcast advertising. But it helps the company develop a close bond with customers that's virtually impossible to achieve through ads.

Distribution-led introductions work best for products with distinctive distribution channels.

Examples: Products for hobbyists and sports enthusiasts.

• *Shrewder information distribution.* Wine marketers, for example, can provide information about which wine to choose with different foods…wine history…wine taste characteristics,

etc. This can be done with printed material, videos or touch screens to create brand recognition that's more effective than that of advertising because it's both immediate and useful.

• *Shrewder customer involvement.* This makes the selling environment personal.

Example: When buying cosmetics in a department store, women can get a personal recommendation from a beauty consultant on the right colors and combinations of makeup. This provides involvement which bonds the customer to the brand.

• *Shrewder entertainment techniques.* The ultimate selling tool. Makers of children's cereals and soft drinks have recognized this for a long time. Now, even retailers of big-ticket items are using it.

Example: Tandy Corp. has invested millions of dollars in stores that provide entertainment value appropriate for consumer electronics, such as giant karaoke screens…kid's video games, etc. And they have invited other manufacturers to participate with their own ideas.

The right time for ads:

While there are innumerable creative ways to bring out new products, advertising still does work best in some cases. Products that have developed a strong customer base without big ad campaigns can often successfully use advertising to expand the line.

Example: Hanes underwear. For years, its products were big sellers despite little advertising. But after the company launched major ad campaigns, it was able to successfully bring out a new line for women.

Advertising can present the brand in a fresh way. This gives the extended products an enormous boost compared with ones that are advertised the same way the original product was.

Source: Hunter Hastings, senior partner, Ryan Management Group, marketing consultants, 33 Riverside Ave., Westport, Connecticut 06880.

Antibiotics Before Surgery

Antibiotics before surgery reduce infection afterward. Using antibiotics two hours or less before an operation is significantly more effective than if the patient is given medication earlier, during the operation or afterward.

Benefits are found in surgery ranging from cardiovascular procedures to labor and deliveries.

Source: David C. Classen, MD, department of clinical epidemiology, LDS Hospital, Salt Lake City, Utah. Dr. Classen led a study of more than 2,800 patients who underwent elective surgery.

Don't Take The Wrong Baby Home From the Hospital

How not to take the wrong baby home from the hospital: Most hospitals simply match the child's wristband with that of the mother's... but a child's wristband can fall off or be removed during his/her hospital stay.

More accurate: Checking the child's footprint and the mother's fingerprint to confirm that they belong together, says Alan Winter, DDS, a dentist in private practice in New York City and author of *Someone Else's Son*, a novel about two children switched at birth.

Most accurate: DNA testing—but this is expensive and takes several weeks for results. *Good news:* While it is easy for mix-ups to occur, they are very rare.

Tungsten-Halogen Lamp Hazard

The bright bulbs emit more ultraviolet radiation than conventional bulbs—and could be harmful to people using them at close range in desk lamps.

Safeguard: A thin glass filter between the bulb and the user—common in tungsten-halogen floor lamps, but not in desk lamps.

Source: Graeme Elliot, scientist at the Australian Radiation Laboratory, Melbourne.

The Electricity/Health Connection

Electric razors may heighten leukemia risk, according to a scary new study—but they aren't the only electrical appliances that could cause cancer. Details of study by the authoritative Batelle Institute show that men who used electric shavers more than 2½ minutes a day were twice as likely to get leukemia as those who didn't.

Probable cause: Electrical fields from plug-in razors disrupt cell division controlled by the pineal gland. This study shows an effect from intermittent electromagnetic fields. Previous studies found higher cancer risk only in people exposed continuously to such fields—at work or at home (power lines, computer terminals, electric blankets, etc.).

Self-defense:

Limit exposure time—or maintain a safe distance from the following sources of electromagnetic fields...

• Electric shavers. Use only if in a rush or away from home.

• Hair dryers. Minimize home use—professional users should avoid holding at chest height.

• Massagers/vibrators. Minimize use.

• Microwave ovens. Pregnant women should avoid standing in front of these during use...all users should stand at least three feet away. Have technician check oven-door seal periodically for radiation leakage.

• TV. To find a safe distance for any set, use a portable AM radio: Tune to a spot between stations to get static...turn up volume...turn on TV and—holding the radio two to three feet away—back up until static starts to fade.

• Laser printers, fax machines, and photocopiers. Should be at least four to six feet from the nearest worker's desk—pregnant women should avoid use entirely.

• Electric blankets. Discard those made before early 1990...look for new models that emit no electromagnetic radiation...or—turn on blanket an hour before bedtime to warm bed, then turn off and unplug the blanket before getting in.

Source: Robert O. Becker, MD, Lowville, New York. He is the author of *Cross Currents*, Jeremy Tarcher, Inc., 9110 Sunset Blvd., Los Angeles 90069. The book is about electromagnetic radiation and your health.

Ammonia and Chlorine Bleach Danger

Never mix these two common household cleaners. Many people do, thinking they will get a more powerful cleaning agent. *Truth:* When mixed, bleach and ammonia produce a noxious—and potentially deadly—gas. Ironically, the combination has virtually no cleaning power compared with the separate liquids.

Source: *Complete Trash: The Best Way to Get Rid of Practically Everything Around the House* by Norm Crampton, secretary, Institute for Solid Wastes of the American Public Works Association, M. Evans and Co., 216 E. 49 St., New York 10017.

Tax-Advantaged Way to Pay For Long-Term Health Care

The unpleasant facts about long-term health care...

• Forty-three percent of all Americans who turn 65 this year will enter a nursing home.

• Most nursing-home care costs $30,000 to $40,000 a year.

• Medicare pays only 2% of the total nursing home charges incurred in the US.

• Forty-nine percent of all long-term care costs are paid out-of-pocket.

• Half of all nursing-home patients are discharged within six months. But the length of stay for the other half averages two and a half years.

• The 85 and older age group will double by the year 2000. So, the need for nursing-home care will accelerate.

Insurance:

People begin to worry about long-term care costs when they're in their 50s and 60s. That's when their parents start going into nursing homes.

The most popular way of paying for long-term-health care is to buy a long-term care insurance policy, which many insurance companies offer. Policies are cheaper for persons in their 50s and 60s than they are for those in their 70s and 80s. But there are problems with these policies...

• *They're expensive.* A husband and wife in their early 60s will pay over $2,500 a year for a long-term-care policy that provides $3,000 a month for coverage. The couple probably won't need coverage for 15 or 20 years. By that time, the coverage will be inadequate because of spiraling health care costs. Most people drop these policies after paying them for only a couple of years. And they lose everything they've spent on the policies.

• *Premiums will rise.* Insurance companies leave themselves the option in these policies for significant rate increases down the line. People may find their premiums going up.

Better way:

A better way of dealing with this problem is to buy a single-premium life insurance policy that provides for payments of long-term care.

How it works: You make a single investment to buy the policy. The minimum deposit is $10,000. Typically people buy these policies with a $50,000 or $100,000 investment. But that's not a lot when you realize that the median expenditure for a 2½-year stay in a nursing home will be $75,000 to $100,000.

Part of what you're buying with your money is a death benefit that's typically two to three times the deposit, depending on your age. A $100,000 deposit might get you a death benefit of $250,000.

The policy provides that you can draw out 2% of the death benefit per month for nursing home care and 1% a month for home health care. This gives you 50 months of nursing home care or 100 months of home health care.

Advantages in this method of paying for long-term care...

• The money accumulates on a tax-deferred basis. Only when you start taking the money out do you pay tax.

• Your deposit earns interest (currently 6.5%). This allows you to accumulate money to counteract the effects of inflation. These policies carry a minimum guaranteed interest rate of 4%. That means that you'll be able to offset the rising cost of long-term health care by at least 4% a year if not more.

• As the value of the policy goes up, so does the death benefit. Both the cash value and the death benefit grow.

• You'll never get back less than 100% of your original investment, plus some interest.

• The biggest part of the payments, when they're taken out for health care, is nontaxable. Withdrawals from the policy are partly a return of your original investment, which is not taxable, and partly a return of interest, which is taxable.

• When you die, the death benefit is paid to your beneficiaries income-tax-free.

Example: A couple, both 64 years old, invests $100,000 in a single-premium health-care policy.

The death benefit on such a policy would currently be $239,212.

This would pay a monthly nursing-home benefit of $4,784 (2% of $239,212), or a monthly home-care benefit of $2,392 (1% of $239,212).

These amounts will grow as the value of the policy increases because of interest buildup. Either spouse, or both, can use the death benefit for health care. They can draw against the death benefit until it's exhausted.

If you do not have a block of cash available for this kind of policy…

• Some insurance companies have developed a way for people to swap an existing annuity for a single-premium life policy via a new annuity. The swap eliminates immediate taxation.

• Arrangements can also be made to roll over an IRA or Keogh into a special annuity from which money is taken to establish a single-premium life-insurance policy for long-term care. The money that comes from the annuity to pay for the life-insurance policy is taxable.

Bottom line: One of the biggest advantages of single premium life policies is that if you decide to cash them in, you are guaranteed to get 100% of your investment back, plus some interest.

Source: Alan Nadolna, president, Associates in Financial Planning, 100 S. Wacker Drive, Chicago 60606.

Mothball Danger

Some moth repellents, particularly camphor balls, contain naphthalene and can be fatal if swallowed by children. Some infant deaths have occurred when babies were merely exposed to clothing and blankets stored with mothballs.

Also dangerous: Mothballs containing para-dichlorobenzene. They're less toxic but may be carcinogenic.

Source: *University of California Berkeley Wellness Letter,* 5 Water Oak, Fernandina Beach, Florida 32034.

Credit-Card Companies' Promises

Beware of credit-card companies' promotional promises to make up the difference if credit-card holders find an item they've purchased at a lower price. *Main problem:* Consumers must put together a lot of paperwork to get a refund, says Gerri Detweiler of Bankcardholders of America in Herndon, Virginia. *Clothing catch:* You may find a coat you bought last month at a lower price, but Citicorp requires a printed advertisement listing the specific item —and that's very hard to find. *Electronics catch:* Major electronic retailers get unique model numbers from manufacturers to prevent price shopping—even if you see your new VCR advertised for less, chances are it will have a different model number.

Arlene Singer Tells All Her Secrets Of How To Take Things Back

Many people mistakenly believe that once you wear a piece of clothing, you cannot return it. But this is simply not so. While I certainly don't suggest returning a cocktail dress that you've bought just to wear to an important party, there's nothing wrong with returning a girdle that doesn't hold you in, or a pair of energized panty hose that sag in the first hour you wear them, or athletic socks with elastic that stretches out after one wearing.

It's quite easy to take almost anything back —off-tasting food, poorly made clothes, difficult appliances, cosmetics or unused concert tickets, etc.

First step: Recognize that you can't return something if you don't try.

Secrets of successful returns:

• Don't feel guilty. Returning merchandise is neither illegal nor immoral. In fact, consumers are far more often the victims of sales and marketing hypes than are the manufacturers and stores who hawk the merchandise. A store can resell merchandise that is returned in good condition, or return damaged merchandise to its suppliers for credit.

Furthermore, losses incurred by stores for merchandise that cannot be sent back represent a legitimate cost of doing business and are already figured into the price of the merchandise. You're actually paying for the right to return. So exercise it.

• Have a valid reason for the return. This can range from a poorly fitting garment, to damaged or defective merchandise, to a gift that is just not your taste.

L.L. Bean, one of the nation's largest mail-order companies, has an exemplary return policy that allows customers to return anything purchased from the company at any time, even years after an item was purchased, and they will replace the item, offer store-credit, or give a refund.

• Be honest. You may be returning an item because you discovered after you bought it that you could get the same thing for less someplace else. If you level with the store, it may be willing to match a competitor's price rather than lose a sale.

• Be polite. It's much more helpful if you are pleasant when making a return, rather than storming in and making a big scene. But that doesn't mean you should immediately cave in if the retailer resists your return.

Just recently, a store manager balked when I was returning something, so I just raised my voice a bit, and was a little more firm. I said—in a voice that all the customers around me could hear—that I couldn't believe the store's inflexible return policy. After he glanced around, and saw the other customers intently listening to us, the manager decided to honor my return request.

• Deal with the person in charge. If a sales clerk is having a bad day, he may refuse a return request that ordinarily would be honored. If you ask to speak with the manager, who usually has a much broader view of the importance of maintaining customers, chances are that you'll get a more sympathetic hearing.

• Vote with your wallet. If a reasonable return request is denied, let the merchant know that you won't shop at the store again. And let the store know that you'll suggest to your friends that they avoid the place as well. Sometimes, the threat of a small-scale boycott will make a store reconsider. Or—the management will reconsider their policy, helping others in the future.

• Beware of discount stores and small boutiques. Such establishments often have very stringent return policies, and may be totally unwilling to negotiate. In general, I find that major department stores have the most lenient return policies. *One standout:* Nordstrom's, which has the return policy of giving the customer what the customer wants. In essence, it means never saying "no" to customers, because satisfied customers will keep coming back.

• Use a charge card. Credit cards give you more leverage in making returns. If a store refuses to honor a reasonable return request, for example, you can threaten to withhold payment. If that doesn't work, go ahead and withhold the payment…but first contact your credit-card issuer in writing and explain your reason for doing so.

•Save receipts. This way you'll have evidence of the date and place of purchase. Should you lose the receipt, don't give up hope. If you've paid by credit card, the card issuer should be able to produce a copy of the original transaction.

•Be sure of a store's return policy before you make your purchase. If you're buying a present for someone months in advance, first find out if there is a time limit for returns. If a store has a 7-day limit, for example, you may do better by taking your business to an establishment with a more lenient policy, particularly if the recipient of the gift is finicky.

•Don't take no for an answer. I once bought an expensive piece of cookware that melted when my husband overheated it on the stove. A pot made for cooking should not melt, even when used by a clumsy husband. The local Bloomingdale's branch refused to exchange the pot for a new one, claiming that the cookware had been abused, so my husband took the melted-down pot to another Bloomingdale's, where they gladly exchanged it for a new one.

•Know your legal rights. Generally, stores are required to post their return policies in a public spot. If they don't, they usually must give you your money back, rather than refuse to accept the return or require you to accept a store credit. If a store won't take back defective merchandise, you can always try to return it to the manufacturer. And if all else fails, you can take the merchant to your local small claims court.

Source: Arlene Singer, a media buyer for an advertising firm in the Washington, DC area and co-author, with Karen Parmet, of the book, *Take It Back! The Art of Returning Almost Anything,* National Press Books, 7200 Wisconsin Ave., Suite 212, Bethesda, Maryland 20814.

What It's Vital to Know Before Your Operation

Each year, tens of thousands of Americans undergo surgery. Fortunately, the vast majority of these operations are successful. Yet several factors—all at least partly avoidable—do sometimes conspire against doctors and patients, resulting in needless pain, longer-than-normal recovery periods, and even fatalities.

Keys to safer surgery:

•Maintain a positive mental attitude. A patient's attitude affects the outcome of surgery almost as much as the surgeon's skill. Many times I've seen terminally ill patients defy the odds and recover fully after a difficult surgery. In contrast, patients with conventionally curable conditions may succumb in surgery—simply because they convince themselves they are doomed.

Key to a speedy recovery: A determination to get out of bed as soon as possible and return to a normal life style.

Patients who just lie in bed following surgery suffer more complications and stay sicker longer than those who resolve to get back on their feet as soon as possible. The longer you remain in bed following surgery, the greater your risk of suffering a chest infection or a deep vein thrombosis (DVT), a potentially fatal disorder if a clot in the leg breaks off and makes its way to the lungs.

Helpful: Imagine yourself coming through surgery with flying colors and then boasting to friends that you had one of the speediest recoveries on record.

•Stay physically fit. Five-mile jogs and strenuous weight-training sessions are not necessary. But, being in shape does reduce the risk of infection and complications resulting from surgery.

Physical fitness also shortens the time needed for recovery—sometimes dramatically. Of course, if you need emergency surgery, there's no time for physical conditioning. But if surgery can safely be postponed for a few weeks, use that time to start an exercise regimen. Do aerobic and strength training. Ask your surgeon to recommend any specific exercises that might prove helpful.

Example: Sit-ups and leg lifts strengthen the stomach muscles, thereby reducing the risk of hernia following abdominal surgery.

Be sure to inform your surgeon beforehand of any physical limitation or health problem that might complicate surgery. If you catch a cold or flu just prior to your operation, phone your doctor to ask if you should postpone the procedure.

•Maintain proper nutrition. Recovery following surgery is a complex process involving tissue repair, replacement of blood and other body fluids, and the fighting of infection.

Poor nutrition hampers the body's ability to perform these functions, placing patients at risk not only of a prolonged recovery, but also of muscle loss, kidney failure, and other potentially serious complications. *Especially important:*

•For blood replacement: Iron, vitamin B$_{12}$, and folate.

•For prevention of bruising and bleeding: Vitamin C and Vitamin K.

•For tissue repair: Zinc.

•For immunity: Copper.

•For prevention of post-surgery constipation: Dietary fiber.

Bottom line: If you believe your diet is lacking in these nutrients, ask your doctor to recommend a daily multivitamin/mineral supplement.

•Maintain proper weight. Being even moderately overweight makes surgery more difficult for surgeons and anesthesiologists, lengthens your recovery period, and boosts your risk of complications.

Recent study: Of 500 patients who recently underwent abdominal surgery in an English hospital, those overweight by 30% or more were almost twice as likely to develop serious infections following surgery than were non-obese patients. If you are overweight—and have the time—lose weight before your operation. Avoid crash diets. Lose weight gradually —no more than two pounds a week.

•Don't smoke. Smoke retards the healing process and interferes with the action of certain important drugs. Smokers are six times more likely to develop chest infections following abdominal surgery than are nonsmokers.

While four to six weeks of abstinence are needed to curb these risks, giving up cigarettes even for a few days or hours prior to surgery is extremely beneficial.

Background: Tobacco smoke contains carbon monoxide, a substance highly toxic to hemoglobin, the blood protein responsible for transporting oxygen throughout the body. Less healthy hemoglobin means slower healing following surgery. Tobacco smoke also contains nicotine, a powerful stimulant that forces the heart to pump faster and to use more oxygen. Though this extra burden does not ordinarily pose a severe problem, it has been known to cause heart attacks in some surgical patients—especially those who have been smoking for many years.

•Limit alcohol consumption. Heavy drinkers—especially those who can "hold their liquor" without becoming visibly drunk—often require more anesthetic than nondrinkers.

This difference poses problems for anesthesiologists who are not forewarned. In addition, heavy drinkers often have nutritional deficiencies that compromise the post-surgery healing process. Finally, heavy drinking irritates the liver, hampering the organ's ability to break down medications and to produce proteins essential to clotting of the blood.

Bottom line: The less you drink, the safer your surgery.

•Check your medications. While most prescription drugs can safely be taken up to and during the period of surgery, others may interfere with safe anesthesia or surgery. Consult your surgeon if you are taking insulin, an anticoagulant, or steroids. The dose will need adjusting for surgery.

In addition, birth control pills containing estrogen raise the risk of deep vein thrombosis during surgery. The Pill should be avoided for at least four weeks prior to major surgery.

Exception: The so-called "minipill" does not contain estrogen and is safe to use prior to surgery.

•Secure loose dental work—and repair decayed teeth. Anesthesia often involves insertion of tubes and instruments into the patient's mouth. If your teeth are loose or badly decayed, or if you have a bridge or other fragile dental work, tell your surgeon well before any surgery.

Danger: Loose teeth or dental work may become lodged in the throat or windpipe, resulting in breathing difficulties. In addition, bacteria present in decayed teeth may spread infection elsewhere in the body following surgery. Cavities should be filled well in advance of surgery.

Source: Robin A. J. Youngson, MD, a Fellow in England's Royal College of Anaesthetists and currently staff anesthesiologist at Auckland Public Hospital, Auckland, New Zealand. Dr. Youngson is the author of *Operation! A Handbook for Surgical Patients,* David & Charles PLC, Brunel House, Newton Abbot, Devon, England.

High-Tech Way To Spot a Liar

Folk wisdom always said you can't trust what people say if they don't look you straight in the eye. But that was before TV. How about the politician who is giving a speech on television and only *seems* to be looking you in the eye? A new generation of candidate watchers has the answer. Watch the speaker's nose. If he rubs it at important moments in the speech, he's probably telling something other than the whole truth. Two Presidents in a row gave themselves away just this way.

Home Medical Tests

Choices: Although some home medical tests are accurate and useful when used as instructed—not all are reliable.

Biggest danger...

False negatives. The test may read "no problem" even though a condition does exist.

Trap: False sense of security and failure to seek timely medical treatment.

Common causes of false negatives:
- The test itself is unreliable.
- Manufacturer's instructions weren't followed correctly.
- The test's shelf life has expired.

To improve accuracy:
- Buy the test from a reliable outlet where inventory turns over quickly.
- Follow manufacturer's instructions.
- If you get a negative reading, repeat the test a few days later to confirm the results.

Reasonably accurate—tests for...
- Pregnancy. However, false negatives do occur.
- Blood glucose. This enables diabetics to monitor blood sugar level and adjust insulin dosages accordingly.
- Ovulation. This test should only be used to assist in achieving pregnancy...not as a contraceptive maneuver.

Recommended with reservation:
- Strep throat. Tests are inaccurate.
- Cholesterol. Further testing and medical history are needed for treatment purposes.
- Stool guaiac. This tests for the presence of blood in the stool, an early symptom of colorectal cancer. Meat in the diet can give a false positive result, causing needless worry. False negatives are also common. A physical exam by a doctor is important in conjunction with the test.

Source: Paul Bachner, MD, chairman of the department of pathology and laboratory medicine at United Hospital in Port Chester, New York 10573. Dr. Bachner is former chairman of the College of American Pathologists' Quality Assurance Committee, which studies factors that improve the accuracy of lab results within hospitals and independent laboratories.

16

Enjoying Your Leisure

New Ways to Have Fun In the 1990's

In the next few years, we'll see dramatic shifts in the way we have fun, whether it's pursuing recreation or being entertained.

Driving the changes: Aging of the baby boom generation, plus a wider rift between those who have money and those who don't...and between those with plenty of spare time and those who don't have enough time to take care of job and family.

What to expect:

•A closer link between health and pleasure. Jogging, for instance, will be on the decline, while aerobic therapy is on the way in. In a sense, pastimes will become more pleasurable.

Reason: Until recently, things we enjoyed often had to with overindulgence and were bad for our health. Today, more pastimes are becoming good for our health, or at least not harmful.

On the way out: Big dinners, evenings of drinking, spending the day at the beach (since

we've learned about the harmful effects of radiation). Shopping for the fun of shopping will also lose much of its appeal since many of us will be under greater economic pressure.

Funtime activities for the future:

Bird watching (already a fast-growing hobby), food gardening, structured relaxation for stress management, and hanging out at "brain bars" (establishments where nonalcoholic drinks are laced with nutrients that supposedly help our cerebral abilities) and networking with people on computer systems.

In the coming years, we'll see a continuation of the trend where some people have a great deal and time and money while others have too little. That means fun will become more closely linked to the ability to find time for it.

Many Americans will have to re-learn the art of having fun with their children, an activity that was largely shoved aside in the last two decades. And most of us will have to take greater care in scheduling a scarcer amount of fun time with family and friends.

The goal: To enjoy taking time off without

losing ground professionally.

Many of us are already relying on new technologies to help with this aspect of time management. Cellular phones, for instance, often show up at football games and restaurants.

Prediction: Most people will soon tire of trying to have fun while they're electronically tethered to the office.

Source: Edith Weiner is president of Weiner, Edrich, Brown, Inc., futurists and strategic planning consultants, 200 E. 33 St., New York 10016.

Super Summertime Drinks...Without Liquor

Teetotaler's Wine can be made in any quantity and is best served in wine glasses. Mix equal parts chilled ginger ale and chilled, unsweetened grape juice. Serves 16.

Ellen's Energizer is a refreshing summer drink as well as a great stomach settler. Combine ½ cup of half-and-half with ½ cup ginger ale...or—if you're counting calories—½ cup skim milk with ½ cup diet ginger ale. Serve over crushed ice. Serves one.

Fast Fruit Punch is a great thirst-quencher and has a pretty purple color. In a punch bowl, combine 1 quart ginger ale, one 46-ounce can pineapple juice, one 32-ounce bottle grape juice, one 6-ounce can frozen orange juice (prepared) and one 6-ounce can frozen lemonade (prepared). Add ice and a fresh fruit garnish. Serves 40.

Festive Punch is a perfect beverage for summer barbecues, brunches or luncheons. You'll need three 6-ounce cans frozen lemonade concentrate (prepared), one 10-ounce package of frozen strawberries (thawed), 1 quart chilled ginger ale, ice, one pint raspberry sherbet and fresh whole raspberries.

Pour lemonade into the punch bowl and stir in strawberries. Just before serving add ginger ale and an ice ring, then stir in sherbet. Place a raspberry in each cup and serve. Serves 10.

Source: Jane Brandt, author of *Drinks Without Liquor,* Workman Publishing, 708 Broadway, New York 10003.

Better Shopping

Department-store fluorescent lighting often distorts colors. *Result:* You may not be able to tell the true color of clothing, lipstick or other merchandise you've purchased until you get it home. *Self-defense:* If what you buy doesn't live up to your expectations, take it back and demand a refund—the store's poor lighting isn't your fault.

Source: *Live Better for Less,* 21 E. Chestnut St., Chicago 60611.

Consumer Credit Doesn't Always Travel Well

So if you're relocating and establishing credit (from home mortgage to credit cards) in a new area, double check your current credit reports to make sure there are no inaccuracies. Don't assume your report is sparkling clean. Occasional late payments, errors and legitimate disputes with creditors can result in a poor rating that may slow or even stop a new credit application. Steps to take: Before moving, get a report from a major credit reporting agency—TRW, Equifax or Trans Union—and clear up any problems.

Source: *Consumer Finance Bulletin,* Education Foundation, 919 18 St. NW, Washington, DC 20006.

Videotaping Basics

To hold the camera as steady as possible, keep your feet apart with your weight evenly distributed between them...tuck elbows into your body for support...for a smooth, side-to-side pan, keep the bottom half of your body still and pivot the upper half, "rolling" your body over a solid support, such as a wall...in windy conditions, find a firm support—wall, railing, car trunk—to lean against.

Source: *John Hedgecoe's Complete Guide to Video* by John Hedgecoe, professor of photography, Royal College of Art, London. Sterling Publishing Co., 387 Park Ave. S., New York 10016.

Shrewder Lottery Playing

Most lottery players either choose their numbers at random or plug in family birth dates. *Their assumption:* Since winning numbers are chosen at random, there is no way to improve a player's chances. In fact, mathematical strategies can make a huge difference in playing the lottery.

Key: Choosing *unpopular* numbers that are unlikely to be selected by other players. *Result:* While your chance of winning the jackpot remains the same, the *amount* you stand to win is much larger…since you'll be splitting your prize with fewer (if any) other players.

In a "6/49" lottery (where the players choose six numbers between 1 and 49), there are about 14 million different combinations available. In a typical game, 20% of those combinations—2.8 million different plays—are selected by no one.

A shrewd lottery strategy will consistently land you within that 20% window…giving you a strong chance of pocketing the entire jackpot should you win.

Better: The larger the jackpot, the better your return on every dollar you wager. *Reason:* A disproportionate number of the extra bettors will be playing combinations that you'll be avoiding.

What are these unpopular numbers that you should be targeting?

•All numbers over 31, for the simple reason that they won't be chosen by anyone playing birth or anniversary dates. At least four of your six choices should be 32 or above.

•Numbers ending in 1, 2, 8, 9…and 0. Most people tend to select numbers ending in 3 through 7. *Especially unpopular:* 10, 20, 30, and 40.

On the other hand, avoid playing the more popular numbers or combinations, including:

•Multiples of 7, which are favored by the superstitious.

•Single-digit numbers (1 through 9). Use no more than one of these among your six choices.

•Numbers that form vertical, horizontal, or diagonal patterns on your bet slip card. These are also quite popular.

•The combination 1-2-3-4-5-6, which may be the most popular of all.

Bottom line: By playing the least popular numbers, you can increase the amount of money you bring home by *more than 600%.*

Source: Alan J. Reiss, president of US Mathematical Labs, 18 Main St., Concord, Massachusetts 01742. His company sells two mathematical tools for lottery players…a computer software program available for IBM or MAC for $104 (please specify 3 1/2" or 5 1/4" disk), and a mechanical "WinWheel" for $21.95…to help people to generate "original" sets of numbers unlikely to be selected by other players.

Nearsighted People Are Smarter?

Nearsighted people on average score six to eight points higher on IQ tests than do members of the general population. They also score higher on college entrance exams…and they get better grades in school. Puzzling: The disparity does not seem to exist because nearsighted people hurt their eyes by reading more. It exists among children who are too young to read, and is reflected in skills that are not related to reading. A genetic cause is suspected, but for now the statistical correlation between nearsightedness and intelligence is unexplained.

Source: Camilla Benbow, psychologist at Iowa State University, quoted in *Hippocrates,* 475 Gate Five Rd., Sausalito, California 94965.

Computer News That You Can Use

Protect computer systems by using modems that will connect with an outside call only if the call comes from an authorized phone number. A hacker trying to gain access to the system won't be at such a number, and so won't be able to succeed.

Source: Eric Paulak, editor, *411* 11300 Rockville Pike, Rockville, Maryland 20852.

How to Prevent Cellular Phone Fraud

Even companies that make minimal use of cellular phones are vulnerable to being ripped off by the growing number of cellular hackers.

Achilles' heel: The phone's electronic serial number (ESN)—embedded on a computer chip inside the phone...and its mobile ID number (MIN)—the telephone number assigned by the cellular phone company.

These numbers can be detected and decoded by criminals equipped with special devices that pick up cellular phone signals and record the two key numbers. These can then be used for illegal cellular service, ending up on the company's bill. They can also be picked up from office files or computers. Self-defense:

•Instruct the cellular carrier to block all international calls—unless you absolutely must use your cellular phone for overseas calling.

•Keep all cellular phone records locked

•Don't keep ESNs and associated MINs on a computer. If a hacker wants your numbers, chances are he'll know his way around computer files as well as he does around the cellular airwaves.

•Don't divulge ESNs and associated MINs to anyone except the person responsible for dealing with the cellular company. The numbers should be in as few hands as possible to maintain maximum security.

•Ask for the most detailed form of billing available from the carrier—so you can carefully scrutinize calling records.

Source: Dick Sharman, The Guidry Group, telecommunications consultants, 1400 Woodloch Forest Dr., Woodlands, Texas 77380, quoted in *411*, 11300 Rockville Pike, Rockville, Maryland 20852.

Diamond Savvy

Beware of a diamond that has been set so that the pavilion (bottom) of the stone is blocked from view or enclosed in metal. A closed back is often a sign that something is being hidden. Examples: The stone may be a rhinestone (glass with a foil back)...a lower quality diamond with a coating to improve its color...a single-cut diamond made to appear like an expensive brilliant-cut diamond.

Source: *The Diamond Ring Buying Guide* by Renée Newman, International Jewelry Publications, Box 13334, Los Angeles 90013.

Rules to Keep a Friendly Poker Game Friendly

Neighborhood poker—exemplified by the guys on *The Odd Couple*—is more than just a game. It's a friendship around a table. And friendship thrives in a comfortable atmosphere where friends show each other consideration. Bottom line: Poker should be fun. To set the scene...

Make it comfortable:

•The room. It should be big enough for a table and at least seven chairs, with plenty of room to get up and leave the table without bumping other players. Important: A window that opens at the top...if there's cigarette and cigar smoke, it has to go somewhere. Provide large ashtrays or your floor will suffer.

•TV. Good for players who drop out of the game...and for everyone when there's a major sports event. It doesn't matter where the TV sits, but keep the sound low—it can be turned up for the exciting moments.

•Music. It's up to the individual group whether to have music...and what kind of music. Play the radio, so that no one has to hop up to change tapes, etc.

•Table. A round table is preferred, but any shape will do. Use a tablecloth to make a smooth, cushioned surface. Chips bounce when tossed on a bare table top.

•Chairs. Use strong, metal folding chairs... wood is not strong enough. Comfort is not a concern in poker games. If you're winning, you'll be very comfortable.

•Cards. Use high-quality cards. Cheap cards crease and bend easily—a card with a folded corner will be a marked card for the rest of evening.

Use two decks at a time, each with a different color backing. While one deck is being dealt, the other can be reshuffled by the player who dealt the previous hand. Hold on to decks from previous weeks in case you need an emergency replacement deck.

•Chips. Have at least three colors—one for each of the minimum and maximum bets, and one for double the maximum. Clay chips handle better than plastic. They're available from gambling supply houses—check your Yellow Pages.*

•Food. Chips, pretzels, popcorn and nuts are the old standbys. Select food that can be eaten with one hand, leaving the other free to hold cards.

Later in the evening something more substantial will be necessary. Cold cuts or pizza work well. Both can sit for a while and remain edible, require few utensils and don't make a mess. Use paper plates, and keep plastic bags handy for garbage. Mistake: Chinese food. It's too messy.

Food should be supplied by the host...but paid for by all. Arrive at a set donation or take a cut from each pot.

•Disaster control. Keep plenty of paper towels and a portable vacuum cleaner handy.

•Clean-up philosophy. Nobody leaves until the garbage is bagged, ashtrays are emptied and the immediate area is made neat.
Playing etiquette:

•Know what you are going to deal when the deck comes to you. Poker has a rhythm. Being indecisive breaks it.

•Turn all your cards face down to indicate you're out of a hand. Or toss them to the dealer or into the pot so they're out of the way. Take care that no one sees your cards. What one player knows, all should know.

•Clean up condensation from beverage bottles and cans. Wet cards ruin the game.

•Be honest. You only have to be caught once to be marked forever.

•Bring enough money to play for at least half the night. The worst thing you can do is quit early and leave only four players. Rule of

thumb: Bring enough money to buy three full stacks of chips.

•If you must leave early, make it known in advance. This gives the other players a chance to find someone else.

•If you drink beer...bring beer. Once it comes into the house, though, it's community property. Note: If you want to drink or eat something different than what is being served, bring it.

•Keep your up cards fully exposed in a stud game so everyone can see them. Players who try to cover up their cards in a stud game are not trusted.

•Announce your ante. Say something like "I'm in" loud enough so that others hear you. Then, if the pot comes up short, you'll have witnesses.

Don't give another player advice on betting, even if asked. Your advice could sabotage a bluffer, or simply be bad advice.

•Once you've dropped out, don't look at another player's hand without permission. And don't react to what you've seen.

•Don't look at another player's hand if you've seen someone else's. Your expression could give something away. Worse: Giving advice to either of the player's whose cards you've seen. Your advice would be based on knowledge of two or three hands (including your own)—knowledge not available to other players.

•Don't call out what cards of possibilities another player has showing. Only the dealer has this right. This is all the more true when you've dropped out.

•Never help another player figure out what he/she has. A player must call his own hand.

•Don't feel sorry for a loser and hold the bet down. It's humiliating for the loser. Play to win big. It's not malicious—it's the game.

•Don't feel sorry for a novice. It's sink or swim. And you could find yourself in the position of carrying a bad player.

•Don't show your complete winning hand if you win the pot by default. You may have been bluffing and that's information no one paid to see...and you don't want anyone to know. Only by calling your final bet do players pay for the privilege of seeing your hand.

*Also available from Gamblers General Store, 800 S. Main St., Las Vegas 89101, 800-322-2447. Prices vary depending on quality.

• Never play poker with someone whose nickname is a city. If he's good enough to be the best in town, he's good enough to beat anyone in your neighborhood.

Source: Stewart Wolpin, author of *The Rules of Neighborhood Poker According to Hoyle,* New Chapter Press, 381 Park Ave. South, New York 10016.

Cycling and Sex

Male bicyclists who ride up to 100 miles a week may become impotent. Repeated thrusting down on the pedals pounds the groin against the seat, damaging the critical arteries and nerves. Initial symptoms: Buttock numbness and difficulty getting an erection for a day or two. Trap: Damage may be irreversible and may not be apparent for years. Self-defense: Padded bike seat and shorts…rise off the seat occasionally, especially when sprinting…a correct size bike—you shouldn't have to shift your body on the downstroke.

Source: Harin Padma-Nathan, assistant professor of urology, University of South Carolina School of Medicine, quoted in *American Health,* 80 Fifth Ave, New York 10011.

The Pleasures Of Organic Gardening

There really is no need to use chemicals and gasoline-powered machines when gardening or tending to your lawn. Organic methods are just as successful and use only fertilizers and pest controls found in nature. Advantages:

• Creates a healthier environment by rebuilding the top soil, protecting ground water, and using less energy.

• Produces homegrown, organic (chemical-free) vegetables—fresher and cheaper than the ones you can buy in natural-foods stores or supermarkets.

Organic fertilizers:

While synthetic fertilizers feed the crop, they deplete the soil, then make future crops dependent on continued applications. Organic fertilizers feed the plants and nourish the soil. All plants need…

• Nitrogen for lush foliage.

Best organic sources: Homemade or bagged compost—decomposed plants or animal wastes rich in nitrogen and other trace minerals. Add up to two inches to each garden bed yearly. For fast results: Use blood meal and dried blood (by-products of slaughterhouses), or cottonseed meal (ground from seeds of the cotton plant).

• Phosphorus for flower and seed production.

Best organic source: Colloidal phosphate, a rock powder, also rich in lime and trace minerals. For fast results: Try bone meal—it's effective, but more expensive.

• Potash (Potassium) for strong roots and solid branches.

Best organic sources: Granite dust (a rock powder) and greensand (a mineral-rich deep sea deposit). For fast results: Try wood ashes left from a wood stove or fireplace.

Important: Soil conditions in your garden—and the specific needs of plants you want to grow—should determine your choice of fertilizer. Your local garden center or the US Department of Agriculture's cooperative extension service can test your soil and recommend the best organic fertilizer for your needs.

Organic pest and weed control:

• Insecticidal soaps: Spray every three to five days for about three weeks to eliminate most pests on specific plants or plant groupings.

Cost: $5 to $7 for 8 oz. of concentrate, which makes 4 gallons of spray covering 1,000 square feet. To deter pests, add onion, hot pepper and/or garlic blended to a pulp and squeezed through cotton cheesecloth.

• Fabric coverings: Sheets of very thin-woven polyester or thin-spun polypropylene, sold as "floating" row covers or super-light insect barriers. Use only for vegetable gardens—not for ornamental plants…make sure plants have enough water—high temperatures under the fabric can make them dry…and remove covers over squashes, melons and cucumbers when the flowers start to bloom—in time for pollination.

Cost: Under $10, for a 10' x 10' sheet of polypropylene or an 8' x 20' sheet of polyester.

•Beneficial insects: Bugs that kill harmful insects that eat your vegetables or plants. They can be purchased at local garden centers or by mail order.*

•Mulching: Cover the earth around each plant or row to deter weeds and conserve water with shredded bark mulch, wood chips, cocoa or buckwheat hulls. (Also use straw and shredded leaves for vegetable plants—but not for ornamentals.) Old mulch decomposes and can be worked into the soil. New mulch is spread after planting.

*Mail-order companies that sell these insects include: Gardens Alive!, 5100 Schenley Pl., Lawrenceburg, Indiana 47025. 812-537-8650...Gardener's Supply Co., 128 Intervale Rd., Burlington, Vermont 05401. 802-863-1700.

Source: Bonnie Wodin, of Golden Yarrow Landscaping, Heath, Massachusetts 01346, designs custom gardens and landscapes. She also lectures frequently on horticulture and landscaping.

How to Make The Most Of Your Time... Without Driving Yourself Crazy

People have less free time than they did a generation ago—37% less than in 1973, according to a recent Harris survey. There is, though, more time available than you think. Three general rules...

•Eliminate slave-of-habit routines. Example: Spending 45 minutes each morning with the daily paper...when you can get the news you need with a quick scan of the front page or 10 minutes with an all-news radio station.

•Change your schedule so that you're at your best for your most important and challenging tasks. Many executives waste the start of their work day—when they may be freshest—by going through their mail. They'd do better by plunging into a tough report and saving the mail for later in the day, when they're slowing down.

•Learn to do two or three things at the same

time. When you go to the bank, always bring something you need to read on the inevitable line. When you make a call and are placed on hold, switch to your speaker phone and take care of some paperwork. When your party comes on the line switch back.

Most time-saving ideas are small in scale—but those minutes add up. In most cases, a newly efficient person can save an hour a day—and that is a significant amount of time. The morning routine:

•Pop out of bed as soon as you wake up, rather than lingering under the covers. Incentive: Think of the most pleasant activity on your schedule that day.

•Plan a pre-breakfast work segment—30 to 60 minutes of uninterrupted concentration in some quiet part of your home.

•Write a "to-do" list in your daily organizer book—a schedule of the high-priority tasks you need to address. Do it the night before. Less urgent tasks should be listed under "Things to Be Done This Week" and "Things for Following Weeks."

•Schedule tasks that require others' actions for early in the day. By reaching people early, you're more likely to get them to do what you need that day.

Organizing your office:

•Angle your desk away from open doorways, busy corridors or windows—all sources of distraction.

•Keep your desk neat. Clear away everything unrelated to the project at hand. To dispose of clutter: Eliminate dispensable items, including photos, gadgets and magazines. Put in a few inexpensive bookshelves you can get to without rising.

•Install the largest wastebasket your office can gracefully contain.

Communications:

•Use a dictation device, rather than a secretary's shorthand. Advantages: More speed and flexibility...simpler changes...enhanced concentration.

•Computerized electronic mail eliminates much time-wasting telephone tag. For maximum efficiency: Note when you'll be available for a return phone call.

•Rely on your answering machine to screen incoming calls. Your highest priority should always be the most important item on your schedule...which is rarely attending to the telephone.

The media:

Read selectively. Concentrate on one general newspaper. Before you start reading: Examine the general and business news indexes for stories of interest.

•If you find an item of interest in a newspaper or magazine, rip it out and read it when appropriate—and throw the rest of the publication away.

•Read for 15 to 30 minutes before bedtime. This is a good time for books that inspire or entertain.

Source: Ray Josephs, public-relations pioneer and author of the newly revised *How to Gain An Extra Hour Every Day.* Penguin USA, 375 Hudson St., New York 10014.

Improved Backswings For Older Golfers

Backswings get shorter as golfers get older. When the swings get too short, you'll lose distance, accuracy and consistency.

Remedies:

Hold the club lightly. Reason: Too tight a grip tenses the arm and shoulder muscles and restricts the backswing.

Put more weight on your right foot, especially on full swings with woods and longer irons. Result: A head start on your swing and less weight to shift.

Turn your chin to the right (or to the left, if you're a southpaw) as you start your backswing. If it throws your timing off, cock your chin in the direction of the backswing before you swing.

Saving Money Each Month

The wheels of commerce turn with predictable regularity on an annual basis. Key: Timing your purchases.

•January. Traditional after-Christmas and New Year's bargains include men's suits, linens (white sales), appliances and furniture.

•February. The season of love brings big reductions on china, glass, silver, mattresses and bedding.

•March. Watch for special pre-season promotions for spring clothing. Ski equipment is at an annual low as well.

•April. Sales begin again after the Easter holiday, especially on clothing.

•May. Spring cleaning means specials on household cleaning products. This also is a good month to shop for carpets and rugs.

•June. Shop for furniture. Semiannual inventory is on its way in, and old items must go.

•July. Most stores liquidate their inventories to make room for fall goods during this month. Sportswear, sporting equipment and garden tools and supplies take noticeable dips.

•August. If you are in the market for a car, August is clearance time on current models. Also, equipment linked to the summer season is marked down. Look for good deals on patio furniture, lawn mowers, yard tools, and barbeque and camping equipment.

•September. The best deals on school clothes are at the end of the month. If you can hold off the "first-day complex" you'll save big on what's "in" this year.

•October. This is the month to do your Christmas shopping. Stores are postured to boost retail sales before the holiday season.

•November. Wool clothes ranging from women's coats to men's suits come down significantly this month as store owners cut their inventories for their second shipment of the season.

•December. Next to August, this month is the best time to buy a new car.

Source: Reprinted with permission from *52 Ways to Stretch a Buck* by Kenny Luck, director, New Life Treatment Centers, Laguna Beach, California. ©1992 Thomas Nelson Publishers, Box 141000, Nashville 37214.

Shopping Much Smarter Now

The old rules of shopping no longer apply. To spend wisely and get the best for the least, take heed of the following changes in shopping rules:

•No longer true: Buy a known brand. Once consumers find a brand name they believe delivers quality, they continue to select that brand with little comparison before purchasing.

Reality: Our research has found that past performance of a brand is a poor predictor of future quality. Better: Check *Consumer Reports* for products that are regularly rated from year to year. There are often good reasons why a brand doesn't maintain the same quality.

•No longer true: Look for a seal of approval. It's fine to look for the seal of approval of Underwriters Laboratories, which assures the safety of electrical products—but some seals don't mean much. Good Housekeeping's seal, for example, only gives assurances of limited refund or replacement by Good Housekeeping.

•No longer true: Buy the top of the line. Many appliances and other durables are marketed in product lines, with a no-frills model at the bottom. Consumers assume that the top-of-the-line model not only has more features but is also of higher quality.

Reality: People who buy top-of-the-line often pay for features they don't want or need. Many of the same features may be offered on lower-priced models of that manufacturer or a competitor. Check!

•No longer true: Price indicates quality. Several studies have demonstrated a poor price-quality correlation and some have even shown a negative relationship—that is, higher prices associated with lower quality. But shoppers don't seem to learn this—even with frequently purchased or big ticket items where they should do more research before buying.

Exercise: Create a simple chart showing prices of all varieties of a product having the same level of quality. You'll quickly see which is the best buy. Of course it becomes more complex in comparing products with many features and product qualities, such as personal stereo systems. But even there, if you plot a chart with price on the vertical scale and quality features on the horizontal scale, you'll be able to quickly spot which models are way out of line.

•No longer true: Larger sizes are better buys. Don't assume that larger sizes of a packaged goods product are a better buy than smaller sizes. Much research has demonstrated that the larger size rule is frequently invalid. Sometimes there's actually a surcharge on the larger size. Quantity discounts, however, are more common than quantity surcharges—and are larger in amount. Consumers generally do get a good deal by buying larger sizes…but there are exceptions.

Bottom line:

If you don't have the time or inclination to research every purchase, and some rules have worked for you, fine. Continue to use them. But pay attention to unit pricing labels in stores and, even with brands that have been satisfactory over time, occasionally check to make sure they're still competitive in quality and price.

Also read labels to make sure you're not getting something you don't want in terms of ingredients or environmental problems.

Helpful resources: The public library is the best place to start on consumer research. It has entire magazines devoted to product categories. People at the library will also know of local consumer-action groups.

Every state has a Cooperative Extension Service, funded partly by the US Dept. of Agriculture and partly by the state and local counties. These are located at land-grant universities. They are a source of useful consumer-buying publications.

Also: Write the Consumer Information Center, Pueblo, Colorado 81009, for a free catalogue of US government pamphlets, many of which are very useful for smart shopping.

Source: Brenda J. Cude, extension specialist and associate professor, family economics, Cooperative Extension Service, University of Illinois at Urbana-Champaign, 271 Bevier Hall, 905 S. Goodwin Ave., Urbana, Illinois 61801.

Computer Glare

Computer glare can be reduced with tinted eyeglass lenses to counteract the VDT's screen color. For a screen with green characters: Use a purplish red tint. For amber letters: Light blue tint. For a black-and-white screen: Light gray tint.

Source: *Healthy Eyes Better Vision*, by Jeffrey Anshel, OD, optometrist in private practice in Del Mar, California, specializing in vision therapy and preventive approaches to eye problems. Corporate Vision Consulting, 2404-A Sacada Circle, La Costa, California 92009.

How Amy Dacyczyn Avoids Overspending At the Supermarket

Although most people go to the supermarket with a budget in mind, they usually spend much more money than they had planned to spend. But by using a variety of strategies, I spend only $180 a month to feed our family of eight.

The first step to saving money at the supermarket is to overcome your most common excuses for why your bill is so high…

The big myths:

•Myth: Never shop with your kids. Reality: If you can't say no to your children, you have a parenting problem, not a shopping problem.

•Myth: Shop the aisles in reverse order to avoid temptation. Reality: If you can't resist temptation, you have a problem with self-discipline, not budgeting.

•Myth: Menus must be planned in advance to save at the supermarket. Reality: Don't plan meals more than one day in advance, or you're likely to spend more at the supermarket.

Example: If you scheduled pork chops and they're too expensive, you'll probably buy them anyway. Better: Stock up on foods that are purchased at a good price. Then prepare meals with the foods you have already bought. There should be pork chops that you bought on sale in your freezer.

Supermarket strategies:

Once you've overcome the myths, you're ready to put serious money-saving strategies into place. My favorites…

•Work on your attitude. Saving money on groceries depends on a consistent attitude toward shopping—every time you shop. It is essential that you enter the supermarket fully conscious and determined about what you will—or will not—buy.

If you are prone to impulse shopping, you must decide to take control of your shopping habits.

Helpful: Practice. Try the strategies listed below, and learn more about what it costs for your family to eat the food you normally buy. Before you know it, nothing on earth could induce you to spend your hard-earned cash on a hamburger mix or sugar-coated cereal.

•Shop with a list. Make a list of specific groceries that you will buy at certain prices…but be flexible. What's on your list may not be on sale, but you may find a great deal on something that's not on your list.

Key: Be steadfast about what you will not buy. Certain products, such as toaster pastries, are too expensive at any price.

•Keep a price book. This strategy helps to save me more time and money than anything else I do.

In fact, comparison shopping is essential, since most people's memory for prices is not as good as they think it is. It's easy to figure out the cheapest can of green beans in one store, but most of us shop at more than one location—supermarkets, wholesale clubs, farmers' markets, natural food stores, discount stores—and foods come in different-sized packages.

To keep track of prices, I carry a small loose-leaf notebook that fits in my purse. On each page, I have listed the prices I've encountered for a specific product, with abbreviations for the store name, brand, item size, price and unit price. The pages are arranged alphabetically by product for easy reference.

Try shopping at a different good value store each week, so that you visit them all within a month. You will soon find patterns emerging.

Example: Cheese is usually a good buy at the wholesale club and seldom on sale at the supermarket.

Added benefit: You'll soon find that not every advertised sale is really a sale. Prices at the same store for the same item may vary from week to week by as much as a third.

Rule of thumb: The items at the front and back of the sale flyers are usually the best deals, though there may be a few on the inside pages.

•Buy groceries in bulk. This does not necessarily mean you have to buy huge quantities. It simply means you must buy enough of each item at its lowest price to provide for your family from sale to sale—or to last until your next trip to the wholesale club. Buying in bulk can save the average family at least $50 a month.

Helpful: Not all food has to be stored in the kitchen. If you were offered $50 a month to rent the space under your bed, would you do it? Use a closet or a shelf in the garage for that bargain case of peanut butter.

For maximum savings: Invest in an extra freezer. For example, the largest Sears model costs less than $6 a month to run. Even apartment dwellers can often arrange to keep locked freezers in the basements of their buildings.

•Determine which products are the least expensive, and how to buy them as inexpensively as possible.

Examples: I calculate which meats are the least expensive based on portion size, and I watch for sales. I generally choose from the lower end of cuts—with occasional treats. I also calculate the cost per gallon of fruit juice, whether it is frozen, bottled or canned.

My family drinks apple, orange or grape juice …or lemonade made from sugar, water and lemon juice concentrate. We don't buy processed blends of fruit juices, which are always more expensive than other juices. We do buy store brands.

Stay away from: Single serving packages, snack packs, lunch sizes…almost anything disposable, except toilet paper and tissues.

Examples: Diapers, paper plates, napkins, tablecloths.

•Set limits on what you are willing to pay for staple food items. Gradually, you will determine realistic upper limits for the items you routinely buy. Stick to your limits.

Example: In my area of the country, I will pay no more than 69 cents a pound for meat on the bone—or $1.20 a pound or less for boneless.

•Buy food in its "original" form. Avoid convenience and processed foods. Pop your own popcorn. Make your own breading for chicken and pork. Buy regular oatmeal rather than processed cereal or "instant" oatmeal.

Source: Amy Dacyczyn, author of *The Tightwad Gazette* (Villard Books), a book of cost-cutting strategies that have appeared in her newsletter of the same name. Rural Route 1, Box 3570, Leeds, Maine 04263.

Dog-Training Basics

•Keep lessons short. Four half-hour lessons will be more productive than one full hour.

•Give lessons at the same time and place each day, in an area where there are no distractions.

•Don't attempt to teach just after the dog has eaten a full meal.

•Keep lessons consistent and interesting.

•Make sure you've got the dog's attention before giving a command.

•Limit commands to one or two words. Use the same tone of voice all the time.

•Praise or blame the dog during an act, not afterward, so it knows what it has done right—or wrong.

•Wait until the dog learns one lesson before moving on.

•Command with firmness and authority, yet with kindness and patience. Do not show displeasure if the dog makes a mistake—stop if you find yourself losing patience.

•Always finish with a game.

Source: *The Howell Book of Dog Care* by Tim Hawcroft, veterinary surgeon in private practice in Sydney, Australia. Howell Book House, 866 Third Ave., New York 10022. 800-257-5755.

Andrew Sarris' Favorite Horror Movies

Ghost and ghoul stories go far back in our civilization to the earliest campfires, where our ancestors tried to exorcise their fears of death, the dark and the unknown.

The gothic horror movie genre originated in the German silent classics—Robert Wiene's *The Cabinet of Dr. Caligari* (1919) and F.W. Murnau's *Nosferatu* (1922)...and the first, though unauthorized, screen adaptation of Bram Stoker's literary vampire classic *Dracula* (1897).

The most famous Hollywood horror films are still James Whale's *Frankenstein* (1931), adapted from Mary Shelley's novel, with Boris Karloff as the Monster...and Tod Browning's authorized version of *Dracula* (1931), with Bela Lugosi as the courtly Count Dracula. Both movies remain profoundly horrific without the sickeningly simulated blood and gore created by today's special-effects technicians.

I would like to recommend a few works in the gothic horror genre that are longer on imagination than sheer exploitation.

• *Carrie* (1976) is the best of the high-school revenge fantasy horror movies, with Sissy Spacek triumphantly punishing all her tormentors and director Brian DePalma adding his stylistic flourishes to the final prom slaughter.

• *Cat People* (1942) was the first of producer Val Lewton and director Jacques Tourneur's efforts to give new life to the horror genre after it had almost drowned in juvenile facetiousness. Simone Simon brings her mesmerizingly feline beauty to her accursed characterization.

• *Dead of Night* (1945) is my all-time favorite, particularly because of Michael Redgrave's terrifying incarnation of a crazed ventriloquist who loses his will and soul to his malignant dummy. Alberto Cavalcanti, Charles Crichton, Basil Dearden and Robert Hamer each direct one of four interlocking supernatural stories that take place in a British country house where the guest-storytellers couldn't be nicer.

• *The Hunger* (1983) is best seen in the privacy of your living room since theater audiences are hopelessly embarrassed by the seductive spectacle of Catherine Deneuve and Susan Sarandon in the most erotic horror film of all time. David Bowie contributes another androgynous curio to his career, and Tony Scott directs in a chillingly fragmented manner.

• *I Walked With a Zombie* (1943) is, despite its lurid come-on title, a truly gothic romance set in the voodoo-drenched Caribbean. Another sensitive and intelligent collaboration between Lewton and Tourneur, plus the bright-eyed beauty of Frances Dee.

• *The Masque of the Red Death* (1964) is Roger Corman's supreme horror film with a superior British cast—Jane Asher, Hazel Court, Patrick Magee—supporting Vincent Price as Edgar Allan Poe's Satanic Prince Prospero who practices the black arts while his people are dying of the plague.

• *Near Dark* (1987) is Kathryn Bigelow's lyrical extension of the vampire genre to roadhouse Middle America, with a Murnau-like metaphorical shadows-into-blazing-sun-contrast, literally pitting light against darkness.

• *The Old Dark House* (1932) is perhaps the best of the lonely-house-on-a-dark-and-stormy-night thrillers and is graced with a remarkable cast headed by Boris Karloff, Charles Laughton, Melvyn Douglas, Ernest Thesiger and Gloria Stuart. Elegantly directed by James Whale, one of the most literate and sophisticated directors of the 1930s.

• *The Shining* (1980) is one of the most underrated horror movies in film history. Director Stanley Kubrick and screenwriter Diane Johnson have transformed Stephen King's novel into the ultimate screen nightmare about writer's block. Jack Nicholson plays the monstrous consequence of literary frustration.

• *The Uninvited* (1944) is my favorite haunted-house movie. Gail Russell searches poignantly for the spirit of her dead mother. Ray Milland and Ruth Hussey as the brother and sister who rent the ghost-ridden dwelling assist in sorting out the tangled past. Lewis Allen directed, but the real auteur is composer Victor Young with his melodious "Stella by Starlight" score.

Source: Andrew Sarris is a professor of film in the School of the Arts at Columbia University, New York, and film critic for *The New York Observer*.

Prehistoric Creatures You Can See for Yourself

The dinosaurs brought to life in the block-buster *Jurassic Park* have been a source of excitement for over 100 years. The best places in the US to see and learn about them...

•American Museum of Natural History is redesigning its world-renowned dinosaur collection right now. It is the largest in the world. The collection includes one of the world's two mummified dinosaur fossils (with the skin dried over the bone) as well as mammoths, saber-toothed cats and hundreds of fossil vertebrates. Visitors can enjoy several changing exhibits before the remodeling is completed.
American Museum of Natural History, Central Park West at 79 St., New York 10024. 212-769-5100.

•Carnegie Museum of Natural History houses the third-largest dinosaur collection in the country. It gives free guided tours of its "Dinosaur Hall" every Saturday and Sunday. You can walk around and under the skeletons of 11 different species and examine about 500 fossil specimens. Most of the museum's dinosaur remains come from the Morrison Formation in Utah, where some of the best big dinosaur remains in the world were preserved.
Carnegie Museum of Natural History, 4400 Forbes Ave., Pittsburgh 15213. 412-622-3131.

•Cincinnati Museum of Natural History. Walk into the ice-blue heart of a glacier and cross into a spring day 19,000 years ago. Meltwater runs over the sides of a simulated glacier into ponds and bogs. You can feel the damp wind on your face and listen to glacial creaks—and roaring Ice Age mammals. Fossils, sculptures, aromas and lighting complete the effect. Children love this simulated trip into the Ice Age.
Cincinnati Museum of Natural History, The Museum Center, 1301 Western Ave., Cincinnati 45203. 513-287-7020.

•Houston Museum of Natural Science is the site of the largest specimen of a flying reptile found to date. The fossil remains of the Quetzalcoatlus northropi suggest a wingspan of nearly 50 feet (larger than that of an F-4 fighter jet). Other exhibits include a huge Diplodocus skeleton, a six-foot armadillo skeleton, saber-toothed cats and early horses.
Houston Museum of Natural Science, 1 Hermann Circle Dr., Houston 77030. 713-639-4600.

•The Mammoth Site of Hot Springs—a huge sinkhole of mammoth fossils preserved in layers of terraced sediments. The bones of an estimated 100 mammoths, a great short-faced bear, an extinct pronghorn and a camel have been found at this site. You can view an assembled mammoth skeleton, life-sized silhouettes of 25 animals and the excavation process. Special opportunity: Hands-on experiences in the screening for fossils.
The Mammoth Site of Hot Springs, Box 606, Hot Springs, South Dakota 57747. 605-745-6017.

•National Museum of Natural History. Part of the Smithsonian Institution, this museum warrants a full afternoon of your time with its skeletons of Albertosaurus, Tyrannosaurus Rex, Maiasaura, Stegosaurus, Triceratops and other well-known dinosaurs. You can run your fingers over mammoth and mastodon teeth—and then watch a slide program on glaciation.
National Museum of Natural History, Smithsonian Institution, 10 St. & Constitution Ave. NW, Washington, DC 20560. 202-357-2700.

•Natural History Museum of Los Angeles County. A three-toed dinosaur footprint, the largest catalogued vertebrate fossil collection in North America, a 72-foot Mamenchisaurus, a Tyrannosaur Rex skull and a Pterosaur with a 23-foot wingspan are among the amazing things you'll see at this popular museum. This museum also operates the fascinating George C. Page Museum at the La Brea Tar Pits in Los Angeles. At the tar pits, you'll see skeletons of a saber-toothed cat and the La Brea Woman (the only human skeleton recovered from the pits). In the summer, you can watch the excavation of plants and animals from 10,000 to 40,000 years ago.
Natural History Museum of Los Angeles County, 900 Exposition Blvd., Los Angeles 90007. 213-744-3466.

•Royal Tyrrell Museum of Palaeontology. More than a half million visitors a year come to Alberta to visit this unique museum in the Red Deer River Valley. The museum has 35 complete dinosaur skeletons and a Palaeoconservatory with more than 110 species of plants. Its Nova Room enables you to examine fossilized insects through a microscope and touch original fossils and casts.
Tyrrell Museum of Palaeontology, Box 7500, Drumheller, Alberta, Canada T0J 0Y0. 403-823-7707.

Source: Richard Will, coauthor of *Dinosaur Digs: Places Where You Can Discover Prehistoric Creatures.* Country Roads Press, Box 286, Castine, Maine 04421. 800-729-9179.

17

Very, Very Smart Education

New Directions In Education

During the next year or two we can expect a backlash against the multicultural push that has been building in recent years. That's because there's a real question about whether young people are getting a solid grounding in reading, writing and math—much less the ability to think, reason and understand ethics and philosophy--all things they need to know to function in the kind of world they'll be moving into.

Multiculturalism has forced distinctions on people and culturally ghettoized what they learned in school. Now more and more educators are coming out and saying that this is not really good education…that individual cultures or points of view don't have to be excluded in the future, but they need to be made part of a broader, more traditional curriculum.

College education—we foresee a shift away from America's traditional democratization, in which anyone, no matter how poor they were born, could aspire to good public college education if they were bright enough and resourceful.

Today, the public education system that fed these kids into public colleges has broken down. The schools have become unsafe and hostile places for children to learn. As a result, most of the brightest young people are being pulled out of public schools and put into the safety of private schools.

So, from a very early age, we're starting to see class distinctions develop in the education system. People who can afford to send their children to private schools or to move to better neighborhoods are leaving the others behind.

At the same time, going to college has become expensive. Even city and state colleges cost from $2,000 to $6,000 a year. Kids without any financial backing simply can't afford to attend college. They have to go to work. The state colleges have become very competitive because so many of the best and brightest of the middle class students are now going there, that marginal students can't get in.

The bottom line is that we are moving toward a patrimonial society in which children will make it depending on whom their parents know and what their parents can afford. To some extent it's always been true that if you were wealthy and well connected you stood a better chance of getting into the very top schools. What's happening now is that the very bright poor student has no place to go. Education is no longer the ticket for the poor or disenfranchised to rise up and better themselves.

And—then even graduates of good colleges today are having a hard time finding jobs. It used to be that if you graduated from a good school with high marks, you were assured of moving into a good job and career.

Right now, one in five college graduates can't find a job. Another one out of five end up employed in a job that doesn't require a college degree. And this situation is going to get worse as downsizing of companies continues in the next few years.

The hard fact today is that landing a job has a lot more to do with whom the parents know and the networking the kids have done throughout their lifetimes than on which college they graduated from, although they do need a college degree.

If you're a parent facing education decisions for your children in the next few years, a very good case can be made for not sending them to the highest priced learning institutions despite the historical status attached to these schools.

A better strategy is to build up your own network of contacts and also to broaden your child's base of contacts and experiences through travel and various extra-curricular activities.

Instead of spending $100,000 for an Ivy League education (often more costly education since many Ivy Leaguers tend to go on to graduate work), it's smarter now to shop around and find the best education value. That's often a state university.

You can then leverage a $40,000 investment with additional expenditures before and after to make sure the child learns vital coping skills such as communications, and that he/she gets any additional training or apprenticeship needed for a specific career. Money saved on the obligatory college education can also be used to help your child start some kinds of entrepreneurial ventures.

Source: Edith Weiner is president of Weiner, Edrich, Brown, Inc., futurists and strategic planning consultants, 200 E. 33 St., New York 10016.

Better Education

Pick your child's classroom carefully. Ask other parents and teachers, too—in the spring—before the next year's class assignments are made. You can then approach the principal with concrete information on why your child will work and learn better in a particular class. If the school doesn't respond, be persistent.

Source: *The Classroom Crucible: What Really Works, What Doesn't and Why* by education-policy analyst Edward Pauly. Basic Books, 10 E. 53 St., New York 10022.

Kids and Reading

Help children learn to read by giving them things they want to read. Examples: Write children notes instead of trying to get them to read from a plodding workbook…read aloud, even to older children…If a child is reading aloud and comes to an unfamiliar word, don't immediately ask him to sound it out. Ask, "What makes sense there?" This helps the child think about what word fits in with what he's reading.

Source: Lawrence Kutner, PhD, child psychologist, syndicated columnist and author of *Parent & Child: Getting Through to Each Other.* Avon Books, 1350 Avenue of the Americas, New York 10019.

Kindergarten Basics

There are two major and quite different approaches to kindergarten education. Academic programs stress intellectual skills through formal instruction. Developmental programs cultivate the whole child. Most schools emphasize one approach while including elements of the other.

Remember: Five-year-olds are not ready to be chained to a desk. Young children learn best from hands-on activities. Bottom line: Choose a program that leaves a major part of the day free for play and child-selected activities.

Source: *Ready for School? What Every Preschooler Should Know* by former teachers and syndicated newspaper columnists Marge Eberts and Peggy Gisler. Meadowbrook Press, 18318 Minnetonka Blvd., Deephaven, Minnesota 55391.

Make Your Baby Smarter

Make your babies smarter simply by talking to them. Example: As you hand a child a wooden spoon, tell him/her what it is, how it feels, what it's used for. Also: Don't use baby talk. Speak correctly, in complete sentences. Speak face-to-face. Continually introduce new words. Once he begins speaking, correct verbal mistakes by repeating what he said, using the correct form. Example: If he says, "I doed it," say, "Yes, you did it!"

Source: *Starting Out Well: A Parents' Approach to Physical Activity and Nutrition* by Lawrence A. Golding, PhD, director of exercise physiology, School of Health and Physical Education, University of Nevada, Las Vegas. Leisure Press, 1607 N. Market St., Champaign, Illinois 61820.

Kids and Losing Gracefully

Children love beating their parents at simple card and board games. But if they always win at home, they develop false expectations about the real world. Best: Let them lose sometimes. It is less threatening at home than at a friend's house. Important: When children come home after games, ask whether they had fun—not whether they won. Purpose: To teach that winning is not the only reason to play.

Source: Lawrence Kutner, PhD, author of *Parent and Child: Getting Through to Each Other*. Avon, 1350 Avenue of the Americas, New York 10019.

Educating at Home

Teaching children at home does not make them social misfits. More than 300,000 US families now educate at home—for religious reasons or from disenchantment with schools in their areas. A major argument against home schooling has been that it deprives children of peer contacts needed for social development. New study: There is no difference in adulthood between personal and social adaptations of home-taught and school-taught children.

Source: Study of more than 50 adults who were taught at home by their parents, led by J. Gary Knowles, EdD, assistant professor of education, University of Michigan at Ann Arbor.

College Bargains

With annual tuition approaching $20,000 for most Ivy League schools, it's reassuring to know that many first-rate colleges remain affordable. Best college values include:

East:

•University of Connecticut. Storrs. 203-486-2000. Rural setting 30 minutes from Hartford. Particularly strong English and economics departments. Student population: 13,000. Student-faculty ratio: 16:1. Faculty holding doctorates: 90%. Library: 2.5 million volumes. Tuition: $11,410*...$4,290 for Connecticut residents.

•State University of New York, Albany. 518-442-3300. The gem of the SUNY system. Top-notch programs in business administration, pre-medicine and political science. Student population: 10,000. Student-faculty ratio: 20:1. Faculty holding doctorates: 96%. Library: 1.5 million volumes. Tuition: $6,550...$2,630 for New York residents.

South:

•The Georgia Institute of Technology. Atlanta. 404-894-2000. One of the nation's great engineering schools. Student population: 12,814. Student-faculty ratio: 21:1. Faculty holding doctorates: 90%. Library: 2.7 million volumes (additional 3.5 million technical documents on
*Tuitions listed may be subject to change.

microfilm). Tuition: $4,266...$2,823 for Georgia residents.

•University of North Carolina. Chapel Hill. 919-962-2211. Arguably the best college buy in the country, with a magnificent campus and first-rate programs in English, psychology and economics. Student population: 15,000. Student-faculty ratio: 16:1. Faculty holding doctorates: 94%. Library: 4.5 million volumes. Tuition: $7,868...$1,248 for North Carolina residents.

Midwest:

•Creighton University. Omaha, Nebraska. 402-280-2700. A Roman Catholic institution with first-rate science programs, especially in biology, psychology and nursing. Student population: 3,500. Student-faculty ratio: 6:1. Faculty holding doctorates: 90%. Library: 750,000 volumes. Tuition: $9,932.

•Miami University. Oxford, Ohio. 513-529-1809. Located an hour away from Cincinnati on a bucolic 2,138-acre campus. Excellent departments of accounting, finance and marketing. Student population: 15,000. Student-faculty ratio: 19:1. Faculty holding doctorates: 95%. Library: 1.2 million volumes. Tuition: $9,060...$2,934 for Ohio residents.

•University of Missouri. Columbia. 314-882-2121. Despite its reputation as a party school, this small-town institution has excellent academics, including first-rate programs in accounting, business administration and journalism. Student population: 17,000. Student-faculty ratio: 11:1. Faculty holding doctorates: 80%. Library: Three million volumes (additional five million in university-wide computer network). Tuition: $8,010...$2,934 for Missouri residents.

West:

•University of Arizona. Tucson. 602-621-2211. Good all-around school in a sun-drenched Southwest city. Good programs in psychology, political science and astronomy. Student population: 23,000. Student-faculty ratio: 19:1. Faculty holding doctorates: 94%. Library: 3.6 million volumes. Tuition: $7,284... $1,778 for Arizona residents.

•University of California, Berkeley. 510-642-6000. Academically one of the finest institutions in the US, Berkeley ranks near Harvard in English, history and political science. Set on a 212-acre campus overlooking San Francisco Bay. Student population: 21,850. Student-faculty ratio: 17:1. Faculty holding doctorates: 99% (including eight Nobel laureates). Library: Eight million volumes. Tuition: $12,033...$4,334 for California residents.

•University of Oregon. Eugene. 503-346-3111. Two hours from Portland, this campus combines a strong intellectual atmosphere and a pleasant college-town setting. Strong business administration, psychology and journalism departments. Active social life, centered upon student organizations. Student population: 13,000. Student-faculty ratio: 18:1. Faculty holding doctorates: 80%. Library: 1.5 million volumes. Tuition: $7,851...$2,721 for Oregon residents.

Source: Stuart Kahan, founder of Kahan College Consulting Service, New York City. He is the author of *Accepted*, a critical survey of US universities. Allworth Press, 10 E. 23 St., New York 10010.

Easier Learning

Make learning easier by not expecting to be perfect right away. Accept your mistakes until you learn to do things well. Benefits: You'll develop a solid foundation on which to build ...you'll wipe out fear of failure...the more you learn about a subject, the easier it is to learn even more.

Source: *The Secret of Getting Straight A's: Learn More in Less Time with Little Effort* by aerospace engineer Brian Marshall. Hathaway International Publications, Box 6543, Buena Park, California 90622.

Learn While You Drive

The average person drives from 12,500 to 25,000 miles each year. Translated into hours, that's one to two college semesters. Helpful: Use time spent behind the wheel listening to creative or self-help tapes or your favorite music. Avoid radio shows that cause you to think negatively.

Source: *101 Simple Ways to Be Good to Yourself: How to Discover Peace and Joy in Your Life* by Oklahoma City stress consultant Donna Watson, PhD. Energy Press, 5275 McCormick Mountain, Austin, Texas 78734.

Auditing Classes

You can still attend college even if you don't want a degree. Even the most prestigious, competitive colleges and universities will allow you to take two or three courses without actually applying to the school. Some let you "audit," or sit in on, classes. You pay a fee but do not have to complete exams or written assignments and, of course, you get no college credit. But auditing a course is a good way to see if you like a particular school, major or course.

Source: *College After 30: It's Never Too Late to Get the Degree You Need!* by college and university consultants Sunny and Kim Baker. Bob Adams, Inc., 260 Center St., Holbrook, Massachusetts 02343.

College Success

Students do much better in college when they form alliances with fellow students, faculty members and student advisers. Recommended: Enrollment in at least one small class every semester. The frequent interaction among students and between students and teacher helps counter the anonymity of large lecture classes.

Source: Five-year study by Harvard University professors, led by Richard J. Light, professor of education, reported in *The New York Times.*

Athletic Scholarships

Athletic scholarships are awarded by even the smallest colleges. But these schools often don't have the budgets to recruit prospects. Assertiveness pays. Helpful: Ask high school coaches for leads...contact college coaches di-

rectly and let them know about your abilities ...write a self-profile, including information about academics, family, athletic ability, honors. Apply during the 10th and 11th grades... senior year may be too late.

Source: Marilyn Shapiro, editor, *College Financial Aid Strategies.* 14609 Woodcrest Dr., Suite 101, Rockville, Maryland 20853.

Children And Reading Basics

Buy a bed lamp so children can read before going to sleep...play word games together... encourage them to contribute lines to letters you write...act out the stories you read together using different voices for different characters...give books as gifts...don't punish children by forcing them to read or write for a set period of time.

Source: Child psychologist Lawrence Kutner, PhD, author of *Parent & Child: Getting Through to Each Other.* Avon Books, 1350 Avenue of the Americas, New York 10019.

Saving for Your Child's Education The Right Way

When saving for children's education, where you put your money is just as important as how much you put away each month.

Given the large sum that you have to raise in 18 years or less, you have to invest your savings in vehicles that will earn you a high rate of return—with as little risk as possible.

As your savings balloon over time, you must know how to best protect that capital. You want to be sure that the funds are there when the time comes to pay the tuition bills.

Common mistakes:

Mistake: Putting the money in the child's name or a custodial account. Both are too risky. Putting the money in the child's hands means the child owns and controls the money immediately with a custodial account. From age 14 on, he/she can petition the court for an accounting on the use of the money. At age 18, the child gets full access to the lump sum.

It's also too risky to keep a college fund in the parents' names. Creditors can go after the money, and, in the case of a divorce, the money may be subject to equitable distribution.

Better way: Set up a trust in the child's name with a parent as co-trustee. It costs about $1,000. When this trust is properly structured, only the IRS will be able to sue for the money.

Meanwhile, trustees can use the money for the health, education and care of the child. And the assets can be distributed to the child in sensible increments so he can learn how to handle the money.

Mistake: Waiting until the child is a few years old to start saving. The sooner you begin saving, the more opportunity the money will have to grow. Best: Begin an investment program when the child is born and contribute to it on a monthly basis.

Mistake: Avoiding the stock market. Equities are the one long-term investment that can defy the ravages of inflation. But the stock market is volatile, so you may want to consider selling part of that stock portfolio and taking profits as your child enters his mid-teens. This will protect what you've made from any sudden drops in the market as your child nears college age.

If you're unfamiliar with investing and don't have a trusted expert to guide you at the time, you can put the money into very conservative products, such as Certificates of Deposits or money-market funds. Then you'll have at least some money saved.

Mistake: Succumbing to yield-greed. Don't be deceived by an investment's *yield*—the money you *regularly receive* from that investment. More important is the total return—the yield plus the increase—or decrease—in the value of your original investment.

In extremely high-risk investments, your yield can be lofty while your total return is shrinking dramatically, because the value of your principal is going down.

Mistake: Not being well-diversified. If you own only a few stocks or bonds, the portfolio can be devastated if just one or two of your holdings hit the skids. Better: Consider buying mutual funds of both stocks and bonds.

Portfolio strategy:

While there is no single "right" portfolio, the best and safest route for most people is a varied portfolio of mutual funds. The mix should depend on how much time you have before your child goes to college. What you really need is two or three different portfolios over the years.

• When the child is young—under age 14. The further away your child is from the first year of college, the more adventurous you can be—within limits. Put a solid chunk of money —60% to 75%—in aggressive growth or small-stock funds. They are volatile but can be highly rewarding if you have the time—and temperament—to ride out market swings. Tax law favors this aggressive strategy if the securities are in a trust in the child's name and you're the co-trustee. When children are under 14, most of their income may be taxed at your own high rate (the kiddie tax).

• When the child gets closer to college age —older than age 14. Veer toward low-volatility assets such as money-market funds and short-term Certificates of Deposit. Don't run the risk of having to sell stocks or funds when they're temporarily depressed in order to meet college bills. When children reach age 14 and their income is taxed at their own relatively low rates, high-yield conservative investments make sense.

A simple portfolio:

A portfolio for people sophisticated enough to know they should own some stock but don't have time to monitor more sophisticated investments is based on the Vanguard family of funds.*

This portfolio consists mostly of no-load index funds, which are not the top performers but regularly rank among the best.

*Vanguard Group, Inc., Box 2600, Valley Forge, Pennsylvania 19482. 800-662-7447. Minimum initial investment: $3,000.

Years to College	Allocation	Investments
10 or more	60% stocks	Vanguard Total Stock Market (30%) Vanguard Pacific (15%) Vanguard Europe (15%)
	40% bonds	Vanguard Bond Market
5 to 9	40% stocks	Preceding Vanguard Stock Funds (20%, 10%, 10%)
	40% bonds	Vanguard Bond Market
	20% cash	Fixed-income investments with maturities of a year or less
1 to 5	10% stocks	Vanguard Total Stock Market
	40% bonds	Vanguard Bond Market
	50% cash	Fixed-income investments with maturities of a year or less

This portfolio is intended only as a guide. Fine-tune it with the investment climate and your own level of sophistication as you become more knowledgeable about investments.

Other choices: Two top-drawer fund families that offer special no-load investment programs for the college-bound:

•Fidelity Investments' College Savings Plan. The several funds include…Cash Reserves/money-market, Blue Chip/conservative stock fund, Growth & Income/conservative stock fund, Asset Manager/market-timing fund. Parents can buy a mix of these funds in any proportion and make automatic investments periodically. Minimum transfer from a checking or money-market account: $100.

Fidelity Distributor Corp., 82 Devonshire St., Boston 02109. 800-544-8888. Minimum initial investment: $1,000.

•Twentieth Century Investors' College Investment Program. While a child is very young, parents can automatically invest as little as $25 monthly in its Select Fund, a stock fund with a good record. As the child gets older (you decide the age), Twentieth Century begins to transfer fixed amounts every month from Select to its money-market fund.

Twentieth Century Investors, 4500 Main St., Box 419200, Kansas City, Missouri 64141. 800-345-2121. No minimum initial investment. A $10 annual fee when it begins switching investments to cash.

•If you want still more flexibility and less paperwork, consider an account at discount broker Charles Schwab, where you can take your pick among more than 600 mutual funds, most of them with no load. Schwab charges no commission on some.

Charles J. Schwab & Co., 800-435-4000, 24 hours a day, 7 days a week. Minimum initial investment depends on funds chosen. Free comparative guide to mutual-fund performance at any Schwab office.

Source: Martin M. Shenkman, a New York attorney specializing in estate, tax and personal planning. He and Warren Boroson, a financial journalist, are the coauthors of *Keys to Investing for Your Child's Future*, Barron's Educational Series, 250 Wireless Blvd., Hauppauge, New York 11788.

College Isn't For All Kids

Creative careers:

•*Designers:* Areas of specialization include industrial, package, textile, set and display, interior and floral design. Most require only two years of post-high-school study. Salaries are as high as $50,000/year. Forty percent of designers are self-employed and can earn far more.

•*Photographers* don't even need a high school diploma…but they must be creative and technically skilled. Experienced photographers make at least $40,000/year…and the self-employed can do much better.

•*Movie-camera operators* with good skills can earn over $50,000/year…and mingle with celebrities.

Health-care careers:

•*Paramedics* take a nine-month program after high school. They earn about $32,000 with experience.

•*Dental hygienists* with a two-year associate degree and a license can work part-time and earn about $15/hour.

•*Laboratory, X-ray and other technicians* usually have a two-year degree, work in hospitals and labs and earn up to $40,000/year.

• *Dispensing opticians* usually learn on the job and can earn up to $100,000/year after gaining enough experience to open their own business.

Technical careers:

• *Broadcast technicians* in the TV and radio industry need an associate degree and an FCC operator license. Technicians at network-owned stations earn $50,000+/year...supervisors make close to $100,000.

• *Air-traffic controllers* take an intensive 11–13 week course at the FAA Academy in Oklahoma City. They average about $40,000/year with experience.

• *Engineering technicians* assist highly qualified scientists and engineers. They have associate degrees and earn up to $40,000/year.

Source: Harlow C. Unger, a former college teacher and placement counselor and author of *But What If I Don't Want to Go to College? A Guide to Successful Careers Through Alternative Education.* Facts on File Inc., 460 Park Ave. South, New York 10016.

Playground Safety

More than a quarter of a million children are injured on playgrounds each year—and there are no federal standards for playground safety. *Watch out for:* Broken equipment or equipment that lets kids climb too high (these account for 75% of playground mishaps)...openings in equipment smaller than 3½ inches by 9 inches in which a child's head can get trapped...broken glass, trash and animal droppings...swings set less than two feet apart...overcrowded conditions. *Important:* At least a six-foot (preferably eight-foot) perimeter around slides and all climbing equipment, including monkey bars. Avoid equipment with missing pieces or sharp edges, splintered wood and damaged hardware.

Source: Mary Ellen Fise, product-safety director at the Consumer Federation of America, which has developed guidelines for safer playgrounds, quoted in *Parents*, 685 Third Ave., New York 10017.

Checklist: Sources of College Money

• *Corporations.* Employee tuition benefits are an underused resource for college money in the US. Thousands of companies have programs that support all or part of employees' tuitions...or of their employees' children.

• *Athletic scholarships.* Millions of dollars in college-sponsored athletic scholarships go unused each year, usually because too few students apply or qualify.

There is money available for archery, badminton, bowling, crew, handball, lacrosse—even synchronized swimming. The State University of New York at Purchase even has a Frisbee scholarship.

• *Special talents.* Students with unusual aptitude in any area of the arts or sciences may find a grant tailored to them.

• *Gender and ethnicity.* Many organizations specify funding for men, women or students of a particular ancestry. Some, such as the United Negro College Fund, are well-known. Others are not.

Examples: The Swiss Benevolent Society of Chicago...The Vatra's Educational Foundation, Boston, for students of Albanian descent.

• *Family affiliations.* Many unions, sororities, fraternities, religious and civic organizations give grants to members and their children.

• *Areas of study.* Countless grants are awarded in specific areas of study.

Examples: The National Press Photographers Foundation for students of photojournalism...the Quota International Fund for those studying education of the hearing impaired.

• *Personal circumstances.* There are scholarships for Jewish orphans, disabled students, daughters of deceased railroad employees, and children of those killed during military action or public service, among others.

•*College students.* Don't forget to apply if you are already in school or are returning to school. Many grants are for upperclassmen.

Example: The AT&T Undergraduate Scholarship for public relations students is for sophomores through seniors.

•*Smaller grants.* Don't neglect the smaller grants—several $500 grants can add up to make the difference between living at home or attending the college of your choice.

Source: Laurie Blum, author of 20 *Free Money* books and a partner in Blum & O'Hara, a Los Angeles fund-raising firm. Among her most recent titles are *Free Money for College* and *Free Money for Foreign Study,* published by Facts On File, 460 Park Ave. S., New York 10016, and *Free Money for Graduate School* and *Free Money for Athletic Scholarships,* Henry Holt & Co., 115 W. 18 St., New York 10011.

18

Consumer Savvy

To Make Wool Garments Last Longer...

Brush wool clothes frequently...rest wool for at least 24 hours before wearing again...refresh it by hanging in a steamy bathroom...use sturdy hangers. Remove spots and stains promptly. *To remove:*

...alcohol or food—place a towel under the area. Sprinkle soda water over it and rub gently toward the center of the spot.

...coffee or tea—sponge with glycerine. If none is available, use warm water.

...grease—sponge with dry-cleaning solvent or spot cleaner.

...ink—immerse in cold water.

...mud—once dry, brush and sponge from back of the garment with soapy water.

...lipstick—rub white bread over the area with a firm, gentle motion.

Source: The Wool Bureau, Inc., 330 Madison Ave., New York 10017.

Supersavers

•When food shopping, weigh produce priced by the bunch, such as carrots, celery, broccoli, onions, and fruit. Buy the heaviest and get extra pounds free.

•Drink water. It takes 15,000 eight-ounce glasses of tap water to equal the cost of a six-pack of soda.

•Freeze your credit card—literally. Freeze in a plastic bag partially filled with water (it will not damage the magnetic strip). In an emergency, thaw.

•Furnish a college student's dorm or apartment with "finds" from garage sales.

•If you have a chronic illness, schedule telephone home visits with your doctor in place of regular office visits. This is a new option you should explore with your doctor.

•Veterans and senior citizens can qualify for an exemption on property taxes. Your local tax office has information on the amount to which you are entitled.

• Make your own stationery. Press small flowers and leaves in a thick phone book. Later glue the dried flowers on paper for an elegant look.

• Enlist your children's help to lower the utility bill. Post last month's bill and let them share any money saved in the future.

• Put summer grass clippings, autumn leaves, and vegetable scraps in a "compost pile." Next spring there will be free mulch and fertilizer for the garden.

• Get a shoe "tune-up." Have the uppers conditioned, attach neoprene protective soles, and apply a sealant to uppers that allows wear in any kind of weather with minimum damage.

• When the supermarket sells out of the loss-leader items, always ask for rain checks and buy at rock-bottom prices when items are back in stock.

• Do your own wallpapering after viewing a do-it-yourself video. Purchase wallpaper at a discount store for additional savings.

• Save on your food budget. Contact the County Cooperative Extension Agent and receive information on gardening in your locale.

Source: Jackie Iglehart, editor of *The Penny Pincher* newsletter, Box 809-BL, Kings Park, New York 11754. 516-724-1868.

Limited-Edition-Collectibles Trap

Very few coins, plates, and artworks touted as rarities make good investments. They are manufactured on assembly lines and sold at high prices by professional direct-marketing firms. Within a couple of years, you can find these items at secondhand stores for a fraction of their original prices.

Source: *Scrooge Investing* by Mark Skousen, PhD, adjunct professor of economics, Dearborn Financial Publishing, Inc., 520 N. Dearborn St., Chicago 60610.

Filing Savvy

File all receipts for returned merchandise with receipts. When you get your credit card statement, make sure you were credited for the returned item. If no credit appears: Contact your credit card company at the 800 number on your bill.

Source: *How to Return Just About Anything* by Patricia Forst, Longwood, Florida-based lecturer on consumer satisfaction, Thomas Nelson Publishers, Box 141000, Nashville, TN 37214.

Beware of Paying Full Price

Never pay full price unless you are sure you have exhausted all other options. Decide if you must have something new, or can buy it used. If you need an item urgently, improvise—try borrowing it instead of rushing out to buy it.

Source: *The Tightwad Gazette: Promoting Thrift as a Viable Alternative Lifestyle* by Amy Dacyczyn, founder, *The Tightwad Gazette* newsletter, Villard Books, 201 E. 50 St., New York 10022.

Avoid Service Contracts

Manufacturers' service contracts are almost never a good buy. Salespeople push them because they carry high sales commissions. But the contracts very rarely pay back their costs—and are usually not renewable when a product has reached the end of its typical useful life—when it might start to need major repairs. Better than a service contract: Pre-purchase research to find reliable, high-quality products.

Source: *100 Ways to Avoid Common Legal Pitfalls Without a Lawyer* by Stephen Christianson, Esq., a Virginia-based lawyer specializing in civil litigation, Citadel Press, 600 Madison Ave., New York 10022.

Better Clothes Buying

To gauge the true cost of a piece of clothing, calculate the price-per-wear. Example: A $200 pair of shoes, worn twice a week for a year, costs about $2 per wear. But a $25 pair, worn for only two special occasions, costs $12.50 per wear—not a bargain. An item's versatility and durability can be more important than its purchase price.

Source: *Out of the Rat Race*, Gregory Communications Group, Box 95341, Seattle 98145.

Pay Special Attention At The Check-Out Counter

Group special sale items together when unloading the grocery cart, along with anything missing a price tag or a tag that may be wrong. Pay special attention when these items are rung up—they are the most likely to be rung incorrectly, even in stores using scanners. Self-defense: Watch closely as all items are rung up—and check your receipt at home.

Source: *Money*, Rockefeller Center, New York 10020.

Lightbulb Savvy

Compact fluorescent bulbs screw into standard lightbulb sockets and give off light that looks like that from incandescent bulbs...but last more than 10 times as long and use only one-quarter the energy. Cost per 60-watt bulb: About $20, plus $10 of electricity over its lifetime. Ten traditional bulbs would cost less (about $10) but use $45 of electricity. Best places to use: Where lights are left on at least two hours per day. Caution: The fluorescent bulbs won't fit all lamps or covered fixtures.

Source: *You Can Change America* by The Earth Works Group, dedicated to facilitating change at a grassroots level, Earthworks Press, 1400 Shattuck Ave., Box 25, Berkeley, California 94709.

Better Shopping

Plan ahead. Do extensive research to find out just what you need. Plan finances so you can pay as much cash as possible.

Source: *The Tightwad Gazette: Promoting Thrift as a Viable Alternative Lifestyle* by Amy Dacyczyn, founder, *The Tightwad Gazette* newsletter. Villard Books, 201 E. 50 St., New York 10022.

Better Kitten Buying

Buy from a busy household with children. Less desirable: Kittens from pet stores or rescue shelters, where infectious diseases are common. Traits to look for: Interest when you play with a moving object...a glossy coat... clean, dry eyes and ears...minimum age: eight to 10 weeks. Warning signs: Nasal discharge or sneezing...diarrhea...black dust in the coat (a sign of fleas).

Source: *A Miscellany of Cat Owners' Wisdom* by Kay White. Running Press, 125 S. 22 St., Philadelphia 19103.

Better Lawn Mowers

Cordless, rechargeable electrics need no oil, gas, starter ropes or tune-ups—and are much quieter than gas-powered mowers. Electrics use far less energy—around $5.50 a year, about the same amount as a toaster. And they generate practically no pollution. Using a gas mower for one hour creates as much pollution as driving a car 50 miles. Cost: $350 to $550—about the same as high-end gas mowers.

Source: Joel Makower, editor, *The Green Consumer Letter*, 1526 Connecticut Ave. NW, Washington, DC 20036.

The Best Exercise Videos

Exercise videotapes are not all alike. A videotape that one person finds highly motivating may prove discouraging—even dangerous—to another.

For a safe and satisfying workout, match the tape to your specific needs*...

•Best for beginning exercisers: *Jingo*, by Debbie and Carlos Rosas. This easy-to-follow video blends non-impact aerobics—no jumping—with elements drawn from dance and martial arts. 60 minutes.

Available from Niawave, Box 712, Portland, Oregon 97207.

•Best for dancers: *The Hip Hop Solution*, by Victoria Jackson. This innovative video affords a good workout and teaches dance steps made famous by pop musicians. 30 minutes.

•Best for "step" enthusiasts: *Step Aerobic and Abdominal Workout*, by Jane Fonda. By far, the best video for users of the popular "step" apparatus. No tricky choreography, just a high-intensity workout. 57 minutes.

•Best for die-hard exercisers: *Firm Arms and Abs* and *Lean Legs and Buns*, both by Karen Voight. Demanding videos for already-fit people who want to boost muscle tone. Users must provide their own dumbbells, ankle weights and weight-lifting bench. 47 minutes/ 51 minutes.

•Best for stress relief: *Yogarobics*, by Larry Lane. Blends gentle exercise with soothing relaxation techniques. 53 minutes.

•Best for overweight people: *Sweatin' to the Oldies*, by Richard Simmons. The first of a four-tape series, this is a fast-paced, effective weight-loss program presented with humor, compassion and—most important—a high-energy band playing hit songs. 43 minutes.

•Best for pregnant women: *Pregnancy Program*, by Kathy Smith. Safe workouts for all stages of pregnancy and the postpartum period. Mixes low-impact aerobics with exercises for flexibility and good posture. 95 minutes.

•Best for kids: *Hip Hop Animal Rock*, by Gilda Marx. Uses animated animals to teach kids proper exercise techniques. Suitable for ages five through 12. 30 minutes.

•Best for persons over age 50: *Positive Moves*, by Angela Lansbury. Great motivation plus gentle strength and stretching exercises from the famous actress. Also includes general tips for active living and recipes. 46 minutes.

•Best for back pain sufferers: *Back Health*, by Joanie Greggains. Pain-free routine for toning muscles in the back, buttocks and legs. Includes tips on pain prevention. 38 minutes.

•Best for disabled people: Exercise tapes for paraplegics, quadriplegics, amputees and persons with cerebral palsy are available from National Handicapped Sports, 451 Hungerford Dr., Suite 100, Rockville, Maryland 20850. 800-966-4647. 30 minutes each.

*Unless otherwise noted, all videotapes are available through videotape stores. A good mail-order source for exercise tapes is Collage Video Specialties, 5390 Main St. NE, Minneapolis 55421. 800-433-6769.

Source: Peg Jordan, RN, author of several books on fitness and editor-in-chief of *American Fitness*, 15250 Ventura Blvd, Sherman Oaks, California 91403.

No-Haggle Trap

Car buyers who shop at one-price "no-haggle" dealerships to avoid the discomfort of negotiating may pay as much as $1,000 more for the convenience. Reason: Prices at no-haggle dealerships are inflexible and typically higher than those that consumers could negotiate for themselves at traditional showrooms.

Source: W. James Bragg is the author of *In the Driver's Seat: The New Car Buyer's Negotiating Bible*. Random House, 201 E. 50 St., New York 10022.

Generic Drug Savings

To save money on drugs, ask your doctor for a generic version of the prescription (at a savings of up to 70%)...comparison shop at pharmacies...consider mail-order (for discounts of up to 40%). Major mail-order pharmacies: Action Mail Order/800-452-1976... Family Pharmaceuticals/800-922-3444...Medi-Mail/800-331-1458.

Source: *Money*, Rockefeller Center, New York 10020.

Latest Car-Repair Scam

Freon theft is on the rise. Freon, used in car cooling systems, is now so expensive—between $12 and $20 per pound, with three to five pounds per car—that shady car-repair companies are stealing it while they service your car. Tip-off: Your car's cooling system doesn't work as well or stops working following other car repairs. Important: Be sure to have your car serviced by someone you trust.

Source: David Solomon is editor of *Nutz & Boltz*®, Box 123, Butler, Maryland 21023. 800-888-0091.

New Gold Card Scam

A caller says you have been pre-approved for a gold card and he/she just needs a little information to send the card to you. He asks for Social Security, checking account and credit card numbers and your mother's birth name. You never get the card. The caller gets information to tap into your bank accounts and credit lines. Self-defense: By law, credit card issuers must have your written approval to send you a card. Tell any caller to send you an application by mail. Or just hang up.

Source: John Barker, National Consumers League, 815 15 St. NW, Washington, DC 20005. 202-639-8140.

Multiple-Deposit Leases

When leasing a car, ask the finance company for a "multiple-deposit lease." It will allow you to leave a larger deposit in exchange for a lower interest rate. Result: Reduced expenses over time. Example: You're told that the minimum deposit for a three-year lease on a $30,000 car is $500, and your monthly payments will be $520. If you leave $4,000 instead, your payments would be $460—or a total savings of $2,160. That's more than 54% return on your investment, since the $4,000 deposit is returned to you at the end of the lease.

Source: Art Spinella, vice president and general manager of CNW Marketing/Research, a Bandon, Oregon firm that tracks car-leasing trends.

Supersavers #2

• Prolong the life of shoes by using an unfinished cedar shoe tree ($10 to $20 per pair). Cedar slowly withdraws moisture from leather, leaving the shoes pliant and looking like new.

• Use a clothesline or drying rack instead of a dryer and save $0.50 to $1 on each load of laundry.

• Water lawns and gardens in the early morning to reduce evaporation and prevent fungus. Just before sunrise is best.

• Shop "high-and-low" at the supermarket. The most expensive items are stocked at eye level. Bend over—or stand on tiptoe—to reach for cheaper items.

• Make your own baby food. Puree home-cooked foods in a food processor, and freeze individual portions in an ice tray. Store food cubes in a plastic bag.

• Buy ready-to-use pizza dough from a pizza shop, add your own toppings and bake at 450 degrees for about 20 minutes.

• Rotate and keep tires properly inflated. Everyone knows tires last longer that way—and you get better gas mileage—but only a small percentage of people follow through.

• Save energy by using a toaster oven for small items. It heats the house less in summer and doesn't need to preheat.

• Decrease excessive use of water and prevent septic system overflow by installing an ultra-low flush toilet, which will cut indoor water usage by 25%. Toilets are the biggest indoor water-wasters.

• Be a shoe tester and earn free shoes. For information, contact Shoe Testers Association, 660 Spartan Blvd. #9, Spartanburg, South Carolina 29301. 803-587-1719.

• Grow your own fruit and save space by planting dwarf fruit trees, which grow to one-third the size of regular fruit trees and produce two-thirds the amount of fruit.

•Assemble a 72-hour emergency kit. Be prepared for hurricanes, earthquakes, tornadoes, etc. A good source for these items is Emergency Essentials, a mail-order company in Orem, Utah. For a free catalog, call 800-999-1863.

•Grow a variety of vegetables in a small space by interplanting—planting seeds of one type of vegetable in between seeds of another. A few good combinations are tomatoes/basil, beans/corn/squash/carrots, and peppers/carrots/onions. For a free list of these combinations, send a self-addressed, stamped, business-sized envelope to *The Penny Pincher*.

Source: Jackie Iglehart, editor of *The Penny Pincher,* Box 809-BL, Kings Park, New York 11754. 516-724-1868.

19

Technology 1994

New VCR Time

Videocassette recorders have been around for more than a decade, yet most people are not fully familiar with how to program them. Many gave up years ago, frustrated by their failed attempts to decipher complex owner's manuals and codes or set the unit's tiny buttons.

Now a new generation of VCR technology is making it easier for consumers to record favorite shows. This user-friendly equipment ranges from hand-held devices to VCR decks —nearly all of the technology is relatively inexpensive.

Add-on devices:

•Panasonic Program Director. This hand-held remote control—a replacement for the one that came with your VCR—works in conjunction with on-screen programming. Recording times, channels and dates are programmed by turning a series of thumbwheels designed to limit frustration. Each wheel controls its own on-screen display. Check the package to see if your VCR is listed before purchasing.

•VCR Voice Programmer.* This hand-held unit lets users enter up to 15 programs over a 60-day period using simple voice commands. The programmer has a built-in microphone, and it recognizes up to four different voices. Compatible with most systems. Toll-free help line provides guidance for the rather complex initial set-up process.

•VCR-Plus. This device lets users program their VCRs by punching in numerical codes that appear in *TV Guide* and many newspapers. Each program has its own unique code.

Easy-to-use VCRs:

•Emerson VCP 680. This bare-bones VCR plays but does not record and is ideal for households that already have a full-function deck. 10" x 13" x 3½".

•Magnavox VR-9140. This full-function unit features on-screen programming. Automatic feature cleans record and playback heads each time a tape is inserted. Records up to

*Available via mail-order only from *Voice Powered Technology*, 17525 Sherman Way, Canoga Park, California 91306. 800-788-0800.

eight events over a one-year period. Monaural sound. 14⅕" x 11⅕" x 3½".

•Panasonic PV-4250. Features on-screen programming, hi-fi stereo, MTS—for full stereo recording of programs broadcast in stereo—and a real-time counter that indicates the time remaining on the tape. Records up to four events over a one-month period. 14⅛" x 11¼" x 3½".

•JVC HR-DX62. Features on-screen programming in both English and Spanish, hi-fi stereo, built-in MTS decoder and hyperbass system for theater-like sound quality. Records up to eight events over a one-year period. 14" x 11" x 4".

•RCA VR-667HF. One of several VCRs now available with VCR-Plus circuitry built in. Features on-screen programming, hi-fi stereo, MTS and automatic head-cleaning. This deck's remote unit controls not only the VCR but also 30 different brands of televisions. 12⅞" x 15¾" x 3½".

•Mitsubishi HS-U67. "Super VHS" circuitry in this top-of-the-line model boosts screen resolution from the standard 240 horizontal lines per inch to more than 400—if you're using a newer model TV set. Result: A picture that's significantly crisper than conventional VHS images. Also features hi-fi stereo, MTS, on-screen programming and "intelligent picture" circuitry, which automatically enhances the picture quality of poorly recorded or heavily worn videocassettes. High-speed rewind mechanism rewinds a two-hour tape in one minute 26 seconds—half the time of a conventional VCR. Records up to eight programs over a one-month period. 16¾" x 13⅞" x 4".

Bottom line: Whatever add-on device or VCR you purchase—shop around. Discounts are widely available. Make sure the salesperson demonstrates it before you leave the store.

Source: Andy Pargh, an independent product reviewer who writes "The Gadget Guru," a nationally syndicated newspaper column. He is also a regular on the *Today* show.

Better Software To Manage Your Money Better

A personal computer can be a valuable tool for managing money and preparing taxes—but only if the personal-finance software that you buy perfectly suits your needs. Two things to consider before purchasing financial software:

•How complex are your finances?

•What format does your computer accept (DOS, Windows or Macintosh)?

Some software programs excel at managing a checkbook, while others can manage a sophisticated investment portfolio. Nearly all will save you time and effort. My favorites…

Checkbook management:

•Microsoft Money 2.0/Windows. Lots of built-in assistance for keeping track of your checkbook and budget. The on-screen graphic resembles a checkbook. Information is filled in, and calculations are done automatically.

The Microsoft Corp., One Microsoft Way, Redmond, Washington 98052. 800-426-9400.

•Quicken 6.0/DOS. Easy to learn and easy to use. Sorts financial information into budget and tax categories for fast analysis and record-keeping. Data can then be transferred to most major tax-preparation software packages.

•Quicken for Windows 2.0 adds a feature at no extra cost called IntelliCharge. Owners of this product can apply for a Visa Gold Card where all charges placed on the card are electronically sent via modem to your computer and are automatically sorted.

•QuickBooks/DOS is much like Quicken, but it is a simple accounting program for those who have home offices or small businesses. Uses the same checkbook-based entry scheme as Quicken but adds business features—invoicing, accounts payable, etc.

Intuit Inc., Box 3014, Menlo Park, California 94026. 800-625-8742.

Financial planning:

•Managing Your Money 9.0/DOS and Managing Your Money 5.0/Macintosh. The most comprehensive financial-planning package.

Besides checkbook and portfolio management, it includes a calendar, to-do list, simple word processor and tax planner. Tracks investments, calculates mortgage payments, even analyzes whether it makes financial sense for you to buy or lease a car or home.

MECA Software Inc. Box 912, 55 Walls Dr., Fairfield, Connecticut 06430. 800-365-1546.

Investing:

•Smart Investor by Money Magazine/DOS. An on-line investing service, which means it requires a phone line and a modem. Maintains, via modem, a research database of stocks, bonds, mutual funds, CDs and money funds. It also provides stock, option and mutual-fund quotes (running on a 15-minute delay) and on-line trading through discount brokers. Its investment-planning assistance tools are quite good.

Reality Technologies Inc., 2200 Renaissance Blvd., King of Prussia, Pennsylvania 19406. 800-346-2024.

•WealthBuilder 3.0 by *Money* Magazine/DOS and WealthBuilder 2.0/Macintosh. These feature-rich programs include Smart Investor (DOS only), which helps users set objectives and manage investments for long-term financial success. Tutorials help novices with the basic concepts of investing.

Reality Technologies Inc.

Taxes:

•Andrew Tobias' TaxCut/DOS, Macintosh, Windows. Question-and-answer format determines which of more than 85 IRS-approved tax forms to use. Then it leads the taxpayer through them with excellent "help" screens. The "shoebox" feature, which keeps track of important receipts and tax information throughout the year, is particularly nice. All versions print IRS-approved forms on any printer.

MECA Software Inc. Box 912, 55 Walls Dr., Fairfield, Connecticut 06430. 800-365-1546.

•MacInTax/Macintosh. Also features a Q&A format and good "help" system. For an extra $19.95, the program allows electronic filing for faster refunds.

ChipSoft Inc., 6256 Greenwich Dr., Suite 100, San Diego 92122. 619-453-4446.

•Prodigy/DOS, Macintosh. Windows version by summer. A general-interest on-line information service with special features for financial planning: Business newswire...a Money Talk bulletin board that offers advice on taxes and investments...on-line financial experts...even on-line banking and bill-paying. Offers hundreds of features for general use, too, including electronic mail, which connects to two million other users.

Prodigy Services Co., 445 Hamilton Ave., White Plains, New York 10601. 800-PRODIGY.

Source: An industry insider who has studied the technology field for 15 years.

Favorite New Electronics

Answering machines:

•Sony IT-A3000 is a digital answering machine that offers voice mail for the home. Callers can direct messages to three "mail boxes." Built-in display shows how many messages are in each mailbox, and security codes prevent someone from listening to or erasing messages. Other features: Digital message shuttle to play back messages at variable speeds, pre-recorded greeting, beep that alerts the user when incoming messages have been received and six-station auto-dialer and 20-number speed dial. Available now.

One Sony Dr. #56, Park Ridge, New Jersey 07656. 800-937-7669.

•Toshiba FT-9003 is an all-digital answering machine—both incoming and outgoing messages are recorded onto chips for immediate access. (No more waiting for the tape to rewind.) The user can erase some messages while keeping others. Built-in cordless phone handset controls all functions remotely. The handset can be used for privacy when listening to messages. Available now.

82 Totowa Rd.,Wayne, New Jersey 07470. 800-631-3811.

Compact-disc player:

•Fisher Studio 24. This CD player/changer lets you insert 24 discs at one time and categorize each one. Users choose from among seven pre-selected categories—rock, jazz, country, etc....or designate them yourself—party mix,

Dad's favorites, etc. The unit can be programmed to play only the music in the category you've selected—no heavy metal surprises during a romantic dinner for two, for example. Includes standard CD features, such as sequential and random play, and remote control. Available now.

21350 Lassen St., Chatsworth, California 91311. 800-209-2424.

Cordless phones:

•The Cobra Intenna 910 has the best sound quality and longest range of any cordless phone on the market—1,500 to 2,200 feet from the base. The antenna, which is usually the first part of a cordless phone to break, is built into the handset. Available now.

6500 W. Cortland St., Chicago 60635. 312-889-8870.

•Panasonic KX-T9900 is a small cordless phone that looks like a watch and can be strapped to your wrist. The sound is surprisingly good, and the unit's range is that of a standard cordless, 300 to 1,000 feet, depending on where you live—rural or urban. You can listen through a tiny speaker or plug in an earphone jack, which allows you to listen in privacy. The built-in display shows the number dialed, the length of time spent on the call and the battery's strength. Available now.

Consumer Affairs Dept., 50 Meadowland Pkwy., Secaucus, New Jersey 07094. 201-348-9090.

•Sony SPP-X90 has two handsets. One is attached to the base and the other is cordless. The cordless handset doubles as a speaker phone—a first. It beeps when the user walks out of range—300 to 400 feet from the base—which limits unexpected disconnections. Available now.

One Sony Dr. #56, Park Ridge, New Jersey 07656. 800-937-7669.

Videocassette recorder:

•JVC HR-J200. Like all of JVC's new VCRs, this model offers a family message center that turns the TV screen into an electronic bulletin board.

How it works: Using the VCR remote, you can type in messages for other family members. When the TV and VCR are turned on, the messages appear on the TV screen. You can type in any message or choose one of nine

pre-programmed notes—"Please call..." "Meet me at..." etc.—and simply fill in the blank. Available now.

41 Slater Dr., Elmwood Park, New Jersey 07407. 800-526-5308.

Source: Andy Pargh, an independent product reviewer. He writes "The Gadget Guru," a nationally syndicated newspaper column and is a contributing correspondent to the NBC *Today* show.

How to Protect Against A Telecommunications Disaster

Telecommunications failures, such as the one that wiped out phone service in all of downtown Manhattan in 1990, will become more frequent as phone companies find it increasingly difficult to keep up with the growing volume of phone traffic.

While there's not much an individual business can do to *prevent* a phone company service outage, it can be prepared for such events—and that can be helpful. It can also take steps to prevent outages caused by its own equipment...

As a precaution for service interruptions caused by the *local* phone company, keep cellular telephones on hand for people who absolutely can't be without phone service.

To minimize problems when the *long-distance* carrier's service is interrupted, establish an account with a second long-distance company—as back-up. In the event the primary long distance company interrupts its service, simply route calls through the back-up.

Prevent problems with the company's equipment:

•Elevation. Don't locate telephone cables or circuits in the basement or on the ground floor. Reason: Telecommunications equipment on the lower floor could be disabled by a flood. At the very least, they should be a minimum of 18 inches above the floor. Install a pump as an extra precaution on any floor that could remotely be affected by floods or leaks. Check the condition of drains.

•Routing. Consider redesigning the telecommunications cable routing outside of the office. Construction workers sometimes inadvertently cut telecommunications cables connecting to local carriers. If a telecommunications outage would mean a major disruption for the company, it might be worthwhile to have cables leaving your premises on two different routes to the local carrier. It's unlikely both would be cut.

Also, because telecommunications cables can be cut by construction workers *inside* the building, have someone in the company monitor any work being done—so the company's cables can be identified and avoided.

•Grounding. Check for proper grounding of telecommunications cables and power lines going into the phone system. Though communications vendors are supposed to do this when they install a system, there are many companies whose telecommunications systems have been destroyed during electrical storms.

•Outside backup. Consider setting up back-up facilities with an outside system. If a telecommunications outage would be devastating, a "hot site" for back-up facilities, such as a suburban warehouse, may pay. Banks, for example, are set up so that in the event that a fire, flood or other disaster knocks out their system, they move their people to the hot site. For this, they pay a fee to an outside vendor, like an insurance premium.

Alternative: Arrange with another company to use their facilities in an emergency. The problem is finding a company which has excess capacity. Many companies might agree to limited use of their facilities for a brief period, but extensive use could disrupt their own operations.

•Vandalism. To prevent vandalism, make sure phone equipment is in a secure location. Limit access to those with a need to enter, such as vendors and repair people. While a company's phone exchange equipment (its PBX) is typically in a cabinet with a lock, often the key for the lock is the same for all of the vendor's systems. Have the lock changed, so you can limit access.

Many PBXs have a feature known as Direct Inward System Access, or DISA, which enables offsite employees, such as salespeople in the field, to call in and place their calls through the system, taking advantage of volume discounts. While access is password-protected, it's commonly broken by hackers. It's much safer to have offsite people use a calling card.

Source: Neil S. Sachnoff, president, TeleCom Clinic, telecommunications research and publishing, 355 South End Ave., Suite 3N, New York 10280. Mr. Sachnoff is the author of *Secrets of Installing a Telephone System*, and *The Definitive Guide to Job Descriptions/Telecommunications Volume.*

How to Play the New Cellular Phone Game

Prices and features of cellular telephones and services have become so confusing that it's easy to pay too much or buy the wrong thing.

Fail-safe purchasing rules:

•Pay as little as possible for the size phone you want, but no more than $125 per phone. Despite what the advertisements say, there's no significant difference in quality between the most expensive model and the cheapest.

By paying top dollar, you'll get features you don't need and probably won't even remember that you have.

Good deals abound. Many dealers have teamed up with cellular phone service companies to offer customers a $300 phone for $50 if they sign up for at least three months of service.

•Buy based on the type of phone you need, not the level of power. People who have read cellular phone ads know that they come with either 0.6 watts or 3 watts of power. But the choice is limited since it's the *type* of cellular phone that governs its power. All auto and transportable phones have 3 watts of power. Hand-held models have 0.6 watts.

The difference: Sound quality is slightly better on 3-watt phones, and they can be used farther from relay stations that are generally in or near urban centers. However, some cities—including parts of New York—have cellular systems that give the user of a 3-watt system absolutely no technical advantage over the user of an 0.6-watt system.

Bottom line: If you want to use a cellular phone in an urban area, carrying it with you around town, an 0.6-watt phone will be powerful enough.

•Don't sign up for long-term cellular service. New pricing schemes will continue, so there's no reason to be locked into a deal longer than three or, at most, six months. Most cellular service now costs $20–$50 a month, plus 25¢–$1 per minute for local calls, depending on the time of day.

It doesn't cost—it pays:

Missing a sale because the salesperson had to drive to a pay phone is far more expensive than any cellular on the market.

Best for them: A cellular phone *and* a beeper. If someone needs to get in touch, he/she can phone the 800 number of the beeper service, which will signal the employee and display the name and number of the person who wants a call-back.

Coming soon:

Two technological developments that will influence which phones the company buys…

•Stationary cellular phones. Just out: Telular (Memphis) makes a small black box called a PhoneCell, which converts over-the-air cellular signals to the standard landline signals your office's PBX, key system, single line phone, fax, modem, voice mail, cash register, cash machine, burglar alarm, pay phone, etc., are accustomed to.

Advantages: You can now put phones where wires won't reach or may be in danger. Riverboats use them for phones in guest rooms. Hospitals have them for doctors to use when landlines break. You can put them in temporary places, where landlines are too expensive to wire or can't be put in fast enough. Police use them at emergency sites.

•Digital technology will replace the current analog cellular system over the next two to five years. Impact: Greatly improved quality and fewer problems in getting a line. In many urban areas, for instance, it has already become difficult to get a cellular line during drive time and other peak hours of usage.

Beware: Don't postpone buying a cellular phone because you're waiting for Personal Communication Services—phones that can be as small as a fountain pen, can be used virtually worldwide and can transmit data as easily as voice. Reality: It may be near the turn of the century before PCSs are widespread.

Source: Harry Newton, publisher, *Teleconnect Magazine*, 12 W. 21 St., New York 10010.

Computer Virus Fallacy

It is *not* true that "shareware"—public domain software—and programs loaded from the outside through modems pose the greatest threat of virus infection. Viruses are spread at the same rate by commercial software packages that come sealed from the manufacturer. The real cause of most virus infections is the casual exchange and copying of disks which spreads a virus from one machine to another, regardless of where the virus originated.

Source: Study by IBM's High Integrity Computing Laboratory, Yorktown Heights, New York, cited in *The Office*, 1600 Summer St., Stamford, Connecticut 06905.

Streamline Computer Hard Drives

Free up memory space by transferring outdated or little-used files to floppy disks or data cartridges. Also, create broad subdirectories and save related files as a group. Color code disk labels for easy use. Example: Red for sales, green for payroll, blue for accounting. Back up files regularly. Use file compression programs to increase available space on the hard drive.

Source: Steven Solomon, vice president, consumer products, Fuji Photo Film U.S.A., writing in *Modern Office Technology*, 1100 Superior Ave., Cleveland 44114.

Reduce Radiation Hazard From Personal Computers

While the danger is still unverified, evidence mounts that video display terminals (VDTs) emit low-frequency electromagnetic fields that are linked to brain tumors, cancer and miscarriages. Apple and Compaq, among others, have introduced low-emission monitors that add $100 to the price and meet Sweden's MPR II guidelines, which have become the *de facto* standard for VDT radiation. When buying a monitor, ask if it meets MPR II standards. For existing monitors, consult a local computer-equipment supplier about inexpensive add-on equipment that reduces emissions. Safety alternatives: Sit at least an arm's length from the front of the screen—the farther the better—or switch to a laptop with a liquid-crystal display.

Source: Robert Dieterich, editor, *VDT News*, quoted in *Business Week*, 1221 Ave. of the Americas, New York 10020, weekly.

Drug Testing By Hair Sample

Drug testing by hair sample is more accurate than conventional urinalysis? One company, for example, found 18% of job applicants tested positive using hair analysis, compared with only 2.7% using urine tests. According to the company, if it relied on urinalysis in pre-employment screening, 15 of every 100 employees would be drug users.

Source: *Marsh & McLennan Companies Substance Abuse Issues*, 1166 Ave. of the Americas, New York 10036, quarterly.

Remote Computing

Many companies have found they need to provide traveling or home-based employees with links to in-house computer systems. Sales personnel who travel often, and executives who prepare for meetings from home often find a need to access the in-house computer system with all of its data and operating programs.

Appropriate access to the company's computing system from the road is easy with the right hardware, software and communication devices.

Example: A salesperson on the road can hook up the notebook computer he travels with to an in-the-office PC to send and receive electronic mail, obtain product information, access new price or inventory figures, or even print out a report to be left in the office for a supervisor. The traveler can also gain access to sophisticated programs on the office computing system, using the notebook as a remote terminal.

Equipment needed:
- Hayes-compatible modems at each end of the transmission. High-speed modems—9600 baud or faster—are needed to minimize program slowdown that occurs when transmitting large amounts of data through phone lines. Cost: About $250 each, although new computers often have modems built in.
- Phone line dedicated to computer access in the office. And, preferably, a dedicated phone line at the remote location. Reason: Call waiting and other voice-oriented phone features can interrupt computer links. Hotels now often offer dedicated phone lines to business travelers.
- Remote access software. Two excellent products are:
- PC Anywhere, which is powerful and easy to use, but which can be difficult to install.
- Carbon Copy, which is easy to install, but a little more difficult to use.

To allow remote access, the office computer must be left on at all times, although the monitor may be turned off. The employee activates the software from the remote location by having his computer call the PC in the office, and then entering a password, which assures that the caller's use is authorized.

Once on-line, the caller has full use of the office PC as if he were sitting in front of it. Security safeguards can limit a caller's access to just certain parts of the system, if this is desired.

Extra benefit: Remote access software also allows rapid transfer of data files between computers located within the office through cable connections. This can be a fast and easy way of transferring large amounts of data compared with swapping and copying numerous floppy disks.

Source: Patricia Robison, president of Computing Independence, 402 W. 20 St., New York 10011.

Sending Important Business Faxes

Send important business faxes directly from a computer with a fax board instead of scanning them into a fax machine in the conventional way. Reason: Scanning degrades the document image. Documents faxed directly from a computer have a much higher image quality than the faxes most people are used to receiving, and produce a favorable impression of the company.

Source: Peter Davidson, Davidson Consulting, Burbank, California, writing in *Office Systems '93*, 941 Danbury Rd., Box 150, Georgetown, Connecticut 06829.

Getting Voice Mail Messages Returned

Leave more than your name and number. Tell what the message is about, and why it is in the other person's interest to return the call. And leave your number twice, so the other person can return the call even if the recording garbles your number the first time.

Source: Harry Newton, publisher, *Teleconnect*, 12 W. 21 St., New York 10010.

Windows Alert!

Windows assumes you always have a mouse installed on the computer. If you unplug the mouse to attach another device—such as a modem or printer—to the same port, Windows will continue sending commands to the mouse. *Trap:* The other device will probably fail. *Self-defense:* Hook the second device to an auxiliary port, or follow Windows operating manual instructions to "uninstall" the mouse and reinstall it later.

Source: *Teleconnect*, 12 W. 21 St., New York 10010.

Electric and Magnetic Fields Paradox

On the one hand, low-frequency electric and magnetic fields (EMFs) are used for healing—for bone fractures that will not knit. On the other hand, chronic exposure to EMFs may have some link with cancer and other diseases. Explanation: Exposure to EMFs for health reasons is very different from the chronic exposure that can be experienced on the job or at home, we hear from EMF researcher Jack Adams. EMF exposure for healing is at a much higher level than the exposure from power lines or an electric blanket, for example. But EMFs for healing are directed at one point in the body and treatments last for a few minutes at a time over a period of months, instead of several hours every day. Research to better understand how EMFs affect the body continues. Those being treated with EMFs for health reasons should not fear exposure during treatment.

Source: Jack Adams, PhD, is a research fellow in the department of engineering and public policy, Carnegie Mellon University, Pittsburgh.

Check the Cables

Check the cables—first—whenever a PC, fax, phone, modem, or other electronic equipment malfunctions. Remove the connecting cables, check terminations, then reconnect. Helpful: Keep on hand a simple cable tester that checks for continuity, reverse polarity and shorts.

Source: *Inbound/Outbound*, 12 W. 21 St., New York 10010.

Anti-Forgery Technology Breakthrough

New ink pen encodes an inventor's or artist's own DNA in the ink, which when used to mark or sign an original piece of work, unalterably authenticates the item. Ink can also be used to mark original industrial equipment—to deter counterfeiting. Cost: Less than $1 to mark a unit, depending on the number of units.

Source: Art Guard, Inc., 5777 W. Century Boulevard, Los Angeles 90045.

Cellular-Phone Self-Defense

While the recent scare that cellular phones may cause brain tumors has not yet been documented, there are ways to protect yourself *now* should the danger prove to be real. Keep conversations short…don't use for routine conversations—keep mainly for emergencies …use a beeper instead. In cars, use a phone with the antenna on the outside of the vehicle…elsewhere, use a "bag phone," which has its antenna on its base, not on the handset.

Source: Arthur Winter, MD, is director, New Jersey Neurological Institute's Memory Enhancement Clinic, and coauthor of *Build Your Own Brain Power*, St. Martin's Press, 175 Fifth Ave., New York 10010.

Better Computing

New software—Stacker 2.0 for PC and Stacker for Mac—only $149, can double hard-drive storage capacity and are much cheaper than buying an expensive add-on hard-disk. Especially suited for notebook or laptop computer users.

Source: Costa Rodis, a New York City computer consultant to businesses and individuals.

Virtual Reality And Real Eye Trouble

Prolonged exposure to stereoscopic visual effects—typical of virtual-reality systems—makes it temporarily difficult for the eye to focus on real objects. Vision quickly returns to normal—but the long-term effects are unknown.

Source: Kageyu Noro, a virtual-reality researcher and professor at Waseda University, Tokyo, quoted in *Business Week*, 1221 Avenue of the Americas, New York 10020.

Car Phones and Driving

Car phones and driving don't mix—unless you follow these safety advisories: Only buy a phone equipped with a hands-free speakerphone feature with a microphone that clips conveniently on the sun visor. Avoid dialing a number while driving. Wait until a stop light or pull over. If you *must* dial while driving, use the phone's autodialer. And for safety's sake, drive in the slow lane.

Source: National Safety Council, Chicago.

Keeping Up

"Reach down" to keep up with company operations—and technology. Savvy managers constantly interview subordinates to find out what is actually taking place. Added advantage: When an employee reverses roles with the boss and acts the teacher, the status gap between the two is narrowed…and morale is significantly improved.

Source: *The Working Leader: The Triumph of High Performance Over Conventional Management Principles* by Leonard R. Sayles, PhD, senior research scientist, Center for Creative Leadership, and professor emeritus, Columbia University Graduate School of Business. *The Free Press*, 866 Third Ave., New York 10022.

700 Phone Number

New 700 phone number service lets important phone calls be forwarded to any number —as you travel. You provide the 700 number, which is unlisted, to only those you want to have it. By dialing an access code, calls to the 700 number can be directed to any desired phone. Thus, calls to an office phone can be directed to a car phone while driving, then to another phone at your destination.

Source: Daria M. Hoffman, managing editor, *Update*, 20 Railroad Ave., Hackensack, New Jersey 07601.

20

Did You Know That...

...good intentions don't count

...in a business relationship? Neither do feelings or attitudes...unless they are reflected in overt action. Relationships are defined by behavior—what each party does for and to the other.

Source: *Overcoming Resistance: A Practical Guide to Producing Change in the Workplace* by management consultant Jerald M. Jellison, PhD, based in Los Angeles. Simon & Schuster, 1230 Avenue of the Americas, New York 10020.

...thumb-sucking is normal

...and harmless in children as old as age four? It may push the child's front baby teeth forward and the lower baby teeth backward but shouldn't affect the place-ment or alignment of the adult teeth, which come in at about age six. *Important:* Frequent thumb-sucking after the child turns four could adversely affect the permanent teeth.

Source: Marc Patenaude, DDS, pediatric specialist in private practice in New York City.

...39,235 people died in 1992

...on US highways? This was the lowest number in 30 years. The fatality rate of 1.8 deaths per 100 million miles driven was the lowest number ever recorded. *Possible reasons for improvement:* Airbags...increased use of seat belts ...fewer alcohol-related deaths.

Source: Statistics from the US Department of Transportation, reported in *Automotive News*, 1400 Woodbridge Ave., Detroit 48207.

311

...the price of a doctor visit

...for an established patient rose 85% between 1983 and 1992—from an average of $25.11 to $46.43? By comparison, the prices of goods and services in the US rose 41% in that time.

Source: American Medical Association, 515 N. State St., Chicago 60610.

...some organically grown fibers

...can be bad for the environment? *Example:* Cotton grown in some areas of the desert. Water to grow it is diverted by man-made channels. The diversion threatens dozens of species.

Source: Jason Makansi, editor, *Common Sense on Energy and Our Environment*, Box 215, Morrisville, Pennsylvania 19067.

...close-up visual activity

—like playing video games or reading—can bring on myopia? Extensive reading and game-playing seem to make nearsightedness likelier. *Reason:* Unknown. *Likely:* Nearsightedness has a strong genetic component that may be triggered or worsened by close-up activity.

Source: Hilda Capó, MD, assistant professor of clinical ophthalmology, Bascom Palmer Eye Institute, University of Miami School of Medicine.

...the most preferred time for sex

...is between the hours of 8 pm and midnight? *Second favorite time:* Before breakfast on the weekends.

Source: Survey of 3,144 men and women, reported in *New Woman*, 215 Lexington Ave., New York 10016.

...nearly 60% of American adults

...rarely, if ever, exercise? *Danger:* Those who do not engage in regular physical activity are at a higher risk of death from coronary heart disease.

Source: Survey of 87,433 people by the State Behavioral Risk Factor Surveillance System and analyzed by the Centers for Disease Control. Reported in *Morbidity and Mortality Weekly Report*, Centers for Disease Control, 1600 Clifton Rd., Mail Stop CO8NE, Atlanta 30333.

...overwatering kills

...more houseplants than anything else? *Symptoms:* Leaves that turn yellow and fall off. To save an overwatered plant, re-pot it...trim back all the damaged parts...place it in indirect sun...remember not to overwater it again.

Source: *Smart Cents: Creative Tips and Quips for Living the Skinflint Way* by *Skinflint News* publishers Ron and Melodie Moore. Price Stern Sloan, Inc., 11150 Olympic Blvd., Suite 650, Los Angeles 90064.

...88% of women wear shoes

...that are too small for their feet? *Result:* 80% of women suffer foot pain...76% have deformities—hammertoes, bunions, etc.

Source: Study of 356 women conducted by the American Orthopaedic Foot and Ankle Society, reported in *Health*, 301 Howard St., San Francisco 94105.

...only 13% of retirees

...will pay higher Social Security taxes under the new tax law? Although the bulk of the new law is retroactive to January 1, 1993, the portion affecting Social Security benefits is not.

Source: Roundup of Social Security experts in *The New York Times*.

...friends are not a luxury

—they're a necessity? We need them to maintain our mental and physical well-being. *Important:* Personal and professional friendships don't just happen—they must be cultivated.

Source: *101 Simple Ways To Be Good to Yourself: How to Discover Peace and Joy in Your Life* by stress consultant Donna Watson, PhD. Energy Press, 5275 McCormick Mountain, Austin 78734.

...dried fruit

...is about as nutritious as fresh fruit? All nutrients remain throughout the drying process—with the exception of Vitamin C. Actually, dried fruit can provide even more nutrients, including iron, magnesium, potassium, Vitamin A, beta-carotene and fiber, because it is generally eaten in greater quantities than fresh fruit.

Source: *Consumer Reports on Health*, 101 Truman Ave., Yonkers, New York 10703.

...contact-lens discomfort

...can result from a woman's menstrual cycle? *Symptoms:* Dry eyes and blurred vision. *Cause:* Varying estrogen levels increase evaporation from the eye's film of tears.

Source: American Optometric Association. 243 N. Lindbergh Blvd., St. Louis 63141.

...working the foot pedals

...on a manual transmission car can strain the lower back?

Source: *The Back Almanac*, Lanier Publishing, Box 20429, Oakland, California 94620.

...sitting on your wallet

...may aggravate the sciatic nerve—which serves the buttock and the back of the thigh and leg—and can be painful? *Better:* Keep your wallet in a front pocket. It's safer there, too.

Source: *The Back Almanac*, Lanier Publishing, Box 20429, Oakland, California 94620.

...the cost of insurance claims

...for car-crash survivors who suffered catastrophic injuries rose 73% during the last three years? In 1988, the average cost was $515,200. In 1991 (the most recent year of available information), it rose to $892,800. *Shocking:* 48% of catastrophically injured people were between the ages of 16 and 30.

Source: Data from the Insurance Research Council, reported in *Nutz & Boltz®*, Box 123, Butler, Maryland 21030.

...down-and-out stocks

...can be super-safe investments—if an investor shows patience? *Low-risk strategy:* When a stock refuses to slide any further after bad news, it's time to buy.

Source: *The Nature of Risk: Stock Market Survival and the Meaning of Life* by financial consultant Justin Mamis. Addison-Wesley, Jacob Way, Reading, Massachusetts 01867.

...soot may kill

...up to 60,000 people each year? *Particularly vulnerable:* The young, the elderly and those who suffer from asthma. *Distressing:* Dangerous soot levels often are well within the limits that are allowed by current air pollution laws.

Source: Studies by the Harvard School of Public Health.

…very large dogs

…are best for young children? Large dogs are unafraid of children, and they don't mind standard roughhousing. *Gentlest breeds:* Old English Sheepdogs and Newfoundlands. *Breeds to avoid for growing families:* All toy dogs. To protect themselves, they'll snap at anyone who so much as tweaks their ears or tails.

Source: *The 125 Most Asked Questions About Dogs (and the Answers)* by John Malone, Lancaster, Pennsylvania-based writer and pet lover. William Morrow and Co., 1350 Avenue of the Americas, New York 10019.

…the retina accounts for 40%

…of all nerve fibers connected to the brain —but only one-millionth of a person's total body weight? Our eyes register 36,000 visual messages each hour…and can perceive about 150 different colors.

Source: *Healthy Eyes, Better Vision: Everyday Eye Care for the Whole Family* by Jeffrey Anshel, OD, optometrist in private practice in Del Mar, California. Corporate Vision Consulting, 2404-A Sacada Circle, LaCosta, California 92009.

…39% of all the paper thrown out

…last year in the US was recycled?

Source: *The Zero Population Growth Reporter*, 1400 16 St. NW, Suite 320, Washington, DC 20036.

…family ties are reinforced

…when family members share the mundane and trivial—as well as the important and pro-

found? *Key:* Expressing a genuine interest in one another's lives.

Source: *Roots and Wings: Discovering and Developing Family Strengths*, by Washington, DC human development counselor Karen Lawrence Allen. The Pilgrim Press, 700 Prospect Ave. E., Cleveland 44115.

…type size is crucial in leases?

…A New York judge ruled that a tenant had not given up her right to a jury trial even though she signed a lease waiving that right. *Reason:* The print on the lease was smaller than the legal minimum. *Key:* Type size must be sufficient to ensure that tenants do not unknowingly give up important rights. *Self-defense:* This decision applies only in New York and may be appealed—but tenants everywhere have the right to insist that leases be legible and clear.

Source: *Old New York One Corp. v. Szabo, No. 100463/92*, New York County, Civil Court, Housing Part 18, reported in *New York Law Journal*, 111 Eighth Ave., New York 10011.

…"legally blind"

…means your vision tests 20/200 or worse… while wearing the best possible corrective lenses? It doesn't matter how poor your eyesight is without glasses or contacts. As long as it's correctable to better than 20/200, you're not legally blind.

Source: *Healthy Eyes, Better Vision: Everyday Eye Care for the Whole Family* by Jeffrey Anshel, OD, optometrist in private practice in Del Mar, California. Corporate Vision Consulting, 2404-A Sacada Circle, LaCosta, California 92009.

…brushing too frequently

…or too vigorously can cause gums to recede and damage the exposed root surfaces of teeth? *Best:* Brush twice a day, floss once a day and have a professional cleaning twice a year.

Source: *Consumer Reports on Health*, 101 Truman Avenue, Yonkers, New York 10703.

...riding against traffic

...is one of the leading causes of death among bicyclists? When drivers turn right onto a road, they look left and pull out when it seems clear. If you bicycle against traffic, these drivers are not likely to see you until it's too late.

Source: *The New Bike Book: How to Get the Most Out of Your New Bicycle* by Jim Langley, a bike mechanic, touring cyclist and contributing editor of Bicycling. Bicycle Books Inc., 32 Glenn Dr., Mill Valley, California 94941.

...doctors do not eat well?

...Most prefer red meat and chicken to fish ...only 20% say they eat the recommended five servings of fruits and vegetables daily... and 55% are overweight.

Source: Nationwide study commissioned by Sudler & Hennessey, the health care and pharmaceuticals advertising division of Young & Rubicam, reported in *Adweek*, 1515 Broadway, New York 10036.

...renovations

...add more to home value than changes that increase the house's size or modernize it? *Most important:* Plumbing, electrical, heating and cooling systems...roof, windows and doors. *Key:* Renovations must improve comfort and convenience. *Big-ticket items that cost more than they add to value:* Swimming pools, hot tubs, outdoor spas, tennis courts, customized or built-in furnishings, deluxe wall and floor coverings.

Source: *The Big Fix-Up: How to Renovate Your Home Without Losing Your Shirt* by Stephen M. Pollan, financial consultant and personal finance commentator for CNBC. Fireside, 1230 Avenue of Americas, New York 10020.

...Americans favor higher taxes

...on alcohol and tobacco? More than 70% of those surveyed favor higher taxes on tobacco and alcohol. *Contrast:* Only 17% favor higher taxes on gasoline...17%/higher taxes on home mortgage deductions...10%/higher taxes on Social Security benefits...6%/higher tax rates on middle-income Americans.

Source: Survey of more than 5,000 US households, conducted for The Conference Board, 845 Third Ave., New York 10022.

...brass faucets can leach lead

...into water, especially when new? *Prevention:* Always run water for one minute before drinking.

Source: University of California, *Berkeley Wellness Letter*, Box 412, Prince St. Station, New York 10012.

...improved office ventilation

...and lighting increases worker productivity? When fresh air intake is limited to save on air conditioning and heating costs, absenteeism soars due to illness. Improper lighting also makes older workers, in particular, less efficient.

Source: *Office Biology* by New York-based consultants Edith Weiner and Arnold Brown. MasterMedia Limited, 17 E. 89 St., New York 10128.

...stock mutual funds

...do not offer safety in a bear market? The fact that a fund invests in many stocks provides diversity, which protects you from taking a big loss if one stock falls. But if the whole market falls, your fund will go with it. *Trap:* Many

315

investors are pouring money into mutual funds only because interest rates paid on other investments are so low. But with the stock market at a historic high level, this can be very risky now.

Source: James B. Stack, editor, *InvesTech Mutual Fund Advisor*, 2472 Birch Glen, Whitefish, Montana 59937.

...300 million cells in your body

...die every minute? They are immediately replaced by the division of living cells, so that the number of cells in your body remains constant throughout adulthood.

Source: *Your Health*, 5401 NW Broken Sound Blvd., Boca Raton, Florida 33487.

...four out of five cars failed

...one or more parts of their annual inspections? More than 25% were low on oil or needed an oil change...20% failed the emissions test...29% had tires with the incorrect inflation pressure and/or unsatisfactory treads...almost 50% had less than the minimum recommended amount of antifreeze protection.

Source: Survey of 12,000 cars at 65 inspection sights around the country, conducted by Automotive Aftermarket Research Council, 10 Laboratory Dr., Box 13966, Research Triangle Park, North Carolina 27709.

...walking up and down two flights

...of stairs every day can burn off as much as six pounds' worth of calories in a year?

Source: *Healthy, Wealthy, & Wise: A Step-By-Step Plan for Success Through Healthful Living* by fitness consultant Krs Edstrom, Prentice-Hall, Route 9W, Englewood Cliffs, New Jersey 07632.

...one of two adult children

...live within 25 miles of their parents...and one of four live within five miles? *Most scattered:* Adult children who went to college... and those who are still single. Marriage tends to move people closer to their parents...and closer still after they have children of their own.

Source: Study of 13,000 American households by Ge Lin, a doctoral student at the State University of New York at Buffalo, reported in *Modern Maturity*, 3200 E. Carson St., Lakewood, California 90712.

...the average school year

...in 1869-1870 was 132.2 days, with average attendance of 78.4 days? *Modern-day comparison:* In 1980-1981 (the most recent complete data available), the average school year was 178.2 days, with 160.7 days' average attendance.

Source: Study by the National Center for Education Statistics, reported in *Education Week*, 4301 Connecticut Ave. NW, Washington, DC 20008.

...couples who argue the most

...are more likely to divorce or separate—whatever form their arguments take? The frequency of arguments matters more than whether the arguments are calm and rational—or explosive and emotional.

Source: Three-year study of nearly 700 married couples, led by Ronald Kessler, PhD, professor of sociology, University of Michigan/Ann Arbor.

...75% of all drowning victims

...are children between the ages of one and three? Two-thirds of these victims are boys.

Seventy-seven percent of victims were missing for five minutes or less. *Crucial:* Never leave a child unattended near any water—a toddler can drown in only a few inches of water.

Source: US Consumer Product Safety Commission statistics, reported in *Your Health*, 5401 NW Broken Sound Blvd., Boca Raton, Florida 33487.

...cavities are contagious?

...The bacteria most responsible for tooth decay originate in mothers' mouths and pass in saliva to their children after first molars come in—around age two. *Recommended:* Mothers of young children should be sure to maintain their own dental health.

Source: Study of children from birth to age five, led by Page Caufield, DDS, PhD, University of Alabama School of Dentistry in Birmingham.

...one trillion is a very big number?

...It would take 11.57 days to count to one million (at a rate of one number per second)... 31.69 years to count to one billion...and 31,688.09 years to count to one trillion.

Source: *American Council on Consumer Interests Newsletter*, 240 Stanley Hall, Columbia, Missouri 65211.

...most heart-disease studies

...are of limited direct value to the public? *Trap:* They reflect limited statistical data rather than proven cause-and-effect relationships. *Examples:* It is unproven that wine or walnuts can prevent heart attacks—or that baldness is a risk factor.

The only established prevention factors: Stop smoking, control high blood pressure, eat to lower cholesterol and avoid obesity, and exer-

cise appropriately. More research is needed to find the best way to prevent the nation's leading killer.

Source: Dr. James Muller, co-director, Institute for Prevention of Cardiovascular Disease at Deaconess Hospital, Boston.

...melanoma kills

...about 7,000 people in the US every year? *Recommended:* More attention to protection from the sun, whose ultraviolet rays could cause or accelerate this fast-spreading and deadly form of skin cancer.

Source: Howard Koh, MD, skin cancer specialist and chairman of the American Academy of Dermatology's Committee of Melanoma/Skin Cancer Screening. Reported by Boston University Medical Center.

...there are no good or bad financial

...markets, only up or down markets? There is no right or wrong in investing, only the opportunity to make money and the risk of losing it. *Key:* Remember that market environments change, and adjust your investment strategy accordingly.

Source: Richard Schmidt, editor and publisher, *The Risk Report*, 999 Ninth St. S., Naples Florida 33940.

...women buckle up

...more than men? More than 60% of women surveyed use safety restraints. Fewer than half the men do. Older drivers are more likely to buckle up. More than 55% of those over age 30 use restraints...compared with 47% of drivers and passengers from ages 16 to 29.

Source: Study of drivers at 240 intersections throughout Michigan, by Frederick M. Streff, PhD, associate research scientist, Transportation Research Institute, University of Michigan.

Did You Know That...

...just because your home phone

...is ringing doesn't mean you have to stop what you're doing to answer it? If you're too busy with other things or simply don't feel like talking, let it ring—or let your answering machine pick up the call. The world won't come to an end. If the call is really important, the other person will try you again.

Source: _101 Simple Ways to be Good to Yourself: How to Discover Peace and Joy in Your Life_ by Oklahoma City stress consultant Donna Watson, PhD. Energy Press, 5275 McCormick Mountain, Austin, Texas 78734.

...men snore louder and longer

...during the summer because of increased absorption of ultraviolet rays? The UV rays produce more relaxation at bedtime. The more relaxed a person is, the stronger the snoring.

Source: _Stop Your Husband From Snoring: A Medically Proven Program to Cure the Night's Worst Nuisance_, by Derek S. Lipman, MD, Portland, Oregon ear, nose and throat specialist. Rodale Press, 33 E. Minor St., Emmaus, Pennsylvania 18098.

...alcohol adds weight?

...Even moderate drinking can increase your waistline. Two cans of beer daily can add 33 pounds in one year...one glass of wine each day can add 10 pounds.

Also: Alcohol inhibits the body's ability to burn fat by about one-third—per three ounces consumed.

Source: _Healthy, Wealthy & Wise: A Step-By-Step Plan for Success Through Healthful Living_ by fitness consultant Krs Edstrom, Prentice-Hall, Route 9W, Englewood Cliffs, New Jersey 07632.

...modern women's bone density

...is significantly less than the bone density of women 200 years ago—making hip fractures from osteoporosis more likely today? _Possible reasons:_ Women did much more physical activity two centuries ago than today...did not smoke, since cigarettes were unknown... and probably drank little if any alcohol.

Source: Analysis of skeletons of women buried between 1729 and 1852 in England, led by Belinda Lees, BSc, Wynn Institute for Metabolic Research, London, England, reported in _The Lancet_, 42 Bedford Square, LondonWC1B 3SL, England.

...teaching children at home

...does not make them social misfits? More than 300,000 US families now educate at home —for religious reasons or from disenchantment with schools in their areas. A major argument against home schooling has been that it deprives children of peer contacts needed for social development. _New study:_ There is no difference in adulthood between personal and social adaptations of home-taught and school-taught children.

Source: Study of more than 50 adults who were taught at home by their parents, led by J. Gary Knowles, EdD, assistant professor of education, University of Michigan at Ann Arbor.

...heart attacks increase

...following holidays? Heart-attack rates are 28% higher the day after Easter...17% higher on July 5...16% higher on January 2. _Also:_ Men are 21% more likely to suffer a heart attack on their birthdays. _Theory:_ Holidays can provoke emotional stress—and overindulgence in drinking and smoking.

Source: A study of 118,966 heart attacks at 90 New Jersey hospitals by Alan Wilson, PhD, of the Robert Wood Johnson Medical School, New Brunswick, New Jersey.

...badminton causes more eye

...injuries than any other racquet sport? Last year 52% of eye injuries from racquet sports came from badminton. *Next:* Tennis with 24% ...and 24% from squash and racquetball. *Important:* Wear eye protection when playing any type of racquet sport.

Source: Michael Easterbrook, MD, Toronto eye surgeon, quoted in *The Medical Post*, 777 Bay St., Toronto, Ontario M5W 1A7.

...sexual intercourse occurs

...more than 100 million times daily around the world? *Results:* 910,000 conceptions... 350,000 cases of sexually transmitted disease.

Source: World Health Organization study, reported in *The New York Times.*

...home diabetes diagnosis

...will soon be possible through high-tech toilets? The Japanese-built toilets will incorporate biosensors that will automatically test for the presence of glucose in urine—an early sign of diabetes. *Status:* Soon to be introduced in Japan. No word on plans for export to the United States.

Source: Research leader: Isao Karube, Research Centre for Advanced Science and Technology, University of Tokyo, reported in *New Scientist*, King's Reach Tower, Stamford St., London SE1 9LS, UK.

...it only takes a speck of dirt

...or dust to muck up a camera's delicate inner workings? Most dirt or dust enters the camera when the back is opened or when a lens is changed, so be particularly careful to shield the interior when changing film or a lens. *Helpful:* A can of compressed air safely removes dirt.

Source: Rick Rankin, co-owner of Professional Camera Repair Service, 37 W. 47 St., New York 10036.

...kids' allowances

...have not gone up over the past five years? Median allowance for children aged nine and 10 is $2...ages 11 through 14, $5—virtually the same for all ages as in 1988.

Source: Survey of almost 700 children, aged nine to 14, by *Zillions: Consumer Reports for Kids*, 101 Truman Ave., Yonkers, New York 10703.

...heavy drinking over age 40

...accelerates the body's natural declines in testosterone level and liver efficiency? *Result:* Heavy drinkers are more likely to lose sexual desire...become impotent...have a lower sperm count...become sterile. *Good news:* Alcohol-induced changes that lower testosterone levels are reversible over time for men who stop drinking. The sooner drinking stops, the less time the body needs to rebound.

Source: *Sex Over 40* by Saul Rosenthal, MD, founder of the Sexual Therapy Clinic of San Antonio, Texas. Jeremy P. Tarcher, Inc., 5858 Wilshire Blvd., Los Angeles 90036.

...siblings need

...equal consideration, not equal treatment? Parents usually say that they treat all their children the same, but this is impossible...and inappropriate. *Better:* Treat each child according to his/her emotional, intellectual and biological maturity. *Helpful:* Encourage your children's differences as well as their similarities...

hold family meetings to clear up gripes, including favoritism. *Important:* Spend private time with each child.

Source: Stephen Bank, PhD, adjunct professor of psychology, Wesleyan University, Middletown, Connecticut, quoted in *The New York Times*.

…high blood pressure

…incidence dropped dramatically in the last decade? Though the population increased by 9.7%, the number of people suffering from hypertension has dipped from 58 million in 1980 to 50 million in 1991—a 14% fall-off. *Key:* Increasing attention to physical fitness, healthier diet, drop in number of smokers and decrease in alcohol consumption.

Source: Survey conducted by the National Heart, Lung, Blood Institute at the National Institutes of Health, 9000 Rockville Pike, Bethesda, Maryland 20892.

…the weight gain

…that is common after a person quits smoking does not last? Smokers typically gain about seven to 10 pounds after quitting. But only two years later, ex-smokers are no more likely than nonsmokers to be overweight.

Source: Study of more than 1,600 people, aged 20 to 65, by researchers at the University of Saskatchewan in Saskatoon, Canada, reported in *The Medical Post*, 777 Bay St., Toronto, Ontario M5W 1A7.

…car renters

…with recent accidents—or drunk-driving convictions—are being rejected by auto-rental firms? In a pilot program that could spread nationally, New York-area firms use drivers'-license numbers to tap publicly available records.

Source: Consensus of car-rental-firm executives and officials of consumer groups, reported in *The Wall Street Journal*.

…women's worst health threat

…is the men they live with? Violence is the leading cause of injury to women aged 15 to 44—more common than car accidents and cancer deaths *combined*. Troubling connection…*violence and televised sports*. Workers at crisis centers report consistent increases in calls on days when major sporting events are on TV.

Source: Reports by the US Surgeon General's office and a consensus of domestic-violence action groups, reported in *The New York Times*.

…moon madness is a myth?

…Despite a longstanding belief in the influence of the full moon on behavior, there is no evidence that crisis centers receive more calls —or calls of a more distressed nature—when the moon is full. Nor is there evidence that suicide, attempted suicide or suicide threats increase at this time.

Source: Analysis of 20 years of calls to crisis centers and 28 years of studies of suicide and attempted suicide, led by I.W. Kelly, PhD, department of educational psychology, University of Saskatchewan, Canada, reported in *Psychological Reports*, Box 9229, Missoula, Montana 59807.

…medium-term bonds

…may soon become much more volatile? Many investors disappointed by CD rates have moved into two-to-five-year bonds—seeking higher interest with safety for their principal. But as US economic activity picks up, these are the bonds that banks will dump to make more profitable loans to growing companies. *Self-defense:* Diversification—some money in short maturities, some in medium-term bonds and some in long-term issues.

Source: James Benham, chairman, The Benham Group, 1665 Charleston Rd., Mountain View, California 94043.

...58% of timeshare owners

...in a recent poll were trying to sell their properties, but only 3% actually had? As the number of long-term timeshare owners increases, selling should become even more difficult. *Good news:* You can probably purchase a timeshare on the secondary market for a much lower price than new.

Source: Survey of 485 timeshare owners by Resort Property Owners Association, reported in *Consumers Digest*, 5705 N. Lincoln Ave., Chicago 60659.

...the gun ownership/ suicide link

...remains unproved? A recent study points to strong evidence that the presence of guns increases the risk of suicide in the home. But the study omits preexisting psychological factors—for example, gun owners may be more likely to have a predisposition to commit suicide.

Source: Gary Kleck, PhD, School of Criminology and Criminal Justice, Florida State University, writing in *The New England Journal of Medicine*, 10 Shattuck St., Boston 02115.

...pharmaceutical companies

...often induce physicians to prescribe their drugs by paying them to participate in dubious studies? *Reality:* Although the doctor provides some data to make the process look scientific, the study is so poorly designed, the results are useless...but the doctor still gets paid as much as $100 per patient enrolled. *Self-defense:* Ask your doctor if he/she receives compensation from the drug company for any study he asks you to participate in. *Reason:* If the study involves Medicaid or Medicare patients he may be in violation of the federal anti-kickback law. Call the Public Citizen Doctor Bribing Hotline: 202-833-3000.

Source: *Health Letter*, 2000 P St. NW, Washington, DC 20036.

...the most fuel-efficient US cars

...sell very poorly? Some US cars are capable of getting up to 55 miles per gallon. But super-high-mileage autos make up less than two percent of all new-car sales. *Reason:* Consumers prefer larger cars, to carry more people and cargo...or cars like Ford's Taurus and GM's Saturn, which trade some fuel efficiency for more luxury features.

Source: US Environmental Protection Agency and the auto-industry-funded Coalition for Vehicle Choice, reported in *The Washington Post*.

...pregnant workers

...on fixed evening and night shifts are more likely to have miscarriages than women working days? *Highest risk:* Shifts starting at 3pm to 4pm. Women on those shifts were four times more likely to miscarry than women working day shifts.

Source: Study of more than 1,300 women, led by Claire Infante-Rivard, MD, PhD, associate professor, McGill University School of Occupational Health and University of Montreal, Canada.

...high-school students with jobs

...do poorer in school, miss class more often and spend less time on homework than those who don't work? The effect is most serious among teens who work more than 15 to 20 hours a week. More than two-thirds of all high-school juniors and seniors are employed.

Source: Study by Laurence Steinberg, PhD, professor of psychology, Temple University, Philadelphia.

...about 1% of adults

...are bed-wetters? *Good news:* Desmopressin (DDAVP), an analogue of antidiuretic hormone, has been successful in treating those who have tried other regimens unsuccessfully for nocturnal enuresis. The drug is used as a nasal spray once a night and no side effects have been reported by users.

Source: Nocturnal-enuresis patient M.J.M. De Graaf, writing in *The Lancet*, 428 E. Preston St., Baltimore 21202.

...hypertension shrinks the brain?

...Men suffering from long-term high blood pressure have larger fluid-filled cavities in their skulls—and smaller brains. *Possible reason:* Over time, hypertension may do slight but irreversible damage to blood vessels in the brain. *Result:* Some brain tissue is slowly starved of oxygen and dies. *Consequences:* Language, memory and other problems in later life.

Source: Research by neuroscientists Judith Salerno and Declan Murphy, National Institute on Aging, reported in *Discover* magazine, 114 Fifth Ave., New York 10011.

...deceit is a normal part of life?

...Social interaction requires some deception, such as polite thank-yous for unwanted gifts or uninteresting parties. All societies and cultures have social codes that govern interactions and hide true feelings behind cordiality.

Source: Donald Norman, PhD, chair, cognitive sciences department, University of California, and author of *Turn Signals Are the Facial Expression of Automobiles*, Addison-Wesley Publishing Co., Jacob Way, Reading, Massachusetts 01867, writing in *Utne Reader*, 1624 Harmon Pl., Minneapolis, Minnesota 55403.

...nearly 60% of American adults

...lead sedentary lives? They spend less than three 20-minute sessions per week at leisure-time physical activity. *Disturbing:* It's a myth that Americans are becoming more physically active. The percentage who are physically active now is about the same as it was in the mid-1980s.

Source: Paul Z. Siegel, MD, medical epidemiologist, Behavioral Risk Factor Surveillance Surveys for the Centers for Disease Control and Prevention.

21

The New Tax Law Loopholes

The New Tax Law

The Clinton tax package has been signed into law, and while it increases taxes generally, it also contains new tax breaks for business. *Major provisions...*

Tax rates:

• The top corporate tax rate rises from 34% to 35%.

• The top rate increases to 39.6% for firms organized as S corporations, proprietorships and partnerships—which have their income taxed on their owners' personal returns. These new higher tax rates are effective retroactively to January 1, 1993.

Opportunity: Businesses that obtained filing extensions for 1992 may not yet have filed their 1992 returns. These businesses may still have the option to cut their tax bills by making elections that accelerate income into 1992 to have it taxed at a lower rate—the reverse of the normal filing strategy, which is to defer income to delay paying tax.

Example: If a property was sold on the installment basis during 1992, the company may elect not to report the sale on the installment basis, so the full gain will be taxed on the 1992 return at a lower tax rate.

Look for other filing opportunities to accelerate income into lower-tax 1992, or delay deductions to be taken in higher-tax 1993.

Intangibles:

One of the most favorable provisions of the new law for business allows the cost of intangible assets that are acquired in a business purchase to be written off through amortization deductions taken over a 15-year period.

The proper tax treatment of intangibles—items such as customer lists, favorable contracts, workforce in place, trademarks and franchise rights—has been one of the most hotly contested areas of dispute between businesses and the IRS in recent years.

The new law sets clear rules for the deduction of intangibles, and even allows amortization of deductions for the cost of goodwill, for which no deduction was allowed in earlier years.

Even better, companies can elect to use the 15-year write-off retroactively for acquisitions made after July 25, 1991.

Strategy: For business acquisitions made between July 25, 1991 and the effective date of the new law, the company can choose which set of deduction rules to apply to intangibles. Old law sometimes allowed write-off periods for intangibles of under 15 years, and thus larger deductions. But the many uncertainties of the old law make an IRS challenge to deductions more likely.

The new law allows deductions to be taken with less risk. So consider the trade-offs.

More help:

• Research and experimentation tax credit has been renewed retroactively to July 1, 1992, when it expired under previous law. Companies should plan to make use of the credit, and review their books to find expenditures incurred during the period since the credit expired that may qualify for the credit.

Note: The IRS has also recently released regulations that may help companies claim larger business expense deductions for research costs. The new rules make it clear that certain restrictive definitions of "research expenditures" that apply when claiming the credit do not apply when claiming expense deductions. Have the company's tax adviser check the details.

• Targeted jobs tax credit has been renewed. This credit encourages companies to hire new employees from specified groups. It provides a tax break of up to $2,400 for hiring new employees from targeted groups. The credit equals 40% of up to the first $6,000 of the new hire's wages.

• Expensing deduction for new business equipment has been increased from $10,000 to $17,500 when a company places less than $200,000 of new equipment in service during the year.

This allows a business to deduct the cost of such equipment immediately, instead of over a period of years through depreciation deductions. The new limit is effective for tax years beginning after December 31, 1992, so companies can take advantage of it now.

• Employer-provided educational assistance receives a renewal of tax-favored treatment. Again, this break expired on July 1, 1992. Employees who received this benefit and included it in income may wish to file amended returns to claim a refund.

• Luxury tax has been repealed on boats, airplanes, furs and jewelry (but not automobiles), retroactive to the beginning of this year. Companies selling these items can now make sales without the luxury tax—and provide refunds to customers who made purchases earlier this year.

• Alternative Minimum Tax (AMT) is modified by adjusting the way depreciation is computed for AMT purposes.

Rules are complicated, but the net effect is that companies facing the AMT may benefit by delaying the date when new equipment is placed in service until after December 1993, when the new rules will become effective. Have the firm's tax adviser check the details.

• Passive loss deduction limits are lifted for real estate professionals who materially participate in the management of rental properties. The passive losses derived from such properties can now be used to offset income from trade or business activity, provided certain tests are satisfied.

Revenue raisers:

• *Benefit programs.* The amount of pay that can be counted when computing qualified retirement plan benefits is reduced to $150,000 from $235,840. This may reduce the benefits available to top-paid employees, so companies may wish to find ways to supplement retirement plan benefits with nonqualified programs.

• *Business meals and entertainment.* The deduction for business meals and entertainment is reduced from 80% to 50% of their cost. Make sure the company's accounting system for business meals is comprehensive, so every eligible deductible dollar is claimed.

Effective date: Tax years beginning after December 31, 1993.

• *Compensation.* A company may lose its deduction for compensation in excess of $1 million annually paid to the CEO and the four other top-paid officers. The deduction disallowance does not apply to compensation that is tied to performance measures, so the company may wish to adopt pay-for-performance programs for very highly paid personnel. Also, the deduction limit does not apply to private companies.

The new rules apply beginning in 1994, so review the company's compensation plans now.

• *Moving expenses.* The new law eliminates moving expense deductions that previously were allowed for the cost of move-related house-hunting trips, temporary lodging near a new work site, meals and costs related to selling an old home or settling an unexpired lease, and buying or leasing a new residence. Since a company that pays such expenses on behalf of an employee cannot deduct them, businesses may wish to review worker-relocation programs.

The new rules apply to expenses incurred after December 31, 1993, so expenses incurred before year-end can still be deducted.

• *Real estate depreciation.* The depreciation period for newly acquired business real estate is increased from 31½ years to 39 years, resulting in smaller annual depreciation deductions. Factor in these reduced deductions when considering the cash-flow cost of a real estate acquisition.

The new rule applies to property acquired on or after May 13, 1993, unless there was a legally binding commitment to acquire the property in effect before that date.

• *Club dues.* The new disallows any deduction for club dues, including not only country clubs and social clubs but also airline and hotel clubs—even though these were exempt from earlier versions of the law because they are not social clubs but provide business travel services.

Effective date: After December 31, 1993. So individuals may still claim deductions for dues paid before year-end.

Note: The company can still deduct club dues paid for an employee so long as the dues are treated as compensation.

• *Business travel.* The law does not allow travel deductions for a spouse or dependent who accompanies an individual on a business trip and helps perform business duties—for example, by acting as a hostess or secretary.

To claim such a deduction now, the accompanying spouse or dependent must be a bona fide employee of the business entity that reimburses expenses.

Effective date: The new rule is effective for travel after December 31, 1993.

• *Lobbying costs.* Deductions for lobbying expenses are generally eliminated.

Effective date: After December 31, 1993.

Source: James C. Godbout, partner, Ernst & Young, 1200 19 St. NW, Washington, DC 20036.

Refund Opportunities

Many of the changes made by the Clinton Tax Act were retroactive. If any of the following changes affect you, call your accountant and discuss whether you may be entitled to a refund:

• Self-employed taxpayers who incurred health insurance costs after July 1, 1992, and filed their tax return without claiming the 25% deduction that was retroactively reinstated to July 1, 1992.

• Employees who received certain employer-provided educational assistance between June 30, 1992, and December 31, 1992, that was included in income. The exclusion for up to $5,250 of such benefits was retroactively reinstated.

• Investors who donated appreciated art works or other tangible personal property to charity between June 30 and December 31, 1992, and treated the appreciation as a tax preference item may be entitled to a refund since this preference item for Alternative Minimum Tax (AMT) purposes was retroactively repealed to June 30, 1992. (Formerly, the appreciation was included in AMT calculations.)

• Investors in low-income housing may qualify for additional low-income housing credits. The credit was retroactively reinstated to June 30, 1992, along with several modifications.

• Employers who paid wages to employees who are members of certain disadvantaged groups between June 30, 1992, and December 31, 1992, may qualify for an increased targeted jobs credit (40% of wages up to $6,000 and

$3,000 for summer youth employees) as a result of the retroactive reinstatement of the credit.

•Homeowners and renters whose principal residence or personal belongings were damaged as a result of a casualty in a presidential-declared disaster area on or after September 1, 1991, may qualify for additional tax benefits where insurance proceeds had created a taxable gain.

•Investors in qualified small issue bonds after June 30, 1992, may qualify for tax benefits.

•Disabled taxpayers who paid the luxury excise tax on a part or accessory installed on a passenger vehicle to enable him/her to operate the vehicle—or to enter or exit the vehicle—where the parts or accessories were not commonly available can obtain a refund of the tax. This change is retroactive to December 31, 1990.

•Consumers who paid the 10% luxury tax on airplanes costing more than $250,000, boats costing more than $100,000, or jewelry/furs costing more than $10,000 on or after January 1, 1993, are entitled to a refund. Contact the merchant who sold you the item.

Source: Martin M. Shenkman, Esq., a New York attorney specializing in estate, tax and personal planning.

Annuities: A Better Investment Under The New Tax Law

For individuals seeking secure income, investments in annuities have been made even more attractive by the new tax law. Today, annuities provide both tax and economic benefits...

•*Tax deferral.* Investment returns earned on an annuity contract aren't taxed until they are withdrawn. This tax-deferred compounding results in your having more money at the end of the investment period than there would be if taxes were withdrawn from investment earnings each year.

•*Higher returns.* During periods of low interest rates, annuities consistently have paid higher returns than have been available from competing income-producing investments offered by banks and money funds.

Planning:

Annuities should be used to provide income after reaching age 59½. Annuity payments received before that age are subject to a 10% penalty on early withdrawals.

More tax breaks:

In addition to tax deferral for investment earnings, annuities offer these tax advantages...

•*Tax break on payouts.* When you receive payments from an annuity, only a portion of each payment is taxable to you. That's because a part of each payment is considered to be a return of your original investment, and thus is tax-free.

The fact that a portion of each payment is tax-free means that the amount of tax you owe on each payment will be much less than the tax you'd owe on a payment of the same dollar size received from a taxable investment.

•*Social Security break.* The new tax law can also make annuities more attractive than alternative investments to many receiving Social Security benefits.

Under the new tax law, persons with incomes greater than specified threshold amounts will have 85% of their Social Security benefits subject to income tax. However, income received from an annuity is not counted when computing whether the Social Security tax income threshold has been reached.

Contrast: Income received from tax-exempt municipal bonds is included in the Social Security tax income computation. Thus, investments in annuities can help head off the 85% tax on Social Security benefits.

Investing:

Annuity programs are available to a variety of individual needs...

•*Immediate annuity:* Purchased with a single up-front payment and begins making periodic payments to you right away. The tax-free portion of each payment will be quite large—depending on the age of the investor, it may be as high as 85%.

•*Deferred annuity:* Set to begin at a future date, such as after retirement. Because your money is invested for a longer period of time, you get a larger benefit from the tax-deferred compounding of investment returns.

• *Split annuity:* Combines the features of immediate and deferred annuities.

• *Variable annuities:* Can provide investors with the flexibility they may desire to maintain in today's markets.

While standard annuities provide a contractually specified rate of return on your investment, a variable annuity lets you invest in a portfolio of stock and bond mutual funds that you can manage yourself. The size of your final benefit will depend on the investment returns you earn.

Best returns and safety:

Comparison shop among different insurance companies for the annuity plan you want to buy—surprisingly large differences may exist in the rates of return offered by different insurers.

Invest only with insurance companies that have earned top ratings for financial strength and safety from the leading insurance industry ratings services—A.M. Best, Moody's, Standard & Poors, and Duff & Phelps. You can find these ratings in your local public library or send a request for a list of recommended annuity carriers to Alan Nadolna, Associates in Financial Planning, 100 S. Wacker Dr., #1650, Chicago 60606.

Source: Alan Nadolna, president, Associates in Financial Planning, 100 S. Wacker Dr., #1650, Chicago 60606.

New Tax Law Loopholes ...And More Loopholes

The Clinton tax changes are now law. The top tax rate has gone up from 31% to 39.6% retroactively to the first of the year.

That's the bad news.

The good news is that there are a number of ways to benefit from the new law. *Loopholes:*

Investments:

The real top tax rate is even higher than 39.6%. It is as high as 44% when you take into account the loss of deductions and personal exemptions that high income taxpayers face.

Tax rates this high make certain investments more attractive than they were before the law changed.

• *Loophole:* Municipal bonds. Higher tax rates enhance the value of tax-free investments. For an investor in the 31% tax bracket, the top rate under the old law, a tax-free investment yielding 5% was the equivalent of a taxable investment yielding 7.2%.

But for an investor paying a top rate of 44% under the new law, a tax-free investment yielding 5% is the equivalent of a taxable investment yielding 8.9%. If you include state taxes, the taxable equivalent yield would be even greater.

• *Loophole:* Invest for capital gains. Under the new law, capital gains are taxed at a maximum of 28%, while salary and other income is taxed at official rates as high as 39.6%. The more income you can take as capital gains, the better.

Bonus I: Capital gains are not taxed until they are realized when you sell an asset.

Bonus II: Capital gains that you hold at your death are not taxed at all.

Retirement plans:

Higher tax rates make retirement plans more valuable. Your deduction for contributions to a retirement plan is worth more at a higher tax rate and the benefit of tax-deferred compounding of money in the plan is also worth more. Contributions to a plan give you current tax deductions at today's high tax rates. Higher current rates make it more likely that you'll be in a lower tax bracket when you retire and take the money out.

• *Loophole:* Contribute the maximum to your 401(k), Keogh plan, and IRA this year and next.

Stock options:

If your company is thinking about giving stock options to its employees, ask them to give incentive stock options (ISOs).

• *Loophole:* ISOs are taxed in a different way than other options. You don't pay tax when you exercise an ISO—the tax is deferred.

When you sell the stock the option is tied to, your gain is a capital gain. Thus, ISOs are a way to convert ordinary income into capital gains. And capital gains are taxed at a very favorable rate under the new law.

S-Corps:

The income of an S-corporation is taxed on the owners personal income tax return. When individual tax rates were lower than corporate tax rates it made sense to convert to an S-corporation.

But under the new law the top corporate tax rate is only 35%, while an individual can be taxed up to 44%.

•*Loophole:* Consider terminating your S-corp election if your income from the business is sufficiently high enough that you pay at the top individual income tax rates—36% or 39.6%.

Downside: If you terminate your S-corp election for this purpose, you'll also lose it for other purposes, such as the benefit of single taxation on the proceeds from the sale of the business.

Real estate:

The new law liberalizes the passive loss rules for individuals in the real estate business. Under the new rules, real estate losses are deductible against salary and other income for certain qualifying real estate professionals. A person qualifies under the new rules if…

•More than half of his/her personal services are performed in real estate trades or businesses.

•He/she spends more than 750 hours a year on such activities.

•He/she materially participates in such activities.

Suppose a husband is a real estate developer who only spends 500 hours in the real estate business. He has substantial losses from real estate and a substantial salary. Under the old rules, the husband can't deduct his losses against his salary. But under the new rules there's a way to make those losses deductible.

•*Loophole:* Put your spouse to work in a real estate business. A husband and wife filing a joint return meet the eligibility requirements for the new law if, during the tax year, one spouse performs more than 750 hours in a real estate trade or business. So, if one spouse puts in 750 hours selling real estate, say, no matter how much that spouse earns, the other spouse's real estate losses would be deductible against the couple's salary and other income.

Caution: The spouse with losses would have to put in 500 hours in the activities he was en-

gaged in and otherwise qualify as a material participant in real estate activities.

Spouses who travel:

The new law prohibits deductions for the travel expenses of a spouse unless the spouse is a bona fide employee of the business paying the expenses and…

•The travel of the spouse is for a bona fide business purpose, and

•The expenses incurred would otherwise be deductible.

•*Loophole:* Consider making your spouse an employee of the business if you have your own business and your spouse frequently travels with you on business.

Downside: You'll have to pay Social Security tax on salary you pay him/her.

Real estate depreciation:

The new law increased the depreciation period for nonresidential real estate from 31.5 years to 39 years for property placed in service on or after May 13, 1993. Rules that ease in the change generally prevent the new period from applying to property placed in service before January 1, 1994, if there was a contract to purchase or construct the property before May 13, 1994. You can use the 31.5 year depreciation period for this property.

Paying the tax:

The extra taxes you owe because of the higher tax rates for 1993 can be paid in three installments, April 15, 1994, April 17, 1995, and April 15, 1996.

Caution: Underpayment of any installment will make the whole of the unpaid tax payable immediately. If you file for an extension of your 1993 return, you will run afoul of the installment rule if your first installment is estimated incorrectly and turns out to be too low.

The thing to do if you owe extra tax is to file your 1993 return on time, estimating amounts, such as income and loss from partnerships, that you're unsure of, and then file an amended return later providing the correct figures. That way you'll pay the first installment of your extra tax on time and will qualify to make further installments.

Source: Edward Mendlowitz, partner, Mendlowitz Weitsen, CPAs, Two Pennsylvania Plaza, New York 10121.

The New Tax On Social Security Benefits

Retirees beware: Uncle Sam will take a bigger bite of your Social Security payments, starting in 1994. But you'll have to struggle to learn exactly how big, because the new rules are very complicated.

Before the Clinton tax law, all retirees paid income taxes on up to one-half of their Social Security benefits when their provisional income* exceeded $32,000 for married couples ($25,000 for single taxpayers). The taxable amount was equal to...one-half of the provisional income above the threshold or one-half of the Social Security benefits, whichever was less.

New law:

Starting next year Social Security benefits will be taxed based on a two-tier system:

• The tax on one-half of the benefits for people with provisional income above the old income thresholds ($32,000/ $25,000) but below the new income thresholds ($44,000/ $34,000) remains.

• A tax on 85% of Social Security benefits for retirees whose provisional income, figured using the same formula explained above, exceeds new thresholds of $44,000 for married taxpayers and $34,000 for single taxpayers.

For taxpayers above the new higher thresholds, taxable income will include the lesser of...

• 85% of Social Security benefits or

• the sum of the following amounts: The smaller of the amount of Social Security benefits included under present law—or inclusion amounts set at $4,500 for single taxpayers...or $6,000 for married couples filing jointly

plus...85% of excess provisional income over the new threshold amounts of $44,000 for couples and $34,000 for singles.

Example: John and Jane have $35,000 of taxable investment and pension income, $20,000 of Social Security benefits and $5,000 of tax-free income. Their provisional income equals $50,000. Under the present law, John and Jane have to include $9,000 of their Social Security benefits in income. This is half of their excess provisional income of $18,000 ($50,000 – $32,000). Since this is less than half of their Social Security benefits ($10,000), they only have to include $9,000 of their benefits in income.

Under the new law, John and Jane's taxable amount of Social Security benefits will be $11,100. Here's how they arrive at that figure...

• First they calculate 85% of their Social Security benefits. In their case this is $17,000 (85% x $20,000).

• Then they determine whether this is larger or smaller than the sum of...

The smaller of the amount of their Social Security benefits included under present law ($9,000)...

...or $6,000 (the married couple's inclusion figure under the new law), plus 85% of their excess provisional income over the new thresholds.

In John and Jane's case, their excess provisional income under the new law is $6,000 ($50,000–$44,000). 85% of $6,000 is $5,100.

So John and Jane will include $11,100 of their benefits in income ($6,000 plus $5,100) because this is smaller than $17,000.

Source: James C. Godbout, partner, Ernst & Young, 1200 19 St. NW, Washington, DC 20036.

Steps to Take Before Year-End to Cut Taxes Under the New Tax Law

Plan now to take action before year-end to cut the taxes you'll pay under the Clinton tax law. Smart planning now enables you to minimize the cost of retroactive tax-rate increases and beat deadlines imposed by other law changes that take effect at year-end.

Executives:

Steps to consider now:

The new tax law has a major impact on executive compensation planning.

• *Bonuses.* People earning more than $135,000 who expect a year-end bonus should consider asking their employers to pay the bonus before year-end, instead of just after it.

The 1.45% Medicare tax on wages currently applies to only the first $135,000 of wages, but will apply to all wages in 1994. So paying the bonus before year-end will avoid the tax, unless you'll be crossing over into the next income tax bracket. And since the company owes a matching 1.45% tax, early payment will cut its tax bill, too—saving 2.9% overall.

•*Retirement plans.* The new law reduces the amount of salary upon which qualified retirement benefits can be based from $235,840 this year to only $150,000 next year.

Therefore, high-salary executives will have their qualified retirement benefits cut. Negotiate now to set up a supplemental nonqualified retirement benefit or some other compensating benefit that will restore the value of your compensation package.

•*Stock compensation.* The new tax law increases the top tax rates (36% and 39.6%) paid on salary income…but sets the top tax rate on long-term capital gains at only 28%. This change, which is effective this year, makes compensation in the form of stock shares more attractive relative to normal salary.

Helpful: Encourage the corporation to set up an incentive stock option (ISO) program. These tax-favored options are not taxed when granted or exercised.

When shares bought with ISOs are sold after being held for more than a year, the entire gain that results is a long-term capital gain. In contrast, the bargain element on a nonqualified stock option is taxable ordinary income when exercised, and only that appreciation that occurs after the exercise of the option is capital gain.

Depending on the exercise price and the dividend yield, you may wish to consider exercising nonqualifieds earlier to minimize the amount taxed as compensation.

If some form of stock compensation is already available to you, look into ways to make the most of it now.

Personal planning:

Be alert to these new-law strategies that affect taxpayers across-the-board…

•*Marriage penalty.* Consider staying single to avoid marriage "penalties" imposed by the new law. *Examples:*

•*Social Security tax.* Two individuals can have up to $68,000 of income before 85% of Social Security benefits become subject to income tax, while a couple can have only $44,000 of income.

•*Income tax.* Two individuals can have up to $500,000 of income before becoming subject to the 39.6% bracket, but a couple can have only $250,000.

•*Deduction disallowance.* Two individuals can have up to $216,900 of Adjusted Gross Income before itemized deductions become reduced by 3% of any excess amount. For a couple, the limit is only $108,450.

Point: If you will be divorced soon, consider finalizing the divorce before year-end to cut the year's taxes.

•*Charitable gifts.* By making a gift of appreciated property to a charity, you can get a deduction for the property's full market value without having to pay tax on its appreciation.

The new tax law facilitates such gifts by eliminating the potential AMT liability that could result from them under the old law. This provision of the new law applies retroactively, so consider making such gifts before year-end to cut this year's tax bill.

•*Reexamine trusts.* Families that use trust arrangements to hold assets and help cut the family tax bill should reexamine them now. The new law increases the tax rates paid by trusts.

Under the new law, a trust must pay 31% tax on income greater than $3,500, 36% tax on income greater than $5,500, and 39.6% tax on income greater than the fairly small amount of $7,500. Take a hard look at family trusts in light of these tax bracket changes.

•*Moving expenses.* The new tax law eliminates moving expense deductions for house-hunting trips, meals, and temporary living expenses. It also increases the minimum distance of a deductible move from 35 miles to 50 miles.

However, the new rules don't apply until after year-end. So, if you are planning to move soon, incur these expenses before year-end to save your deduction for them.

Investors:

Steps to consider now...

Planning to earn long-term capital gains will become more important to investors in coming years.

• With interest rates at long-term lows, stocks and mutual funds that provide potentially higher returns through capital gains become relatively more attractive investments.

• The new tax law sets a favorable maximum tax rate on capital gains—only 28%, even when ordinary income is taxed at rates as high as 39.6%. This change is in effect for 1993, so gains can be taken at a favorable rate now.

Caution: Persons who are used to investing in interest-bearing securities should remember that stocks and mutual funds can go down in value as well as up, and not risk money they will need to use in the near term.

Traps in investing for capital gains:

• *Interest deduction limit.* Investment interest is deductible to the extent that you have investment income. But the new law cuts back this deduction by removing long-term capital gains from the definition of investment income. This change was placed in effect retroactively for all of 1993.

Danger: Persons who have borrowed to carry investments, such as those who invest through margin accounts, may lose interest deductions they expected to claim for interest paid on their borrowings.

Investors should review their debt structure to check the status of interest deductions. Do so now while there is still time to act to save deductions before year-end.

Escape: The new law says that capital gains may be included in investment income to support an interest deduction if you elect not to use the favorable 28% tax rate for capital gain income.

• *Alternative Minimum Tax (AMT).* Large amounts of long-term capital gains may make you subject to the AMT, and this may cause you to lose other tax benefits you were expecting to claim.

Example: State and local income taxes are not deductible under AMT rules, so taking large capital gains could increase the bottom line cost of local taxes paid by people who live in high tax states, particularly New York.

Project your AMT liability for the year now, while there is still time to take action before year-end. Avoid unpleasant surprises.

Self-employeds:

Steps to consider now:

Special consideration applies to small businesses.

• *Equipment expensing.* The new law increases the amount of newly acquired business equipment (property placed in service of less than $200,000 for 1993) that can be expensed —that is deducted immediately instead of over a period of years through depreciation—from $10,000 to $17,500.

This increase is available in 1993, so don't waste it. Make qualifying purchases before year-end.

• *Form of organization.* Under the new tax law, owners of partnerships and S corporations may pay taxes on business income at a higher rate than owners of regular corporations— which have a top tax rate of only 35%. Of course, many factors affect the best choice of business organization. But now consider the tax penalty that can apply to income earned by partnerships and S corporations when deciding what form of organization to use.

• *Small business stock.* The new tax law creates a 50% tax exemption for capital gains earned on the stock of certain new businesses when it is held for more than five years. If you are planning on starting a new business, you may be able to use this stock to attract investors. Or, if you are planning to back a new business being started by a family member or friend, you may wish to obtain this stock. Consult your tax adviser for details.

• *Retirement benefits.* The reduction of the amount of income on which retirement benefits may be based to only $150,000, discussed above, applies to self-employeds and family businesses, too. This may reduce the amount of a Keogh contribution you are able to make.

What to do: Consider adopting an "age-weighted" retirement plan. An age-weighted plan lets larger contributions be made to the accounts of older plan participants. This can be very advantageous in the case of a family business, where the biggest earner and business manager is likely to be the oldest participant, while younger family members or outsiders provide clerical and support functions. Consult with your tax adviser for details.

Source: Nadine Gordon Lee, Ernst & Young.

Myths About the New Tax Law— And the Truth You Should Know

Many myths and misconceptions exist about the new Clinton tax law. Here are some of the most mistaken myths and the truth about them...

Myth: Only the very rich—the top 1% of income earners —are affected by the new law.

Truth: The new tax law can have a significant impact on almost anyone. It creates new restrictions on deductions for moving expenses, business meal and entertainment costs, business travel costs and investment interest expenses. Those apply regardless of income level—and the restrictions are explained further on in this article.

Myth: The law creates just two new tax "brackets"—36% and 39.6%.

Truth: The new law creates a whole series of income thresholds in which various extra tax liabilities now begin to apply. *When you report more than...*

- $44,000 of "provisional" income—defined as Adjusted Gross Income (AGI) plus tax-exempt income, plus half of social security benefits—on a joint return, or $34,000 on a single return, 85% of Social Security benefits are subject to income tax.
- $108,450 of AGI on either a joint or single return, total itemized deductions are reduced by 3% of the excess—except deductions for medical expenses, casualty and theft losses, and investment interest.
- $135,000 of wages, you will incur the 1.45% Medicare tax on all wages over this amount

starting in 1994. The tax rate is 2.9% for self-employed persons.

- $140,000 of taxable income on a joint return, or $115,000 on a single return, you incur the new 36% tax rate.
- $162,700 of AGI on a joint return, or $108,450 on a single return, you lose 2% of your personal exemptions for every $2,500 (or portion thereof) by which AGI exceeds the threshold amount.
- $250,000 of taxable income on either a joint or single return, you are subject to the 39.6% income tax rate.

Myth: The top new tax rate is 39.6%.

Truth: After the 39% tax rate for income-related disallowances of itemized deductions and dependency exemptions (which are described above)...and the Medicare tax...it is easy to see that the real top personal tax rate can be much higher.

Example: A self-employed person with a family of four in the 39.6% tax bracket may effectively be subject to approximately a 1% deduction disallowance, a 2% exemption disallowance and the 2.9% Medicare tax, creating a total tax rate approaching 46%.

Because these other tax provisions can also apply to persons with less than $250,000 of income, individuals in the new "stated" 36% tax bracket may, in fact, find themselves paying a real marginal tax rate that is higher than the supposedly top rate of 39.6%.

And when you add state and local income taxes, many individuals may find themselves paying a real effective marginal tax rate exceeding 50%.

Myth: The tax law is retroactive so you can't do anything about it.

Truth: Not all the provisions in the new tax law are retroactive. In many cases, it is possible to take tax-saving steps before year-end.

- *Moving expenses.* The new law increases the distance you must move to qualify for this deduction from 35 miles to 50 miles and eliminates deductions for pre-move house-hunting trips, meals incurred while traveling or living in temporary quarters and costs related to selling (or disposing of the lease on) an old residence, or buying (or leasing) a new residence. But you can still deduct these items in 1993 if you incur them before year-end.

•*Meals and entertainment*. The deduction for meals and entertainment is reduced from 80% of cost to 50% of cost. No deduction is allowed for club dues—including social, business, luncheon, athletic, airline and hotel clubs.

However, if you entertain before year-end, you can still deduct 80% of the cost. And in 1993, you can deduct the cost of prepaying club dues for fiscal 1994.

•*Business travel*. The new tax law disallows any business expense deduction for the cost of a spouse or dependent who accompanies you on a business trip, unless the other person is a bona fide employee of the party paying the expenses and is traveling with a genuine business purpose. But it may still be possible to arrange to pay for such deductible travel through December 31, 1993.

Also, the extension of the Medicare tax to wages over $135,000 is not effective until 1994, so it is possible to avoid the tax by accelerating the receipt of income from next year to this year—perhaps by taking a bonus before year-end.

And the tax new law reduces the amount of wage income that can be used as a basis for making retirement plan contributions from $235,840 this year to $150,000—effective in plan years beginning after December 31, 1993. So employees and self-employed persons with income over these amounts may wish to "max out" deductible plan contributions for 1993. *Aim:* To put money in the plan that they will not be able to put in in 1994 and later.

Myth: There's no way to plan around the impact of the new higher tax rates.

Truth: The new law makes tax planning more important than ever. *Where it can pay off...*

•*Investments*. The maximum tax rate on long-term capital gains under the new law is 28%, compared to the 31%, 36% or 39.6% "stated" rates that many people will be paying on ordinary income. Review investment strategies to take advantage of the increased value of long-term gains.

On the downside, the new tax law retroactively restricts the deduction for investment interest—which normally is deductible to the extent you have investment income—by removing long-term capital gains from the definition of investment income.

If you were planning to take a large investment interest deduction for this year, review your situation now to see if you should modify your debt structure and investment portfolio.

•*Deferred compensation*. With higher tax rates imposed on higher income levels, it now can make more sense to enter a deferred compensation program with your employer. Then, salary will be received in a later year—such as after retirement—when your income may be lower so you will be in a lower tax bracket.

•*Threshold planning*. Be aware of how different marginal tax rates take effect at different income thresholds, as mentioned above.

Project expected income for this year and for 1994. If you expect to move into a higher threshold next year, it can pay to reverse conventional tax-planning strategy by accelerating income into this year, when your tax rate will be lower...or postponing deductions into next year, when your tax rate may be higher.

Myth: Investments in real estate now are more attractive. The new tax law lets passive losses from real estate investments be deducted against other income.

Truth: The provisions of the new tax law that allow for greater deductibility of passive losses apply only to real estate professionals—persons who spend more than 50% of their working hours in the active management of real estate.

The liberalization of the rules does not apply to the typical individual who owns real estate property, such as a house or vacation property, as an investment.

For persons who are not real estate professionals, all the old deduction restrictions on passive losses still apply.

Myth: The new tax law eliminates any tax benefit from club memberships.

Truth: The new law eliminates only the deduction club dues—including those for social, business, luncheon, athletic, airline and hotel clubs.

However, the law does not eliminate deductions for other kinds of club expenses that qualified for deduction under the old law.

Thus, if you pay for business meals or entertain at your club, these are still deductible (subject to the 50%-of-cost limit). Similarly, if you obtain travel services through an airline or hotel club, the cost of these services remains deductible as before.

Source: George E.L. Barbee, executive director of client services, Price Waterhouse. He is a contributor to the firm's books on taxes, investing and retirement.

Index

Z